Deviant Behavior

A TEXT-READER IN
THE SOCIOLOGY OF DEVIANCE

FOURTH EDITION

Deviant Behavior

A TEXT-READER IN THE SOCIOLOGY OF DEVIANCE

FOURTH EDITION

Delos H. Kelly

CALIFORNIA STATE UNIVERSITY, LOS ANGELES

ST. MARTIN'S PRESS
NEW YORK

To Jane, Brett Alan, Erin Lynn, and Alison Michele

Editor: Louise H. Waller
Manager, publishing services: Emily Berleth
Project management: Pat Kennedy, Publication Services
Cover design: Tom McKeveny

Library of Congress Catalog Card Number: 92-50055

Manufactured in the United States of America.
76543
fedcba

For information, write:
St. Martin's Press, Inc.
175 Fifth Avenue
New York, NY 10010

ISBN: 0-312-08034-4

ACKNOWLEDGMENTS

Acknowledgments and copyrights are continued at the back of the book on pages 655–656, which constitute an extension of the copyright page.

Jack P. Gibbs, "Conceptions of Deviant Behavior: The Old and the New," *Pacific Sociological Quarterly,* pp. 9–11 (Spring, 1966). Reprinted by permission of JAI Press.
Howard S. Becker, "Moral Entrepreneurs: The Creation and Enforcement of Deviant Categories," reprinted with the permission of The Free Press, a Division of Macmillan, Inc. from OUTSIDERS by Howard S. Becker. Copyright © 1963 by The Free Press.
Troy Duster, "The Legislation of Morality: Creating Drug Laws," reprinted with the permission of The Free Press, a Division of Macmillan, Inc. from THE LEGISLATION OF MORALITY by Troy Duster. Copyright © 1970 by the Free Press.
Peter Conrad, "The Discovery of Hyperkinesis: Notes on the Medicalization of Deviant Behavior," © 1975 by the Society for the Study of Social Problems. Reprinted from *Social Problems,* Vol. 23, No. 1, October 1975, pp. 12–21, by permission.
Emile Durkheim, "The Normal and the Pathological," reprinted with the permission of The Free Press, a Division of Macmillan, Inc. From THE RULES OF SOCIOLOGICAL METHOD by Emile Durkheim, translated by Sarah A. Solvey and John H. Mueller. Edited by George E. G. Catlin. Copyright © 1938 by George E. G. Catlin; copyright renewed 1966 by Sarah A. Solvey, John H. Mueller, George E. G. Catlin.
Kai T. Erikson, "On the Sociology of Deviance," reprinted with the permission of Macmillan Publishing Company from WAYWARD PURITANS by Kai Erikson. Copyright © 1966 by Macmillan Publishing Company.
Thorsten Sellin, "The Conflict of Conduct Norms," a report of the subcommittee on Delinquency of the Committee on Personality and Culture, Social Science Research Council Bulletin 41 (New York, 1938).

Preface

Some anthologies dealing with the subject of deviance emphasize the ways in which society responds to deviant behavior. Others, by examining why certain individuals violate the social norm, focus on the motivational element. A few trace the evolution of deviant categories. *Deviant Behavior* has been designed to integrate and balance these concerns in a single volume—to explore, through carefully selected readings, the ramifications of deviance for the individual (the *actor*) and for society.

Part 1 considers the ways society defines deviance and the deviant. Of particular interest is the role that specific individuals—especially those who hold political power or who serve as enforcers of the law—play in the labeling of actors and acts as deviant. It will become clear to the reader that no individual and no behavior is inherently deviant: it is society's perception of an actor or an act as deviant that affixes the label. Deviance, in other words, is in the eye of the beholder.

Why does socially prohibited behavior occur—and persist, despite society's efforts to eliminate or discourage it? How can we make sense of deviance? Sociologists approach these questions from a number of different theoretical perspectives. Part 2 presents readings by major theorists representing the most important of these perspectives. The introduction to the section furnishes students with the theoretical framework upon which to build an understanding and an appreciation of these key thinkers.

Part 3 follows the *career* of the social deviant: it traces the steps by which he or she becomes identified by society as a deviant. It depicts, for example, how a relative attempts to cope with increasingly bizarre or violent behavior of a family member. Frequently, attempts to manage or control the deviant at home fail, and the family turns to institutions and agencies of social control for help.

Once deviants have been institutionalized, their career is determined, to a great extent, by their experiences within the institution. Part 4 explores the workings of several people-processing and people-changing facilities—ranging from the courts to the mental hospital—to examine how such structures deal with clients and how clients, in turn, may adapt their behavior and their personal identity to their surroundings.

For certain types of deviance, institutional controls are far less significant than the traditions and norms of deviant subcultures. Part 5 examines the ways in which such structures shape the career of the male prostitute, the drug dealer, the house prostitute, and others.

Part 6 analyzes the processes by which deviant categories, actors, and structures can be altered or transformed. The first two selections offer contemporary accounts of how selected deviant conceptions and categories have undergone significant changes. Clearly, if the underlying content of the prevailing images changes, then so, too, must the picture of deviance change. Thus activities that may have been seen as "deviant" at one time may now be perceived as "acceptable" or even "normal" by various audiences. Adler and Adler's research on "tinydopers" (i.e., marijuana-smoking children under nine years old) offers an excellent illustration of this process. The next two readings describe various personal and institutional barriers that confront those who desire to move from a deviant to a nondeviant status—in particular, society's reluctance to accept as "normal" anyone who has borne the stigma of deviance. The remaining two pieces outline specific ways in which deviant organizations, decision makers, and structures could be controlled, sanctioned, or even rehabilitated.

Overall, then, this book explores the establishment and maintenance of deviant categories; the motivations behind deviant behavior; the identification as deviant of individuals and of particular segments of society, by formal and informal means; the effects of institutionalization upon the deviant; and the efforts of deviants to eradicate the label society has placed upon them. Analysis is also given to the ways in which deviant categories and structures can be altered.

I would like to thank many people for their help in preparing the fourth edition of this book, particularly my editors, Louise Waller and Huntley McNair Funsten. Decisions about adding and deleting material from edition to edition are always made with apprehension. It is difficult to presume to make the right choices for both the people you hope will give your book a fresh examination, and the people who have been loyal and contented users of previous editions. Suggestions from the following individuals helped make my deliberations considerably easier: Thomas F. Arcaro, Elon College; Stephen T. Cassano, Manchester Community College; Susan Caulfield, SUNY-Albany; Virginia Cranston, Stockton State College; Donna K. Darden, University of Arkansas; John D. Delamater, University of Wisconsin; Richard K. Edwards, Northeastern University; Jonathan Freedman, Syracuse University; Doris B. Griscom, Eastern Connecticut State University; Charles Hanna, Duquesne University; Darnell F. Hawkins, University of Illinois, Chicago; John Heeren, California State University, San Bernadino; Trudy K. Henson, University of South Carolina, Aiken; Penelope Honke, Auburn University; Christopher Hunter, Grinnell College; Gary Jaworski, Fairleigh Dickinson; John M. Johnson, Arizona State University; Maureen Kelleher, Northeastern University; Deborah K. King, Dartmouth College; Marianna King, California State University, Los Angeles; Matthew C. Leone, University of California, Irvine; Richard F. Lowy, University of California, Riverside; Patrick T. Macdonald, University of California, Davis; Lyn Markham, SUNY-Albany; H. Gilman McCann, University of Vermont; Ron Miller, Chadron State College; Andre Modigliani, University of Michigan; Eugene Obidinski, SUNY College-Oneonta; Richard O'Toole, Kent State University Main Campus; Warren R. Paap, California State College, Bakersfield; Eugenia Patru, Our Lady of Holy Cross College; Thomas A. Petee, Auburn University; Henry Pontell, University of California, Irvine;

Susan P. Robbins, University of Houston; F. Burke Rochford, Middlebury College; Ruth Seydlitz, University of New Orleans; Thomas Shey, California State University-Los Angeles; Joseph Sheley, Tulane University; Beverly Smirni, Empire State College; J. William Spencer, Purdue University; Robert E. Stanfield, University of Vermont; M. F. Stuck, SUNY College-Oswego; John R. Sutton, Princeton University; Carol Anne Warren, University of Kansas; Martin S. Weinberg, Indiana University; Thomas S. Weinberg, SUNY College-Buffalo; Rose Weitz, Arizona State University; Ron Weitzer, University of Puget Sound; and J. D. Wemhaner, Tulsa Junior College.

Delos H. Kelly

Contents

General Introduction 1

Part 1 / Creating Deviance 11

Introduction
Conceptions, Images, and Entrepreneurs

1 / Conceptions of Deviant Behavior: The Old and the New,
JACK P. GIBBS 15

2 / Moral Entrepreneurs: The Creation and Enforcement of Deviant Categories,
HOWARD S. BECKER 21

Deviant Categories and Actors

3 / The Legislation of Morality: Creating Drug Laws,
TROY DUSTER 29

4 / The Discovery of Hyperkinesis: Notes on the Medicalization of Deviant Behavior,
PETER CONRAD 40

Part 2 / Understanding Deviance: Theories and Perspectives 51

Introduction
The Functionalist Perspective

5 / The Normal and the Pathological,
EMILE DURKHEIM 61

6 / On the Sociology of Deviance,
KAI T. ERIKSON 66

The Culture Conflict Perspective

7 / The Conflict of Conduct Norms,
THORSTEN SELLIN 74

8 / Outlaw Motorcyclists:
An Outgrowth of Lower Class Cultural Concerns,
J. MARK WATSON 79

Cultural Transmission Theory

9 / Techniques of Neutralization:
A Theory of Delinquency,
GRESHAM M. SYKES AND DAVID MATZA 93

10 / Convicted Rapists' Vocabulary of Motive:
Excuses and Justifications,
DIANA SCULLY AND JOSEPH MAROLLA 99

Anomie or Opportunity Theory

11 / Social Structure and Anomie,
ROBERT K. MERTON 119

12 / Differential Opportunity
and Delinquent Subcultures,
RICHARD A. CLOWARD
AND LLOYD E. OHLIN 130

Radical-Conflict Theory

13 / A Radical Perspective on Crime,
JEFFREY H. REIMAN 141

14 / A Sociological Analysis
of the Law of Vagrancy,
WILLIAM J. CHAMBLISS 151

Control Theory

15 / A Control Theory of Delinquency,
TRAVIS HIRSCHI 164

16 / The Socially Bounded Decision Making
of Persistent Property Offenders,
NEAL SHOVER AND DAVID HONAKER 173

*The Interactionist, Societal Reactions,
or Labeling Perspective*

17 / Primary and Secondary Deviation,
EDWIN M. LEMERT 192

18 / Career Deviance,
HOWARD S. BECKER 197

Part 3 / Becoming Deviant 201

Introduction

19 / In the Closet with Illness: Epilepsy, Stigma Potential and Information Control, JOSEPH W. SCHNEIDER AND PETER CONRAD *205*

20 / Living with the Stigma of AIDS, ROSE WEITZ *222*

21 / The Adjustment of the Family to the Crisis of Alcoholism, JOAN K. JACKSON *237*

22 / How Women Experience Battering: The Process of Victimization, KATHLEEN J. FERRARO AND JOHN M. JOHNSON *256*

Part 4 / Institutional Deviance 273

Introduction

Typing by Agents of Social Control

23 / The Societal Reaction to Deviance: Ascriptive Elements in the Psychiatric Screening of Mental Patients in a Midwestern State, THOMAS J. SCHEFF AND DANIEL M. CULVER *281*

24 / Normal Rubbish: Deviant Patients in Casualty Departments, ROGER JEFFERY *297*

Social-Control Agents and the Amplification of Deviance

25 / Ironies of Social Control: Authorities as Contributors to Deviance through Escalation, Nonenforcement, and Covert Facilitation, GARY T. MARX *313*

26 / The Social Context of Police Lying, JENNIFER HUNT AND PETER K. MANNING *333*

Sanctioning and Treatment

27 / Accounts, Attitudes, and Solutions: Probation Officer–Defendant Negotiations of Subjective Orientations,
JACK W. SPENCER *351*

28 / Court Responses to Skid Row Alcoholics,
JACQUELINE P. WISEMAN *368*

Effects of Institutional Processing

29 / The Moral Career of the Mental Patient,
ERVING GOFFMAN *377*

30 / Illness Career Descent in Institutions for the Elderly,
BRADLEY J. FISHER *395*

Part 5 / Noninstitutional Deviance 407

Introduction

Structures and Organizational Components

31 / The Social Organization of Deviants,
JOEL BEST AND DAVID F. LUCKENBILL *415*

32 / Deviant Career Mobility: The Case of Male Prostitutes,
DAVID F. LUCKENBILL *433*

Entering and Learning Deviant Cultures

33 / Drifting into Dealing: Becoming a Cocaine Seller,
SHEIGLA MURPHY, DAN WALDORF, AND CRAIG REINARMAN *451*

34 / The Madam as Teacher: The Training of House Prostitutes,
BARBARA SHERMAN HEYL *473*

Patterns and Variations

35 / State-Organized Crime,
WILLIAM J. CHAMBLISS *487*

36 / Corporations, Organized Crime, and the Disposal of Hazardous Waste: An Examination of the Making of a Criminogenic Regulatory Structure,
ANDREW SZASZ 507

The Effects of Deviant Careers

37 / Handling the Stigma of Handling the Dead: Morticians and Funeral Directors,
WILLIAM E. THOMPSON 524

38 / Good People Doing Dirty Work: A Study of Social Isolation,
DAVID S. DAVIS 545

Part 6 / Changing Deviance 561

Introduction
Deviant Conceptions and Categories

39 / Reform the Law: Decriminalization,
SAMUEL WALKER 569

40 / Tinydopers: A Case Study of Deviant Socialization,
PATRICIA A. ADLER AND PETER ADLER 580

Deviant Actors

41 / The Identity Change Process: A Field Study of Obesity,
DOUGLAS DEGHER AND GERALD HUGHES 597

42 / Suspended Identity: Identity Transformation in a Maximum Security Prison,
THOMAS J. SCHMID AND RICHARD S. JONES 610

Deviant Organizations, Decision Makers, and Structures

43 / The Impact of Publicity on Corporate Offenders: The Ford Motor Company and the Pinto Papers,
BRENT FISSE AND JOHN BRAITHWAITE 627

44 / Rehabilitating Social Systems and Institutions,
DELOS H. KELLY 641

Deviant Behavior

A TEXT-READER IN THE SOCIOLOGY OF DEVIANCE

FOURTH EDITION

General Introduction

We all carry in our minds images of deviance and the deviant. To some, deviants are murderers and rapists. Others would include in the list prostitutes, child molesters, wife beaters, and homosexuals. With regard to the motivations behind deviant behavior, some of us would place the blame on the family, while others would emphasize genetic or social factors, especially poverty.

CREATING DEVIANCE

Regardless of what kinds of behavior we consider deviant or what factors we believe cause deviance, we must recognize that deviance *and* the deviant emerge out of a continuous process of interaction among people. For deviance to become a public fact, however, several conditions need to be satisfied: (1) some deviant category (e.g., mores and laws) must exist; (2) a person must be viewed as violating the category; and (3) someone must attempt to enforce this violation of the category. If the individuals demanding enforcement are successful in their efforts to label the violator, the social deviant has been created.

The Creation of Deviant Categories

As far as deviant categories are concerned, relatively little attention has been focused on their evolution. Formal and informal codes of conduct are generally accepted as "givens," and investigators concentrate on the examination of *why* the categories are violated and *how* they are enforced. An approach of this kind is inadequate, however, particularly in view of the fact that new categories are continually evolving and old ones are being modified. Obviously, as the definitions or categories of deviance change, the picture of deviance must also be altered. The changing content of the laws governing cocaine provides an example. If there are no penalties for possessing and using cocaine, one cannot be formally charged and processed for doing so.

In studying deviance, then, a central question needs to be raised: How (and why) do *acts* become defined as deviant?[1] Providing answers to this question requires an examination of how deviance is defined, how the definitions are maintained, and how violators of the definitions are processed and treated. This entails a historical and ongoing analysis of those legislative and political processes that affect the evolution, modification, and enforcement of deviant categories. Central focus must be placed on those who possess the power and resources not only to define deviance but also to apply a label of deviance to a violator and to make the label stick. These processes are highlighted in Part 1 and will be evident in the discussion of the "conflict model" in Part 2.

Reactions to Violators of Deviant Categories

In terms of the *actor*, an equally important question can be asked: How (and why) do violators of various types of deviant categories (mores, laws, and regulations) become labeled as deviant? Answering this question requires an examination of the interaction occurring between an *actor* and an *audience*. A simple paradigm (Figure 1) can illustrate how the deviant is reacted to and thus socially created. This paradigm can be applied to most of the selections in this volume.

The Interactional Paradigm: A young man (the social *actor*) is seen selling or snorting cocaine (the *act*, a violation of a deviant category) by a police officer (a social *audience*, an enforcer of the deviant category) and is arrested. The youth's deviation thus becomes a matter of public record, and a deviant career is initiated—a career that may be solidified and perpetuated by legal and institutional processing. Another officer, however, might ignore the offense. In the first case, then, the violator is initially labeled as a "deviant," whereas in the second he is not. Figure 1 indicates that audience response not only is critical, but depends on several factors. The example also helps to underscore the fact that there is nothing inherently deviant about any act or actor—their meanings are derived from the interpretations *others* place on them. Hence the notion is put forth that "deviance lies in the eyes of the beholder." This example can be extended by considering the fourth element of the paradigm: *third parties*, or witnesses. Specifically, a young man may be observed selling or snorting cocaine by a peer, and the peer may choose to ignore the offense. Another peer, however, may not only

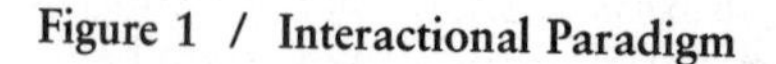

Figure 1 / Interactional Paradigm

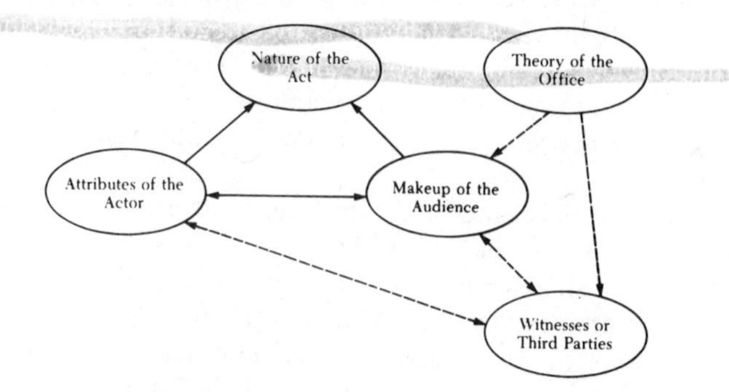

consider the act illegal or deviant but may decide to do something about it. The peer lacks the power to arrest; he can, however, bring in third parties in an effort to create a shared attitude toward the cocaine user—namely, that is he a "criminal" or "deviant." The peer may turn to other peers, and they may decide to call the police and have the user arrested. If this happens, the person's "deviance" becomes a public fact.

Thus, the label "deviant" is a status conferred on a person by an observer or observers. Although an understanding of this process requires an examination of the way the four basic elements of the paradigm interact with one another, such an examination is not sufficient. An awareness of the *theory of the office* that a particular agent or audience operates out of is also necessary, especially if the occupant of the office is an agent of social control. The preceding example, as well as the "organizational paradigm" highlighted in Figure 2, can be used to illustrate this requirement. This paradigm represents a refinement of the "interactional paradigm" described in Figure 1. Here I am focusing on the audience, particularly in terms of how an institution expects certain outcomes on the part of its agents. This paradigm will be generally applied throughout this volume.

The Organizational Paradigm: Although it might be assumed that the police officer in our examples operates on the basis of his or her own initiative, this is frequently far from the truth. The officer, like any institutional or bureaucratic agent concerned with the processing (through the courts) or rehabilitating (in correctional facilities) of clients, is guided and generally constrained by a theory of the office, or "working ideology." The officer, through informal (contacts with other officers) and formal (police academies) socialization experiences, learns how to identify and classify deviants or suspected deviants. These institutional, or "diagnostic," stereotypes (Scheff, 1966) constitute a basic ingredient of a department's official perspective. The officer, for example, learns how to recognize the "typical"

Figure 2 / Organizational Paradigm

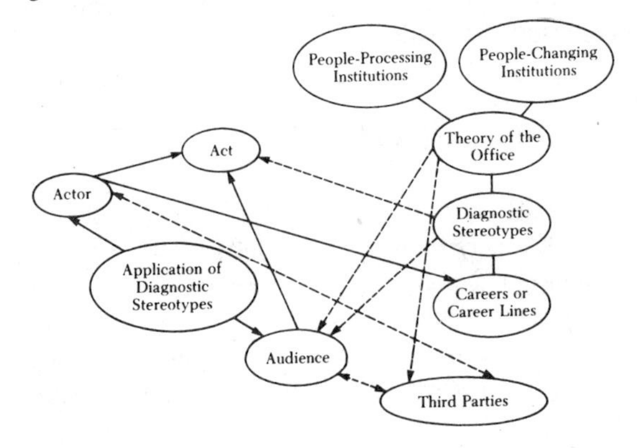

case of child molestation, runaway, or rape. These "normal crimes" (Sudnow, 1965), or "social type designations," not only help the officer make sense out of events; they also provide criteria upon which a suspect can be initially identified, classified, and then selected out to play the role of the deviant.

An institution's stereotypes are basic to the *rate production process*—the creation of a body of institutional statistics. If, for example, a police chief feels that homosexual behavior is morally wrong or criminal, not only will this one individual's conception become embedded within the theory of the office, but the officers will be required to zero in on such activity. This response will produce a set of crime statistics exhibiting an unusually high arrest rate for homosexual exchanges. Similarly, if a police chief formally or informally communicates to his department personnel that African-Americans, Hispanics, Native Americans, and other minorities constitute the "real" deviants, delinquents, and criminals, such people will be disproportionately selected out to play the role of the deviant—that is, they will become more vulnerable to institutional processing. This, too, will produce a set of statistics reflecting a heavy concentration of these individuals. The statistics can, in turn, serve as justification for heavy and continued surveillance in areas containing such groups. Examples of this phenomenon abound.

If we are to approach an understanding of what causes deviance, and particularly of the ways in which institutional careers arise and are perpetuated, then we need initially to analyze and dissect the existing structure of the institutions of social control. To obtain an understanding of how institutions operate requires, as suggested by Figure 2, sensitization to several basic organizational elements and processes: (1) the institution's theory of the office, (2) the content of the institutional stereotypes embedded within the theory of the office and used to identify clients for typing and processing, (3) the existing careers or career lines (and associated role expectations) into which the identified clients are placed, (4) the socialization of institutional agents and their application of diagnostic stereotypes to clients, and (5) the effects of institutional typing and processing, from the perspectives of both the client and the institution.

UNDERSTANDING DEVIANCE

In the discussion of the creation of deviance it was argued that some deviant category must exist, a person must be viewed as violating the category, and someone must make a demand for enforcement. Thus far, too, the focus has been upon the evolution and change of deviant categories, as well as on the interactional aspects—how and why violators of categories may be reacted to. Missing from this analysis, however, is a concern for the motivational aspects—the reasons why people may violate deviant categories. This concern has been generally ignored by the labeling or interactionist proponents. Their main interest revolves around examining audience reactions and the impact of those reactions on people. Implicit in such a stand is the idea that the reasons for behavior are relatively unimportant. If, however, we are to approach a more complete understanding of deviance from a dynamic perspective, attention must also be given to motivation. Such a view provides us with an opportunity continually to analyze how behavior and labels interact with each other.

Violations of Deviant Categories

Traditionally, writers have concentrated on trying to explain why people may violate various types of deviant categories. Some have spent their time trying to explain group or structural rates of deviance, and others have concentrated on those processes by which individuals learn culture and traditions. These efforts have produced many schools of thought, each with its own set of assumptions. The "anomie" theorists, for example, argue that blocked opportunity can produce a tendency or strain toward deviation. The "conflict" theorists, by contrast, contend that the powerless may consciously violate the laws formulated by the powerful. Understanding deviance, then, requires that we investigate those reasons why people may violate deviant categories and by their violations bring upon themselves a particular labeling. The selections in Part 2 offer some representative attempts to explore this question.

BECOMING DEVIANT

With regard to the process of becoming deviant, an initial distinction can be made between *private* and *public* settings. A husband may violate a particular set of expectations by acting strangely. The wife may try to make sense out of such behavior by rationalizing it away or neutralizing it. She may argue to herself and others that her husband has experienced some personal setbacks and that the peculiar behavior will pass. At this stage the wife is trying to develop a counterdefinition of the situation, and she is also refusing to impute a deviant label to her spouse. The husband's behavior may grow increasingly violent, though, to the point where the wife finds it necessary to bring in agents of social control. She may call the police (third parties) or ultimately have her husband committed to a mental institution. If this should happen, not only have the wife's tolerance limits been exceeded but her attempts at various strategies of *accommodation* (e.g., neutralization or rationalization) have failed. The husband may then be typed as, for example, a schizophrenic and processed in accordance with the establishment's expectations of what the schizophrenic career should entail. The patient is expected, thereafter, to live up to his institutional role—to accept the label and act accordingly. The case of McMurphy in *One Flew Over the Cuckoo's Nest* (Kesey, 1962) describes what may happen when a patient protests against his assigned label. Because McMurphy rejects the "sick role," he becomes embroiled in a running battle with Big Nurse, the institution's agent. In our example, a similar situation may evolve with respect to the husband's response: he may repudiate the institutional tag, he may try to ignore it, or he may accept it. His response, like the responses of observers, is frequently difficult to predict.

In private settings, attempts may be made to regulate and control behavior, and these efforts may be successful. However, once third parties or social-control agents (e.g., the police or psychiatrists) are called in, the individual is frequently on his or her way to becoming an institutional deviant—that is, the organizational paradigm becomes operative, not only from the institution's viewpoint but from the actor's perspective. In particular, if a mental institution is involved, the client becomes viewed as a "mental patient"; this label becomes the patient's *master status* (Becker, 1963), and people will then often react to the person on the basis of the label rather than regarding him or her as sane or "normal." The changing of one's status, or the *status degradation ceremony* (Garfinkel, 1956), also affects the views others have of the "deviant" (one's public identity), as well as how the actor views himself or herself (one's personal identity). The change frequently affects the person's self-esteem (how one views self, positively or negatively, relative to others on selected criteria).

INSTITUTIONAL AND NONINSTITUTIONAL CAREERS

An important distinction should be made between *institutional* and *noninstitutional* careers. A noninstitutional career is one that a person pursues primarily as a matter of choice. The individual takes an active role in structuring and presenting a specific image of self to others. The bookie, gambler, con artist, nudist, skid row alcoholic, and homosexual provide examples. Such individuals generally progress through some semblance of a career: once they gain entry or exposure, they begin to learn the existing culture and traditions. The bookie, for instance, may start out as a runner, "learn the ropes," and then move into other phases of the bookmaking operation. Similarly, the skid row alcoholic who wants to become an accepted member of the "bottle-gang culture" will become familiar with the norms prevalent among the skid row inhabitants, particularly norms that relate to the procurement and consumption of alcohol. Violations of the normative code frequently cause a person to be excluded from the group (Rubington,

1973). As with the sanctioning of "deviants" by "nondeviants," the "labeled deviants" have ways of punishing those who deviate from their own code.

Institutional careers, by contrast, involve those in which the individual plays a relatively passive role. Here, the career is initiated and perpetuated by some socializing or social-control institution; this process was briefly noted in the discussion of how one becomes deviant. The careers of the "school misfit," mental patient, delinquent, and criminal are of this type. The major difference between institutional careers and noninstitutional careers concerns the role of the actor, particularly in the matter of choice and in the means of gaining entry. Once the institutional career begins, though, the mental patient, like the skid row alcoholic, is expected to learn and act in accordance with the existing subculture and its traditions.

Institutional and noninstitutional careers are not mutually exclusive. Frequently, a degree of overlap exists between the two. The skid row alcoholic, for example, may be arrested and sent to an alcoholic ward, where his or her behavior becomes subject to institutional or bureaucratic control. Similarly, the prostitute may be arrested and taken to jail. In both instances the activities become a matter of institutional knowledge and record. A secret homosexual, by contrast, may never directly experience the effects of institutional processing.

The Effects of Institutional and Noninstitutional Careers

The distinction between institutional and noninstitutional careers provides a backdrop against which a person's reactions can be assessed. How, for example, is a person likely to respond to institutional typing and processing as a deviant? Will he or she reject or accept the institutional label? Answering these questions requires a consideration of how the "status degradation ceremony" affects an actor's personal and public identity. If the deviant rejects the label, a discrepancy (or *identity crisis*) occurs between one's personal and public identities—that is, between one's view of self as normal and the institution's view of one as a deviant. Obviously, unless some personal gain can be realized, such as the enhancement of one's prestige or status in the eyes of others, most persons will reject a deviant label imputed to them. Maintaining an image of self that is at odds with the institution's image is not without its costs, though, and eventually the individual may come to accept the label and bring his or her behavior into line with institutional expectations. Lemert (1951) argues that *acceptance of the label* is a critical step on the way to secondary or *career* deviance. Not only do some individuals change their view of self—for instance, from that of "normal" to that of "schizophrenic"—but they often change their mode of dress, mannerisms, and circle of acquaintances. Acceptance of the label, it should be noted, is an important precondition to being certified as "sane" or "rehabilitated" by institutions.

Involvement in noninstitutional careers or activities affects both the participants and other members of society. The covert gay or lesbian teacher, for example, engages in sexual activity that some would consider deviant, and a discrepancy may evolve between her personal and public identities. Privately she may view herself as gay and a normal female, but publicly she is viewed and responded to as a heterosexual teacher. As with the institutional deviant, however, an identity crisis may arise. She may decide to "come out" and admit her sexual preference to others. Such a strategy is not without its costs. She may be ostracized by her family, friends, and acquaintances; and, more than likely, she will be either discriminated against on her job or fired. In view of these possibilities, she may decide to keep her sexual preference hidden and perhaps become involved in a gay subculture. Such involvement can provide her with a degree of social support, as well as appropriate rationalizations to legitimize her way of life. Still, she (and other noninstitutional deviants) is aware not only that she is engaging in potentially discrediting behavior but also that she must operate in a society in which many hostile elements remain.

CHANGING DEVIANCE

Identity problems do not cease when one leaves an institution or decides to "go straight." Public or known ex-deviants, whether of the institutional or noninstitutional variety, continue to be viewed as deviants. What Simmons (1969) calls a "lingering of traces" quite frequently occurs, especially among those who carry an institutionally bestowed label. Institutions, it has been pointed out, are most efficient in assigning deviant labels; they are notoriously inefficient when it comes to removing labels and their associated stigma (Goffman, 1963). Former deviants must continue to bear the brunt of the label—with the result that their behavioral patterns are much less likely to change.

The probability of rehabilitating someone who does not view his or her activity or career as deviant is poor. Many noninstitutional deviants—such as prostitutes, gamblers, and homosexuals—feel little need to "repent"; they believe that the pressures they face and the difficulties they experience result from the intolerance of society. In fact, many of these individuals feel strongly that it is society that should be rehabilitated. On the other hand, some noninstitutional deviants—as well as some institutional deviants, such as mental patients, criminals, and delinquents—may try to transform their "deviant" identity. If they do, they can expect to encounter certain barriers. Job applications, for example, frequently require prospective employees to list any arrests, convictions, or periods of institutionalization—circumstances that bar entry into many occupations. Such roadblocks can produce feelings of frustration and inferiority. What many ex-deviants soon realize is that even if they change, they will still be effectively discriminated against because of past activities or involvement with stigmatizing institutions. They also learn very quickly that the social and political establishment is virtually unchanging—that the burden of change falls upon *them.*

SUMMARY AND ORGANIZATION OF THIS VOLUME

This book explores the subject of deviance in a number of ways—by focusing in turn on society, on the individual, and on institutions of control and rehabilitation. Part 1 describes how deviant categories evolve and how people who violate these categories become defined as social deviants. Part 2 analyzes why people may elect to violate deviant categories—violations that can initiate the defining or labeling process. Part 3 deals with the deviant career, particularly as it arises in private, noninstitutional settings. Part 4 describes how careers may become initiated and perpetuated by institutions, while Part 5 examines the rise and furtherance of noninstitutional careers. Finally, Part 6 discusses how conceptions, careers, and organizational structures may be altered. Throughout, a major focus is on the impact that involvement in institutional as well as noninstitutional activities and careers has upon actors, audiences, and third parties.

Note

1. For an excellent discussion of questions such as these, see particularly Ronald L. Akers, "Problems in the Sociology of Deviance: Social Definitions and Behavior." *Social Forces*, 46 (June 1968), 455–465.

References

Becker, Howard S. *Outsiders: Studies in the Sociology of Deviance.* New York: Free Press, 1963.

Garfinkel, Harold. "Conditions of Successful Degradation Ceremonies." *American Journal of Sociology*, 61 (March 1956), 420–424.

Goffman, Erving. *Stigma: Notes on the Management of Spoiled Identity.* Englewood Cliffs, N.J.: Prentice-Hall, 1963.

—— The Moral Career of the Mental Patient," *Psychiatry*, 22 (1959), 123–142.

Kesey, Ken. *One Flew Over the Cuckoo's Nest.* New York: Viking, 1962.

Lemert, Edwin. *Social Pathology*. New York: McGraw-Hill, 1951.

Rubington, Earl. "Variations in Bottle-Gang Controls." In Earl Rubington and Martin S. Weinberg, eds., *Deviance: The Interactionist Perspective.* New York: Macmillan, 1973.

Scheff, Thomas J. "Typification in the Diagnostic Practices of Rehabilitation Agencies." In Marvin B. Sussman, ed., *Sociology and Rehabilitation.* Washington, D.C.: American Sociological Association, 1966.

Simmons, J. L. *Deviants.* Berkeley: Glendessary, 1969.

Sudnow, David. "Normal Crimes: Sociological Features of the Penal Code," *Social Problems*, 12 (Winter 1965), 255–270.

Part 1 / Creating Deviance

As noted in the general introduction, approaching an understanding of deviance requires an examination of several interrelated factors. An initial concern involves the way in which the subject matter is to be approached, viewed, and subsequently defined. Does the theorist or researcher, for example, conceptualize and define deviance and the deviant in individual terms, or does he or she invoke some type of structural view? Similarly, is there something inherently deviant about certain acts or actors, or do their meanings derive from the interpretations and reactions of others? If the latter, then not only should the student of deviance be aware that a specific image is being advanced (i.e., the notion that deviance and the deviants are social constructs), but he or she must also recognize the need to examine the evolution of deviant categories and the ways in which violators of the categories may be perceived and responded to. As noted earlier, for deviance to become a social fact, a person must be viewed as violating some deviant category and thereafter be labeled as deviant by a social observer.

The initial two selections in this part introduce, in a general way, the major conceptual and definitional issues in the field of deviance. Some important tools are also introduced. The selections that follow offer illustrations of how the concepts are utilized. In addition, more systematic attention is given to the basic processes involved in the construction of the social deviant: (1) the creation of deviant categories and (2) the reactions to violators of deviant categories.

CONCEPTIONS, IMAGES, AND ENTREPRENEURS

The idea that deviant categories can be viewed as social constructs represents a particular image of deviance. Such a view also suggests the possibility of competing conceptions. Jack P. Gibbs, in "Conceptions of Deviant Behavior: The Old and the New," acknowledges these points but stresses that the prevailing conceptions continue to dominate. How one comes to "think about" a specific phenomenon influences the definitions that are developed, as well as the theory or explanation that may result. For example, in the area of deviance, do we locate pathological or deviant-producing stimuli within the actor or do we look elsewhere, perhaps to society in general? Gibbs maintains that the former viewpoint is favored in the fields of crime and deviance. Historically, the dominant conception has been one of individual pathology. Gibbs then proceeds to compare what he terms the "older conceptions" (e.g., the idea that deviants or criminals possess some *internal* trait that distinguishes them from nondeviants) with the "new conception" (i.e., the view that the essential characteristic of a deviant or deviant act is *external* to the actor and the act). This new perspective emphasizes the *character of the reaction* that a specific act or actor may elicit. If the responses are of a certain kind, deviance comes into being. Gibbs then offers several criticisms of the new conception. Is, for example, this perspective intended to be a substantive theory of deviant behavior, or is it primarily a definitional/conceptual treatment of it? Even if the perspective is viewed as an explanatory framework, Gibbs maintains that several questions have not been answered adequately. "Why," for example, "is the act in question considered deviant and/or criminal in some societies but not in others?"

The Gibbs piece sensitizes one to the fact that the underlying images and conceptions of deviance have changed, and it also helps to highlight the manner in which social observers—either individually or collectively—ascribe meaning to the actions of others. Thus, deviance is very much a product of initiative on the part of observers. Logically, then, the reactors and decision makers must become the object of direct study. What, for example, can we say about the content of their conceptions and belief systems? The selection by Howard S. Becker, "Moral Entrepreneurs: The Creation and Enforcement of Deviant Categories," adds some refinements to these issues. Becker also provides an excellent general overview of how deviant categories, particularly rules, evolve. Central to his analysis is the role of *moral entrepreneurs*, whom he categorizes into *rule creators* and *rule enforcers*. Rule creators are individuals who see some "evil" in society and feel that the evil can be corrected only by legislating against it. Frequently their efforts result in the passage of a new law—that is, the creation of a new deviant category. Becker offers several interesting examples that describe this legislative-political phenomenon. He argues that a successful crusade will not only result in "the creation of a new set of rules" but will often give rise to "a new set of enforcement agencies and officials." It becomes the function of these officials to enforce the new rules. Becker concludes his analysis by offering several comments relating to rule enforcers. He contends, for example, that enforcers are concerned primarily with enforcing the law and not its contents; they are also interested in justifying their own position in the organization, as well as in gaining respect from their clients. Many of these same phenomena can be observed in several other selections, especially those that deal with institutional incarceration and deviance.

DEVIANT CATEGORIES AND ACTORS

Quite clearly, in cases where the moral entrepreneurs and their crusades succeed, society is often confronted with a new deviant category and a corresponding enforcement or social-control apparatus. Becker's general discussion of the dynamics behind the passage of various laws (e.g., the Eighteenth Amendment and sexual psychopath laws) offers illustrations of this. Troy Duster, in "The Legislation of Morality: Creating Drug Laws," presents a more detailed account of how specific laws, or deviant categories, were created. His focus is primarily on the Harrison Narcotics Act of 1914.

Duster argues initially that there is often an intertwining between law and morality. He then proceeds to document his case. He begins by noting that, even though the public has been concerned primarily with LSD and marijuana, it is the drug opium that has dominated our conception of narcotics. Morphine, an opium-based pain reliever, was widely used during the Civil War, and for some years afterward, and there were no state or federal laws regulating the sale and distribution of the drug. Pharmacists sold it at will. Duster estimates that 3 percent of the population was probably addicted to morphine around the turn of the century; this began to produce alarm among members of the medical profession. During this period, heroin, a morphine derivative, was also produced. Unlike morphine, heroin was at first thought to be nonaddictive. It was not until five years after it was discovered in 1898 that serious warnings about heroin's addictive features appeared in an American medical journal. However, the warnings spread slowly, and heroin, like morphine, became very popular. In fact, Duster states that, during the period from 1865 to 1900, addiction was probably eight times greater than it is today. If he is correct, then why is addiction today viewed as being of far greater moral, legal, and social significance?

Duster hypothesizes that the major factor accounting for the differing conceptions of addiction has been the dramatic shift of addicts from one social category to another. Although most people today believe that addiction is mainly a lower-class problem, this has not always been the case. In fact, up until 1914, the middle and upper classes had the largest numbers of addicts. As Duster's quotes from medical journals show, lower-class addicts were regarded as mental and moral defectives, while upper-class addicts were equated with ministers, judges, and senators. A similar shift occurred with respect to age (i.e., from predominantly middle-aged to the young) and sex (i.e., from predominantly female to male). Associated with these shifts and changing moral interpretations were attempts, primarily by doctors, to have laws passed that would regulate the manufacture and distribution of narcotics. Many states did pass individual laws. On the national level, Congress ratified the Harrison Narcotics Act in 1914.

Peter Conrad, in "The Discovery of Hyperkinesis: Notes on the Medicalization of Deviant Behavior," provides another historical account of how conceptions of behavior can change. His initial comments are given to the ways in which selected forms of behavior (e.g., alcoholism and drug addiction) become defined as a medical problem or illness and how, thereafter, the medical profession is mandated or licensed to provide the appropriate treatment. Conrad's focus is given to hyperkinesis, particularly its discovery. In his analysis, he describes the various *clinical* (e.g., the effects of amphetamine drugs on children's behavior) and *social* (e.g., the pharmaceutical revolution and associated government action) factors that gave rise to the creation of this new medical diagnostic category. He then moves to a discussion of how deviant behavior on the part of children became conceptualized as a medical problem, as well as why this happened. Conrad concludes with a discussion of some of the important implications that flow from the medicalization of deviant behavior. For example, the medical profession "has not only a monopoly on anything that can be conceptualized as illness," but also the power to define deviant behavior as a medical problem, so that certain procedures can be done that otherwise would not be allowed (e.g., cutting on the body). Moreover, society has a tendency to individualize social problems. Instead of looking to defects of social systems for causes and solutions, we look within the individuals or, instead of analyzing the social situation that affects a perceived difficult child, we prescribe a stimulant medication. Such a treatment strategy, Conrad asserts, deflects our attention away from the real possibility that the family or classroom situation may be the problem. This tendency to characterize problems in individual, clinical, or medical terms, will be given additional attention in Part 6, especially those selections dealing with the rehabilitation of social structures.

The selections by Duster and Conrad illustrate how, as a result of changing perceptions, behavior may not only become increasingly defined as deviant but may also become criminalized or medicalized. When this occurs, we can speak of the creation of deviant, criminal, or medical categories. And once the categories are in place, we can begin to analyze how others react to the violators of the categories. Many of the selections in Part 4 and Part 5 offer specific illustrations of how actors may be responded to.

1 / Conceptions of Deviant Behavior: The Old and the New

JACK P. GIBBS

The ultimate end of substantive theory in any science is the formulation of empirical relations among classes of phenomena, e.g., X varies directly with Y, X is present if and only if Y is present. However, unless such propositions are arrived at by crude induction of sheer intuition, there is a crucial step before the formulation of a relational statement. This step can be described as the way the investigator comes to perceive or "think about" the phenomena under consideration. Another way to put it is the development of a "conception."

There is no clear-cut distinction between, on the one hand, a conception of a class of phenomena and, on the other, formal definitions and substantive theory. Since a conception emphasizes the predominant feature of a phenomenon, it is not entirely divorced from a definition of it; but the former is not identical with the latter. Thus, for example, the notion of exploitation looms large in the Marxian conception of relations among social classes; but exploitation is or may be only one feature of class relations, and it does not serve as a formal definition of them. Further, in certain fields, particularly the social sciences, a conception often not only precedes but also gives rise to operational definitions. As the case in point, if an operational definition of social class relies on the use of "reputational technique," the investigator's conception of social class is in all probability non-Marxian.

What has been said of the distinction between definitions and conceptions holds also for the relation between the latter and substantive theory. A conception may generate a particular theory, but it is not identical with it. For one thing, a conception contains definitional elements and is therefore partially tautological, which means that in itself a conception is never a clear-cut empirical proposition. Apart from its tautological character, a conception is too general to constitute a testable idea. Nonetheless, a conception may generate substantive theory, and it is certainly true that theories reflect conceptions. Durkheim's work is a classic illustration. His theory on suicide clearly reflects his view of society and social life generally.

In a field without consensus as to operational definitions and little in the way of systematic substantive theory, conceptions necessarily occupy a central position. This condition prevails in most of the social sciences. There, what purport to be definitions of classes of phenomena are typically general and inconsistent to the point of lacking empirical applicability (certainly in the operational sense of the word). Moreover, what passes for a substantive theory in the social sciences is more often than not actually a loosely formulated conception. These observations are not intended to deride the social sciences for lack of progress. All fields probably go through a "conceptions" stage; it is only more apparent in some than in others.

Of the social sciences, there is perhaps no better clear-cut illustration of the importance of conceptions than in the field identified as criminology and the study of deviant behavior. As we shall see, the history of the field can be described best in terms of changing conceptions of crime, criminals, deviants, and deviation. But the purpose of this paper is not an historical account of major trends in the field. If it is true that conceptions give rise to formal definitions and substantive theory, then a critical appraisal of conceptions is important in its own right. This is all the more true in the case of criminology and the study of deviant behavior, where conceptions are frequently confused with substantive theories, and the latter so clearly reflect the former.

OLDER CONCEPTIONS

In recent years there has been a significant change in the prevailing conception of deviant behavior and deviants. Prior to what is designated here as the "new perspective," it commonly was assumed that there is something inherent in deviants which distinguishes them from non-deviants.[1] Thus, from Lombroso to Sheldon, criminals were viewed as biologically distinctive in one way or another.[2] The inadequacies of this conception are now obvious. After decades of research, no biological characteristic which distinguishes criminals has been discovered, and this generalization applies even to particular types of criminals (e.g., murderers, bigamists, etc.). Consequently, few theorists now even toy with the notion that all criminals are atavistic, mentally defective, constitutionally inferior. But the rejection of the biological conception of crime stems from more than research findings. Even casual observation and mild logic cast doubt on the idea. Since legislators are not geneticists, it is difficult to see how they can pass laws in such a way as to create "born criminals." Equally important, since most if not all "normal" persons have violated a law at one time or another,[3] the assertion that criminals are so by heredity now appears most questionable.

Although the biological conception generally has been rejected, what is here designated as the analytic conception of criminal acts largely has escaped criticism. Rather than view criminal acts as nothing more or less than behavior contrary to legal norms, the acts are construed as somehow injurious to society. The shift from the biological to the analytical conception is thus from the actors to the characteristics of their acts, with the idea being that some acts are inherently "criminal" or at least that criminal acts share intrinsic characteristics in common.

The analytical conception is certainly more defensible than the biological view, but it is by no means free of criticism. Above all, the "injurious" quality of some deviant acts is by no means conspicuous, as witness Durkheim's observation:

> ...there are many acts which have been and still are regarded as criminal without in themselves being harmful to society. What social danger is there in touching a tabooed object, an impure animal or man, in letting the sacred fire die down, in eating certain meats, in failure to make the traditional sacrifice over the grave of parents, in not exactly pronouncing the ritual formula, in not celebrating holidays, etc.?[4]

Only a radical functionalism would interpret the acts noted by Durkheim as literally injuring society in any reasonable sense of the word. The crucial point is that, far from actually injuring society or sharing some intrinsic feature in common, acts may be criminal or deviant because and only because they are proscribed legally and/or socially. The proscription may be irrational in that members of the society cannot explain it, but it is real nonetheless. Similarly, a law may be "arbitrary" in that it is imposed by a powerful minority and, as a consequence, lacks popular support and is actively opposed. But if the law is consistently enforced (i.e., sanctions are imposed regularly on violators), it is difficult to see how it is not "real."

The fact that laws may appear to be irrational and arbitrary has prompted attempts to define crime independently of legal criteria, i.e., analytically. The first step in this direction was Garofalo's concept of natural crime—acts which violate prevailing sentiments of pity and probity.[5] Garofalo's endeavor accomplished very little. Just as there is probably no act which is contrary to law universally, it is equally true that no act violates sentiments of pity and probity in all societies. In other words, cultural relativity defeats any attempt to compile a list of acts which are crimes universally. Also, it is hard to see why the violation of a rigorously enforced traffic regulation is not a crime even though unrelated to sentiments of pity and probity. If it is not a crime, what is it?

The search for an analytic identification of crime continued in Sellin's proposal to abandon legal criteria altogether in preference for "conduct norms."[6] The rationale for the proposal is simple. Because laws vary and may be "arbitrary" in any one society, a purely legal definition of crime is not suited for scientific study. But Sellin's observations on the arbitrariness of laws apply in much the same way to conduct norms. Just as the content of criminal law varies from one society to the next and from time to time, so does the content of extra-legal norms. Further, the latter may be just as arbitrary as criminal laws. Even in a highly urbanized society such as the United States, there is evidently no rationale or utilitarian reason for all of the norms pertaining to mode of dress. True, there may be much greater conformity to conduct norms than to some laws, but the degree of conformity is hardly an adequate criterion of the "reality" of norms, legal or extra-legal. If any credence whatever can be placed in the Kinsey report, sexual taboos may be violated frequently and yet remain as taboos. As a case in point, even if adultery is now common in the United States, it is significant that the participants typically attempt to conceal their acts. In brief, just as laws may be violated frequently and are "unreal" in that sense, the same applies to some conduct norms; but in neither case do they cease to be norms. They would cease to be norms if and only if one defines deviation in terms of statistical regularities in behavior, but not even Sellin would subscribe to the notion that normative phenomena can or should be defined in statistical terms.

In summary, however capricious and irrational legal and extra-legal norms may appear to be, the inescapable conclusion is that some acts are criminal or deviant for the very simple reason that they are proscribed.

THE NEW CONCEPTION

Whereas both the pathological and the analytical conceptions of deviation assume that some intrinsic feature characterizes deviants and/or deviant acts, an emerging perspective in sociology flatly rejects any such assumption. Indeed, as witness the following statements by Kitsuse, Becker, and Erikson, exactly the opposite position is taken.

Kitsuse: Forms of behavior *per se* do not differentiate deviants from non-deviants; it is the responses of the conventional and conforming members of the society who identify and interpret behavior as defiant which sociologically transform persons into deviants.[7]

Erikson: From a sociological standpoint, deviance can be defined as conduct which is generally thought to require the attention of social control agencies—that is, conduct about which "something should be done." Deviance is not a property *inherent in* certain forms of behavior; it is a property *conferred upon* these forms by the audiences which directly or indirectly witness them. Sociologically, then, the critical variable in the study of deviance is the social *audience* rather than individual *person*, since it is the audience which eventually decides whether or not any given action or actions will become a visible case of deviation.[8]

Becker: From this point of view, deviance is *not* a quality of the act a person commits, but rather a consequence of the application by others of rules and sanctions to an "offender." The deviant is one to whom that label has successfully been applied; deviant behavior is behavior that people so label.[9]

The common assertion in the above statements is that acts can be identified as deviant or criminal only by reference to the character of reaction to them by the public or by the official agents of a politically organized society. Put simply, if the reaction is of a certain kind, then and only then is the act deviant. The crucial point is that the essential feature of a defiant or deviant act is *external* to the actor and the act. Further, even if the act or actors share some feature in common other than social reactions to them, the feature neither defines nor completely explains deviation. To take the extreme case, even if Lombroso had been correct in his assertion that criminals are biologically distinctive, the biological factor neither identifies the criminal nor explains criminality. Purely biological variables may explain why some persons commit certain acts, but they do not explain why the acts are crimes. Consequently, since criminal law is spatially and temporally relative, it is impossible to distinguish criminals from noncriminals (assuming that the latter do exist, which is questionable) in terms of biological characteristics. To illustrate, if act X is a crime in society A but not a crime in society B, it follows that, even assuming Lombroso to have been correct, the anatomical features which distinguish the criminal in society A may characterize the noncriminal in society B. In both societies some persons may be genetically predisposed to commit act X, but the act is a crime in one society and not in the other. Accordingly, the generalization that all persons with certain anatomical features are criminals would be, in this instance, false. True, one may assert that the "born criminal" is predisposed to violate the laws of his own society, but this assumes either that "the genes" know what the law is or that the members of the legislature are geneticists (i.e., they deliberately enact laws in such a way that the "born criminal" will violate them). Either assumption taxes credulity.

The new perspective of deviant behavior contradicts not only the biological but also the analytical conception. Whereas the latter seeks to find something intrinsic in deviant or, more specifically, criminal acts, the new conception denies any such characterization. True, the acts share a common denominator—they are identified by the character of reaction to them—but this does not mean that the acts are "injurious" to society or that they are in any way inherently abnormal. The new conception eschews the notion that some acts are deviant or criminal in all societies. For that matter, the reaction which identifies a deviant act may not be the same from one society or social group to the next. In general, then, the new conception of deviant behavior is relativistic in the extreme.

* * *

Notes

1. Throughout this paper crime is treated as a sub-class of deviant behavior. Particular issues may be discussed with reference to crime, but on the whole the observations apply to deviant behavior generally.
2. Although not essential to the argument, it is perhaps significant that the alleged biological differentiae of criminals have been consistently viewed as "pathological" in one sense or another.

3. See Edwin H. Sutherland and Donald R. Cressey, *Principles of Criminology*, 6th ed., Chicago: J.B. Lippincott, 1960, p. 39.
4. Emile Durkheim, *The Division of Labor in Society*, trans. George Simpson, Glencoe, Illinois: The Free Press, 1949, p. 72.
5. Raffaele Garofalo, *Criminology*, Boston: Little, Brown, & Co., 1914, Chapter I.
6. Thorsten Sellin, *Culture Conflict and Crime*, New York: Social Science Research Council, Bulletin 41, 1938.
7. John I. Kitsuse, "Societal Reaction to Deviant Behavior: Problems of Theory and Method," *Social Problems*, 9 (Winter, 1962), p. 253.
8. Kai T. Erikson, "Notes on the Sociology of Deviance," *Social Problems*, 9 (Spring, 1962), p. 308.
9. Howard S. Becker, *Outsiders*, New York: The Free Press of Glencoe, 1963, p. 9.

2 / Moral Entrepreneurs: The Creation and Enforcement of Deviant Categories

HOWARD S. BECKER

RULE CREATORS

The prototype of the rule creator, but not the only variety as we shall see, is the crusading reformer. He is interested in the content of rules. The existing rules do not satisfy him because there is some evil which profoundly disturbs him. He feels that nothing can be right in the world until rules are made to correct it. He operates with an absolute ethic; what he sees is truly and totally evil with no qualification. Any means is justified to do away with it. The crusader is fervent and righteous, often self-righteous.

It is appropriate to think of reformers as crusaders because they typically believe that their mission is a holy one. The prohibitionist serves as an excellent example, as does the person who wants to suppress vice and sexual delinquency or the person who wants to do away with gambling.

These examples suggest that the moral crusader is a meddling busybody, interested in forcing his own morals on others. But this is a one-sided view. Many moral crusades have strong humanitarian overtones. The crusader is not only interested in seeing to it that other people do what he thinks [is] right. He believes that if they do what is right it will be good for them. Or he may feel that his reform will prevent certain kinds of exploitation of one person by another. Prohibitionists felt that they were not simply forcing their morals on others, but attempting to provide the conditions for a better way of life for people prevented by drink from realizing a truly good life. Abolitionists were not simply trying to prevent slave owners from doing the wrong thing; they were trying to help slaves achieve a better life. Because of the importance of the humanitarian motive, moral crusaders (despite their relatively single-minded devotion to their particular cause) often lend their support to other humanitarian crusades. Joseph Gusfield has pointed out that:

> The American temperance movement during the 19th century was a part of a general effort toward the improvement of the worth of the human being through improved morality as well as economic conditions. The mixture of the religious,

> the equalitarian, and the humanitarian was an outstanding facet of the moral reformism of many movements. Temperance supporters formed a large segment of movements such as sabbatarianism, abolition, woman's rights, agrarianism, and humanitarian attempts to improve the lot of the poor....
>
> In its auxiliary interests the WCTU revealed a great concern for the improvement of the welfare of the lower classes. It was active in campaigns to secure penal reform, to shorten working hours and raise wages for workers, and to abolish child labor and in a number of other humanitarian and equalitarian activities. In the 1880's the WCTU worked to bring about legislation for the protection of working girls against the exploitation by men.[1]

As Gusfield says,[2] "Moral reformism of this type suggests the approach of a dominant class toward those less favorably situated in the economic and social structure." Moral crusaders typically want to help those beneath them to achieve a better status. That those beneath them do not always like the means proposed for their salvation is another matter. But this fact—that moral crusades are typically dominated by those in the upper levels of the social structure—means that they add to the power they derive from the legitimacy of their moral position, the power they derive from their superior position in society.

Naturally, many moral crusades draw support from people whose motives are less pure than those of the crusader. Thus, some industrialists supported Prohibition because they felt it would provide them with a more manageable labor force.[3] Similarly, it is sometimes rumored that Nevada gambling interests support the opposition to attempts to legalize gambling in California because it would cut so heavily into their business, which depends in substantial measure on the population of Southern California.[4]

The moral crusader, however, is more concerned with ends than with means. When it comes to drawing up specific rules (typically in the form of legislation to be proposed to a state legislature or the Federal Congress), he frequently relies on the advice of experts. Lawyers, expert in the drawing of acceptable legislation, often play this role. Government bureaus in whose jurisdiction the problem falls may also have the necessary expertise, as did the Federal Bureau of Narcotics in the case of the marihuana problem.

As psychiatric ideology, however, becomes increasingly acceptable, a new expert has appeared—the psychiatrist. Sutherland, in his discussion of the natural history of sexual psychopath laws, pointed to the psychiatrist's influence.[5] He suggests the following as the conditions under which the sexual psychopath law, which provides that a person "who is diagnosed as a sexual psychopath may be confined for an indefinite period in a state hospital for the insane,"[6] will be passed.

> First, these laws are customarily enacted after a state of fear has been aroused in a community by a few serious sex crimes committed in quick succession. This is illustrated in Indiana, where a law was passed following three or four sexual attacks in Indianapolis, with murder in two. Heads of families bought guns and

watch dogs, and the supply of locks and chains in the hardware stores of the city was completely exhausted....

A second element in the process of developing sexual psychopath laws is the agitated activity of the community in connection with the fear. The attention of the community is focused on sex crimes, and people in the most varied situations envisage dangers and see the need of and possibility for their control....

The third phase in the development of those sexual psychopath laws has been the appointment of a committee. The committee gathers the many conflicting recommendations of persons and groups of persons, attempts to determine "facts," studies procedures in other states, and makes recommendations, which generally include bills for the legislature. Although the general fear usually subsides within a few days, a committee has the formal duty of following through until positive action is taken. Terror which does not result in a committee is much less likely to result in a law.[7]

In the case of sexual psychopath laws, there usually is no government agency charged with dealing in a specialized way with sexual deviations. Therefore, when the need for expert advice in drawing up legislation arises, people frequently turn to the professional group most closely associated with such problems:

In some states, at the committee stage of the development of a sexual psychopath law, psychiatrists have played an important part. The psychiatrists, more than any others, have been the interest group back of the laws. A committee of psychiatrists and neurologists in Chicago wrote the bill which became the sexual psychopath law of Illinois; the bill was sponsored by the Chicago Bar Association and by the state's attorney of Cook County and was enacted with little opposition in the next session of the State Legislature. In Minnesota all the members of the governor's committee except one were psychiatrists. In Wisconsin the Milwaukee Neuropsychiatric Society shared in pressing the Milwaukee Crime Commission for the enactment of a law. In Indiana the attorney-general's committee received from the American Psychiatric Association copies of all the sexual psychopath laws which had been enacted in other states.[8]

The influence of psychiatrists in other realms of the criminal law has increased in recent years.

In any case, what is important about this example is not that psychiatrists are becoming increasingly influential, but that the moral crusader, at some point in the development of his crusade, often requires the services of a professional who can draw up the appropriate rules in an appropriate form. The crusader himself is often not concerned with such details. Enough for him that the main point has been won; he leaves its implementation to others.

By leaving the drafting of the specific rule in the hands of others, the crusader opens the door for many unforeseen influences. For those who draft legislation for crusaders have their own interests, which may affect the legislation they prepare. It is likely that the sexual psychopath laws drawn by psychiatrists contain many features never intended by the citizens who spearheaded the drives to "do something about sex crimes," features which do however reflect the professional interests of organized psychiatry.

* * *

RULE ENFORCERS

The most obvious consequence of a successful crusade is the creation of a new set of rules. With the creation of a new set of rules we often find that a new set of enforcement agencies and officials is established. Sometimes, of course, existing agencies take over the administration of the new rule, but more frequently a new set of rule enforcers is created. The passage of the Harrison Act presaged the creation of the Federal Narcotics Bureau, just as the passage of the Eighteenth Amendment led to the creation of police agencies charged with enforcing the Prohibition Laws.

With the establishment of organizations of rule enforcers, the crusade becomes institutionalized. What started out as a drive to convince the world of the moral necessity of a new rule finally becomes an organization devoted to the enforcement of the rule. Just as radical political movements turn into organized political parties and lusty evangelical sects become staid religious denominations, the final outcome of the moral crusade is a police force. To understand, therefore, how the rules creating a new class of outsiders are applied to particular people we must understand the motives and interests of police, the rule enforcers.

Although some policemen undoubtedly have a kind of crusading interest in stamping out evil, it is probably much more typical for the policeman to have a certain detached and objective view of his job. He is not so much concerned with the content of any particular rule as he is with the fact that it is his job to enforce the rule. When the rules are changed, he punishes what was once acceptable behavior just as he ceases to punish behavior that has been made legitimate by a change in the rules. The enforcer, then, may not be interested in the content of the rule as such, but only in the fact that the existence of the rule provides him with a job, a profession, and a *raison d'être*.

Since the enforcement of certain rules provides justification for his way of life, the enforcer has two interests which condition his enforcement activity: first, he must justify the existence of his position and, second, he must win the respect of those he deals with.

These interests are not peculiar to rule enforcers. Members of all occupations feel the need to justify their work and win the respect of others. Musicians would like to do this but have difficulty finding ways of successfully impressing their worth on customers. Janitors fail to win their tenants' respect, but develop an ideology which stresses the quasi-professional responsibility they have to keep confidential the intimate knowledge of tenants they acquire in the course of their work.[9] Physicians, lawyers, and other professionals, more successful in winning the respect of clients, develop elaborate mechanisms for maintaining a properly respectful relationship.

In justifying the existence of his position, the rule enforcer faces a double problem. On the one hand, he must demonstrate to others that the problem still exists: the rules he is supposed to enforce have some point, because infractions occur. On the other hand, he must show that his attempts at enforcement are effective and worthwhile, that the evil he is supposed to deal with is in fact being dealt with adequately. Therefore, enforcement organizations, particularly when they are seeking funds, typically oscillate between two kinds of claims. First, they say that by reason of their efforts the problem they deal with is approaching solution. But, in the same breath, they say the problem is perhaps worse than ever (though through no fault of their own) and requires renewed and increased effort to keep it under control. Enforcement officials can be more vehement than anyone else in their insistence that the problem they are supposed to deal with is still with us, in fact is more with us than ever before. In making these claims, enforcement officials provide good reason for continuing the existence of the position they occupy.

We may also note that enforcement officials and agencies are inclined to take a pessimistic view of human nature. If they do not actually believe in original sin, they at least like to dwell on the difficulties in getting people to abide by rules, on the characteristics of human nature that lead people toward evil. They are skeptical of attempts to reform rule-breakers.

The skeptical and pessimistic outlook of the rule enforcer, of course, is reinforced by his daily experience. He sees, as he goes about his work, the evidence that the problem is still with us. He sees the people who continually repeat offenses, thus definitely branding themselves in his eyes as outsiders. Yet it is not too great a stretch of the imagination to suppose that one of the underlying reasons for the enforcer's pessimism about human nature and the possibilities of reform is that fact that if human nature were perfectible and people could be permanently reformed, his job would come to an end.

In the same way, a rule enforcer is likely to believe that it is necessary for the people he deals with to respect him. If they do not, it will be very difficult to do his job; his feeling of security in his work will be lost. Therefore, a good deal of enforcement activity is devoted not to the actual enforcement of rules, but to coercing respect from the people the enforcer deals with. This means that one may be labeled as deviant not because he has actually broken a rule, but because he has shown disrespect to the enforcer of the rule.

Westley's study of policemen in a small industrial city furnishes a good example of this phenomenon. In his interview, he asked policemen, "When do you think a policeman is justified in roughing a man up?" He found that "at least 37% of the men believed that it was legitimate to use violence to coerce respect."[10] He gives some illuminating quotations from his interviews:

> Well, there are cases. For example, when you stop a fellow for a routine questioning, say a wise guy, and he starts talking back to you and telling you you are no good and that sort of thing. You know you can take a man in on a disorderly conduct charge, but you can practically never make it stick. So what you do in a case like that is to egg the guy on until he makes a remark where you can justifiably slap him and, then, if he fights back, you can call it resisting arrest.
>
> Well, a prisoner deserves to be hit when he goes to the point where he tries to put you below him.
>
> You've gotta get rough when a man's language becomes very bad, when he is trying to make a fool of you in front of everybody else. I think most policemen try to treat people in a nice way, but usually you have to talk pretty rough. That's the only way to set a man down, to make him show a little respect.[11]

What Westley describes is the use of an illegal means of coercing respect from others. Clearly, when a rule enforcer has the option of enforcing a rule or not, the difference in what he does may be caused by the attitude of the offender toward him. If the offender is properly respectful, the enforcer may smooth the situation over. If the offender is disrespectful, then sanctions may be visited on him. Westley has shown that this differential tends to operate in the case of traffic offenses, where the policeman's discretion is perhaps at a maximum.[12] But it probably operates in other areas as well.

Ordinarily, the rule enforcer has a great deal of discretion in many areas, if only because his resources are not sufficient to cope with the volume of rule-breaking he is supposed to deal with. This means that he cannot tackle everything at once and to this extent must temporize with evil. He cannot do the whole job and knows it. He takes his time, on the assumption that the problems he deals with will be around for a long while. He establishes priorities, dealing with things in their turn, handling the most pressing problems immediately and leaving others for later. His attitude toward his work, in short, is professional. He lacks the naive moral fervor characteristic of the rule creator.

If the enforcer is not going to tackle every case he knows of at once, he must have a basis for deciding when to enforce the rule, which persons committing which acts to label as deviant. One criterion for selecting people is the "fix." Some people have sufficient political influence or know-how to be able to ward off attempts at enforcement, if not at the time of apprehension then at a later stage in the process. Very often, this function is professionalized; someone performs the job on a full-time basis, available to anyone who wants to hire him. A professional thief described fixers this way:

> There is in every large city a regular fixer for professional thieves. He has no agents and does not solicit and seldom takes any case except that of a profes-

sional thief, just as they seldom go to anyone except him. This centralized and monopolistic system of fixing for professional thieves is found in practically all of the large cities and many of the small ones.[13]

Since it is mainly professional thieves who know about the fixer and his operations, the consequence of this criterion for selecting people to apply the rules to is that amateurs tend to be caught, convicted, and labeled deviant much more frequently than professionals. As the professional thief notes:

> You can tell by the way the case is handled in court when the fix is in. When the copper is not very certain he has the right man, or the testimony of the copper and the complainant does not agree, or the prosecutor goes easy on the defendant, or the judge is arrogant in his decisions, you can always be sure that someone has got the work in. This does not happen in many cases of theft, for there is one case of a professional to twenty-five or thirty amateurs who know nothing about the fix. These amateurs get the hard end of the deal every time. The coppers bawl out about the thieves, no one holds up his testimony, the judge delivers an oration, and all of them get credit for stopping a crime wave. When the professional hears the case immediately preceding his own, he will think, "He should have got ninety years. It's the damn amateurs who cause all the heat in the stores." Or else he thinks, "Isn't it a damn shame for that copper to send that kid away for a pair of hose, and in a few minutes he will agree to a small fine for me for stealing a fur coat?" But if the coppers did not send the amateurs away to strengthen their records of convictions, they could not sandwich in the professionals whom they turn loose.[14]

Enforcers of rules, since they have no stake in the content of particular rules themselves, often develop their own private evaluation of the importance of various kinds of rules and infractions of them. This set of priorities may differ considerably from those held by the general public. For instance, drug users typically believe (and a few policemen have personally confirmed it to me) that police do not consider the use of marihuana to be as important a problem or as dangerous a practice as the use of opiate drugs. Police base this conclusion on the fact that, in their experience, opiate users commit other crimes (such as theft or prostitution) in order to get drugs, while marihuana users do not.

Enforcers then, responding to the pressures of their own work situation, enforce rules and create outsiders in a selective way. Whether a person who commits a deviant act is in fact labeled a deviant depends on many things extraneous to his actual behavior: whether the enforcement official feels that at this time he must make some show of doing his job in order to justify his position, whether the misbehaver shows proper deference to the enforcer, whether the "fix" has been put in, and where the kind of act he has committed stands on the enforcer's list of priorities.

The professional enforcer's lack of fervor and routine approach to dealing with evil may get him into trouble with the rule creator. The rule creator, as we have said, is concerned with the content of the rules that interest him.

He sees them as the means by which evil can be stamped out. He does not understand the enforcer's long-range approach to the same problems and cannot see why all the evil that is apparent cannot be stamped out at once.

When the person interested in the content of a rule realizes or has called to his attention the fact that enforcers are dealing selectively with the evil that concerns him, his righteous wrath may be aroused. The professional is denounced for viewing the evil too lightly, for failing to do his duty. The moral entrepreneur, at whose instance the rule was made, arises again to say that the outcome of the last crusade has not been satisfactory or that the gains once made have been whittled away and lost.

Notes

1. Joseph R. Gusfield, "Social Structure and Moral Reform: A Study of the Woman's Christian Temperance Union," *American Journal of Sociology*, LXI (November, 1955), 223.
2. *Ibid.*
3. See Raymond G. McCarthy, editor, *Drinking and Intoxication* (New Haven and New York: Yale Center of Alcohol Studies and The Free Press of Glencoe, 1959), pp. 395–396.
4. This is suggested in Oscar Lewis, *Sagebrush Casinos: The Story of Legal Gambling in Nevada* (New York: Doubleday and Co., 1953), pp. 223–234.
5. Edwin H. Sutherland, "The Diffusion of Sexual Psychopath Laws," *American Journal of Sociology*, LVI (September, 1950), 142–148.
6. *Ibid.*, pp. 142.
7. *Ibid.*, pp. 143–145.
8. *Ibid.*, pp. 145–146.
9. See Ray Gold, "Janitors Versus Tenants: A Status-Income Dilemma," *American Journal of Sociology*, LVII (March, 1952), 486–493.
10. William A. Westley, "Violence and the Police," *American Journal of Sociology*, LIX (July, 1953), 39.
11. *Ibid.*
12. See William A. Westley, "The Police: A Sociological Study of Law, Custom, and Morality" (unpublished Ph.D. dissertation, University of Chicago, Department of Sociology, 1951).
13. Edwin H. Sutherland (editor), *The Professional Thief* (Chicago: University of Chicago Press, 1937), pp. 87–88.
14. *Ibid.*, pp. 91–92.

3 / The Legislation of Morality: Creating Drug Laws

TROY DUSTER

INTRODUCTION

The relationship between law and morality is both complicated and subtle. This is true even in a situation where a society is very homogeneous and where one might find a large degree of consensus about moral behavior. Those who argue that law is simply the empirical operation of morality are tempted to use homogeneous situations as examples. In discussing this relationship, Selznick asserts that laws are secondary in nature.[1] They are secondary in the sense that they obtain their legitimacy in terms of some other more primary reference point.

> The distinctively legal emerges with the development of secondary rules, that is, rules of authoritative determination. These rules, selectively applied, "raise up" the primary norms and give them a legal status.... The appeal from an *asserted* rule, however, coercively enforced, to a justified rule is the elementary legal act. This presumes at least a dim awareness that some reason lies behind the impulse to conform, a reason founded not in conscience, habit, or fear alone, but in the decision to uphold an authoritative order. The rule of legal recognition may be quite blunt and crude: the law is what the king or priest says it is. But this initial reference of a primary norm to a ground of obligation breeds the complex elaboration of authoritative rules that marks a developed legal order.[2]

The most primary of reference points is, of course, the moral order. One can explain why he does something for just so long, before he is driven to a position where he simply must assert that it is "right" or "wrong." With narcotics usage and addiction, the issue in contemporary times is typically raised in the form of a moral directive, irrespective of the physiological and physical aspects of addiction. The laws concerning narcotics usage may now be said to be a secondary set held up against the existing primary or moral view of drugs. However, the drug laws have been on the books for half a century, during which time, as we shall see, this country has undergone a remarkable transformation in its moral interpretation of narcotics usage. Clearly, if we want to understand the ongoing relationship between the law and morality, we are misled by assuming one has some fixed relationship to the other. To put it another way, if a set of laws remains unchanged while the moral order undergoes a drastic transformation, it follows that the relationship of law to morality must be a changing thing, and cannot be static. If narcotics law was simply the empirical element of narcotics morality, a change in the moral judgment of narcotics use should be accompanied by its counterpart in the law, and vice versa. As Selznick points out:

> In recent years, the great social effects of legal change have been too obvious to ignore. The question is no longer *whether* law is a significant vehicle of social change but rather *how* it so functions and what special problems arise.[3]

Selznick goes on to suggest explorations into substantive problems of "change." The connection of law to change is clearly demonstrable. If a society undergoes rapid technological development, new social relationships will emerge, and so too, will a set of laws to handle them. The gradual disintegration of the old caste relationships in India has been and will be largely attributable to the development of new occupations which contain no traditional forms regulating how one caste should respond to another.

The relationship of law to morality is not quite so clear. It is more specific, but more abstract. The sociological study of the narcotics problem is critical to discussion of this relationship, because it provides a specific empirical case where one can observe historically the interplay between the two essential components. More than any other form of deviance, the history of drug use contains an abundance of material on both questions of legislation and morality, and of the relationship between them.

BACKGROUND AND SETTING

Despite the public clamor of the 1960s about LSD and marijuana, the drug that has most dominated and colored the American conception of narcotics is opium. Among the most effective of painkillers, opium has been known and used in some form for thousands of years. Until the middle of the nineteenth century, opium was taken orally, either smoked or ingested. The Far East monopolized both production and consumption until the hypodermic needle was discovered as an extremely effective way of injecting the drug instantly into the bloodstream. It was soon to become a widely used analgesic. The first hypodermic injections of morphine, an opium derivative used to relieve pain, occurred in this country in 1856.[4]

Medical journals were enthusiastic in endorsing the new therapeutic usages that were possible, and morphine was the suggested remedy for an endless variety of physical sufferings. It was during the Civil War, however, that morphine injection really spread extensively. Then wholesale usage and addiction became sufficiently pronounced so that one could speak of an American problem for the first time.[5] Soldiers were given morphine to deaden the pain from all kinds of battle injuries and illnesses. After the war, ex-soldiers by the thousands continued using the drug, and recommending it to friends and relatives.

Within a decade, medical companies began to include morphine in a vast number of medications that were sold directly to consumers as household remedies. This was the period before governmental regulation, and the layman was subjected to a barrage of newspaper and billboard advertisements claiming cures for everything from the common cold to cholera. "Soothing Syrups" with morphine often contained no mention of their contents, and many men moved along the path to the purer morphine through this route.

> It is not surprising that many persons became dependent on these preparations and later turned to the active drug itself when accidentally or otherwise they learned of its presence in the "medicine" they had been taking.... The peak of the patent medicine industry was reached just prior to the passage of the Pure Food and Drug Act in 1906.[6]

It must be remembered that there were no state or federal laws concerning the sale and distribution of medicinal narcotic drugs during this period under discussion, and pharmacists sold morphine simply when it was requested by a customer. There is no way to accurately assess the extent of addiction at that time, nor is there now, for that matter. However, there are some informed estimates by scholars who have studied many facets of the period. Among the better guesses many will settle for is that from 2 to 4 percent of the population was addicted in 1895.[7] Studies of pharmaceutical dispensaries, druggists, and physicians' records were carried out in the 1880s and 1890s which relate to this problem. The widespread use of morphine was demonstrated by Hartwell's survey of Massachusetts druggists in 1888,[8] Hull's study of Iowa druggists in 1885,[9] Earle's work in Chicago in 1880,[10] and Grinnell's survey of Vermont in 1900.[11] The methodological techniques of investigation do not meet present-day standards, but even if certain systematic biases are assumed, the 3 percent figure is an acceptable guess of the extent of addiction.

The large numbers of addicts alarmed a growing number of medical men. The American press, which had been so vocal in its denunciation of the sensational but far less common opium smoking in opium dens in the 1860s and 1870s, was strangely if typically silent on morphine medication and its addicting effects. Just as the present-day press adroitly avoids making news of very newsworthy government proceedings on false advertising (an issue in which there may also be some question of the accomplice), newspapers of that time did not want to alienate the advertisers, because they were a major source of revenue. Nonetheless, the knowledge of the addicting qualities of morphine became more and more common among a sizable minority of physicians.

It was in this setting, in 1898, that a German pharmacological researcher named Dreser produced a new substance from a morphine base, diacetylmorphin, otherwise known as heroin. The medical community was enthusiastic in its reception of the new drug. It had three times the strength of morphine, and it was believed to be free from addicting qualities. The most respectable medical journals of Germany and the United States carried articles and reports lauding heroin as a cure for morphine addiction.[12]

Within five short years, the first definitive serious warnings about the addicting qualities of heroin appeared in an American medical journal.[13] The marvelous success of heroin as a painkiller and sedative, however, made the drug popular with both physician and patient. It should be remembered that one did not need a prescription to buy it. The news of the new warnings traveled slowly, and heroin joined morphine as one of the most frequently used pain remedies for the ailing and suffering.

From 1865 to 1900, then, addiction to narcotics was relatively widespread. This is documented in an early survey of material by Terry and Pellens, a treatise which remains the classic work on late nineteenth- and early twentieth-century problems of addiction.[14] In proportion to the population, addiction was probably eight times more prevalent then than now, despite the large increase in the general population.

It is remarkable, therefore, that addiction is regarded today as a problem of far greater moral, legal, and social significance than it was then. As we shall see directly, the problem at the turn of the century was conceived in very different terms, treated in a vastly different manner, and located in opposite places in the social order.

The first task is to illustrate how dramatic and complete was the shift of addicts from one social category to another during a critical twenty-year period. The second task is to examine the legal activity which affected that shift. Finally, the task will be to examine the changing moral judgments that coincided with these developments.

It is now taken for granted that narcotic addicts come primarily from the working and lower classes.... This has not always been true. The evidence clearly indicates that the upper and middle classes predominated among narcotic addicts in the period up to 1914. In 1903, the American Pharmaceutical Association conducted a study of selected communities in the United States and Canada. They sent out mailed questionnaires to physicians and druggists, and from the responses, concluded that

> while the increase is most evident with the lower classes, the statistics of institutes devoted to the cure of habitues show that their patients are principally drawn form those in the higher walks of life....[15]

From a report on Massachusetts druggists published in 1889 and cited by Terry and Pellens, the sale of opium derivatives to those of higher incomes exceeded the amount sold to lower-income persons.[16] This is all the more striking if we take into account the fact that the working and lower classes comprised a far greater percentage of the population of the country in 1890 than they do today. (With the 1960 census figures, the population of the United States becomes predominantly white collar for the first time in history.) In view of the fact that the middle class comprised proportionately less of the population, the incidence of its addiction rate can be seen as even more significant.

It was acknowledged in medical journals that a morphine addict could not be detected as an addict so long as he maintained his supply.[17] Some of the most respectable citizens of the community, pillars of middle-class morality, were addicted. In cases where this was known, the victim was regarded as one afflicted with a physiological problem, in much the same way as we presently regard the need of a diabetic for insulin. Family histories later indicated that many went through their daily tasks, their occupations, completely undetected by friends and relatives.[18]

There are two points of considerable significance that deserve more careful consideration. The first is the fact that some friends and relatives could and did know about an addiction and still did not make a judgment, either moral or psychological, of the person addicted. The second is that the lower classes were not those primarily associated with morphine or heroin usage in 1900.

The moral interpretation of addiction in the twentieth century is especially interesting in view of the larger historical trend. Western man has, on the whole, developed increasing tolerance and compassion for problems that were previously dogmatically treated as moral issues, such as epilepsy, organic and functional mental disorders, polio, diabetes, and so on. There was a time when most were convinced that the afflicted were possessed by devils, were morally evil, and inferior. Both medical opinion and literature of the eighteenth and nineteenth centuries were replete with the moral interpretation of countless physiological problems which have now been reinterpreted in an almost totally nonmoral fashion. The only moral issue now attendant to these questions is whether persons suffering should receive treatment from physicians. Even venereal diseases, which retain a stigma, are unanimously conceived as physiological problems that should be treated physiologically irrespective of the moral conditions under which they were contracted.

The narcotic addict of the 1890s was in a situation almost the reverse of those suffering from the above problems. His acquaintances and his community could know of his addiction, feel somewhat sorry for his dependence upon *medication*, but admit him to a position of respect and authority. If the heroin addict of 1900 was getting a willful thrill out of his injection, no one was talking about either the willful element or the thrill, not even the drug companies. If the thrill was to be had, there was no reason for manufacturers not to take advantage of this in their advertisements. They had no moral compunctions about patently false claims for a cure, or about including an opium derivative without so stating on the label.

Despite that fact that all social classes had their share of addicts, there was a difference in the way lower-class addicts were regarded. This difference was exacerbated when legislation drove heroin underground, predominantly to the lower classes. Writing in the *American Journal of Clinical Medicine* in 1918, G. Swaine made an arbitrary social classification of addicts, about which he offered the following distinction:

> In Class one, we can include all of the physical, mental and moral defectives, the tramps, hoboes, idlers, loaders, irresponsibles, criminals, and denizens of the underworld. . . . In these cases, morphine addiction is a vice, as well as a disorder resulting from narcotic poisoning. These are the "drug fiends." In Class two, we have many types of good citizens who have become addicted to the use of the drug innocently, and who are in every sense of the word "victims." Morphine is no respecter of persons, and the victims are doctors, lawyers, ministers, artists, actors, judges, congressmen, senators, priests, authors, women, girls, all of who realize their conditions and want to be cured. In these cases, morphine-addiction is not a vice, but, an incubus, and, when they are cured they stay cured.[19]

This may seem to jump ahead of the task of this section which is simply to portray as accurately as possible the dramatic shift of addicts from one social category to another during this period. However, the shift itself carried with it more than a description. These were the beginnings of moral interpretations for the meaning of that shift. By 1920, a medical journal reported cases treated at Riverside Hospital in New York City in the following manner:

> Drug addicts may be divided into two general classes. The first class is composed of people who have become addicted to the use of drugs through illness, associated probably with an underlying neurotic temperament. The second class, which is *overwhelmingly in the majority* [italics mine], is at the present time giving municipal authorities the greatest concern. These persons are largely from the underworld, or channels leading directly to it. They have become addicted to the use of narcotic drugs largely through association with habitues and they find in the drug a panacea for the physical and mental ills that are the result of the lives they are leading. Late hours, dance halls, and unwholesome cabarets do much to bring about this condition of body and mind. . . .[20]

Whereas in 1900 the addict population was spread relatively evenly over the social classes (with the higher classes having slightly more), by 1920, medical journals could speak of the "overwhelming" majority from the "unrespectable" parts of society. The same pattern can be seen with the shift from the predominantly middle-aged to the young, and with the shift from a predominance of women to an overwhelming majority of men.

In a study reported in 1880 and cited by Terry and Pellens, addiction to drugs was said to be "a vice of middle life, the larger number, by far, being from 30 to 40 years of age."[21] By 1920, Hubbard's study of New York's clinic could let him conclude that:

> Most, in fact 70 percent of the addicts in our clinic, are young people . . . the one and only conclusion that we can arrive at, is that acquirements of this practice—drug addiction—is incident to propinquity, bad associates, taken together with

> weak vacillating dispositions, making a successful combination in favor of the acquirement of such a habit.[22]

A report of a study of addiction to the Michigan State Board of Health in 1878 stated that, of 1,313 addicts, 803 were females, 510 males.[23] This is corroborated by Earle's study of Chicago, reported in 1880:

> Among the 235 habitual opium-eaters, 169 were found to be females, a proportion of about 3-to-1. Of these 169 females, about one-third belong to that class known as prostitutes. Deducting these, we still have among those taking the different kinds of opiates, 2 females to 1 male.[24]

Similarly, a report by Hull in 1885 on addiction in Iowa lists the distribution by sex as two-thirds female, and Terry's research in Florida in 1913 reported that 60 percent of the cases were women.[25] Suddenly, as if in magical correspondence to the trend cited above on social class and age, the sex distribution reversed itself, and in 1914, McIver and Price report[ed] that 70 percent of the addicts at Philadelphia General Hospital were males.[26] A governmental report to the Treasury Department in 1918 found addicts about equally divided between both sexes in the country, but a 1920 report for New York conclusively demonstrated that males were by then the predominant sex among drug addicts. Hubbard's report indicated that almost 80 percent of the New York Clinic's population of addicts were male.[27] The Los Angeles Clinic had a similar distribution for 1920 and 1921. The picture is clear. Taking only the three variables of age, sex, and social class into account, there is a sharp and remarkable transformation to be noticed in the two-decade period at the turn of the century. Let us examine now the legal turn of events of the period.

Prior to 1897, there was no significant legislation in any state concerning the manufacture or distribution of narcotics. As we have seen, the medical profession was becoming increasingly aware of the nature of morphine addiction when heroin was discovered in 1898. The alarm over the common practice of using morphine for a myriad of ills was insufficient to stem the tide of great enthusiasm with which physicians greeted heroin. Nonetheless, a small band of dedicated doctors who had been disturbed by the widespread ignorance of morphine in the profession (warnings about addiction did not appear in medical texts until about 1900) began to agitate for governmental intervention and regulation.[28]

From 1887 to 1908, many states passed individual laws aimed at curbing some aspect of the distribution of narcotics. Opium smoking was a favorite target of most of these laws, a development occasioned by the more concentrated treatment given this issue in the American press. Nonetheless, many of the state legislatures listened to medical men who insisted on the need for more control on the widespread distribution of the medicinally used opium derivatives. New York's state legislature passed the first comprehensive piece of legislation in the country concerning this problem in 1904, the Boylan Act.

As with many other problems of this kind, the lack of uniform state laws meant that control was virtually impossible. There is great variety in the law-making ability of each state, and sometimes it seems as though each state reviews the others carefully in order not to duplicate the provisions of their laws. If New York wanted registration of pharmacists, Massachusetts would want the registration of the central distributing warehouses, Illinois might want only the physician's prescriptions, and so forth. It soon became clear that only national and even international centralized control would be effective.

At the request of the United States, an international conference on opium was called in early 1909. Among countries accepting the invitation to this convention held in Shanghai were China, Great Britain, France, Germany, Italy, Russia, and Japan. Prior to this time, there had been a few attempts at control by individual nations in treaties, but this was the first concerted action on a truly international level. The major purpose of this first conference, as well as two other international conventions that were called within the next four years, was to insure that opium and related drugs be distributed only for expressly medical purposes, and ultimately distributed to the consumer through medical channels. The conferences called for regulation of the traffic at ports of entry, especially, but also tried to deal with the complicated problem of mail traffic. The handful of nations represented at the first Shanghai conference recognized the need for obtaining agreement and compliance from every nation in the world. The United States found itself in the embarrassing position of being the only major power without any control law covering distribution of medicinal narcotics within its borders. (The 1909 federal law was directed at opium smoking.) It was very much as a direct result of participation in the international conventions, then, that this country found itself being pressed for congressional action on the problem.

In this climate of both internal and international concern for the medicinal uses of the opium derivatives, Congress passed the Harrison Narcotic Act, approved December 17, 1914.

The Harrison Act stipulated that anyone engaged in the production or distribution of narcotics must register with the federal government and keep records of all transactions with drugs. This was the first of the three central provisions of the act. It gave the government precise knowledge of the legal traffic, and for the first time, the various uses and avenues of distribution could be traced.

The second major provision required that all parties handling the drugs through either purchase or sale pay a tax. This was a critical portion, because it meant that enforcement would reside with the tax collector, the Treasury Department, and more specifically, its Bureau of Internal Revenue. The Bureau set up a subsidiary organization to deal with affairs related to surveillance of activities covered by the new law. The immediate task was to insure that drugs were registered and passed through legitimate channels, beginning with importation and ending with the consumer. Since everyone was required to keep a record, the Bureau could demand and survey documentary material at every stage of the market operation.

Finally, the third major provision of the Harrison Act was a subtle "sleeper" that was not to obtain importance until the Supreme Court made a critical interpretation in 1919. This was the provision that unregistered persons could purchase drugs only upon the prescription of a physician, and that such a prescription must be for legitimate medical use. It seemed innocent enough a provision, one that was clearly included so that the physician retained the only control over the dispensation of narcotics to the consumer. As such, the bill was designed by its framers to place the addict completely in the hands of the medical profession.

It is one of those ironic twists that this third provision, intended for one purpose, was to be used in such a way as to thwart that purpose. As a direct consequence of it, the medical profession abandoned the drug addict. The key revolved around the stipulation that doctors could issue a prescription only to addicts for *legitimate* medical purposes. The decision about what is legitimate medical practice rests ultimately outside the medical profession in the moral consensus which members of society achieve about legitimacy. Even if the medical profession were to agree that experimental injections of a new drug on a random sample of babies would do most to advance medical science, the moral response against experimentation would be so strong as to destroy its claim to legitimacy. Thus, it is only in arbitrary and confined hypothetical instances that we can cogently argue that the medical profession determines legitimate practice.

So it was that the germ of a moral conception, the difference between good and evil or right and wrong, was to gain a place in the exercise of the new law.

Since the Harrison Act said nothing explicitly about the basis upon which physicians could prescribe narcotics for addicts, the only theoretical change that was forseeable was the new status of the prescription at the drug counter. All sales were to be registered, and a signed prescription from a physician was required. But when the physician became the only legal source of the drug supply, hundreds of thousands of law-abiding addicts suddenly materialized outside of doctors' offices. It was inconceivable that the relatively small number of doctors in the country could so suddenly handle over half a million new patients in any manner, and certainly it was impossible that they might handle them individually. The doctor's office became little more than a dispensing station for the addict, with only an infinitesimal fraction of addicts receiving personal care. In most cases, this was simply a continuation of the small number who had already been under regular care.

In New York City for example, it was impossible for a doctor with even a small practice to do anything more than sign prescriptions for his suddenly created large clientele. The government agents were alarmed at what they regarded as cavalier treatment of the prescription by the medical profession, and were concerned that the spirit and intent of the new drug law were being violated. They decided to prosecute some physicians who were prescribing to addicts en masse. They succeeded in convicting them, and appeals took the cases up to the Supreme Court. In a remarkable case (*Webb vs. U.S.*, 1919) the Supreme Court made a decision that was to have far-reaching effects on the narcotics traffic, ruling that:

> a prescription of drugs for an addict "not in the course of professional treatment in the attempted cure of the habit, but being issued for the purpose of providing the user with morphine sufficient to keep him comfortable by maintaining his customary use" was not a prescription in the meaning of the law and was not included within the exemption for the doctor-patient relationship.[29]

Doctors who continued to prescribe to addicts on anything but the most personal and individual basis found themselves faced with the real, demonstrated possibility of fines and prison sentences. As I have indicated, there were hundreds of thousands of addicts, and only a few thousand physicians to handle them. If there were thirty or forty addicts outside a doctor's office waiting for prescriptions, *or even waiting for a chance to go through withdrawal*, the Supreme Court decision and the Treasury Department's actions made it almost certain that the doctor would turn them away. A minority of doctors, some for humanitarian reasons, some from the profit-motive of a much higher fee, continued to prescribe. Scores of them were arrested, prosecuted, fined, imprisoned, and set forth as an example to others. The addict found himself being cut off gradually but surely from all legal sources, and he began to turn gradually but surely to the welcome arms of the black marketeers.

And so it was that the law and its interpretation by the Supreme Court provided the final condition and context for a moral reassessment of what had previously been regarded as a physiological problem. The country could begin to connect all addicts with their newfound underworld associates, and could now begin to talk about a different class of men who were consorting with criminals. The step was only a small one to the imputation of criminal intent. The bridge between law and morality was drawn.

Notes

1. Philip Selznick, "Sociology of Law" (mimeographed, Center for the Study of Law and Society, University of California, Berkeley), April, 1965. Prepared for the *International Encyclopedia of the Social Sciences*.
2. *Ibid.*
3. *Ibid.*, p. 23.
4. Charles E. Terry and Mildred Pellens, *The Opium Problem* (New York: Bureau of Social Hygiene, 1928), p. 66.
5. *Ibid.*, p. 69.
6. *Ibid.*, p. 75.
7. Marie Nyswander, *The Drug Addict as a Patient* (New York: Grune & Stratton, 1956), pp. 1–13.

8. B. H. Hartwell, "The Sale and Use of Opium in Massachusetts," *Annual Report Massachusetts State Board of Health*, 1889.
9. Terry and Pellens, *op. cit.*, p. 17.
10. C. W. Earle, "The Opium Habit," *Chicago Medical Review*, 2 (1880), 442–490.
11. A. P. Grinnell, "A Review of Drug Consumption and Alcohol as Found in Proprietary Medicine," *Medical Legal Journal*, 1905, pp. 426–589.
12. A much longer list of references is cited by Terry and Pellens, *op. cit.*, and the following are only a small but representative portion: H. Dreser, the man credited with the discovery of heroin, writing of his own findings in an Abstract to the *Journal of the American Medical Association*, 1898; two reports by M. Manges in the *New York Medical Journal*, November 26, 1898 and January 20, 1900.
13. G. E. Pettey, "The Heroin Habit, Another Curse," *Alabama Medical Journal*, 15 (1902–1903), 174–180.
14. Terry and Pellens, *op. cit.*
15. E. G. Eberle, "Report of Committee on Acquirement of Drug Habits," *American Journal of Pharmacology*, October, 1903, p. 481.
16. Terry and Pellens, *op. cit.*, p. 468.
17. C. S. Pearson, "A Study of Degeneracy as Seen Among Addicts," *New York Medical Journal*, November 15, 1919, pp. 805–808.
18. For example, cf. T. S. Blair, "Narcotic Drug Addiction as Regulated by a State Department of Health," *Journal of the American Medical Association*, 72 (May 17, 1919), 1442–1444.
19. G. D. Swaine, "Regarding the Luminal Treatment of Morphine Addiction," *American Journal of Clinical Medicine*, 25 (August, 1918), 611.
20. Terry and Pellens, *op. cit.*, p. 499.
21. *Ibid.*, p. 475.
22. S. D. Hubbard, "The New York City Narcotic Clinic and Differing Points of View on Narcotic Addiction," *Monthly Bulletin of the Department of Health, City of New York*, February, 1920.
23. Terry and Pellens, *op. cit.*, p. 11.
24. Earle, *op. cit.*
25. Terry and Pellens, *op. cit.*, pp. 470–471.
26. J. McIver and G. E. Price, "Drug Addiction," *Journal of the American Medical Association*, 66 (February 12, 1916), 477.
27. Hubbard, *op. cit.*
28. Nyswander, *op. cit.*
29. Alfred R. Lindesmith, *The Addict and the Law* (Bloomington: Indiana University Press, 1965), p. 6.

4 / The Discovery of Hyperkinesis: Notes on the Medicalization of Deviant Behavior

PETER CONRAD

INTRODUCTION

The increasing medicalization of deviant behavior and the medical institution's role as an agent of social control has gained considerable notice (Freidson, 1970; Pitts, 1971; Kittrie, 1971; Zola, 1972). By medicalization we mean defining behavior as a medical problem or illness and mandating or licensing the medical profession to provide some type of treatment for it. Examples include alcoholism, drug addiction and treating violence as a genetic or brain disorder. This redefinition is not a new function of the medical institution: psychiatry and public health have always been concerned with social behavior and have traditionally functioned as agents of social control (Foucault, 1965; Szasz, 1970; Rosen, 1972)....

This paper describes how certain forms of behavior in children have become defined as a medical problem and how medicine has become a major agent for their social control since the discovery of hyperkinesis. By discovery we mean both origin of the diagnosis and treatment for this disorder; and discovery of children who exhibit this behavior. The first section analyzes the discovery of hyperkinesis and why it suddenly became popular in the 1960's. The second section will discuss the medicalization of deviant behavior and its ramifications.

THE MEDICAL DIAGNOSIS OF HYPERKINESIS

Hyperkinesis is a relatively recent phenomenon as a medical diagnostic category. Only in the past two decades has it been available as a recognized diagnostic category and only in the last decade has it received widespread notice and medical popularity. However, the roots of the diagnosis and treatment of this clinical entity are found earlier.

Hyperkinesis is also known as Minimal Brain Dysfunction, Hyperactive Syndrome, Hyperkinetic Disorder of Childhood, and by several other diagnostic categories. Although the symptoms and the presumed etiology vary, in general the behaviors are quite similar and greatly overlap.[1] Typical symptom patterns for diagnosing the disorder include: extreme excess of motor activity (hyperactivity); very short attention span (the child flits from activity to activity); restlessness; fidgetiness; often wildly oscillating mood swings (he's fine one day, a terror the next); clumsiness; aggressive-like behavior; impulsivity; in school he cannot sit still, cannot comply with rules, has low frustration level; frequently there may be sleeping problems and acquisition of speech may be delayed (Stewart, 1966, 1970; Wendy, 1971). Most of the symptoms for the disorder are deviant behaviors.[2] It is six times as prevalent among boys as among girls. We use the term hyperkinesis to represent all the diagnostic categories of this disorder.

THE DISCOVERY OF HYPERKINESIS

It is useful to divide the analysis into what might be considered *clinical factors* directly related to the diagnosis and treatment of hyperkinesis and *social factors* that set the context for the emergence of the new diagnostic category.

Clinical Factors

Bradley (1937) observed that amphetamine drugs had a spectacular effect in altering the behavior of school children who exhibited behavior disorders or learning disabilities. Fifteen of the thirty children he treated actually became more subdued in their behavior. Bradley termed the effect of this medication paradoxical, since he expected that amphetamines would stimulate children as they stimulated adults. After the medication was discontinued the children's behavior returned to premedication level.

A scattering of reports in the medical literature on the utility of stimulant medications for "childhood behavior disorders" appeared in the next two decades. The next significant contribution was the work of Strauss and his associates (Strauss and Lehtinen, 1947) who found certain behavior (including hyperkinesis behaviors) in postencephaletic children suffering from what they called minimal brain injury (damage). This was the first time these behaviors were attributed to the new organic distinction of minimal brain damage.

This disorder still remained unnamed or else it was called a variety of names (usually just "childhood behavior disorder"). It did not appear as a specific diagnostic category until Laufer, et al. (1957) described it as the "hyperkinetic impulse disorder" in 1957. Upon finding "the salient characteristics of the behavior pattern . . . are strikingly similar to those with clear cut organic causation" these researchers described a disorder with no clear-cut history or evidence for organicity (Laufer, et al., 1957).

In 1966 a task force sponsored by the U.S. Public Health Service and the National Association for Crippled Children and Adults attempted to clarify the ambiguity and confusion in terminology and symptomology in diagnosing children's behavior and learning disorders. From over three dozen diagnoses, they agreed on the term "minimal brain dysfunction" as an overriding diagnosis that would include hyperkinesis and other disorders (Clements, 1966). Since this time M.B.D. has been the primary formal diagnosis or label.

In the middle 1950's a new drug, Ritalin, was synthesized, that has many qualities of amphetamines without some of their more undesirable side effects. In 1961 this drug was approved by the F.D.A. for use with children. Since this time there has been much research published on the use of Ritalin in the treatment of childhood behavior disorders. This medication became the "treatment of choice" for treating children with hyperkinesis.

Since the early sixties, more research appeared on the etiology, diagnosis and treatment of hyperkinesis (cf. DeLong, 1972; Grinspoon and Singer, 1973; Cole, 1975)—as much as three-quarters concerned with drug treatment of the disorder. There had been increasing publicity of the disorder in the mass media as well. The *Reader's Guide to Periodical Literature* had no articles on hyperkinesis before 1967, one each in 1968 and 1969, and a total of forty for 1970 through 1974 (a mean of eight per year).

Now hyperkinesis has become the most common child psychiatric problem (Gross and Wilson, 1974:142); special pediatric clinics have been established to treat hyperkinetic children, and substantial federal funds have been invested in etiological and treatment research. Outside the medical profession, teachers have developed a working clinical knowledge of hyperkinesis' symptoms and treatment (cf. Robin and Bosco, 1973); articles appear regularly in mass circulation magazines and newspapers so that parents often come to clinics with knowledge of this diagnosis. Hyperkinesis is no longer the relatively esoteric diagnostic category it may have been twenty years ago, it is now a well-known clinical disorder.

Social Factors

The social factors affecting the discovery of hyperkinesis can be divided into two areas: (1) The Pharmaceutical Revolution; (2) Government Action.

(1) The Pharmaceutical Revolution. Since the 1930's the pharmaceutical industry has been synthesizing and manufacturing a large number of psychoactive drugs, contributing to a virtual revolution in drug making and drug taking in America (Silverman and Lee, 1974).

Psychoactive drugs are agents that affect the central nervous system. Benzedrine, Ritalin, and Dexedrine are all synthesized psychoactive stimulants which were indicated for narcolepsy, appetite control (as "diet pills"), mild depression, fatigue, and more recently hyperkinetic children.

Until the early sixties there was little or no promotion and advertisement of any of these medications for use with childhood disorders.[3] Then two major pharmaceutical firms (Smith, Kline and French, manufacturer of Dexedrine and CIBA, manufacturer of Ritalin) began to advertise in medical journals and through direct mailing and efforts of the "detail men." Most of this advertising of the pharmaceutical treatment of hyperkinesis was directed to the medical sphere; but some of the promotion was targeted for the educational sector also (Hentoff, 1972). This promotion was probably significant in disseminating information concerning the diagnosis and treatment of this newly discovered disorder.[4] Since 1955 the use of psychoactive medications (especially phenothiazines) for the treatment of persons who are mentally ill, along with the concurrent dramatic decline in inpatient populations, has made psychopharmacology an integral part of treatment for mental disorders. It has also undoubtedly increased the confidence in the medical profession for the pharmaceutical approach to mental and behavioral problems.

(2) **Government Action.** Since the publication of the U.S.P.H.S. report on M.B.D. there have been at least two significant governmental reports on treating school children with stimulant medications for behavior disorders. Both of these came as a response to the national publicity created by the *Washington Post* report (1970) that five to 10 percent of the 62,000 grammar school children in Omaha, Nebraska were being treated with "behavior modification drugs to improve deportment and increase learning potential" (quoted in Grinspoon and Singer, 1973). Although the figures were later found to be a little exaggerated, it nevertheless spurred a Congressional investigation (U.S. Government Printing Office, 1970) and a conference sponsored by the Office of Child Development (1971) on the use of stimulant drugs in the treatment of behaviorally disturbed school children.

The Congressional Subcommittee on Privacy chaired by Congressman Cornelius E. Gallagher held hearings on the issue of prescribing drugs for hyperactive school children. In general, the committee showed great concern over the facility in which the medication was prescribed; more specifically that some children at least were receiving drugs from general practitioners whose primary diagnosis was based on teachers' and parents' reports that the child was doing poorly in school. There was also a concern with the absence of follow-up studies on the long-term effects of treatment.

The H.E.W. committee was a rather hastily convened group of professionals (a majority were M.D.'s) many of whom already had commitments to drug treatment for children's behavior problems. They recommended that only M.D.'s make the diagnosis and prescribe treatment, that the pharmaceutical companies promote the treatment of the disorder only through medical channels, that parents should not be coerced to accept any particular treatment and that long-term follow-up research should be done. This report served as blue ribbon approval for treating hyperkinesis with psychoactive medications.

DISCUSSION

We will focus discussion on three issues: How children's deviant behavior became conceptualized as a medical problem; why this occurred when it did; and what are some of the implications of the medicalization of deviant behavior.

How does deviant behavior become conceptualized as a medical problem? We assume that before the discovery of hyperkinesis this type of deviance was seen as disruptive, disobedient, rebellious, anti-social or deviant behavior. Perhaps the label "emotionally disturbed" was sometimes used, when it was in vogue in the early sixties, and the child was usually managed in the context of the family or the school or in extreme cases, the child guidance clinic. How then did this constellation of deviant behaviors become a medical disorder?

The treatment was available long before the disorder treated was clearly conceptualized. It was twenty years after Bradley's discovery of the "paradoxical effect" of stimulants on certain deviant children that Laufer named the disorder and described its characteristic symptoms. Only in the late fifties were both the diagnostic label and the pharmaceutical treatment available. The pharmaceutical revolution in mental health and the increased interest in child psychiatry provided a favorable background for the dissemination of knowledge about this new disorder. The latter probably made the medical profession more likely to consider behavior problems in children as within their clinical jurisdiction.

There were agents outside the medical profession itself that were significant in "promoting" hyperkinesis as a disorder within the medical framework. These agents might be conceptualized in Becker's terms as "moral entrepreneurs," those who crusade for creation and enforcement of the rules (Becker, 1963).[5] In this case the moral entrepreneurs were the pharmaceutical companies and the Association for Children with Learning Disabilities.

The pharmaceutical companies spent considerable time and money promoting stimulant medications for this new disorder. From the middle 1960's on, medical journals and the free "throwaway" magazines contained elaborate advertising for Ritalin and Dexedrine. These ads explained the utility of treating hyperkinesis and urged the physician to diagnose and treat hyperkinetic children. The ads run from one to six pages. For example, a two-page ad in 1971 stated:

> MBD...MEDICAL MYTH OR DIAGNOSABLE DISEASE ENTITY What medical practioner has not, at one time or another, been called upon to examine an impulsive, excitable hyperkinetic child? A child with difficulty in concentrating. Easily frustrated. Unusually aggressive. A classroom rebel. In the absence of any organic pathology, the conduct of such children was, until a few short years ago, usually dismissed as...spunkiness, or evidence of youthful vitality. But it is now evident that in many of these children the hyperkinetic syndrome exists as a distinct medical entity. This syndrome is readily diagnosed through patient histories, neurologic signs, and psychometric testing—has been classified by an expert panel convened by the United States Department of Health, Education and Welfare as Minimal Brain Dysfunction, MBD.

The pharmaceutical firms also supplied sophisticated packets of "diagnostic and treatment" information on hyperkinesis to physicians, paid for professional conferences on the subject, and supported research in the identification and treatment of the disorder. Clearly these corporations had a vested interest in the labeling and treatment of hyperkinesis; CIBA had $13 million profit from Ritalin alone in 1971, which was 15 percent of the total gross profits (Charles, 1971; Hentoff, 1972).

The other moral entrepreneur, less powerful than the pharmaceutical companies, but nevertheless influential, is the Association for Children with Learning Disabilities. Although their focus is not specifically on hyperkinetic children, they do include it in their conception of Learning Disabilities along with aphasia, reading problems like dyslexia and perceptual motor problems. Founded in the early 1950's by parents and professionals, it has functioned much as the National Association for Mental Health does for mental illness: promoting conferences, sponsoring legislation, providing social support. One of the main functions has been to disseminate information concerning this relatively new area in education, Learning Disabilities. While the organization does have a more educational than medical perspective, most of the literature indicates that for hyperkinesis members have adopted the medical model and the medical approach to the problem. They have sensitized teachers and schools to the conception of hyperkinesis as a medical problem.

The medical model of hyperactive behavior has become very well accepted in our society. Physicians find treatment relatively simple and the results sometimes spectacular. Hyperkinesis minimizes parents' guilt by emphasizing "it's not their fault, it's an organic problem" and allows for nonpunitive management or control of deviance. Medication often makes a child less disruptive in the classroom and sometimes aids a child in learning. Children often like their "magic pills" which make their behavior more socially acceptable and they probably benefit from a reduced stigma also.

THE MEDICALIZATION OF DEVIANT BEHAVIOR

Pitts has commented that "medicalization is one of the most effective means of social control and that it is destined to become the main mode of *formal* social control" (1971:391). Kittrie (1971) has termed it "the coming of the therapeutic state."

Medicalization of mental illness dates at least from the seventeenth century (Foucault, 1965; Szasz, 1970). Even slaves who ran away were once considered to be suffering from the disease *drapedomania* (Chorover, 1973). In recent years alcoholism, violence, and drug addiction as well as hyperactive behavior in children have all become defined as medical problems, both in etiology or explanation of the behavior and the means of social control or treatment.

There are many reasons why this medicalization has occurred. Much scientific research, especially in pharmacology and genetics, has become technologically more sophisticated, and found more subtle correlates with human behavior. Sometimes these findings (as in the case of XYY chromosomes and violence) become etiological explanations for deviance. Pharmacological technology that makes new discoveries affecting behavior (e.g., antabuse, methadone and stimulants) are used as treatment for deviance. In part this application is encouraged by the prestige of the medical profession and its attachment to science. As Freidson notes, the medical profession has first claim to jurisdiction over anything that deals with the functioning of the body and especially anything that can be labeled illness (1970:251). Advances in genetics, pharmacology and "psychosurgery" also may advance medicine's jurisdiction over deviant behavior.

Second, the application of pharmacological technology is related to the humanitarian trend in the conception and control of deviant behavior. Alcoholism is no longer sin or even moral weakness, it is now a disease. Alcoholics are no longer arrested in many places for "public drunkenness," they are now somehow "treated," even if it is only to be dried out. Hyperactive children are now considered to have an illness rather than to be disruptive, disobedient, overactive problem children. They are not as likely to be the "bad boy" of the classroom; they are children with a medical disorder. Clearly there are some real humanitarian benefits to be gained by such a medical conceptualization of deviant behavior. There is less condemnation of the deviants (they have an illness, it is not their fault) and perhaps less social stigma. In some cases, even the medical treatment itself is more humanitarian social control than the criminal justice system.

There is, however, another side to the medicalization of deviant behavior. The four aspects of this side of the issue include (1) the problem of expert control; (2) medical social control; (3) the individualization of social problems; and (4) the "depoliticization" of deviant behavior.

1. *The problem of expert control.* The medical profession is a profession of experts; they have a monopoly on anything that can be conceptualized as illness. Because of the way the medical profession is organized and the mandate it has from society, decisions related to medical diagnoses and treatment are virtually controlled by medical professionals.

Some conditions that enter the medical domain are not *ipso facto* medical problems, especially deviant behavior, whether alcoholism, hyperactivity or drug addiction. By defining a problem as medical it is removed from the public realm where there can be discussion by ordinary people and put on a plane where only medical people can discuss it. As Reynolds states,

> The increasing acceptance, especially among the more educated segments of our populace, of technical solutions—solutions administered by disinterested politically and morally neutral experts—results in the withdrawal of more and more areas of human experience from the realm of public discussion. For when drunkenness, juvenile delinquency, sub par performance and extreme political beliefs are seen as symptoms of an underlying illness or biological defect the merits and drawbacks of such behavior or beliefs need not be evaluated (1973:200–221).

The public may have their own conceptions of deviant behavior but that of the experts is usually dominant.

2. *Medical social control.* Defining deviant behavior as a medical problem allows certain things to be done that could not otherwise be considered; for example, the body may be cut open or psychoactive medications may be given. This treatment can be a form of social control.

In regard to drug treatment Lennard points out: "Psychoactive drugs, especially those legally prescribed, tend to restrain individuals from behavior and experience that are not complementary to the requirements of the dominant value system" (1971:57). These forms of medical social control presume a prior definition of deviance as a medical problem. Psychosurgery on an individual prone to violent outbursts requires a diagnosis that there was something wrong with his brain or nervous system. Similarly, prescribing drugs to restless, overactive and disruptive school children requires a diagnosis of hyperkinesis. These forms of social control, what Chorover (1973) has called "psychotechnology," are very powerful and often very efficient means of controlling deviance. These relatively new and increasingly popular forms of social control could not be utilized without the medicalization of deviant behavior. As it suggested from the discovery of hyperkinesis, if a mechanism of medical social control seems useful, then the deviant behavior it modifies will develop a medical label or diagnosis. No overt malevolence on the part of the medical profession is implied: rather it is part of a complex process, of which the medical profession is only a part. The larger process might be called the individualization of social problems.

3. *The individualization of social problems.* The medicalization of deviant behavior is part of a larger phenomenon that is prevalent in our society, the individualization of social problems. We tend to look for causes and

solutions to complex social problems in the individual rather than in the social system. This view resembles Ryan's (1971) notion of "blaming the victim"; seeing the causes of the problem in individuals rather than in the society where they live. We then seek to change the "victim" rather than the society. The medical perspective of diagnosing an illness in an individual lends itself to the individualization of social problems. Rather than seeing certain deviant behaviors as symptomatic of problems in the social system, the medical perspective focuses on the individual diagnosing and treating the illness, generally ignoring the social situation.

Hyperkinesis serves as a good example. Both the school and the parents are concerned with the child's behavior; the child is very difficult at home and disruptive in school. No punishments or rewards seem consistently to work in modifying the behavior; and both parents and school are at their wits' end. A medical evaluation is suggested. The diagnoses of hyperkinetic behavior leads to prescribing stimulant medications. The child's behavior seems to become more socially acceptable, reducing problems in school and at home.

But there is an alternate perspective. By focusing on the symptoms and defining them as hyperkinesis we ignore the possibility that behavior is not an illness but an adaption to a social situation. It diverts our attention from the family or school and from seriously entertaining the idea that the "problem" could be in the structure of the social system. And by giving medications we are essentially supporting the existing systems and do not allow this behavior to be a factor of change in the system.

4. *The depoliticization of deviant behavior.* Depoliticization of deviant behavior is a result of both the process of medicalization and individualization of social problems. To our western world, probably one of the clearest examples of such a depoliticization of deviant behavior occurred when political dissenters in the Soviet Union where declared mentally ill and confined in mental hospitals (cf. Conrad, 1972). This strategy served to neutralize the meaning of political protest and dissent, rendering it the ravings of mad persons.

The medicalization of deviant behavior depoliticizes deviance in the same manner. By defining the overactive, restless and disruptive child as hyperkinetic we ignore the meaning of behavior in the context of the social system. If we focused our analysis on the school system we might see the child's behavior as symptomatic of some "disorder" in the school or classroom situation, rather than symptomatic of an individual neurological disorder.

CONCLUSION

I have discussed the social ramifications of the medicalization of deviant behavior, using hyperkinesis as the example. A number of consequences of this medicalization have been outlined, including the depoliticization of deviant behavior, decision-making power of experts, and the role of medicine as an agent of social control. In the last analysis medical social control may be the central issue, as in this role medicine becomes a *de facto* agent of the *status quo*. The medical profession may not have entirely sought this role, but its members have been, in general, disturbingly unconcerned and unquestioning in their acceptance of it. With the increasing medical knowledge and technology it is likely that more deviant behavior will be medicalized and medicine's social control function will expand.

Notes

1. The U.S.P.H.S. report (Clements, 1966) included 38 terms that were used to describe or distinguish the conditions that it labeled Minimal Brain Dysfunction. Although the literature attempts to differentiate M.B.D., hyperkinesis, hyperactive syndrome, and several other diagnostic labels, it is our belief that in practice they are almost interchangeable.

2. For a fuller discussion of the construction of the diagnosis of hyperkinesis, see Conrad (1976), especially Chapter 6.

3. The American Medical Association's change in policy is accepting more pharmaceutical advertising in the late fifties may have been important. Probably the F.D.A. approval of the use of Ritalin for children in 1961 was more significant. Until 1970, Ritalin was advertised for treatment of "functional behavior problems in children." Since then, because of an F.D.A. order, it has only been promoted for treatment of M.B.D.

4. The drug industry spends fully 25 percent of its budget on promotion and advertising. See Coleman et al. (1966) for the role of the detail men and how physicians rely upon them for information.

5. Freidson also notes the medical professional role as moral entrepreneur in this process also:

> The profession does treat the illnesses laymen take to it, but it also seeks to discover illness of which the laymen may not even be aware. One of the greatest ambitions of the physician is to discover and describe a "new" disease or syndrome... (1970:252).

References

Becker, Howard S. 1963. *Outsiders: Studies in the Sociology of Deviance.* New York: Free Press.

Bradley, Charles. 1937. "The Behavior of Children Receiving Benzedrine." *American Journal of Psychiatry,* 94 (March): 577–585.

Charles, Alan. 1971. "The Case of Ritalin." *New Republic,* 23 (October): 17–19.

Chorover, Stephen L. 1973. "Big Brother and Psychotechnology." *Psychology Today* (October): 43–54.

Clements, Samuel D. 1966. "Task Force I: Minimal Brain Dysfunction in Children." National Institute of Neurological Diseases and Blindness, Monograph no. 3. Washington, D.C.: U.S. Department of Health, Education and Welfare.

Cole, Sherwood. 1975. "Hyperactive Children: The Use of Stimulant Drugs Evaluated." *American Journal of Orthopsychiatry,* 45 (January): 28–37.

Coleman, James, Elihu Katz, and Herbert Menzel. 1966. *Medical Innovation.* Indianapolis: Bobbs-Merrill.

Conrad, Peter. 1972. "Ideological Deviance: An Analysis of the Soviet Use of Mental Hospitals for Political Dissenters." Unpublished manuscript.

Conrad, Peter. 1976. *Identifying Hyperactive Children: A Study in the Medicalization of Deviant Behavior.* Lexington, Mass.: D.C. Heath and Co.

DeLong, Arthur R. 1972. "What Have We Learned from Psychoactive Drugs Research with Hyperactives?" *American Journal of Diseases in Children,* 123 (February): 177–180.

Foucault, Michel. 1965. *Madness and Civilization,* New York: Pantheon.

Freidson, Eliot. 1970. *Profession of Medicine: A Study of the Sociology of Applied Knowledge.* New York: Dodd, Mead.

Grinspoon, Lester and Susan Singer. 1973. "Amphetamines in the Treatment of Hyperactive Children." *Harvard Educational Review,* 43 (November): 515–555.

Gross, Mortimer B. and William E. Wilson. 1974. *Minimal Brain Dysfunction.* New York: Brunner Mazel.

Hentoff, Nat. 1972. "Drug Pushing in the Schools: The Professionals." *The Village Voice,* 22 (May): 21–23.

Kittrie, Nicholas. 1971. *The Right to Be Different.* Baltimore: Johns Hopkins Press.

Laufer, M. W., Denhoff, E., and Solomons, G. 1975. "Hyperkinetic Impulse Disorder in Children's Behavior Problems." *Psychosomatic Medicine,* 19 (January): 38–49.

Lennard, Henry L. and Associates. 1971. *Mystification and Drug Misuse.* New York: Harper and Row.

Office of Child Development. 1971. "Report of the Conference on the Use of Stimulant Drugs in Treatment of Behaviorally Disturbed Children." Washington, D.C.: Office of Child Development, Department of Health, Education and Welfare, January 11–12.

Pitts, Jesse. 1968. "Social Control: The Concept." In David Sills (ed.), *International Encyclopedia of the Social Sciences.* Vol. 14. New York: Macmillan.

Reynolds, Janice M. 1973. "The Medical Institution." In Larry T. Reynolds and James M. Henslin, *American Society: A Critical Analysis.* New York: David McKay.

Robin, Stanley S. and James J. Bosco. 1973. "Ritalin for School Children: The Teacher's Perspective." *Journal of School Health,* 47 (December): 624–628.

Rosen, George. 1972. "The Evolution of Social Medicine." In Howard E. Freeman, Sol Levine, and Leo Reeder, *Handbook of Medical Sociology.* Englewood Cliffs, N.J.: Prentice-Hall.

Ryan, William. 1970. *Blaming the Victim.* New York: Vintage.

Silverman, Milton and Philip R. Lee. 1974. *Pills, Profits and Politics.* Berkeley: University of California Press.

Sroufe, L. Alan and Mark Stewart. 1973. "Treating Problem Children with Stimulant Drugs." *New England Journal of Medicine,* 289 (August 23): 407–421.

Stewart, Mark A. 1970. "Hyperactive Children." *Scientific American,* 222 (April): 794–798.

Stewart, Mark A., A. Ferris, N. P. Pitts, and A. G. Craig. 1966. "The Hyperactive Child Syndrome." *American Journal of Orthopsychiatry,* 36 (October): 861–867.

Strauss, A. A. and L. E. Lehtinen. 1947. *Psychopathology and Education of the Brain-Injured Child.* Vol. 1. New York: Grune and Stratton.

U.S. Government Printing Office. 1970. "Federal Involvement in the Use of Behavior Modification Drugs on Grammar School Children of the Right to Privacy Inquiry: Hearing Before a Subcommittee of the Committee on Government Operations." Washington, D.C.: 91st Congress, 2nd session (September 29).

Wender, Paul. 1971. *Minimal Brain Dysfunction in Children.* New York: John Wiley and Sons.

Zola, Irving. 1972. "Medicine as an Institution of Social Control." *Sociological Review,* 20 (November): 487–504.

Part 2 / Understanding Deviance: Theories and Perspectives

In Part 1 I introduced a specific concern for the ways in which deviant categories arise, as well as the ways in which violators of existing categories may be reacted to. Missing from this introduction was a concern for *why* actors may exhibit behavior in violation of established norms, rules, regulations, and laws—violations that may cause them to be initially labeled as deviants. I have argued previously that if we are to approach a more complete understanding of deviance in terms of social processes, we must not only analyze the creation of deviant categories and the reactions to violators of categories; we must also examine the motivations for deviance. The selections in this part represent some of the major attempts to accomplish this goal.

Explanations of the motivations for deviance have taken various forms. Some observers would place the blame on a defective family structure or arrested personality adjustment; others would emphasize such conditions as poverty or racism; and there are proponents of the thesis that individuals are born deviant. It should be recognized, however, that no single factor can adequately explain why actors commit deviant acts. For example, findings in the area of delinquency research generally conclude that a combination of family, school, and peer variables is the most likely source of motivations for youth crime and deviance.

The actual attempts at understanding or explaining motivations for deviancy can, for our purposes, be roughly grouped into seven categories: (1) functionalist, (2) culture conflict, (3) cultural transmission, (4) anomie, (5) radical-conflict, (6) control, and (7) interactionist. Of these particular approaches, it should be noted that functionalism, culture conflict, control theory, and anomie are basically structural. Some structuralists seek to explain why crime and deviance exist in the social system, whereas others analyze societal-structural conditions that seem to produce pressures toward deviation. The cultural transmission view is concerned primarily with how, through social-psychological-symbolic processes, actors learn existing cultures and traditions. The radical-conflict theorists, by contrast, investigate how the powerful influence the creation of deviant categories and point out the frequent application of such categories to the less powerful. Finally, the interactionists analyze the labeling ceremony and its impact on individuals. Although each of these approaches explicitly emphasizes certain underlying themes, concepts, or processes, there is frequently an implied or direct overlap among the various models. Such linkages are evident in the subsequent discussions of each model.

THE FUNCTIONALIST PERSPECTIVE

Social scientists who use a functionalist model contend that deviance is an integral part of any social system and that such behavior satisfies some societal need. In terms of sociological analysis, advocates of this model maintain that deviance serves the important function of demarcating and maintaining current boundaries of acceptable behavior. These particular conceptions are embedded in Emile Durkheim's work.

In his statement "The Normal and the Pathological," Durkheim argues that crime not only inheres in all societies but also serves a useful function for the collective conscience, particularly in maintaining the social system. And although forms and definitions of criminal and deviant behavior (i.e., the *collective types* or deviant categories) may vary from society to society, such behaviors do provide members with a basis for punishing violators of the prevailing normative codes. Punishment serves as an important reminder to others that certain behaviors are acceptable while others are not. Thus, achievement of an understanding of deviance and its categories requires an examination of the prevailing definitions of conformity.

In "On the Sociology of Deviance," Kai T. Erikson argues that behavior that may be acceptable within a family setting may not be perceived as such by the larger community. Furthermore, conduct that may be viewed unfavorably by the community may actually go unnoticed in other parts of the culture. In varying situations, then, different standards are used to assess whether or not an actor's behavior exceeds a social unit's "tolerance limits." If it does, the violator may be sanctioned negatively. In a sense, a community or social unit is concerned with the maintenance of its boundaries. Erikson argues that interactions occurring between a potential deviant and a community's official agents play an especially important role in "locating and publicizing the group's outer edges." Such confrontations are not without their individual and structural ramifications, however. Not only may a social actor be selected out, formally processed, and cast into a new status (e.g., that of a criminal), but if the violator is a member of a deviant group, the confrontation and resultant sanctioning may operate in such a way as to actually enhance an actor's esteem in the eyes of his or her peers, as well as to solidify and make more obvious the underlying structure, identity, and character of the group. Erikson goes on to offer some interesting observations. For example, he comments on the fact that even though selected institutions have been created to combat deviance, they, like many deviant groups, often operate in such a way as to encourage, promote, and perpetuate it.

It should be noted that Erikson, given his primary focus on the maintenance and operation of normative systems, is not concerned specifically with explaining why actors engage in activities that may cause them to be labeled as deviants by others. The next perspective, however, considers the question of motivation more directly; in doing so, it enters the realm of social-psychological, or interactional, processes, particularly those aspects involved with the inculcation of values and traditions within members of society.

THE CULTURE CONFLICT PERSPECTIVE

A basic premise underlying this perspective is the notion that, because socializing influences and experiences vary a great deal, people are frequently confronted with conflicting definitions of a situation. Furthermore, if they act in accordance with their own values, they may be defined as deviants by those who are operating from a different set of values.

These ideas are elaborated upon by Thorsten Sellin. In "The Conflict of Conduct Norms," he argues that actors are members of numerous groups and are, therefore, exposed to many different sets of conduct norms and values. Among those who migrate from one society to another, the sense of cultural conflict may be particularly severe. Migrants frequently find themselves constrained and regulated by a new and unfamiliar set of values. Sellin cites, as an example, the case in which a father kills the seducer of his daughter. In Sicily, killing a seducer is acceptable; in the United States it is considered murder. A lack of consensus with respect to existing norms, then, may not only give rise to cultural conflicts of various types but may also result in the application of deviant labels to those who violate deviant categories.

J. Mark Watson, in "Outlaw Motorcyclists: An Outgrowth of Lower Class Cultural Concerns," provides another illustration of the culture conflict model. Watson focuses on outlaw motorcyclists—a subculture that he studied as a participant-observer over a period of three years. He begins by describing the biker subculture and the associated outlaw lifestyle. Of interest are the ways in which the outlaw bikers view the world and themselves. They tend to see the world as "hostile, weak, and effeminate" while viewing themselves as "outsiders." Watson concludes with an analysis of how the biker subculture, in its operation, compares with a typology of "focal concerns" (e.g., the emphasis that is placed on "trouble," "toughness," "smartness," and "excitement") developed by Walter Miller. For example, trouble is more than a major theme; it serves important functions for the group (e.g., it provides an opportunity for demonstrating masculinity and helps to enforce group solidarity). The selection gives an excellent feel for how a particular subculture operates in a larger, dominant culture—a culture that possesses the power and resources to tag people as "outsiders."

CULTURAL TRANSMISSION THEORY

A central tenet underlying the cultural transmission model is the idea that one learns cultural traditions and values through symbolic communication with others. Two of the more famous representatives of this position are Gresham M. Sykes and David Matza.

In "Techniques of Neutralization: A Theory of Delinquency," Sykes and Matza argue that juveniles do not really reject middle-class values. Rather, because the existing normative structure has a certain flexibility, actors can "bend" the laws to fit their needs. Also basic to this thesis is the idea that when actors contemplate the commission of a delinquent or criminal act, they must come to grips with any immediate or potential threats to their identity. Developing an effective system of "neutralization" or rationalization is one way of accomplishing this. Sykes and Matza assert, moreover, that this attitude of self-justification is operative during and after the commission of an offense as well. The writers make the additional point that we all use rationalizations, whether we are involved in deviant activities or not.

Diana Scully and Joseph Marolla, in "Convicted Rapists' Vocabulary of Motive: Excuses and Justifications," focus on rape. Their basic assumption is that, contrary to many of the individualistic notions that are advanced to explain it (e.g., rapists are propelled by "irresistible impulses" or "diseased minds"), rape is behavior that is learned in interaction with others. And similar to the Sykes-Matza position, a portion of this learning entails acquiring those attitudes, motives, and actions that are conducive to the sexual assault of women. The researchers, in their interviews with 114 convicted rapists, offer evidence in support of this thesis. They observe that their sample can be divided into two basic categories of rapists: the admitters and the deniers. The "deniers" attempt to justify their rapes by casting aspersions on the victim; in doing so, they often invoke selected cultural stereotypes (e.g., women are seductresses, women really mean "yes" when they say "no," nice girls don't get raped, and the like). The "admitters," by contrast, regard their behavior as wrong, not justifiable, and frequently blame themselves instead of the victim; they use various appeals to excuse their rapes (e.g., drugs, alcohol, emotional problems, and so on).

Several of the articles discussed thus far (e.g., the one by Sykes and Matza) have been concerned rather directly with the way in which socialization processes may bring about behavior that can be labeled as deviant. However, with one notable exception (Watson's theory), none of these writers has systematically examined the conditions that may lead to an exploration of nonconformist adaptations. The next perspective offers a more specific attempt to do so.

ANOMIE OR OPPORTUNITY THEORY

Those who subscribe to anomie theory are concerned primarily with the social conditions that may produce a strain toward deviation. Of particular focus is the way actors posture themselves relative to the existing social structure. Robert K. Merton's article, "Social Structure and Anomie," represents what many consider the classic study, within anomie theory, of the emergence of deviant behavior.

Basic to Merton's explanation is the contention that any society can be characterized in terms of its structure, particularly its goals and its means. A well-integrated society, he reasons, displays a balance between these elements. In such a society, when people want to obtain societal goals, they will use the appropriate institutionalized means for doing so. American society, according to Merton, does not maintain this sort of balance. It is a society in which emphasis is placed almost exclusively on the achievement of goals—regardless of the methods used to attain them. Those affected the most by the imbalance are the *lower classes*. Most members of the lower classes accept the American dream of attaining success; when they attempt to realize their goals through legitimate means, however, they find themselves blocked, mainly because they do not possess the necessary resources. They may substitute other means—for instance, stealing or robbing. Merton refers to these individuals as "innovators." He argues, further, that when there is a disjunction between goals and means, the result may be cultural chaos, or *anomie*. In this situation, the predictability and regulation of behavior become tenuous.

Richard A. Cloward and Lloyd E. Ohlin, in "Differential Opportunity and Delinquent Subcultures," extend Merton's theory by incorporating the notion of *illegitimate opportunity structures;* they also make a significant contribution to the literature on the formation of deviant subcultures. The authors argue specifically that, just as there are differentials in access to legitimate means (Merton), so there are differentials in access to illegitimate means. Hence, illegitimate avenues are not necessarily open or freely available to all those unable to obtain goals through legitimate channels. Not everyone, for instance, can become a successful con artist or embezzler. Cloward and Ohlin substantiate their thesis by showing how status-deprived, lower-class males learn the necessary skills associated with a particular type of criminal activity. Whether a specific activity or subculture evolves, however, is a function of the existing structure of the neighborhood, especially the relative availability of legitimate and illegitimate opportunity structures. For example, in a setting that exhibits a high degree of integration, or interplay, between legitimate and illegitimate structures, a criminal subculture is likely to evolve. Such a subculture furnishes the deprived with a source of material gain and provides them with a setting in which they can become socialized into the ways of an existing culture and traditions.

Although several of the statements thus far have offered hypotheses as to why deviance exists in a social system—and why actors commit deviant acts—none has provided an overall framework that can be used to understand how deviant categories arise, why they are violated, and how they are enforced. (The major exception is Becker's general statement in Part 1.) The next perspective addresses these concerns in a more systematic, integrated manner.

RADICAL-CONFLICT THEORY

Radical-conflict theorists study groups, particularly the ways in which their interests and needs influence the definitions, laws, and policies that evolve. Jeffrey H. Reiman, in "A Radical Perspective on Crime," offers a contemporary statement on the conflict model. He maintains that laws and the associated criminal justice system operate in such a manner as to support the established social and economic order. Concentrating on the individual wrongdoer, Reiman argues, is a particularly effective way of attaining this end. By blaming the individual, the criminal justice system simultaneously diverts our attention away from the possible evils of the social order and acquits society of any criminality or injustice. Further, Reiman argues that various types of social arrangements actually sustain and benefit from the perpetuation of the ideology of individual failure or blame. Reiman uses portions of Cloward and Ohlin's theory to buttress his case. For example, even though people are encouraged to succeed, many do fail, and especially those from the lower classes. As Reiman puts it: "... many are called but few are chosen." Involvement in criminal activities does offer an outlet for those experiencing failure and frustration. Thus, not only is society structured in such a way as to actually produce crime, but those who "reap the benefits of the competition for success" (i.e., those who enjoy a high standard of living) do not have to pay for the costs of this competition. The bill is paid by the poor. In fact, the affluent, Reiman argues, deny that they benefit from an economic system that produces a high degree of suffering and frustration for the poor.

This bias against the poor is manifested in other ways. Reiman speaks specifically of the bonuses associated with such a bias. For example, an image is conveyed that the real threat to a decent society comes from the poor. Another important bonus for the powerful is that the bias generates persistent hostility toward the poor. Reiman then notes some of the indignities that the poor suffer at the hands of the welfare system and its agents. Aid, instead of being viewed as an act of justice, is perceived as an act of charity. Many of these points, I might add, will be elaborated on in Part 6, particularly in my discussion of the need to rehabilitate institutions and social systems.

William J. Chambliss, in "A Sociological Analysis of the Law of Vagrancy," provides an interesting account of how selected vagrancy laws came into being. He focuses initially on those social conditions that produced the first full-fledged vagrancy law. This statute, passed in England in 1349, was a partial outgrowth of the Black Death that struck in 1348. Probably the most significant economic effect produced by this pestilence was the decimation of the labor force. At least 50 percent of the population died at a time when the English economy was dependent on a cheap source of labor. Even prior to the Black Death, obtaining an adequate supply of cheap labor was becoming a problem. It was in conditions such as these that the first vagrancy laws emerged. Chambliss maintains that the statutes were actually designed for one express purpose: to force laborers to accept employment under conditions favorable to the landowners. The laws also effectively curtailed the geographical mobility of laborers. In time, such curtailment was no longer necessary. However, the statutes were not eliminated or negated; rather, they underwent some notable alterations. For example, a modification passed in England in 1530 shifted society's focus from laborers to criminals. Chambliss ends by presenting a general discussion of vagrancy laws in the United States—many of which are adoptions of English laws.

CONTROL THEORY

A central feature of control theory is the view that various levels and types of societal commitment, when coupled with other factors, are often important precursors to the commission of deviant acts. Travis Hirschi offers a well-known statement of this position.

In "A Control Theory of Delinquency," he notes that control theorists assume that delinquency will result when an actor's bond to society is weakened or broken. He then proceeds to discuss and analyze the various elements that comprise the bond of society, particularly as they relate to the question of motivation. For example, the "commitment" element refers to the idea that most people invest a great deal of time and energy in conventional lines of activity (e.g., educational and occupational pursuits). When deviant behavior is contemplated, the risks of such deviation must be considered. The guiding assumption is that involvement in deviance or crime would jeopardize one's investments. Hirschi concludes with a section on "belief," another major element of the bond to society. The underlying premise is that society is characterized by a common value system. If this is correct—and if, further, one retains some type of allegiance to established values—then a basic question presents itself: "Why does a man violate the rules in which he believes?" Hirschi, in his attempt to answer this question, rejects the view that an actor must rationalize or neutralize his or her behavior. Hirschi prefers, instead, the notion that the weakness of one's beliefs can be used to explain motivation. When a person's belief in the validity of norms is weakened, the probability of delinquency and deviance increases.

Neal Shover and David Honaker, in "The Socially Bounded Decision Making of Persistent Property Offenders," offer another variant of this position. The researchers are concerned specifically with analyzing the criminal decision-making processes used by persistent property offenders. A central focus, then, becomes the matter of *choice*. Do, for example, prior offenders, in their pursuit of financial or criminal gain, actually "discount or ignore the formal risks of crime?" Shover and Honaker attempt to shed some light on this concern. They offer interview data obtained from 60 career criminals—all of whom had been out of prison at least seven months. The subjects were asked to recount the crimes they had committed subsequent to their release, as well as how the decision was made to commit the crime. Of concern were their assessments of the potential risks and awards associated with the commission of an illegal act. Some interesting findings emerged. For example, the majority gave little thought to the possibility of arrest or subsequent incarceration. The researchers go on to argue that it is useful to examine the decision-making process of offenders within the context of their lifestyle. A central characteristic of this process is referred to as the *life as party* syndrome—a lifestyle that in addition to promoting the notion of "good times," exhibits little concern for those commitments that go beyond one's present social setting. Shover and Honaker conclude by discussing various implications of their results. Risk perceptions, it is suggested, should be analyzed in terms of the various situations or contexts that affect people.

The last perspective to be considered in this section—the interactionist view—is not specifically concerned with the evolution or violation of deviant categories. Rather, this model explores the ways in which people who violate deviant categories (for whatever reasons) are responded to by formal and informal agents of social control. In this respect, definitional and interactional processes are given central focus. As explicated and refined by the interactional and organizational paradigms in the general introduction, this perspective is applied systematically throughout the remainder of this volume.

THE INTERACTIONIST, SOCIETAL REACTIONS, OR LABELING PERSPECTIVE

Individuals who subscribe to the interactionist, or labeling, school examine those social and psychological, or interactional, processes that take place among actors, audiences, and third parties, particularly in terms of their impact on the personal and social-public identity of the actor. The main concern of these proponents, then, is definitional processes and products, and their effects.

Edwin M. Lemert, in "Primary and Secondary Deviation," is concerned with the "sequence of interaction" that takes place between actors and audiences—especially those aspects that ultimately give rise to secondary or career deviance. Central to this process are the actor's perception of and reactions to the negative social reactions he or she encounters. Quite often the actor's response to negative sanctions (or punishments) leads to the application of additional penalties. This type of reciprocal relationship can gradually deteriorate until the deviant actually accepts the imputed status or label. The acceptance of this particular status and its associated label frequently results in other significant changes. The deviant may, for example, buy new clothes and change his or her speech, posture, and mannerisms to fit the new role.

Howard S. Becker has explored the concept of career, the major orienting focus of this volume, in some depth. He also introduces some important analytical distinctions. In "Career Deviance," he argues that public labeling is generally the most crucial step in building a long-term deviant career. Not only does being branded a deviant affect one's continued social participation, but it frequently produces notable changes in the actor's self-image. The most drastic change, however, seems to occur with respect to the actor's public identity—that is, how others view him or her. Suddenly, in the eyes of others he or she has become a different person; this new status can be effectively referred to as a *master status*. In offering an important distinction between master and subordinate statuses, Becker argues that master statuses assume a certain priority and appear to override most other status considerations.

The status of a deviant is one such status. In relating to a deviant, people will frequently respond to the label and not to the individual. Treatment of an actor in this fashion—as if he or she is generally deviant and not specifically deviant—can serve as a self-fulfilling prophecy whereby attempts are made to mold the actor into the image others have of him or her. Deliberate attempts may be made, for example, to exclude the deviant from any meaningful social intercourse. The actor may respond negatively to such treatment, and, over time, exclusion and its associated reactions can actually give rise to more deviance. The treatment situation, Becker claims, is especially likely to produce such a result. Many of these processes, as well as those described by Lemert, will become even more evident in my discussion of the initiation and perpetuation of deviant careers, particularly those careers that are subject to institutional processing (Part 4).

5 / The Normal and the Pathological

EMILE DURKHEIM

Crime is present not only in the majority of societies of one particular species but in all societies of all types. There is no society that is not confronted with the problem of criminality. Its form changes; the acts thus characterized are not the same everywhere; but, everywhere and always, there have been men who have behaved in such a way as to draw upon themselves penal repression. If, in proportion as societies pass from the lower to the higher types, the rate of criminality, i.e., the relation between the yearly number of crimes and the population, tended to decline, it might be believed that crime, while still normal, is tending to lose this character of normality. But we have no reason to believe that such a regression is substantiated. Many facts would seem rather to indicate a movement in the opposite direction. From the beginning of the [nineteenth] century, statistics enable us to follow the course of criminality. It has everywhere increased. In France the increase is nearly 300 per cent. There is, then, no phenomenon that presents more indisputably all the symptoms of normality, since it appears closely connected with the conditions of all collective life. To make of crime a form of social morbidity would be to admit that morbidity is not something accidental, but, on the contrary, that in certain cases it grows out of the fundamental constitution of the living organism; it would result in wiping out all distinction between the physiological and the pathological. No doubt it is possible that crime itself will have abnormal forms, as, for example, when its rate is unusually high. This excess is, indeed, undoubtedly morbid in nature. What is normal, simply, is the existence of criminality, provided that it attains and does not exceed, for each social type, a certain level, which it is perhaps not impossible to fix in conformity with the preceding rules.[1]

Here we are, then, in the presence of a conclusion in appearance quite paradoxical. Let us make no mistake. To classify crime among the phenomena of normal sociology is not to say merely that it is an inevitable, although regrettable phenomenon, due to the incorrigible wickedness of men; it is to affirm that it is a factor in public health, an integral part of all healthy societies. This result is, at first glance, surprising enough to have puzzled even ourselves for a long time. Once this first surprise has been overcome, however, it is not difficult to find reasons explaining this normality and at the same time confirming it.

In the first place crime is normal because a society exempt from it is utterly impossible. Crime, we have shown elsewhere, consists of an act that offends certain very strong collective sentiments. In a society in which criminal acts are no longer committed, the sentiments they offend would have to be found without exception in all individual consciousnesses, and they must be found to exist with the same degree as sentiments contrary to them. Assuming that this condition could actually be realized, crime would not thereby disappear; it would only change its form, for the very cause which would thus dry up the sources of criminality would immediately open up new ones.

Indeed, for the collective sentiments which are protected by the penal law of a people at a specified moment of its history to take possession of the public conscience or for them to acquire a stronger hold where they have an insufficient grip, they must acquire an intensity greater than that which they had hitherto had. The community as a whole must experience them more vividly, for it can acquire from no other source the greater force necessary to control these individuals who formerly were the most refractory. For murderers to disappear, the horror of bloodshed must become greater in those social strata from which murderers are recruited; but, first it must become greater throughout the entire society. Moreover, the very absence of crime would directly contribute to produce this horror; because any sentiment seems much more respectable when it is always and uniformly respected.

One easily overlooks the consideration that these strong states of the common consciousness cannot be thus reinforced without reinforcing at the same time the more feeble states, whose violation previously gave birth to mere infraction of convention—since the weaker ones are only the prolongation, the attenuated form, of the stronger. Thus robbery and simple bad taste injure the same single altruistic sentiment, the respect for that which is another's. However, this same sentiment is less grievously offended by bad taste than by robbery; and since, in addition, the average consciousness has not sufficient intensity to react keenly to the bad taste, it is treated with greater tolerance. That is why the person guilty of bad taste is merely blamed, whereas the thief is punished. But, if this sentiment grows stronger, to the point of silencing in all consciousnesses the inclination which disposes man to steal, he will become more sensitive to the offenses which, until then, touched him but lightly. He will react against them, then, with more energy; they will be the object of greater opprobrium, which will transform certain of them from the simple moral faults that they were and give them the quality of crimes. For example, improper contracts, or contracts improperly executed, which only incur public blame or civil damages, will become offenses in law.

Imagine a society of saints, a perfect cloister of exemplary individuals. Crimes, properly so called, will there be unknown; but faults which appear venial to the layman will create there the same scandal that the ordinary offense does in ordinary consciousnesses. If, then, this society has the power to judge and punish, it will define these acts as criminal and will treat them as such. For the same reason, the perfect and upright man judges his smallest failings with a severity that the majority reserve for acts more truly in the nature of an offense. Formerly, acts of violence against persons were more frequent than they are today, because respect for individual dignity was less strong. As this has increased, these crimes have become more rare; and also, many acts violating this sentiment have been introduced into the penal law which were not included there in primitive times.[2]

In order to exhaust all the hypotheses logically possible, it will perhaps be asked why this unanimity does not extend to all collective sentiments without exception. Why should not even the most feeble sentiment gather enough energy to prevent all dissent? The moral consciousness of the society would be present in its entirety in all the individuals, with a vitality sufficient to prevent all acts offending it—the purely conventional faults as well as the crimes. But a uniformity so universal and absolute is utterly impossible; for the immediate physical milieu in which each one of us is placed, the hereditary antecedents, and the social influences vary from one individual to the next, and consequently diversify consciousnesses. It is impossible for all to be alike, if only because each one has his own organism and that these organisms occupy different areas in space. That is why, even among the lower peoples, where individual originality is very little developed, it nevertheless does exist.

Thus, since there cannot be a society in which the individuals do not differ more or less from the collective type, it is also inevitable that, among these divergences, there are some with a criminal character. What confers this character upon them is not the intrinsic quality of a given act but that definition which the collective conscience lends them. If the collective conscience is stronger, if it has enough authority practically to suppress these divergences, it will also be more sensitive, more exacting; and, reacting against the slightest deviations with the energy it otherwise displays only against more considerable infractions, it will attribute to them the same gravity as formerly to crimes. In other words, it will designate them as criminal.

Crime is, then, necessary; it is bound up with fundamental conditions of all social life, and by that very fact it is useful, because these conditions of which it is part are themselves indispensable to the normal evolution of morality and law.

Indeed, it is no longer possible today to dispute the fact that law and morality vary from one social type to the next, nor that they change within the same type if the conditions of life are modified. But, in order that these transformations may be possible, the collective sentiments at the basis of morality must not be hostile to change, and consequently must have but moderate energy. If they were too strong, they would no longer be plastic. Every pattern is an obstacle to new patterns, to the extent that the first pattern is inflexible. The better a structure is articulated, the more it offers a healthy resistance to all modification; and this is equally true of functional, as of anatomical, organization. If there were no crimes, this condition could not have been fulfilled; for such a hypothesis presupposes that collective sentiments have arrived at a degree of intensity unexampled in history. Nothing is good indefinitely and to an unlimited extent. The authority which the moral conscience enjoys must not be excessive; otherwise no one would dare criticize it, and it would too easily congeal into an immutable form. To make progress, individual originality must be able to express itself. In order that the originality of the idealist whose dreams transcend his century may find expression, it is necessary that the originality of the criminal, who is below the level of his time, shall also be possible. One does not occur without the other.

Nor is this all. Aside from this indirect utility, it happens that crime itself plays a useful role in this evolution. Crime implies not only that the way remains open to necessary changes but that in certain cases it directly prepares these changes. Where crime exists, collective sentiments are sufficiently flexible to take on a new form, and crime sometimes helps to determine the form they will take. How many times, indeed, it is only an anticipation of future morality—a step toward what will be! According to Athenian law, Socrates was a criminal, and his condemnation was no more than just. However, his crime, namely, the independence of his thought, rendered a service not only to humanity but to his country. It served to prepare a new morality and faith which the Athenians needed, since the traditions by which they had lived until then were no longer in harmony with the current conditions of life. Nor is the case of Socrates unique; it is reproduced periodically in history. It would never have been possible to establish the freedom of thought we now enjoy if the regulations prohibiting it had not been violated before being solemnly abrogated. At that time, however, the violation was a crime, since it was an offense against sentiments still very keen in the average conscience. And yet this crime was useful as a prelude to reforms which daily became more necessary. Liberal philosophy had as its precursors the heretics of all kinds who were justly punished by secular authorities during the entire course of the Middle Ages and until the eve of modern times.

From this point of view the fundamental facts of criminality present themselves to us in an entirely new light. Contrary to current ideas, the criminal no longer seems a totally unsociable being, a sort of parasitic element, a strange and unassimilable body, introduced into the midst of society.[3] On the contrary, he plays a definite role in social life. Crime, for its part, must no longer be conceived as an evil that cannot be too much suppressed. There is no occasion for self-congratulation when the crime rate drops noticeably below the average level, for we may be certain that this apparent progress is associated with some social disorder. Thus, the number of assault cases never falls so low as in times of want.[4] With the drop in the crime rate, and as a reaction to it, comes a revision, or the need of a revision in the theory of punishment. If, indeed, crime is a disease, its punishment is its remedy and cannot be otherwise conceived; thus, all the discussions it arouses bear on the point of determining what the punishment must be in order to fulfil this role of remedy. If crime is not pathological at all, the object of punishment cannot be to cure it, and its true function must be sought elsewhere.

Notes

1. From the fact that crime is a phenomenon of normal sociology, it does not follow that the criminal is an individual normally constituted from the biological and psychological points of view. The two questions are independent of each other. This independence will be better understood when we have shown, later on, the difference between psychological and sociological facts.

2. Calumny, insults, slander, fraud, etc.

3. We have ourselves committed the error of speaking thus of the criminal, because of a failure to apply our rule (*Division du travail social,* pp. 395–96).

4. Although crime is a fact of normal sociology, it does not follow that we must not abhor it. Pain itself has nothing desirable about it; the individual dislikes it as society does crime, and yet it is a function of normal physiology. Not only is it necessarily derived from the very constitution of every living organism, but it plays a useful role in life, for which reason it cannot be replaced. It would, then, be a singular distortion of our thought to present it as an apology for crime. We would not even think of protesting against such an interpretation, did we not know to what strange accusations and misunderstandings one exposes oneself when one undertakes to study moral facts objectively and to speak of them in a different language from that of the layman.

6 / On the Sociology of Deviance

KAI T. ERIKSON

Human actors are sorted into various kinds of collectivity, ranging from relatively small units such as the nuclear family to relatively large ones such as a nation or culture. One of the most stubborn difficulties in the study of deviation is that the problem is defined differently at each one of these levels: behavior that is considered unseemly within the context of a single family may be entirely acceptable to the community in general, while behavior that attracts severe censure from the members of the community may go altogether unnoticed elsewhere in the culture. People in society, then, must learn to deal separately with deviance at each one of these levels and to distinguish among them in his own daily activity. A man may disinherit his son for conduct that violates old family traditions or ostracize a neighbor for conduct that violates some local custom, but he is not expected to employ either of these standards when he serves as a juror in a court of law. In each of the three situations he is required to use a different set of criteria to decide whether or not the behavior in question exceeds tolerable limits.

In the next few pages we shall be talking about deviant behavior in social units called "communities," but the use of this term does not mean that the argument applies only at that level of organization. In theory, at least, the argument being made here should fit all kinds of human collectivity—families as well as whole cultures, small groups as well as nations—and the term "community" is only being used in this context because it seems particularly convenient.[1]

The people of a community spend most of their lives in close contact with one another, sharing a common sphere of experience which makes them feel that they belong to a special "kind" and live in a special "place." In the formal language of sociology, this means that communities are boundary maintaining: each has a specific territory in the world as a whole, not only in the sense that it occupies a defined region of geographical space but also in the sense that it takes over a particular niche in what might be called cultural space and develops its own "ethos" or "way" within that compass. Both of these dimensions of group space, the geographical and the cultural, set the community apart as a special place and provide an important point of reference for its members.

When one describes any system as boundary maintaining, one is saying that it controls the fluctuation of its consistent parts so that the whole retains a limited range of activity, a given pattern of constancy and stability, within the larger environment. A human community can be said to maintain boundaries, then, in the sense that its members tend to confine themselves to a particular radius of activity and to regard any conduct which drifts outside that radius as somehow inappropriate or immoral. Thus the group retains a kind of cultural integrity, a voluntary restriction on its own potential for expansion, beyond that which is strictly required for accommodation to the environment. Human behavior can vary over an enormous range, but each community draws a symbolic set of parentheses around a certain segment of that range and limits its own activities within that narrower zone. These parentheses, so to speak, are the community's boundaries.

Now people who live together in communities cannot relate to one another in any coherent way or even acquire a sense of their own stature as group members unless they learn something about the boundaries of the territory they occupy in social space, if only because they need to sense what lies beyond the margins of the group before they can appreciate the special quality of the experience which takes place within it. Yet how do people learn about the boundaries of their community? And how do they convey this information to the generations which replace them?

To begin with, the only material found in a society for marking boundaries is the behavior of its members—or rather, the networks of interaction which link these members together in regular social relations. And the interactions which do the most effective job of locating and publicizing the group's outer edges would seem to be those which take place between deviant persons on the one side and official agents of the community on the other. The deviant is a person whose activities have moved outside the margins of the group, and when the community calls him to account for that vagrancy it is making a statement about the nature and placement of its boundaries. It is declaring how much variability and diversity can be tolerated within the group before it begins to lose its distinctive shape, its unique identity. Now there may be other moments in the life of the group which perform a similar service: wars, for instance, can publicize a group's boundaries by drawing attention to the line separating the group from an adversary, and certain kinds of religious ritual, dance ceremony, and other traditional pageantry can dramatize the difference between "we" and "they" by portraying a symbolic encounter between the two. But on the whole, members of a community inform one another about the placement of their boundaries by participating in the confrontations which occur when persons who venture out to the edges of the group are met by policing agents whose special business it is to guard the cultural integrity of the community. Whether these confrontations take the form of criminal trials, excommunication hearings, courts-martial, or even psychiatric case conferences, they act as boundary-maintaining devices in the sense that they demonstrate to whatever audience is concerned where the line is drawn between behavior that belongs in the special universe of the group and behavior that does not. In general, this kind of information is not easily relayed by the straightforward use of language. Most readers of this paragraph, for instance, have a fairly clear idea of the line separating theft from more legitimate forms of commerce, but few of them have ever seen a published statute describing these differences. More likely than not, our information on the subject has been drawn from publicized instances in which the relevant laws were applied—and for that matter, the law itself is largely a collection of past cases and decisions, a synthesis of the various confrontations which have occurred in the life of the legal order.

It may be important to note in this connection that confrontations between deviant offenders and the agents of control have always attracted a good deal of public attention. In our own past, the trial and punishment of offenders were staged in the market place and afforded the crowd a chance to participate in a direct, active way. Today, of course, we no longer parade deviants in the town square or expose them to the carnival atmosphere of a Tyburn, but it is interesting that the "reform" which brought about this change in penal practice coincided almost exactly with the development of newspapers as a medium of mass information. Perhaps this is no more than an accident of history, but it is nonetheless true that newspapers (and now radio and television) offer much the same kind of entertainment as public hangings or a Sunday visit to the local gaol. A considerable portion of what we call "news" is devoted to reports about deviant behavior and its consequences, and it is no simple matter to explain why these items should be considered newsworthy or why they should command the extraordinary attention they do. Perhaps they appeal to a number of psychological perversities among the mass audience, as commentators have suggested, but at the same time they constitute one of our main sources of information about the normative outlines of society. In a figurative sense, at least, morality and immorality meet at the public scaffold, and it is during this meeting that the line between them is drawn.

Boundaries are never a fixed property of any community. They are always shifting as the people of the group find new ways to define the outer limits of their universe, new ways to position themselves on the larger cultural map. Sometimes changes occur within the structure of the group which require its members to make a new survey of their territory—a change of leadership, a shift of mood. Sometimes changes occur in the surrounding environment, altering the background against which the people of the group have measured their own uniqueness. And always, new generations are moving in to take their turn guarding old institutions and need to be informed about the contours of the world they are inheriting. Thus single encounters between the deviant and his community are only fragments of an ongoing social process. Like an article of common law, boundaries remain a meaningful point of reference only so long as they are repeatedly tested by persons on the fringes of the group and repeatedly defended by persons chosen to represent the group's inner morality. Each time the community moves to censure some act of deviation, then, and convenes a formal ceremony to deal with the responsible offender, it sharpens the authority of the violated norm and restates where the boundaries of the group are located.

For these reasons, deviant behavior is not a simple kind of leakage which occurs when the machinery of society is in poor working order, but may be, in controlled quantities, an important condition for preserving the stability of social life. Deviant forms of behavior, by marking the outer edges of group life, give the inner structure its special character and thus supply the framework within which the people of the group develop an orderly sense of their own cultural identity. Perhaps this is what Aldous Huxley had in mind when he wrote:

> Now tidiness is undeniably good—but a good of which it is easily possible to have too much and at too high a price.... The good life can only be lived in a society in which tidiness is preached and practised, but not too fanatically, and where efficiency is always haloed, as it were, by a tolerated margin of mess.[2]

This raises a delicate theoretical issue. If we grant that human groups often derive benefit from deviant behavior, can we then assume that they are organized in such a way as to promote this resource? Can we assume, in other words, that forces operate in the social structure to recruit offenders and to commit them to long periods of service in the deviant ranks? This is not a question which can be answered with our present store of empirical data, but one observation can be made which gives the question an interesting perspective—namely, that deviant forms of conduct often seem to derive nourishment from the very agencies devised to inhibit them. Indeed, the agencies built by society for preventing deviance are often so poorly equipped for the task that we might well ask why this is regarded as their "real" function in the first place.

It is by now a thoroughly familiar argument that many of the institutions designed to discourage deviant behavior actually operate in such a way as to perpetuate it. For one thing, prisons, hospitals, and other similar agencies provide aid and shelter to large numbers of deviant persons, sometimes giving them a certain advantage in the competition for social resources. But beyond this, such institutions gather marginal people into tightly segregated groups, give them an opportunity to teach one another the skills and attitudes of a deviant career, and even provoke them into using these skills by reinforcing their sense of alienation from the rest of society.[3] Nor is this observation a modern one:

> The misery suffered in gaols is not half their evil; they are filled with every sort of corruption that poverty and wickedness can generate; with all the shameless and profligate enormities that can be produced by the impudence of ignominy, the range of want, and the malignity of dispair. In a prison the check of the public

> eye is removed; and the power of the law is spent. There are few fears, there are no blushes. The lewd inflame the more modest; the audacious harden the timid. Everyone fortifies himself as he can against his own remaining sensibility; endeavoring to practise on others the arts that are practised on himself; and to gain the applause of his worst associates by imitating their manners.[4]

These lines, written almost two centuries ago, are a harsh indictment of prisons, but many of the conditions they describe continue to be reported in even the most modern studies of prison life. Looking at the matter from a long-range historical perspective, it is fair to conclude that prisons have done a conspicuously poor job of reforming the convicts placed in their custody; but the very consistency of this failure may have a peculiar logic of its own. Perhaps we find it difficult to change the worst of our penal practices because we *expect* the prison to harden the inmate's commitment to deviant forms of behavior and draw him more deeply into the deviant ranks. On the whole, we are a people who do not really expect deviants to change very much as they are processed through the control agencies we provide for them, and we are often reluctant to devote much of the community's resources to the job of rehabilitation. In this sense, the prison which graduates long rows of accomplished criminals (or, for that matter, the state asylum which stores its most severe cases away in some back ward) may do serious violence to the aims of its founders; but it does very little violence to the expectations of the population it serves.

These expectations, moreover, are found in every corner of society and constitute an important part of the climate in which we deal with deviant forms of behavior.

To begin with, the community's decision to bring deviant sanctions against one of its members is not a simple act of censure. It is an intricate rite of transition, at once moving the individual out of his ordinary place in society and transferring him into a special deviant position.[5] The ceremonies which mark this change of status, generally, have a number of related phases. They supply a formal stage on which the deviant and his community can confront one another (as in the criminal trial); they make an announcement about the nature of his deviancy (a verdict or diagnosis, for example); and they place him in a particular role which is thought to neutralize the harmful effects of his misconduct (like the role of prisoner or patient). These commitment ceremonies tend to be occasions of wide public interest and ordinarily take place in a highly dramatic setting.[6] Perhaps the most obvious example of a commitment ceremony is the criminal trial, with its elaborate formality and exaggerated ritual, but more modest equivalents can be found wherever procedures are set up to judge whether or not someone is legitimately deviant.

Now an important feature of these ceremonies in our own culture is that they are almost irreversible. Most provisional roles conferred by society—those of the student or conscripted soldier, for example—include some kind of terminal ceremony to mark the individual's movement back out of the role once its temporary advantages have been exhausted. But the roles allotted the deviant seldom make allowance for this type of passage. He is ushered into the deviant position by a decisive and often dramatic ceremony, yet is retired from it with scarcely a word of public notice. And as a result, the deviant often returns home with no proper license to resume a normal life in the community. Nothing has happened to cancel out the stigmas imposed upon him by earlier commitment ceremonies; nothing has happened to revoke the verdict or diagnosis pronounced upon him at that time. It should not be surprising, then, that the people of the community are apt to greet the returning deviant with a considerable degree of apprehension and distrust, for in a very real sense they are not at all sure who he is.

A circularity is thus set into motion which has all the earmarks of a "self-fulfilling prophesy," to use Merton's fine phrase. On the one hand, it seems quite obvious that the community's apprehensions help reduce whatever chances the deviant might otherwise have had for a successful return home. Yet at the same time, everyday experience seems to show that these suspicions are wholly reasonable, for it is a well-known and highly publicized fact that many if not most ex-convicts return to crime after leaving prison and that large numbers of mental patients require further treatment after an initial hospitalization. The common feeling that deviant persons never really change, then, may derive from a faulty premise; but the feeling is expressed so frequently and with such conviction that it eventually creates the facts which later "prove" it to be correct. If the returning deviant encounters this circularity often enough, it is quite understandable that he, too, may begin to wonder whether he has fully graduated from the deviant role, and he may respond to the uncertainty by resuming some kind of deviant activity. In many respects, this may be the only way for the individual and his community to agree what kind of person he is.

Moreover this prophesy is found in the official policies of even the most responsible agencies of control. Police departments could not operate with any real effectiveness if they did not regard ex-convicts as a ready pool of suspects to be tapped in the event of trouble, and psychiatric clinics could not do a successful job in the community if they were not always alert to the possibility of former patients suffering relapses. Thus the prophesy gains currency at many levels within the social order, not only in the poorly informed attitudes of the community at large, but in the best informed theories of most control agencies as well.

In one form or another this problem has been recognized in the West for many hundreds of years, and this simple fact has a curious implication. For if our culture has supported a steady flow of deviation throughout long periods of historical change, the rules which apply to any kind of evolutionary thinking would suggest that strong forces must be at work to keep the flow intact—and this because it contributes in some important way to the survival of the culture as a whole. This does not furnish us with sufficient warrant to declare that deviance is "functional" (in any of the many senses of that term), but it should certainly make us wary of the assumption so often made in sociological circles that any well-structured society is somehow designed to prevent deviant behavior from occurring.[7]

It might be then argued that we need new metaphors to carry our thinking about deviance onto a different plane. On the whole, American sociologists have devoted most of their attention to those forces in society which seem to assert a centralizing influence on human behavior, gathering people together into tight clusters called "groups" and bringing them under the jurisdiction of governing principles called "norms" or "standards." The questions which sociologists have traditionally asked of their data, then, are addressed to the uniformities rather than the divergencies of social life: how is it that people learn to think in similar ways, to accept the same group moralities, to move by the same rhythms of behavior, to see life with the same eyes? How is it, in short, that cultures accomplish the incredible alchemy of making unity out of diversity, harmony out of conflict, order out of confusion? Somehow we often act as if the differences between people can be taken for granted, being too natural to require comment, but that the symmetry which human groups manage to achieve must be explained by referring to the molding influence of the social structure.

But variety, too, is a product of the social structure. It is certainly remarkable that members of a culture come to look so much alike; but it is also remarkable that out of all this sameness a people can develop a complex division of labor, move off into diverging career lines, scatter across the surface of the territory they share in common, and create so many differences of temper, ideology, fashion, and mood. Perhaps we can conclude, then, that two separate yet often competing currents are found in any society: those forces which promote a high degree of conformity among the people of the community so that they know what to expect from one another, and those forces which encourage a certain degree of diversity so that people can be deployed across the range of group space to survey its potential, measure its capacity, and, in the case of those we call deviants, patrol its boundaries. In such a scheme, the deviant would appear as a natural product of group differentiation. He is not a bit of debris spun out by faulty social machinery, but a relevant figure in the community's overall division of labor.

Notes

1. In fact, the first statement of the general notion presented here was concerned with the study of small groups. See Robert A. Dentler and Kai T. Erikson, "The Functions of Deviance in Groups," *Social Problems*, VII (Fall 1959), pp. 98–107.

2. Aldous Huxley, *Prisons: The "Carceri" Etchings by Piranesi* (London: The Trianon Press, 1949), p. 13.

3. For a good description of this process in the modern prison, see Gresham Sykes, *The Society of Captives* (Princeton, N.J.: Princeton University Press, 1958). For discussions of similar problems in two different kinds of mental hospital, see Erving Goffman, *Asylums* (New York: Bobbs-Merrill, 1962) and Kai T. Erikson, "Patient Role and Social Uncertainty: A Dilemma of the Mentally Ill," *Psychiatry*, XX (August 1957), pp. 263–274.

4. Written by "a celebrated" but not otherwise identified author (perhaps Henry Fielding) and quoted in John Howard, *The State of the Prisons*, London, 1777 (London: J. M. Dent and Sons, 1929), p. 10.

5. The classic description of this process as it applies to the medical patient is found in Talcott Parsons, *The Social System* (Glencoe, Ill.: The Free Press, 1951).

6. See Harold Garfinkel, "Successful Degradation Ceremonies," *American Journal of Sociology*, LXI (January 1956), pp. 420–424.

7. Albert K. Cohen, for example, speaking for a dominant strain in sociological thinking, takes the question quite for granted: "It would seem that the control of deviant behavior is, by definition, a culture goal." See "The Study of Social Disorganization and Deviant Behavior" in Merton, et al., *Sociology Today* (New York: Basic Books, 1959), p. 465.

7 / The Conflict of Conduct Norms

THORSTEN SELLIN

CULTURE CONFLICTS AS CONFLICTS OF CULTURAL CODES

...There are social groups on the surface of the earth which possess complexes of conduct norms which, due to differences in the mode of life and the social values evolved by these groups, appear to set them apart from other groups in many or most respects. We may expect conflicts of norms when the rural dweller moves to the city, but we assume that he has absorbed the basic norms of the culture which comprises both town and country. How much greater is not the conflict likely to be when Orient and Occident meet, or when the Corsican mountaineer is transplanted to the lower East Side of New York. Conflicts of cultures are inevitable when the norms of one cultural or subcultural area migrate to or come in contact with those of another.

Conflicts between the norms of divergent cultural codes may arise

1. when these codes clash on the border of contiguous culture areas;
2. when, as may be the case with legal norms, the law of one cultural group is extended to cover the territory of another; or
3. when members of one cultural group migrate to another.[1]

Speck, for instance, notes that "where the bands popularly known as Montagnais have come more and more into contact with Whites, their reputation has fallen lower among the traders who have known them through commercial relationships within that period. The accusation is made that they have become less honest in connection with their debts, less trustworthy with property, less truthful, and more inclined to alcoholism and sexual freedom as contacts with the frontier towns have become easier for them. Richard White reports in 1933 unusual instances of Naskapi breaking into traders' store houses."[2]

Similar illustrations abound in the works of the cultural anthropologists. We need only to recall the effect on the American Indian of the culture conflicts induced by our policy of acculturation by guile and force. In this instance, it was not merely contact with the white man's culture, his religion, his business methods, and his liquor, which weakened the tribal mores. In addition, the Indian became subject to the white man's law and this brought conflicts as well, as has always been the case when legal norms have been imposed upon a group previousy ignorant of them. Maunier[3] in discussing the diffusion of French law in Algeria, recently stated: "In introducing the *Code Penal* in our colonies, as we do, we transform into offenses the ancient usages of the inhabitants which their customs permitted or imposed. Thus, among the Khabyles of Algeria, the killing of adulterous wives is ritual murder committed by the father or brother of the wife and not by her husband, as elsewhere. The woman having been sold by her family to her husband's family, the honor of her relatives is soiled by her infidelity. Her father or brother has the right and the duty to kill her in order to cleanse by her blood the honor of her relatives. Murder in revenge is also a duty, from family to family, in case of murder of or even in case of insults to a relative: the vendetta, called the *rekba* in Khabylina, is imposed by the law of honor. But these are crimes in French law! Murder for revenge, being premeditated and planned, is assassination, punishable by death! ... What happens, then, often when our authorities pursue the criminal, guilty of an offense against public safety as well as against morality: public enemy of the French order, but who has acted in accord with a respected custom? The witnesses of the assassination, who are his relatives, or neighbors, fail to lay charges against the assassin; when they are questioned, they pretend to know nothing; and the pursuit is therefore useless. A French magistrate has been able to speak of the conspiracy of silence among the Algerians; a conspiracy aiming to preserve traditions, always followed and obeyed, against their violation by our power. This is the tragic aspect of the conflict of laws. A recent decree forbids the husband among the Khabyles to profit arbitrarily by the power given him according to this law to repudiate his wife, demanding that her new husband pay an exorbitant price for her—this is the custom of the *lefdi*. Earlier, one who married a repudiated wife paid nothing to the former husband. It appears that the first who tried to avail himself of the new law was killed for violating the old custom. The abolition of the ancient law does not always occur without protest or opposition. That which is a crime was a duty; and the order which we cause to reign is sometimes established to the detriment of 'superstition'; it is the gods and the spirits, it is believed, that would punish any one who fails to revenge his honor."

When Soviet law was extended to Siberia, similar effects were observed. Anossow[4] and Wirschubski[5] both relate that women among the Siberian tribes, who, in obedience to the law, laid aside their veils, were killed by their relatives for violating one of the most sacred norms of their tribes.

We have noted that culture conflicts are the natural outgrowth of processes of social differentiation, which produce an infinity of social groupings, each with its own definitions of life situations, its own interpretations of social relationships, its own ignorance or misunderstanding of the social values of other groups. The transformation of a culture from a homogeneous and well-integrated type to a heterogeneous and disintegrated type is therefore accompanied by an increase of conflict situations. Conversely, the operation of integrating processes will reduce the number of conflict situations. Such conflicts within a changing culture may be distinguished from those created when different cultural systems come in contact with one another, regardless of the character or stage of development of these systems. In either case, the conduct of members of a group involved in the conflict of codes will in some respects be judged abnormal by the other group.

THE STUDY OF CULTURE CONFLICTS

In the study of culture conflicts, some scholars have been concerned with the effect of such conflicts on the conduct of specific persons, an approach which is naturally preferred by psychologists and psychiatrists and by sociologists who have used the life history technique. These scholars view the conflict as internal. Wirth[6] states categorically that a culture "conflict can be said to be a factor in delinquency only if the individual feels it or acts as if it were present." Culture conflict is mental conflict, but the character of this conflict is viewed differently by the various disciplines which use this term. Freudian psychiatrists[7] regard it as a struggle between deeply rooted biological urges which demand expression and the culturally created rules which give rise to inhibitive mechanisms which thwart this expression and drive them below the conscious level of the mind, whence they rise either by ruse in some socially acceptable disguise, as abnormal conduct when the inhibiting mechanism breaks down, or as neuroses when it works too well. The sociologist, on the other hand, thinks of mental conflict as being primarily the clash between antagonistic conduct norms incorporated in personality. "Mental conflict in the person," says Burgess in discussing the case presented by Shaw in *The Jack-Roller*, "may always be explained in terms of the conflict of divergent cultures."[8]

If this view is accepted, sociological research on culture conflict and its relationships to abnormal conduct would have to be strictly limited to a study of the personality of cultural hybrids. Significant studies could be conducted only by the life-history case technique applied to persons in whom the conflict is internalized, appropriate control groups being utilized, of course....

The absence of mental conflict, in the sociological sense, may, however, be well studied in terms of culture conflict. An example may make this clear. A few years ago a Sicilian father in New Jersey killed the sixteen-year-old seducer of his daughter, expressing surprise at his arrest since he had merely defended his family honor in a traditional way. In this case a mental conflict in the sociological sense did not exist. The conflict was external and occurred between cultural codes or norms. We may assume that where such conflicts occur violations of norms will arise merely because persons who have absorbed the norms of one cultural group or area migrate to another and that such conflict will continue so long as the acculturation process has not been completed.... Only then may the violations be regarded in terms of mental conflict.

If culture conflict may be regarded as sometimes personalized, or mental, and sometimes as occurring entirely in an impersonal way solely as a conflict of group codes, it is obvious that research should not be confined to the investigation of mental conflicts and that contrary to Wirth's categorical statement that it is impossible to demonstrate the existence of a culture conflict "objectively... by a comparison between two cultural codes"[9] this procedure has not only a definite function, but may be carried out by researchers employing techniques which are familiar to the sociologist.

The emphasis on the life history technique has grown out of the assumption that "the experiences of one person at the same time reveals the life activities of his group" and that "habit in the individual is an expression of custom in society."[10] This is undoubtedly one valid approach. Through it we may hope to discover generalizations of a scientific nature by studying persons who (1) have drawn their norms of conduct from a variety of groups with conflicting norms, or (2) who possess norms drawn from a group whose code is in conflict with that of the group which judges the conduct. In the former case alone can we speak of mental or internal culture conflict; in the latter, the conflict is external.

If the conduct norms of a group are, with reference to a given life situation, inconsistent, or if two groups possess inconsistent norms, we may assume that the members of these various groups will individually reflect such group attitudes. Paraphrasing Burgess, the experiences of a group will reveal the life activities of its members. While these norms can, no doubt, be best established by a study of a sufficient number of representative group members, they may for some groups at least be fixed with sufficient certainty to serve research purposes by a study of the social institutions, the administration of justice, the novel, the drama, the press, and other expressions of group attitudes. The identification of the groups in question having been made, it might be possible to determine to what extent such conflicts are reflected in the conduct of their members. Comparative studies based on the violation rates of the members of such groups, the trends of such rates, etc., would dominate this approach to the problem.

In conclusion, then, culture conflict may be studied either as mental conflict or as a conflict of cultural codes. The criminologist will naturally tend to concentrate on such conflicts between legal and nonlegal conduct norms. The concept of conflict fails to give him more than a general framework of reference for research. In practice, it has, however, become nearly synonymous with conflicts between the norms of cultural systems or areas. Most researches which have employed it have been done on immigrant or race groups in the United States, perhaps due to the ease with which such groups may be identified, the existence of more statistical data recognizing such groupings, and the conspicuous differences between some immigrant norms and our norms.

Notes

1. This is unfortunately not the whole story, for with the rapid growth of impersonal communication, the written (press, literature) and the spoken word (radio, talkie), knowledge concerning divergent conduct norms no longer grows solely out of direct personal contact with their carriers. And out of such conflicts grow some violations of custom and of law which would not have occurred without them.

2. Speck, Frank G. "Ethical Attributes of the Labrador Indians." *American Anthropologist*. N. S. 35:559–94. October–December 1933. P. 559.

3. Maunier, René, "La diffusion du droit français en Algérie." Harvard Tercentenary Publications, *Independence, Convergence, and Borrowing in Institutions, Thought, and Art*. Cambridge: Harvard University Press. 1937. Pp. 84–85.

4. Anossow, J. J. "Die volkstümlichen Verbrechen im Strafkodex der USSR." *Monatsschrift für Kriminalpsychologie und Strafrechtsreform*. 24:534–37. September 1933.

5. Wirschubski, Gregor. "Der Schutz der Sittlichkeit im Sowjetstrafrecht." *Zeitschrift für die gesamte Strafrechtswissenschaft*. 51:317–28. 1931.

6. Wirth, Louis. "Culture Conflict and Misconduct." *Social Forces*. 9:484–92. June 1931. P. 490. Cf. Allport, Floyd H. "Culture Conflict versus the Individual as Factors in Delinquency." *Ibid*. Pp. 493–97.

7. White, William A. *Crimes and Criminals*. New York: Farrar & Rinehart. 1933. Healy, William. *Mental Conflict and Misconduct*. Boston: Little, Brown & Co. 1917. Alexander, Franz and Healy, William. *Roots of Crime*. New York: Alfred A. Knopf. 1935.

8. Burgess, Ernest W. in Clifford R. Shaw's *The Jack-Roller*. Chicago: University of Chicago Press. 1930. Pp. 184–197, p. 186.

9. Wirth, Louis. *Op. cit*. P. 490. It should be noted that Wirth also states that culture should be studied "on the objective side" and that "the sociologist is not primarily interested in personality but in culture."

10. Burgess, Ernest W. *Op. cit*. P. 186.

8 / Outlaw Motorcyclists: An Outgrowth of Lower Class Cultural Concerns

J. MARK WATSON

INTRODUCTION

Walter Miller's (1958) typology of focal concerns of lower class culture as a generating milieu for gang delinquency is by most standards a classic in explaining gang behavior among juvenile males. Its general heuristic value is here demonstrated by the striking parallel between this value system and that of adult outlaw motorcyclists.

The reader may remember Miller's general schema, which concerned the strain between the value system of youthful lower class males and the dominant, middle class value system of those in a position to define delinquent behavior. Miller, by describing these values (he used the term "focal concerns"), anticipated conflict theory, without directly pointing out the conflicting values of the middle class definers of delinquent behavior. Although there have been some disagreements surrounding details of Miller's description of the functioning of adolescent gangs, the basic focal concerns described in the typology have been relatively free of criticism as to their validity in describing the values of young lower class males. Some questions have been raised about the degree to which these values actually are in contrast with those of middle class adolescents, however (see, for example, Gordon et al., 1963). Because the typology itself is contained in the discussion of biker values, it will not be discussed separately here.

METHODOLOGY

The findings of the paper are based on my 3 years of participant observation in the subculture of outlaw motorcyclists. Although I am not a member of any outlaw clubs, I am or have been acquainted with members and officers of various clubs, as well as more loosely organized groups of motorcyclists for 10 years. I am myself a motorcycle enthusiast, which facilitated a natural entry into the biker scene. I both build and ride bikes and gained direct access to local biker groups by frequenting places where bikers congregate to work on their bikes. Building a bike gave me legitimation and access to local biker groups and eventually led to contact with other bikers, including outlaws. Groups observed varied from what could be classified as clubs to loose-knit groups of associated motorcyclists. Four groups were studied in depth. Two small local groups in middle Tennessee were subjects of direct participation. Here they are given the fictional names of the Brothers and the Good Old Boys. In addition, one regional group from North Carolina, given the fictional name of Bar Hoppers, was studied through interviews with club officers and members. One national-level group, one of the largest groups of outlaw motorcyclists, was extensively observed and interviewed, primarily at regional and national events. This group is given the fictional name of the Convicts. Additional information was also gathered by attempting to interview at regional and national events members and officers of a wide range of clubs. This was easily done by simply looking at club "colors" (patches) and seeking out members of clubs that were not already represented in the study. This technique was used primarily to check for the representativeness of behavior, values, beliefs, and other characteristics observed in in-depth studies of the four clubs mentioned above. Another source of validation of conclusions was extensive use of biker literature such as magazines and books by or about bikers.

Data were collected by means of interviews conducted from January 1977 to March 1980. Interviews were informally administered in the sense that no formal interview schedule was used. Instead, bikers were queried in the context of what would pass for normal conversation. Extensive observations of behavior were made while directly participating in the activities of the groups, everyday events such as hanging out and from building bikes to "runs," (trips), swap meets, and cult events, such as speed week at Daytona Beach, Florida, and the National Motorcycle Drag Championships at Bowling Green, Kentucky. Such events led to contact with bikers from all over the United States, inasmuch as these events attract a national sample of dedicated bikers, including the whole range of types from simple enthusiasts to true outlaws. Notes and impressions were taken at night and/or after the events. Groups and individuals were generally not aware that they were being studied, although I made no attempt to hide my intentions. Some bikers who came to know me were curious about a university professor participating in such activities and accordingly were told that a study was being conducted. This honesty was prompted by fear of being suspected of being a narcotics agent. Such self-revelation was rarely necessary as the author affected the clothing and jargon of bikers and was accepted as such. Frequent invitations to engage in outrageous and illegal behavior (e.g., drug use and purchase of stolen parts) that would not be extended to outsiders were taken as a form of symbolic acceptance. My demeanor and extensive association with lower class gangs in adolescence combined with the type of mechanical skills necessary to build bikes mentioned earlier may have contributed to an ability to blend in. Reactions to self-revelation, when necessary, generally ranged from amazement to amusement. I suspect that, as is true with the general population, most bikers had no idea what a sociologist was, but the presence of a professor in their midst was taken as a sort of legitimation for the group.

Observations and conclusions were cross-checked on an ongoing basis with a group of five biker informants whom I knew well, including members of the Brothers, Good Old Boys, and the Convicts who lived in the mid-Tennessee area. Informants were selected on the basis of several criteria. First, informants had to know and be known well enough by me to establish a trusting relationship. This limited informants to local bikers found in my area of residence. As mentioned above, outlaw motorcyclists are not particularly trusting, and this obstacle had to be overcome. Second, informants had to be articulate enough to communicate such concepts as values. Most bikers are not particularly articulate, so this criterion eliminated many members of local groups whom I knew well. Third, informants had to have extensive experience in biker subculture. Consequently, informants were limited to bikers who had traveled and lived in a wide geographic area and had experience wider than that represented by the mid-South region. Consequently, informants were generally older than the typical biker population, varying in age from the early 30s to the mid-40s. Three of the informants were former or current owners of custom motorcycle shops that catered to biker clientele. All were what might be defined as career bikers. Finally, all informants had to possess enough objectivity about the biker lifestyle to be willing to read and comment on the author's conclusions. Many of these conclusions, though valid and objective, one hopes, are not particularly flattering to participants in the outlaw motorcyclists subculture. One informant was lost because of obvious antagonism generated by some conclusions. In addition, conversations with hundreds of unsuspecting bikers were held in order to ascertain the generalizability of observations. The latter technique involved appearing to be ignorant or confused and simply asking for a definition of the situation, for example, "What's happening?" or, "What are they doing?" or even venturing an evaluation such as, "That's stupid; Why do they do that?" all in order to elicit a response from an observer of some act. It must be kept in mind that research conducted with this kind of deviant subculture can be dangerous. Because many outlaws do not welcome scrutiny and carefully avoid those whom they feel may not be trusted, which includes most nonbikers, I remained as unobtrusive as possible. Consequently, the methodology was adapted to the setting. Generally, I felt my presence was accepted. Throughout the study I sensed no change in the cyclists' behavior over time by my presence. This acceptance can be symbolized by my receiving a nickname (Doc) and eventually being defined as an expert in a certain type of obsolete motorcycle (the Harley-Davidson 45-cubic-inch side-valve model). I assumed the role of an inside outsider.

THE BIKER SUBCULTURE

We may locate outlaw bikers in the general spectrum of bikers as the most "outrageous" (their own term, a favorite modifier indicating something distinctively appealing to their own jaded sense of values) on the continuum of bikers, which extends from housewives on mopeds to clubs that actually engage in illegal behavior with a fair degree of frequency, thus the term "outlaws" (Thompson, 1967:9). Outlaws generally adopt certain symbols and lead a lifestyle that is clearly defined and highly visible to other bikers. Symbols include extensive tattooing, beard, dirty jeans, earrings, so-called stroker caps and quasi-military pins attached, engineer's boots, and cut-off jackets with club emblems, called "colors," sewn on the back. Weapons, particularly buck knives and guns of any sort, and chains (motorcycle or other types) are favorite symbols as well (Easyriders, February, 1977:28, 29, 55). By far the most important symbol, however, is the Harley-Davidson V-twin motorcycle.[1] It should be kept in mind that many other motorcyclists affect these symbols, although they are by no means outlaws. Outlaws almost always belong to clubs, whereas many motorcyclists who do not belong to the clubs use them as reference groups and attempt to imitate some aspects of their behavior. These symbols and the basic lifestyle are generalizable to a wide range of bikers and may even be found among British and European bikers, with the exception of the Harley-Davidson motorcycle (Choppers, April 1980:12).

OUTLAW LIFESTYLE

For the outlaw, his lifestyle takes on many of the characteristics of dedication to a religious sect (Watson, 1979). This lifestyle is in many respects a lower class variation of bohemian, "dropout" subcultures. Such similarities include frequent unemployment and disdain for cleanliness, orderliness, and other concerns of conventional culture. For example, I have observed bikes being built and stored in living rooms or kitchens, two non-essential rooms in the subculture. This is apparently a common practice. Parts may be stored in an oil bath in the bathtub, also a nonessential device. The biker and other bohemian subcultures may appear similar on the basis of casual observations, but some outlaw biker values are strikingly different from the beatnik or hippy subcultures of the 1950s and 1960s. Other bohemian subcultures emphasized humanistic values, whereas the outlaw bikers' values emphasize male dominance, violence, force, and racism (Easyriders, October 1977:15). Although individual freedom and choice are also emphasized, the clubs actually suppress individual freedom, while using the value to defend their lifestyle from outsiders. For example, when the Convicts take a club trip called a "run," all members must participate. Those whose bikes are "down" for repairs are fined and must find a ride in a truck with the women. Many club rules require members to follow orders as prescribed by club decisions upon threat of violence and expulsion. Club rules generally include a constitution and bylaws that are surprisingly elaborate and sophisticated for groups of this nature. Many club members express pride in their written regulations. It seems likely that the basic format is borrowed from that developed by the Hell's Angels (Thompson, 1967:72). Most club decisions are made in a democratic way, but minority rights are not respected. Once such a decision is made, it is imperative to all members, with risk of physical retribution for failure to conform. Typical rules include care of colors, which are to never touch the ground or be washed. They are treated essentially as a flag. Other rules mentioned above and below have to do with following group decisions without dissent and such requirements as defending club honor through unanimous participation in avenging affronts to other clubs' members. Club rules may be enforced by self-appointed committees or by formally designated sergeants at arms or enforcers. One informant expressed it this way: "They'll take your bike, your old lady, and stomp the shit out of you if you make 'em look bad." This particular expression related to some prospective "probate" members and their failure to live up to club rules requiring violent reactions to challenges to club honor. The observation came from a retired club member when I queried him about an almost surreal conflict over the wearing of a club symbol by a nonmember.

Use of mind-altering drugs is another area of overlap between biker and bohemian subcultures. Outlaw bikers will take or drink almost anything to alter their consciousness (Easyriders, May 1978:24, 25). The groups studied regularly used "uppers," "downers," and marijuana but rarely used hallucinogens. One informant explained that the latter "fuck you up so you can't ride, so we don't use it much." Apparently, one can ride on uppers, downers, or when drunk but not when hallucinating. Curiously enough, the most commonly used drug is alcohol taken in the rather mild form of beer (though in great quantity). Where there are outlaw bikers one will usually find drugs, but one will almost always find beer.

Outsider status, the use of drugs, and the seeking of cheap rent result in frequent overlap between outlaw bikers and other bohemian types, in both territory and interpersonal relations. The bikers usually tolerate the other bohemians, because the latter share an interest in and serve as a source of supply of, or customers for, drugs. Bikers, however, view them with contempt because they are not masculine enough. Hippies, dopers, and fairies are similar types as far as bikers are concerned. Masculinity as a dominant value is expressed in many ways, including toughness and a general concern with looking mean, dirty, and "outrageous." When asked about a peripheral member of a local group, one informant replied, "He's a hippy, but he don't ride. We put up with him because he has good dope. I feel sorry for him because he's just a fucked-up puke."

Some other biker-associated values include racism, concern with Nazism, and in-group superiority. "Righteousness" is achieved through adherence to these values. One celebrity member of the Brothers had been convicted of killing a young black man in a street confrontation. He is reported to have jumped bail and lived with a Nazi couple in South America, where he worked as a ranch hand. This particular member spoke some German and frequently spouted racist and Nazi doctrine. A typical righteous outlaw belongs to a club, rides an American-made motorcycle, is a white male, displays the subculture's symbols, hates most if not all nonwhites and Japanese motorcycles, works irregularly at best, dresses at all times in dirty jeans, cut-off denim jacket, and engineer's boots, drinks beer, takes whichever drugs are available, and treats women as objects of contempt.

OUTLAW BIKER WORLD VIEW AND SELF-CONCEPT

The outlaw biker generally views the world as hostile, weak, and effeminate. Perhaps this view is a realistic reaction to a working-class socialization experience. However, the reaction contains certain elements of a self-fulfilling prophecy. Looking dirty, mean, and generally undesirable may be a way of frightening others into leaving one alone, although, in many senses such an appearance arouses anger, hostility, and related emotions in the observer and results in the persecution that such qualities are intended to protect one from.

Bikers tend to see the world in terms of here and now. They are not especially hostile toward most social institutions such as family, government, and education. Most of the local group members had finished high school and had been employed from time to time, and some had been college students. Some were veterans, and nearly all had been married more than once. Few had been successful in these endeavors, however. They are generally not capable of establishing the temporal commitments necessary for relating to such institutions. For example, marriages and similar relationships rarely last more than a few years, and education requires concentrated effort over a time span that they are generally not willing or in many cases not capable of exerting. Most of them drift from one job to another or have no job at all. Simply keeping up with where the informants were living proved to be a challenge. I frequently had a call from a local biker relating that he was "on his way over" only to find that he did not arrive at all or arrived hours or days later. I have been on runs that were to depart in the early morning and that did not in fact depart until hours later. The biker's sense of time and commitment to it is not only lower class, but more typical of preliterate societies. The result is frequent clashes with bureaucratically organized institutions, such as government and economy, which are oriented toward impulse control, commitment, and punctuality, and failure in organizations that require long-term commitments or interpersonal relations, such as family and education.

A similar view of regulation causes frequent conflicts. Bikers are not basically violent but are impulsive. Regulations that conflict with their impulses are ignored. Attempts to enforce such regulations (generally by law enforcement officers) are viewed not as legal regulation but as unreasonable demands (harassment). Of course, this impulsiveness can be destructive and self-defeating. I have seen bikers destroy engines they spent hundreds of dollars on by simply overreving them. I have also seen doors, jukeboxes, bike gas tanks, and other items destroyed in an impulsive moment—sometimes in rage, sometimes in humor, or out of boredom. Bikers demand freedom to follow these impulses, which often involve behavior defined by the observer as outrageous. Occasionally bikers reinforce this conception by conforming to the stereotype and deliberately shocking more conventional people, especially if they feel their social space is being invaded. An illustrative incidence occurred in 1978 at the National Championship Drag Races, an event for motorcycles in Bowling Green, Kentucky. An area of a local amusement park was designated "for bikers only." This area was clearly marked with large signs. Occasionally local citizens and outraged tourists insisted on driving through to see the scene. Bikers had begun "partying" and engaging in heavy drinking, drug use, and generally impulsive behavior, including frequent male and female nudity, which occasioned some notice but no shock to other bikers. However, when outsiders drove through, they were deliberately exposed to substantial nudity and what were no doubt interpreted as obscene and disgusting displays by those viewing them. The result was that the city of Bowling Green declined future events of that nature. The races have been held elsewhere in subsequent years.

Outlaw bikers generally view themselves as outsiders. I have on occasion invited local bikers to settings that would place them in contact with members of the middle class. Their frequent response is that they would "not fit in" or would "feel out of place." Basically, they seem to feel that they cannot compete with what sociologists define as the middle class although I have never heard the term used by bikers. Outlaws see themselves as losers, as symbolized by tatoos, patches, and even their humor, which portrays them as ignorant. "One percenter" is a favorite patch, referring to its wearers as the most deviant fraction of the biker fraternity. In effect, the world that they create for themselves is an attempt to suspend the rules of competition that they cannot win by and create a world where one does not compete but simply exists (Montgomery, 1976, 1979). Pretense and self-importance are ways to lose acceptance quickly in such a situation. One does not compete with or "put down" a fellow biker, for he is a "brother."

It is not that bikers are uniformly hostile toward the outside world; they are indifferent toward, somewhat threatened by, and contemptuous of it.

MILLER'S FOCAL CONCERNS AS EXPRESSED IN OUTLAW BIKER CULTURE

Trouble

Trouble is a major theme of the outlaw biker culture as illustrated by the very use of the term "outlaw." The term refers to one who demonstrates his distinctiveness (righteousness) by engaging in outrageous and even illegal behavior. Trouble seems to serve several purposes in this subculture. First, flirting with trouble is a way of demonstrating masculinity—trouble is a traditionally male prerogative. Trouble also enforces group solidarity through emphasizing the outsider status of the outlaw, a status that can be sustained only by the formation of counterculture. Given the outlaw biker's world view and impulsiveness, trouble comes without conscious effort. Trouble may come over drug use, stolen bikes or parts, possession of firearms, or something as simple as public drunkenness. Some of the local bikers whom I knew well had prison records for manslaughter (defined as self-defense by the subjects), receiving stolen property, drug possession, statutory rape, and assault on an officer. All saw these sentences as unjust and claimed that the behavior was justifiable or that they were victims of a case of overzealous regulation of everyday activities or deliberate police harassment.

Trouble used to take the form of violence between biker clubs and groups (Easyriders, April 1977:13, 41). Most of this activity was generated by issues of club honor involving the stealing of women or perceived wrongs by members of other clubs. The general motivation for this activity seemed to be an opportunity to demonstrate toughness (see below). The only open conflict that I saw was an incident, mentioned earlier, between the Brothers and the Convicts over the right of the other groups to wear a one percenter badge as part of their club colors. In recent years most groups have abandoned the practice of interclub violence and emphasize instead the conflict between group members and police. An issue that is a current example of this conflict and that therefore serves this unifying purpose is the mandatory helmet laws in many states and the related attempts of the federal Department of Transportation to regulate modification by owners of motorcycles (Supercycle, May 1979:4, 14–15, 66).

Organized reaction to trouble in the sense of attempts to regulate motorcycles and motorcyclists is probably as close to political awareness and class consciousness as bikers come. Outlaw types, however, generally have little to do with these activities, partly because they view them as hopeless and partly because they correctly perceive their support and presence at such activities as unwelcome and poor public relations.

Toughness

In addition to trouble, toughness is at the heart of the biker emphasis on masculinity and outrageousness. To be tough is to experience trouble without showing signs of weakness. Therefore, the objective of trouble is to demonstrate the masculine form of toughness. Bikers have contempt for such comforts as automobiles or even devices that increase biking comfort or safety such as eye protection, helmets, windshields, farings or even frames with spring rear suspension (a so-called hardtail is the preferred frame). Bikers wear denim or leather, but the sleeves are generally removed to show contempt for the danger of "road rash," abrasions caused by contact with the road surface at speed, which protective material can prevent. Part of toughness is the prohibition against expressing love for women and children in any but a possessive way. Women are viewed with contempt and are regarded as a necessary nuisance (generally referred to as "cunts," "whores," or "sluts"), as are children ("rug rats"). Curiously, bikers seem to attract an adequate supply of women despite the poor treatment they receive from them in such a situation. One informant expressed his contempt for women in this way, "Hell, if I could find a man with a pussy, I wouldn't fuck with women. I don't like 'em. They're nothing but trouble." When asked about the female's motivation for participation in the subculture, one (male) informant stated simply "they're looking for excitement." The women attracted to such a scene are predictably tough and hard-bitten themselves. Not all are unattractive, but most display signs of premature aging typical of lower class and deviant lifestyles. All work to keep up their mate and his motorcycle. I must admit that my interviews with biker women were limited lest my intentions be misinterpreted. I could have hired some of them under sexual pretenses, as many may be bought, but ethical and financial considerations precluded this alternative. My general impression is that these women generally come from lower class families in which the status of the female is not remarkably different from that they currently enjoy. Being a biker's "old lady" offers excitement and opportunities to engage in exhibitionist and outlandish behavior that in their view contrasts favorably with the lives of their mothers. Many are mothers of illegitimate children before they resort to bikers and may view themselves as fallen women who have little to lose in terms of respectability. Most seem to have fairly low self-concepts, which are compatible with their status as bikers' old ladies.

Of course, the large, heavy motorcycles bikers ride are symbolic of their toughness as well. Not everyone can ride such a machine because of its sheer weight. Many models are "kick start," and require some strength and skill just to start. A certain amount of recklessness is also used to express toughness. To quote Bruce Springsteen: "It's a death trap, a suicide rap" (Springsteen, 1975), and the ability to ride it, wreck it, and survive demonstrates toughness in a very dramatic way. An example of my experience in this regard may be illuminating. Although I had ridden motorcycles for years, I became aware of the local biker group while building my first Harley-Davidson. Full acceptance by this group was not extended until my first and potentially fatal accident, however. Indeed, local bikers who had only vaguely known me offered the gift of parts and assistance in reconstructing my bike and began to refer to me by a new nickname, "Doc." I sensed and was extended a new degree of acceptance after demonstrating my "toughness" by surviving the accident. Toughness, in this sense, is a combination of stupidity and misfortune, and hardly relates to any personal virtue.

Smartness

On this characteristic, biker values seem to diverge from general lower class values as described by Miller. The term "dumb biker" is frequently used as a self-description. Given the choice of avoiding, outsmarting, or confronting an opponent, the biker seems to prefer avoidance or confrontation. Confrontation gives him the opportunity to demonstrate toughness by generating trouble. Avoidance is not highly valued, but no one can survive all the trouble he could generate, and the stakes are frequently the highest—life itself or at least loss of freedom. The appearance of toughness and outlandishness mentioned above make confrontation a relatively infrequent occurrence, as few outsiders will challenge a group of outlaw bikers unless the issue is of great significance. Smartness, then, does not seem to be an emphasized biker value or characteristic. Gambling on outsmarting an opponent is for low stakes such as those faced by the adolescents Miller studied.

Excitement

One of the striking things about the outlaw lifestyle is its extremes. Bikers hang out at chopper (motorcycle) shops, clubhouses, or bars during the day, except when they are in prison or jail, which is not uncommon. Places frequented by bikers are generally located in lower class neighborhoods. A clubhouse, for example, is generally a rented house which serves as a headquarters, party location, and place for members to "crash" when they lack more personal accommodations. They are not unlike a lower class version of a fraternity house. Outlaws tend to designate bars as their own. This involves taking over bars to the exclusion of their usual lower or working-class clientele. Such designations are frequently short-lived as the bars may be closed as a public nuisance or the proprietor may go out of business for economic or personal reasons as a result of the takeover. I know of at least one such bar that was burned by local people to rid the neighborhood of the nuisance. Its owner relocated the business some 40 miles away.

Local bikers who worked generally had unskilled and semi-skilled jobs, which are dull in themselves. Examples include laborers, factory workers, construction workers, and hospital orderlies. Many do not work regularly, being supported by their women.[2] In any case, most of their daylight hours are spent in a deadly dull environment, where the most excitement may be a mechanical problem with a bike. Escape from this dull lifestyle is dramatic in its excesses. Drugs, alcohol, and orgiastic parties are one form of escape. Other escapes include the run or simply riding the bikes for which the subculture is named. Frequently both forms of escape are combined, and such events as the Daytona and Sturgis runs are remarkable, comparing favorably to Mardi Gras as orgiastic events. Living on the edge of trouble, appearing outlandish, fierce, and tough, itself yields a form of self-destructive excitement, especially when it can be used to outrage others. Unlike the situation that Miller studied, excitement and trouble rarely seem to center around women, as their status among bikers is even lower than in the lower class in general. I have never seen a conflict over a woman among bikers and am struck by the casual manner in which they move from one biker to another. The exchange of women seems to be the male's prerogative, and women appear to be traded or given away as casually as pocket knives are exchanged among old men. I have on occasion been offered the use of a female for the duration of a run. This offer was always made by the male and was made in the same manner that one might offer the use of a tool to a neighbor. (I have never been offered the loan of a bike, however.) The low regard for women combined with the traditional biker's emphasis on brotherhood seem to minimize conflicts over women. Those conflicts that do occur over women seem to occur between clubs and are a matter of club honor rather than jealousy or grief over the loss of a relationship.

Fate

Because bikers do not emphasize smartness to the extent that Miller perceived it among the lower class, the role of fate in explaining failure to succeed is somewhat different for them. In Miller's analysis fate was a rationalization used when one was outsmarted. The biker's attitude toward fate goes much deeper and could be described as figuratively and literally fatalistic. The theme of death is central to their literature and art.[3] A biker who becomes economically successful or who is too legitimate is suspect. He is no longer one of them. He has succeeded in the outside and in a sense has sold out. His success alone shows his failure to subscribe to the basic values that they hold. He is similar to a rich Indian—no longer an Indian but a white man with red skin. Members of local groups, the Brothers and the Good Old Boys, came and went. Membership fluctuated. Few members resigned because of personal difficulty. However, many former members were still around. The single characteristic that they all shared was economic success. Although these former members tended to be older than the typical member, many current members were as old or older. Success in small businesses were typical. Some former members had been promoted to lower management positions in local factories and related businesses, apparently were no longer comfortable in their former club roles, and so resigned. Some kept their bikes, others exchanged them for more respectable touring bikes, and others sold their bikes. In any case, although some maintained limited social contact and others participated in occasional weekend runs, their success appeared to make them no longer full participants in group activities and resulted ultimately in their formal resignation from the clubs. Bikers basically see themselves as losers and affect clothing, housing, and other symbols of the embittered and dangerous loser. They apparently no longer dream the unrealistic adolescent dreams of the "big break." Prison and death are seen as natural concomitants of the biker lifestyle. Fate is the grim reaper that so often appears in biker art.

Autonomy

Autonomy in the form of freedom is central to the outlaw biker expressed philosophy and in this respect closely parallels the lower class themes outlined by Miller. A studied insistence that they be left alone by harassing law enforcement agencies and overregulating bureaucrats is a common theme in biker literature and personal expressions. The motorcycle itself is an individual thing, begrudgingly including an extra seat for an "old lady" or "down" brother. Ironically, the outlaw biker lifestyle is so antisocial vis-à-vis the wider society that it cannot be pursued individually. A lone outlaw knows he is a target, an extremely visible and vulnerable one. Therefore, for purposes of self-protection, the true outlaw belongs to a club and rarely makes a long trip without the company of several brothers.

Outlaw clubs are themselves both authoritarian and democratic. Members may vote on issues or at least select officers,[4] but club policy and rules are absolute and may be enforced with violence (Choppers, March 1978:36–39). Antisocial behavior associated with the outlaw lifestyle itself frequently results in loss of autonomy. Most prisons of any size not only contain a substantial biker population but may contain local (prison) chapters of some of the larger clubs (Life, August 1979:80–81). Easyriders, a biker magazine, regularly contains sections for pen pals and other requests from brothers in prison (Easyriders, October 1977:16–19, 70). So, although autonomy in the form of the right to be different is pursued with a vengeance, the ferocity with which it is pursued ensures its frequent loss.

Miller noted an ambivalent attitude among lower class adolescents toward authority: they both resented it and sought situations in which it was forced on them. The structure of outlaw clubs and the frequent incarceration that is a result of their lifestyle would seem to be products of a similar ambivalence. Another loss of autonomy that Miller noted among lower class gangs was a dependence on females that caused dissonance and was responsible for lower class denigration of female status. Outlaws take the whole process a step further, however. Many of their women engage in prostitution, topless waitressing, or menial, traditionally female labor. Some outlaws live off the income of several women and in this sense are dependent on them but only in the sense that a pimp is dependent on his string of girls. From their point of view, the females see themselves as protected by and dependent on the male rather than the other way around.

CONCLUSION

Miller's typology of lower class focal concerns appears to be a valid model for analyzing outlaw biker cultures, just as it was for analyzing some forces behind juvenile gang delinquency. Although there are some differences in values and their expression, the differences are basically those occurring by the transferring of the values from street-wise adolescents to adult males. Both groups could be described as lower class, but my experiences with bikers indicate a working-class family background with downward mobility. A surprising proportion of the bikers interviewed indicated respectable working-class or lower middle-class occupations for their fathers. Examples included postal worker, forestry and lumber contractor, route sales business owner, and real estate agency owner. They are definitely not products of multigenerational poverty. I would classify them as nonrespectable working-class marginals.

The study is presented primarily as an ethnographic description of a difficult and sometimes dangerous subculture to study, which when viewed from the outside appears as a disorganized group of deviants but when studied carefully with some insider's insights is seen to have a coherent and reasonably consistent value system and a lifestyle based on that value system.

Notes

1. A favorite T-shirt observed at cult events is one saying, "If you ain't a Harley rider, you ain't shit!"

2. Outlaw bikers sometimes support themselves by dealing in drugs, bootleg liquor, and prostitution of their women.

3. Of the fiction in the entire 1977 issue of Easyriders, 40% of the articles concerned themselves with death.

4. Officer selection may be based on many processes, some of which would hardly be recognized as democratic by those outside the subculture. Leaders are popularly selected, however. Physical prowess may be the basis of selection, for example.

References

Choppers
1978 "Club profile: Northern Indiana Invaders M/C." (March):36–39.

Choppers
1980 "Mailbag." (April):12.

Easyriders
1977 "Gun nut report." (February):28, 29, 55.

Easyriders
1977 "Gang wars are a thing of the past." (April):13, 41.

Easyriders
1977 "Man is the ruler of woman." (October):15.

Easyriders
1977 "Jammin in the joint." (October):16–19, 70 (Also "Mail call").

Easyriders
1978 "The straight dope on Quaaludes." (May):24–25.

Gordon, Robert A., Short, Jr., James F., Cartwright, Desmond, and Strodtbeck, Fred
1963 "Values and gang delinquency." American Journal of Sociology 69:109–128.

Life
1979 "Prison without stripes." (August):80–81.

Miller, Walter B.
1958 "Lower class culture as a generating milieu for gang delinquency." Journal of Social Issues 14:5–19.

Montgomery, Randall
1976 "The outlaw motorcycle subculture." Canadian Journal of Criminology and Corrections 18.

Montgomery, Randall
1979 "The outlaw motorcycle subculture II." Canadian Journal of Criminology and Corrections 19.

Springsteen, Bruce
1975 "Born to run." Columbia Records.

Supercycle
1979 "On reserve." (May):4, 14–15, 66.

Thompson, Hunter
1967 Hell's Angels: A strange and terrible saga. New York: Random House.

Watson, John M.
1979 "Righteousness on two wheels: Bikers as a secular sect." Unpublished paper read at the Southwestern Social Science Association, March 1979.

9 / Techniques of Neutralization: A Theory of Delinquency

GRESHAM M. SYKES
DAVID MATZA

As Morris Cohen once said, one of the most fascinating problems about human behavior is why men violate the laws in which they believe. This is the problem that confronts us when we attempt to explain why delinquency occurs despite a greater or lesser commitment to the usages of conformity. A basic clue is offered by the fact that social rules or norms calling for valued behavior seldom if ever take the form of categorical imperatives. Rather, values or norms appear as *qualified* guides for action, limited in their applicability in terms of time, place, persons, and social circumstances. The moral injunction against killing, for example, does not apply to the enemy during combat in time of war, although a captured enemy comes once again under the prohibition. Similarly, the taking and distributing of scarce goods in a time of acute social need is felt by many to be right, although under other circumstances private property is held inviolable. The normative system of a society, then, is marked by what Williams has termed *flexibility*; it does not consist of a body of rules held to be binding under all conditions.[1]

This flexibility is, in fact, an integral part of the criminal law in that measures for "defenses to crimes" are provided in pleas such as non-age, necessity, insanity, drunkenness, compulsion, self-defense, and so on. The individual can avoid moral culpability for his criminal action—and thus avoid the negative sanctions of society—if he can prove that criminal intent was lacking. *It is our argument that much delinquency is based on what is essentially an unrecognized extension of defenses to crimes, in the form of justifications for deviance that are seen as valid by the delinquent but not by the legal system or society at large.*

These justifications are commonly described as rationalizations. They are viewed as following deviant behavior and as protecting the individual from self-blame and the blame of others after the act. But there is also reason to believe that they precede deviant behavior and make deviant behavior possible. It is this possibility that Sutherland mentioned only in passing and that other writers have failed to exploit from the viewpoint of sociological theory. Disapproval flowing from internalized norms and conforming others in the social environment is neutralized, turned back, or deflected in advance. Social controls that serve to check or inhibit deviant motivational patterns are rendered inoperative, and the individual is freed to engage in delinquency without serious damage to his self-image. In this sense, the delinquent both has his cake and eats it too, for he remains committed to the dominant normative system and yet so qualifies its imperatives that violations are "acceptable" if not "right." Thus the delinquent represents not a radical opposition to law-abiding society but something more like an apologetic failure, often more sinned against than sinning in his own eyes. We call these justifications of deviant behavior techniques of neutralization; and we believe these techniques make up a crucial component of Sutherland's "definitions favorable to the violation of law." It is by learning these techniques that the juvenile becomes delinquent, rather than by learning moral imperatives, values, or attitudes standing in direct contradiction to those of the dominant society. In analyzing these techniques, we have found it convenient to divide them into five major types.

THE DENIAL OF RESPONSIBILITY

Insofar as the delinquent can define himself as lacking responsibility for his deviant actions, the disapproval of self or others is sharply reduced in effectiveness as a restraining influence. As Justice Holmes has said, even a dog distinguishes between being stumbled over and being kicked, and modern society is no less careful to draw a line between injuries that are unintentional, i.e., where responsibility is lacking, and those that are intentional. As a technique of neutralization, however, the denial of responsibility extends much further than the claim that deviant acts are an "accident" or some similar negation of personal accountability. It may also be asserted that delinquent acts are due to forces outside of the individual and beyond his control such as unloving parents, bad companions, or a slum neighborhood. In effect, the delinquent approaches a "billiard ball" conception of himself in which he sees himself as helplessly propelled into new situations. From a psychodynamic viewpoint, this orientation toward one's own actions may represent a profound alienation from self, but it is important to stress the fact that interpretations of responsibility are cultural constructs and not merely idiosyncratic beliefs. The similarity between this mode of justifying illegal behavior assumed by the delinquent and the implications of a "sociological" frame of reference or a "humane" jurisprudence is readily apparent.[2] It is not the validity of this orientation that concerns us here, but its function of deflecting blame attached to violations of social norms and its relative independence of a particular personality structure.[3] By learning to view himself as more acted upon than acting, the delinquent prepares the way for deviance from the dominant normative system without the necessity of a frontal assault on the norms themselves.

THE DENIAL OF INJURY

A second major technique of neutralization centers on the injury or harm involved in the delinquent act. The criminal law has long made a distinction between crimes which are *mala in se* and *mala prohibita*—that is, between acts that are wrong in themselves and acts that are illegal but not immoral—and the delinquent can make the same kind of distinction in evaluating the wrongfulness of his behavior. For the delinquent, however, wrongfulness may turn on the question of whether or not anyone has clearly been hurt by his deviance, and this matter is open to a variety of interpretations. Vandalism, for example, may be defined by the delinquent simply as "mischief"—after all, it may be claimed, the persons whose property has been destroyed can well afford it. Similarly, auto theft may be viewed as "borrowing," and gang fighting may be seen as a private quarrel, an agreed upon duel between two willing parties, and thus of no concern to the community at large. We are not suggesting that this technique of neutralization, labeled the denial of injury, involves an explicit dialectic. Rather, we are arguing that the delinquent frequently, and in a hazy fashion, feels that his behavior does not really cause any great harm despite the fact that it runs counter to law. Just as the link between the individual and his acts may be broken by the denial of responsibility, so may the link between acts and their consequences be broken by the denial of injury. Since society sometimes agrees with the delinquent, e.g., in matters such as truancy, "pranks," and so on, it merely reaffirms the idea that the delinquent's neutralization of social controls by means of qualifying the norms is an extension of common practice rather than a gesture of complete opposition.

THE DENIAL OF THE VICTIM

Even if the delinquent accepts the responsibility for his deviant actions and is willing to admit that his deviant actions involve an injury or hurt, the moral indignation of self and others may be neutralized by an insistence that the injury is not wrong in light of the circumstances. The injury, it may be claimed, is not really an injury; rather, it is a form of rightful retaliation or punishment. By a subtle alchemy the delinquent moves himself into the position of an avenger and the victim is transformed into a wrong-doer. Assaults on homosexuals or suspected homosexuals, attacks on members of minority groups who are said to have gotten "out of place," vandalism as revenge on an unfair teacher or school official, thefts from a "crooked" store owner—all may be hurts inflicted on a transgressor, in the eyes of the delinquent. As Orwell has pointed out, the type of criminal admired by the general public has probably changed over the course of years and Raffles no longer serves as a hero;[4] but Robin Hood, and his latter-day derivatives such as the tough detective seeking justice outside the law, still capture the popular imagination, and the delinquent may view his acts as part of a similar role.

To deny the existence of the victim, then, by transforming him into a person deserving injury is an extreme form of a phenomenon we have mentioned before, namely, the delinquent's recognition of appropriate and inappropriate targets for his delinquent acts. In addition, however, the existence of the victim may be denied for the delinquent, in a somewhat different sense, by the circumstances of the delinquent act itself. Insofar as the victim is physically absent, unknown, or a vague abstraction (as is often the case in delinquent acts committed against property), the awareness of the victim's existence is weakened. Internalized norms and anticipations of the reactions of others must somehow be activated if they are to serve as guides for behavior; and it is possible that a diminished awareness of the victim plays an important part of determining whether or not this process is set in motion.

THE CONDEMNATION OF THE CONDEMNERS

A fourth technique of neutralization would appear to involve a condemnation of the condemners or, as McCorkle and Korn have phrased it, a rejection of the rejectors.[5] The delinquent shifts the focus of attention from his own deviant acts to the motives and behavior of those who disapprove of his violations. His condemners, he may claim, are hypocrites, deviants in disguise, or impelled by personal spite. This orientation toward the conforming world may be of particular importance when it hardens into a bitter cynicism directed against those assigned the task of enforcing or expressing the norms of the dominant society. Police, it may be said, are corrupt, stupid, and brutal. Teachers always show favoritism and parents always "take it out" on their children. By a slight extension, the rewards of conformity—such as material success—become a matter of pull or luck, thus decreasing still further the stature of those who stand on the side of the law-abiding. The validity of this jaundiced viewpoint is not so important as its function in turning back or deflecting the negative sanctions attached to violations of the norms. The delinquent, in effect, has changed the subject of the conversation in the dialogue between his own deviant impulses and the reactions of others; and by attacking others, the wrongfulness of his own behavior is more easily repressed or lost to view.

THE APPEAL TO HIGHER LOYALTIES

Fifth, and last, internal and external social controls may be neutralized by sacrificing the demands of the larger society for the demands of the smaller social groups to which the delinquent belongs, such as the sibling pair, the gang, or the friendship clique. It is important to note that the delinquent does not necessarily repudiate the imperatives of the dominant normative system, despite his failure to follow them. Rather, the delinquent may see himself as caught up in a dilemma that must be resolved, unfortunately, at the cost of violating the law. One aspect of this situation has been studied by Stouffer and Toby in their research on the conflict between particularistic and universalistic demands, between the claims of friendship and general social obligations, and their results suggest that "it is possible to classify people according to a predisposition to select one or the other horn of a dilemma in role conflict."[6] For our purposes, however, the most important point is that deviation from certain norms may occur not because the norms are rejected but because others' norms, held to be more pressing or involving a higher loyalty, are accorded precedence. Indeed, it is the fact that both sets of norms are believed in that gives meaning to our concepts of dilemma and role conflict.

The conflict between the claims of friendship and the claims of law, or a similar dilemma, has of course long been recognized by the social scientist (and the novelist) as a common human problem. If the juvenile delinquent frequently resolves his dilemma by insisting that he must "always help a buddy" or "never squeal on a friend," even when it throws him into serious difficulties with the dominant social order, his choice remains familiar to the supposedly law-abiding. The delinquent is unusual, perhaps, in the extent to which he is able to see the fact that he acts in behalf of the smaller social groups to which he belongs as a justification for violations of society's norms, but it is a matter of degree rather than of kind.

"I didn't mean it." "I didn't really hurt anybody." "They had it coming to them." "Everybody's picking on me." "I didn't do it for myself." These slogans or their variants, we hypothesize, prepare the juvenile for delinquent acts. These "definitions of the situation" represent tangential or glancing blows at the dominant normative system rather than the creation of an opposing ideology; and they are extensions of patterns of thought prevalent in society rather than something created *de novo*.

Techniques of neutralization may not be powerful enough to fully shield the individual from the force of his own internalized values and the reactions of conforming others, for as we have pointed out, juvenile delinquents often appear to suffer from feelings of guilt and shame when called into account for their deviant behavior. And some delinquents may be so isolated from the world of conformity that techniques of neutralization need not be called into play. Nonetheless, we would argue that techniques of neutralization are critical in lessening the effectiveness of social controls and that they lie behind a large share of delinquent behavior. Empirical research in this area is scattered and fragmentary at the present time, but the work of Redl,[7] Cressey,[8] and others has supplied a body of significant data that has done much to clarify the theoretical issues and enlarge the fund of supporting evidence. Two lines of investigation seem to be critical at this stage. First, there is need for more knowledge concerning the differential distribution of techniques of neutralization, as operative patterns of thought, by age, sex, social class, ethnic group, etc. On a priori grounds it might be assumed that these justifications for deviance will be more readily seized by segments of society for whom a discrepancy between common social ideals and social practice is most apparent. It is also possible, however, that the habit of "bending" the dominant normative system—if not "breaking" it—cuts across our cruder social categories and is to be traced primarily to patterns of social interaction within the familial circle. Second, there is need for a greater understanding of the internal structure of techniques of neutralization, as a system of beliefs and attitudes, and its relationship to various types of delinquent behavior. Certain techniques of neutralization would appear to be better adapted to particular deviant acts than to others, as we have suggested, for example, in the case of offenses against property and the denial of the victim. But the issue remains far from clear and stands in need of more information.

In any case, techniques of neutralization appear to offer a promising line of research in enlarging and systematizing the theoretical grasp of juvenile delinquency. As more information is uncovered concerning techniques of neutralization, their origins, and their consequences, both juvenile delinquency in particular and deviation from normative systems in general may be illuminated.

Notes

1. Cf. Robin Williams, Jr., *American Society*, New York: Knopf, 1951, p. 28.
2. A number of observers have wryly noted that many delinquents seem to show a surprising awareness of sociological and psychological explanations for their behavior and are quick to point out the causal role of their poor environment.
3. It is possible, of course, that certain personality structures can accept some techniques of neutralization more readily than others, but this question remains largely unexplored.
4. George Orwell, *Dickens, Dali, and Others*, New York: Reynal, 1946.
5. Lloyd W. McCorkle and Richard Korn, "Resocialization Within Walls," *The Annals of the American Academy of Political and Social Science*, 293 (May, 1954), pp. 88–98.
6. See Samuel A. Stouffer and Jackson Toby, "Role Conflict and Personality," in *Toward a General Theory of Action*, edited by Talcott Parsons and Edward A. Shils, Cambridge, Mass.: Harvard University Press, 1951, p. 494.
7. See Fritz Redl and David Wineman, *Children Who Hate*, Glencoe, Ill.: The Free Press, 1956.
8. See D. R. Cressey, *Other People's Money*, Glencoe, Ill.: The Free Press, 1953.

10 / Convicted Rapists' Vocabulary of Motive: Excuses and Justifications

DIANA SCULLY
JOSEPH MAROLLA

Psychiatry has dominated the literature on rapists since "irresistible impulse" (Glueck, 1925:323) and "disease of the mind" (Glueck, 1925:243) were introduced as the causes of rape. Research has been based on small samples of men, frequently the clinicians' own patient population. Not surprisingly, the medical model has predominated: rape is viewed as an individualistic, idiosyncratic symptom of a disordered personality. That is, rape is assumed to be a psychopathologic problem and individual rapists are assumed to be "sick." However, advocates of this model have been unable to isolate a typical or even predictable pattern of symptoms that are causally linked to rape. Additionally, research has demonstrated that fewer than 5 percent of rapists were psychotic at the time of their rape (Abel *et al.*, 1980).

We view rape as behavior learned socially through interaction with others; convicted rapists have learned the attitudes and actions consistent with sexual aggression against women. Learning also includes the acquisition of culturally derived vocabularies of motive, which can be used to diminish responsibility and to negotiate a non-deviant identity.

Sociologists have long noted that people can, and do, commit acts they define as wrong and, having done so, engage various techniques to disavow deviance and present themselves as normal. Through the concept of "vocabulary of motive," Mills (1940:904) was among the first to shed light on this seemingly perplexing contradiction. Wrong-doers attempt to reinterpret their actions through the use of a linguistic device by which norm breaking conduct is socially interpreted. That is, anticipating the negative consequences of their behavior, wrong-doers attempt to present the act in terms that are both culturally appropriate and acceptable.

Following Mills, a number of sociologists have focused on the types of techniques employed by actors in problematic situations (Hall and Hewitt, 1970; Hewitt and Hall, 1973; Hewitt and Stokes, 1975; Sykes and Matza, 1957). Scott and Lyman (1968) describe excuses and justifications, linguistic "accounts" that explain and remove culpability for an untoward act after it has been committed. *Excuses* admit the act was bad or inappropriate but deny full responsibility, often through appeals to accident, or biological drive, or through scapegoating. In contrast, *justifications* accept responsibility for the act but deny that it was wrong—that is, they show in this situation the act was appropriate. *Accounts* are socially approved vocabularies that neutralize an act or its consequences and are always a manifestation of an underlying negotiation of identity.

Stokes and Hewitt (1976:837) use the term "aligning actions" to refer to those tactics and techniques used by actors when some feature of a situation is problematic. Stated simply, the concept refers to an actor's attempt, through various means, to bring his or her conduct into alignment with culture. Culture in this sense is conceptualized as a "set of cognitive constraints—objects—to which people must relate as they form lines of conduct" (1976:837), and includes physical constraints, expectations and definitions of others, and personal biography. Carrying out aligning actions implies both awareness of those elements of normative culture that are applicable to the deviant act and, in addition, an actual effort to bring the act into line with this awareness. The result is that deviant behavior is legitimized.

This paper presents an analysis of interviews we conducted with a sample of 114 convicted, incarcerated rapists. We use the concept of accounts (Scott and Lyman, 1968) as a tool to organize and analyze the vocabularies of motive which this group of rapists used to explain themselves and their actions. An analysis of their accounts demonstrates how it was possible for 83 percent (n = 114)[1] of these convicted rapists to view themselves as non-rapists.

When rapists' accounts are examined, a typology emerges that consists of admitters and deniers. Admitters (n = 47) acknowledged that they had forced sexual acts on their victims and defined the behavior as rape. In contrast, deniers[2] either eschewed sexual contact or all association with the victim (n = 35),[3] or admitted to sexual acts but did not define their behavior as rape (n = 32).

The remainder of this paper is divided into two sections. In the first, we discuss the accounts which the rapists used to justify their behavior. In the second, we discuss those accounts which attempted to excuse the rape. By and large, the deniers used justifications while the admitters used excuses. In some cases, both groups relied on the same themes, stereotypes, and images: some admitters, like most deniers, claimed that women enjoyed being raped. Some deniers excused their behavior by referring to alcohol or drug use, although they did so quite differently than admitters. Through these narrative accounts, we explore convicted rapists' own perceptions of their crimes.

METHODS AND VALIDITY

From September, 1980, through September, 1981, we interviewed 114 male convicted rapists who were incarcerated in seven maximum or medium security prisons in the Commonwealth of Virginia. All of the rapists had been convicted of the rape or attempted rape (n = 8) of an adult woman, although a few had teenage victims as well. Men convicted of incest, statutory rape, or sodomy of a male were omitted from the sample.

Twelve percent of the rapists had been convicted of more than one rape or attempted rape, 39 percent also had convictions for burglary or robbery, 29 percent for abduction, 25 percent for sodomy, and 11 percent for first or second degree murder. Eighty-two percent had a previous criminal history but only 23 percent had records for previous sex offenses. Their sentences for rape and accompanying crimes ranged from 10 years to an accumulation by one man of seven life sentences plus 380 years; 43 percent of the rapists were serving from 10 to 30 years and 22 percent were serving at least one life term. Forty-six percent of the rapists were white and 54 percent were black. Their ages ranged from 18 to 60 years; 88 percent were between 18 and 35 years. Forty-two percent were either married or cohabitating at the time of their offense. Only 20 percent had a high school education or better, and 85 percent came from working-class backgrounds. Despite the popular belief that rape is due to a personality disorder, only 26 percent of these rapists had any history of emotional problems. When the rapists in this study were compared to a statistical profile of felons in all Virginia prisons, prepared by the Virginia Department of Corrections, rapists who volunteered for this research were disproportionately white, somewhat better educated, and younger than the average inmate.

All participants in this study were volunteers. We sent a letter to every inmate (n = 3500) at each of the seven prisons. The letters introduced us as professors at a local university, described our research as a study of men's attitudes toward sexual behavior and women, outlined our procedures for ensuring confidentiality, and solicited volunteers from all criminal categories. Using one follow-up letter, approximately 25 percent of all inmates, including rapists, indicated their willingness to be interviewed by mailing an information sheet to us at the university. From this pool of volunteers, we constructed a sample of rapists based on age, education, race, severity of current offenses, and previous criminal records. Obviously, the sample was not random and thus may not be representative of all rapists.

Each of the authors—one woman and one man—interviewed half of the rapists. Both authors were able to establish rapport and obtain information. However, the rapists volunteered more about their feelings and emotions to the female author and her interviews lasted longer.

All rapists were given an 89-page interview, which included a general background, psychological, criminal, and sexual history, attitude scales, and 30 pages of open-ended questions intended to explore their perceptions of their crimes, their victims, and theirselves. Because a voice print is an absolute source of identification, we did not use tape recorders. All interviews were hand recorded. With some practice, we found it was possible to record much of the interview verbatim. While hand recording inevitably resulted in some lost data, it did have the advantage of eliciting more confidence and candor in the men.

Interviews with the rapists lasted from three hours to seven hours; the average was about four-and-one-half hours. Most of the rapists were reluctant to end the interview. Once rapport had been established, the men wanted to talk, even though it sometimes meant, for example, missing a meal.

Because of the reputation prison inmates have for "conning," validity was a special concern in our research. Although the purpose of the research was to obtain the men's own perceptions of their acts, it was also necessary to establish the extent to which these perceptions deviated from other descriptions of their crimes. To establish validity, we used the same technique others have used in prison research: comparing factual information, including details of the crime, obtained in the interview with pre-sentence reports on file at the prisons (Athens, 1977; Luckenbill, 1977; Queen's Bench Foundation, 1976). Pre-sentence reports, written by a court worker at the time of conviction, usually include general background information, a psychological evaluation, the offender's version of the details of the crime, and the victim's or police's version of the details of the crime. Using these records allowed us to clarify two important issues: first, the amount of change that had occurred in rapists' accounts from pre-sentencing to the time when we interviewed them; and, second, the amount of discrepancy between rapists' accounts, as told to us, and the victims' and/or police versions of the crime, contained in the pre-sentence reports.

The time between pre-sentence reports and our interviews (in effect, the amount of time rapists had spent in prison before we interviewed them) ranged from less than one year to 20 years; the average was three years. Yet despite this time lapse, there were no significant changes in the way rapists explained their crimes, with the exception of 18 men who had denied their crimes at their trials but admitted them to us. There were no cases of men who admitted their crime at their trial but denied them when talking to us.

However, there were major differences between the accounts we heard of the crimes from rapists and the police's and victim's versions. Admitters (including deniers turned admitters) told us essentially the same story as the police and victim versions. However, the admitters subtly understated the force they had used and, though they used words such as *violent* to describe their acts, they also omitted reference to the more brutal aspects of their crime.

In contrast, deniers' interview accounts differed significantly from victim and police versions. According to the pre-sentence reports, 11 of the 32 deniers had been acquainted with their victim. But an additional four deniers told us they had been acquainted with their victims. In the pre-sentence reports, police or victim versions of the crime described seven rapes in which the victim had been hitchhiking or was picked up in a bar; but deniers told us this was true of 20 victims. Weapons were present in 21 of the 32 rapes according to the pre-sentence reports, yet only nine men acknowledged the presence of a weapon and only two of the nine admitted they had used it to threaten or intimidate their victim. Finally, in at least seven of the rapes, the victim had been seriously injured,[4] but only three men admitted

Table 1 / Comparison of Admitter's and Denier's Crimes Police/Victim Versions in Pre-Sentence Reports

Characteristics	*Percent Admitters* $n = 47$	*Percent Deniers* $n = 32$
White Assailant	57	41
Black Assailant	43	59
Group Rape	23	13
Multiple Rapes	43	34
Assailant a Stranger	72	66
Controversial Situation	06	22
Weapon and/or Injury Present (includes victim murdered)	74	69

injury. In two of the three cases, the victim had been murdered; in these cases the men denied the rape but not the murder. Indeed, deniers constructed accounts for us which, by implicating the victim, made their own conduct appear to have been more appropriate. They never used words such as *violent*, choosing instead to emphasize the sexual component of their behavior.

It should be noted that we investigated the possibility that deniers claimed their behavior was not criminal because, in contrast to admitters, their crimes resembled what research has found the public define as a controversial rape, that is, victim an acquaintance, no injury or weapon, victim picked up hitchhiking or in a bar (Burt, 1980; Burt and Albin, 1981; Williams, 1979). However, as Table 1 indicates, the crimes committed by deniers were only slightly more likely to involve these elements.

This contrast between pre-sentence reports and interviews suggest several significant factors related to interview content validity. First, when asked to explain their behavior, our sample of convicted rapists (except deniers turned admitters) responded with accounts that had changed surprisingly little since their trials. Second, admitters' interview accounts were basically the same as others' versions of their crimes, while deniers systematically put more blame on the victims.

JUSTIFYING RAPE

Deniers attempted to justify their behavior by presenting the victim in a light that made her appear culpable, regardless of their own actions. Five themes run through attempts to justify their rapes: (1) women as seductresses; (2) women mean "yes" when they say "no"; (3) most women eventually relax and enjoy it; (4) nice girls don't get raped; and (5) guilty of a minor wrongdoing.

1) Women as Seductresses

Men who rape need not search far for cultural language which supports the premise that women provoke or are responsible for rape. In addition to common cultural stereotypes, the fields of psychiatry and criminology (particularly the subfield of victimology) have traditionally provided justifications for rape, often by portraying raped women as the victims of their own seduction (Albin, 1977; Marolla and Scully, 1979). For example, Hollander (1924:130) argues:

> Considering the amount of illicit intercourse, rape of women is very rare indeed. Flirtation and provocative conduct, i.e., tacit (if not actual) consent is generally the prelude to intercourse.

Since women are supposed to be coy about their sexual availability, refusal to comply with a man's sexual demands lacks meaning and rape appears normal. The fact that violence and, often, a weapon are used to accomplish the rape is not considered. As an example, Abrahamsen (1960:61) writes:

> The conscious or unconscious biological or psychological attraction between man and woman does not exist only on the part of the offender toward the woman but, also, on her part toward him, which in many instances may, to some extent, be the impetus for his sexual attack. Often a woman [sic] unconsciously wishes to be taken by force—consider the theft of the bride in Peer Gynt.

Like Peer Gynt, the deniers we interviewed tried to demonstrate that their victims were willing and, in some cases, enthusiastic participants. In these accounts, the rape became more dependent upon the victim's behavior than upon their own actions.

Thirty-one percent (n = 10) of the deniers presented an extreme view of the victim. Not only willing, she was the aggressor, a seductress who lured them, unsuspecting, into sexual action. Typical was a denier convicted of his first rape and accompanying crimes of burglary, sodomy, and abduction. According to the pre-sentence reports, he had broken into the victim's house and raped her at knife point. While he admitted to the breaking and entry, which he claimed was for altruistic purposes ("to pay for the prenatal care of a friend's girlfriend"), he also argued that when the victim discovered him, he had tried to leave but she had asked him to stay. Telling him that she cheated on her husband, she had voluntarily removed her clothes and seduced him. She was, according to him, an exemplary sex partner who "enjoyed it very much and asked for oral sex.[5] Can I have it now?" he reported her as saying. He claimed they had spent hours in bed, after which the victim had told him he was good looking and asked to see him again. "Who would believe I'd meet a fellow like this?" he reported her as saying.

In addition to this extreme group, 25 percent (n = 8) of the deniers said the victim was willing and had made some sexual advances. An additional 9 percent (n = 3) said the victim was willing to have sex for money or drugs. In two of these three cases, the victim had been either an acquaintance or picked up, which the rapists said led them to expect sex.

2) Women Mean "Yes" When They Say "No"

Thirty-four percent (n = 11) of the deniers described their victim as unwilling, at least initially, indicating either that she had resisted or that she had said no. Despite this, and even though (according to pre-sentence reports) a weapon had been present in 64 percent (n = 7) of these 11 cases, the rapists justified their behavior by arguing that either the victim had not resisted enough or that her "no" had really meant "yes." For example, one denier who was serving time for a previous rape was subsequently convicted of attempting to rape a prison hospital nurse. He insisted he had actually completed the second rape, and said of his victim: "She semi-struggled but deep down inside I think she felt it was a fantasy come true." The nurse, according to him, had asked a question about his conviction for rape, which he interpreted as teasing. "It was like she was saying, 'rape me.' " Further, he stated that she had helped him along with oral sex and "from her actions, she was enjoying it." In another case, a 34-year-old man convicted of abducting and raping a 15-year-old teenager at knife point as she walked on the beach, claimed it was a pickup. This rapist said women like to be overpowered before sex, but to dominate after it begins.

> A man's body is like a coke bottle, shake it up, put your thumb over the opening and feel the tension. When you take a woman out, woo her, then she says "no, I'm a nice girl," you have to use force. All men do this. She said "no" but it was a societal no, she wanted to be coaxed. All women say "no" when they mean "yes" but its a societal no, so they won't have to feel responsible later.

Claims that the victim didn't resist or, if she did, didn't resist enough, were also used by 24 percent (n = 11) of admitters to explain why, during the incident, they believed the victim was willing and that they were not raping. These rapists didn't redefine their acts until some time after the crime. For example, an admitter who used a bayonet to threaten his victim, an employee of the store he had been robbing, stated:

> At the time I didn't think it was rape. I just asked her nicely and she didn't resist. I never considered prison. I just felt like I had met a friend. It took about five years of reading and going to school to change my mind about whether it was rape. I became familiar with the subtlety of violence. But at the time, I believed that as long as I didn't hurt anyone it wasn't wrong. At the time, I didn't think I would go to prison. I thought I would beat it.

Another typical case involved a gang rape in which the victim was abducted at knife point as she walked home about midnight. According to two of the rapists, both of whom were interviewed, at the time they had thought the victim had willingly accepted a ride from the third rapist (who was not interviewed). They claimed the victim didn't resist and one reported her as saying she would do anything if they would take her home. In this rapist's view, "She acted like she enjoyed it, but maybe she was just acting. She wasn't crying, she was engaging in it." He reported that she had been friendly to the rapist who abducted her and, claiming not to have a home phone, she gave him her office number—a tactic eventually used to catch the three. In retrospect, this young man had decided, "She was scared and just relaxed and enjoyed it to avoid getting hurt." Note, however, that while he had redefined the act as rape, he continued to believe she enjoyed it.

Men who claimed to have been unaware that they were raping viewed sexual aggression as a man's prerogative at the time of the rape. Thus they regarded their act as little more than a minor wrongdoing even though most possessed or used a weapon. As long as the victim survived without major physical injury, from their perspective, a rape had not taken place. Indeed, even U.S. courts have often taken the position that physical injury is a necessary ingredient for a rape conviction.

3) Most Women Eventually Relax and Enjoy It

Many of the rapists expected us to accept the image, drawn from cultural stereotype, that once the rape began, the victim relaxed and enjoyed it.[6] Indeed, 69 percent (n = 22) of deniers justified their behavior by claiming not only that the victim was willing, but also that she enjoyed herself, in some cases to an immense degree. Several men suggested that they had fulfilled their victims' dreams. Additionally, while most admitters used adjectives such as "dirty," "humiliated," and "disgusted," to describe how they thought rape made women feel, 20 percent (n = 9) believed that their victim enjoyed herself. For example, one denier had posed as a salesman to gain entry to his victim's house. But he claimed he had had a previous sexual relationship with the victim, that she agreed to have sex for drugs, and that the opportunity to have sex with him produced "a glow, because she was really into oral stuff and fascinated by the idea of sex with a black man. She felt satisfied, fulfilled, wanted me to stay, but I didn't want her." In another case, a denier who had broken into his victim's house but who insisted the victim was his lover and let him in voluntarily, declared "She felt good, kept kissing me and wanted me to stay the night. She felt proud after sex with me." And another denier, who had hid in his victim's closet and later attacked her while she slept, argued that while she was scared at first, "once we got into it, she was ok." He continued to believe he hadn't committed rape because "she enjoyed it and it was like she consented."

4) Nice Girls Don't Get Raped

The belief that "nice girls don't get raped" affects perception of fault. The victim's reputation, as well as characteristics or behavior which violate normative sex role expections, are perceived as contributing to the commission of the crime. For example, Nelson and Amir (1975) defined hitchhike rape as a victim-precipitated offense.

In our study, 69 percent (n = 22) of deniers and 22 percent (n = 10) of admitters referred to their victims' sexual reputation, thereby evoking the stereotype that "nice girls don't get raped." They claimed that the victim was known to have been a prostitute, or a "loose" woman, or to have had a lot of affairs, or to have given birth to a child out of wedlock. For example, a denier who claimed he had picked up his victim while she was hitchhiking stated, "To be honest, we [his family] knew she was a damn whore and whether she screwed one or 50 guys didn't matter." According to pre-sentence reports this victim didn't know her attacker and he abducted her at knife point from the street. In another case, a denier who claimed to have known his victim by reputation stated:

> If you wanted drugs or a quick piece of ass, she would do it. In court she said she was a virgin, but I could tell during sex [rape] that she was very experienced.

When other types of discrediting biographical information were added to these sexual slurs, a total of 78 percent (n = 25) of the deniers used the victim's reputation to substantiate their accounts. Most frequently, they referred to the victim's emotional state or drug use. For example, one denier claimed his victim had been known to be loose and, additionally, had turned state's evidence against her husband to put him in prison and save herself from a burglary conviction. Further, he asserted that she had met her current boyfriend, who was himself in and out of prison, in a drug rehabilitation center where they were both clients.

Evoking the stereotype that women provoke rape by the way they dress, a description of the victim as seductively attired appeared in the accounts of 22 percent (n = 7) of deniers and 17 percent (n = 8) of admitters. Typically, these descriptions were used to substantiate their claims about the victim's reputation. Some men went to extremes to paint a tarnished picture of the victim, describing her as dressed in tight black clothes and without a bra; in one case, the victim was portrayed as sexually provocative in dress and carriage. Not only did she wear short skirts, but she was observed to "spread her legs while getting out of cars." Not all of the men attempted to assassinate their victim's reputation with equal vengeance. Numerous times they made subtle and offhand remarks like, "She was a waitress and you know how they are."

The intent of these discrediting statements is clear. Deniers argued that the woman was a "legitimate" victim who got what she deserved. For example, one denier stated that all of his victims had been prostitutes; pre-sentence reports indicated they were not. Several times during his interview, he referred to them as "dirty sluts," and argued "anything I did to them was justified." Deniers also claimed their victim had wrongly accused them and was the type of woman who would perjure herself in court.

5) Only a Minor Wrongdoing

The majority of deniers did not claim to be completely innocent and they also accepted some accountability for their actions. Only 16 percent (n = 5) of deniers argued that they were totally free of blame. Instead, the majority of deniers pleaded guilty to a lesser charge. That is, they obfuscated the rape by pleading guilty to a less serious, more acceptable charge. They accepted being over-sexed, accused of poor judgment or trickery, even some violence, or guilty of adultery or contributing to the delinquency of a minor, charges that are hardly the equivalent of rape.

Typical of this reasoning is a denier who met his victim in a bar when the bartender asked him if he would try to repair her stalled car. After attempting unsuccessfully, he claimed the victim drank with him and later accepted a ride. Out riding, he pulled into a deserted area "to see how my luck would go." When the victim resisted his advances, he beat her and he stated:

> I did something stupid. I pulled a knife on her and I hit her as hard as I would hit a man. But I shouldn't be in prison for what I did. I shouldn't have all this time [sentence] for going to bed with a broad.

This rapist continued to believe that while the knife was wrong, his sexual behavior was justified.

In another case, the denier claimed he picked up his under-age victim at a party and that she voluntarily went with him to a motel. According to pre-sentence reports, the victim had been abducted at knife point from a party. He explained:

> After I paid for a motel, she would have to have sex but I wouldn't use a weapon. I would have explained I spent money and, if she still said no, I would have forced her. If it had happened that way, it would have been rape to some people but not to my way of thinking. I've done that kind of thing before. I'm guilty of sex and contributing to the delinquency of a minor, but not rape.

In sum, deniers argued that, while their behavior may not have been completely proper, it should not have been considered rape. To accomplish this, they attempted to discredit and blame the victim while presenting their own actions as justified in the context. Not surprisingly, none of the deniers thought of himself as a rapist. A minority of the admitters attempted to lessen the impact of their crime by claiming the victim enjoyed being raped. But despite this similarity, the nature and tone of admitters' and deniers' accounts were essentially different.

EXCUSING RAPE

In stark contrast to deniers, admitters regarded their behavior as morally wrong and beyond justification. They blamed themselves rather than the victim, although some continued to cling to the belief that the victim had contributed to the crime somewhat, for example, by not resisting enough.

Several of the admitters expressed the view that rape was an act of such moral outrage that it was unforgivable. Several admitters broke into tears at intervals during their interviews. A typical sentiment was,

> I equate rape with someone throwing you up against a wall and tearing your liver and guts out of you. . . . Rape is worse than murder . . . and I'm disgusting.

Another young admitter frequently referred to himself as repulsive and confided:

> I'm in here for rape and in my own mind, its the most disgusting crime, sickening. When people see me and know, I get sick.

Admitters tried to explain their crime in a way that allowed them to retain a semblance of moral integrity. Thus, in contrast to deniers' justifications, admitters used excuses to explain how they were compelled to rape. These excuses appealed to the existence of forces outside of the rapists' control. Through the use of excuses, they attempted to demonstrate that either intent was absent or responsibility was diminished. This allowed them to admit rape while reducing the threat to their identity as a moral person. Excuses also permitted them to view their behavior as idiosyncratic rather than typical and, thus, to believe they were not "really" rapists. Three themes run through these accounts: (1) the use of alcohol and drugs; (2) emotional problems; and (3) nice guy image.

1) The Use of Alcohol and Drugs

A number of studies have noted a high incidence of alcohol and drug consumption by convicted rapists prior to their crime (Groth, 1979; Queen's Bench Foundation, 1976). However, more recent research has tentatively concluded that the connection between substance use and crime is not as direct as previously thought (Ladouceur, 1983). Another facet of alcohol and drug use mentioned in the literature is its utility in disavowing deviance. McCaghy (1968) found that child molesters used alcohol as a technique for neutralizing their deviant identity. Marolla and Scully (1979), in a review of psychiatric literature, demonstrated how alcohol consumption is applied differently as a vocabulary of motive. Rapists can use alcohol both as an excuse for their behavior and to discredit the victim and make her more responsible. We found the former common among admitters and the latter common among deniers.

Alcohol and/or drugs were mentioned in the accounts of 77 percent (n = 30) of admitters and 84 percent (n = 21) of deniers and both groups were equally likely to have acknowledged consuming a substance—admitters, 77 percent (n = 30); deniers, 72 percent (n = 18). However, admitters said they had been affected by the substance; if not the cause of their behavior, it was at least a contributing factor. For example, an admitter who estimated his consumption to have been eight beers and four "hits of acid" reported:

> Straight, I don't have the guts to rape. I could fight a man but not that. To say, "I'm going to do it to a woman," knowing it will scare and hurt her, takes guts or you have to be sick.

Another admitter believed that his alcohol and drug use,

> ...brought out what was already there but in such intensity it was uncontrollable. Feelings of being dominant, powerful, using someone for my own gratification, all rose to the surface.

In contrast, deniers' justifications required that they not be substantially impaired. To say that they had been drunk or high would cast doubt on their ability to control themself or to remember events as they actually happened. Consistent with this, when we asked if the alcohol and/or drugs had had an effect on their behavior, 69 percent (n = 27) of admitters, but only 40 percent (n = 10) of deniers, said they had been affected.

Even more interesting were references to the victim's alcohol and/or drug use. Since admitters had already relieved themselves of responsibility through claims of being drunk or high, they had nothing to gain from the assertion that the victim had used or been affected by alcohol and/or drugs. On the other hand, it was very much in the interest of deniers to delcare that their victim had been intoxicated or high: that fact lessened her credibility and made her more responsible for the act. Reflecting these observations, 72 percent (n = 18) of deniers and 26 percent (n = 10) of admitters maintained that alcohol or drugs had been consumed by the victim. Further, while 56 percent (n = 14) of deniers declared she had been affected by this use, only 15 percent (n = 6) of admitters made a similar claim. Typically, deniers argued that the alcohol and drugs had sexually aroused their victim or rendered her out of control. For example, one denier

Table 2 / Rapists' Accounts of Own and Victims' Alcohol and/or Drug (A/D) Use and Effect

	Admitters n = 39 %	*Deniers* n = 25 %
Neither Self nor Victim Used A/D	23	16
Self Used A/D	77	72
Of Self Used, no Victim Use	51	12
Self Affected by A/D	69	40
Of Self Affected, no Victim Use or Affect	54	24
Self A/D Users who were Affected	90	56
Victim Used A/D	26	72
Of Victim Used, no Self Use	0	0
Victim Affected by A/D	15	56
Of Victim Affected, no Self Use or Affect	0	40
Victim A/D Users who were Affected	60	78
Both Self and Victim Used and Affected by A/D	15	16

insisted that his victim had become hysterical from drugs, not from being raped, and it was because of the drugs that she had reported him to the police. In addition, 40 percent (n = 10) of deniers argued that while the victim had been drunk or high, they themselves either hadn't ingested or weren't affected by alcohol and/or drugs. None of the admitters made this claim. In fact, in all of the 15 percent (n = 6) of cases where an admitter said the victim was drunk or high, he also admitted to being similarly affected.

These data strongly suggest that whatever role alcohol and drugs play in sexual and other types of violent crime, rapists have learned the advantage to be gained from using alcohol and drugs as an account. Our sample was aware that their victim would be discredited and their own behavior excused or justified by refering to alcohol and/or drugs.

2) Emotional Problems

Admitters frequently attributed their acts to emotional problems. Forty percent (n = 19) of admitters said they believe an emotional problem had been at the root of their rape behavior, and 33 percent (n = 15) specifically related the problem to an unhappy, unstable childhood or a marital-domestic situation. Still others claimed to have been in a general state of unease. For example, one admitter said that at the time of the rape he had been depressed, feeling he couldn't do anything right, and that something had been missing from his life. But he also added, "being a rapist is not part of my personality." Even admitters who could locate no source for an emotional problem evoked the popular image of rapists as the product of disordered personalities to argue they also must have problems:

> The fact that I'm a rapist makes me different. Rapists aren't all there. They have problems. It was wrong so there must be a reason why I did it. I must have a problem.

Our data do indicate that a precipitating event, involving an upsetting problem of everyday living, appeared in the accounts of 80 percent (n = 38) of admitters and 25 percent (n = 8) of deniers. Of those experiencing a precipitating event, including deniers, 76 percent (n = 35) involved a wife or girlfriend. Over and over, these men described themselves as having been in a rage because of an incident involving a woman with whom they believed they were in love.

Frequently, the upsetting event was related to a rigid and unrealistic double standard for sexual conduct and virtue which they applied to "their" woman but which they didn't expect from men, didn't apply to themselves, and, obviously, didn't honor in other women. To discover that the "pedestal" didn't apply to their wife or girlfriend sent them into a fury. One especially articulate and typical admitter described his feeling as follows. After serving a short prison term for auto theft, he married his "childhood sweetheart" and secured a well-paying job. Between his job and the volunteer work he was doing with an ex-offender group, he was spending long hours away from home, a situation that had bothered his wife. In response to her request, he gave up his volunteer work, though it was clearly meaningful to him. Then, one day, he discovered his wife with her former boyfriend "and my life fell apart." During the next several days, he said his anger had made him withdraw into himself and, after three days of drinking in a motel room, he abducted and raped a stranger. He stated:

> My parents have been married for many years and I had high expectations about marriage. I put my wife on a pedestal. When I walked in on her, I felt like my life had been destroyed, it was such a shock. I was bitter and angry about the fact that I hadn't done anything to my wife for cheating. I didn't want to hurt her [victim], only to scare and degrade her.

It is clear that many admitters, and a minority of deniers, were under stress at the time of their rapes. However, their problems were ordinary—the types of upsetting events that everyone experiences at some point in life. The overwhelming majority of the men were not clinically defined as mentally ill in court-ordered psychiatric examinations prior to their trials. Indeed, our sample is consistent with Abel *et al.* (1980) who found fewer than 5 percent of rapists were psychotic at the time of their offense.

As with alcohol and drug intoxication, a claim of emotional problems works differently depending upon whether the behavior in question is being justified or excused. It would have been counter-productive for deniers to have claimed to have had emotional problems at the time of the rape. Admitters used psychological explanations to portray themselves as having been temporarily "sick" at the time of the rape. Sick people are usually blamed for neither the cause of their illness nor for acts committed while in that state of diminished capacity. Thus, adopting the sick role removed responsibility by excusing the behavior as having been beyond the ability of the individual to control. Since the rapists were not "themselves," the rape was idiosyncratic rather than typical behavior. Admitters asserted a non-deviant identity despite their self-proclaimed disgust with what they had done. Although admitters were willing to assume the sick role, they did not view their problem as a chronic condition, nor did they believe themselves to be insane or permanently impaired. Said one admitter, who believed that he needed psychological counseling: "I have a mental disorder, but I'm not crazy." Instead, admitters viewed their "problem" as mild, transient, and curable. Indeed, part of the appeal of this excuse was that not only did it relieve responsibility, but, as with alcohol and drug addiction, it allowed the rapist to "recover." Thus, at the time of their interviews, only 31 percent (n = 14) of admitters indicated that "being a rapist" was part of their self-concept. Twenty-eight percent (n = 13) of admitters stated they had never thought of themselves as rapists, 8 percent (n = 4) said they were unsure, and 33 percent (n = 16) asserted they had been a rapist at one time but now were recovered. A multiple "exrapist," who believed his "problem" was due to "something buried in my subconscious" that was triggered when his girlfriend broke up with him, expressed a typical opinion:

> I was a rapist, but not now. I've grown up, had to live with it. I've hit the bottom of the well and it can't get worse. I feel born again to deal with my problems.

3) Nice Guy Image

Admitters attempted to further neutralize their crime and negotiate a nonrapist identity by painting an image of themselves as a "nice guy." Admitters projected the image of someone who had made a serious mistake but, in every other respect, was a decent person. Fifty-seven percent (n = 27) expressed regret and sorrow for their victim indicating that they wished there were a way to apologize for or amend their behavior. For example, a participant in a rape-murder, who insisted his partner did the murder, confided, "I wish there was something I could do besides saying 'I'm sorry, I'm sorry.' I live with it 24 hours a day and, sometimes, I wake up crying in the middle of the night because of it."

Schlenker and Darby (1981) explain the significance of apologies beyond the obvious expression of regret. An apology allows a person to admit guilt while at the same time seeking a pardon by signalling that the event should not be considered a fair representation of what the person is really like. An apology separates the bad self from the good self, and promises more acceptable behavior in the future. When apologizing, an individual is attempting to say: "I have repented and should be forgiven," thus making it appear that no further rehabilitation is required.

The "nice guy" statements of the admitters reflected an attempt to communicate a message consistent with Schlenker's and Darby's analysis of apologies. It was an attempt to convey that rape was not a representation of their "true" self. For example,

> It's different from anything else I've ever done. I feel more guilt about this. It's not consistent with me. When I talk about it, it's like being assaulted myself. I don't know why I did it, but once I started, I got into it. Armed robbery was a way of life for me, but not rape. I feel like I wasn't being myself.

Admitters also used "nice guy" statements to register their moral opposition to violence and harming women, even though, in some cases, they had seriously injured their victims. Such was the case of an admitter convicted of a gang rape:

> I'm against hurting women. She should have resisted. None of us were the type of person that would use force on a woman. I never positioned myself on a woman unless she showed an interest in me. They would play to me, not me to them. My

> weakness is to follow. I never would have stopped, let alone pick her up without the others. I never would have let anyone beat her. I never bothered women who didn't want sex; never had a problem with sex or getting it. I loved her—like all women.

Finally, a number of admitters attempted to improve their self-image by demonstrating that, while they had raped, it could have been worse if they had not been a "nice guy." For example, one admitter professed to being especially gentle with his victim after she told him she had just had a baby. Others claimed to have given the victim money to get home or make a phone call, or to have made sure the victim's children were not in the room. A multiple rapist, whose pattern was to break in and attack sleeping victims in their homes, stated:

> I never beat any of my victims and I told them I wouldn't hurt them if they cooperated. I'm a professional thief. But I never robbed the women I raped because I felt so bad about what I had already done to them.

Even a young man, who raped his five victims at gun point and then stabbed them to death, attempted to improve his image by stating:

> Physically they enjoyed the sex [rape]. Once they got involved, it would be difficult to resist. I was always gentle and kind until I started to kill them. And the killing was always sudden, so they wouldn't know it was coming.

SUMMARY AND CONCLUSIONS

Convicted rapists' accounts of their crimes include both excuses and justifications. Those who deny what they did was rape justify their actions; those who admit it was rape attempt to excuse it or themselves. This study does not address why some men admit while others deny, but future research might address this question. This paper does provide insight on how men who are sexually aggressive or violent construct reality, describing the different strategies of admitters and deniers.

Admitters expressed the belief that rape was morally reprehensible. But they explained themselves and their acts by appealing to forces beyond their control, forces which reduced their capacity to act rationally and thus compelled them to rape. Two types of excuses predominated: alcohol/drug intoxication and emotional problems. Admitters used these excuses to negotiate a moral identity for themselves by viewing rape as idiosyncratic rather than typical behavior. This allowed them to reconceptualize themselves as recovered or "exrapists," someone who had made a serious mistake which did not represent their "true" self.

In contrast, deniers' accounts indicate that these men raped because their value system provided no compelling reason not to do so. When sex is viewed as a male entitlement, rape is no longer seen as criminal. However, the deniers had been convicted of rape, and like the admitters, they attempted to negotiate an identity. Through justifications, they constructed a "controversial" rape and attempted to demonstrate how their behavior, even if not quite right, was appropriate in the situation. Their denials, drawn from common cultural rape stereotypes, took two forms, both of which ultimately denied the existence of a victim.

The first form of denial was buttressed by the cultural view of men as sexually masterful and women as coy but seductive. Injury was denied by portraying the victim as willing, even enthusiastic, or as politely resistant at first but eventually yielding to "relax and enjoy it." In these accounts, force appeared merely as a seductive technique. Rape was disclaimed: rather than harm the woman, the rapist had fulfilled her dreams. In the second form of denial, the victim was portrayed as the type of woman who "got what she deserved." Through attacks on the victim's sexual reputation and, to a lesser degree, her emotional state, deniers attempted to demonstrate that since the victim wasn't a "nice girl," they were not rapists. Consistent with both forms of denial was the self-interested use of alcohol and drugs as a justification. Thus, in contrast to admitters, who accentuated their own use as an excuse, deniers emphasized the victim's consumption in an effort to both discredit her and make her appear more responsible for the rape. It is important to remember that deniers did not invent these justifications. Rather, they reflect a belief system which has historically victimized women by promulgating the myth that women both enjoy and are responsible for their own rape.

While admitters and deniers present an essentially contrasting view of men who rape, there were some shared characteristics. Justifications particularly, but also excuses, are buttressed by the cultural view of women as sexual commodities, dehumanized and devoid of autonomy and dignity. In this sense, the sexual objectification of women must be understood as an important factor contributing to an environment that trivializes, neutralizes, and, perhaps, facilitates rape.

Finally, we must comment on the consequences of allowing one perspective to dominate thought on a social problem. Rape, like any complex continuum of behavior, has multiple causes and is influenced by a number of social factors. Yet, dominated by psychiatry and the medical model, the underlying assumption that rapists are "sick" has pervaded research. Although methodologically unsound, conclusions have been based almost exclusively on small clinical populations of rapists—that extreme group of rapists who seek counseling in prison and are the most likely to exhibit psychopathology. From this small, atypical group of men, psychiatric findings have been generalized to all men who rape. Our research, however, based on volunteers from the entire prison population, indicates that some rapists, like deniers, viewed and understood their behavior from a popular cultural perspective. This strongly suggests that cultural perspectives, and not an idiosyncratic illness, motivated their behavior. Indeed, we can argue that the psychiatric perspective has contributed to the vocabulary of motive that rapists use to excuse and justify their behavior (Scully and Marolla, 1984).

Efforts to arrive at a general explanation for rape have been retarded by the narrow focus of the medical model and the preoccupation with clinical populations. The continued reduction of such complex behavior to a singular cause hinders, rather than enhances, our understanding of rape.

Notes

This research was supported by a grant (R01 MH33013) from the National Center For the Prevention and Control of Rape, National Institute of Mental Health. The authors thank the Virginia Department of Corrections for their cooperation and assistance in this research. Correspondence to: Department of Sociology and Anthropology, Virginia Commonwealth University, 312 Shafer Court, Richmond, VA 23284.

1. These numbers include pretest interviews. When the analysis involves either questions that were not asked in the pretest or that were changed, they are excluded and thus the number changes.

2. There is, of course, the possibility that some of these men really were innocent of rape. However, while the U.S. criminal justice system is not without flaw, we assume that it is highly unlikely that this many men could have been unjustly convicted of rape, especially since rape is a crime with traditionally low conviction rates. Instead, for purposes of this research, we assume that these men were guilty as charged and that their attempt to maintain an image of non-rapist springs from some psychologically or sociologically interpretable mechanism.

3. Because of their outright denial, interviews with this group of rapists did not contain the data being analyzed here and, consequently, they are not included in this paper.

4. It was sometimes difficult to determine the full extent of victim injury from the pre-sentence reports. Consequently, it is doubtful that this number accurately reflects the degree of injuries sustained by victims.

5. It is worth noting that a number of deniers specifically mentioned the victim's alleged interest in oral sex. Since our interview questions about sexual history indicated that the rapists themselves found oral sex marginally acceptable, the frequent mention is probably another attempt to discredit the victim. However, since a tape recorder could not be used for the interviews and the importance of these claims didn't emerge until the data was being coded and analyzed, it is possible that it was mentioned even more frequently but not recorded.

6. Research shows clearly that women do not enjoy rape. Holmstrom and Burgess (1978) asked 93 adult rape victims, "How did it feel sexually?" Not one said they enjoyed it. Further, the trauma of rape is so great that it disrupts sexual functioning (both frequency and satisfaction) for the overwhelming majority of victims, at least during the period immediately following the rape and, in fewer cases, for an extended period of time (Burgess and Holmstrom, 1979; Feldman-Summers *et al.*, 1979). In addition, a number of studies have shown that rape victims experience adverse consequences prompting some to move, change jobs, or drop out of school (Burgess and Holmstrom, 1974; Kilpatrick *et al.*, 1979; Ruch *et al.*, 1980; Shore, 1979).

References

Abel, Gene, Judith Becker, and Linda Skinner
1980 "Aggressive behavior and sex." Psychiatric Clinics of North America 3(2):133–151.

Abrahamsen, David
1960 The Psychology of Crime. New York: John Wiley.

Albin, Rochelle
1977 "Psychological studies of rape." Signs 3(2):423–435.
Athens, Lonnie
1977 "Violent crimes: A symbolic interactionist study." Symbolic Interaction 1(1):56–71.
Burgess, Ann Wolbert, and Lynda Lytle Holmstrom
1974 Rape: Victims of Crisis. Bowie: Robert J. Brady.
1979 "Rape: Sexual disruption and recovery." American Journal of Orthopsychiatry 49(4):648–657.
Burt, Martha
1980 "Cultural myths and supports for rape." Journal of Personality and Social Psychology 38(2):217–230.
Burt, Martha, and Rochelle Albin
1981 "Rape myths, rape definitions, and probability of conviction." Journal of Applied Psychology 11(3):212–230.
Feldman-Summers, Shirley, Patricia E. Gordon, and Jeanette R. Meagher
1979 "The impact of rape on sexual satisfaction." Journal of Abnormal Psychology 88(1):101–105.
Glueck, Sheldon
1925 Mental Disorders and the Criminal Law. New York: Little Brown.
Groth, Nicholas A.
1979 Men Who Rape. New York: Plenum Press.
Hall, Peter M., and John P. Hewitt
1970 "The quasi-theory of communication and the management of dissent." Social Problems 18(1):17–27.
Hewitt, John P., and Peter M. Hall
1973 "Social problems, problematic situations, and quasi-theories." American Journal of Sociology 38(3):367–374.
Hewitt, John P., and Randall Stokes
1975 "Disclaimers." American Sociological Review 40(1):1–11.
Hollander, Bernard
1924 The Psychology of Misconduct, Vice, and Crime. New York: Macmillan.
Holmstrom, Lynda Lytle, and Ann Wolbert Burgess
1978 "Sexual behavior of assailant and victim during rape." Paper presented at the annual meetings of the American Sociological Association, San Francisco, September 2–8.
Kilpatrick, Dean G., Lois Veronen, and Patricia A. Resnick
1979 "The aftermath of rape: Recent empirical findings." American Journal of Orthopsychiatry 49(4):658–669.
Ladouceur, Patricia
1983 "The relative impact of drugs and alcohol on serious felons." Paper presented at the annual meetings of the American Society of Criminology, Denver, November 9–12.
Luckenbill, David
1977 "Criminal homicide as a situated transaction." Social Problems 25(2): 176–187.
McCaghy, Charles
1968 "Drinking and deviance disavowal: The case of child molesters." Social Problems 16(1):43–49.

Marolla, Joseph, and Diana Scully
1979 "Rape and psychiatric vocabularies of motive." Pp. 301–318 in Edith S. Gomberg and Violet Franks (eds.), Gender and Disordered Behavior: Sex Differences in Psychopathology. New York: Brunner/Mazel.
Mills, C. Wright
1940 "Situated actions and vocabularies of motive." American Sociological Review 5(6):904–913.
Nelson, Steve, and Menachem Amir
1975 "The hitchhike victim of rape: A research report." Pp. 47–65 in Israel Drapkin and Emilio Viano (eds.), Victimology: A New Focus. Lexington, KY: Lexington Books.
Queen's Bench Foundation
1976 Rape; Prevention and Resistance. San Francisco: Queen's Bench Foundation.
Ruch, Libby O., Susan Meyers Chandler, and Richard A. Harter
1980 "Life change and rape impact." Journal of Health and Social Behavior 21(3):248–260.
Schlenker, Barry R., and Bruce W. Darby
1981 "The use of apologies in social predicaments." Social Psychology Quarterly 44(3):271–278.
Scott, Marvin, and Stanford Lyman
1968 "Accounts." American Sociological Review 33(1):46–62.
Scully, Diana, and Joseph Marolla
1984 "Rape and psychiatric vocabularies of motive: Alternative perspectives." In Ann Wolbert Burgess (ed.), Handbook on Rape and Sexual Assault. New York: Garland Publishing.
Shore, Barbara K.
1979 "An examination of critical process and outcome factors in rape." Rockville, MD: National Institute of Mental Health.
Stokes, Randall, and John P. Hewitt
1976 "Aligning actions." American Sociological Review 41(5):837–849.
Sykes, Gresham M., and David Matza
1957 "Techniques of neutralization." American Sociological Review 22(6): 664–670.
Williams, Joyce
1979 "Sex role stereotypes, women's liberation, and rape: A cross-cultural analysis of attitude." Sociological Symposium 25 (Winter):61–97.

11 / Social Structure and Anomie

ROBERT K. MERTON

There persists a notable tendency in sociological theory to attribute the malfunctioning of social structure primarily to those of man's imperious biological drives which are not adequately restrained by social control. In this view, the social order is solely a device for "impulse management" and the "social processing" of tensions. These impulses which break through social control, be it noted, are held to be biologically derived. Nonconformity is assumed to be rooted in original nature.[1] Conformity is by implication the result of a utilitarian calculus or unreasoned conditioning. This point of view, whatever its other deficiencies, clearly begs one question. It provides no basis for determining the nonbiological conditions which induce deviations from prescribed patterns of conduct. In this paper, it will be suggested that certain phases of social structure generate the circumstances in which infringement of social codes constitutes a "normal" response.[2]

The conceptual scheme to be outlined is designed to provide a coherent, systematic approach to the study of socio-cultural sources of deviate behavior. Our primary aim lies in discovering how some social structures *exert a definite pressure* upon certain persons in the society to engage in noncomformist rather than conformist conduct. The many ramifications of the scheme cannot all be discussed; the problems mentioned outnumber those explicitly treated.

Among the elements of social and cultural structure, two are important for our purposes. These are analytically separable although they merge imperceptibly in concrete situations. The first consists of culturally defined goals, purposes, and interests. It comprises a frame of aspirational reference. These goals are more or less integrated and involve varying degrees of prestige and sentiment. They constitute a basic, but not the exclusive, component of what Linton aptly has called "designs for group living." Some of these cultural aspirations are related to the original drives of man, but they are not determined by them. The second phase of the social structure defines, regulates, and controls the acceptable modes of achieving these goals. Every social group invariably couples its scale of desired ends with moral or institutional regulation of permissible and required procedures for attaining these ends. These regulatory norms and moral imperatives do not necessarily coincide with technical or efficiency norms. Many procedures which from the standpoint of *particular individuals* would be most efficient in securing desired values, e.g., illicit oil-stock schemes, theft, fraud, are ruled out of the institutional area of permitted conduct. The choice of expedients is limited by the institutional norms.

To say that these two elements, culture goals and institutional norms, operate jointly is not to say that the ranges of alternative behaviors and aims bear some constant relation to one another. The emphasis upon certain goals may vary independently of the degree of emphasis upon institutional means. There may develop a disproportionate, at times, a virtually exclusive, stress upon the value of specific goals, involving relatively slight concern with the institutionally appropriate modes of attaining these goals. The limiting case in this direction is reached when the range of alternative procedures is limited only by technical rather than institutional considerations. Any and all devices which promise attainment of the all important goal would be permitted in this hypothetical polar case.[3] This constitutes one type of cultural malintegration. A second polar type is found in groups where activities originally conceived as instrumental are transmuted into ends in themselves. The original purposes are forgotten, and ritualistic adherence to institutionally prescribed conduct becomes virtually obsessive.[4] Stability is largely ensured while change is flouted. The range of alternative behaviors is severely limited. There develops a tradition-bound, sacred society characterized by neophobia. The occupational psychosis of the bureaucrat may be cited as a case in point. Finally, there are the intermediate types of groups where a balance between culture goals and institutional means is maintained. These are the significantly integrated and relatively stable, though changing, groups.

An effective equilibrium between the two phases of the social structure is maintained as long as satisfactions accrue to individuals who conform to both constraints, viz., satisfactions from the achievement of the goals and satisfactions emerging directly from the institutionally canalized modes of striving to attain these ends. Success, in such equilibrated cases, is twofold. Success is reckoned in terms of the product and in terms of the process, in terms of the outcome and in terms of activities. Continuing satisfactions must derive from sheer *participation* in a competitive order as well as from eclipsing one's competitors if the order itself is to be sustained. The occasional sacrifices involved in institutionalized conduct must be compensated by socialized rewards. The distribution of statuses and roles through competition must be so organized that positive incentives for conformity to roles and adherence to status obligations are provided *for every position* within the distributive order. Aberrant conduct, therefore, may be viewed as a symptom of dissociation between culturally defined aspirations and socially structured means.

Of the types of groups which result from the independent variation of the two phases of the social structure, we shall be primarily concerned with the first, namely, that involving a disproportionate accent on goals.

This statement must be recast in a proper perspective. In no group is there an absence of regulatory codes governing conduct, yet groups do vary in the degree to which these folkways, mores, and institutional controls are effectively integrated with the more diffuse goals which are part of the culture matrix. Emotional convictions may cluster about the complex of socially acclaimed ends, meanwhile shifting their support from the culturally defined implementation of these ends. As we shall see, certain aspects of the social structure may generate countermores and antisocial behavior precisely because of differential emphases on goals and regulations. In the extreme case, the latter may be so vitiated by the goal-emphasis that the range of behavior is limited only by considerations of technical expediency. The sole significant question then becomes, which available means is most efficient in netting the socially approved value?[5] The technically most feasible procedure, whether legitimate or not, is preferred to the institutionally prescribed conduct. As this process continues, the integration of the society becomes tenuous and anomie ensues.

Thus, in competitive athletics, when the aim of victory is shorn of its institutional trappings and success in contests becomes construed as "winning the game" rather than "winning through circumscribed modes of activity," a premium is implicitly set upon the use of illegitimate but technically efficient means. The star of the opposing football team is surreptitiously slugged; the wrestler furtively incapacitates his opponent through ingenious but illicit techniques; university alumni covertly subsidize "students" whose talents are largely confined to the athletic field. The emphasis on the goal has so attenuated the satisfactions deriving from sheer participation in the competitive activity that these satisfactions are virtually confined to a successful outcome. Through the same process, tension generated by the desire to win in a poker game is relieved by successfully dealing oneself four aces, or, when the cult of success has become completely dominant, by sagaciously shuffling the cards in a game of solitaire. The faint twinge of uneasiness in the last instance and the surreptitious nature of public delicts indicate clearly that the institutional rules of the game are *known* to those who evade them, but that the emotional supports of these rules are largely vitiated by cultural exaggeration of the success-goal.[6] They are microcosmic images of the social macrocosm.

Of course, this process is not restricted to the realm of sport. The process whereby exaltation of the end generates a *literal demoralization*, i.e., a deinstitutionalization, of the means is one which characterizes many[7] groups in which the two phases of the social structure are not highly integrated. The extreme emphasis upon the accumulation of wealth as a symbol of success[8] in our own society militates against the completely effective control of institutionally regulated modes of acquiring a fortune.[9] Fraud, corruption, vice, crime, in short, the entire catalogue of proscribed behavior, becomes increasingly common when the emphasis on the *culturally induced* success-goal becomes divorced from a coordinated institutional emphasis.

This observation is of crucial theoretical importance in examining the doctrine that antisocial behavior most frequently derives from biological drives breaking through the restraints imposed by society. The difference is one between a strictly utilitarian interpretation which conceives man's ends as random and an analysis which finds these ends deriving from the basic values of the culture.[10]

Our analysis can scarcely stop at this juncture. We must turn to other aspects of the social structure if we are to deal with the social genesis of the varying rates and types of deviate behavior characteristic of different societies. Thus far, we have sketched three ideal types of social orders constituted by distinctive patterns of relations between culture ends and means. Turning from these types of *culture patterning*, we find five logically possible, alternative modes of adjustment or adaptation *by individuals* within the culture-bearing society or group.[11] These are schematically presented in the following table, where (+) signifies "acceptance," (−) signifies "elimination," and (±) signifies "rejection and substitution of new goals and standards."

	Culture Goals	*Institutionalized Means*
I. Conformity	+	+
II. Innovation	+	−
III. Ritualism	−	+
IV. Retreatism	−	−
V. Rebellion[12]	±	±

Our discussion of the relation between these alternative responses and other phases of the social structure must be prefaced by the observation that persons may shift from one alternative to another as they engage in different social activities. These categories refer to role adjustments in specific situations, not to personality *in toto*. To treat the development of this process in various spheres of conduct would introduce a complexity unmanageable within the confines of this paper. For this reason, we shall be concerned primarily with economic activity in the broad sense, "the production, exchange, distribution, and consumption of goods and services" in our competitive society, wherein wealth has taken on a highly symbolic cast. Our task is to search out some of the factors which exert pressure upon individuals to engage in certain of these logically possible alternative responses. This choice, as we shall see, is far from random.

In every society, Adaptation I (conformity to both culture goals and means) is the most common and widely diffused. Were this not so, the stability and continuity of the society could not be maintained. The mesh of expectancies which constitutes every social order is sustained by the modal behavior of its members falling within the first category. Conventional role behavior oriented toward the basic values of the group is the rule rather than the exception. It is this fact alone which permits us to speak of a human aggregate as comprising a group or society.

Conversely, Adaptation IV (rejection of goals and means) is the least common. Persons who "adjust" (or maladjust) in this fashion are, strictly speaking, *in* the society but not *of* it. Sociologically, these constitute the true "aliens." Not sharing the common frame of orientation, they can be included within the societal population merely in a fictional sense. In this category are *some* of the activities of psychotics, psychoneurotics, chronic autists, pariahs, outcasts, vagrants, vagabonds, tramps, chronic drunkards, and drug addicts.[13] These have relinquished, in certain spheres of activity, the culturally defined goals, involving complete aim-inhibition in the polar case, and their adjustments are not in accord with institutional norms. This is not to say that in some cases the source of their behavioral adjustments is not in part the very social structure which they have in effect repudiated nor that their very existence within a social area does not constitute a problem for the socialized population.

This mode of "adjustment" occurs, as far as structural sources are concerned, when both the culture goals and institutionalized procedures have been assimilated thoroughly by the individual and imbued with affect and high positive value, but where those institutionalized procedures which promise a measure of successful attainment of the goals are not available to the individual. In such instances, there results a two-fold mental conflict insofar as the moral obligation for adopting institutional means conflicts with the pressure to resort to illegitimate means (which may attain the goal) and inasmuch as the individual is shut off from means which are both legitimate *and* effective. The competitive order is maintained, but the frustrated and handicapped individual who cannot cope with this order drops out. Defeatism, quietism, and resignation are manifested in escape mechanisms which ultimately lead the individual to "escape" from the requirements of the society. It is an expedient which arises from continued failure to attain the goal by legitimate measures and from an inability to adopt the illegitimate route because of internalized prohibitions and institutionalized compulsives, *during which process the supreme value of the success-goal has as yet not been renounced*. The conflict is resolved by eliminating *both* precipitating elements, the goals and means. The escape is complete, the conflict is eliminated, and the individual is associated.

Be it noted that where frustration derives from the inaccessibility of effective institutional means for attaining economic or any other type of highly valued "success," that Adaptations II, III, and V (innovation, ritualism, and rebellion) are also possible. The result will be determined by the particular personality, and thus, the *particular* cultural background, involved. Inadequate socialization will result in the innovation response whereby the conflict and frustration are eliminated by relinquishing the institutional means and retaining the success-aspiration; an extreme assimilation of institutional demands will lead to ritualism wherein the goal is dropped as beyond one's reach but conformity to the mores persists; and rebellion occurs when emancipation from the reigning standards, due to frustration or to marginalist perspectives, leads to the attempt to introduce a "new social order."

Our major concern is with the illegitimacy adjustment. This involves the use of conventionally proscribed but frequently effective means of attaining at least the simulacrum of culturally defined success—wealth, power, and the like. As we have seen, this adjustment occurs when the individual has assimilated the cultural emphasis on success without equally internalizing the morally prescribed norms governing means for its attainment. The question arises, Which phases of our social structure predispose toward this mode of adjustment? We may examine a concrete instance, effectively analyzed by Lohman,[14] which provides a clue to the answer. Lohman has shown that specialized areas of vice in the near north side of Chicago constitute a "normal" response to a situation where the cultural emphasis upon pecuniary success has been absorbed, but where there is little access to conventional and legitimate means for attaining such success. The conventional occupational opportunities of persons in this area are almost completely limited to manual labor. Given our cultural stigmatization of manual labor, and its correlate, the prestige of white collar work, it is clear that the result is a strain toward innovational practices. The limitation of opportunity to unskilled labor and the resultant low income cannot compete *in terms of conventional standards of achievement* with the high income from organized vice.

For our purposes, this situation involves two important features. First, such antisocial behavior is in a sense "called forth" by certain conventional values of the culture *and* by the class structure involving differential access to the approved opportunities for legitimate, prestige-bearing pursuit of the culture goals. The lack of high integration between the means-and-end elements of the cultural pattern and the particular class structure combine to favor a heightened frequency of antisocial conduct in such groups. The second consideration is of equal significance. Recourse to the first of the alternative responses, legitimate effort, is limited by the fact that actual advance toward desired success-symbols through conventional channels is, despite our persisting open-class ideology,[15] relatively rare and difficult for those handicapped by little formal education and few economic resources. The dominant pressure of group standards of success is, therefore, on the gradual attenuation of legitimate, but by and large ineffective, strivings and the increasing use of illegitimate, but more or less effective, expedients of vice and crime. The cultural demands made on persons in this situation are incompatible. On the one hand, they are asked to orient their conduct toward the prospect of accumulating wealth and on the other, they are largely denied effective opportunities to do so institutionally. The consequences of such structural inconsistency are psychopathological personality, and/or antisocial conduct, and/or revolutionary activities. The equilibrium between culturally designated means and ends becomes highly unstable with the progressive emphasis on attaining the prestige-laden ends by any means whatsoever. Within this context, Capone represents the triumph of amoral intelligence over morally prescribed "failure," when the channels of vertical mobility are closed or narrowed[16] *in a society which places a high premium on economic affluence and social ascent for* all *its members.*[17]

This last qualification is of primary importance. It suggests that other phases of the social structure besides the extreme emphasis on pecuniary success must be considered if we are to understand the social sources of antisocial behavior. A high frequency of deviate behavior is not generated simply by "lack of opportunity" or by this exaggerated pecuniary emphasis. A comparatively rigidified class structure, a feudalistic or caste order, may limit such opportunities far beyond the point which obtains in our society today. It is only when a system of cultural values extols, virtually above all else, certain *common* symbols of success *for the population at large* while its social structure rigorously restricts or completely eliminates access to approved modes of acquiring these symbols *for a considerable part of the same population* that antisocial behavior ensues on a considerable scale. In other words, our egalitarian ideology denies by implication the existence of noncompeting groups and individuals in the pursuit of pecuniary success. The same body of success-symbols is held to be desirable for all. These goals are held to *transcend class lines*, not to be bounded by them, yet the actual social organization is such that there exist class differentials in the accessibility of these *common* success-symbols. Frustration and thwarted aspiration lead to the search for avenues of escape from a culturally induced intolerable situation; or unrelieved ambition may eventuate in illicit attempts to acquire the dominant values.[18] The American stress on pecuniary success and ambitiousness for all thus invites exaggerated anxieties, hostilities, neuroses, and antisocial behavior.

This theoretical analysis may go far toward explaining the varying correlations between crime and poverty.[19] Poverty is not an isolated variable. It is one in a complex of interdependent social and cultural variables. When viewed in such a context, it represents quite different states of affairs. Poverty as such, and consequent limitation of opportunity, are not sufficient to induce a conspicuously high rate of criminal behavior. Even the often mentioned "poverty in the midst of plenty" will not necessarily lead to this result. Only insofar as poverty and associated disadvantages in competition for the culture values approved for *all* members of the society are linked with the assimilation of a cultural emphasis on monetary accumulation as a symbol of success is antisocial conduct a "normal" outcome. Thus, poverty is less highly correlated with crime in southeastern Europe than in the United States. The possibilities of vertical mobility in these

European areas would seem to be fewer than in this country, so that neither poverty *per se* nor its association with limited opportunity is sufficient to account for the varying correlations. It is only when the full configuration is considered, poverty, limited opportunity, and a commonly shared system of success-symbols, that we can explain the higher association between poverty and crime in our society than in others where rigidified class structure is coupled with *differential class symbols of achievement.*

In societies such as our own, then, the pressure of prestige-bearing success tends to eliminate the effective social constraint over means employed to this end. "The-end-justifies-the-means" doctrine becomes a guiding tenet for action when the cultural structure unduly exalts the end and the social organization unduly limits possible recourse to approved means. Otherwise put, this notion and associated behavior reflect a lack of cultural coordination. In international relations, the effects of this lack of integration are notoriously apparent. An emphasis upon national power is not readily coordinated with an inept organization of legitimate, i.e., internationally defined and accepted, means for attaining this goal. The result is a tendency toward the abrogation of international law, treaties become scraps of paper, "undeclared warfare" serves as a technical evasion, the bombing of civilian populations is rationalized,[20] just as the same societal situation induces the same sway of illegitimacy among individuals.

The social order we have described necessarily produces this "strain toward dissolution." The pressure of such an order is upon outdoing one's competitors. The choice of means within the ambit of institutional control will persist as long as the sentiments supporting a competitive system, i.e., deriving from the possibility of outranking competitors and hence enjoying the favorable response of others, are distributed throughout the entire system of activities and are not confined merely to the final result. A stable social structure demands a balanced distribution of affect among its various segments. When there occurs a shift of emphasis from the satisfactions deriving from competition itself to almost exclusive concern with successful competition, the resultant stress leads to the breakdown of the regulatory structure.[21] With the resulting attenuation of the institutional imperatives, there occurs an approximation of the situation erroneously held by utilitarians to be typical of society generally wherein calculations of advantage and fear of punishment are the sole regulating agencies. In such situations, as Hobbes observed, force and fraud come to constitute the sole virtues in view of their relative efficiency in attaining goals—which were for him, of course, not culturally derived.

It should be apparent that the foregoing discussion is not pitched on a moralistic plane. Whatever the sentiments of the writer or reader concerning the ethical desirability of coordinating the means-and-goals phases of the social structure, one must agree that lack of such coordination leads to anomie. Insofar as one of the most general functions of social organization is to provide a basis for calculability and regularity of behavior, it is increasingly limited in effectiveness as these elements of the structure become dissociated. At the extreme, predictability virtually disappears and what may be properly termed cultural chaos or anomie intervenes.

This statement, being brief, is also incomplete. It has not included an exhaustive treatment of the various structural elements which predispose toward one rather than another of the alternative responses open to individuals; it has neglected, but not denied the relevance of, the factors determining the specific incidence of these responses; it has not enumerated the various concrete responses which are constituted by combinations of specific values of the analytical variables; it has omitted, or included only by implication, any consideration of the social functions performed by illicit responses; it has not tested the full explanatory power of the analytical scheme by examining a large number of group variations in the frequency of deviate and conformist behavior; it has not adequately dealt with rebellious conduct which seeks to refashion the social framework radically; it has not examined the relevance of cultural conflict for an analysis of culture-goal and institutional-means malintegration. It is suggested that these and related problems may be profitably analyzed by this scheme.

Notes

1. E.g., Ernest Jones, *Social Aspects of Psychoanalysis*, 28, London, 1924. If the Freudian notion is a variety of the "original sin" dogma, then the interpretation advanced in this paper may be called the doctrine of "socially derived sin."

2. "Normal" in the sense of a culturally oriented, if not approved, response. This statement does not deny the relevance of biological and personality differences which may be significantly involved in the *incidence* of deviate conduct. Our focus of interest is the social and cultural matrix; hence we abstract from other factors. It is in this sense, I take it, that James S. Plant speaks of the "normal reaction of normal people to abnormal conditions." See his *Personality and the Cultural Pattern*, 248, New York, 1937.

3. Contemporary American culture has been said to tend in this direction. See André Siegfried, *America Comes of Age*, 26–37, New York, 1927. The alleged extreme(?) emphasis on the goals of monetary success and material prosperity leads to dominant concern with technological and social instruments designed to produce the desired result, inasmuch as institutional controls become of secondary importance. In such a situation, innovation flourishes as the *range of means* employed is broadened. In a sense, then, there occurs the paradoxical emergence of "materialists" from an "idealistic" orientation. Cf. Durkheim's analysis of the cultural conditions which predispose toward crime and innovation, both of which are aimed toward efficiency, not moral norms. Durkheim was one of the first to see that "contrairement aux idées courantes le criminel n'apparait plus comme un être radicalement insociable, comme une sorte d'elément parasitaire, de corps étranger et inassimilable, introduit au sein de la société; c'est un agent régulier de la vie sociale." See *Les Règles de la Méthode Sociologique*, 86–89, Paris, 1927.

4. Such ritualism may be associated with a mythology which rationalizes these actions so that they appear to retain their status as means, but the dominant pressure is in the direction of strict ritualistic conformity, irrespective of such rationalizations. In this sense, ritual has proceeded farthest when such rationalizations are not even called forth.

5. In this connection, one may see the relevance of Elton Mayo's paraphrase of the title of Tawney's well-known book. "Actually the problem *is not that of the sickness of an acquisitive society; it is that of the acquisitiveness of a sick society.*" *Human Problems of an Industrial*

Civilization, 153, New York, 1933. Mayo deals with the process through which wealth comes to be a symbol of social achievement. He sees this as arising from a state of anomie. We are considering the unintegrated montary-success goal as an element in producing anomie. A complete analysis would involve both phases of this system of interdependent variables.

6. It is unlikely that interiorized norms are completely eliminated. Whatever residuum persists will induce personality tensions and conflict. The process involves a certain degree of ambivalence. A manifest rejection of the institutional norms is coupled with some latent retention of their emotional correlates. "Guilt feelings," "sense of sin," "pangs of conscience" are obvious manifestations of this unrelieved tension; symbolic adherence to the nominally repudiated values or rationalizations constitute a more subtle variety of tensional release.

7. "Many," and not all, unintegrated groups, for the reason already mentioned. In groups where the primary emphasis shifts to institutional means, i.e., when the range of alternatives is very limited, the outcome is a type of ritualism rather than anomie.

8. Money has several peculiarities which render it particularly apt to become a symbol of prestige divorced from institutional controls. As Simmel emphasized, money is highly abstract and impersonal. However acquired, through fraud or institutionally, it can be used to purchase the same goods and services. The anonymity of metropolitan culture, in conjunction with this peculiarity of money, permits wealth, the sources of which may be unknown to the community in which the plutocrat lives, to serve as a symbol of status.

9. The emphasis upon wealth as a success-symbol is possibly reflected in the use of the term "fortune" to refer to a stock of accumulated wealth. This meaning becomes common in the late sixteenth century (Spenser and Shakespeare). A similar usage of the Latin *fortuna* comes into prominence during the first century B.C. Both these periods were marked by the rise to prestige and power of the "bourgeoisie."

10. See Kingsley Davis, "Mental Hygiene and the Class Structure," *Psychiatry*, 1928, 1:esp. 62–63; Talcott Parsons, *The Structure of Social Action*, 59–60, New York, 1937.

11. This is a level intermediate between the two planes distinguished by Edward Sapir; namely, culture patterns and personal habit systems. See his "Contribution of Psychiatry to an Understanding of Behavior in Society," *Amer. J. Sociol.*, 1937, 42:862–870.

12. This fifth alternative is on a plane clearly different from that of the others. It represents a *transitional* response which seeks to *institutionalize* new procedures oriented toward revamped cultural goals shared by the members of the society. It thus involves efforts to *change* the existing structure rather than to perform accommodative actions *within* this structure, and introduces additional problems with which we are not at the moment concerned.

13. Obviously, this is an elliptical statement. These individuals may maintain some orientation to the values of their particular differentiated groupings within the larger society or, in part, of the conventional society itself. Insofar as they do so, their conduct cannot be classified in the "passive rejection" category (IV). Nels Anderson's description of the behavior and attitudes of the bum, for example, can readily be recast in terms of our analytical scheme. See *The Hobo*, 93–98, *et passim*, Chicago, 1923.

14. Joseph D. Lohman, "The Participant Observer in Community Studies," *Amer. Sociol. Rev.*, 1937, 2:890–898.

15. The shifting historical role of this ideology is a profitable subject for exploration. The "office-boy-to-president" stereotype was once in approximate accord with the facts. Such vertical mobility was probably more common then than now, when the class structure is more rigid. (See the following note.) The ideology largely persists, however, possibly because it still performs a useful function for maintaining the *status quo*. For insofar as it is accepted by the "masses," it constitutes a useful sop for those who might rebel against the entire structure, were this consoling hope removed. This ideology now serves to lessen the probability of Adaptation V. In short, the role of this notion has changed from that of an approximately valid empirical theorem to that of an ideology, in Mannheim's sense.

16. There is a growing body of evidence, though none of it is clearly conclusive, to the effect that our class structure is becoming rigidified and that vertical mobility is declining. Taussig and Joslyn found that American business leaders are being *increasingly* recruited from the upper ranks of our society. The Lynds have also found a "diminished chance to get ahead" for the working classes in Middletown. Manifestly, these objective changes are not alone significant; the individual's subjective evaluation of the situation is a major determinant of the response. The extent to which this change in opportunity for social mobility has been recognized by the least advantaged classes is still conjectural, although the Lynds present

some suggestive materials. The writer suggests that a case in point is the increasing frequency of cartoons which observe in a tragi-comic vein that "my old man says everybody can't be President. He says if ya can get three days a week steady on W.P.A. work ya ain't doin' so bad either." See F. W. Taussig and C. S. Joslyn, *American Business Leaders*, New York, 1932; R. S. and H. M. Lynd, *Middletown in Transition*, 67 ff., chap. 12, New York, 1937.

17. The role of the Negro in this respect is of considerable theoretical interest. Certain elements of the Negro population have assimilated the dominant caste's values of pecuniary success and social advancement, but they also recognize that social ascent is at present restricted to their own caste almost exclusively. The pressures upon the Negro which would otherwise derive from the structural inconsistencies we have noticed are hence not identical with those upon lower class whites. See Kingsley Davis, *op. cit.*, 63; John Dollard, *Caste and Class in a Southern Town*, 66 ff., New Haven, 1936; Donald Young, *American Minority Peoples*, 581, New York, 1932.

18. The psychical coordinates of these processes have been partly established by the experimental evidence concerning *Anspruchsniveaus* and levels of performance. See Kurt Lewin, *Vorsatz, Willie and Bedurfnis*, Berlin, 1926; N. F. Hoppe, "Erfolg und Misserfolg," *Psychol. Forschung*, 1930, 14:1–63; Jerome D. Frank, "Individual Differences in Certain Aspects of the Level of Aspiration," *Amer. J. Psychol.*, 1935, 47:119–128.

19. Standard criminology texts summarize the data in this field. Our scheme of analysis may serve to resolve some of the theoretical contradictions which P. A. Sorokin indicates. For example, "not everywhere nor always do the poor show a greater proportion of crime... many poorer countries have had less crime than the richer countries.... The [economic] improvement in the second half of the nineteenth century, and the beginning of the twentieth, has not been followed by a decrease of crime." See his *Contemporary Sociological Theories*, 560–561, New York, 1928. The crucial point is, however, that poverty has varying social significance in different social structures, as we shall see. Hence, one would not expect a linear correlation between crime and poverty.

20. See M. W. Royse, *Aerial Bombardment and the International Regulation of War*, New York, 1928.

21. Since our primary concern is with the socio-cultural aspects of this problem, the psychological correlates have been only implicitly considered. See Karen Horney, *The Neurotic Personality of Our Time*, New York, 1937, for a psychological discussion of this process.

12 / Differential Opportunity and Delinquent Subcultures

RICHARD A. CLOWARD
LLOYD E. OHLIN

THE AVAILABILITY OF ILLEGITIMATE MEANS

Social norms are two-sided. A prescription implies the existence of a prohibition, and *vice versa*. To advocate honesty is to demarcate and condemn a set of actions which are dishonest. In other words, norms that define legitimate practices also implicitly define illegitimate practices. One purpose of norms, in fact, is to delineate the boundary between legitimate and illegitimate practices. In setting this boundary, in segregating and classifying various types of behavior, they make us aware not only of behavior that is regarded as right and proper but also of behavior that is said to be wrong and improper. Thus the criminal who engages in theft or fraud does not invent a new way of life; the possibility of employing alternative means is acknowledged, tacitly at least, by the norms of the culture.

This tendency for proscribed alternatives to be implicit in every prescription, and *vice versa*, although widely recognized, is nevertheless a reef upon which many a theory of delinquency has foundered. Much of the criminological literature assumes, for example, that one may explain a criminal act simply by accounting for the individual's readiness to employ illegal alternatives of which his culture, through its norms, has already made him generally aware. Such explanations are quite unsatisfactory, however, for they ignore a host of questions regarding the *relative availability* of illegal alternatives to various potential criminals. The aspiration to be a physician is hardly enough to explain the fact of becoming a physician; there is much that transpires between the aspiration and the achievement. This is no less true of the person who wants to be a successful criminal. Having decided that he "can't make it legitimately," he cannot simply choose among an array of illegitimate means, all equally available to him. As we have noted earlier, it is assumed in the theory of anomie that access to conventional means is differentially distributed, that some individuals, because of their social class, enjoy certain advantages that are denied to those elsewhere in the class structure. For example, there are variations in the degree to which members of various classes are fully exposed to and thus acquire the values, knowledge, and skills that facilitate upward mobility. It should not be startling, therefore, to suggest that there are socially structured variations in the availability of illegitimate means as well. In connection with delinquent subcultures, we shall be concerned principally with differentials in access to illegitimate means within the lower class.

Many sociologists have alluded to differentials in access to illegitimate means without explicitly incorporating this variable into a theory of deviant behavior. This is particularly true of scholars in the "Chicago tradition" of criminology. Two closely related theoretical perspectives emerged from this school. The theory of "cultural transmission," advanced by Clifford R. Shaw and Henry D. McKay, focuses on the development in some urban neighborhoods of a criminal tradition that persists from one generation to another despite constant changes in population.[1] In the theory of "differential association," Edwin H. Sutherland described the processes by which criminal values are taken over by the individual.[2] He asserted that criminal behavior is learned, and that it is learned in interaction with others who have already incorporated criminal values. Thus the first theory stresses the value systems of different areas; the second, the systems of social relationships that facilitate or impede the acquisition of these values.

Scholars in the Chicago tradition, who emphasized the processes involved in learning to be criminal, were actually pointing to differentials in the availability of illegal means—although they did not explicitly recognize this variable in their analysis. This can perhaps best be seen by examining Sutherland's classic work, *The Professional Thief*. "An inclination to steal," according to Sutherland, "is not a sufficient explanation of the genesis of the professional thief."[3] The "self-made" thief, lacking knowledge of the ways of securing immunity from prosecution and similar techniques of defense, "would quickly land in prison; . . . a person can be a professional thief only if he is recognized and received as such by other professional thieves." But recognition is not freely accorded: "Selection and tutelage are the two necessary elements in the process of acquiring recognition as a professional thief. . . . A person cannot acquire recognition as a professional thief until he has had tutelage in professional theft, *and tutelage is given only to a few persons selected from the total population.*" For one thing, "the person must be appreciated by the professional thieves. He must be appraised as having an adequate equipment of wits, front, talking-ability, honesty, reliability, nerve and determination." Furthermore, the aspirant is judged by high standards of performance, for only "a very small percentage of those who start on this process ever reach the stage of professional thief. . . . " Thus motivation and pressures toward deviance do not fully account for deviant behavior any more than motivation and pressures toward conformity account for conforming behavior. The individual must have access to a learning environment and, once having been trained, must be allowed to perform his role. Roles, whether conforming or deviant in content, are not necessarily freely available; access to them depends upon a variety of factors, such as one's socioeconomic position, age, sex, ethnic affiliation, personality characteristics, and the like. The potential thief, like the potential physician, finds that access to his goal is governed by many criteria other than merit and motivation.

What we are asserting is that access to illegitimate roles is not freely available to all, as is commonly assumed. Only those neighborhoods in which crime flourishes as a stable, indigenous institution are fertile criminal learning environments for the young. Because these environments afford integration of different age-levels of offender, selected young people are exposed to "differential association" through which tutelage is provided and criminal values and skills are acquired. To be prepared for the role may not, however, ensure that the individual will ever discharge it. One important limitation is that more youngsters are recruited into these patterns of differential associations than the adult criminal structure can possibly absorb. Since there is a surplus of contenders for these elite positions, criteria and mechanisms of selection must be evolved. Hence a certain proportion of those who aspire may not be permitted to engage in the behavior for which they have prepared themselves.

Thus we conclude that access to illegitimate roles, no less than access to legitimate roles, is limited by both social and psychological factors. We shall here be concerned primarily with socially structured differentials in illegitimate opportunities. Such differentials, we contend, have much to do with the type of delinquent subculture that develops.

LEARNING AND PERFORMANCE STRUCTURES

Our use of the term "opportunities," legitimate or illegitimate, implies access to both learning and performance structures. That is, the individual must have access to appropriate environments for the acquisition of the values and skills associated with the performance of a particular role, and he must be supported in the performance of the role once he has learned it.

Tannenbaum, several decades ago, vividly expressed the point that criminal role performance, no less than conventional role performance, presupposes a patterned set of relationships through which the requisite values and skills are transmitted by established practitioners to aspiring youth:

> It takes a long time to make a good criminal, many years of specialized training and much preparation. But training is something that is given to people. People learn in a community where the materials and the knowledge are to be had. A craft needs an atmosphere saturated with purpose and promise. The community

> provides the attitudes, the point of view, the philosophy of life, the example, the motive, the contacts, the friendships, the incentives. No child brings those into the world. He finds them here and available for use and elaboration. The community gives the criminal his materials and habits, just as it gives the doctor, the lawyer, the teacher, and the candlestick-maker theirs.[4]

Sutherland systematized this general point of view, asserting that opportunity consists, at least in part, of learning structures. Thus "criminal behavior is learned" and, furthermore, it is learned "in interaction with other persons in a process of communication." However, he conceded that the differential-association theory does not constitute a full explanation of criminal behavior. In a paper circulated in 1944, he noted that "criminal behavior is partially a function of opportunities to commit [*i.e.*, to perform] specific classes of crime, such as embezzlement, bank burglary, or illicit heterosexual intercourse." Therefore, "while opportunity may be partially a function of association with criminal patterns and of the specialized techniques thus acquired, it is not determined entirely in that manner, and consequently differential association is not the sufficient cause of criminal behavior."[5]

To Sutherland, then, illegitimate opportunity included conditions favorable to the performance of a criminal role as well as conditions favorable to the learning of such a role (differential associations). These conditions, we suggest, depend upon certain features of the social structure of the community in which delinquency arises.

We believe that each individual occupies a position in both legitimate and illegitimate opportunity structures. This is a new way of defining the situation. The theory of anomie views the individual primarily in terms of the legitimate opportunity structure. It poses questions regarding differentials in access to legitimate routes to success-goals; at the same time it assumes either that illegitimate avenues to success-goals are freely available or that differentials in their availability are of little significance. This tendency may be seen in the following statement by Merton:

> Several researches have shown that specialized areas of vice and crime constitute a "normal" response to a situation where the cultural emphasis upon pecuniary success has been absorbed, but where there is little access to conventional and legitimate means for becoming successful. The occupational opportunities of people in these areas are largely confined to manual labor and the lesser white-collar jobs. Given the American stigmatization of manual labor *which has been found to hold rather uniformly for all social classes,* and the absence of realistic opportunities for advancement beyond this level, the result is a marked tendency toward deviant behavior. The status of unskilled labor and the consequent low income cannot readily compete *in terms of established standards of worth* with the promises of power and high income from organized vice, rackets and crime.... [Such a situation] leads toward the gradual attenuation of legitimate, but by and large ineffectual, strivings and the increasing use of illegitimate, but more or less effective, expedients.[6]

The cultural-transmission and differential-association tradition, on the other hand, assumes that access to illegitimate means is variable, but it does not recognize the significance of comparable differentials in access to legitimate means. Sutherland's "ninth proposition" in the theory of differential association states:

> *Though criminal behavior is an expression of general needs and values, it is not explained by those general needs and values since non-criminal behavior is an expression of the same needs and values.* Thieves generally steal in order to secure money, but likewise honest laborers work in order to secure money. The attempts by many scholars to explain criminal behavior by general drives and values, such as the happiness principle, striving for social status, the money motive, or frustration, have been and must continue to be futile since they explain lawful behavior as completely as they explain criminal behavior.[7]

In this statement, Sutherland appears to assume that people have equal and free access to legitimate means regardless of their social position. At the very least, he does not treat access to legitimate means as variable. It is, of course, perfectly true that "striving for social status," "the money motive," and other socially approved drives do not fully account for either deviant or conforming behavior. But if goal-oriented behavior occurs under conditions in which there are socially structured obstacles to the satisfaction of these drives by legitimate means, the resulting pressures, we contend, might lead to deviance.

The concept of differential opportunity structures permits us to unite the theory of anomie, which recognizes the concept of differentials in access to legitimate means, and the "Chicago tradition," in which the concept of differentials in access to illegitimate means is implicit. We can now look at the individual, not simply in relation to one or the other system of means, but in relation to both legitimate and illegitimate systems. This approach permits us to ask, for example, how the relative availability of illegitimate opportunities affects the resolution of adjustment problems leading to deviant behavior. We believe that the way in which these problems are resolved may depend upon the kind of support for one or another type of illegitimate activity that is given at different points in the social structure. If, in a given social location, illegal or criminal means are not readily available, then we should not expect a criminal subculture to develop among adolescents. By the same logic, we should expect the manipulation of violence to become a primary avenue to higher status only in areas where the means of violence are not denied to the young. To give a third example, drug addiction and participation in subcultures organized around the consumption of drugs presuppose that persons can secure access to drugs and knowledge about how to use them. In some parts of the social structure, this would be very difficult; in others, very easy. In short, there are marked differences from one part of the social structure to another in the types of illegitimate adaptation that are available to persons in search of solutions to problems of adjustment arising from the restricted availability of legitimate means.[8] In this sense, then, we can think of individuals as being located in two opportunity structures—one legitimate, the other illegitimate. Given limited access to success-goals by legitimate means, the nature of the delinquent response that may result will vary according to the availability of various illegitimate means.[9]

VARIETIES OF DELINQUENT SUBCULTURE

As we have noted, there appear to be three major types of delinquent subculture typically encountered among adolescent males in lower-class areas of large urban centers. One is based principally upon criminal values; its members are organized primarily for the pursuit of material gain by such illegal means as extortion, fraud, and theft. In the second, violence is the keynote; its members pursue status ("rep") through the manipulation of force or threat of force. These are the "warrior" groups that attract so much attention in the press. Finally, there are subcultures which emphasize the consumption of drugs. The participants in these drug subcultures have become alienated from conventional roles, such as those required in the family or the occupational world. They have withdrawn into a restricted world in which the ultimate value consists in the "kick." We call these three subcultural forms "criminal," "conflict," and "retreatist," respectively.[10]

These shorthand terms simply denote the *principal* orientation of each form of adaptation from the perspective of the dominant social order; although one can find many examples of subcultures that fit accurately into one of these three categories, subcultures frequently appear in somewhat mixed form. Thus members of a predominantly conflict subculture may also on occasion engage in systematic theft; members of a criminal subculture may sometimes do combat in the streets with rival gangs. But this should not obscure the fact that these subcultures tend to exhibit essentially different orientations.

The extent to which the delinquent subculture organizes and controls a participant's allegiance varies from one member to another. Some members of the gang are almost totally immersed in the perspectives of the subculture and bring them into play in all their contacts; others segregate this aspect of their lives and maintain other roles in the family, school, and church. The chances are relatively slight, however, that an adolescent can successfully segregate delinquent and conforming roles for a long period of time. Pressures emanate from the subculture leading its members to adopt unfavorable attitudes toward parents, school teachers, policemen, and other adults in the conventional world. When he is apprehended for delinquent acts, the possibility of the delinquent's maintaining distinctly separate role involvements breaks down, and he is confronted with the necessity of choosing between law-abiding and delinquent styles of life. Since family, welfare, religious, educational, law-enforcement, and correctional institutions are arrayed against the appeal of his delinquent associates, the decision is a difficult one, frequently requiring either complete acceptance or complete rejection of one or the other system of obligations.[11]

At any one point in time, however, the extent to which the norms of the delinquent subculture control behavior will vary from one member to another. Accordingly, descriptions of these subcultures must be stated in terms of the fully indoctrinated member rather than the average member. Only in this way can the distinctiveness of delinquent styles of life be made clear. It is with this understanding that we offer the following brief empirical characterizations of the three main types of delinquent subculture.

The Criminal Pattern

The most extensive documentation in the sociological literature of delinquent behavior patterns in lower-class culture describes a tradition which integrates youthful delinquency with adult criminality.[12] In the central value orientation of youths participating in this tradition, delinquent and criminal behavior is accepted as a means of achieving success-goals. The dominant criteria of in-group evaluation stress achievement, the use of skill and knowledge to get results. In this culture, prestige is allocated to those who achieve material gain and power through avenues defined as illegitimate by the larger society. From the very young to the very old, the successful "haul"—which quickly transforms the penniless into a man of means—is an ever-present vision of the possible and desirable. Although one may also achieve material success through the routine practice of theft or fraud, the "big score" remains the symbolic image of quick success.

The means by which a member of a criminal subculture achieves success are clearly defined for the aspirant. At a young age, he learns to admire and respect older criminals and to adopt the "right guy" as his role-model. Delinquent episodes help him to acquire mastery of the techniques and orientation of the criminal world and to learn how to cooperate successfully with others in criminal enterprises. He exhibits hostility and distrust toward representatives of the larger society. He regards members of the conventional world as "suckers," his natural victims, to be exploited when possible. He sees successful people in the conventional world as having a "racket"—*e.g.*, big businessmen have huge expense accounts, politicians get graft, etc. This attitude successfully neutralizes the controlling effect of conventional norms. Toward the in-group the "right guy" maintains relationships of loyalty, honesty, and trustworthiness. He must prove himself reliable and dependable in his contacts with his criminal associates although he has no such obligations toward the out-group of noncriminals.

One of the best ways of assuring success in the criminal world is to cultivate appropriate "connections." As a youngster, this means running with a clique composed of other "right guys" and promoting an apprenticeship or some other favored relationship with older and successful offenders. Close and dependable ties with income-producing outlets for stolen goods, such as the wagon peddler, the junkman, and the fence, are especially useful. Furthermore, these intermediaries encourage and protect the young delinquent in a criminal way of life by giving him a jaundiced perspective on the private morality of many functionaries in conventional society. As he matures, the young delinquent becomes acquainted with a new world made up of predatory bondsmen, shady lawyers, crooked policemen, grafting politicians, dishonest businessmen, and corrupt jailers. Through "connections" with occupants of these half-legitimate, half-illegitimate roles and with "big shots" in the underworld, the aspiring criminal validates and assures his freedom of movement in a world made safer for crime.

The Conflict Pattern[13]

The role-model in the conflict pattern of lower-class culture is the "bopper" who swaggers with his gang, fights with weapons to win a wary respect from other gangs, and compels a fearful deference from the conventional adult world by his unpredictable and destructive assaults on persons and property. To other gang members, however, the key qualities of the bopper are those of the successful warrior. His performance must reveal a willingness to defend his personal integrity and the honor of the gang. He must do this with great courage and displays of fearlessness in the face of personal danger.

The immediate aim in the world of fighting gangs is to acquire a reputation for toughness and destructive violence. A "rep" assures not only respectful behavior from peers and threatened adults but also admiration for the physical strength and masculinity which it symbolizes. It represents a way of securing access to the scarce resources for adolescent pleasure and opportunity in underprivileged areas.

Above all things, the bopper is valued for his "heart." He does not "chicken out," even when confronted by superior force. He never defaults in the face of a personal insult or a challenge to the integrity of his gang. The code of the bopper is that of the warrior who places great stress on courage, the defense of his group, and the maintenance of honor.

Relationships between bopping gang members and the adult world are severely attenuated. The term that the bopper uses most frequently to characterize his relationships with adults is "weak." He is unable to find appropriate role-models that can designate for him a structure of opportunities leading to adult success. He views himself as isolated and the adult world as indifferent. The commitments of adults are to their own interests and not to his. Their explanations of why he should behave differently are "weak," as are their efforts to help him.

Confronted by the apparent indifference and insincerity of the adult world, the ideal bopper seeks to win by coercion the attention and opportunities he lacks and cannot otherwise attract. In recent years the street-gang worker who deals with the fighting gang on its own "turf" has come to symbolize not only a recognition by conventional adult society of the gang's toughness but also a concession of opportunities formerly denied. Through the alchemy of competition between gangs, this gesture of attention by the adult world to the "worst" gangs is transformed into a mark of prestige. Thus does the manipulation of violence convert indifference into accommodation and attention into status.

The Retreatist Pattern

Retreatism may include a variety of expressive, sensual, or consummatory experiences, alone or in a group. In this analysis, we are interested only in those experiences that involve the use of drugs and that are supported by a subculture. We have adopted these limitations in order to maintain our focus on subcultural formations which are clearly recognized as delinquent, as drug use by adolescents is. The retreatist preoccupation with expressive experiences creates many varieties of "hipster" cult among lower-class adolescents which foster patterns of deviant but not necessarily delinquent conduct.

Subcultural drug-users in lower-class areas perceive themselves as culturally and socially detached from the life-style and everyday preoccupations of members of the conventional world. The following characterization of the "cat" culture, observed by Finestone in a lower-class Negro area in Chicago, describes drug use in the more general context of "hipsterism."[14] Thus it should not be assumed that this description in every respect fits drug cultures found elsewhere. We have drawn heavily on Finestone's observations, however, because they provide the best descriptions available of the social world in which lower-class adolescent drug cultures typically arise.

The dominant feature of the retreatist subculture of the "cat" lies in the continuous pursuit of the "kick." Every cat has a kick—alcohol, marijuana, addicting drugs, unusual sexual experiences, hot jazz, cool jazz, or any combination of these. Whatever its content, the kick is a search for ecstatic experiences. The retreatist strives for an intense awareness of living and a sense of pleasure that is "out of this world." In extreme form, he seeks an almost spiritual and mystical knowledge that is experienced when one comes to know "it" at the height of one's kick. The past and the future recede in the time perspective of the cat, since complete awareness in present experience is the essence of the kick.

The successful cat has a lucrative "hustle" which contrasts sharply with the routine and discipline required in the ordinary occupational tasks of conventional society. The many varieties of the hustle are characterized by a rejection of violence or force and a preference for manipulating, persuading, outwitting, or "conning" others to obtain resources for experiencing the kick. The cat begs, borrows, steals, or engages in some petty con-game. He caters to the illegitimate cravings of others by peddling drugs or working as a pimp. A highly exploitative attitude toward women permits the cat to view pimping as a prestigeful source of income. Through the labor of "chicks" engaged in prostitution or shoplifting, he can live in idleness and concentrate his entire attention on organizing, scheduling, and experiencing the esthetic pleasure of the kick. The hustle of the cat is secondary to his interest in the kick. In this respect the cat differs from his fellow delinquents in the criminal subculture, for whom income-producing activity is a primary concern.

The ideal cat's appearance, demeanor, and taste can best be characterized as "cool." The cat seeks to exhibit a highly developed and sophisticated taste for clothes. In his demeanor, he struggles to reveal a self-assured and unruffled manner, thereby emphasizing his aloofness and "superiority" to the "squares." He develops a colorful, discriminating vocabulary and ritualized gestures which express his sense of difference from the conventional world and his solidarity with the retreatist subculture.

The word "cool" also best describes the sense of apartness and detachment which the retreatist experiences in his relationships with the conventional world. His reference group is the "society of cats," an "elite" group in which he becomes isolated from conventional society. Within this group, a new order of goals and criteria of achievement are created. The cat does not seek to impose this system of values on the world of the square. Instead, he strives for status and deference within the society of cats by cultivating the kick and the hustle. Thus the retreatist subculture provides avenues to success-goals, to the social admiration and the sense of well-being or oneness with the world which the members feel are otherwise beyond their reach.

Notes

1. See esp. C. R. Shaw, *The Jack-Roller* (Chicago: University of Chicago Press, 1930); Shaw, *The Natural History of a Delinquent Career* (Chicago: University of Chicago Press, 1931); Shaw *et al.*, *Delinquency Areas* (Chicago: University of Chicago Press, 1940); and Shaw and H. D. McKay, *Juvenile Delinquency and Urban Areas* (Chicago: University of Chicago Press, 1942).

2. E. H. Sutherland, ed., *The Professional Thief* (Chicago: University of Chicago Press, 1937); and Sutherland, *Principles of Criminology*, 4th Ed. (Philadelphia: Lippincott, 1947).

3. All quotations on this page are from *The Professional Thief*, pp. 211–13. Emphasis added.

4. Frank Tannenbaum, "The Professional Criminal," *The Century*, Vol. 110 (May–Oct. 1925), p. 577.

5. See A. K. Cohen, Alfred Lindesmith, and Karl Schuessler, eds., *The Sutherland Papers* (Bloomington, Ind.: Indiana University Press, 1956), pp. 31–35.

6. R. K. Merton, *Social Theory and Social Structure*, Rev. and Enl. Ed. (Glencoe, Ill.: Free Press, 1957), pp. 145–46.

7. *Principles of Criminology, op. cit.*, pp. 7–8.

8. For an example of restrictions on access to illegitimate roles, note the impact of racial definitions in the following case: "I was greeted by two prisoners who were to be my

cell buddies. Ernest was a first offender, charged with being a 'hold-up' man. Bill, the other buddy, was an older offender, going through the machinery of becoming a habitual criminal, in and out of jail. . . . The first thing they asked me was, 'What are you in for?' I said, 'Jack-rolling.' The hardened one (Bill) looked at me with a superior air and said, 'A hoodlum, eh? An ordinary sneak thief. Not willing to leave jack-rolling to the niggers, eh? That's all they're good for. Kid, jack-rolling's not a white man's job.' I could see that he was disgusted with me, and I was too scared to say anything." (Shaw, *The Jack-Roller, op. cit.*, p. 101).

9. For a discussion of the way in which the availability of illegitimate means influences the adaptations of inmates to prison life, see R. A. Cloward, "Social Control in the Prison," *Theoretical Studies of the Social Organization of the Prison*, Bulletin No. 15 (New York: Social Science Research Council, March 1960), pp. 20–48.

10. It should be understood that these terms characterize these delinquent modes of adaptation from the reference position of conventional society; they do not necessarily reflect the attitudes of members of the subcultures. Thus the term "retreatist" does not necessarily reflect the attitude of the "cat." Far from thinking of himself as being in retreat, he defines himself as among the elect.

11. Tannenbaum summarizes the community's role in this process of alienation by the phrase "dramatization of evil" (Frank Tannenbaum, *Crime and the Community* [New York: Columbia University Press, 1938], pp. 19–21). For a more detailed account of this process, see Chap. 5, *infra*.

12. See esp. C. R. Shaw, *The Jack-Roller* (Chicago: University of Chicago Press, 1930); Shaw, *The Natural History of a Delinquent Career* (Chicago: University of Chicago Press, 1940); Shaw and H. D. McKay, *Juvenile Delinquency and Urban Areas* (Chicago: University of Chicago Press, 1942); E. H. Sutherland, ed., *The Professional Thief* (Chicago: University of Chicago Press, 1937); Sutherland, *Principles of Criminology*, 4th ed. (Philadelphia: J. P. Lippincott Co., 1947); and Sutherland, *White Collar Crime* (New York: Dryden Press, 1949).

13. For descriptions of conflict groups, see Harrison Salisbury, *The Shook-up Generation* (New York: Harper & Bros., 1958); *Reaching the Unreached*, a Publication of the New York City Youth Board, 1952; C. K. Myers, *Light the Dark Streets* (Greenwich, Conn.: Seabury Press, 1957); Walter Bernstein, "The Cherubs Are Rumbling," *The New Yorker*, Sept. 21, 1957; Sam Glane, "Juvenile Gangs in East Side Los Angeles," *Focus*, Vol. 29 (Sept. 1959), pp. 136–41; Dale Kramer and Madeline Karr, *Teen-Age Gangs* (New York: Henry Holt, 1953); S. V. Jones, "The Cougars—Life with a Brooklyn Gang," *Harper's*, Vol. 209 (Nov. 1954), pp. 35–43; P. C. Crawford, D. I. Malamud, and J. R. Dumpson, *Working with Teen-Age Gangs* (New York Welfare Council, 1950); Dan Wakefield, "The Gang That Went Good," *Harper's*, Vol. 216 (June 1958), pp. 36–43.

14. Harold Finestone, "Cats, Kicks and Color," *Social Problems*, Vol. 5 (July 1957), pp. 3–13.

13 / A Radical Perspective on Crime

JEFFREY H. REIMAN

THE IMPLICIT IDEOLOGY OF CRIMINAL JUSTICE

Every criminal justice system conveys a subtle, yet powerful message in support of established institutions. It does this for two interconnected reasons.

First, because it concentrates on *individual* wrongdoers. This means that *it diverts our attention away from our institutions, away from consideration of whether our institutions themselves are wrong or unjust or indeed "criminal."*

Second, because the criminal law is put forth as the *minimum neutral ground rules* for any social living. We are taught that no society can exist without rules against theft and violence, and thus the criminal law is put forth as politically neutral, as the minimum requirements of *any* society, as the minimum obligations that any individual owes his fellows to make social life of any decent sort possible. Thus, it not only diverts our attention away from the possible injustice of our social institutions, but *the criminal law bestows upon those institutions the mantle of its own neutrality.* Since the criminal law protects the established institutions (e.g., the prevailing economic arrangements are protected by laws against theft, etc.), attacks on those established institutions become equivalent to violations of the minimum requirements for any social life at all. In effect, *the criminal law enshrines the established institutions as equivalent to the minimum requirements for* any *decent social existence—and it brands the individual who attacks those institutions as one who has declared war on* all *organized society and who must therefore be met with the weapons of war.*

This is the powerful magic of criminal justice. By virtue of its focus on *individual* criminals, it diverts us from the evils of the *social* order. By virtue of its presumed neutrality, it transforms the established social (and economic) order from being merely *one* form of society open to critical comparison with others into *the* conditions of *any* social order and thus immune from criticism. Let us look more closely at this process.

What is the effect of focusing on individual guilt? Not only does this divert our attention from the possible evils in our institutions, but it puts forth half the problem of justice as if it were the *whole* problem. To focus on individual guilt is to ask whether or not the individual citizen has fulfilled his obligations to his fellow citizens. *It is to look away from the issue of whether his fellow citizens have fulfilled their obligations to him.*

To look only at individual responsibility is to look away from social responsibility. To look only at individual criminality is to close one's eyes to social injustice and to close one's ears to the question of whether our social institutions have exploited or violated the individual. *Justice is a two-way street—but criminal justice is a one-way street.*

Individuals owe obligations to their fellow citizens because their fellow citizens owe obligations to them. Criminal justice focuses on the first and looks away from the second. *Thus, by focusing on individual responsibility for crime, the criminal justice system literally acquits the existing social order of any charge of injustice!*

This is an extremely important bit of ideological alchemy. It stems from the fact [that] the same act can be criminal or not, unjust or just, depending on the conditions in which it takes place. Killing someone is ordinarily a crime. But if it is in self-defense or to stop a deadly crime, it is not. Taking property by force is usually a crime. But if the taking is just retrieving what has been stolen, then no crime has been committed. Acts of violence are ordinarily crimes. But if the violence is provoked by the threat of violence or by oppressive conditions, then, like the Boston Tea Party, what might ordinarily be called criminal is celebrated as just. This means that when we call an act a crime *we are also making an implicit judgment about the conditions in response to which it takes place.* When we call an act a crime, we are saying that the conditions in which it occurs are not themselves criminal or deadly or oppressive or so unjust as to make an extreme response reasonable or justified, that is, to make such a response non-criminal.

This means that when the system holds an individual responsible for a crime, *it is implicitly conveying the message that the social conditions in which the crime occurred are not responsible for the crime,* that they are not so unjust as to make a violent response to them excusable. The criminal justice system conveys as much by what it does not do as by what it does. By holding the individual responsible, *it literally acquits the society of criminality or injustice.*

Judges are prone to hold that an individual's responsibility for a violent crime is diminished if it was provoked by something that might lead a "reasonable man" to respond violently and that criminal responsibility is eliminated if the act was in response to conditions so intolerable that any "reasonable man" would have been likely to respond in the same way. In this vein, the law acquits those who kill or injure in self-defense and treats lightly those who commit a crime when confronted with extreme provocation. The law treats leniently the man who kills his wife's lover and the woman who kills her brutal husband, even when neither has acted directly in self-defense. By this logic, when we hold an individual completely responsible for a crime, we are saying that the conditions in which it occurred are such that a "reasonable man" should find them tolerable. In other words, by focusing on individual responsibility for crimes, *the criminal justice system broadcasts the message that the social order itself is reasonable and not intolerably unjust.*

Thus the criminal justice system serves to focus moral condemnation on individuals and to deflect it away from the social order that may have either violated the individual's rights or dignity or literally pushed him or her to the brink of crime. This not only serves to carry the message that our social institutions are not in need of fundamental questioning, but it further suggests that the justice of our institutions is obvious, not to be doubted. Indeed, since it is deviations from these institutions that are crimes, the established institutions become the implicit standard of justice from which criminal deviations are measured.

This leads to the second way in which a criminal justice system always conveys an implicit ideology. It arises from the presumption that the criminal law is nothing but the politically neutral minimum requirements of any decent social life. What is the consequence of this?

Obviously, as already suggested, this presumption transforms the prevailing social order into justice incarnate and all violations of the prevailing order into injustice incarnate. This process is so obvious that it may be easily missed.

Consider, for example, the law against theft. It does indeed seem to be one of the minimum requirements of social living. As long as there is scarcity, any society—capitalist or socialist—will need rules preventing individuals from taking what does not belong to them. But the law against theft is more: it is a law against stealing what individuals *presently* own. *Such a law has the effect of making present property relations a part of the criminal law.*

Since stealing is a violation of the law, this means that present property relations become the implicit standard of justice against which criminal deviations are measured. Since criminal law is thought of as the minimum requirements of any social life, this means that present property relations become equivalent to the minimum requirements of *any* social life. And the criminal who would alter the present property relations becomes nothing less than someone who is declaring war on all organized society. The question of whether this "war" is provoked by the injustice or brutality of the society is swept aside. Indeed, this suggests yet another way in which the criminal justice system conveys an ideological message in support of the established society.

Not only does the criminal justice system acquit the social order of any charge of injustice, it specifically cloaks the society's own crime-producing tendencies. I have already observed that by blaming the individual for a crime, the society is acquitted of the charge of injustice. I would like to go further now and argue that by blaming the individual for a crime, the society is acquitted of the charge of complicity in that crime! This is a point worth developing, since many observers have maintained that modern competitive societies such as our own have structural features that tend to generate crime. Thus, holding the individual responsible for his or her crime serves the function of taking the rest of society off the hook for their role in sustaining and benefiting from social arrangements that produce crime. Let us take a brief detour to look more closely at this process.

Cloward and Ohlin argue in their book *Delinquency and Opportunity*[1] that much crime is the result of the discrepancy between social goals and the legitimate opportunities available for achieving them. Simply put, in our society everyone is encouraged to be a success, but the avenues to success are open only to some. The conventional wisdom of our free enterprise democracy is that anyone can be a success if he or she has the talent and the ambition. Thus, if one is not a success, it is because of their own shortcomings: laziness or lack of ability or both. On the other hand, opportunities to achieve success are not equally open to all. Access to the best schools and the best jobs is effectively closed to all but a few of the poor and begins to open wider only as one goes up the economic ladder. The result is that many are called but few are chosen. And many who have taken the bait and accepted the belief in the importance of success and the belief that achieving success is a result of individual ability must cope with the feelings of frustration and failure that result when they find the avenues to success closed. Cloward and Ohlin argue that one method of coping with these stresses is to develop alternative avenues to success. Crime is such an alternative. Crime is a means by which people who believe in the American dream pursue it when they find the traditional routes barred. Indeed, it is plain to see that the goals pursued by most criminals are as American as apple pie. I suspect that one of the reasons that American moviegoers enjoy gangster films—movies in which gangsters such as Al Capone, Bonnie and Clyde, or Butch Cassidy and the Sundance Kid are the heroes, as distinct from police and detective films whose heroes are defenders of the law—is that even where they deplore the hero's methods, they identify with his or her notion of success, since it is theirs as well, and respect the courage and cunning displayed in achieving that success.

It is important to note that the discrepancy between success goals and legitimate opportunities in America is not an aberration. It is a structural feature of modern competitive industrialized society, a feature from which many benefits flow. Cloward and Ohlin write that

> ...a crucial problem in the industrial world...is to locate and train the most talented persons in every generation, irrespective of the vicissitudes of birth, to occupy technical work roles.... Since we cannot know in advance who can best fulfill the requirements of the various occupational roles, the matter is presumably settled through the process of competition. But how can men throughout the social order be motivated to participate in this competition?...
>
> One of the ways in which the industrial society attempts to solve this problem is by defining success-goals as potentially accessible to all, regardless of race, creed, or socioeconomic position.[2]

But since these universal goals are urged to encourage a competition to weed out the best, there are necessarily fewer openings than seekers. And since those who achieve success are in a particularly good position to exploit their success to make access for their own children easier, the competition is rigged to work in favor of the middle and upper classes. As a result, "many lower-class persons... are the victims of a contradiction between the goals toward which they have been led to orient themselves and socially structured means of striving for these goals."[3]

> [The poor] experience desperation born of the certainty that their position in the economic structure is relatively fixed and immutable—a desperation made all the more poignant by their exposure to a cultural ideology in which failure to orient oneself upward is regarded as a moral defect and failure to become mobile as proof of it.[4]

The outcome is predictable. "Under these conditions, there is an acute pressure to depart from institutional norms and to adopt illegitimate alternatives."[5]

In brief, this means that the very way in which our society is structured to draw out the talents and energies that go into producing our high standard of living has a costly side effect: it produces crime. But by holding individuals responsible for this crime, those who enjoy that high standard of living can have their cake and eat it. They can reap the benefits of the competition for success and escape the responsibility of paying for the costs of that competition. By holding the poor crook legally and morally guilty, the rest of society not only passes the costs of competition on to the poor, but they effectively deny that they (the affluent) are the beneficiaries of an economic system that exacts such a high toll in frustration and suffering.

Willem Bonger, the Dutch Marxist criminologist, maintained that competitive capitalism produces egotistic motives and undermines compassion for the misfortunes of others and thus makes human beings literally *more capable of crime*—more capable of preying on their fellows without moral inhibition or remorse—than earlier cultures that emphasized cooperation rather than competition.[6] Here again, the criminal justice system relieves those who benefit from the American economic system of the costs of that system. By holding criminals morally and individually responsible for their crimes, we can forget that the motives that lead to crime—the drive for success at any cost, linked with the beliefs that success means outdoing others and that violence is an acceptable way of achieving one's goals—are the same motives that powered the drive across the American continent and that continue to fuel the engine of America's prosperity.

David Gordon, a contemporary political economist, maintains "that nearly all crimes in capitalist societies represent perfectly *rational* responses to the structure of institutions upon which capitalist societies are based."[7] That is, like Bonger, Gordon believes that capitalism tends to provoke crime in all economic strata. This is so because most crime is motivated by a desire for property or money and is an understandable way of coping with the pressures of inequality, competition, and insecurity, all of which are essential ingredients of capitalism. Capitalism depends, Gordon writes,

> ...on basically competitive forms of social and economic interaction and upon substantial inequalities in the allocation of social resources. Without inequalities, it would be much more difficult to induce workers to work in alienating environments. Without competition and a competitive ideology, workers might not be inclined to struggle to improve their relative income and status in society by working harder. Finally, although rights of property are protected, capitalist societies do not guarantee economic security to most of their individual members. Individuals must fend for themselves, finding the best available opportunities to provide for themselves and their families.... Driven by the fear of economic insecurity and by a competitive desire to gain some of the goods unequally distributed throughout the society, many individuals will eventually become "criminals."[8]

To the extent that a society makes crime a reasonable alternative for a large number of its members from all classes, that society is itself not very reasonably or humanely organized and bears some degree of responsibility for the crime it encourages. Since the criminal law is put forth as the minimum requirements that can be expected of any "reasonable man," its enforcement amounts to a denial of the real nature of the social order to which Gordon and the others point. Here again, by blaming the individual criminal, the criminal justice system serves implicitly but dramatically to acquit the society of its criminality.

THE BONUS OF BIAS

We turn now to consideration of the additional ideological bonus that is derived from the criminal justice system's bias against the poor. This bonus is a product of the association of crime and poverty in the popular mind. This association, the merging of the "criminal classes" and the "lower classes" into the "dangerous classes," was not invented in America. The word "villain" is derived from the Latin *villanus*, which means a farm servant. And the term "villein" was used in feudal England to refer to a serf who farmed the land of a great lord and who was literally owned by that lord.[9] In this respect, our present criminal justice system is heir to a long and hallowed tradition.

The value of this association was already seen when we explored the "average citizen's" concept of the Typical Criminal and the Typical Crime. It is quite obvious that throughout the great mass of middle America, far more fear and hostility are directed toward the predatory acts of the poor than the rich. Compare the fate of politicians in recent history who call for tax reform, income redistribution, prosecution of corporate crime, and any sort of regulation of business that would make it better serve American social goals with that of politicians who erect their platform on a call for "law and order," more police, less limits on police power, and stiffer prison sentences for criminals—and consider this in light of what we have already seen about the real dangers posed by corporate crime and business-as-usual.

In view of all that has been said already, it seems clear that Americans have been systematically deceived as to what are the greatest dangers to their lives, limbs and possessions. The very persistence with which the system functions to apprehend and punish poor crooks and ignore or slap on the wrist equally or more dangerous individuals is testimony to the sticking power of this deception. That Americans continue to tolerate the gentle treatment meted out to white-collar criminals, corporate price fixers, industrial polluters, and political-influence peddlers, while voting in droves to lock up more poor people faster and longer, indicates the degree to which they harbor illusions as to who most threatens them. It is perhaps also part of the explanation for the continued dismal failure of class-based politics in America. American workers rarely seem able to forget their differences and unite to defend their shared interests against the rich whose wealth they produce. Ethnic divisions serve this divisive function well, but undoubtedly the vivid portrayal of the poor—and, of course, the blacks—as hovering birds of prey waiting for the opportunity to snatch away the workers' meager gains serves also to deflect opposition away from the upper class. A politician who promises to keep their communities free of blacks and their prisons full of them can get their votes even if the major portion of his or her policies amount to continuation of favored treatment of the rich at their expense. Surely this is a minor miracle of mind control.

The most important "bonus" derived from the identification of crime and poverty is that it paints the picture that the threat to decent middle Americans comes from those below them on the economic ladder, not those above. For this to happen the system must not only identify crime and poverty, but *it must also fail to reduce crime so that it remains a real threat.* By doing this, it deflects the fear and discontent of middle Americans, and their possible opposition, away from the wealthy. The two politicians who most clearly gave voice to the discontent of middle Americans in the post-World War II period were George Wallace and Spiro Agnew. Is it any accident that their politics were extremely conservative and their anger reserved for the poor (the welfare chiselers) and the criminal (the targets of law and order)?

There are other bonuses as well. For instance, if the criminal justice system functions to send out a message that bestows legitimacy on present property relations, the dramatic impact is mightily enhanced if the violator of the present arrangements is propertyless. In other words, the crimes of the well-to-do "redistribute" property among the haves. In that sense, they do not pose a symbolic challenge to the larger system in which some have much and many have little or nothing. If the criminal threat can be portrayed as coming from the poor, then the punishment of the poor criminal becomes a morality play in which the sanctity of legitimacy of the system in which some have plenty and others have little or nothing is dramatically affirmed. It matters little who the poor criminals really rip off. What counts is that middle Americans come to fear that those poor criminals are out to steal what they own.

There is yet another and, I believe, still more important bonus for the powerful in America, produced by the identification of crime and poverty. It might be thought that the identification of crime and poverty would produce sympathy for the criminals. My suspicion is that it produces or at least reinforces the reverse: *hostility toward the poor.*

Indeed, there is little evidence that Americans are very sympathetic to criminals or poor people. I have already pointed to the fact that very few Americans believe poverty to be a cause of crime. Other surveys find that most Americans believe that police should be tougher than they are now in dealing with crime (83 percent of those questioned in a 1972 survey); that courts do not deal harshly enough with criminals (75 percent of those questioned in a 1969 survey); that a majority of Americans would like to see the death penalty for convicted murderers (57 percent of those questioned in November 1972); and that most would be more likely to vote for a candidate who advocated tougher sentences for law-breakers (83 percent of those questioned in a 1972 survey).[10] Indeed, the experience of Watergate seems to suggest that sympathy for criminals begins to flower only when we approach the higher reaches of the ladder of wealth and power. For some poor ghetto youth who robs a liquor store, five years in the slammer is our idea of tempering justice with mercy. When a handful of public officials try to walk off with the U.S. Constitution, a few months in a minimum security prison will suffice. If the public official is high enough, resignation from office and public disgrace tempered with a $60,000-a-year pension is punishment enough.

My view is that since the criminal justice system—in fact and fiction—deals with *individual legal* and *moral guilt*, the association of crime with poverty does not mitigate the image of individual moral responsibility for crime, the image that crime is the result of an individual's poor character. My suspicion is that it does the reverse: it generates the association of poverty and individual moral failing and thus *the belief that poverty itself is a sign of poor or weak character*. The clearest evidence that Americans hold this belief is to be found in the fact that attempts to aid the poor are regarded as acts of charity rather than as acts of justice. Our welfare system has all the demeaning attributes of an institution designed to give handouts to the undeserving and none of the dignity of an institution designed to make good on our responsibilities to our fellow human beings. If we acknowledged the degree to which our economic and social institutions themselves breed poverty, we would have to recognize our own responsibilities toward the poor. If we can convince ourselves that the poor are poor because of their own shortcomings, particularly moral shortcomings like incontinence or indolence, then we need acknowledge no such responsibility to the poor. Indeed, we can go further and pat ourselves on the back for our generosity and handing out the little that we do, and of course, we can make our recipients go through all the indignities that mark them as the undeserving objects of our benevolence. By and large, this has been the way in which Americans have dealt with their poor.[11] It is a way that enables us to avoid asking the question of why the richest nation in the world continues to produce massive poverty. It is my view that this conception of the poor is subtly conveyed by the way our criminal justice system functions.

Obviously, no ideological message could be more supportive of the present social and economic order than this. It suggests that poverty is a sign of individual failing, not a symptom of social or economic injustice. It tells us loud and clear that massive poverty in the midst of abundance is not a sign pointing toward the need for fundamental changes in our social and economic institutions. It suggests that the poor are poor because they deserve to be poor, or at least because they lack the strength of character to overcome poverty. When the poor are seen to be poor in character, then economic poverty coincides with moral poverty and the economic order coincides with the moral order—as if a divine hand guided its workings, capitalism leads to everyone getting what they morally deserve!

If this association takes root, then when the poor individual is found guilty of a crime, the criminal justice system acquits the society of its responsibility not only for the crime *but for poverty as well.*

With this, the ideological message of criminal justice is complete. The poor rather than the rich are seen as the enemies of the mass of decent middle Americans. Our social and economic institutions are held to be responsible for neither crime nor poverty and thus are in need of no fundamental questioning or reform. The poor are poor because they are poor of character. The economic order and the moral order are one. And to the extent that this message sinks in, the wealthy can rest easily—even if they cannot sleep the sleep of the just.

Thus, we can understand why the criminal justice system creates the image of crime as the work of the poor and fails to stem it so that the threat of crime remains real and credible. The result is ideological alchemy of the highest order. The poor are seen as the real threat to decent society. The ultimate sanctions of criminal justice dramatically sanctify the present social and economic order, and *the poverty of criminals makes poverty itself an individual moral crime!*

Such are the ideological fruits of a losing war against crime whose distorted image is reflected in the criminal justice carnival mirror and widely broadcast to reach the minds and imaginations of America.

Notes

1. Richard A. Cloward and Lloyd E. Ohlin, *Delinquency and Opportunity: A Theory of Delinquent Gangs* (New York: The Free Press, 1960), esp. pp. 77–107.
2. Ibid., p. 81.
3. Ibid., p. 105.
4. Ibid., p. 107.
5. Ibid., p. 105.
6. Willem Bonger, *Criminality and Economic Conditions*, abridged and with an introduction by Austin T. Turk (Bloomington, Indiana: Indiana University Press, 1969), pp. 7–12, 40–47. Willem Adriaan Bonger was born in Holland in 1876 and died by his own hand in 1940 rather than submit to the Nazis. His *Criminalité et conditions économiques* first appeared in 1905. It was translated into English and published in the United States in 1916. Ibid., pp. 3–4.
7. David M. Gordon, "Capitalism, Class and Crime in America," *Crime and Delinquency* (April 1972), p. 174.
8. Ibid., p. 174.
9. William and Mary Morris, *Dictionary of Word and Phrase Origins*, II (New York: Harper & Row, 1967), p. 282.
10. *Sourcebook*, pp. 203, 204, 223, 207; see also p. 177.
11. Historical documentation of this can be found in David J. Rothman, *The Discovery of the Asylum: Social Order and Disorder in the New Republic* (Boston: Little, Brown, 1971); and in Frances Fox Piven and Richard A. Cloward, *Regulating the Poor: The Functions of Public Welfare* (New York: Pantheon, 1971), which carries the analysis up to the present.

14 / A Sociological Analysis of the Law of Vagrancy

WILLIAM J. CHAMBLISS

With the outstanding exception of Jerome Hall's analysis of theft[1] there has been a severe shortage of sociologically relevant analyses of the relationship between particular laws and the social setting in which these laws emerge, are interpreted, and take form. The paucity of such studies is somewhat surprising in view of widespread agreement that such studies are not only desirable but absolutely essential to the development of a mature sociology of law.[2] A fruitful method of establishing the direction and pattern of this mutual influence is to systematically analyze particular legal categories, to observe the changes which take place in the categories and to explain how these changes are themselves related to and stimulate changes in the society. This chapter is an attempt to provide such an analysis of the law of vagrancy in Anglo-American Law.

LEGAL INNOVATION: THE EMERGENCE OF THE LAW OF VAGRANCY IN ENGLAND

There is general agreement among legal scholars that the first full fledged vagrancy statute was passed in England in 1349. As is generally the case with legislative innovations, however, this statute was preceded by earlier laws which established a climate favorable to such change. The most significant forerunner to the 1349 vagrancy statute was in 1274 when it was provided:

> Because that abbies and houses of religion have been overcharged and sore grieved, by the resort of great men and other, so that their goods have not been sufficient for themselves, whereby they have been greatly hindered and impoverished, that they cannot maintain themselves, nor such charity as they have been accustomed to do; it is provided, that none shall come to eat or lodge in any house of religion, or any other's foundation than of his own, at the costs of the house, unless he be required by the governor of the house before his coming hither.[3]

Unlike the vagrancy statutes this statute does not intend to curtail the movement of persons from one place to another, but is solely designed to provide the religious houses with some financial relief from the burden of providing food and shelter to travelers.

The philosophy that the religious houses were to give alms to the poor and to the sick and feeble was, however, to undergo drastic change in the next fifty years. The result of this changed attitude was the establishment of the first vagrancy statute in 1349 which made it a crime to give alms to any who were unemployed while being of sound mind and body. To wit:

> Because that many valiant beggars, as long as they may live of begging, do refuse to labour, giving themselves to idleness and vice, and sometimes to theft and other abominations; it is ordained, that none, upon pain of imprisonment shall, under the colour of pity or alms, give anything to such which may labour, or presume to favour them towards their desires; so that thereby they may be compelled to labour for their necessary living.[4]

It was further provided by this statute that:

> ...every man and woman, of what condition he be, free or bond, able in body, and within the age of threescore years, not living in merchandize nor exercising any craft, nor having of his own whereon to live, nor proper land whereon to occupy himself, and not serving any other, if he in convenient service (his estate considered) be required to serve, shall be bounded to serve him which shall him require.... And if any refuse, he shall on conviction by two true men,... be commited to gaol till he find surety to serve.
>
> And if any workman or servant, of what estate or condition he be, retained in any man's service, do depart from the said service without reasonable cause or license, before the term agreed on, he shall have pain of imprisonment.[5]

There was also in this statute the stipulation that the workers should receive a standard wage. In 1351 this statute was strengthened by the stipulation:

> And none shall go out of the town where he dwelled in winter, to serve the summer, if he may serve in the same town.[6]

By 34 Ed. 3 (1360) the punishment for these acts became imprisonment for fifteen days and if they "do not justify themselves by the end of that time, to be sent to gaol till they do."

A change in official policy so drastic as this did not, of course, occur simply as a matter of whim. The vagrancy statutes emerged as a result of changes in other parts of the social structure. The prime-mover for this legislative innovation was the Black Death which struck England about 1348. Among the many disastrous consequences this had upon the social structure was the fact that it decimated the labor force. It is estimated that by the time the pestilence had run its course at least fifty per cent of the population of England had died from the plague. This decimation of the labor force would necessitate rather drastic innovations in any society but its impact was heightened in England where, at this time, the economy was highly dependent upon a steady supply of cheap labor.

Even before the pestilence, however, the availability of an adequate supply of cheap labor was becoming a problem for the landowners. The crusades and various wars had made money necessary to the lords and, as a result, the lord frequently agreed to sell the serfs their freedom in order to obtain the needed funds. The serfs, for their part, were desirous of obtaining their freedom (by "fair means" or "foul") because the larger towns which were becoming more industrialized during this period could offer the serf greater personal freedom as well as a higher standard of living. This process is nicely summarized by Bradshaw:

> By the middle of the 14th century the outward uniformity of the manorial system had become in practice considerably varied... for the peasant had begun to drift to the towns and it was unlikely that the old village life in its unpleasant aspects should not be resented. Moreover the constant wars against France and Scotland were fought mainly with mercenaries after Henry III's time and most villages contributed to the new armies. The bolder serfs either joined the armies or fled to the towns, and even in the villages the free men who held by villein tenure were as eager to commute their services as the serfs were to escape. Only the amount of "free" labor available enabled the lord to work his demesne in many places.[7]

And he says regarding the effect of the Black Death:

> ...in 1348 the Black Death reached England and the vast mortality that ensued destroyed that reserve to labor which alone had made the manorial system even nominally possible.[8]

The immediate result of these events was of course no surprise: Wages for the "free" man rose considerably and this increased, on the one hand, the landowner's problems and, on the other hand, the plight of the unfree tenant. For although wages increased for the personally free laborers, it of course did not necessarily add to the standard of living of the serf, if anything it made his position worse because the landowner would be hard pressed to pay for the personally free labor which he needed and would thus find it more and more difficult to maintain the standard of living for the serf which he had heretofore supplied. Thus the serf had no alternative but flight if he chose to better his position. Furthermore, flight generally meant both freedom and better conditions since the possibility of work in the new weaving industry was great and the chance of being caught small.[9]

It was under these conditions that we find the first vagrancy statutes emerging. There is little question but that these statutes were designed for one express purpose: to force laborers (whether personally free or unfree) to accept employment at a low wage in order to insure the landowner an adequate supply of labor at a price he could afford to pay. Caleb Foote concurs with this interpretation when he notes:

> The anti-migratory policy behind vagrancy legislation began as an essential complement of the wage stabilization legislation which accompanied the breakup of feudalism and the depopulation caused by the Black Death. By the Statutes of

> Labourers in 1349–1351, every able-bodied person without other means of support was required to work for wages fixed at the level preceding the Black Death; it was unlawful to accept any more, or to refuse an offer to work, or to flee from one country to another to avoid offers of work or to seek higher wages, or go give alms to able-bodied beggars who refused to work.[10]

In short, as Foote says in another place, this was "an attempt to make the vagrancy statutes a substitute for serfdom."[11] This same conclusion is equally apparent from the wording of the statute where it is stated:

> Because great part of the people, and especially of workmen and servants, late died in pestilence; many seeing the necessity of masters, and great scarcity of servants, will not serve without excessive wages, and some rather willing to beg in idleness than by labour to get their living: it is ordained, that every man and woman, of what condition he be, free or bond, able in body and within the age of threescore years, not living in merchandize, (etc.) be required to serve....

The innovation in the law, then, was a direct result of the aforementioned changes which had occurred in the social setting. In this case these changes were located for the most part in the economic institution of the society. The vagrancy laws were designed to alleviate a condition defined by the lawmakers as undesirable. The solution was to attempt to force a reversal, as it were, of a social process which was well underway; that is, to curtail mobility of laborers in such a way that labor would not become a commodity for which the landowners would have to compete.

Statutory Dormancy: A Legal Vestige

In time, of course, the curtailment of the geographical mobility of laborers was no longer requisite. One might well expect that when the function served by the statute was no longer an important one for society, the statutes would be eliminated from the law. In fact, this has not occurred. The vagrancy statutes have remained in effect since 1349. Furthermore, as we shall see in some detail later, they were taken over by the colonies and have remained in effect in the United States as well.

The substance of the vagrancy statutes changed very little for some time after the first ones in 1349–1351 although there was a tendency to make punishments more harsh than originally. For example, in 1360 it was provided that violators of the statute should be imprisoned for fifteen days,[12] and in 1388 the punishment was to put the offender in the stocks and to keep him there until "he find surety to return to his service."[13] That there was still, at this time, the intention of providing the landowner with labor is apparent from the fact that this statute provides:

> ...and he or she which use to labour at the plough and cart, or other labour and service of husbandry, till they be of the age of 12 years, from thenceforth shall abide at the same labour without being put to any mistery or handicraft: and any covenant of apprenticeship to the contrary shall be void.[14]

The next alteration in the statutes occurs in 1495 and is restricted to an increase in punishment. Here it is provided that vagrants shall be "set in stocks, there to remain by the space of three days and three nights, and there to have none other sustenance but bread and water; and after the said three days and nights, to be had out and set at large, and then to be commanded to void the town."[15]

The tendency to increase the severity of punishment during this period seems to be the result of a general tendency to make finer distinctions in the criminal law. During this period the vagrancy statutes appear to have been fairly inconsequential in either their effect as a control mechanism or as a generally enforced statute.[16] The processes of social change in the culture generally and the trend away from serfdom and into a "free" economy obviated the utility of these statutes. The result was not unexpected. The judiciary did not apply the law and the legislators did not take it upon themselves to change the law. In short, we have here a period of dormancy in which the statute is neither applied nor altered significantly.

A SHIFT IN FOCAL CONCERN

Following the squelching of the Peasant's Revolt in 1381, the services of the serfs to the lord "...tended to become less and less exacted, although in certain forms they lingered on till the seventeenth century....By the sixteenth century few knew there were any bondmen in England...and in 1575 Queen Elizabeth listened to the prayers of almost the last serfs in England...and granted them manumission."[17]

In view of this change we would expect corresponding changes in the vagrancy laws. Beginning with the lessening of punishment in the statute of 1503 we find these changes. However, instead of remaining dormant (or becoming more so) or being negated altogether, the vagrancy statutes experienced a shift in focal concern. With this shift the statutes served a new and equally important function for the social order or England. The first statute which indicates this change was in 1530. In this statute (22 H. 8. c. 12 1530) it was stated:

> If any person, being whole and mighty in body, and able to labour, be taken in begging, or be vagrant and can give no reckoning how he lawfully gets his living;...and all other idle persons going about, some of them using divers and subtil crafty and unlawful games and plays, and some of them feigning themselves to have knowledge of...crafty sciences...shall be punished as provided.

What is most significant about this statute is the shift from an earlier concern with laborers to a concern with *criminal* activities. To be sure, the stipulation of persons "being whole and mighty in body, and able to labour, be taken in begging, or be vagrant" sounds very much like the concerns of the earlier statutes. Some important differences are apparent however when the rest of the statute includes those who "...can give no reckoning how he lawfully gets his living"; "some of them using divers and subtil crafty and unlawful games and plays." This is the first statute which specifically focuses upon these kinds of criteria for adjudging someone a vagrant.

It is significant that in this statute the severity of punishment is increased so as to be greater not only than provided by the 1503 statute but the punishment is more severe than that which had been provided by *any* of the pre-1503 statutes as well. For someone who is merely idle and gives no reckoning of how he makes his living the offender shall be:

> ...had to the next market town, or other place where they [the constables] shall think most convenient, and there to be tied to the end of a cart naked, and to be beaten with whips throughout the same market town or other place, till his body be bloody by reason of such whipping.[18]

But, for those who use "divers and subtil crafty and unlawful games and plays," etc., the punishment is "...whipping at two days together in manner aforesaid."[19] For the second offense, such persons are:

> ...scourged two days, and the third day to be put upon the pillory from nine of the clock till eleven before noon of the same day and to have one of his ears cut off.[20]

And if he offend the third time "...to have like punishment with whipping, standing on the pillory and to have his other ear cut off."

This statute (1) makes a distinction between types of offenders and applies the more severe punishment to those who are clearly engaged in "criminal" activities, (2) mentions a specific concern with categories of "unlawful" behavior, and (3) applies a type of punishment (cutting off the ear) which is generally reserved for offenders who are defined as likely to be a fairly serious criminal.

Only five years later we find for the first time that the punishment of death is applied to the crime of vagrancy. We also note a change in terminology in the statute:

> and if any ruffians...after having been once apprehended...shall wander, loiter, or idle use themselves and play the vagabonds...shall be eftfoons not only whipped again, but shall have the gristle of his right ear clean cut off. And if he shall again offend, he shall be committed to gaol till the next sessions; and being their convicted upon indictment, he shall have judgements to suffer pains and execution of death, as a felon, as an enemy of the commonwealth.[21]

It is significant that the statute now makes persons who repeat the crime of vagrancy a felon. During this period then, the focal concern of the vagrancy statutes becomes a concern for the control of felons and is no longer primarily concerned with the movement of laborers.

These statutory changes were a direct response to changes taking place in England's social structure during this period. We have already pointed out that feudalism was decaying rapidly. Concomitant with the breakup of feudalism was an increased emphasis upon commerce and industry. The commercial emphasis in England at the turn of the sixteenth century is of particular importance in the development of vagrancy laws. With commercialism came considerable traffic bearing valuable items. Where there were 169 important merchants in the middle of the fourteenth century there were 3,000 merchants engaged in foreign trade alone at the beginning of the sixteenth century.[22] England became highly dependent upon commerce for its economic support. Italians conducted a great deal of the commerce in England during this early period and were held in low repute by the populace. As a result, they were subject to attacks by citizens and, more important, were frequently robbed of their goods while transporting them. "The general insecurity of the times made any transportation hazardous. The special risks to which the alien merchant was subjected gave rise to the royal practice of issuing formally executed covenants of safe conduct through the realm."[23]

Such a situation not only called for the enforcement of existing laws but also called for the creation of new laws which would facilitate the control of persons preying upon merchants transporting goods. The vagrancy statutes were revived in order to fulfill just such a purpose. Persons who had committed no serious felony but who were suspected of being capable of doing so could be apprehended and incapacitated through the application of vagrancy laws once these laws were refocused so as to include "... any ruffians... [who] shall wander, loiter, or idle use themselves and play the vagabond...."[24]

The new focal concern is continued in 1 Ed. 6. c. 3 (1547) and in fact is made more general so as to include:

> Whoever man or woman, being not lame, impotent, or so aged or diseased that he or she cannot work, not having whereon to live, shall be lurking in any house, or loitering or idle wandering by the highway side, or in streets, cities, towns, or villages, not applying themselves to some honest labour, and so continuing for three days; or running away from their work; every such person shall be taken for a vagabond. And... upon conviction of two witnesses... the same loiterer (shall) be marked with a hot iron in the breast with the letter V, and adjudged him to the person bringing him, to be his slave for two years....

Should the vagabond run away, upon conviction, he was to be branded by a hot iron with the letter S on the forehead and to be thenceforth declared a slave forever. And in 1571 there is modification of the punishment to be inflicted, whereby the offender is to be "branded on the chest with the letter V" (for vagabond). And, if he is convicted the second time, the brand is to be made on the forehead. It is worth noting here that this method of punishment, which first appeared in 1530 and is repeated here with somewhat more force, is also an indication of a change in the type of person to whom the law is intended to apply. For it is likely that nothing so permanent as branding would be applied to someone who was wandering but looking for work, or at worst merely idle and not particularly dangerous *per se*. On the other hand, it could well be applied to someone who was likely to be engaged in other criminal activities in connection with being "vagrant."

By 1571 in the statute of 14 Ed. c. 5 the shift in focal concern is fully developed:

> All rogues, vagabonds, and sturdy beggers shall . . . be committed to the common gaol . . . he shall be grievously whipped, and burnt thro' the gristle of the right ear with a hot iron of the compass of an inch about. . . . And for the second offense, he shall be adjudged a felon, unless some person will take him for two years in to his service. And for the third offense, he shall be adjudged guilty of felony without benefit of clergy.

And there is included a long list of persons who fall within the statute: "proctors, procurators, idle persons going about using subtil, crafty and unlawful games or plays; and some of them feigning themselves to have knowledge of . . . absurd sciences . . . and all fencers, bearwards, common players in interludes, and minstrels . . . all juglers, pedlars, tinkers, petty chapmen . . . and all counterfeiters of licenses, passports and users of the same." The major significance of this statute is that it includes all the previously defined offenders and adds some more. Significantly, those added are more clearly criminal types, counterfeiters, for example. It is also significant that there is the following qualification of this statute: "Provided also, that this act shall not extend to cookers, or harvest folks, that travel for harvest work, corn or hay."

That the changes in this statute were seen as significant is indicated by the following statement which appears in the statute:

> And whereas by reason of this act, the common gaols of every shire are like to be greatly pestered with more number of prisoners than heretofore hath been, for that the said vagabonds and other lewd persons before recited shall upon their apprehension be committed to the said gaols; it is enacted. . . .[25]

And a provision is made for giving more money for maintaining the gaols. This seems to add credence to the notion that this statute was seen as being significantly more general than those previously.

It is also of importance to note that this is the first time the term *rogue* has been used to refer to persons included in the vagrancy statutes. It seems, *a priori*, that a "rogue" is a different social type than is a "vagrant" or a "vagabond"; the latter terms implying something more equivalent to the idea of a "tramp" whereas the former (rogue) seems to imply a more disorderly and potentially dangerous person.

The emphasis upon the criminalistic aspect of vagrants continues in Chapter 17 of the same statute:

> Whereas divers *licentious* persons wander up and down in all parts of the realm, to countenance their *wicked behavior*; and do continually assemble themselves

> armed in the highways, and elsewhere in troops, *to the great terror* of her majesty's true subjects, *the impeachment of her laws*, and the disturbance of the peace and tranquility of the realm; and whereas many outrages are daily committed by these dissolute persons, and more are likely to ensure if speedy remedy be not provided. (Italics added.)

With minor variations (e.g., offering a reward for the capture of a vagrant) the statutes remained essentially of this nature until 1743. In 1743 there was once more an expansion of the types of persons included such that "all persons going about as patent gatherers, or gatherers of alms, under pretense of loss by fire or other casualty; or going about as collectors for prisons, gaols, or hospitals; all persons playing or betting at any unlawful games; and all persons who run away and leave their wives or children... all persons wandering abroad, and lodging in alehouses, barns, outhouses, or in the open air, not giving good account of themselves," were types of offenders added to those already included.

By 1743 the vagrancy statutes had apparently been sufficiently reconstructed by the shifts of concern so as to be once more a useful instrument in the creation of social solidarity. This function has apparently continued down to the present day in England and the changes from 1743 to present have been all in the direction of clarifying or expanding the categories covered but little has been introduced to change either the meaning or the impact of this branch of the law.

We can summarize this shift in focal concern by quoting from Halsbury. He has noted that in the vagrancy statutes:

> ...elaborate provision is made for the relief and incidental control of destitute wayfarers. These latter, however, form but a small portion of the offenders aimed at by what are known as the Vagrancy Laws,...many offenders who are in no ordinary sense of the word vagrants, have been brought under the laws relating to vagrancy, and the great number of the offenses coming within the operation of these laws have little or no relation to the subject of poor relief, but are more properly directed towards the prevention of crime, the preservation of good order, and the promotion of social economy.[26]

Before leaving this section it is perhaps pertinent to make a qualifying remark. We have emphasized throughout this section how the vagrancy statutes underwent a shift in focal concern as the social setting changed. The shift in focal concern is not meant to imply that the later focus of the statutes represents a completely new law. It will be recalled that even in the first vagrancy statute there was reference to those who "do refuse labor, giving themselves to idleness and vice and sometimes to theft and other abominations." Thus the possibility of criminal activities resulting from persons who refuse to labor was recognized even in the earliest statute. The fact remains, however, that the major emphasis in this statute and in the statutes which followed the first one was always upon the "refusal to labor" or "begging." The "criminalistic" aspect of such persons was relatively unimportant. Later, as we have shown, the criminalistic potential becomes of paramount importance. The thread runs back to the earliest statute but the reason for the statutes' existence as well as the focal concern of the statutes is quite different in 1743 than it was in 1349.

VAGRANCY LAWS IN THE UNITED STATES

In general, the vagrancy laws of England, as they stood in the middle eighteenth century, were simply adopted by the states. There were some exceptions to this general trend. For example, Maryland restricted the application of vagrancy laws to "free" Negroes. In addition, for *all* states the vagrancy laws were even more explicitly concerned with the control of criminals and undesirables than had been the case in England. New York, for example, explicitly defines prostitutes as being a category of vagrants during this period. These exceptions do not, however, change the general picture significantly and it is quite appropriate to consider the U.S. vagrancy laws as following from England's of the middle eighteenth century with relatively minor changes. The control of criminals and undesirables was the *raison d'ětre* of the vagrancy laws in the U.S. This is as true today as it was in 1750. As Caleb Foote's analysis of the application of vagrancy statutes in the Philadelphia court shows, these laws are presently applied indiscriminately to persons considered a "nuisance." Foote suggests that "... the chief significance of this branch of the criminal law lies in its quantitative impact and administration usefulness."[27] Thus it appears that in America the trend begun in England in the sixteenth, seventeenth and eighteenth centuries has been carried to its logical extreme and the laws are now used principally as a mechanism for "clearing the streets" of the derelicts who inhabit the "skid rows" and "Bowerys" of our large urban areas.

Since the 1800's there has been an abundant source of prospects to which the vagrancy laws have been applied. These have been primarily those persons deemed by the police and the courts to be either actively involved in criminal activities or at least peripherally involved. In this context, then, the statutes have changed very little. The functions served by the statutes in England of the late eighteenth century are still being served today in both England and the United States. The locale has changed somewhat and it appears that the present day application of vagrancy statutes is focused upon the arrest and confinement of the "down and outers" who inhabit certain sections of our larger cities but the impact has remained constant. The lack of change in the vagrancy statutes, then, can be seen as a reflection of the society's perception of a continuing need to control some of its "suspicious" or "undesirable" members.[28]

A word of caution is in order lest we leave the impression that this administrative purpose is the sole function of vagrancy laws in the U.S. today. Although it is our contention that this is generally true it is worth remembering that during certain periods of our recent history, and to some extent today, these laws have also been used to control the movement of workers. This was particularly the case during the depression years and California is of course infamous for its use of vagrancy laws to restrict the admission of migrants from other states.[29] The vagrancy statutes, because of their history, still contain germs within them which make such effects possible. Their main purpose, however, is clearly no longer the control of laborers but rather the control of the undesirable, the criminal and the "nuisance."

DISCUSSION

The foregoing analysis of the vagrancy laws has demonstrated that these laws were a legislative innovation which reflected the socially perceived necessity of providing an abundance of cheap labor to landowners during a period when serfdom was breaking down and when the pool of available labor was depleted. With the eventual breakup of feudalism the need for such laws eventually disappeared and the increased dependence of the economy upon industry and commerce rendered the former use of the vagrancy statutes unnecessary. As a result, for a substantial period the vagrancy statutes were dormant, undergoing only minor changes and, presumably, being applied infrequently. Finally, the vagrancy laws were subjected to considerable alteration through a shift in the focal concern of the statutes. Whereas in their inception the laws focused upon the "idle" and "those refusing to labor" after the turn of the sixteenth century the emphasis came to be upon "rogues," "vagabonds," and others who were suspected of being engaged in criminal activities. During this period the focus was particularly upon "road men" who preyed upon citizens who transported goods from one place to another. The increased importance of commerce to England during this period made it necessary that some protection be given persons engaged in this enterprise and the vagrancy statutes provided one source for such protection by refocusing the acts to be included under the statutes.

Comparing the results of this analysis with the findings of Hall's study of theft we see a good deal of correspondence. Of major importance is the fact that both analyses demonstrate the truth of Hall's assertion that "The functioning of courts is significantly related to concomitant cultural needs, and this applies to the law of procedure as well as to substantive law."[30]

Our analysis of the vagrancy laws also indicates that when changed social conditions create a perceived need for legal changes that these alterations will be effected through the revision and refocusing of existing statutes. This process was demonstrated in Hall's analysis of theft as well as in our analysis of vagrancy. In the case of vagrancy the laws were dormant when the focal concern of the laws was shifted so as to provide control over potential criminals. In the case of theft the laws were re-interpreted (interestingly, by the courts and not by the legislature) so as to include persons who were transporting goods for a merchant but who absconded with the contents of the packages transported.

It also seems probable that when the social conditions change and previously useful laws are no longer useful there will be long periods when these laws will remain dormant. It is less likely that they will be officially negated. During this period of dormancy it is the judiciary which has principal responsibility for *not* applying the statutes. It is possible that one finds statutes being negated only when the judiciary stubbornly applies laws which do not have substantial public support. An example of such laws in contemporary times would be the "Blue Laws." Most states still have laws prohibiting the sale of retail goods on Sunday yet these laws are rarely applied. The laws are very likely to remain but to be dormant unless a recalcitrant judge or a vocal minority of the population insists that the laws be applied. When this happens we can anticipate that the statutes will be negated.[31] Should there arise a perceived need to curtail retail selling under some special circumstances, then it is likely that these laws will undergo a shift in focal concern much like the shift which characterized the vagrancy laws. Lacking such application the laws will simply remain dormant except for rare instances where they will be negated.

This analysis of the vagrancy statutes (and Hall's analysis of theft as well) has demonstrated the importance of "vested interest" groups in the emergence and/or alteration of laws. The vagrancy laws emerged in order to provide the powerful landowners with a ready supply of cheap labor. When this was no longer seen as necessary and particularly when the landowners were no longer dependent upon cheap labor nor were they a powerful interest group in the society the laws became dormant. Finally a new interest group emerged and was seen as being of great importance to the society and the laws were then altered so as to afford some protection to this group. These findings are thus in agreement with Weber's contention that "status groups" determine the content of the law.[32] The findings are inconsistent, on the other hand, with the perception of the law as simply a reflection of "public opinion" as is sometimes found in the literature.[33] We should be cautious in concluding, however, that either of these positions is necessarily correct. The careful analysis of other laws, and especially of laws which do not focus so specifically upon the "criminal," are necessary before this question can be finally answered.

In conclusion, it is hoped that future analyses of changes within the legal structure will be able to benefit from this study by virtue of (1) the data provided and (2) the utilization of a set of concepts (innovation, dormancy, concern and negation) which have proved useful in the analysis of the vagrancy law. Such analyses should provide us with more substantial grounds for rejecting or accepting as generally valid the description of some of the processes which appear to characterize changes in the legal system.

Notes

1. Hall, J., *Theft, Law and Society* (Bobbs-Merrill, 1939). See also, Alfred R. Lindesmith, "Federal Law and Drug Addiction," *Social Problems*, Vol. 7, No. 1, 1959, p. 48.
2. See, for examples, Rose, A., "Some Suggestions for Research in the Sociology of Law," *Social Problems*, Vol. 9, No. 3, 1962, pp. 281–283, and Geis, G., "Sociology, Criminology, and Criminal Law," *Social Problems*, Vol. 7, No. 1, 1959, pp. 40–47. For a more complete listing of most of the statutes dealt with in this report the reader is referred to Burn, *The History of the Poor Laws*. Citations of English statutes should be read as follows: 3 Ed. 1. c. 1. refers to the third act of Edward the first, chapter one, etc.
3. 3 Ed. 1. c. 1.
4. 35 Ed. 1. c. 1.
5. 23 Ed. 3.
6. 25 Ed. 3 (1351).
7. Bradshaw, F., *A Social History of England*, p. 54.
8. *Ibid.*
9. *Ibid.*, p. 57.
10. Foote, C., "Vagrancy Type Law and Its Administration," *Univ. of Pennsylvania Law Review* (104), 1056, p. 615.
11. *Ibid.*
12. 34 Ed. 3 (1360).
13. 12 R. 2 (1388).
14. *Ibid.*
15. 11 H. & C. 2 (1495).
16. As evidenced for this note the expectation that "...the common gaols of every shire are likely to be greatly pestered with more numbers of prisoners than heretofore..." when the statutes were changed by the statute of 14 Ed. c. 5 (1571).
17. Bradshaw, *op. cit.*, p. 61.
18. 22 H. 8. c. 12 (1530).
19. *Ibid.*
20. *Ibid.*
21. 27 H. 8. c. 25 (1535).
22. Hall, *op. cit.*, p. 21.
23. *Ibid.*, p. 23.
24. 27 H. 8. c. 25 (1535).
25. 14 E., c. 5. (1571).
26. Earl of Halsbury, *The Laws of England* (Butterworth & Co., Bell Yard, Temple Bar, 1912), pp. 606–607.
27. Foote, *op. cit.*, p. 613. Also see in this connection, Irwin Deutscher; "The Petty Offender," *Federal Probation*, XIX, June, 1955.
28. It is on this point that the vagrancy statutes have been subject to criticism. See for example, Lacey, Forrest W., "Vagrancy and Other Crimes of Personal Condition," *Harvard Law Review* (66), p. 1203.
29. *Edwards v. California*, 314 S. 160 (1941).
30. Hall, *op. cit.*, p. XII.
31. Negation, in this instance, is most likely to come about by the repeal of the statute. More generally, however, negation may occur in several ways including the declaration of a statute as unconstitutional. This later mechanism has been used even for laws which have been "on the books" for long periods of time. Repeal is probably the most common, although not the only, procedure by which a law is negated.
32. Rheinstein, M., *Max Weber on Law in Economy and Society* (Harvard University Press, 1954).
33. Friedman, N., *Law in a Changing Society* (Berkeley and Los Angeles: University of California Press, 1959).

15 / A Control Theory of Delinquency

TRAVIS HIRSCHI

Control theories assume that delinquent acts result when an individual's bond to society is weak or broken. Since these theories embrace two highly complex concepts, the *bond* of the individual to *society*, it is not surprising that they have at one time of another formed the basis of explanations of most forms of aberrant or unusual behavior. It is also not surprising that control theories have described the elements of the bond to society in many ways, and that they have focused on a variety of units as the point of control....

ELEMENTS OF THE BOND

Attachment

In explaining conforming behavior, sociologists justly emphasize sensitivity to the opinion of others.[1] Unfortunately,... they tend to suggest that man *is* sensitive to the opinion of others and thus exclude sensitivity from their explanations of deviant behavior. In explaining deviant behavior, psychologists, in contrast, emphasize insensitivity to the opinion of others.[2] Unfortunately, they too tend to ignore variation, and, in addition, they tend to tie sensitivity inextricably to other variables, to make it part of a syndrome or "type," and thus seriously to reduce its value as an explanatory concept. The psychopath is characterized only in part by "deficient attachment to or affection for others, a failure to respond to the ordinary motivations founded in respect or regard for one's fellow";[3] he is also characterized by such things as "excessive aggressiveness," "lack of superego control," and "an infantile level of response."[4] Unfortunately, too, the behavior that psychopathy is used to explain often becomes part of the *definition* of psychopathy. As a result, in Barbara Wootton's words: "[The psychopath] is... *par excellence*, and without shame or qualification, the model of the circular process by which mental abnormality is inferred from anti-social behavior while anti-social behavior is explained by mental abnormality."[5]

The problems of diagnosis, tautology, and name-calling are avoided if the dimensions of psychopathy are treated as causally and therefore problematically interrelated, rather than as logically and therefore necessarily bound to each other. In fact, it can be argued that all of the characteristics attributed to the psychopath follow from, are effects of, his lack of attachment to others. To say that to lack attachment to others is to be free from moral restraints is to use lack of attachment to explain the guiltlessness of the psychopath, the fact that he apparently has no conscience or superego. In this view, lack of attachment to others is not merely a symptom of psychopathy, it *is* psychopathy; lack of conscience is just another way of saying the same thing; and the violation of norms is (or may be) a consequence. For that matter, given that man is an animal, "impulsivity" and "aggressiveness" can also be seen as natural consequences of freedom from moral restraints. However, since the view of man as endowed with natural propensities and capacities like other animals is peculiarly unpalatable to sociologists, we need not fall back on such a view to explain the amoral man's aggressiveness.[6] The process of becoming alienated from others often involves or is based on active interpersonal conflict. Such conflict could easily supply a reservoir of *socially derived* hostility sufficient to account for the aggressiveness of those whose attachments to others have been weakened.

Durkheim said it many years ago: "We are moral beings to the extent that we are social beings."[7] This may be interpreted to mean that we are moral beings to the extent that we have "internalized the norms" of society. But what does it mean to say that a person has internalized the norms of society? The norms of society are by definition shared by the members of society. To violate a norm is, therefore, to act contrary to the wishes and expectations of other people. If a person does not care about the wishes and expectations of other people—that is, if he is insensitive to the opinion of others—then he is to that extent not bound by the norms. He is free to deviate.

The essence of internalization of norms, conscience, or superego thus lies in the attachment of the individual to others.[8] This view has several advantages over the concept of internalization. For one, explanations of deviant behavior based on attachment do not beg the question, since the extent to which a person is attached to others can be measured independently of his deviant behavior. Furthermore, change or variation in behavior is explainable in a way that it is not when notions of internalization or superego are used. For example, the divorced man is more likely after divorce to commit a number of deviant acts, such as suicide or forgery. If we explain these acts by reference to the superego (or internal control), we are forced to say that the man "lost his conscience" when he got a divorce; and, of course, if he remarries, we have to conclude that he gets his conscience back.

This dimension of the bond to conventional society is encountered in most social control-oriented research and theory. F. Ivan Nye's "internal control" and "indirect control" refer to the same element, although we avoid the problem of explaining changes over time by locating the "conscience" in the bond to others rather than making it part of the personality.[9] Attachment to others is just one aspect of Albert J. Reiss's "personal controls"; we avoid his problems of tautological empirical *observations* by making the relationship between attachment and delinquency problematic rather than definitional.[10] Finally, Scott Briar and Irving Piliavin's "commitment" or "stake in conformity" subsumes attachment, as their discussion illustrates, although the terms they use are more closely associated with the next element to be discussed.[11]

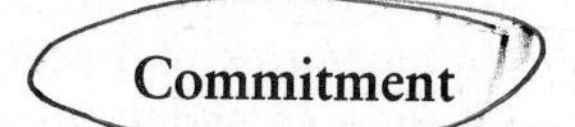

Commitment

"Of all passions, that which inclineth men least to break the laws, is fear. Nay, excepting some generous natures, it is the only thing, when there is the appearance of profit or pleasure by breaking the laws, that makes men keep them."[12] Few would deny that men on occasion obey the rules simply from fear of the consequences. This rational component in conformity we label commitment. What does it mean to say that a person is committed to conformity? In Howard S. Becker's formulation it means the following:

> First, the individual is in a position in which his decision with regard to some particular line of action has consequences for other interests and activities not necessarily [directly] related to it. Second, he has placed himself in that position by his own prior actions. A third element is present though so obvious as not to be apparent; the committed person must be aware [of these other interests] and must recognize that his decision in this case will have ramifications beyond it.[13]

The idea, then, is that the person invests time, energy, himself, in a certain line of activity—say, getting an education, building up a business, acquiring a reputation for virtue. When or whenever he considers deviant behavior, he must consider the costs of this deviant behavior, the risk he runs of losing the investment he has made in conventional behavior.

If attachment to others is the sociological counterpart of the superego or conscience, commitment is the counterpart of the ego or common sense. To the person committed to conventional lines of action, risking one to ten years in prison for a ten-dollar holdup is stupidity, because to the committed person the costs and risks obviously exceed ten dollars in value. (To the psychoanalyst, such an act exhibits failure to be governed by the "reality-principle.") In the sociological control theory, it can be and is generally assumed that the decision to commit a criminal act may well be rationally determined—that the actor's decision was not irrational given the risks and costs he faces. Of course, as Becker points out, if the actor is capable of in some sense calculating the costs of a line of action, he is also capable of calculational errors: ignorance and error return, in the control theory, as possible explanations of deviant behavior.

The concept of commitment assumes that the organization of society is such that the interest of most persons would be endangered if they were to engage in criminal acts. Most people, simply by the process of living in an organized society, acquire goods, reputations, prospects that they do not want to risk losing. These accumulations are society's insurance that they will abide by the rules. Many hypotheses about the antecedents of delinquent behavior are based on this premise. For example, Arthur L. Stinchcombe's hypothesis that "high school rebellion... occurs when future status is not clearly related to present performance"[14] suggests that one is committed to conformity not only by what one has but also by what one hoped to obtain. Thus "ambition" and/or "aspiration" play an important role in producing conformity. The person becomes committed to a conventional line of action, and he is therefore committed to conformity.

Most lines of action in a society are of course conventional. The clearest examples are educational and occupational careers. Actions thought to jeopardize one's chances in these areas are presumably avoided. Interestingly enough, even nonconventional commitments may operate to produce conventional conformity. We are told, at least, that boys aspiring to careers in the rackets or professional thievery are judged by their "honesty" and "reliability"—traits traditionally in demand among seekers of office boys.[15]

Involvement

Many persons undoubtedly owe a life of virtue to a lack of opportunity to do otherwise. Time and energy are inherently limited: "Not that I would not, if I could, be both handsome and fat and well dressed, and a great athlete, and make a million a year, be a wit, a bon vivant, and a lady killer, as well as a philosopher, a philanthropist, a statesman, warrior, and African explorer, as well as a 'tone-poet' and saint. But the thing is simply impossible."[16] The things that William James here says he would like to be or do are all, I suppose, within the realm of conventionality, but if he were to include illicit actions he would still have to eliminate some of them as simply impossible.

Involvement or engrossment in conventional activities is thus often part of a control theory. The assumption, widely shared, is that a person may be simply too busy doing conventional things to find time to engage in deviant behavior. The person involved in conventional activities is tied to appointments, deadlines, working hours, plans, and the like, so the opportunity to commit deviant acts rarely arises. To the extent that he is engrossed in conventional activities, he cannot even think about deviant acts, let alone act out his inclinations.[17]

This line of reasoning is responsible for the stress placed on recreational facilities in many programs to reduce delinquency, for much of the concern with the high school dropout, and for the idea that boys should be drafted into the army to keep them out of trouble. So obvious and persuasive is the idea that involvement in conventional activities is a major deterrent to delinquency that it was accepted even by Sutherland: "In the general area of juvenile delinquency it is probable that the most significant difference between juveniles who engage in delinquency and those who do not is that the latter are provided abundant opportunities of a conventional type for satisfying their recreational interests, while the former lack those opportunities or facilities."[18]

The view that "idle hands are the devil's workshop" has received more sophisticated treatment in recent sociological writings on delinquency. David Matza and Gresham M. Sykes, for example, suggest that delinquents have the values of a leisure class, the same values ascribed by Veblen to *the* leisure class: a search for kicks, disdain of work, a desire for the big score, and acceptance of aggressive toughness as proof of masculinity.[19] Matza and Sykes explain delinquency by reference to this system of values, but they note that adolescents at all class levels are "to some extent" members of a leisure class, that they "move in a limbo between earlier parental domination and future integration with the social structure through the bonds of work and marriage."[20] In the end, then, the leisure of the adolescent produces a set of values, which, in turn, leads to delinquency.

Belief

Unlike the cultural deviance theory, the control theory assumes the existence of a common value system within the society or group whose norms are being violated. If the deviant is committed to a value system different from that of conventional society, there is, within the context of the theory, nothing to explain. The question is, "Why does a man violate the rules in which he believes?" It is not, "Why do men differ in their beliefs about what constitutes good and desirable conduct?" The person is assumed to have been socialized (perhaps imperfectly) into the group whose rules he is violating; deviance is not a question of one group imposing its rules on the members of another group. In other words, we not only assume the deviant *has* believed the rules, we assume he believes the rules even as he violates them.

How can a person believe it is wrong to steal at the same time he is stealing? In the strain theory, this is not a difficult problem. (In fact, the strain theory was devised specifically to deal with this question.) The motivation to deviance adduced by the strain theorist is so strong that we can well understand the deviant act even assuming the deviator believes strongly that it is wrong.[21] However, given the control theory's assumptions about motivation, if both the deviant and the nondeviant believe the deviant act is wrong, how do we account for the fact that one commits it and the other does not?

Control theories have taken two approaches to this problem. In one approach, beliefs are treated as mere words that mean little or nothing if the other forms of control are missing. "Semantic dementia," the dissociation between rational faculties and emotional control which is said to be characteristic of the psychopath, illustrates this way of handling the problem.[22] In short, beliefs, at least insofar as they are expressed in words, drop out of the picture; since they do not differentiate between deviants and nondeviants, they are in the same class as "language" or any other characteristic common to all members of the group. Since they represent no real obstacle to the commission of delinquent acts, nothing need be said about how they are handled by those committing such acts. The control theories that do not mention beliefs (or values), and many do not, may be assumed to take this approach to the problem.

The second approach argues that the deviant rationalizes his behavior so that he can at once violate the rule and maintain his belief in it. Donald R. Cressey had advanced this argument with respect to embezzlement,[23] and Sykes and Matza have advanced it with respect to delinquency.[24] In both Cressey's and Sykes and Matza's treatments, these rationalizations (Cressey calls them "verbalizations," Sykes and Matza term them "techniques of neutralization") occur prior to the commission of the deviant act. If the neutralization is successful, the person is free to commit the act(s) in question. Both in Cressey and in Sykes and Matza, the strain that prompts the effort at neutralization also provides the motive force that results in the subsequent deviant act. Their theories are thus, in this sense, strain theories. Neutralization is difficult to handle within the context of a theory that adheres closely to control theory assumptions, because in the control theory there is no special motivational force to account for the neutralization. This difficulty is especially noticeable in Matza's later treatment of this topic, where the motivational component, the "will to delinquency," appears *after* the moral vacuum has been created by the techniques of neutralization.[25] The question thus becomes: Why neutralize?

In attempting to solve a strain-theory problem with control-theory tools, the control theorist is thus led into a trap. He cannot answer the crucial question. The concept of neutralization assumes the existence of moral obstacles to the commission of deviant acts. In order plausibly to account for a deviant act, it is necessary to generate motivation to deviance that is at least equivalent in force to the resistance provided by these moral obstacles. However, if the moral obstacles are removed, neutralization and special motivation are no longer required. We therefore follow the implicit logic of control theory and remove these moral obstacles by hypothesis. Many persons do not have an attitude of respect toward the rules of society; many persons feel no moral obligation to conform regardless of personal advantage. Insofar as the values and beliefs of these persons are consistent with their feelings, and there should be a tendency toward consistency, neutralization is unnecessary; it has already occurred.

Does this merely push the question back a step and at the same time produce conflict with the assumption of a common value system? I think not. In the first place, we do not assume, as does Cressey, that neutralization occurs in order to make a specific criminal act possible.[26] We do not assume, as do Sykes and Matza, that neutralization occurs to make many delinquent acts possible. We do not assume, in other words, that the person constructs a system of rationalizations in order to justify commission of acts he *wants* to commit. We assume, in contrast, that the beliefs that free a man to commit deviant acts are *unmotivated* in the sense that he does not construct or adopt them in order to facilitate the attainment of illicit ends. In the second place, we do not assume, as does Matza, that "delinquents concur in the conventional assessment of delinquency."[27] We assume, in contrast, that there is *variation* in the extent to which people believe they should obey the rules of society, and, furthermore, that the less a person believes he should obey the rules, the more likely he is to violate them.[28]

In chronological order, then, a person's beliefs in the moral validity or norms are, for no teleological reason, weakened. The probability that he will commit delinquent acts is therefore increased. When and if he commits a delinquent act, we may justifiably use the weakness of his beliefs in explaining it, but no special motivation is required to explain either the weakness of his beliefs or, perhaps, his delinquent act.

The keystone of this argument is of course the assumption that there is variation in belief in the moral validity of social rules. This assumption is amenable to direct empirical test and can thus survive at least until its first confrontation with data. For the present, we must return to the idea of a common value system with which this section was begun.

The idea of a common (or perhaps better, a single) value system is consistent with the fact, or presumption, of variation in the strength of moral beliefs. We have not suggested that delinquency is based on beliefs counter to conventional morality; we have not suggested that delinquents do not believe delinquent acts are wrong. They may well believe these acts are wrong, but the meaning and efficacy of such beliefs are contingent on other beliefs and, indeed, on the strength of other ties to the conventional order.[29]

Notes

1. Books have been written on the increasing importance of interpersonal sensitivity in modern life. According to this view, controls from within have become less important than controls from without in *producing* conformity. Whether or not this observation is true as a description of historical trends, it is true that interpersonal sensitivity has become more important in *explaining* conformity. Although logically it should also have become more important in explaining nonconformity, the opposite has been the case, once again showing that Cohen's observation that an explanation of conformity should be an explanation of deviance cannot be translated as "an explanation of conformity has to be an explanation of deviance." For the view that interpersonal sensitivity currently plays a greater role than formerly in producing conformity, see William J. Goode, "Norm Commitment and Conformity to Role-Status Obligations," *American Journal of Sociology*, LXVI (1960), 246–258. And, of course, also see David Riesman, Nathan Glazer, and Rouel Denney, *The Lonely Crowd* (Garden City, New York: Doubleday, 1950), especially Part I.

2. The literature on psychopathy is voluminous. See William McCord and Joan McCord, *The Psychopath* (Princeton: D. Van Nostrand, 1964).

3. John M. Martin and Joseph P. Fitzpatrick, *Delinquent Behavior* (New York: Random House, 1964), p. 130.

4. *Ibid.* For additional properties of the psychopath, see McCord and McCord, *The Psychopath*, pp. 1–22.

5. Barbara Wootton, *Social Science and Social Pathology* (New York: Macmillan, 1959), p. 250.

6. "The logical untenability [of the position that there are forces in man 'resistant to socialization'] was ably demonstrated by Parsons over 30 years ago, and it is widely recognized that the position is empirically unsound because it assumes [!] some universal biological drive system distinctly separate from socialization and social context—a basic and intransigent human nature" (Judith Blake and Kingsley Davis, "Norms, Values, and Sanctions," *Handbook of Modern Sociology*, ed. Robert E. L. Faris [Chicago: Rand McNally, 1964], p. 471).

7. Emile Durkheim, *Moral Education*, trans. Everett K. Wilson and Herman Schnurer (New York: The Free Press, 1961), p. 64.

8. Although attachment alone does not exhaust the meaning of internalization, attachments and beliefs combined would appear to leave only a small residue of "internal control" not susceptible in principle to direct measurement.

9. F. Ivan Nye, *Family Relationships and Delinquent Behavior* (New York: Wiley, 1958), pp. 5–7.

10. Albert J. Reiss, Jr., "Delinquency as the Failure of Personal and Social Controls," *American Sociological Review*, XVI (1951), 196–207. For example, "Our observations show . . . that delinquent recidivists are less often persons with mature ego ideals or nondelinquent social roles" (p. 204).

11. Scott Briar and Irving Piliavin, "Delinquency, Situational Inducements, and Commitment to Conformity," *Social Problems*, XIII (1965), 41–42. The concept "stake in conformity" was introduced by Jackson Toby in his "Social Disorganization and Stake in Conformity: Complementary Factors in the Predatory Behavior of Hoodlums," *Journal of Criminal Law, Criminology and Police Science*, XLVIII (1957), 12–17. See also his "Hoodlum or Business Man: An American Dilemma," *The Jews*, ed. Marshall Sklare (New York: The Free Press, 1958), pp. 542–550. Throughout the text, I occasionally use "stake in conformity" in speaking in general of the strength of the bond to conventional society. So used, the concept is somewhat broader than is true for either Toby or Briar and Piliavin, where the concept is roughly equivalent to what is here called "commitment."

12. Thomas Hobbes, *Leviathan* (Oxford: Basil Blackwell, 1957), p. 195.

13. Howard S. Becker, "Notes on the Concept of Commitment," *American Journal of Sociology*, LXVI (1960), 35–36.

14. Arthur L. Stinchcombe, *Rebellion in a High School* (Chicago: Quadrangle, 1964), p. 5.

15. Richard A. Cloward and Lloyd E. Ohlin, *Delinquency and Opportunity* (New York: The Free Press, 1960), p. 147, quoting Edwin H. Sutherland, ed., *The Professional Thief* (Chicago: University of Chicago Press, 1937), pp. 211–213.

16. William James, *Psychology* (Cleveland: World Publishing Co., 1948), p. 186.

17. Few activities appear to be so engrossing that they rule out contemplation of alternative lines of behavior, at least if estimates of the amount of time men spend plotting sexual deviations have any validity.

18. *The Sutherland Papers*, ed. Albert K. Cohen et al. (Bloomington: Indiana University Press, 1956), p. 37.

19. David Matza and Gresham M. Sykes, "Juvenile Delinquency and Subterranean Values," *American Sociological Review*, XXVI (1961), 712–719.

20. *Ibid.*, p.718.

21. The starving man stealing the loaf of bread is the image evoked by most strain theories. In this image, the starving man's belief in the wrongness of his act is clearly not something that must be explained away. It can be assumed to be present without causing embarrassment to the explanation.

22. McCord and McCord, *The Psychopath*, pp. 12–15.

23. Donald R. Cressey, *Other People's Money* (New York: The Free Press, 1953).

24. Gresham M. Sykes and David Matza, "Techniques of Neutralization: A Theory of Delinquency," *American Sociological Review*, XXII (1957), 664–670.

25. David Matza, *Delinquency and Drift* (New York: Wiley, 1964), pp. 181–191.

26. In asserting that Cressey's assumption is invalid with respect to delinquency, I do not wish to suggest that it is invalid for the question of embezzlement, where the problem faced by the deviator is fairly specific and he can reasonably be assumed to be an upstanding citizen.

(Although even here the fact that the embezzler's nonsharable financial problem often results from some sort of hanky-panky suggests that "verbalizations" may be less necessary than might otherwise be assumed.)

27. *Delinquency and Drift*, p. 43.

28. This assumption is not, I think, contradicted by the evidence presented by Matza against the existence of a delinquent subculture. In comparing the attitudes and actions of delinquents with the picture painted by delinquent subculture theorists, Matza emphasizes—and perhaps exaggerates—the extent to which delinquents are tied to the conventional order. In implicitly comparing delinquents with a supermoral man, I emphasize—and perhaps exaggerate—the extent to which they are not tied to the conventional order.

29. The position taken here is therefore somewhere between the "semantic dementia" and the "neutralization" positions. Assuming variation, the delinquent is, at the extremes, freer than the neutralization argument assumes. Although the possibility of wide discrepancy between what the delinquent professes and what he practices still exists, it is presumably much rarer than is suggested by studies of articulate "psychopaths."

16 / The Socially Bounded Decision Making of Persistent Property Offenders

NEAL SHOVER
DAVID HONAKER

The 1970s were marked by the eclipse of labeling theory as the dominant individual-level criminological theory and by the reappearance of interest in approaches originally advanced by classical theorists. Economists and cognitive psychologists along with many in the criminological mainstream advanced an interpretation of crime as *choice*, offering models of criminal decision making grounded in the assumption that the decision to commit a criminal act springs from the offender's assessment of its anticipated net utilities (e.g., Becker 1968; Heinke 1978; Carroll 1978; Reynolds 1985). This movement in favor of rational-choice approaches to crime spurred empirical investigation of problems that previously were limited primarily to studies of the death penalty and its impact on the homicide rate.

Early investigations of a rational choice interpretation of crime reported a weak but persistent relationship between the certainty of punishment and rates of serious property crimes (Blumstein, Cohen, and Nagin 1978). It was recognized, however, that an understanding of criminal decision making also requires knowledge about individual perceptions and beliefs about legal threats and other constraints on decision making (e.g., Manski 1978). Investigators moved on two main fronts to meet this need. Some used survey methods to explore differential involvement in minor forms of deviance in samples of restricted age ranges, typically high school and college students (e.g., Waldo and Chiricos 1972). Alternatively they examined the link between risk assessments and criminal participation in samples more representative of the general population (e.g., Tittle 1980). Serious shortcomings of these studies are that most either ignore the potential rewards of crime entirely or they fail to examine its emotional and interpersonal utilities. Still other investigators turned attention to serious criminal offenders and began expanding the narrow existing knowledge base (e.g., Claster 1967), chiefly through the use of cross sectional research designs and survey methods.

For more than a decade now, investigators have studied offenders' attitudes toward legitimate and criminal pursuits, their perceptions of and beliefs about the risks of criminal behavior, and their estimates of the payoffs from conventional and criminal pursuits (e.g., Petersilia et al. 1978; Peterson & Braiker 1980). These studies raise serious questions about the fit between offenders' calculus and a priori assumptions about their utilities and criminal decision making. One investigation of 589 incarcerated property offenders concluded, for example, that the subjects apparently do not utilize "a sensible cost-benefit analysis" when weighing the utilities of crime (Figgie 1988, p. 25). They substantially underestimate the risk of arrest for most crimes, routinely overestimate the monetary benefit they expect, and seem to have "grossly inaccurate perceptions of the costs and benefits associated with property crime" (Figgie 1988, p. 81). Unfortunately, both design and conceptual problems undermine confidence in the findings of this and similar studies. Cross sectional survey methods, for example, are poorly suited for examining dynamic decision-making *processes*. Most such studies also fail to examine offenders' estimates of the likely payoffs from noncriminal alternatives or their non-monetary utilities, such as emotional satisfaction (Katz 1988).

As newer, empirically-based models of criminal decision making have been developed (e.g., Clarke and Cornish 1985; Cornish and Clarke 1986), a growing number of investigators are using ethnographic methods to examine the offender's criminal calculus, often in real or simulated natural settings (e.g., Carrol 1982; Carrol and Weaver 1986). The research reported here continues this line of ethnographic inquiry by using retrospective interviews to examine criminal decision making by serious and persistent property offenders. The focus of our attention is the decision to commit a crime rather than the target-selection decision that has received substantial attention elsewhere (e.g., Scar 1973; Repetto 1974; Maguire 1982; Bennett and Wright 1984a; Rengert and Wasilchick 1985; Cromwell, Olson, and Avary 1991). The first objective is to examine how closely the decision to commit crime conforms to a classical rational choice model in which decisions assumedly are based largely on an assessment of potential returns from alternative courses of action and the risk of legal sanctions. A second objective is to examine the influence of the lifestyle pursued by many persistent property offenders on the salience of their utilities and the risks they assess in criminal decision making.

METHODS AND MATERIALS

The materials for analysis were collected during 1987–1988 as part of a larger study of crime desistance. From the population of all men incarcerated in Tennessee state prisons during 1987 we selected a sample of recidivists with a demonstrated preference for property crimes who were also nearing release from confinement. To select the sample, members of the research team first examined Tennessee Board of Paroles records to identify offenders incarcerated in Tennessee state prisons whose parole was imminent. We then used Department of Corrections records to cull the list of all but those (1) with at least one prior felony confinement, and (2) whose previous or current confinement was for serious property crime. Next the researchers visited prisons, primarily those located in the mid- and eastern areas of the state, and explained the study to and requested research participation from potential subjects. After meeting individually with approximately 75 inmates we reached our sample size objective of 60 subjects. Fifty-eight members of the sample had served at least one prior prison sentence and the remaining two had served one or more jail sentences. They had served time primarily for armed robbery, burglary, or theft. By limiting the sample as outlined we sought to approximate a population of career criminals, a type of offender that has received substantial attention from scholars and policy makers (Petersilia 1980; Blumstein et al. 1988). Subjects ranged from 23 to 70 years of age, with an average age of 34.1 years. In addition to the sample's adult criminal and incarceration profile, 47 percent (n = 28) of the men had also served one or more terms of juvenile confinement. Every member of the sample was interviewed approximately one month prior to release from prison. All data used in the present study, however, were collected in post-release interviews with the men.

Seven to 10 months after their release from prison we successfully traced, contacted, and interviewed 46 of the original sample of 60 men (76.7 percent). (In addition, we established contact with one subject who declined our request for an interview, and with close relatives of another who failed to respond to repeated requests that he contact us.) Semi-structured ethnographic interviews were the principal data-collection technique. The interview included questions about the former prisoners' activities and living arrangements following release, self-report items measuring postrelease criminal participation, and questions about the context of reinvolvement in crime. They were paid $100 for completing the interviews, all of which were audiotape recorded and transcribed for subsequent analysis. Fourteen subjects were in jail or prison again when interviewed, but most were interviewed in their former or newly established home communities.

Part of the interviews produced detailed descriptions of the most recent, easily recalled property crime that each subject had committed in the free world prior to the interview. They described either crimes they had committed prior to incarceration or, for those subjects who were locked up when interviewed, their return to jail or prison. Our objective was to gain through the repeat offender's eyes an understanding of the decision to commit specific criminal acts. We asked our subjects to focus their recollection on how the decision was made, and to provide a detailed account of the potential risks and rewards they assessed while doing so. The result was 40 usable descriptions of crimes and attempted crimes, which included 15 burglaries, 12 armed robberies, 5 grand larcenies, 4 unarmed robberies, 2 auto thefts, 1 series of check forgeries, and 1 case of receiving and concealing stolen property. Transcripts of the interviews were analyzed using *The Ethnograph,* a software package for use on text-based data (Seidel, Kjolseth, and Seymour 1988). Use of this software enabled us to code and to retrieve for analysis segments of interview text.

FINDINGS

Analysis reveals the most striking aspect of the subjects' decision making for the crimes they described is that a majority gave little or no thought to the possibility of arrest and confinement. Of 34 subjects who were asked specifically whether they considered the risk of arrest or who spontaneously indicated whether they did so, 21 (62 percent) said they did not. The comments of two subjects are typical:

Q: Did you think about . . . getting caught?
A: No.
Q: [H]ow did you manage to put that out of your mind?
A: [It] never did come into it.
Q: Never did come into it?
A: Never did, you know. It didn't bother me.

Q: Were you thinking about bad things that might happen to you?
A: None whatsoever.
Q: No?
A: I wasn't worried about getting caught or anything, you know. I was a positive thinker through everything, you know. I didn't have no negative thoughts about it whatsoever.

The 13 remaining subjects (38%) acknowledged they gave some thought to the possibility of arrest but most said they managed to dismiss it easily and to carry through with their plans:

Q: Did you worry much about getting caught? On a scale of one to ten, how would you rank your degree of worry that day?
A: [T]he worry was probably a one. You know what I mean? The worry was probably one. I didn't think about the consequences, you know. I know it's stupidity, but it didn't—that [I] might go to jail, I mean—it crossed my mind but it didn't make much difference.

Q: As you thought about doing that [armed robbery], were there things that you were worried about?
A: Well, the only thing that I was worried about was— . . . getting arrested didn't even cross my mind—just worrying about getting killed is the only thing, you know, getting shot. That's the only thing. . . . But, you know, . . . you'd have to be really crazy not to think about that . . . you could possibly get in trouble. It crossed my mind, but I didn't worry about it all that much.

Some members of our sample said they managed deliberately and consciously to put out of mind all thoughts of possible arrest:

When I went out to steal, I didn't think about the negative things. 'Cause if you think negative, negative things are going to happen. And that's the way I looked at it.... I done it just like it was a job or something. Go out and do it, don't think about getting caught, 'cause that would make you jumpy, edgy, nervous. If you looked like you were doing something wrong, then something wrong is 'gonna happen to you.... You just, you just put [the thought of arrest] out of your mind, you know.

Q: Did you think about [the possibility of getting caught] very much that night?
A: I didn't think about it that much, you know.... [I]t comes but, you know, you can wipe it away.
Q: How do you wipe it away?
A: You just blank it out. You blank it out.

Another subject said simply that "I try to put that [thought of arrest] the farthest thing from my mind that I can."

Many subjects attribute their ability to ignore or to dismiss all thought of possible arrest to a state of intoxication or drug-altered consciousness:

Q: You didn't think about going to prison?
A: Never did. I guess it was all that alcohol and stuff, and drugs.... The day I pulled that robbery?—no. I was so high I didn't think about nothing.

Another subject told us that he had been drinking the entire day that he committed the crime and, by the time it occurred, he was in "nightlight city."

While it is clear that the formal risks of crime were not considered carefully by most members of the sample, equally striking is the finding that very few thought about or assessed legitimate alternatives before opting to commit a criminal act. Of 22 subjects who were asked specifically whether they had done so, 16 indicated that they gave no thought whatsoever to legitimate alternatives. The six subjects who did either ignored or quickly dismissed them as inapplicable, given their immediate circumstances.

We recognize the methodological shortcomings of the descriptions of criminal decision making and behavior used as data for this study. Since the subjects were questioned in detail only about specific offenses they could remember well, the sample of descriptions may not be representative of the range of crimes they committed. By definition, they are memorable ones. Moreover, the recall period for these crimes ranged from one to 15 years, raising the possibility of errors caused by selective recall. Whether or not this could have produced systematic bias in the data is unknown. We cannot rule out the possibility that past crimes are remembered as being less rational than they actually were at the time of commission. Such a tendency could account in part for our interpretation of the data and our description of their style of decision making. The fact that we limited the sample to recidivists means also that we cannot determine how much their behavior may reflect either innate differences (Gottfredson and Hirschi 1990) or experiential effects, i.e., the effects of past success in committing crime and avoiding arrest (Nagin and Paternoster 1991). It could be argued that the behavior of our subjects, precisely because they had demonstrated a willingness to commit property crimes and had done so in the past, limits the external validity of their reports. Given sample selection criteria and these potential data problems, generalizations beyond the study population must be made with caution.

This said, we believe that the remarkable similarity between our findings and the picture of criminal decision making reported by others who have studied serious property offenders strengthens their credibility significantly. A study of 83 imprisoned burglars revealed that 49 percent did not think about the chances of getting caught for any particular offense during their last period of offending. While 37 percent of them did think about it, most thought there was little or no chance it would happen (Bennett and Wright 1984a, Table A14). Interviews with 113 men convicted of robbery or an offense related to robbery revealed that "over 60 percent... said they had not even thought about getting caught." Another 17 percent said that they had thought about the possibility but "did not believe it to be a problem" (Feeney 1986, p. 59–60). Analysis of prison interviews with 77 robbers and 45 burglars likewise revealed their "general obliviousness toward the consequences [of their crimes] and no thought of being caught" (Walsh 1986, p. 157). In sum, our findings along with the findings from other studies suggest strongly that many serious property offenders seem to be remarkably casual in weighing the formal risks of criminal participation. As one of our subjects put it, "you think about going to prison about like you think about dying, you know." The impact of alcohol and drug use in diminishing concern with possible penalties also has been reported by many others (e.g., Bennett and Wright 1984b; Cromwell, Olson, and Avary 1991).

If the potential legal consequences of crime do not figure prominently in crime commission decision making by persistent thieves, what *do* they think about when choosing to commit crime? Walsh (1980; 1986) shows that typically they focus their thoughts on the money that committing a crime may yield and the good times they expect to have with it when the crime is behind them. Carroll's data (1982) likewise indicate that the amount of gain offenders expect to receive is "the most important dimension" in their decision making, while the certainty of punishment is the least important of the four dimensions on which his subjects assessed crime opportunities. Our findings are consistent with these reports; our subjects said that they focused on the expected gains from their crimes:

> I didn't think about nothing but what I was going to do when I got that money, how I was going to spend it, what I was going to do with it, you know.

> See, you're not thinking about those things [possibility of being arrested]. You're thinking about that big paycheck at the end of thirty to forty-five minutes worth of work.

> [A]t the time [that you commit crime], you throw all your instincts out the window.... Because you're just thinking about money, and money only. That's all that's on your mind, because you want that money. And you throw, you block everything off until you get the money.

Although confidence in our findings is bolstered by the number of points on which they are similar to reports by others who have explored crime commission decision making, they do paint a picture of decision making that is different from what is known about the way at least some offenders make target selection decisions. Investigators (e.g., Cromwell, Olson, and Avary 1991) have shown that target decisions approximate simple commonsense conceptions of rational behavior (Shover 1991). A resolution of the problem presented by these contradictory findings is suggested by others (Cromwell, Olson, and Avary 1991) and is also apparent in our data: Criminal participation often results from a *sequence* of experientially and analytically discrete decisions, all of potentially varying degrees of intentional rationality. Thus, once a *motivational* crime commission decision has been made, offenders may move quickly to selecting, or to exploiting, an apparently suitable target. At this stage of the criminal participation process, offenders are preoccupied with the *technical* challenge of avoiding failure at what now is seen as a *practical task*. As one subject put it, "you don't think about getting caught, you think about how in hell you're going to do it *not* to get caught, you know." His comments were echoed by another man: "The only thing you're thinking about is looking and acting and trying *not* to get caught." Last, consider the comments of a third subject: "I wasn't afraid of getting caught, but I was cautious, you know. Like I said, I was thinking only in the way to prevent me from getting caught." Just as bricklayers do not visualize graphically or deliberate over the bodily carnage that could follow from a collapsed scaffold *once there is a job to be done,* many thieves apparently do not dwell at length on the likelihood of arrest or on the pains of imprisonment when proceeding to search out or exploit suitable criminal opportunities.

The accumulated evidence on crime commission decision making by persistent offenders is substantial and persuasive: the rationality they employ is limited or bounded severely (e.g., Carroll 1982; Cromwell, Olson, and Avary 1991). While unsuccessful persistent offenders may calculate potential benefits and costs before committing criminal acts, they apparently do so differently or weigh utilities differently than as sketched in a priori decision-making models. As Walsh (1980, p. 141) suggests, offenders' "definitions of costs and rewards seem to be at variance with society's estimates of them." This does not mean their decision making is *irrational,* but it does point to the difficulties of understanding it and then refining theoretical models of the process. Our objective in the remainder of this paper is an improved understanding of criminal decision making based on analysis of the socially anchored purposes, utilities, and risks of the acts that offenders commit. Put differently, we explore the contextual origins of their bounded rationality.

LIFESTYLE, UTILITIES, AND RISK

It is instructive to examine the decision making of persistent property offenders in context of the lifestyle that is characteristic of many in their ranks: *life as party*. The hallmark of life as party is the enjoyment of "good times" with minimal concern for the obligations and commitments that are external to the person's immediate social setting. It is a lifestyle distinguished in many cases by two repetitively cyclical phases and correspondingly distinctive approaches to crime. When offenders' efforts to maintain the lifestyle (i.e., their party pursuits) are largely successful, crimes are committed in order to sustain circumstances or a pattern of activities they experience as pleasurable. As Walsh (1986, p. 15) puts it, crimes committed under these circumstances are "part of a continuing satisfactory way of life." By contrast, when offenders are less successful at party pursuits, their crimes are committed in order to avoid circumstances experienced as threatening, unpleasant, or precarious. Corresponding to each of these two phases of party pursuits is a distinctive set of utilities and stance toward legal risk.

Life as Party

Survey and ethnographic studies alike show that persistent property offenders spend much of their criminal gains on alcohol and other drugs (Petersilia et al. 1978; Maguire 1982; Gibbs and Shelley 1982; Figgie 1988; Cromwell, Olson, and Avary 1991). The proceeds of their crimes, as Walsh has noted (1986, p. 72), "typically [are] used for personal, non-essential consumption (e.g., 'nights out'), rather than, for example, to be given to family or used for basic needs." Thieves spend much of their leisure hours enjoying good times. Our subjects were no different in this regard. For example,

> I smoked an ounce of pot in a day, a day and a half. Every other day I had to go buy a bag of pot, at the least. And sometimes I've went two or three days in a row.... And there was never a day went by that I didn't [drink] a case, case and a half of beer. And [I] did a 'script of pills every two days.

While much of their money is consumed by the high cost of drugs, a portion may be used for ostentatious enjoyment and display of luxury items and activities that probably would be unattainable on the returns from blue-collar employment:

> [I]t was all just, it was all just a big money thing to me at the time, you know. Really, what it was was impressing everybody, you know. "Here Floyd is, and he's never had nothing in his life, and now look at him: he's driving new cars, and wearing jewelry," you know.

Life as party is enjoyed in the company of others. Typically it includes shared consumption of alcohol or other drugs in bars and lounges, on street corners, or while cruising in automobiles. In these venues, party pursuers celebrate and affirm values of spontaneity, autonomy, independence, and resourcefulness. Spontaneity means that rationality and long-range planning are eschewed in favor of enjoying the moment and permitting the day's activities and pleasures to develop in an unconstrained fashion. This may mean, for example, getting up late, usually after a night of partying, and then setting out to contact and enjoy the company of friends and associates who are known to be predisposed to partying:

I got up around about eight-thirty that morning....

Q: Eight-thirty? Was that the usual time that you got up?

A: Yeah, if I didn't have a hangover from the night before....

Q: What kind of drugs were you doing then?

A: I was doing... Percadans, Dilauds, taking Valiums, drinking.... [A]nyway, I got up that morning about eight-thirty, took me a bath, put on some clothes and... decided to walk [over to his mother's home]. [T]his particular day,... my nephew was over [there].... We was just sitting in the yard and talking and drinking beer, you know.... It was me, him, and my sister. We was sitting out there in the yard talking. And this guy that we know,... he came up, he pulled up. So my nephew got in the car with him and they left. So, you know, I was sitting there talking to my sister.... And then, in the meantime, while we was talking, they come back, about thirty minutes later with a case of beer, some marijuana and everything,... and there was another one of my nephews in the car with them. So me, two of my sisters, and two of my nephews, we got in the car with this guy here and we just went riding. So we went to Hadley Park and... we stayed out there. There were so many people out there, they were parked on the grass and things, and the vice squad come and run everybody away. So when they done that, we left.... So we went back out [toward his mother's home] but instead of going over to my mother's house we went to this little joint [tavern]. Now we're steady drinking and smoking weed all during this day. So when we get there, we park and get out and see a few friends. We [were] talking and getting high, you know, blowing each other a shotgun [sharing marijuana].

Enjoyment of party pursuits in group context is enhanced through the collective emphasis on personal autonomy. Because it is understood by all that participants are free to leave if they no longer enjoy or do not support group activities, the continuing presence of each participant affirms for the remainder the pleasures of the lifestyle. Uncoerced participation thus reinforces the shared assumption that group activities are appropriate and enjoyable. The behavioral result of the emphasis on autonomy is acceptance of or acquiescence in group decisions and activities.

Party pursuits also appeal to offenders because they permit conspicuous display of independence (Persson 1981). This generally means avoidance of the world of routine work and freedom from being "under someone's thumb." It also may include being free to avoid or to escape from restrictive routines:

I just wanted to be doing something. Instead of being at home, or something like that. I wanted to be running, I wanted to be going to clubs, and picking up

> women, and shooting pool. And I liked to go to [a nearby resort community] and just drive around over there. A lot of things like that.... I was drinking two pints or more a day.... I was doing Valiums and I was doing Demerol.... I didn't want to work.

The proper pursuit and enjoyment of life as party is expensive, due largely to the costs of drugs. As one of our subjects remarked: "We was doing a lot of cocaine, so cash didn't last long, you know. If we made $3,000, two thousand of it almost instantly went for cocaine." Some party pursuers must meet other expenses as well if the lifestyle is to be maintained:

> Believe it or not, I was spending [$700] a day.
> Q: On what?
> A: Pot, alcohol, women, gas, motel rooms, food.
> Q: You were living in hotels, motels?
> A: Yeah, a lot of times, I was. I'd take a woman to a motel. I bought a lot of clothes. I used to like to dress pretty nicely, I'd buy suits.

Party pursuits require continuous infusions of money, and no single method of generating funds allows enjoyment of it for more than a few days. Consequently, the emphasis on spontaneity, autonomy, and independence is matched by the importance attached to financial resourcefulness. This is evidenced by the ability to sustain the lifestyle over a period of time. Doing so earns for offenders a measure of respect from peers for their demonstrated ability to "get over." It translates into "self-esteem... as a folk hero beating the bureaucratic system of routinized dependence" (Walsh 1986, p. 16). The value of and respect for those who demonstrate resourcefulness means that criminal acts, as a means of sustaining life as party, generally are not condemned by the offender's peers.

The risks of employing criminal solutions to the need for funds are approached blithely but confidently in the same spontaneous and playful manner as are the rewards of life as party. In fact, avoidance of careful and detailed planning is a way of demonstrating possession of valued personal qualities and commitment to the lifestyle. Combined with the twin assumptions that peers have chosen freely and that one should not interfere with their autonomy, avoidance of rational planning finds expression in a reluctance to suggest that peers should weigh carefully the possible consequences of whatever they choose to do. Thus, the interaction that precedes criminal incidents is distinguished by circumspection and the use of linguistic devices that relegate risk and fear to the background of attention. The act of stealing, for example, is referred to obliquely but knowingly as "doing something" or as "making money":

> [After a day of partying,] I [got] to talking about making some money, because I didn't have no money. This guy that we were riding with, he had all the money.... So me and him and my nephew, we get together, talking about making some money. This guy tells me, he said, "man, I know where there's a good place at."

Q: Okay, so you suggested you all go somewhere and rob?
A: Yeah, "make some"—well, we called it "making money."

Q: Okay. So, then you and this fellow met up in the bar.... Tell me about the conversation?
A: Well, there wasn't much of a conversation to it, really.... I asked him if he was ready to go, if he wanted to go do something, you know. And he knew what I meant. He wanted to go make some money somehow, any way it took.

To the external observer, inattention to risk at the moment when it would seem most appropriate may seem to border on irrationality. For the offender engaged in party pursuits, however, it is but one aspect of behaviors that are rational in other respects. It opens up opportunities to enjoy life as party and to demonstrate commitment to values shared by peers. Resourcefulness and disdain for conventional rationality affirm individual character and style, both of which are important in the world of party pursuits (Goffman 1967).

Party Pursuits and Eroding Resources

Paradoxically, the pursuit of life as party can be appreciated and enjoyed to the fullest extent only if participants moderate their involvement in it while maintaining identities and routines in the straight world. Doing so maintains "escape value" but it also requires an uncommon measure of discipline and forbearance. The fact is that extended and enthusiastic enjoyment of life as party threatens constantly to deplete irrevocably the resources needed to sustain measured enjoyment of its pleasures. Three aspects of the life-as-party lifestyle can contribute to this end.

First, some offenders become ensnared increasingly by the chemical substances and drug using routines that are common there. In doing so, the meaning of drug consumption changes:

> See, I was doing drugs every day. It just wasn't every other day, it was to the point that, after the first few months doing drugs, I would have to do "X amount" of drugs, say, just for instance, just to feel like I do now. Which is normal.

Once the party pursuer's physical or psychological tolerance increases significantly, drugs are consumed not for the high they once produced but instead to maintain a sense of normality by avoiding sickness or withdrawal.

Second, party pursuits erode legitimate fiscal and social capital. They can not be sustained by legitimate employment and they may in fact undermine both one's ability and inclination to hold a job. Even if offenders are willing to work at the kinds of employment available to them, and evidence suggests that many are not (Cromwell, Olson, and Avary 1991), the time schedules of work and party pursuits conflict. The best times of the day for committing many property crimes are also the times the offender would be at work, and it is nearly impossible to do both consistently and well. For those who pursue life as a party, legitimate employment often is foregone or sacrificed (Rengert and Wasilchick 1985). The absence of income from noncriminal sources reinforces the need to find other sources of money.

Determined pursuit of life as party also may affect participants' relationships with legitimate significant others. Many offenders manage to enjoy the lifestyle successfully only by exploiting the concern and largesse of family and friends. This may take the form of repeated requests for and receipt of personal loans that go unreturned, occasional thefts, or other forms of exploitation:

> I lived well for awhile. I lived well . . . until I started shooting cocaine real bad, intravenously. . . . [A]nd then everything, you know, went up in smoke, you know. Up my arm. The watches, the rings, . . . the car, you know. I used to have a girl, man, and her daddy had two horses. I put them in my arm. You know what I mean? . . . I made her sell them horses. My clothes and all that stuff, a lot of it, they went up in smoke when I started messing with that cocaine.

Eventually, friends and even family members may come to believe that they have been exploited or that continued assistance will only prolong a process that must be terminated. As one subject told us, "Oh, I tried to borrow money, and borrow money and, you know, nobody would loan it to me. Because they knew what I was doing." After first refusing further assistance, acquaintances, friends, and even family members may avoid social contacts with the party pursuer or sever ties altogether. This dialogue occurred between the interviewer and one of our subjects.

Q: [B]esides doing something wrong, did you think of anything else that you could do to get money? . . . Borrow it?

A: No, I'd done run that in the ground. See, you burn that up. That's burned up, right there, borrowing, you know. . . . Once I borrow, you know, I might get $10 from you today and, see, I'll be expecting to be getting $10 tomorrow, if I could. And then, when I see you [and] you see me coming, you say, "no, I don't have none." . . . [A]s the guys in the penitentiary say, "you absorb all of your remedies," you see. And that's what I did: I burned my remedies up, you know.

Last, when party pursuits are not going well, feelings of shame and self-disgust are not uncommon (Frazier and Meisenhelder 1985). Unsuccessful party pursuers as a result may take steps to reduce these feelings by distancing themselves voluntarily from conventional others:

Q: You were married to your wife at that time?

A: Yeah, I was married . . .

Q: Where was she living then?

A: I finally forced her to go home, you know . . . I made her go home, you know. And it caused an argument, for her to go home to her mother's. I felt like that was the best thing I did for her, you know. She hated me . . . for it at the time, didn't understand none of it. But, really, I intentionally made her go. I really spared her the misery that we were going to have. And it came. It came in bundles.

When party pursuers sustain severe losses of legitimate income and social resources, regardless of how it occurs, they grow increasingly isolated from conventional significant others. The obvious consequence is that this reduces interpersonal constraints on their behavior.

As their pursuit of life as party increasingly assumes qualities of difficulty and struggle, offenders' utilities and risk perceptions also change. Increasingly, crimes are committed not to enhance or sustain the lifestyle so much as to forestall unpleasant circumstances. Those addicted to alcohol or other drugs, for example, must devote increasing time and energy to the quest for monies to purchase their chemicals of choice. Both their drug consumption and the frequency of their criminal acts increase (Ball et al. 1983; Johnson et al. 1985). For them, as for others, inability to draw on legitimate or low-risk resources may precipitate a crisis. One of our respondents retold how, facing a court appearance on a burglary charge, he needed funds to hire an attorney:

> I needed some money bad or if I didn't, if I went to court the following day, I was going to be locked up. The judge was going to lock me up. Because I didn't have no lawyer. And I had went and talked to several lawyers and they told me... they wanted a thousand dollars, that if I couldn't come up with no thousand dollars, they couldn't come to court with me.... [S]o I went to my sister. I asked my sister, I said, "look here, what about letting me have seven or eight hundred dollars"—which I knowed she had the money because she... had been in a wreck and she had gotten some money out of a suit. And she said, "well, if I give you the money you won't do the right thing with it." And I was telling her, "no, no, I need a lawyer." But I couldn't convince her to let me have the money. So I left.... I said, shit, I'm fixin' to go back to jail.... [S]o as I left her house and was walking—I was going to catch the bus—the [convenience store] and bus stop was right there by each other. So, I said I'm going to buy me some gum.... [A]nd in the process of me buying the chewing gum, I seen two ladies, they was counting money. So I figured sooner or later one of them was going to come out with the money.... I waited on them until... one came out with the money, and I got it.

Confronted by crisis and preoccupied with relieving immediate distress, the offender eventually may experience and define himself as propelled by forces beyond his control. Behavioral options become dichotomized into those that hold out some possibility of relief, however risky, and those that promise little but continued pain. Legitimate options are few and are seen as unlikely solutions. A criminal act may offer some hope of relief, however temporary. The offender may imbue the criminal option with almost magical prospects for ending or reversing the state of discomfort:

> I said, "well, look at it like this": if I don't do it, then tomorrow morning I've got the same [problems] that I've got right now. I could be hungry. I'm going to want food more. I'm going to want cigarettes more. I'm going to want everything more. [But] if I do it, and if I make it, then I've got all I want.

Acts that once were the result of blithe unconcern with risk can over time come to be based on a personal determination to master or reverse what is experienced as desperately unpleasant circumstances. As a result, inattention to risk in the offender's decision making may give way to the perception that he has *nothing to lose:*

> It . . . gets to the point that you get into such a desperation. You're not working, you can't work. You're drunk as hell, been that way two or three weeks. You're no good to yourself, and you're no good to anybody else. Self-esteem is gone [and] spiritually, mentally, physically, financially bankrupt. You ain't got nothing to lose.

Desperate to maintain or reestablish a sense of normality, the offender pursues emotional relief with a decision to act decisively, albeit in the face of legal odds recognized as narrowing. By acting boldly and resolutely to make the best of a grim situation, one gains a measure of respect, if not from others, then at least from oneself.

> I think, when you're doing . . . drugs like I was doing, I don't think you tend to rationalize much at all. I think it's just a decision you make. You don't weigh the consequences, the pros and the cons. You just do it.

> You know, all kinds of things started running through my mind. If I get caught, then there, there I am with another charge. Then I said, well if I don't do something, I'm going to be in jail. And I just said, "I'm going to do it."

The fact that sustained party pursuits often cause offenders to increase the number of offenses they commit and to exploit criminal opportunities that formerly were seen as risky should not be interpreted as meaning they believe they can continue committing crime with impunity. The opposite is true. Many offenders engaged in crimes intended to halt or reverse eroding fortunes are aware that eventually they will be arrested if they continue doing so:

> Q: How did you manage not to think about, you know, that you could go to prison?
>
> A: Well, you think about it afterwards. You think, "wow, boy, I got away with it again." But you know, sooner or later, the law of averages is gonna catch up with you. You just can't do it [commit crime] forever and ever and ever. And don't think you're not gonna get caught, cause you will.

Bennett and Wright (1984a) likewise show that a majority of persistent offenders endorse the statement that they will be caught "eventually." The cyclical transformation of party pursuits from pleasant and enjoyable to desperate and tenuous is one reason they are able to commit crimes despite awareness of inevitable and potentially severe legal penalties.

The threat posed by possible arrest and imprisonment, however, may not seem severe to some desperate offenders. As compared to their marginal and precarious existence, it may be seen as a form of relief:

> [When he was straight], I'd think about [getting caught]: I could get this, and that [penalties]. . . . [A]nd then I would think, well, I know this is going to

end one day, you know. But, you know, you get so far out there, and get so far off into it that it really don't matter, you know. But you think about that.... I knew, eventually, I would get caught, you know.... I was off into drugs and I just didn't care if I got caught or not.

When I [got] caught—and they caught me right at the house—it's kind of like, you feel good, because you're glad it's over, you know. I mean, a weight being lifted off your head. And you say, well, I don't have to worry about this shit no more, because they've caught me. And it's over, you know.

In sum, due to offenders' eroding access to legitimately secured funds, their diminishing contact with and support from conventional significant others, and their efforts to maintain drug consumption habits, crimes that once were committed for recreational purposes increasingly become desperate attempts to forestall or reverse uncomfortable or frustrating situations. Pursuing the short term goal of maximizing enjoyment of life, legal threats can appear to the offender either as remote and improbable contingencies when party pursuits fulfill their recreational purposes or as an acceptable risk in the face of continued isolation, penury, and desperation.

We analyzed the descriptions of crime provided by our subjects, and their activities on the day the crime occurred. We focused specifically on: (1) the primary purpose of their crimes, i.e., whether they planned to use the proceeds of crime for pleasure or to cope with unpleasant contingencies, and (2) the extent and subjective meaning of their drug use at the time they decided to commit the crime in question. Based on the analysis, we classified the crimes of 15 subjects as behaviors committed in the enjoyment of life as party and 13 as behaviors committed in order to enhance or restore enjoyment of this lifestyle. The 12 remaining offenders could not be classified because of insufficient information in the crime descriptions or they are isolated criminal acts that do not represent a specific lifestyle. Two subjects, for example, described crimes that were acts of vengeance directed at the property of individuals who had treated them or their relatives improperly. One of the men related how he decided to burglarize a home for reasons of revenge:

I was mad.... When I was in the penitentiary, my wife went to his house for a party and he give her a bunch of cocaine.... It happened, I think, about a week before I got out.... I just had it in my mind what I wanted to do: I wanted to hurt him like I was hurt.... I was pretty drunk, when I went by [his home], and I saw there wasn't no car there. So, I just pulled my car in.

The other subject told how an acquaintance had stolen drugs and other possessions from his automobile. In response the subject "staked out the places where he would be for several days before I caught him, at gun point, [and] made him take me to his home, [which] I ransacked, and found some of the narcotics that he had stolen from me." Although neither of these crimes was committed in pursuit of life as party, other crimes committed by both these subjects during their criminal careers did occur as part of that lifestyle. Other investigators have similarly reported that revenge is the dominant motive in a minority of property offenses (e.g., Cromwell, Olson, and Avary 1991, p. 22).

IMPLICATIONS

We have suggested that daily routines characteristic of the partying lifestyle of persistent and unsuccessful offenders may modify both the salience of their various decision utilities and their perceptions of legal risk in the process of their crime commission decisions. This is not to say that these decisions are irrational, only that they do not conform to decision making as sketched by rational choice theories. Our objective was not to falsify the rational choice approach to criminal decision making, for we know of no way this could be accomplished. Whatever it is, moreover, rationality is not a dichotomous variable. Indeed, offenders' target selection decision making appears more rational in the conventional sense than do crime commission decisions.

The lesson here for theories of criminal decision making is that while utilities and risk assessment may be properties of individuals, they are also shaped by the social and personal contexts in which decisions are made. Whether their pursuit of life as party is interpreted theoretically as the product of structural strain, choice, or even happenstance is of limited importance to an understanding of offenders' discrete criminal forays. What is important is that their lifestyle places them in situations that may facilitate important transformations in the utilities of prospective actions. If nothing else, this means that some situations more than others make it possible to discount or ignore risk. We are not the first to call attention to this phenomenon:

> [The] situational nature of sanction properties has escaped the scales and indicators employed in official record and self-report survey research. In this body of research an arrest and a year in prison are generally assumed to have the same meaning for all persons and across all situations. The situational grounding of sanction properties suggests[, however,] that we look beyond official definitions of sanctions and the attitudinal structure of individuals to the properties of situations (Ekland-Olson et al. 1984, p. 174).

Along the same line, the longitudinal survey of adult offenders concludes that decision making "may be conditioned by elements within the immediate situation confronting the individual... [such that] perceptions of the opportunity, returns, and support for crime within a given situation may influence... perceptions of risks and the extent to which those risks are discounted" (Piliavin et al. 1986, p. 115). The same interpretation has been suggested by Shover and Thompson (1992) for their failure to find an expected positive relationship between risk estimates and crime desistance among former prison inmates.

In light of the sample and data limitations of this study we cannot and have not argued that the lifestyle we described *generates* or *produces* the characteristic decision-making behaviors of persistent property offenders. The evidence does not permit such interpretive liberties. It does seem reasonable to suggest, however, that the focal concerns and shared perspectives of those who pursue life as party may function to *sustain* offenders' free-wheeling, but purposeful, decision-making style. Without question there is a close *correspondence* between the two. Our ability to explain and predict decision making requires that we gain a better understanding of how utilities and risk perceptions are constrained by the properties of situations encountered typically by persons in their daily rounds. In other words, we must learn more about the daily worlds that comprise the immediate contexts of criminal decision-making behavior.

Note

This research was supported by grant #86-IJ-CX-0068 from the U.S. Department of Justice, National Institute of Justice (Principal Investigator: Neal Shover). Points of view or opinions expressed here do not necessarily reflect the official position or policies of the Department of Justice. For their critical comments while the paper was in gestation we are grateful to Derek Cornish and to participants in a March 1991 colloquium at the Centre for Socio-Legal Studies, Wolfson College, University of Oxford. Werner Einstadter, Michael Levi, Mike Maguire, and anonymous reviewers also provided helpful comments.

References

Ball J. C., Shaffer, J. W. and Nurco, D. N. (1983) "The day-to-day criminality of heroin addicts in Baltimore: A study in the continuity of offense rates," *Drug and Alcohol Dependence, 12,* 119–142.

Becker, G. (1968) "Crime and punishment: An economic approach," *Journal of Political Economy,* 76, 169–217.

Bennett, T. and Wright, R. (1984a) *Burglars on Burglary,* Hampshire, U.K.: Gower.

—— (1984b) "The relationship between alcohol use and burglary," *British Journal of Addiction,* 79, 431–437.

Blumstein, A., Cohen, J. and Nagin, D., editors (1978) *Deterrence and Incapacitation: Estimating the Effects of Criminal Sanctions on Crime Rates,* Washington, D.C.: National Academy of Sciences.

Carroll, J. S. (1978) "A psychological approach to deterrence: The evaluation of crime opportunities," *Journal of Personality and Social Psychology, 36,* 1512–1520.

—— (1982) "Committing a crime: The offender's decision," in: J. Konecni and E. B. Ebbesen (Eds.), *The Criminal Justice System: A Social-Psychological Analysis,* San Francisco: W. H. Freeman.

Carroll, J. S. and Weaver, F. (1986) "Shoplifters' perceptions of crime opportunities: A process-tracing study," in: D. B. Cornish and R. V. Clarke (Eds.), *The Reasoning Criminal: Rational Choice Perspectives on Offending,* New York: Springer-Verlag.

Clarke, R. V. and Cornish, D. B. (1985) "Modeling offenders' decisions: A framework for research and policy," in: M. Tonry and N. Morris (Eds.), *Crime and Justice: A Review of Research,* Vol. 4, Chicago: University of Chicago Press.

Claster, D. S. (1967) "Comparison of risk perception between delinquents and nondelinquents," *Journal of Criminal Law, Criminology, and Police Science, 58*, 80–86.

Cornish, D. B. and Clarke, R. V., editors (1986) *The Reasoning Criminal: Rational Choice Perspectives on Offending*, New York: Springer-Verlag.

Cromwell, P. F., Olson, J. N. and Avary, D. W. (1991) *Breaking and Entering: An Ethnographic Analysis of Burglary*, Newbury Park, Calif.: Sage.

Ekland-Olson, S., Lieb, J. and Zurcher, L. (1984) "The paradoxical impact of criminal sanctions: Some microstructural findings," *Law & Society Review, 18*, 159–178.

Feeney, F. (1986) "Robbers as decision-makers," in: D. B. Cornish and R. V. Clarke (Eds.), *The Reasoning Criminal: Rational Choice Perspectives on Offending*, New York: Springer-Verlag.

Figgie International (1988) *The Figgie Report Part VI—The Business of Crime: The Criminal Perspective*, Richmond, Va.: Figgie International, Inc.

Frazier, C. E. and Meisenholder, T. (1985) "Criminality and emotional ambivalence: Exploratory notes on an overlooked dimension," *Qualitative Sociology, 8*, 266–284.

Gibbs, J. J. and Shelley, P. L. (1982) "Life in the fast lane: A retrospective view by commercial thieves," *Journal of Research in Crime and Delinquency, 19*, 299–330.

Goffman, E. (1967) *Interaction Ritual*, Garden City, N.Y.: Anchor.

Gottfredson, M. R. and Hirschi, T. (1990) *A General Theory of Crime*, Stanford, Calif.: Stanford University Press.

Heineke, J. M., editor (1978) *Economic Models of Criminal Behavior*, Amsterdam: North-Holland.

Johnson, B. D., Goldstein, P. J., Preble, E., Schmeidler, J., Lipton, D. D., Spunt, B. and Miller, T. (1985) *Taking Care of Business: The Economics of Crime by Heroin Addicts*, Lexington, Mass.: D.C. Heath.

Katz, J. (1988) *Seductions of Crime*, New York: Basic Books.

Maguire, M. in collaboration with T. Bennett (1982) *Burglary in a Dwelling*, London: Heinemann.

Manski, C. F. (1978) "Prospects for inference on deterrence through empirical analysis of individual criminal behavior," in: A. Blumstein, J. Cohen, and D. Nagin (Eds.), *Deterrence and Incapacitation: Estimating the Effects of Criminal Sanctions on Crime Rates*, Washington, D.C.: National Academy of Sciences.

Nagin, D. S. and Paternoster, R. (1991) "On the relationship of past to future participation in delinquency," *Criminology, 29*, 163–189.

Persson, M. (1981) "Time-perspectives amongst criminals," *Acta Sociologica, 24*, 149–165.

Petersilia, J. (1980) "Criminal career research: A review of recent evidence," in: N. Morris and M. Tonry (Eds.), *Crime and Justice: An Annual Review of Research*, Vol. 2, Chicago: University of Chicago Press.

—— Greenwood, P. W. and Lavin, M. (1978) *Criminal Careers of Habitual Felons*, Washington, D.C.: U.S. Department of Justice, National Institute of Law Enforcement and Criminal Justice.

Peterson, M. A. and Braiker, H. B. (1980) *Doing Crime: A Survey of California Prison Inmates*, Santa Monica, Calif.: Rand Corporation.

Piliavin, I., Gartner, R. and Matsueda, R. (1986) "Crime, deterrence, and rational choice," *American Sociological Review, 51*, 101–119.

Rengert, G. F. and Wasilchick, J. (1985) *Suburban Burglary,* Springfield, Ill.: Charles C. Thomas.

Repetto, T. A. (1974) *Residential Crime,* Cambridge, Mass.: Ballinger.

Reynolds, M. O. (1985) *Crime by Choice: An Economic Analysis,* Dallas: Fisher Institute.

Scarr, H. A. (1973) *Patterns of Burglary* (second edition), Washington, D.C.: U.S. Department of Justice, National Institute of Law Enforcement and Criminal Justice.

Seidel, J. V., Kjolseth, R. and Seymour, E. (1988) *The Ethnograph: A User's Guide* (Version 3.0), Littleton, Col.: Qualis Research Associates.

Shover, N. (1991) "Burglary," in: M. Tonry (Ed.), *Crime and Justice: An Annual Review of Research,* Vol. 14, Chicago: University of Chicago Press.

Shover, N. and Thompson, C. Y. (1992) "Age, differential expectations, and crime desistance," *Criminology, 30*, 89–109.

Waldo, G. P. and Chiricos, T. G. (1972) "Perceived penal sanction and self-reported criminality: A neglected approach to deterrence research," *Social Problems, 19*, 522–540.

Walsh, D. (1980) *Break-Ins: Burglary from Private Houses,* London: Constable.

—— (1986) *Heavy Business,* London: Routledge & Kegan Paul.

17 / Primary and Secondary Deviation

EDWIN M. LEMERT

SOCIOPATHIC INDIVIDUATION

The deviant person is a product of differentiating and isolating processes. Some persons are individually differentiated from others from the time of birth onward, as in the case of a child born with a congenital physical defect or repulsive appearance, and as in the case of a child born into a minority racial or cultural group. Other persons grow to maturity in a family or in a social class where pauperism, begging, or crime are more or less institutionalized ways of life for the entire group. In these latter instances the person's sociopsychological growth may be normal in every way, his status as a deviant being entirely caused by his maturation within the framework of social organization and culture designated as "patholog-ical" by the larger society. This is true of many delinquent children in our society.[1]

> It is a matter of great significance that the delinquent child, growing up in the delinquency areas of the city, has very little access to the cultural heritages of the larger conventional society. His infrequent contacts with this larger society are for the most part formal and external. Quite naturally his conception of moral values is shaped and molded by the moral code prevailing in his play groups and the local community in which he lives ... the young delinquent has very little appreciation of the meaning of the traditions and formal laws of society. ... Hence the conflict between the delinquent and the agencies of society is, in its broader aspects, a conflict of divergent cultures.

The same sort of gradual, unconscious process which operates in the socialization of the deviant child may also be recognized in the acquisition of socially unacceptable behavior by persons after having reached adult-hood. However, with more verbal and sophisticated adults, step-by-step violations of societal norms tend to be progressively rationalized in the light of what is socially acceptable. Changes of this nature can take place at the level of either overt or covert behavior, but with a greater likelihood that adults will preface overt behavior changes with projective symbolic departures from society's norms. When the latter occur, the subsequent overt changes may appear to be "sudden" personality modifications. How-ever, whether these changes are completely radical ones is to some extent a moot point. One writer holds strongly to the opinion that sudden and dramatic shifts in behavior from normal to abnormal are seldom the case, that a sequence of small preparatory transformations must be the prelude to such apparently sudden behavior changes. This writer is impressed by the day-by-day growth of "reserve potentialities" within personalities of all individuals, and he contends that many normal persons carry potentialities for abnormal behavior, which, given proper conditions, can easily be called into play.[2]

Personality Changes Not Always Gradual

This argument is admittedly sound for most cases, but it must be taken into consideration that traumatic experiences often speed up changes in personality.[3] Nor can the "trauma" in these experiences universally be attributed to the unique way in which the person conceives of the experience subjectively. Cases exist to show that personality modifications can be telescoped or that there can be an acceleration of such changes caused largely by the intensity and variety of the social stimulation. Most soldiers undoubtedly have entirely different conceptions of their roles after intensive combat experience. Many admit to having "lived a lifetime" in a relatively short period of time after they have been under heavy fire in battle for the first time. Many generals have remarked that their men have to be a little "shooted" or "blooded" in order to become good soldiers. In the process of group formation, crises and interactional amplification are vital requisites to forging true, role-oriented group behavior out of individuated behavior.[4]

The importance of the person's conscious symbolic reactions to his or her own behavior cannot be overstressed in explaining the shift from normal to abnormal behavior or from one type of pathological behavior to another, particularly where behavior variations become systematized or structured into pathological roles. This is not to say that conscious choice is a determining factor in the differentiating process. Nor does it mean that the awareness of the self is a purely conscious perception. Much of the process of self-perception is doubtless marginal from the point of view of consciousness.[5] But however it may be perceived, the individual's self-definition is closely connected with such things as self-acceptance, the subordination of minor to major roles, and with the motivation involved in learning the skills, techniques, and values of a new role. *Self-definitions or self-realizations are likely to be the result of sudden perceptions and they are especially significant when they are followed immediately by overt demonstrations of the new role they symbolize.* The self-defining junctures are critical points of personality genesis and in the special case of the atypical person they mark a division between two different types of deviation.

Primary and Secondary Deviation

There has been an embarrassingly large number of theories, often without any relationship to a general theory, advanced to account for various specific pathologies in human behavior. For certain types of pathology, such as alcoholism, crime, or stuttering, there are almost as many theories as there are writers on these subjects. This has been occasioned in no small way by the preoccupation with the origins of pathological behavior and by the fallacy of confusing *original* causes with *effective* causes. All such theories have elements of truth, and the divergent viewpoints they contain can be reconciled with the general theory here if it is granted that original causes or antecedents of deviant behaviors are many and diversified. This holds especially for the psychological processes leading to similar pathological behavior, but it also holds for the situational concomitants of the initial aberrant conduct. A person may come to use excessive alcohol not only for a wide variety of subjective reasons but also because of diversified situational influences, such as the death of a loved one, business failure, or participating in some sort of organized group activity calling for heavy drinking of liquor. Whatever the original reasons for violating the norms of the community, they are important only for certain research purposes, such as assessing the extent of the "social problem" at a given time or determining the requirements for a rational program of social control. From a narrower sociological viewpoint the deviations are not significant until they are organized subjectively and transformed into active roles and become the social criteria for assigning status. The deviant individuals must react symbolically to their own behavior aberrations and fix them in their sociopsychological patterns. The deviations remain primary deviations or symptomatic and situational as long as they are rationalized or otherwise dealt with as functions of a socially acceptable role. Under such conditions normal and pathological behaviors remain strange and somewhat tensional bedfellows in the same person. Undeniably a vast amount of such segmental and partially integrated pathological behavior exists in our society and has impressed many writers in the field of social pathology.

Just how far and for how long a person may go in dissociating his sociopathic tendencies so that they are merely troublesome adjuncts of normally conceived roles is not known. Perhaps it depends upon the number of alternative definitions of the same overt behavior that he can develop; perhaps certain physiological factors (limits) are also involved. However, if the deviant acts are repetitive and have a high visibility, and if there is a severe societal reaction, which, through a process of identification is incorporated as part of the "me" of the individual, the probability is greatly increased that the integration of existing roles will be disrupted and that reorganization based upon a new role or roles will occur. (The "me" in this context is simply the subjective aspect of the societal reaction.) Reorganization may be the adoption of another normal role in which the tendencies previously defined as "pathological" are given a more acceptable social expression. The other general possibility is the assumption of a deviant role, if such exists; or, more rarely, the person may organize an aberrant sect or group in which he creates a special role of his own. *When a person begins to employ his deviant behavior or a role based upon it as a means of defense, attack, or adjustment to the overt and covert problems created by the consequent societal reaction to him, his deviation is secondary.* Objective evidences of this change will be found in the symbolic appurtenances of the new role, in clothes, speech, posture, and mannerisms, which in some cases heighten social visibility, and which in some cases serve as symbolic cues to professionalization.

Role Conceptions of the Individual Must Be Reinforced by Reactions of Others

It is seldom that one deviant act will provoke a sufficiently strong societal reaction to bring about secondary deviation, unless in the process of introjection the individual imputes or projects meanings into the social situation which are not present. In this case anticipatory fears are involved. For example, in a culture where a child is taught sharp distinctions between "good" women and "bad" women, a single act of questionable morality might conceivably have a profound meaning for the girl so indulging. However, in the absence of reactions by the person's family, neighbors, or the larger community, reinforcing the tentative "bad-girl" self-definition, it is questionable whether a transition to secondary deviation would take place. It is also doubtful whether a temporary exposure to a severe punitive reaction by the community will lead a person to identify himself with a pathological role, unless, as we have said, the experience is highly traumatic. Most frequently there is a progressive reciprocal relationship between the deviation of the individual and the societal reaction, with a compounding of the societal reaction out of the minute accretions in the deviant behavior, until a point is reached where ingrouping and outgrouping between society and the deviant is manifest.[6] At this point a stigmatizing of the deviant occurs in the form of name calling, labeling, or stereotyping.

The sequence of interaction leading to secondary deviation is roughly as follows: (1) primary deviation; (2) social penalties; (3) further primary deviation; (4) stronger penalties and rejections; (5) further deviation, perhaps with hostilities and resentment beginning to focus upon those doing the penalizing; (6) crisis reached in the tolerance quotient, expressed in formal action by the community stigmatizing of the deviant; (7) strengthening of the deviant conduct as a reaction to the stigmatizing and penalties; (8) ultimate acceptance of deviant social status and efforts at adjustment on the basis of the associated role.

As an illustration of this sequence the behavior of an errant schoolboy can be cited. For one reason or another, let us say excessive energy, the schoolboy engages in a classroom prank. He is penalized for it by the teacher. Later, due to clumsiness, he creates another disturbance and again he is reprimanded. Then, as sometimes happens, the boy is blamed for something he did not do. When the teacher uses the tag "bad boy" or "mischief maker" or other invidious terms, hostility and resentment are excited in the boy, and he may feel that he is blocked in playing the role expected of him. Thereafter, there may be a strong temptation to assume his role in the class as defined by the teacher, particularly when he discovers that there are rewards as well as penalties deriving from such a role. There is, of course, no implication here that such boys go on to become delinquents or criminals, for the mischief-maker role may later become integrated with or retrospectively rationalized as part of a role more acceptable to school authorities.[7] If such a boy continues this unacceptable role and becomes delinquent, the process must be accounted for in the light of the general theory of this volume. There must be a spreading corroboration of a sociopathic self-conception and societal reinforcement at each step in the process.

The most significant personality changes are manifest when societal definitions and their subjective counterpart become generalized. When this happens, the range of major role choices becomes narrowed to one general class.[8] This was very obvious in the case of a young girl who was the daughter of a paroled convict and who was attending a small Middle Western college. She continually argued with herself and with the author, in whom she had confided, that in reality she belonged on the "other side of the railroad tracks" and that her life could be enormously simplified by acquiescing in this verdict and living accordingly. While in her case there was a tendency to dramatize her conflicts, nevertheless there was enough societal reinforcement of her self-conception by the treatment she received in her relationship with her father and on dates with college boys to lend it a painful reality. Once these boys took her home to the shoddy dwelling in a slum area where she lived with her father, who was often in a drunken condition, they abruptly stopped seeing her again or else became sexually presumptive.

Notes

1. Shaw, C., *The Natural History of a Delinquent Career*, Chicago, 1941, pp. 75–76. Quoted by permission of the University of Chicago Press, Chicago.
2. Brown, L. Guy, *Social Pathology*, 1942, pp. 44–45.
3. Allport, G., *Personality, A Psychological Interpretation*, 1947, p. 57.
4. Slavson, S. R., *An Introduction to Group Psychotherapy*, 1943, pp. 10, 229*ff*.
5. Murphy, G., *Personality*, 1947, p. 482.
6. Mead G., "The Psychology of Punitive Justice," *American Journal of Sociology*, 23 March, 1918, pp. 577–602.
7. Evidence for fixed or inevitable sequences from predelinquency to crime is absent. Sutherland, E. H., *Principles of Criminology*, 1939, 4th ed., p. 202.
8. Sutherland seems to say something of this sort in connection with the development of criminal behavior. *Ibid*., p. 86.

18 / Career Deviance

HOWARD S. BECKER

One of the most crucial steps in the process of building a stable pattern of deviant behavior is likely to be the experience of being caught and publicly labeled as a deviant. Whether a person takes this step or not depends not so much on what he does as on what other people do, on whether or not they enforce the rule he has violated. . . . First of all, even though no one else discovers the nonconformity or enforces the rules against it, the individual who has committed the impropriety may himself act as an enforcer. He may brand himself as deviant because of what he has done and punish himself in one way or another for his behavior. This is not always or necessarily the case, but may occur. Second, there may be cases like those described by psychoanalysts in which the individual really wants to get caught and perpetrates his deviant act in such a way that it is almost sure he will be.

In any case, being caught and branded as deviant has important consequences for one's further social participation and self-image. The most important consequence is a drastic change in the individual's public identity. Committing the improper act and being publicly caught at it place him in a new status. He has been revealed as a different kind of person from the kind he was supposed to be. He is labeled a "fairy," "dope fiend," "nut," or "lunatic," and treated accordingly.

In analyzing the consequences of assuming a deviant identity let us make use of Hughes' distinction between master and auxiliary status traits.[1] Hughes notes that most statuses have one key trait which serves to distinguish those who belong from those who do not. Thus the doctor, whatever else he may be, is a person who has a certificate stating that he has fulfilled certain requirements and is licensed to practice medicine; this is the master trait. As Hughes points out, in our society a doctor is also informally expected to have a number of auxiliary traits: most people expect him to be upper middle class, white, male, and Protestant. When he is not there is a sense that he has in some way failed to fill the bill. Similarly, though skin color is the master status trait determining who is Negro and who is white, Negroes are informally expected to have certain status traits and not to have others; people are surprised and find it anomalous if a Negro turns out to be a doctor or a college professor. People often have the master status trait but lack some of the auxiliary, informally expected characteristics; for example, one may be a doctor but be female or Negro.

Hughes deals with this phenomenon in regard to statuses that are well thought of, desired and desirable (noting that one may have the formal qualifications for entry into a status but be denied full entry because of lack of the proper auxiliary traits), but the same process occurs in the case of deviant statuses. Possession of one deviant trait may have a generalized symbolic value, so that people automatically assume that its bearer possesses other undesirable traits allegedly associated with it.

To be labeled a criminal one need only commit a single criminal offense, and this is all the term formally refers to. Yet the word carries a number of connotations specifying auxiliary traits characteristic of anyone bearing the label. A man who has been convicted of housebreaking and thereby labeled criminal is presumed to be a person likely to break into other houses; the police, in rounding up known offenders for investigation after a crime has been committed, operate on this premise. Further, he is considered likely to commit other kinds of crimes as well, because he has shown himself to be a person without "respect for the law." Thus, apprehension for one deviant act exposes a person to the likelihood that he will be regarded as deviant or undesirable in other respects.

There is one other element in Hughes' analysis we can borrow with profit: the distinction between master and subordinate statuses.[2] Some statuses, in our society as in others, override all other statuses and have a certain priority. Race is one of these. Membership in the Negro race, as socially defined, will override most other status considerations in most other situations; the fact that one is a physician or middle-class or female will not protect one from being treated as a Negro first and any of these other things second. The status of deviant (depending on this kind of deviance) is this kind of master status. One receives the status as a result of breaking a rule, and the identification proves to be more important than most others. One will be identified as a deviant first, before other identifications are made. The question is raised: "What kind of person would break such an important rule?" And the answer is given: "One who is different from the rest of us, who cannot or will not act as a moral human being and therefore might break other important rules." The deviant identification becomes the controlling one.

Treating a person as though he were generally rather than specifically deviant produces a self-fulfilling prophecy. It sets in motion several mechanisms which conspire to shape the person in the image people have of him.[3] In the first place, one tends to be cut off, after being identified as deviant, from participation in more conventional groups, even though the specific consequences of the particular deviant activity might never of themselves have caused the isolation had there not also been the public knowledge and reaction to it. For example, being a homosexual may not affect one's ability to do office work, but to be known as a homosexual in an office may make it impossible to continue working there. Similarly, though the effects of opiate drugs may not impair one's working ability, to be known as an addict will probably lead to losing one's job. In such cases, the individual finds it difficult to conform to other rules which he had no intention or desire to break, and perforce finds himself deviant in these areas as well. The homosexual who is deprived of a "respectable" job by the discovery of his deviance may drift into unconventional, marginal occupations where it does not make so much difference. The drug addict finds himself forced into other illegitimate kinds of activity, such as robbery and theft, by the refusal of respectable employers to have him around.

When the deviant is caught, he is treated in accordance with the popular diagnosis of why he is that way, and the treatment itself may likewise produce increasing deviance. The drug addict, popularly considered to be a weak-willed individual who cannot forego the indecent pleasures afforded him by opiates, is treated repressively. He is forbidden to use drugs. Since he cannot get drugs legally, he must get them illegally. This forces the market underground and pushes the price of drugs up far beyond the current legitimate market price into a bracket that few can afford on an ordinary salary. Hence the treatment of the addict's deviance places him in a position where it will probably be necessary to resort to deceit and crime in order to support his habit.[4] The behavior is a consequence of the public reaction to the deviance rather than a consequence of the inherent qualities of the deviant act.

Notes

1. Everett C. Hughes, "Dilemmas and Contradictions of Status," *American Journal of Sociology*, L (March, 1945), 353–359.
2. *Ibid.*
3. See Marsh Ray, "The Cycle of Abstinence and Relapse Among Heroin Addicts," *Social Problems*, 9 (Fall, 1961), 132–140.
4. See *Drug Addiction: Crime or Disease?* Interim and Final Reports of the Joint Committee of the American Bar Association and the American Medical Association on Narcotic Drugs (Bloomington, Indiana: Indiana University Press, 1961).

Part 3 / Becoming Deviant

In Part 1, I made some general statements about the way deviant categories arise and the way violators of these categories may be reacted to. In Part 2, I explored some of the major theories and perspectives that serve to explain why actors may commit deviant acts. In this part of the book, I will deal more systematically with reactions that may bring about early stages of deviant careers—careers which may ultimately become subject to institutional control and regulation (Part 4).

In the general introduction, a distinction was made between the initiation of the labeling ceremony in a private domain and initiation in the public domain. I also noted how those engaged in deviant pursuits attempt to manage their behavior and attitudes in such a way as to avoid detection by socially significant "straights," especially formal agents of social control. This avoidance clearly indicates both the existence of some potentially stigmatizing or discreditable feature of their biography and the knowledge that detection is frequently associated with a range of personal and social costs. As an example, the drug pusher runs the risk of being sanctioned by the courts. It is conceivable, of course, that the pusher may never experience any direct contact with the social-control apparatus. In such a case he or she would remain what I have termed a noninstitutional deviant. Still, the pusher is aware of the potentially damaging nature of his or her activities and realizes that if authorities became aware of those activities, that knowledge could be used to initiate some type of institutional career.

In the analysis of strategies for information control and management, it is useful, therefore, to think in terms of actor *and* audience response. The pusher, in an effort to protect his or her self-image and identity cluster, as well as to reduce the odds of being officially designated as a deviant, may employ certain strategies (e.g., denying to self and others that he or she is a pusher). Similarly, those who must deal with actual or potential deviance often invoke various types of coping or accommodative strategies. A wife, for example, may try to accommodate herself to her husband's increasingly violent behavior. If she is successful, the deviance will remain primarily a matter of private knowledge, regulation, and management—although the wife herself may consider her husband to be deviant. If, on the other hand, the wife's accommodative strategies (e.g., attempts at neutralization or rationalization) fail, she may find it necessary to bring in third parties (e.g., social-control agents like the police) to regulate her husband's behavior. Not only have the wife's "tolerance limits" been exceeded in this case, but behavior that had been managed in the private setting now becomes subject to institutional control. And the husband may be typed, processed, and responded to as an involuntary mental patient.

The selections that follow explore the ways in which strategies for management and accommodation operate in private settings. The first selections deal primarily with how actors attempt to manage and control potentially discrediting information about themselves. The remaining selections illustrate how audiences may respond to deviant or increasingly violent behavior on the part of significant and generalized others. These articles offer excellent illustrations of the usefulness of many of the basic concepts and processes introduced in Parts 1 and 2. For example, Ferraro and Johnson, in their analysis of spouse battering, rely very heavily on Sykes and Matza's neutralization techniques.

Joseph W. Schneider and Peter Conrad, in their article "In the Closet with Illness: Epilepsy, Stigma Potential and Information Control," provide an interesting account of how people attempt to manage what they view as discreditable information about themselves. These writers focus on a sample of eighty epileptics, none of whom has a history of long-term institutionalization. The researchers, in their reliance on the metaphor of the closet, initially advance the concept of "stigma potential" to emphasize the fact that epilepsy is a trait that causes one's identity to be discredited. The characterization of the stigma as "potential," they argue, rests on two basic assumptions: (1) that knowledge of the attribute (i.e., epilepsy) be limited to a few people, and (2) that if the trait were to become more widely known, significant changes in self, along with various controls of behavior, might result. Schneider and Conrad cite several examples that underscore the stigma potential of epilepsy (e.g., being discriminated against in the area of employment and being prohibited from marrying in some states). The authors then assert that stigma is not an automatic result of possessing some discreditable trait. Rather, the significance of "'having' epilepsy is a product of a collective definitional process"—one in which the actor and others participate. A discreditable trait or performance becomes relevant to self only if it is perceived as such by the actor. How might the potentially stigmatized feel that others think about them, and how might others react to disclosure? Schneider and Conrad note that our understanding of an actor's *perception of stigma* is limited. They then discuss various strategies relative to concealment and disclosure (i.e., whether, and under what conditions, one will come out of the closet or not). For example, parental training regarding the stigma of epilepsy is often very important. Not only do parents frequently serve as coaches but, as they do so, the children learn how to deal with the fact that they are potentially discreditable.

Other people also teach the importance of concealment. The authors end by discussing the strategies of selective concealment and instrumental telling.

Rose Weitz, in "Living with the Stigma of AIDS," continues this theme. She presents data illustrating how twenty-three gay and bisexual men with AIDS are affected by and attempt to manage the stigma associated with their illnesses. For example, in an effort to reduce, assuage, or avoid the actual or potential stigma associated with AIDS, they may conceal their illnesses to others, as well as change their range of social networks. They may, like the people discussed in the Schneider-Conrad piece, learn whom they can trust with the knowledge of their affliction. Efforts may also be made to educate others about AIDS.

"The Adjustment of the Family to the Crisis of Alcoholism," by Joan K. Jackson, provides an excellent account of how family members, particularly wives, try to adjust to a husband's alcoholism. Jackson's article offers a fruitful examination of how the accommodative process actually works. A wife may at first deny that a drinking problem exists by rationalizing it away, and she may be successful in her attempts. However, it may happen that not only does the drinking become progressively worse, but a family crisis develops. The wife may then decide that there is no real hope for the marriage and leave. Jackson maintains that even though many wives do leave their husbands, they frequently return; their return is often prompted by an increased understanding of alcoholism and by the need to lessen their feelings of guilt at leaving a sick man. When a wife returns, she will attempt to reorganize the family while still relying upon accommodative strategies as necessary.

Kathleen J. Ferraro and John M. Johnson, in "How Women Experience Battering: The Process of Victimization," present some recent evidence on the battering of women. The accounts of 120 battered women provide the major data source. The researchers are concerned specifically with identifying those conditions that keep women locked in abusive relationships. What they discover is that instead of seeking help or escaping, most women initially rationalize the violence that is perpetrated upon them by their husbands. Ferraro and Johnson cite several reasons why battered women resort to rationalization. The main one involves the relative lack of institutional, legal, and cultural supports. Thus, practical and social constraints, when coupled with the factors of commitment and love, prompt the use of rationalizations. Ferraro and Johnson, in extending Sykes and Matza's "techniques of neutralization," develop a six-category typology of rationalizations. Each woman in their study used at least one of these techniques, and some used more than one. In terms of the specific rationalizations, women who invoke "the denial of victimization" technique often blame themselves, thereby neutralizing the spouse's responsibility. Some felt that if they had been more passive or conciliatory, the violence could have been avoided.

Rationalizations may be effective for some; however, when battered women cease to rationalize and begin to acknowledge their abuse, the process of feeling victimized begins. The researchers discuss six catalysts that bring about this redefinition of abuse (e.g., a change in the level of abuse, a change in resources, and a change in the visibility of violence). Ferraro and Johnson conclude with a discussion of what they term the emotional career of victimization; they also comment on the aftermath of leaving.

19 / In the Closet with Illness: Epilepsy, Stigma Potential and Information Control

JOSEPH W. SCHNEIDER
PETER CONRAD

The metaphor of the closet has been used frequently to discuss how people avoid or pursue "deviant" identities. Formulated originally in the homosexual subculture, to be "in the closet" has meant to be a secret or covert homosexual. Sociologists have adopted the notion of "coming out" of the closet to describe the development of a gay identity, focusing on self-definition and "public" disclosure as important elements of identity formation (Dank, 1971; Humphreys, 1972; Warren, 1974; Ponse, 1976). Kitsuse (1980) recently has extended the concept of coming out to refer to the "social affirmation of the self" for a wide variety of disvalued groups, including feminists, elderly people, blacks, prostitutes, marijuana users, American Nazis, and many others. In arguing against an "oversocialized" view of deviants encouraged by some narrow labeling interpretations, Kitsuse suggests that increasing numbers of disvalued people in American society have "come out" to affirm their identities as legitimate grounds for the dignity, worth and pride they believe is rightfully theirs.

This link between the closet metaphor and the development of identity is premised, however, on the assumption that in "coming out" there is indeed something to come out to; that there are some developed or developing social definitions that provide the core of this new, open and proud self. Certainly in the case of homosexuality, abandoning the closet of secrecy and concealment was facilitated greatly by the availability of a public identity as "gay and proud." But what of those disvalued by some attribute, performance, or legacy for whom there is no alternate new and proud identity? And what of those for whom even the existence of some "old" and "spoiled" identity may be questionable? In such cases where there may be no clear identity to move from or to, the closet metaphor may seem to lack insight and hence be of little use. We believe, however, that this metaphor taps a more fundamental sociological problem that may, but need not, be linked to the formation of identity.

In this paper we argue that the metaphor of the closet, entry into and exit from it, may be used to focus on the more general sociological problem of how people attempt to manage what they see as discreditable information about themselves. We draw on depth interview data from a study of people with epilepsy—a stigmatized illness (see also Schneider and Conrad, 1979). We try to see how people attempt to maintain favorable or at least neutral definitions of self, given a condition for which no "new" readily available supportive identity or subculture yet exists, and which most of the time—except for the occurrence of periodic seizures—is invisible. By extending the metaphor of the closet to describe this situation, we hope both to increase its analytic utility and learn more about how people manage nondeviant yet stigmatized conditions.[1]

Our sample of 80 people is divided roughly equally by sex, ranging in age from 14 to 54. Most of the respondents come from a metropolitan area of the midwest and none have a history of long-term institutionalization for epilepsy. Interviews were conducted over a two and a half year period beginning in mid-1976, and respondents were selected on the basis of availability and willingness to participate. We used a snowball sampling technique, relying on advertisements in local newspapers, invitation letters passed anonymously by common acquaintances, and names obtained from local social agencies, self-help groups, and health workers. No pretense to statistical representativeness is intended nor was it sought. Due to official restrictions and perceived stigma associated with epilepsy, a population listing from which to draw such a sample does not exist. Our intention was to develop a sample from which theoretical insights would emerge (see Glaser and Strauss, 1967).

We will try here to provide an "insider's" view[2] of 1) how people with epilepsy themselves define their condition as undesirable and discreditable, and, hence, grounds for being "in the closet"; and of 2) how they attempt to manage this discreditable information in such a way as to protect their reputations and rights as normal members of society. We first discuss epilepsy as a potentially stigmatized condition, then move to illustrations of how people perceive the stigma of epilepsy and adopt various strategies of concealment and (paradoxically) selective disclosure, all directed toward protecting what they believe to be a threatened self.

THE STIGMA POTENTIAL OF EPILEPSY

We suggest the concept "stigma potential" to emphasize the significance of epilepsy as an attribute discreditable to one's personal identity (cf. Goffman, 1963:157). Description of the stigma as "potential" rests on two assumptions: 1) that knowledge of one's epilepsy be limited to relatively few others, and 2) that if it were to become more widely known, significant redefinition of self, accompanied by various restrictions and regulation of conduct, might well follow. Although Goffman suggests that possession of such discreditable attributes weighs heavily and shamefully on one's own definitions of self, whether others have the same knowledge or not, we prefer to make that an empirical question. Like Goffman's discreditable person, Becker's (1963, 1973) secret or potential deviant recognizes his or her own acts, qualities and characteristics, *and* is aware of certain relevant prohibitions in the larger cultural and social setting. Given this knowledge, the potential deviant is one who concludes that there is at least some probability that disclosure would lead to discrediting and undesirable consequences. Becker is more equivocal on the issue of self-derogation and shame, requiring only that the actor be aware that rules do exist which may be applied and enforced if others become aware of the hidden practice or attribute. Although shame is an important phenomenon, it is not necessary to the rise of information control strategies. It is of both theoretical and practical interest that epilepsy is an attribute that would seem to create precisely this kind of potentially deviant or stigmatized person.

Like leprosy and venereal disease, epilepsy is an illness with an ancient associated stigma. Furthermore, epileptic seizures—which can range from nearly imperceptible "spacing out" to the more common, dramatic and bizarre grand mal convulsions—constitute violations of taken-for-granted expectations about the competence of actors in social settings, and are thus likely candidates for becoming "deviant behaviors." Although physicians have been defining and treating it for centuries (Temkin, 1971), epilepsy has long been associated with disreputability, satanic possession, and evil (Lennox and Lennox, 1960). Nineteenth century medical and psychiatric research, including that of Maudsley and Lombroso, suggested a causal link between epilepsy and violent crime[3] and encouraged myths about the relation of epilepsy, violent behavior and mental illness. This research supported placing epileptics in colonies and later special hospitals, excluding them from jobs, from entering the United States as immigrants, and sometimes even from marrying and having children.

The advent of anticonvulsant medications (e.g., phenobarbital in 1912 and Dilantin in 1938) allowed for greater medical control of seizures, enabling epileptics to live more conventional lives. Modern medical conceptualizations of epilepsy as a seizure disorder produced by "intermittent electrochemical impulses in the brain" (U.S. Dept. HEW-NIH, 1975) are far removed from the earlier morally-tinged interpretations. But historical residues of the deviant status of epilepsy remain central to the condition's current social reality. The stigma potential of epilepsy is well-documented. In a fairly recent review of the literature, Arangio (1975, 1976) found that stigma was still pervasive. It was manifested in various forms of social discrimination: difficulty in obtaining a driver's license; until 1965, prohibitions (in some states) against marrying; discrimination in obtaining employment (e.g., until 1959 epileptics were not hired for federal civil service positions); difficulties in obtaining all types of insurance; laws (in nine states) that permit sterilization of epileptics under some conditions; and laws (in 17 states) that allow for institutionalization of epileptics (Arangio, 1975). Researchers using intermittent Gallup poll data over the 25-year period 1949 to 1974 found a decrease in attitudinal prejudice toward epileptics, although 20 percent of the population in 1974 still maintained that epileptics should not be employed (Caveness *et al.*, 1974).

Such attitudes and official regulations are, of course, not lost on people with epilepsy. A recent nationwide survey found that one quarter of all epileptics do not tell their employers about epilepsy, and half indicated that having epilepsy created problems in getting a job (Perlman, 1977). While these and other "objective" aspects of prejudice and discrimination toward people with epilepsy have been documented, the ways in which such features of the larger cultural and social world are given meaning in people's subjective experience is less accessible and relatively unexplored.

THE PERCEPTION OF STIGMA

Stigma is by no means an automatic result of possessing some discreditable attribute. The significance of "having" epilepsy is a product of a collective definitional process in which the actor's perspective occupies a central place. As suggested earlier, a discreditable attribute or performance becomes relevant to self only if the individual perceives it as discreditable, whether or not such perceptions are actually applied by others to self or simply considered as a relevant "object" in the environment that must be taken into account. The actor has an important part in the construction of the meaning of epilepsy and of illness generally. It is of course logically possible that people otherwise deemed "ill" are unaware of what their conditions mean to the others with whom they interact: for example, a person surprised by sympathetic reactions to his or her disclosure of cancer, or a young "tough" who in polite society wears venereal disease as a badge of sexual prowess.

Most sociological work on stigma assumes that the stigmatized learn the meaning of their attribute or performance primarily through direct exposure to rejection and disapproval from others. Less understood is the place of the *perception of stigma*—of what the putatively stigmatized think others think of them and "their kind" and about how these others might react to disclosure. This brings us back to the situation of Goffman's discreditable actor, but makes actors' definitions central and problematic. Such actor definitions of epilepsy provide the foundation on which the stigma of epilepsy is constructed.

Over and over in our interviews, people with epilepsy told us that they "have" something that others "don't understand," and that this lack of understanding and knowledge of "what epilepsy is" is a fundamental source of what they see as an actual or potentially negative reaction. They believe that what little information others have about epilepsy is probably incorrect and stereotypical, sometimes incorporating elements of madness and evil. Adjectives such as "frightened" and "scared" were used to describe others' views of epilepsy. One woman, whose epilepsy had been diagnosed at middle age and who had lost a teaching job because of seizures at work, said:

> Well, I understand it now and *I'm* not afraid of it. But most people are unless they've experienced it, and so you just don't talk to other people about it, and if you do, never use the word "epilepsy." The word itself, I mean job-ways, insurance-ways... anything, the hang-ups there are on it. There's just too much prejudice so the less said about it the better.

One man compared others' ignorance and fear of epilepsy to similar reactions to leprosy: "The public is so ill educated toward an epileptic. It's like someone with leprosy walking into a room. You see a leper and you run because you're afraid of it." And another woman spoke of epilepsy's "historical implications":

> The fact of having epilepsy. It isn't the seizures. I think they are a very minor part of it. Its implications are so *enormous*. The historical implications of epilepsy are fantastic. I'm lucky to have been born when I was. If I was born at the beginning of this century I would have been discarded... probably locked away somewhere.

In these and similar ways, people recognize that ignorance and fear taint public images of epilepsy. They then take such recognitions into account in their own strategies and decisions about how to control such discrediting information.

Seizures in social situations are an important aspect of this discrediting perception of epilepsy. Seizures might be seen as sociologically akin to such involuntary *faux pas* as breaking wind or belching. Farts or belches, however, are reasonably familiar and normalized in middle-class society, but people with epilepsy believe that others ordinarily consider seizures as beyond the boundaries of undesirable but nevertheless "normal" conduct. One woman suggested seizures are "like having your pants fall down" in public. Another described how she believed others see seizures: "I can't use the word 'horrible,' but they think... it's *ugly*. It is. It's strange. It's something you're not used to seeing." People with epilepsy believe that others see the actual behaviors associated with seizures—including unconsciousness, violent muscle contractions, falling to the ground, or simply being "absent" from the social scene—as objective grounds for a more fundamental, "essential" disreputability. The stigma was described this way by another woman:

> It's one of those fear images; it's something that people don't know about and it has strong negative connotations in people's minds. It's a bad image, something scary, sort of like a beggar; it's dirty, the person falling down and frothing at the

mouth and jerking and the bystanders not knowing what to do. It's something that happens in public which isn't "nice."

As these data suggest, aside from the question of shame of self-labeling, people who have epilepsy perceive the social meanings attached to it and to seizures as threats to their status as normal and competent members of society.

COACHES FOR CONCEALMENT: LEARNING TO BE DISCREDITABLE

How do people construct these views of others' perceptions? As we suggested, conventional sociological wisdom has emphasized direct disvaluing treatment by others. While this interactive experience is undoubtedly important to study, our data strongly suggest that people with epilepsy also learn such views from significant and supportive others, particularly from parents. Parental training in the stigma of epilepsy is most clear for people who were diagnosed when they were children, but stigma coaches were also identified by those who were diagnosed when they were adults.[4]

Our data indicate that the more the parents convey a definition of epilepsy as something "bad," and the less willing they are to talk about it with their children, the more likely the child is to see it as something to be concealed. One thirty-four-year-old woman had maintained a strategy of tightly controlled secrecy from the time she was diagnosed as having epilepsy at age fourteen. She recalled her parents' reaction:

> Complete disbelief. You know, "We've never had anything like that in our family." I can remember that was very plainly said, almost like I was something... something was wrong. They did not believe it. In fact, we went to another doctor and then it was confirmed.

These parents proceeded to manage their daughter's epilepsy by a combination of silence and maternal "coaching" on how to conceal it from others. When asked if she told her husband of her epilepsy before they were married, the same woman said:

> I talked to Mom about it. She said, "Don't tell him because some people don't understand. He may not understand. That's not something you talk about." I asked her, "Should I talk to him about passing out?" She said, "Never say 'epilepsy.' It's not something we talk about."

She had learned her "lesson" well and concealed her illness for almost twenty years.

Family silence about epilepsy can itself be a lesson in stigma. One middle-aged woman who was just beginning to "break through" (cf. Davis, 1961) such silence, said that her parents had never told her she had epilepsy: "They just told me I suffered from fainting fits." She had filled this vacuum of silence by concluding that she must be "going mad." Throughout her childhood, and even in her present relationship with her parents, epilepsy had been "brushed under the carpet": "It's not nice to talk about those things." Like sexual variety in the late nineteenth century, epilepsy was obviously something "bad" because it was something "people just didn't (i.e., shouldn't) talk about."

Parents are not the only coaches for secrecy. Close associates, friends, and even professionals sometimes suggest concealment as a strategy for dealing with epilepsy, particularly in circumstances where it is believed to be a disqualifying characteristic. One woman described such advice by a physician-medical examiner who said he "had to" fire her from a teaching job because of her seizures: "He advised me to lie about it. He said, 'If you don't miss work from it and it's not visible to anybody, lie about it.' And I've been doing that since and I've been able to work since."

As the literature on subcultures makes clear, stigmatized people can learn practical survival strategies from others' experience. A supportive subculture surrounding epilepsy is only in its infancy, as is true for most illnesses,[5] but various self-help groups do exist through which people with epilepsy may learn relevant coping skills (see Borman *et al.*, 1980). In the absence of a developed subculture for people like themselves, some people with epilepsy learn the importance of concealment from people with other illnesses. As one woman said of her diabetic husband's experience:

> He didn't know. He hadn't gone through this [or] met other diabetics. He didn't know how to carry out a lie. One of the things that we learned, again from the diabetes, was how [to] lie if they asked for a urine sample. We now have met, through the rap sessions, people who said, "You bring somebody else's urine!" Well, that's a pretty shocking thing to have to do. Yeah, there are times when you gotta lie.

The importance of others as coaches for concealment is clear. Through this "diabetes underground" her husband learned how to lie, then taught it to her.

Some significant others, however, including some parents, adopt strategies of openness, honesty and neutralization. Parents who define their child's epilepsy "just like any other medical problem" and "certainly nothing to be ashamed of" apparently encourage their children to have a much more neutral view and a more open informational control strategy. One successful businessman credited his parents with managing epilepsy so as to minimize it and prevent him from using it as a "crutch" or "excuse":

> The parents of an epileptic child are the key to the whole ball of wax, in recognizing that you have a problem in the family but not to let that control the total actions and whole livelihood and whole future of the family. Accept it and go about doing what has to be done to maintain an even keel.

The themes of "taking epilepsy in stride," not "using" it as a "cop-out" are reminiscent of the cautions against the temptation to use medical excuses which Parsons (1951) analyzed (cf. Waitzkin and Waterman, 1974). They were common to the accounts given to us by people who seemed to portray their epilepsy as "no big thing," partly from concern that such comments might be interpreted by others as requests for "sympathy" and "special treatment." Parents who cautioned against such "special pleading" uses of epilepsy also typically were recalled as having taught their children the values of self-reliance, independence and achievement—as another way of overcoming an emphasis on epilepsy and its significance. Learning that epilepsy need not be a barrier to personal or social acceptance led individuals to be more "out" of than "in" the closet of epilepsy; learning to believe that epilepsy was a shameful flaw encouraged, understandably, the development of just the opposite strategy.

STRATEGIES OF SELECTIVE CONCEALMENT: THE CLOSET OF EPILEPSY HAS A REVOLVING DOOR

Most discussions of the self and the "closet" assume that one can only be in or out, and that being out must follow a period of being in. As we learned more about how people experience epilepsy, we realized that such a view of the closet of epilepsy was much too simple. Sometimes people conceal their epilepsy, sometimes they do not, and the same persons can be both "open" and "closed" during the same period in their lives. In short, both concealment and disclosure proved to be quite complex and selective strategies of information management.

A part of the "wisdom" of the world of epilepsy is that there are some people you can tell about your illness and others you cannot (cf. Goffman, 1963). Even the most secretive (and twelve of our respondents said we were the first people they had told about their epilepsy except for their physician and immediate family) had told at least several other people about their condition. Close friends and family members are perhaps the most clear instance of "safe others," but "people I feel comfortable with" and those who "won't react negatively to epilepsy" are also sometimes told. Such persons are often used to test reactions: "I think the first couple of times I mentioned it was with my very closest friends to sort of test the water and when it wasn't any problem, then I began to feel freer to mention it."

The development of more diffuse disclosure or "coming out" seemed contingent on how these early disclosures went. Just as perceived "positive" results may encourage people to come out more, perceived "negative" consequences from trial disclosures may encourage a return to concealment as the predominant way to control personal and social impacts. As one woman put it:

> I tried to get a driver's license when I was 18 or 19, after I was married. We were living in Mississippi and I put it on [the form] that I was epileptic, only because I was afraid if I pass out and I'm drivin' a car, well, that's dangerous. I took the thing up there and they said, "Epileptics can't—you have to have a doctor's thing." We moved about two months later to California. I got my driver's license and didn't put it down.

Later on she made another attempt at disclosure, this time on an application to live in a college dormitory. After being disqualified from living on campus and then declining a scholarship, she decided that secrecy was the only strategy by which she could minimize the risk of rejection and differential treatment. In retrospect, she concluded: "I don't know if maybe I wasn't testing... at the time, you know, well, is it okay? If things had been different, maybe I could have talked about it." When asked if she discussed epilepsy with new people she meets, another woman spoke specifically of this "risk":

> It depends. I still find it hard, but I'm trying to. I have to trust somebody a lot before I'll tell them in terms of a friendship basis. All my close friends know, but in terms of my work, forget it. This is a risk I can't take after the previous experience. I still have great in-built fears about losing a job from it. I'm not ready to put myself at that risk.

An upwardly-mobile young administrator said he lost his driver's license as a result of disclosing his epilepsy. He recalled that experience and what he had "learned" from it: "I started out tryin' to be honest about it and got burned. So I gave up bein' honest about it in that circumstance." Although this man did disclose his epilepsy to a wide variety of others, including his employer, he said he regularly lied about it on driver's license forms.

Such data clearly suggest that people can and do maintain carefully segregated and selective strategies of managing the stigma potential of epilepsy. Some situations were considered considerably more "high risk" than others. In employment, for example, concealment, including lying on initial employment applications, was thought to be the best general strategy. Because they thought there would be reprisals if their employers subsequently learned of their epilepsy, respondents who advocated such concealment typically said they adopted a monitoring or "see how it's going" approach to possible later disclosure. If they saw approval in others' reactions to them during initial contacts, they could attempt disclosure. One young woman who said she had not had a seizure for 19 years and took no medication was still very sensitive about her "past" when applying for a job:

> Well, employers are the only thing I haven't been open with. On an application, I will not write it. If I feel I have a chance for a job and I'm gonna make it, I'll bring it up. But to put it on that application—because employers, they look at it, they see that thing checked; it just gives me a feeling that they don't give you a chance.

Although she said she never had experienced discriminatory treatment in employment, this woman said she usually waits "until I get into that interview and sell myself first. Then I'll come out and say, 'There's one more point. . . .' " Another respondent said he would wait until "I have my foot in the door and they said, 'Hey, he's doing okay' " before disclosing his epilepsy to his employers. People who had tried this strategy of gradual disclosure after employer approval of their work were often surprised that others made so little of their condition. As a result of such experiences they proceeded to redefine some aspects of their own "theories" of others' reactions to epilepsy.

Finally, concealing epilepsy—staying in the closet—was believed important in situations where others might be predisposed to criticize. One woman, who said she was open to friends, commented that she wouldn't want others "in the neighborhood" to know. She explained; "At this point I'm not involved in quarrels. I would think that if I got into a quarrel or feuding situation, it [the epilepsy] would be something that would be used against me." The same view of epilepsy as ammunition for critics was expressed by a man who defined his work as "very political." He thought that if others learned of his epilepsy, they would "add that on as an element of my character that makes [me] undesirable." Sometimes this "closing ranks" against adversaries can even exclude those who otherwise would be told. One woman said that because her brother married a woman "I don't particularly care for," she had decided simply not to tell him of her diagnosis. Her sister-in-law was "the type that would say, you know, 'You're crazy because you have it,' or 'There's something wrong with you.' And she would probably laugh." Even a physician may be seen more as a gatekeeper than an advocate and counselor. One man expressed this theme in many of our interviews quite clearly:

> If he is going to go running to the state and tell the state every time I have a seizure, I don't feel I can be honest with that doctor. He is not keeping his part of the bargain. Everything on my medical records is supposed to be sacred.

Taken together, these data suggest that the process of information management used by people with epilepsy is much more complex than the now-familiar metaphor of being either "in or out of the closet" would lead us to believe. They also indicate that, in strategies of disclosure and concealment of potentially stigmatizing attributes, being out of or in the closet of *epilepsy* may often have much less to do with one's "identity" than with the more practical matter of preventing others from applying limiting and restrictive rules that disqualify one from normal social roles. Epilepsy is something that is hidden at some times and in some places and disclosed quite readily at other times and in other places. Such disclosure and concealment appear contingent upon a complex interaction of one's learned perceptions of the stigma of epilepsy, actual "test" experiences with others before and/or after disclosure, and the nature of the particular relationships involved.

INSTRUMENTAL TELLING: DISCLOSING AS A MANAGEMENT STRATEGY

Information management may include disclosure as well as concealment, even when the information is potentially discreditable. Except for the respondents who adopted rigidly secretive strategies, the people we spoke to said they "usually" or "always" told certain others of their epilepsy under certain circumstances. In this final section we discuss two types of such telling that emerged in our data: telling as "therapy" and "preventive telling." Both involve disclosure but, like concealment, are conscious attempts to mitigate the potentially negative impact of epilepsy on one's self and daily round.

Telling as Therapy

Disclosing feelings of guilt, culpability, and self-derogation can be cathartic, as we know from a variety of social science research. Particularly for those who have concealed what they see as some personal blemish or flaw, such telling can serve a "therapeutic" function for the self by sharing or diffusing the burden of such information. It can free the energy used to control information for other social activities. Such relief, however, requires a properly receptive audience: that is, listeners who are supportive, encouraging, empathetic, and nonjudgmental. Such occasions of telling and hearing cannot only be cathartic, they also can encourage people with epilepsy to define their condition as a nonremarkable and neutral facet of self, perhaps even an "interesting" one, as one man told us. This sort of "telling as therapy" is akin to what Davis (1961) described as the relief associated with breaking through the collectively created and negotiated silence surrounding the physical disabilities of polio victims when they interacted with normals.

Such therapeutic telling seems instrumental primarily in its impact on the actor's self-definition: at the minimum, it simply externalizes what is believed to be significant information about self that has been denied one's intimates and associates. Many of the people we interviewed, in recalling such experiences of "coming out" to select and safe audiences, emphasized the importance of talk as therapy. One woman said of such talking: "It's what's got me together about it [the epilepsy]." And a man recalled how telling friends about epilepsy allowed him to minimize it in his own mind:

> I think in talking to them [friends] I would try to convince myself that it didn't have to be terribly important. Now that I think more about it, I was probably just defiant about it: "I ain't gonna let this Goddamned thing get in my way, period."

For a final example, one of the few respondents, who in keeping with her mother's careful coaching had told virtually no one, insightfully suggested how she might use the interview itself as grounds for redefining her epilepsy and self:

> It just seems so weird now that I've—because I'm talking to you about it, and I've never talked to anybody about it. It's really not so bad. You know it hasn't affected me that much, but no one wants to talk about it.... [Talking about epilepsy] makes me feel I'm really not so bad off. Just because I can't find answers to those questions, cuz like I think I feel sorry for myself. I can sit around the house and just dream up all these things, you know, why I'm persecuted and [all].

Such selection disclosure to supportive and nonjudgmental others can thus help "banish the ghosts" that flourish in secrecy and isolation. It allows for feedback and the renegotiation of the perception of stigma. Through externalizing what is believed to be a potentially negative feature of self, people with epilepsy *and* their audiences can redefine this attribute as an "ordinary" or "typical" part of themselves (Dingwall, 1976). As we have already indicated, however, this strategy appears to be effective primarily among one's intimates and close friends. When facing strangers or those whose reactions cannot be assumed supportive, such as prospective employers, the motor vehicle bureau, or virtually any bureaucracy's application form, such openness can be set aside quickly.

Preventive Telling

Another kind of instrumental telling we discovered in our data could be called "preventive": disclosure to influence others' actions and/or ideas toward self and toward epileptics in general. One variety of such preventive telling occurs when actors think it probable that others, particularly others with whom they share some routine, will witness their seizures. The grounds cited for such disclosure are that others then "will know what it is" and "won't be scared." By "knowing what it is," respondents mean other define "it"—the epilepsy and seizure—as a *medical* problem, thereby removing blame and responsibility from the actor for the aberrant conduct in question. The actors assume that others should not be "frightened" if they too learn that "it" is a medical problem.

To engage such anticipatory preventive telling is to offer a kind of "medical disclaimer" (cf. Hewitt and Stokes, 1975) intended to influence others' reactions should a seizure occur. By bringing a blameless, beyond-my-control medical interpretation to such potentially discrediting events, people attempt to reduce the risk that more morally disreputable interpretations might be applied by naive others witnessing one's seizures. One young woman recalled that she felt "great" when her parents told her junior high teachers about epilepsy, because "I'd rather have them know than think I was a dummy or something... or think I was having... you know, *problems.*" Reflecting the power of medical excuses (as well as a relative hierarchy of legitimacy among medical excuses), a middle-aged man who described himself as an "alcoholic" told of how he would disclose epilepsy to defuse others' complaints about his drinking:

> I'd say, "I have to drink. It's the only way I can maintain.... I have seizures you know"... and this kind of thing. People would then feel embarrassed. Or you'd say, "I'm epileptic," then they'd feel embarrassed and say, "Oh, well, gee, we're sorry, that's right. We forgot about that."

Such accounts illustrate the kind of social currency that medical definitions possess in general and in particular with respect to epilepsy. As with all currency, however, its effectiveness as a medium of acceptable exchange rests on its mutual validation by those who give and receive it, what others in fact think of such accounts remains largely unknown.

Beyond providing a medical frame of reference through which others may interpret seizures, such preventive telling may also include specific instructions about what others should do when seizures do occur. Because people with epilepsy believe others are almost totally ignorant of what seizures are, they similarly assume that others have little idea of how to react to seizures. By providing what in effect are directions for others to follow, people who do preventive telling believe they are protecting not only their body but their self. As the young administrator we quoted earlier put it:

> Down the road, I'll usually make a point to tell someone I'm around a lot because I know that it's frightening. So I will, partly for my own purposes, tell them I've got it; if I have one [seizure] that it's nothing to worry about. And don't take me to the hospital even if I ask you to. I always tell people that I work with because I presume I'll be with them for some long period of time. And I may have a seizure and I want them to know what *not* to do, in particular.

Through such telling, people solve some of the problems that a seizure represents for naive others. While these others then have the task of carrying out such instructions—which typically are "do nothing," "make me comfortable," "don't call the ambulance," and "keep me from hurting myself"—the authority, and therefore responsibility, for such reaction rests with the individual giving the instructions.

Disclosure of one's epilepsy may depend also on the anticipation of rejection at some subsequent telling or disclosure occasion. "Coming out" to those who appear to be candidates for "close" relationships is a strategy for minimizing the pain of later rejection. As one man said, "If they're going to leave [because of epilepsy] better it be sooner than later." Another spoke of such telling as a "good way of testing" what kind of friend such persons would be. "Why go through all the trauma of falling in love with someone if they are going to hate your guts once they find out you're an epileptic?"

We discovered that people also disclose their epilepsy when they feel it necessary or important to "educate" others. While this strategy is sometimes mediated and supported through participation in various self-help groups, some individuals initiated it themselves. One young man who became active in a local self-help group described his "rap" on epilepsy as follows:

> It's a good manner, I use it quite a bit. I'll come through and say epilepsy is a condition, not a disease. I can throw out all the statistics. I usually say most people are not in wheelchairs or in bed because of epilepsy, they're walking the streets just like I am and other people. Anything like that to make comparisons, to get a point across.

Another respondent, who believed she had benefited greatly by an early talk with a veteran epileptic, spoke of the importance of such education: "That's why I think it is important to come out of the closet to some extent. Because once people have met an epileptic and found out that it's a *person* with epilepsy, that helps a lot." Exposure to a person who "has epilepsy" but is conventional in all other ways may stimulate others to redefine their image of "epileptics."

CONCLUSION

Illness is an individualizing and privatizing experience. As Parsons (1951) argued, occupants of the sick role are not only dissuaded from "enjoying" the exemptions associated with their state but are segregated and separated from other sick people. When individuals desire to be "normal" and lead conventional lives the potential of stigma is isolating; persons fear disclosure of discreditable information and may limit their contacts or connections with others. As Ponse observes, "The veils of anonymity are often as effective with one's own as with those from whom one wishes to hide. Thus, an unintended consequence of secrecy is that it isolates members from one another" (1976:319). Persons with stigmatized illnesses like epilepsy, and perhaps with other illness as well, are doubly insulated from one another, at least in one very important sense. Because there is no illness subculture they are separate, alone and unconnected with others sharing the same problems (for an unusual exception, see Gussow and Tracey, 1968). And this very desire to lead conventional and stigma-free lives further separates and isolates them from each other. It is not surprising that the vast majority of people with epilepsy we interviewed did not know a single other epileptic.

Returning to our metaphor of the closet, we can now see that the potential of stigma certainly leads some people to create the closet as a secret and safe place. And usually, whether with homosexuality or epilepsy, people are in the closet alone. There are important differences, however. Few people in the closet with epilepsy even have any idea where other closets may be. Because there is usually no supportive subculture (a few recent and important self-help groups are notable exceptions) there is no place for a person with epilepsy to get insider information or to test the possible effects of coming out. Since most people with epilepsy want to be considered conventional people with a medical disorder, there is little motivation to come out and develop an epileptic identity. It is little wonder, then, that the closet of epilepsy has a revolving door.

To summarize: for those who possess some discreditable feature of self, some generally hidden "fact" or quality, the disclosure of which they believe will bring undesired consequences, the attempt to control information is a major strategy. We have described several ways people with epilepsy engage in such management work. Our data have suggested that the idea of being "in the closet" and that of being a "secret deviant" need to be extended to incorporate the complex reality of how people very selectively disclose or withhold discreditable information about themselves. Finally, we have shown how disclosing can serve the same ends as concealing. In addition, we suggest that sociological explorations into the experience of illness may well lend new dimensions to old concepts and give us greater understanding of the ways people manage such discomforting and vulnerable parts of their lives.

References

Anspach, Renee R.
1979 "From stigma to identity politics: Political activism among the physically disabled and former mental patients." Social Science and Medicine 13A:766–73.

Arangio, Anthony J.
1975 Behind the Stigma of Epilepsy. Washington, D.C.: Epilepsy Foundation of America.
1976 "The stigma of epilepsy." American Rehabilitation 2 (September/October): 4–6.

Becker, Howard S.
1963 Outsiders. New York: Macmillan.
1973 "Labeling theory reconsidered." Pp. 177–208 in Howard S. Becker, Outsiders, New York: Free Press.

Borman, Leonard D., James Davies and David Droge
1980 "Self-help groups for persons with epilepsy." In B. Hermann [ed.], A Multidisciplinary Handbook of Epilepsy. Springfield, Ill.: Thomas.

Caveness, W. F., H. Houston Merritt and G. H. Gallup, Jr.
1974 "A survey of public attitudes towards epilepsy in 1974 with an indication of trends over the past twenty-five years." Epilepsia 15:523–36.

Conrad, Peter and Joseph W. Schneider
1980 Deviance and Medicalization: From Badness to Sickness. St. Louis, Missouri: Mosby.

Dank, Barry M.
1971 "Coming out in the gay world." Psychiatry 34 (May): 180–97.

Davis, Fred
1961 "Deviance disavowal: The management of strained interaction by the visibly handicapped." Social Problems 9 (Fall):120–32.
Dingwall, Robert
1976 Aspects of Illness. New York: St. Martin's.
Fabrega, Horacio, Jr.
1972 "The study of disease in relation to culture." Behavioral Science 17: 183–200.
1979 "The ethnography of illness." Social Science and Medicine 13A:565–76.
Freidson, Eliot
1966 "Disability as social deviance." Pp. 71–99 in M. Sussman [ed.], Sociology and Rehabilitation. Washington, D.C.: The American Sociological Association.
1970 Profession of Medicine. New York: Dodd, Mead.
Glaser, Barney G. and Anselm L. Strauss
1967 The Discovery of Grounded Theory. Chicago: Aldine.
Goffman, Erving
1963 Stigma. Englewood Cliffs, N.J.: Prentice-Hall.
Gussow, Zachary, and George S. Tracey
1968 "Status, ideology and adaptation to stigmatized illness: A study of leprosy." Human Organization 27 (4):316–25.
Hewitt, John P. and Randall Stokes
1975 "Disclaimers." American Sociological Review 40:1–11.
Humphreys, Laud
1972 Out of the Closets. Englewood Cliffs, N.J.: Prentice-Hall.
Idler, Ellen L.
1979 "Definitions of health and illness in medical sociology." Social Science and Medicine 13A:723–31.
Kitsuse, John I.
1980 "Coming out all over: Deviants and the politics of social problems." Social Problems 28:1.
Lennox, Gordon W. and Margaret A. Lennox
1960 Epilepsy and related disorders, Volume I. Boston: Little, Brown.
Mark, Vernon H. and Frank R. Ervin
1970 Violence and the Brain. New York: Harper & Row.
Parsons, Talcott
1951 The Social System. New York: Free Press.
Perlman, Leonard G.
1977 The Person With Epilepsy: Life Style, Needs, Expectations. Chicago: National Epilepsy League.
Ponse, Barbara
1976 "Secrecy in the lesbian world." Urban Life 5 (October): 313–38.
Schneider, Joseph W. and Peter Conrad
1979 "Medical and sociological typologies: The case of epilepsy." Unpublished manuscript, Drake University, Des Moines, Iowa.
Strauss, Anselm L. and Barney G. Glaser
1975 Chronic Illness and the Quality of Life. St. Louis, Missouri: Mosby.
Temkin, Oswei
1971 The Falling Sickness, Second edition. Baltimore, Maryland: Johns Hopkins Press.

U.S. Department of Health Education and Welfare—National Institute of Health
1975 The NINCDS Epilepsy Research Program. Washington, D.C.: U.S. Government Printing Office.

Waitzkin, H. K. and B. Waterman
1974 The Exploitation of Illness in Capitalist Society. Indianapolis: Bobbs-Merrill.

Warren, Carol A. B.
1974 Identity and Community in the Gay World. New York: Wiley.

West, Patrick B.
1979a "Making sense of epilepsy." Pp. 162–69 in D. J. Osborne, M. M. Gruneberg and J. R. Eiser (eds.), Research in Psychology and Medicine, Volume 2. New York: Academic.
1979b "An investigation into the social construction and consequences of the label epilepsy." Sociological Review 27:719–41.

Notes

1. The moral parallel between illness and deviance has been well-recognized in the sociological literature. Parsons (1951) first noted that illness and crime are analytically similar because they both represent threats to effective role performance and are "dysfunctional" for society, calling forth appropriate mechanisms of social control. Freidson (1966, 1970) addressed this moral parallel more directly, by arguing that both illness and deviance are disvalued and disvaluing attributes variously attached to actors and situations believed to challenge preferred and dominant definitions of appropriate conduct and "health." More recently, Dingwall (1976) has advocated a phenomenological, insider's approach to illness as lived experience. He suggests that illness might be considered deviance (1) to the extent that it involves behavior perceived by others as "out of the ordinary" or unusual, and (2) if sufficient intentionality or willfulness can be attributed to the ill/deviant actor for the conduct in question (see also Conrad and Schneider, 1980). While we stop short of concluding that epilepsy is "deviant," it seems clear from our data that it is stigmatized, at least in the eyes of those who have it.

2. While there is a relative imbalance of sociological "insider" accounts of being deviant, such work is even more rare for the experience of illness. We have few sociological studies of what it is like *to be* sick, to *have* cancer, diabetes, schizophrenia, heart disease, and so on (for exceptions see Davis, 1961; Gussow and Tracey, 1968; Strauss and Glaser, 1975). This may be due in part to the historic dominance of professional medical definitions of health and illness. We agree with Dingwall (1976), Fabrega (1972, 1979), and Idler (1979), that more research is needed into how these and other illnesses are experienced as social phenomena.

3. For a more current version of the argument linking the biophysiology of the brain and violence, see Mark and Ervin (1970).

4. See West's (1979a, b) discussion of 24 British families containing a child with epilepsy and how parents managed negative stereotypes of epilepsy in light of their child's diagnosis.

5. For an interesting discussion of some exceptions, see Anspach's (1979) analysis of the "identity politics" of the physically disabled and former mental patients. As we suggest, the availability of a new and positive identity is crucial to the development of the kind of politics Anspach describes.

20 / Living with the Stigma of AIDS

ROSE WEITZ

INTRODUCTION

In his classic work on the subject (1963:4), Goffman identified three types of stigma:

> First there are abominations of the body—the various physical deformities. Next there are blemishes of individual character..., these being inferred from a known record of, for example,...homosexuality, unemployment, suicidal attempts, and radical political behavior. Finally, there are the tribal stigma of race, nation, and religion, these being stigma that can be transmitted through lineages...

All three types of stigma can affect the lives of persons with AIDS (PWAs as they call themselves). Many PWAs experience stigma because they cannot meet cultural expectations for physical appearance or ability. As the disease progresses, PWAs may become emaciated, exhausted, and, in some cases, covered by disfiguring rashes or cancer lesions. Eventually, they may become unable to walk, talk, see, or care for themselves.

PWAs also may experience stigma because others believe that AIDS is a sign of a "blemished character." Currently, public health officials believe that 89 percent of reported cases of AIDS in the United States have occurred among persons who appear to have contracted AIDS through male homosexual activity or illegal intravenous drug use (AIDS Program, 1989). Because so many PWAs contract AIDS through socially unacceptable activities, even PWAs who have contracted AIDS in other ways frequently find that other people stigmatize them and consider their illness a deserved and divine punishment.

In almost half of all U.S. cases, this stigma is further heightened by notions of inferior or tainted lineage. To date, 41 percent of AIDS cases have occurred among persons already stigmatized because they were born black or hispanic. Another one percent have occurred among hemophiliacs and one percent among children who have contracted AIDS in utero. In these cases, others may stigmatize the individual not only for having AIDS but for having inherited somehow tainted or inferior blood.

Goffman's typology of stigma does not acknowledge the additional stigma which accompanies "abominations of the body" that are fatal, contagious, and still considered mysterious by much of the public. In past centuries, life was short and death was an accepted part of life. Now that early death is a rare and terrifying event, dying patients regardless of diagnosis often experience social rejection (Charmaz, 1980:159–61). In addition, because AIDS was identified so recently, members of the public may fear that AIDS will prove more readily contagious than physicians now believe. A recent national survey found that, despite the contrary evidence, 22% of adults believe that it is somewhat or very likely that a person can get AIDS from insects. Similarly, 23% feared getting AIDS from "eating in a restaurant where the cook has AIDS virus" (National Center for Health Statistics, 1988). Those fears, reinforced by sources as disparate as fundamentalist ministers and Masters and Johnson (1988), lead many individuals to shun PWAs.

Despite the mass media's extensive coverage of AIDS, few sociologists have yet written about the experience of having AIDS and none have focused on how stigma affects PWAs. However, researchers have investigated how people with other illnesses are affected by and manage stigma. Studies suggest that ill people try to avoid stigma either by revealing their illnesses, so that others will not be shocked or confused by their unusual behaviors, or by concealing their illnesses, so that their differences will not lead others to reject them (Schneider and Conrad, 1983; Hilbert, 1984; Boutte, 1987; Brooks and Matson, 1987). Ill persons also can try to reduce stigma by teaching others the biology of their illnesses and arguing against punitive theological explanations for illness (Gussow and Tracy, 1968).

This article describes how stigma affects PWAs' relationships with families, friends, lovers, colleagues, and health care workers. It explores how PWAs avoid or reduce stigma by concealing their illnesses, learning when and to whom they should reveal their illnesses, changing their social networks, educating others about AIDS, developing nonstigmatizing theories of illness causation, and using bravado to convince others that they are still functioning social beings.

METHODS AND SAMPLE

This article draws on interviews I conducted between July, 1986 and March, 1987 with 23 Arizona residents who either had AIDS or AIDS-Related Complex (ARC). For this analysis, I have combined persons with AIDS and persons with ARC because I could not consistently separate the two according to either medical diagnosis or self-diagnosis. For similar reasons, the U.S. Centers for Disease Control recently changed its definition of AIDS to subsume most cases previously considered ARC. Although the prognosis for persons with AIDS is grimmer than that for persons with ARC, some persons with AIDS survive longer and with less disability than some persons with ARC. Moreover, some individuals are told by their physicians that they have ARC when they clearly have AIDS and some are told they have AIDS when they appear to have ARC. Some believe that the two diseases are essentially identical while others believe that they are very different. Finally, some people vacillate in their statements about what disease they have and what its prognosis is. Thus, I could not consistently sort cases by either actual or perceived health status.

All respondents discussed in this article were men who described themselves as gay or bisexual (although none mentioned any recent relationships with women). Three of the men had used drugs as well. I also interviewed two heterosexual women who had used intravenous drugs and one man who was seropositive for HIV antibodies but had not yet been diagnosed as having AIDS or ARC. Because I interviewed only two women and one seropositive but asymptomatic individual, I have only limited understanding of how such individuals' experiences might differ from that of gay or bisexual PWAs. Consequently, I present in this article only data from the interviews with gay and bisexual men.

When my study began, the Arizona Department of Health Services believed that approximately 40 of the 110 known AIDS cases in the state were still living. To contact these and other PWAs, I posted signs in gay bars; announced the study in gay and mainstream newspapers and AIDS political action groups; asked physicians, AIDS support group leaders, and other respondents to inform PWAs of the study; and had non-profit groups which offer emotional or financial support to PWAs send letters describing the study to their clients. Eighteen of the 23 subjects learned of the study through the non-profit groups, two from friends, two from a political action group, and one from a notice in a gay newspaper.

The sample is comparable to the Arizona population in terms of religion and to the state's reported AIDS cases at the time of the study in terms of sex, geographical location (overwhelmingly urban), and mode of transmission (Arizona Dept. of Health Services, February 2, 1987). Because participating in the interviews required mental competence and some physical stamina, the sample undoubtedly underrepresents the most seriously ill PWAs. It also underrepresents persons with Kaposi's sarcoma (1 percent of the sample, but 21 percent of reported cases), even though they tend to be less ill than other PWAs, perhaps because these individuals do not want a stranger to see the disfiguring lesions which Kaposi's sarcoma can cause. In addition, the sample underrepresents nonwhites (0 percent of the sample but 13 percent of reported cases), who typically are less integrated into the AIDS support networks and therefore were less likely to have heard of the study. Finally, the sample overrepresents persons in their thirties (60 percent of the sample, but 42 percent of reported cases) and underrepresents older persons.

The data for this paper were obtained through semistructured interviews. I began with a set list of questions, but during each interview also probed into any unexpected topics that seemed potentially significant. These new topics were then incorporated into subsequent interviews. Thus, all the interviews covered the same basic questions, but the later interviews also included additional ones which emerged as significant in the earlier interviews. Interviews ranged from two to five hours in length, averaging about three hours, and were audiotaped and transcribed. Interviews took place at respondents' homes unless they preferred another location (usually my home).

I analyzed the data using themes which emerged from the respondents' statements. With each interview, I began to develop themes which I followed up in subsequent interviews. After completing the interviews, I reread them all to identify additional critical concepts. I then sorted the interview materials according to these concepts to see what patterns emerged. These patterns were used to develop the structure of my analysis in this article.

The Impact of Stigma

Given the extensive media coverage of AIDS, PWAs cannot avoid knowing that many people condemn them and consider AIDS a divine punishment for sin. Several of my subjects described PWAs as the modern world's equivalent of lepers. A few mentioned their fears that they would be quarantined or even killed if the public learned they had AIDS. One expressed the fear that if the "rednecks living across the street... found out a gay person was over here with AIDS, they may decide to get drunk one night and come over and kill the faggot." The sense of stigma was so strong that another said he would rather die than be cured for if he were cured he would have to live the rest of his life with the stigma of having once had AIDS.

The following sections describe how this sense of stigma develops, and how stigma pervades PWAs' relationships with family, friends, lovers, health care workers, and fellow workers. The final section discusses how PWAs cope with this stigma.

Family All PWAs run a risk that their families will reject them, either because of their illness *per se* or because their illness exposes or emphasizes that they are gay or use drugs. One of the men I spoke with was a 27 year old computer operator whose parents lived in a small town in another state. He felt he had a good relationship with his parents, but had never told them of his sexual orientation. When asked how he thought his family would react to news of his diagnosis, he said:

> You just can't predict. They might find it so disgusting that you'll basically lose them. They'll be gone. Or they'll go through the adjustment period and not mind. You really don't know.

Virtually every respondent reported that at least one family member had ceased contact with him after learning of his illness. One source of this rejection is that diagnosis with AIDS can reinforce families' belief that homosexuality is immoral. Families who had always questioned the morality of homosexuality may interpret an individual's illness as divine punishment, regarding it as proof that homosexual behavior should not be tolerated. For example, a 26 year old tailor from a fundamentalist Christian family, whose relatives had not known he was gay, described how AIDS forced him to reveal his sexual orientation and thus "put a wedge" between him and his family. His family considered homosexuality sinful and questioned whether they should help him with his health problems if he would not change his behaviors. He was still in contact with his parents, even though his mother had told him that his homosexuality was an "embarrassment" to her. But he had stopped talking to his sister because he could not abide her constant admonitions "to repent" and "to confess sin."

Even PWAs whose families in the past appeared to accept their lifestyles may find that their families reject them once their diagnosis becomes known. When questioned about this, the PWAs suggested that somehow AIDS made their homosexuality more real and salient to their families. Just as pregnancy forces parents to recognize their daughters are not just living with men but having sex, diagnosis with AIDS apparently forces families to recognize that their sons or brothers are not simply gay in some abstract way, but actually engage or engaged in homosexual activities. As a result, families who have tolerated their relatives' homosexuality despite deep reservations about its morality find that they can no longer do so. A 38 year old business manager reported that when he first told his parents he was gay "their reaction, while it wasn't initially effusive, at least it was grudgingly accepting." Now, however, he felt that his parents had "used this whole AIDS thing against me" by telling him that AIDS was "just desserts for the homosexuality community." Similarly, a 29 year old blue collar worker recounted how his mother, who previously had seemed to tolerate his lifestyle, responded to news of his diagnosis by telling him "I think your lifestyle is vulgar. I have never understood, I've never accepted it.... Your lifestyle repulses me." She subsequently refused to let him in her house or help him obtain medical insurance.

Even when families do not overtly reject ill relatives, their behavior may still create a sense of stigma. This can happen when families either hide news of their relatives' illnesses from others altogether or tell others that their relatives have some less stigmatized disease. A 39 year old floral designer, whose Catholic family had all known he was gay before he became ill, reported that his mother refused to tell his brothers and sisters that he had AIDS, and ordered him not to tell them as well. When his siblings finally were told, they in turn would not tell their spouses. Such behavior forces PWAs to recognize that, as one fundamentalist Christian said, "it was an embarassment to [the family]... that I was gay and... that I have AIDS." This imposed secrecy places heavy burdens on individuals who subsequently must "live a lie."

Families may reinforce a sense of stigma by adopting extreme and medically unwarranted anti-contagion measures. One family brought their own sheets when visiting their ill son's home. Others refused to allow PWAs to touch any food, share their bathrooms, or come closer than an arm's length away. A 29 year old Mormon salesperson, whose family believed he deserved AIDS as punishment for his sins, reported that initially his family "wouldn't come in the room unless they had gloves and a mask and they wouldn't touch me.... [And] for a time I couldn't go over to somebody's house for dinner. And they still use paper plates [when I eat there]." Even PWAs who feel such precautions are necessary still miss the experience of physical warmth and intimacy. They report feeling stigmatized, isolated, and contaminated.

Although PWAs fear that their families will reject them once their illness becomes known, they also hope that news of their illness will bring their families closer together. A 38 year old store manager who had never had a particularly close relationship with his family described his fantasy "that something like this—an experience where you come this close to death or the reality of death—is when you realize what's really important and not who's right and who's wrong."

For the lucky ones, this fantasy materializes. The oldest man I interviewed, a 57 year old lawyer, had always considered his father a cold and selfish man, and had never been on good terms with him. This situation changed, at least partially, when he became ill. As he described it:

> We've gotten closer.... There's the verbal "I love you," there's the letters. One of the nicest things that's ever happened to me... is my father sent me a personal card. In the inside he wrote "God bless you. I love you son".... It meant the world to me.

Another man described how, despite their disapproval of his lifestyle, his fundamentalist Christian family had provided him with housing, money, and emotional support once they learned of his illness. As he described it, in his family, when "little brother needed help... that took priority over all the other bullshit. They were right there."

Diagnosis can also bring families together by ending previous sources of conflict. Whether to preserve their own health, protect others from infection, or because they simply lose interest in sex once diagnosed with a deadly, sexually transmitted disease, PWAs may cease all sexual activity. For health reasons, PWAs may also stop smoking and drinking. As a result, families that previously had disapproved of PWAs' lifestyles may stop considering them "sick" or "sinful," even if the PWAs continue to consider themselves gay. Consequently, some PWAs achieve a new acceptance from relatives who attach less stigma to AIDS than to their former behaviors.

Friends and Lovers At the time of diagnosis, only 7 of the 23 men had lovers (as opposed to sexual partners with whom they had no ongoing relationship). These seven naturally turned to their lovers as well as their families for emotional support. The two whose lovers were also HIV infected did, indeed, receive support from their lovers, as did one man whose lover was HIV negative and two whose lovers do not know their HIV status. The remaining two men, however, were almost immediately abandoned by their lovers.

The PWAs' friends have proven considerably less sympathetic. Typically, PWAs reported that some friends "are very supportive, come around, enjoy coming over here, whatever. But most of them have backed off." A young blue collar worker described how, when his best friend learned of his diagnosis:

> He couldn't get me out of his apartment fast enough.... It was to the point (my friends) didn't even want to be in same room with me.... It was just like "don't call us, we'll call you...." They stopped returning calls. When I would see them out [at bars], they would see me coming and they would head out in the other direction.

Because housemates, like other friends, may also reject PWAs once they learn about their illness, PWAs may have to make new housing arrangements shortly after receiving their diagnoses. Some housemates left or asked the PWA to leave as soon as they learned that he had AIDS. In other cases, housemates asked the PWAs to leave once the housemates learned that they too were being shunned by others as possible sources of infection. Because of limited financial resources and social stigma, PWAs who need new housing may be forced to move in with their families or with other PWAs. Those who move in with their families risk retreating into a childlike dependency, while those who live with other PWAs must cope with their housemates' illnesses as well as their own.

Although rejection by friends and lovers is common, it is not universal. In fact, some men received acceptance and caring from friends and lovers beyond anything they had expected. The 57 year old lawyer quoted above had received many offers of support from friends. He told me, "I never knew I was [so] loved." Similar experiences led the 38 year old business manager described above to conclude "that family are those people who you can really love and trust and care for" and not necessarily one's blood relations.

Health Care Workers That persons who lack medical training should fear or abhor the victims of a new and deadly disease may not seem surprising. Yet even many health care professionals shun PWAs (Katz et al., 1987; Kelly et al., 1987). In Arizona, as in many other places, no nursing home or after-care facility, only a handful of dentists and ambulance services, and relatively few physicians will care for PWAs. Some respondents had experienced discrimination from professionals directly, while more knew of the problem from talking to others.

Through trial and error, most PWAs eventually find primary practitioners who, they believe, provide good and nonjudgmental care. They still face potential stigma, however, whenever they need specialist or hospital care. It may take several phone calls to find a willing specialist. If hospitalization is needed, the problem is less access to care than quality of care. Hospital staff usually cannot refuse to provide care, but they can make their ignorance and prejudice painfully obvious. One man described how hospital nurses made his friends and family "protect themselves" by donning isolation garb, even though his infection could not be transmitted through casual contact. He reported:

> A lot of the nurses were very nervous. It was obvious. Some of them double gloved and some wouldn't come in at all. I mean, they would if you forced them to, but they weren't going to just drop in and see how you were doing and stuff.

Other PWAs mentioned social workers who refused to enter their hospital rooms and hospital staff who disappeared suddenly once their diagnoses became known. One man first realized that he had AIDS when he suddenly found himself under the care of a new hospital staff team, all of whom appeared gay.

Work By the time individuals receive diagnoses of AIDS, many are physically incapable of working. Others, faced with catastrophic medical bills, must quit their jobs to qualify for state-financed medical assistance.

PWAs who continue working risk additional stigma and discrimination if others learn of their illnesses. Although most courts have rules that PWAs are disabled and thus qualify for protection under anti-discrimination laws (Leonard, 1987), in practice employers can fire PWAs with impunity because few PWAs have the time, money, or stamina to sue successfully (personal communication, Jane Aiken, Arizona Governor's Task Force on AIDS).

Only one man, a mechanic for a large public institution with an established AIDS policy, described his working situation as satisfactory. Every other PWA who revealed his illness was either fired immediately or forced to quit when colleagues or employers made his situation intolerable. An outgoing and amiable young man who had worked as a tailor said that his fellow workers initially responded well, taking only reasonable precautions, such as not sharing drinking glasses.

> Then little things happened.... If a pin came from [my department] they would immediately throw it away because [they thought] if they poked themselves, they could get AIDS... [Then they developed] a list of things for me to do at the end of the day like wipe down the scissors and the table and everything that I touched with a weak solution of ten-to-one [bleach].... With all that happening, I kind of lost the desire to work.

He quit his job soon thereafter. Although he appeared to have a strong legal case, he (like all the others in similar situations) decided he did not have the energy, funds, or time to sue.

Managing the Stigma of AIDS

Avoiding Stigma To maintain as much of their pre-diagnosis lives as possible, PWAs must find ways to avoid or reduce stigma. One basic strategy used by PWAs as well as by people with other stigmatized illnesses (Boutte, 1987; Hilbert, 1984; Schneider and Conrad, 1983) is to hide the nature of their illness.

Hiding can begin at the time of diagnosis. Since AIDS was first identified, federal law has required physicians to report all cases to the government. A new Arizona law (enacted during the study period) requires physicians to report persons who have ARC or who test positive for HIV, the virus that causes AIDS. Although laws supposedly protect the confidentiality of these reports, physicians and patients fear that the information will leak out. As a result, to protect clients from possible legal, social, and financial repercussions, physicians may circumvent the reporting law. One man, for example, described how his physician diagnosed his illness as ARC rather than AIDS to avoid the stigma which the physician believed would result from diagnosis of AIDS and the necessity to report him to the state. The physician told him:

> "If you diagnosed a person with AIDS, people really do back off from that one, I don't care how knowledgeable people are.... We don't want to diagnose people with AIDS if we don't have to diagnose." He [the physician] said, "the first time you go to the hospital with pneumonia or the cancer lesions and stuff like that," he said, "then we got no choice and it has to be reported to the state. But as ARC we don't really have to report ARC cases."

Other physicians avoid reporting by using highly restrictive definitions of AIDS. One physician decided that only his client's pharynx and not his esophagus was infected with candidiasis. This slim distinction allowed the physician to conclude that the client had ARC rather than AIDS and hence did not have to be reported. Physicians can also diagnose each opportunistic infection a client contracts rather than diagnosing AIDS as the underlying cause of those infections.

Fearing that disclosure might result in loss of employment or insurance, PWAs and their physicians also used these tactics to hide diagnoses from insurance companies (and indirectly from employers). A computer operator who was well-read on the biology of AIDS and active in an AIDS political action group described how he and his physician avoided telling his insurance company he had ARC or AIDS:

> [We have] been very careful, even so far, never to put the three big letters [ARC] or four big letters [AIDS] on the [insurance] papers. It's always been just candidiasis or anemia or something ridiculous.... Anything but. And I prefer to keep it that way, and I think probably even [the physician's] notes reflect that.

For the same reason, and as long as they can afford it, PWAs may only request insurance reimbursement for treatments that will not trigger questions about whether they have AIDS.

In addition to hiding their illness from unknown bureaucrats, PWAs may also hide it from families, friends, and sexual partners as well. Shame about his sexuality had led one 41 year old Catholic man to sever all contact with his ex-wife and young children when he started having gay relationships years ago. After he received his diagnosis, and despite his realization that he was dying, he continued this silence:

> I haven't seen my kids for almost 12 years and when AIDS came down, I didn't know how to handle it. How do you tell your kids 2,000 miles away that you're not only homosexual, but you're dying from a killer disease, the "gay plague" as I call it? How do you do that? How do you explain a lifetime in a thirty minute telephone conversation? So I chose not to.

Others chose not to tell their families because they assumed their families would reject them or because the PWAs could not cope with the anguish their news would bring.

Deciding whether to inform sexual partners with whom they were not in continuing relationships was more complex, for it raised the question not only of how to protect oneself from stigma but also how to protect others from infection. This was not an issue for the five men who were in continuing relationships with lovers who knew of their illness. Nor was it an issue for the 14 men who either had sex or had sex only on rare occasions when they were too drunk to make any conscious decisions. Of the remaining four men, two always told their lovers because they felt obliged to inform anyone whom they might infect that they were at risk. The other two disagreed, arguing that they need not disclose their diagnosis as long as they limited themselves to activities unlikely to transmit the virus. Besides, they argued, most gay or bisexual men already had been exposed to the virus. The well-informed computer operator described above stated that he felt no ethical obligation to reveal his diagnosis to sexual partners because "the level of infection in that group is so high that if, in fact, *you* are careful not to exchange body fluids to *them,* then their level of risk out of this encounter is much lower than what they probably did the week before. And they found *that* acceptable." (emphasis in original.)

PWAs use a variety of methods to hide their illnesses from people around them. One man routinely transferred his pills of zidovudine (formerly called azidothymidine or AZT) to an unmarked bottle because he feared others would recognize the drug as one used to treat AIDS. Some selected clothing or used make-up to hide their emaciation or skin problems. Men whose tongues showed the tell-tale whitish spots of candidiasis (an infection that frequently accompanies AIDS) closed their mouths partially while smiling or talking.

Most importantly, PWAs learned to gauge how sick they looked. Whenever possible, they tried to look healthy when out in public. A 23 year old salesperson who had always enjoyed going to bars and never enjoyed solitude described how "Every time I go out [to a bar] I try to hide it. I try to act energetic and normal and I always have them put a squeeze of lime in my drinks so it's like a mixed drink." When their health made it impossible to appear normal, PWAs stayed home. As another man explained, "There are days that I really feel shitty and I look bad and I won't let anybody see me. I won't go around anybody. And then there are days I really force myself to put myself together so I will look decent and I'm not afraid to go out then."

This strategy is no help, however, when PWAs must go out despite visible physical problems. To protect their secret in these circumstances, PWAs may devise plausible alternative explanations for their symptoms. One man explained his weight loss by telling co-workers that he had begun marathon training. Others attributed their physical problems to less stigmatized illnesses, such as leukemia or cancer.

Although hiding one's illness gives PWAs some protection against rejection, it carries a high price. PWAs who hide their illness from employers may lose their jobs when they cannot explain their increased absences and decreased productivity. Those who choose not to tell friends or relatives must endure their illness alone and in silence, without support they might otherwise receive. They must also endure the emotional strain caused by the secretiveness itself. As one man said, "I want to tell. I'm not used to hiding everything from everybody. . . . I'm a basically honest person and I don't like to lie." Finally, PWAs who keep their illnesses secret risk hearing painfully disparaging comments about how AIDS "serves those queers right." On such occasions, PWAs may feel that they cannot respond without risking exposure. A 33 year old salesperson involved with an AIDS political action group said:

> I was at my desk and three secretaries telling AIDS jokes were standing right behind me. It cut and it hurt. I grit my teeth and said nothing. . . . [Occasionally] I try and slide in a little bit of education . . . but I don't push it to the point where they go, "how come he knows so much?"

To avoid questions about why they don't find AIDS jokes humorous, some PWAs even feel obliged to join in the laughter.

Because both concealing and revealing one's illness can create problems, it is difficult for a PWA to decide what to do. To deal with this dilemma, PWAs learn to predict how various others may react to news of their illness. For example, a PWA can tell a relative that he volunteers for an AIDS education group or that a friend of his has AIDS. The relative's reaction can help the PWA decide whether to tell of his own illness.

PWAs also learn not only whom to tell but when to tell of their illness. A 24 year old blue collar worker who had been abandoned by several close friends said, "I used to tell people up front about my diagnosis, but I don't anymore. I let them get to know me, because I really want them to get to know me before they pass judgment on me." A few PWAs whose families lived out of state had decided not to disclose their illness until they could see their families in person. Others, who expected their diagnosis to precipitate family crises, decided not to tell until death appeared imminent.

In the aftermath of disclosure, PWAs can avoid further stigma by reducing contact with friends and relatives who prove unsupportive. As a result, however, their social lives shrink significantly. The man who put lime in his water at bars said:

> [Before getting AIDS] I was out all the time, I loved to be around people. I hated to be by myself. But now, I find that I don't like to be around people that much except if it's people I know that are not going to reject me because I don't want the rejection. I don't want to be hurt; I'm tired of being hurt.

To replace their former social networks, PWAs can join support groups organized for persons who have this illness. These groups afford them a social life without the risk of rejection or social awkwardness. One man who had experienced painful rejections explained that he socialized mostly with other PWAs "mainly because I guess I'm still afraid of people's reactions" but also "because I think they [other PWAs] can understand more what your feelings are, what is going through your head. It's a lot easier to sit around and have a conversation with someone who is also ill with this disease and you don't have to worry about avoiding certain topics." Similarly, the 39 year old floral designer described above, whose mother had refused to tell his siblings of his illness, experienced further trauma when most of his friends abandoned him. He told me of the pleasure he obtained from a recent potluck social for PWAs:

> I was not alone . . . I met a lot of really beautiful people, a lot of really nice friends. They took your phone number, they call you, socialize with you, you go to the show with them. You do things with them. If you need any help or whatever, they're there. . . . I went through hiding myself in my house and every time the facial sores started I would be afraid to go out and let people see me. These people don't care. You're not the only one that's had the facial sores and they don't care. You're welcome there. . . . Nobody [at the potluck] was afraid because a person with ARC or AIDS made a dish. We all rather enjoyed the food. It was like all the barriers went down when you were with these other people.

Although socializing with PWAs solves some problems, it creates others. First, PWAs may find that they have nothing but their illness in common. As a result, the relationships they develop are likely to be superficial and unrewarding. Second, as one man explained, these social circles do not permit the PWA "to get away from AIDS and be myself at the same time." Only with other PWAs can they act truly naturally. Yet when they are with other PWAs, they cannot avoid at least thinking about their illness. Third, PWAs who develop new friendships in these circles must then cope with their friends' illnesses and dying as well as their own. Thus seeking friendship from other PWAs in the end can increase their own sorrow.

Reducing Stigma Although hiding one's illness and restricting one's social circle help PWAs to avoid stigma, they will not reduce that stigma. Some PWAs therefore consider these strategies inadequate and choose, at least in some situations, to attack the roots of the stigma.

To reduce the stigma of AIDS, PWAs may "come out of the closet" about their illness—working for community organizations that provide services to PWAs, becoming "resources" for acquaintances who have unanswered questions about AIDS, or even speaking for the media about having AIDS. PWAs who take this course believe it is the only way truly to improve their situation. For example, the man whose mother refused to help him obtain health insurance subsequently became an active speaker about AIDS. He explained, "the only way that I could see getting rid of that stigma is to stick up for myself and become publicly known, to say it's okay to be my friend, it's okay to hug me, it's okay to sit down on a couch with me and watch TV." Other PWAs continue to conceal their diagnosis but nonetheless try to teach people around them that PWAs should not be shunned. One man described a confrontation with a neighbor who accused him of having AIDS and asked him not to use the pool in their apartment complex. The PWA denied that he had AIDS, but told the neighbor "ignorance is no excuse. You ought to read up on AIDS, you can't get it that way."

To reduce stigma, PWAs must go beyond educating others about the biology of the disease to challenging the idea that AIDS is a deserved punishment for sin. They do so in two ways. First, PWAs can argue that God is the source of love and not of punishment and that God would not have created gay people only to reject them as sinners. Second, they can argue that all illnesses are biological phenomena, not signs of divine judgment, and that it was simply bad luck that the first Americans affected by AIDS were gay. Several of the men stressed their belief that AIDS had originated among heterosexuals in Africa and thus could not be punishment for homosexuality. As one 28 year old construction worker said, "It didn't start out as a homosexual disease and it's not going to finish that way."

These alternative explanations for AIDS allow PWAs to reject their rejectors as prejudiced or ignorant. The construction worker just quoted went on to describe his reaction to Jerry Falwell's statements that AIDS is God's punishment for sin:

> Somebody like that really ought to be put away. He's doing so much damage, it's pathetic and he doesn't know what he's talking about and that's real sad. And we don't need that—we need understanding.

Other PWAs, however, themselves believe that they deserve AIDS (Weitz, 1989). In these circumstances, they can reduce stigma only by accepting responsibility for their actions, forswearing their former activities, and asking forgiveness from their families, churches, and God.

Finally, PWAs can reduce stigma through bravado—putting on what amounts to a show in order to convince others of the reality that they are functioning and worthwhile human beings. The man who chastised his neighbor for being ignorant about AIDS told how he and other PWAs occasionally go to a bar to "show these people that we can live with AIDS. That we can have a good time. That we can dance, that we can socialize, that we're not people with plagues." Describing a recent visit to his neighborhood bar, he said:

> I just walked in, put my arms around somebody, said "Hi, how're you doing? Everything going ok with you?" and he said, "Well, how are you doing?" and I said, "Well, ARC hasn't gotten me down yet, I don't think it will." I said, "I'm going to beat this thing." And I just acted like nothing was wrong.

CONCLUSIONS

Almost by definition, "to define something as a disease or illness is to deem it undesirable" (Conrad and Schneider, 1980:36). By the same token, to say that someone has a disease or (more strongly) is diseased implies that the person is less whole, functioning, or worthy than "normal" people. Consequently, all chronically ill persons must struggle against stigma.

At present, however, no other physical illness in American society carries stigma as severe as AIDS. For example, while some people believe that herpes or leprosy are divine punishments for sin, far more people believe that AIDS is a divine punishment. Similarly, some health care workers provide only grudging, low quality care to patients whom they consider demanding hypochondriacs, such as people who suffer chronic pain with no clear cause. Few if any health care workers, however, refuse to provide care to such persons. Yet many refuse to provide care to PWAs. The stigma of AIDS reflects the fact that it is contagious, deforming, fatal, imperfectly understood, and associated with already stigmatized groups.

Despite the differences between AIDS and other illnesses, however, PWAs manage stigma in much the same way as other chronically ill people. To avoid stigma, PWAs do not disclose their illness if it is invisible, mask the signs of illness if they are visible, lie about those signs if they cannot be masked, and minimize contact with people who reject them when their illness becomes known. Alternatively, PWAs can reveal their illness and either challenge their detractor's theological and biological assumptions or ask forgiveness for their former deviant conduct. In these ways, PWAs, like people with other illnesses, can limit the impact of illness on their social lives.

Acknowledgments

This research was made possible by a grant from the Arizona Disease Control Research Commission and by a small grant from Arizona State University College of Liberal Arts and Sciences. I also wish to thank Rochelle Kern, Karolynn Siegel and Peter Conrad for their comments on earlier drafts of this paper.

References

AIDS Program (1989). AIDS Weekly Surveillance Report—United States, February 20, 1989. Center for Infectious Diseases, Centers for Disease Control.

Boutte, Marie I. (1987). "'The stumbling disease': A case study of stigma among Azorean-Portuguese." *Social Science and Medicine 24(3),* 209–217.

Brooks, Nancy A., and Ronald R. Matson (1987). "Managing multiple sclerosis." *Research in the Sociology of Health Care 6,* 73–106.

Charmaz, Kathy (1980). *The Social Reality of Death.* Reading, MA: Addison-Wesley.

Conrad, Peter, and Joseph Schneider (1980). Deviance and medicalization: From badness to sickness. St. Louis: C. V. Mosby.

Goffman, Erving (1963). *Stigma: Notes on the Management of Spoiled Identity.* Englewood Cliffs, NJ: Prentice-Hall.

Gussow, Zachary, and George S. Tracy (1968). "Status, ideology, and adaptation to stigmatized illness: A study of leprosy." *Human Organization 27,* 316–325.

Hilbert, Richard A. (1984). "The acultural dimensions of chronic pain: Flawed reality construction and the problem of meaning." *Social Problems 31,* 365–78.

Katz, Irwin, R. Glen Hass, Nina Parisi, Janetta Astone, and Denise McEvaddy (1987). "Lay people's and health care personnel's perceptions of cancer, AIDS, cardiac, and diabetic patients." *Psychological Reports 60,* 615–629.

Kelly, Jeffrey A., Janet S. St. Lawrence, Steve Smith, Harold V. Hood, and Donna J. Cook (1987). "Stigmatization of AIDS patients by physicians." *American Journal of Public Health 77,* 789–791.

Leonard, Arthur S. (1987). "AIDS in the workplace." pp. 109–125 in Harlon L. Dalton, Scott Burris, and the Yale AIDS Law Project (eds.), *AIDS and the Law: A Guide for the Public.* New Haven: Yale University Press.

Masters, William H., Virginia E. Johnson, and Robert E. Kolodny (1988). *Crisis: Heterosexual Behavior in the Age of AIDS.* New York: Grove Press.

National Center for Health Statistics, D. A. Dawson (1988). "AIDS knowledge and attitudes for July 1988, Provisional data from the National Health Interview Survey." *Advance Data from Vital and Health Statistics,* No. 161. DHHS Pub. No. 89-1250. Hyattsville, Md.: Public Health Service.

Schneider, Joseph, and Peter Conrad (1983). *Having Epilepsy.* Philadelphia: Temple University Press.

Weitz, Rose (1989). "Uncertainty and the lives of persons with AIDS." *Journal of Health and Social Behavior 30,* 270–81.

21 / The Adjustment of the Family to the Crisis of Alcoholism

JOAN K. JACKSON

...Over a 3-year period, the present investigator has been an active participant in the Alcoholics Anonymous Auxiliary in Seattle. This group is composed partly of women whose husbands are or were members of Alcoholics Anonymous, and partly of women whose husbands are excessive drinkers but have never contacted Alcoholics Anonymous. At a typical meeting one-fifth would be the wives of Alcoholics Anonymous members who have been sober for some time; the husband of another fifth would have recently joined the fellowship; the remainder would be equally divided between those whose husbands were "on and off" the Alcoholics Anonymous program and those whose husbands had as yet not had any contact with Alcoholics Anonymous.

At least an hour and a half of each formal meeting of this group is taken up with a frank discussion of the current family problems of the members. As in other meetings of Alcoholics Anonymous the questions are posed by describing the situation which gives rise to the problem, and the answers are a narration of the personal experiences of other wives who have had a similar problem, rather than direct advice. Verbatim shorthand notes have been taken of all discussions, at the request of the group, who also make use of the notes for the group's purposes. Informal contact has been maintained with past and present members. In the past 3 years 50 women have been members of this group.

The families represented by these women are at present in many different stages of adjustment and have passed through several stages during the past few years. The continuous contact over a prolonged period permits generalizations about processes and changes in family adjustments.

In addition, in connection with research on hospitalized alcoholics, many of their wives have been interviewed. The interviews with the hospitalized alcoholics, as well as with male members of Alcoholics Anonymous, have also provided information on family interactions. Further information has been derived from another group of wives, not connected with Alcoholics Anonymous, and from probation officers, social workers and court officials.

The following presentation is limited insofar as it deals only with families seeking help for the alcoholism of the husband. Other families are known to have solved the problem through divorce, often without having attempted to help the alcoholic member first. Others never seek help and never separate. There were no marked differences between the two groups seeking help, one through the hospital and one through the A.A. Auxiliary. The wives of hospitalized alcoholics gave a history of the family crisis similar to that given by women in the Auxiliary.

A second limitation is that only the families of male alcoholics are dealt with. It is recognized that the findings cannot be generalized to the families of alcoholic women without further research. Due to differences between men and women in their roles in the family as well as in the pattern of drinking, it would be expected that male and female alcoholics would in some ways have a different effect on family structure and function.

A third limitation is imposed for the sake of clarity and brevity: only the accounts of the wives of their attempts to stabilize their family adjustments will be dealt with. For any complete picture, the view of the alcoholic husband would also have to be included.

It must be emphasized that this paper deals with the definitions of the family situations by the wives, rather than with the actual situation. It has been noted that frequently wife and husband do not agree on what has occurred. The degree to which the definition of the situation by the wife or husband correlates with actual behavior is a question which must be left for further research.

The families represented in this study are from the middle and lower classes. The occupations of the husbands prior to excessive drinking include small business owners, salesmen, business executives, skilled and semiskilled workers. Prior to marriage the wives have been nurses, secretaries, teachers, saleswomen, cooks, or waitresses. The economic status of the childhood families of these husbands and wives ranged from very wealthy to very poor.

Method

From the records of discussions of the Alcoholics Anonymous Auxiliary, the statements of each wife were extracted and arranged in a time sequence. Notes on informal contacts were added at the point in the sequence where they occurred. The interviews with the wives of hospitalized alcoholics were similarly treated. These working records on individual families were then examined for uniformities of behavior and for regularities in changes over time.

The similarities in the process of adjustment to an alcoholic family member are presented here as stages of variable duration. It should be stressed that only the similarities are dealt with. Although the wives have shared the patterns dealt with here, there have been marked differences in the length of time between stages, in the number of stages passed through up to the present time, and in the relative importance to the family constellation of any one type of behavior. For example, all admitted nagging, but the amount of nagging was variable.

When the report of this analysis was completed it was read before a meeting of the Auxiliary with a request for correction of any errors in fact or interpretation. Corrections could be presented either anonymously or publicly from the floor. Only one correction was suggested and has been incorporated. The investigator is convinced that her relationship with the group is such that there would be no reticence about offering corrections. Throughout her contact with this group her role has been that of one who is being taught, very similar to the role of the new member. The overall response of the group to the presentation indicated that the members individually felt that they had been portrayed accurately.

The sense of having similar problems and similar experiences is indicated also in the reactions of new members to the Auxiliary's summarization of the notes of their discussions. Copies of these summaries are given to new members, who commonly state that they find it a relief to see that their problems are far from unique and that there are methods which successfully overcome them.

Statement of the Problem

For purposes of this presentation, the family is seen as involved in a cumulative crisis. All family members behave in a manner which they hope will resolve the crisis and permit a return to stability. Each member's action is influenced by his previous personality structure, by his previous role and status in the family group, and by the history of the crisis and its effects on his personality, roles and status up to that point. Action is also influenced by the past effectiveness of that particular action as a means of social control before and during the crisis. The behavior of family members in each phase of the crisis contributes to the form which the crisis takes in the following stages and sets limits on possible behavior in subsequent stages.

Family members are influenced, in addition, by the cultural definitions of alcoholism as evidence of weakness, inadequacy, or sinfulness; by the cultural prescriptions for the roles of family members; and by the cultural values of family solidarity, sanctity, and self-sufficiency. Alcoholism in the family poses a situation defined by the culture as shameful but for the handling of which there are no prescriptions which are effective or which permit direct action not in conflict with other cultural prescriptions. While in crises such as illness or death the family members can draw on cultural definitions of appropriate behavior for procedures which will terminate the crisis, this is not the case with alcoholism in the family. The cultural view has been that alcoholism is shameful and should not occur. Only recently has any information been offered to guide families in their behavior toward their alcoholic member and, as yet, this information resides more in technical journals than in the media of mass communication. Thus, in facing alcoholism, the family is in an unstructured situation and must find the techniques for handling it through trial and error.

STAGES IN FAMILY ADJUSTMENT TO AN ALCOHOLIC MEMBER

The Beginning of the Marriage

At the time marriage was considered, the drinking of most of the men was within socially acceptable limits. In a few cases the men were already alcoholics but managed to hide this from their fiancées. They drank only moderately or not at all when on dates and often avoided friends and relatives who might expose their excessive drinking. The relatives and friends who were introduced to the fiancée were those who had hopes that "marriage would straighten him out" and thus said nothing about the drinking. In a small number of cases the men spoke with their fiancées of their alcoholism. The women had no conception of what alcoholism meant, other than that it involved more than the usual frequency of drinking, and they entered the marriage with little more preparation than if they had known nothing about it.

Stage 1. Incidents of excessive drinking begin and, although they are sporadic, place strains on the husband-wife interaction. In attempts to minimize drinking, problems in marital adjustment not related to the drinking are avoided.

Stage 2. Social isolation of the family begins as incidents of excessive drinking multiply. The increasing isolation magnifies the importance of family interactions and events. Behavior and thought become drinking-centered. Husband-wife adjustment deteriorates and tension rises. The wife begins to feel self-pity and to lose her self-confidence as her behavior fails to stabilize her husband's drinking. There is an attempt still to maintain the original family structure, which is disrupted anew with each episode of drinking, and as a result the children begin to show emotional disturbance.

Stage 3. The family gives up attempts to control the drinking and begins to behave in a manner geared to relieve tension rather than achieve long-term ends. The disturbance of the children becomes more marked. There is no longer an attempt to support the alcoholic in his roles as husband and father. The wife begins to worry about her own sanity and about her inability to make decisions or act to change the situation.

Stage 4. The wife takes over control of the family and the husband is seen as a recalcitrant child. Pity and strong protective feelings largely replace the earlier resentment and hostility. The family becomes more stable and organized in a manner to minimize the disruptive behavior of the husband. The self-confidence of the wife begins to be rebuilt.

Stage 5. The wife separates from her husband if she can resolve the problems and conflicts surrounding this action.

Stage 6. The wife and children reorganize as a family without the husband.

Stage 7. The husband achieves sobriety and the family, which had become organized around an alcoholic husband, reorganizes to include a sober father and experiences problems in reinstating him in his former roles.

Stage 1. Attempts to Deny the Problem

Usually the first experience with drinking as a problem arises in a social situation. The husband drinks in a manner which is inappropriate to the social setting and the expectations of others present. The wife feels embarrassed on the first occasion and humiliated as it occurs more frequently. After several such incidents she and her husband talk over his behavior. The husband either formulates an explanation for the episode and assures her that such behavior will not occur again, or he refuses to discuss it at all. For a time afterward he drinks appropriately and drinking seems to be a problem no longer. The wife looks back on the incidents and feels that she has exaggerated them, feels ashamed of herself for her disloyalty and for her behavior. The husband, in evaluating the incident, feels shame also and vows such episodes will not recur. As a result, both husband and wife attempt to make it up to the other and, for a time, try to play their conceptions of the ideal husband and wife roles, minimizing or avoiding other difficulties which arise in the marriage. They thus create the illusion of a "perfect" marriage.

Eventually another inappropriate drinking episode occurs and the pattern is repeated. The wife worries but takes action only in the situations in which inappropriate drinking occurs, as each long intervening period of acceptable drinking behavior convinces her that a recurrence is unlikely. As time goes on, in attempting to cope with individual episodes, she runs the gamut of possible trial and error behaviors, learning that none is permanently effective.

If she speaks to other people about her husband's drinking, she is usually assured that there is no need for concern, that her husband can control his drinking and that her fears are exaggerated. Some friends possibly admit that his drinking is too heavy and give advice on how they handled similar situations with their husbands. These friends convince her that her problem will be solved as soon as she hits upon the right formula for dealing with her husband's drinking.

During this stage the husband-wife interaction is in no way "abnormal." In a society in which a large proportion of men drink, most wives have at some time had occasion to be concerned, even though only briefly, with an episode of drinking which they considered inappropriate (2). In a society in which the status of the family depends on that of the husband, the wife feels threatened by any behavior on his part which might lower it. Inappropriate drinking is regarded by her as a threat to the family's reputation and standing in the community. The wife attempts to exert control and often finds herself blocked by the sacredness of drinking behavior to men in America. Drinking is a private matter and not any business of the wife's. On the whole, a man reacts to his wife's suggestion that he has not adequately controlled his drinking with resentment, rebelliousness, and a display of emotion which makes rational discussion difficult. The type of husband-wife interaction outlined in this stage has occurred in many American families in which the husband never became an excessive drinker.

Stage 2. Attempts to Eliminate the Problems

Stage 2 begins when the family experiences social isolation because of the husband's drinking. Invitations to the homes of friends become less frequent. When the couple does visit friends, drinks are not served or are limited, thus emphasizing the reason for exclusion from other social activities of the friendship group. Discussions of drinking begin to be sidestepped awkwardly by friends, the wife, and the husband.

By this time the periods of socially acceptable drinking are becoming shorter. The wife, fearing that the full extent of her husband's drinking will become known, begins to withdraw from social participation, hoping to reduce the visibility of his behavior, and thus the threat to family status.

Isolation is further intensified because the family usually acts in accordance with the cultural dictate that it should be self-sufficient and manage to resolve its own problems without recourse to outside aid. Any experiences which they have had with well-meaning outsiders, usually relatives, have tended to strengthen this conviction. The husband has defined such relatives as interfering and the situation has deteriorated rather than improved.

With increasing isolation, the family members begin to lose perspective on their interaction and on their problems. Thrown into closer contact with one another as outside contacts diminish, the behavior of each member assumes exaggerated importance. The drinking behavior becomes the focus of anxiety. Gradually all family difficulties become attributed to it. (For example, the mother who is cross with her children will feel that, if her husband had not been drinking, she would not have been so tense and would not have been angry.) The fear that the full extent of drinking may be discovered mounts steadily; the conceptualization of the consequences of such a discovery becomes increasingly vague and, as a result, more anxiety-provoking. The family feels different from others and alone with its shameful secret.

Attempts to cover up increase. The employer who calls to inquire about the husband's absence from work is given excuses. The wife is afraid to face the consequences of loss of the husband's pay check in addition to her other concerns. Questions from the children are evaded or they are told that their father is ill. The wife lives in terror of the day when the children will be told by others of the nature of the "illness." She is also afraid that the children may describe their father's symptoms to teachers or neighbors. Still feeling that the family must solve its own problems, she keeps her troubles to herself and hesitates to seek outside help. If her husband beats her, she will bear it rather than call in the police. (Indeed, often she has no idea that this is even a possibility.) Her increased isolation has left her without the advice of others as to sources of help in the community. If she knows of them, an agency contact means to her an admission of the complete failure of her family as an independent unit. For the middle-class woman particularly, recourse to social agencies and law enforcement agencies means a terrifying admission of loss of status.

During this stage, husband and wife are drawing further apart. Each feels resentful of the behavior of the other. When this resentment is expressed, further drinking occurs. When it is not, tension mounts and the next drinking episode is that much more destructive of family relationships. The reasons for drinking are explored frantically. Both husband and wife feel that if only they could discover the reason, all members of the family could gear their behavior to making drinking unnecessary. The discussions become increasingly unproductive, as it is the husband's growing conviction that his wife does not and cannot understand him.

On her part, the wife begins to feel that she is a failure, that she has been unable to fulfill the major cultural obligations of a wife to meet her husband's needs. With her increasing isolation, her sense of worth derives almost entirely from her roles as wife and mother. Each failure to help her husband gnaws away at her sense of adequacy as a person.

Periods of sobriety or socially acceptable drinking still occur. These periods keep the wife from making a permanent or stable adjustment. During them her husband, in his guilt, treats her like a queen. His behavior renews her hope and rekindles positive feelings toward him. Her sense of worth is bolstered temporarily and she grasps desperately at her husband's reassurance that she is really a fine person and not a failure and an unlovable shrew. The periods of sobriety also keep her family from facing the inability of the husband to control his drinking. The inaccuracies of the cultural stereotype of the alcoholic—particularly that he is in a constant state of inebriation—also contribute to the family's rejection of the idea of alcoholism, as the husband seems to demonstrate from time to time that he can control his drinking.

Family efforts to control the husband become desperate. There are no culturally prescribed behavior patterns for handling such a situation and the family is forced to evolve its own techniques. Many different types of behavior are tried but none brings consistent results; there seems to be no way of predicting the consequences of any action that may be taken. All attempts to stabilize or structure the situation to permit consistent behavior fail. Threats of leaving, hiding his liquor away, emptying the bottles down the drain, curtailing his money, are tried in rapid succession, but none is effective. Less punitive methods, as discussing the situation when he is sober, babying him during hangovers, and trying to drink with him to keep him at home, are attempted and fail. All behavior becomes oriented around the drinking, and the thought of family members becomes obsessive on this subject. As no action seems to be successful in achieving its goal, the wife persists in trial-and-error behavior with mounting frustration. Long-term goals recede into the background and become secondary to just keeping the husband from drinking today.

There is still an attempt to maintain the illusion of husband-wife-children roles. When father is sober, the children are expected to give him respect and obedience. The wife also defers to him in his role as head of the household. Each drinking event thus disrupts family functioning anew. The children begin to show emotional disturbances as a result of the inconsistencies of parental behavior. During periods when the husband is drinking the wife tries to shield them from the knowledge and effects of his behavior, at the same time drawing them closer to herself and deriving emotional support from them. In sober periods, the father tries to regain their favor. Due to experiencing directly only pleasant interactions with their father, considerable affection is often felt for him by the children. This affection becomes increasingly difficult for the isolated wife to tolerate, and an additional source of conflict. She feels that she needs and deserves the love and support of her children and, at the same time, she feels it important to maintain the children's picture of their father. She counts on the husband's affection for the children to motivate a cessation of drinking as he comes to realize the effects of his behavior on them.

In this stage, self-pity begins to be felt by the wife, if it has not entered previously. It continues in various degrees throughout the succeeding stages. In an attempt to handle her deepening sense of inadequacy, the wife often tries to convince herself that she is right and her husband wrong, and this also continues through the following stages. At this point the wife often resembles what Whalen (1) describes as "The Sufferer."

Stage 3. Disorganization

The wife begins to adopt a "What's the use?" attitude and to accept her husband's drinking as a problem likely to be permanent. Attempts to understand one another become less frequent. Sober periods still engender hope, but hope qualified by skepticism; they bring about a lessening of anxiety and this is defined as happiness.

By this time some customary patterns of husband-wife-children interaction have evolved. Techniques which have had some effectiveness in controlling the husband in the past or in relieving pent-up frustration are used by the wife. She nags, berates or retreats into silence. Husband and wife are both on the alert, the wife watching for increasing irritability and restlessness which mean a recurrence of drinking, and the husband for veiled aspersions on his behavior or character.

The children are increasingly torn in their loyalties as they become tools in the struggle between mother and father. If the children are at an age of comprehension, they have usually learned the true nature of their family situation, either from outsiders or from their mother, who has given up attempts to bolster her husband's position as father. The children are often bewildered but questioning their parents brings no satisfactory answers as the parents themselves do not understand what is happening. Some children become terrified; some have increasing behavior problems within and outside the home; others seem on the surface to accept the situation calmly.[1]

During periods of the husband's drinking, the hostility, resentment and frustrations felt by the couple is allowed expression. Both may resort to violence—the wife in self-defense or because she can find no other outlet for her feelings. In those cases in which the wife retaliates to violence in kind, she feels a mixture of relief and intense shame at having deviated so far from what she conceives to be "the behavior of a normal woman."

When the wife looks at her present behavior, she worries about her "normality." In comparing the person she was in the early years of her marriage with the person she has become, she is frightened. She finds herself nagging and unable to control herself. She resolves to stand up to her husband when he is belligerent but instead finds herself cringing in terror and then despises herself for her lack of courage. If she retaliates with violence, she is filled with self-loathing at behaving in an "unwomanly" manner. She finds herself compulsively searching for bottles, knowing full well that finding them will change nothing, and is worried because she engages in such senseless behavior. She worries about her inability to take constructive action of any kind. She is confused about where her loyalty lies, whether with her husband or her children. She feels she is a failure as a wife, mother and person. She believes she should be strong in the face of adversity and instead feels herself weak.

The wife begins to feel herself avoiding sexual contact with her husband when he has been drinking. Sex under these circumstances, she feels, is sex for its own sake rather than an indication of affection for her. Her husband's lack of consideration of her needs to be satisfied leaves her feeling frustrated. The lack of sexual responsiveness reflects her emotional withdrawal from him in other areas of family life. Her husband, on his part, feels frustrated and rejected; he accuses her of frigidity and this adds to her concern about her adequacy as a woman.[2]

By this time the opening wedge has been inserted into the self-sufficiency of the family. The husband has often been in difficulty with the police and the wife has learned that police protection is available. An emergency has occurred in which the seeking of outside help was the only possible action to take; subsequent calls for aid from outsiders do not require the same degree of urgency before they can be undertaken. However, guilt and a lessening of self-respect and self-confidence accompany this method of resolving emergencies. The husband intensifies these feelings by speaking of the interference of outsiders, or of his night in jail.

In Stage 3 all is chaos. Few problems are met constructively. The husband and wife both feel trapped in an intolerable, unstructured situation which offers no way out. The wife's self-assurance is almost completely gone. She is afraid to take action and afraid to let things remain as they are. Fear is one of the major characteristics of this stage: fear of violence, fear of personality damage to the children, fear for her own sanity, fear that relatives will interfere, and fear that they will not help in an emergency. Added to this, the family feels alone in the world and helpless. The problems, and the behavior of family members in attempting to cope with them, seem so shameful that help from others is unthinkable. They feel that attempts to get help would meet only with rebuff, and that communication of the situation will engender disgust.

At this point the clinical picture which the wife presents is very similar to what Whalen (1) has described as "The Waverer."

Stage 4. Attempts to Reorganize in Spite of the Problems

Stage 4 begins when a crisis occurs which necessitates that action be taken. There may be no money or food in the house; the husband may have been violent to the children; or life on the level of Stage 3 may have become intolerable. At this point some wives leave, thus entering directly into Stage 5.

The wife who passes through Stage 4 usually begins to ease her husband out of his family roles. She assumes husband and father roles. This involves strengthening her role as mother and putting aside her role as wife. She becomes the manager of the home, the discipliner of the children, the decision-maker; she becomes somewhat like Whalen's (1) "Controller." She either ignores her husband as much as possible or treats him as her most recalcitrant child. Techniques are worked out for getting control of his pay check, if there still is one, and money is doled out to her husband on the condition of his good behavior. When he drinks, she threatens to leave him, locks him out of the house, refuses to pay his taxi bills, leaves him in jail overnight rather than pay his bail. Where her obligations to her husband conflict with those to her children, she decides in favor of the latter. As she views her husband increasingly as a child, pity and a sense of being desperately needed by him enter. Her inconsistent behavior toward him, deriving from the lack of predictability inherent in the situation up to now, becomes reinforced by her mixed feelings toward him.

In this stage the husband often tries to set his will against hers in decisions about the children. If the children have been permitted to stay with a friend overnight, he may threaten to create a scene unless they return immediately. He may make almost desperate efforts to gain their affection and respect, his behavior ranging from getting them up in the middle of the night to fondle them to giving them stiff lectures on children's obligations to fathers. Sometimes he will attempt to align the males of the family with him against the females. He may openly express resentment of the children and become belligerent toward them physically or verbally.

Much of the husband's behavior can be conceptualized as resulting from an increasing awareness of his isolation from the other members of the family and their steady withdrawal of respect and affection. It seems to be a desperate effort to regain what he has lost, but without any clear idea of how this can be accomplished—an effort to change a situation in which everyone is seen as against him; and, in reality, this is becoming more and more true. As the wife has taken over control of the family with some degree of success, he feels, and becomes, less and less necessary to the ongoing activity of the family. There are fewer and fewer roles left for him to play. He becomes aware that members of the family enjoy each other's company without him. When he is home he tries to enter this circle of warmth or to smash it. Either way he isolates himself further. He finds that the children discuss with the mother how to manage him and he sees the children acting on the basis of their mother's idea of him. The children refuse to pay attention to his demands: they talk back to him in the same way that they talk back to one another, adding pressure on him to assume the role of just another child. All this leaves him frustrated and, as a result, often aggressive or increasingly absent from home.

The children, on the whole, become more settled in their behavior as the wife takes over the family responsibilities. Decisions are made by her and upheld in the face of their father's attempts to interfere. Participation in activities outside the home is encouraged. Their patterns of interaction with their father are supported by the mother. Whereas in earlier stages the children often felt that there were causal connections between their actions and their father's drinking, they now accept his unpredictability. "Well," says a 6-year-old, "I'll just have to get used to it. I have a drunken father."

The family is more stabilized in one way but in other ways insecurities are multiplied. Pay checks are received less and less regularly. The violence or withdrawal of the father increases. When he is away the wife worries about automobile accidents or injury in fights, which become more and more probable as time passes. The husband may begin to be seriously ill from time to time; his behavior may become quite bizarre. Both of these signs of increasing illness arouse anxiety in the family.

During this stage hopes may rise high for father's "reform" when he begins to verbalize wishes to stop drinking, admits off and on his inability to stop, and sounds desperate for doing something about his drinking. Now may begin the trek to sanitariums for the middle-class alcoholic, to doctors, or to Alcoholics Anonymous. Where just the promise to stop drinking has failed to revive hope, sobriety through outside agencies has the ability to rekindle it brightly. There is the feeling that at last he is "taking really constructive action." In failure the discouragement is deeper. Here another wedge has been inserted into the self-sufficiency of the family.

By this time the wedges are many. The wife, finding she has managed to bring some semblance of order and stability to her family, while not exactly becoming a self-assured person, has regained some sense of worth which grows a little with each crisis she meets successfully. In addition, the very fact of taking action to stabilize the situation brings relief. On some occasion she may be able to approach social agencies for financial help, often during a period when the husband has temporarily deserted or is incarcerated. She may have gone to the family court; she may have consulted a lawyer about getting a restraining order when the husband was in a particularly belligerent state. She has begun to learn her way around among the many agencies which offer help.

Often she has had a talk with an Alcoholics Anonymous member and has begun to look into what is known about alcoholism. If she has attended a few Alcoholics Anonymous meetings, her sense of shame has been greatly alleviated as she finds so many others in the same boat. Her hopes rise as she meets alcoholics who have stopped drinking, and she feels relieved at being able to discuss her problems openly for the first time with an audience which understands fully. She begins to gain perspective on her problem and learns that she herself is involved in what happens to her husband, and that she must change. She exchanges techniques of management with other wives and receives their support in her decisions.

She learns that her husband is ill rather than merely "ornery," and this often serves to quell for the time being thoughts about leaving him which have begun to germinate as she has gained more self-confidence. She learns that help is available but also that her efforts to push him into help are unavailing. She is not only supported in her recently evolved behavior of thinking first of her family, but now this course also emerges from the realm of the unconceptualized and is set in an accepted rationale. She feels more secure in having a reason and a certainty that the group accepts her as "doing the right thing." When she reports deviations from what the group thinks is the "right way," her reasons are understood; she receives solid support, but there is also pressure on her to alter her behavior again toward the acceptable. Blaming and self-pity are actively discouraged. In group discussions she still admits to such feelings but learns to recognize them as they arise and to go beyond them to more productive thinking.

How much her altered behavior changes the family situation is uncertain, but it helps her and gives her security from which to venture forth to further actions of a consistent and constructive type, constructive at least from the point of view of keeping her family on as even a keel as possible in the face of the disruptive influence of the husband. With new friends whom she can use as a sounding board for plans, and with her growing acquaintance with the alternatives and possible patterns of behavior, her thinking ceases to be circular and unproductive. Her anxiety about her own sanity is alleviated as she is reassured by others that they have experienced the same concern and that the remedy is to get her own life and her family under better control. As she accomplishes this, the difference in her feelings about herself convinces her that this is so.

Whether or not she has had a contact with wives of Alcoholics Anonymous members or other wives who have been through a similar experience and have emerged successfully, the very fact of taking hold of her situation and gradually making it more manageable adds to her self-confidence. As her husband is less and less able to care for himself or his family, she begins to feel that he needs her and that without her he would be destroyed. Such a feeling makes it difficult for her to think of leaving him. His almost complete social isolation at this point and his cries for help reinforce this conviction of being needed.

The drinking behavior is no longer hidden. Others obviously know about it, and this becomes accepted by the wife and children. Already isolated and insulated against possible rejection, the wife is often surprised to find that she has exaggerated her fears of what would happen were the situation known. However, the unpredictability of her husband's behavior makes her reluctant to form social relationships which could be violently disrupted or to involve others in the possible consequences of his behavior.

Stage 5. Efforts to Escape the Problems

Stage 5 may be the terminal one for the marriage. In this stage the wife separates from her husband. Sometimes the marriage is re-established after a period of sobriety, when it appears certain that the husband will not drink again. If he does revert to drinking, the marriage is sometimes finally terminated but with less emotional stress than the first time. If the husband deserts, being no longer able to tolerate his lack of status in his family, Stage 6 may be entered abruptly.

The events precipitating the decision to terminate the marriage may be near-catastrophic, as when there is an attempt by the husband to kill the wife or children, or they may appear trivial to outsiders, being only the last straw to an accumulation of years.

The problems in coming to the decision to terminate the marriage cannot be underestimated. Some of these problems derive from emotional conflicts; some are related to very practical circumstances in the situation; some are precipitated by the conflicting advice of outsiders. With several children dependent on her, the wife must decide whether the present situation is more detrimental to them than future situations she can see arising if she should leave her husband. The question of where the money to live on will come from must be thought out. If she can get a job, will there be enough to provide for child care also while she is away from home? Should the children, who have already experienced such an unsettled life, be separated from her to be cared for by others? If the family still owns its own home, how can she retain control of it? If she leaves, where can she go? What can be done to tide the family over until her first earnings come in? How can she ensure her husband's continued absence from the home and thus be certain of the safety of individuals and property in her absence? These are only a small sample of the practical issues that must be dealt with in trying to think her way through to a decision to terminate the marriage.

Other pressures act on her to impede the decision-making process. "If he would only stay drunk till I carry out what I intend to do," is a frequent statement. When the husband realizes that his wife really means to leave, he frequently sobers up, watches his behavior in the home, plays on her latent and sometimes conscious feelings of her responsibility for the situation, stresses his need for her and that without her he is lost, tears away at any confidence she has that she will be able to manage by herself, and threatens her and the children with injury or with his own suicide if he carries out her intention.

The children, in the meantime, are pulling and pushing on her emotions. They think she is "spineless" to stay but unfair to father's chances for ultimate recovery if she leaves. Relatives, who were earlier alienated in her attempts to shield her family but now know of the situation, do not believe in its full ramifications. They often feel she is exaggerating and persuade her to stay with him. Especially is this true in the case of the "solitary drinker." His drinking has been so well concealed that the relatives have no way of knowing the true nature of the situation. Other relatives, afraid that they will be called on for support, exert pressure to keep the marriage intact and the husband thereby responsible for debts. Relatives who feel she should leave him overplay their hands by berating the husband in such a manner as to evoke her defense of him. This makes conscious the positive aspects of her relationship with him, causing her to waver in her decision. If she consults organized agencies, she often gets conflicting advice. The agencies concerned with the well-being of the family may counsel leaving; those concerned with rehabilitating the husband may press her to stay. In addition, help from public organizations almost always involves delay and is frequently not forthcoming at the point where she needs it most.

The wife must come to terms with her own mixed feelings about her husband, her marriage and herself before she can decide on such a step as breaking up the marriage. She must give up hope that she can be of any help to her husband. She must command enough self-confidence, after years of having it eroded, to be able to face an unknown future and leave the security of an unpalatable but familiar past and present. She must accept that she has failed in her marriage, not an easy thing to do after having devoted years to stopping up the cracks in the family structure as they appeared. Breaking up the marriage involves a complete alteration in the life goals toward which all her behavior has been oriented. It is hard for her to rid herself of the feeling that she married him and he is her responsibility. Having thought and planned for so long on a day-to-day basis, it is difficult to plan for a long-term future.

Her taking over the family raises her self-confidence but failure to carry through on decisions undermines the new gains that she has made. Vacillation in her decisions tends to exasperate the agencies trying to help her, and she begins to feel that help from them may not be forthcoming if she finally decides to leave.

Some events, however, help her to arrive at a decision. During the absences of her husband she has seen how manageable life can be and how smoothly her family can run. She finds that life goes on without him. The wife who is working comes to feel that "my husband is a luxury I can no longer afford." After a few short-term separations in which she tries out her wings successfully, leaving comes to look more possible. Another step on the path to leaving is the acceptance of the idea that, although she cannot help her husband, she can help her family. She often reaches a state of such emotional isolation from her husband that his behavior no longer disturbs her emotionally but is only something annoying which upsets daily routines and plans.

Stage 6. Reorganization of Part of the Family

The wife is without her husband and must reorganize her family on this basis. Substantially the process is similar to that in other divorced families, but with some additions. The divorce rarely cuts her relationships to her husband. Unless she and her family disappear, her husband may make attempts to come back. When drunk, he may endanger her job by calls at her place of work. He may attempt violence against members of the family, or he may contact the children and work to gain their loyalty so that pressure is put on the mother to accept him again. Looking back on her marriage, she forgets the full impact of the problem situation on her and on the children and feels more warmly toward her husband, and these feelings can still be manipulated by him. The wide circulation of information on alcoholism as an illness engenders guilt about having deserted a sick man. Gradually, however, the family becomes reorganized.

Stage 7. Recovery and Reorganization of the Whole Family

Stage 7 is entered if the husband achieves sobriety, whether or not separation has preceded. It was pointed out that in earlier stages most of the problems in the marriage were attributed to the alcoholism of the husband, and thus problems in adjustment not related directly to the drinking were unrecognized and unmet. Also, the "sober personality" of the husband was thought of as the "real" personality, with a resulting lack of recognition of other factors involved in his sober behavior, such as remorse and guilt over his actions, leading him to act to the best of his ability like "the ideal husband" when sober. Irritation or other signs of growing tension were viewed as indicators of further drinking, and hence the problems giving rise to them were walked around gingerly rather than faced and resolved. Lack of conflict and lack of drinking were defined as indicating a perfect adjustment. For the wife and husband facing a sober marriage after many years of an alcoholic marriage, the expectations of what marriage without alcoholism will be are unrealistically idealistic, and the reality of marriage almost inevitably brings disillusionments. The expectation that all would go well and that all problems be resolved with the cessation of the husband's drinking cannot be met and this threatens the marriage from time to time.

The beginning of sobriety for the husband does not bring too great hope to the family at first. They have been through this before but are willing to help him along and stand by him in the new attempt. As the length of sobriety increases, so do the hopes for its permanence and efforts to be of help. The wife at first finds it difficult to think more than in terms of today, waking each morning with fear of what the day will bring and sighing with relief at the end of each sober day.

With the continuation of sobriety, many problems begin to crop up. Mother has for years managed the family, and now father again wishes to be reinstated in his former roles. Usually the first role reestablished is that of breadwinner, and the economic problems of the family begin to be alleviated as debts are gradually paid and there is enough left over for current needs. With the resumption of this role, the husband feels that the family should also accept him at least as a partner in the management of the family. Even if the wife is willing to hand over some of the control of the children, for example, the children often are not able to accept this change easily. Their mother has been both parents for so long that it takes time to get used to the idea of consulting their father on problems and asking for his decisions. Often the father tries too hard to manage this change overnight, and the very pressure put on the children toward this end defeats him. In addition, he is unable to meet many of the demands the children make on him because he has never really become acquainted with them or learned to understand them and is lacking in much necessary background knowledge of their lives.

The wife, who finds it difficult to conceive of her husband as permanently sober, feels an unwillingness to let control slip from her hands. At the same time she realizes that reinstatement of her husband in his family roles is necessary to his sobriety. She also realizes that the closer his involvement in the family the greater the probability of his remaining sober. Yet she remembers events in the past in which his failure to handle his responsibilities was catastrophic to the family. Used to avoiding anything which might upset him, the wife often hesitates to discuss problems openly. At times, if she is successful in helping him to regain his roles as father, she feels resentful of his intrusion into territory which she has come to regard as hers. If he makes errors in judgment which affect the family adversely, her former feelings of being his superior may come to the fore and affect her interaction with him. If the children begin to turn to him, she may feel a resurgence of self-pity at being left out and find herself attempting to swing the children back toward herself. Above all, however, she finds herself feeling resentful that some other agency achieved what she and the children could not.

Often the husband makes demands for obedience, for consideration and for pampering which members of the family feel unable to meet. He may become rather euphoric as his sobriety continues and feel superior for a time.

Gradually, however, the drinking problem sinks into the past and marital adjustment at some level is achieved. Even when this has occurred, the drinking problem crops up occasionally, as when the time comes for a decision about whether the children should be permitted to drink. The mother at such times becomes anxious, sees in the child traits which remind her of her husband, worries whether these are the traits which mean future alcoholism. At parties, at first, she is watchful and concerned about whether her husband will take a drink or not. Relatives and friends may, in a party mood, make the husband the center of attention by emphasizing his nondrinking. They may unwittingly cast aspersions on his character by trying to convince him that he can now "drink like a man." Some relatives and friends have gone so far as secretly to "spike" a nonalcoholic drink and then cry "bottoms up!" without realizing the risk of reactivating patterns from the past.

If sobriety has come through Alcoholics Anonymous, the husband frequently throws himself so wholeheartedly into A.A. activities that his wife sees little of him and feels neglected. As she worries less about his drinking, she may press him to cut down on these activities. That this is dangerous, since A.A. activity is correlated with success in Alcoholics Anonymous, has been shown by Lahey (4). Also, the wife discovers that, though she has a sober husband, she is by no means free of alcoholics. In his Twelfth Step work, he may keep the house filled with men he is helping. In the past her husband has avoided self-searching; and now he may become excessively introspective, and it may be difficult for her to deal with this.

If the husband becomes sober through Alcoholics Anonymous and the wife participates actively in groups open to her, the thoughts of what is happening to her, to her husband and to her family will be verbalized and interpreted within the framework of the Alcoholics Anonymous philosophy and the situation will probably be more tolerable and more easily worked out.

SUGGESTIONS FOR FURTHER RESEARCH

The above presentation has roughly delineated sequences and characteristics of family adjustment to an alcoholic husband. A more detailed delineation of the stages is required. The extent to which these findings, based on families seeking help, can be generalized to other families of alcoholics needs to be determined, and differences between these families and others specified. Consideration should be given to the question of correspondence between the wife's definition of the situation and that which actually occurs.

Further research is needed on the factors which determine the rate of transition through the stages, and on the factors which retard such a transition, sometimes to the extent that the family seems to remain in the same stage almost permanently. In the group studied, the majority passed from one stage to the next but took different lengths of time to make the transition. Those wives whose husbands have been sober a long time had all passed through all the stages. None of the long-term members remained in the same stage throughout the time that the group was under study.

Other problems which require clarification are: (*a*) What are the factors within families which facilitate a return to sobriety or hamper it? (*b*) What variations in family behavior are determined by social class? (*c*) What problems are specific to the different types of drinking patterns of the husband—for example, the periodic drinker, the steady drinker, the solitary drinker, the sociable drinker, the drinker who becomes belligerent, and the drinker who remains calm? There are indications in the data gathered in the present study that such specific problems arise.

SUMMARY

The onset of alcoholism in a family member has been viewed as precipitating a cumulative crisis for the family. Seven critical stages have been delineated. Each stage affects the form which the following one will take. The family finds itself in an unstructured situation which is undefined by the culture. Thus it is forced to evolve techniques of adjustment by trial and error. The unpredictability of the situation, added to its lack of structure, engenders anxiety in family members which gives rise to personality difficulties. Factors in the culture, in the environment, and within the family situation prolong the crisis and deter the working out of permanent adjustment patterns. With the arrest of the alcoholism, the crisis enters its final stage. The family attempts to reorganize to include the ex-alcoholic and makes adjustments to the changes which have occurred in him.

It has been suggested that the clinical picture presented by the wife to helping agencies is not only indicative of a type of basic personality structure but also of the stage in family adjustment to an alcoholic. That the wives of alcoholics represent a rather limited number of personality types can be interpreted in two ways, which are not mutually exclusive.

(*a*) That women with certain personality attributes tend to select alcoholics or potential alcoholics as husbands in order to satisfy unconscious personality needs;

(*b*) That women undergoing similar experiences of stress, within similarly unstructured situations, defined by the culture and reacted to by members of the society in such a manner as to place limits on the range of possible behavior, will emerge from this experience showing many similar neurotic personality traits. As the situation evolves some of these personality traits will also change. Changes have been observed in the women studied which correlate with altered family interaction patterns. This hypothesis is supported also by observations on the behavior of individuals in other unstructured situations, in situations involving conflicting goals and loyalties, and in situations in which they were isolated from supporting group interaction. It is congruent also with the theory of reactions to increased and decreased stress.

Notes

1. Some effects of alcoholism of the father on children have been discussed by Newell (3).

2. It is of interest here that marriage counselors and students of marital adjustment are of the opinion that unhappy marriage results in poor sexual adjustment more often than poor sexual adjustment leads to unhappy marriage. If this proves to be true, it would be expected that most wives of alcoholics would find sex distasteful while their husbands are drinking. The wives of the inactive alcoholics report that their sexual adjustments with their husbands are currently satisfactory; many of those whose husbands are still drinking state that they enjoyed sexual relationships before the alcoholism was established.

References

1. Whalen, T. Wives of alcoholics: four types observed in a family service agency. Quart. J. Stud. Alc. 14:632–641, 1953.
2. Club and Educational Bureaus of Newsweek. Is alcoholism everyone's problem? Platform, N.Y., p. 3, Jan. 1950.
3. Newell, N. Alcoholism and the father-image. Quart. J. Stud. Alc. 11:92–96, 1950.
4. Lahey, W. W. A comparison of social and personal factors identified with selected members of Alcoholics Anonymous. Master's Thesis; University of Southern California; 1950.

22 / How Women Experience Battering: The Process of Victimization

KATHLEEN J. FERRARO
JOHN M. JOHNSON

On several occasions since 1850, feminists in Britain and the United States have initiated campaigns to end the battering of women by husbands and lovers, but have received little sympathy or support from the public (Dobash and Dobash, 1979). Sociologists systematically ignored the existence of violence against women until 1971, when journal articles and conferences devoted to the topic of domestic violence began to appear (Gelles, 1974; O'Brien, 1971; Steinmetz and Straus, 1974). Through the efforts of grass-roots activists and academics, battering has been recognized as a widespread social problem (Tierney, 1982). In 1975 a random survey of U.S. families found that 3.8 percent of women experienced severe violence in their marriage (Strauss *et al.,* 1980). The National Crime Survey of 1976 found that one-fourth of all assaults against women who had ever been married were committed by their husbands or ex-husbands (Gacquin, 1978). Shelters providing services to battered women in the United States have not been able to keep pace with requests for assistance (Colorado Association for Aid to Battered Women, 1978; Ferraro, 1981a; Roberts, 1981; Women's Advocates, 1980).

Although the existence of violence against women is now publicly acknowledged, the experience of being battered is poorly understood. Research aimed at discovering the incidence and related social variables has been based on an operational definition of battering which focuses on the violent act. The Conflict Tactic Scales (CTS) developed by Straus (1979), for example, is based on the techniques used to resolve family conflicts. The Violence Scale of the CTS ranks eight violent behaviors, ranging in severity from throwing something at the other person to using a knife or gun (Straus, 1979). The scale is not designed to explore the context of violent actions, or their meanings for the victim or perpetrator. With notable exceptions (Dobash and Dobash, 1979), the bulk of sociological research on battered women has focused on quantifiable variables (Gelles, 1974, 1976; O'Brien, 1971; Steinmetz, 1978; Straus, 1978).

Interviews with battered women make it apparent that the experience of violence inflicted by a husband or lover is shocking and confusing. Battering is rarely perceived as an unambiguous assault demanding immediate action to ensure future safety. In fact, battered women often remain in violent relationships for years (Pagelow, 1981).

Why do battered women stay in abusive relationships? Some observers answer facilely that they must like it. The masochism thesis was the predominant response of psychiatrists writing about battering in the 1960s (Saul, 1972; Snell *et al.*, 1964). More sympathetic studies of the problem have revealed the difficulties of disentangling oneself from a violent relationship (Hilberman, 1980; Martin, 1976; Walker, 1979). These studies point to the social and cultural expectations of women and their status within the nuclear family as reasons for the reluctance of battered women to flee the relationship. The socialization of women emphasizes the primary value of being a good wife and mother, at the expense of personal achievement in other spheres of life. The patriarchal ordering of society assigns a secondary status to women, and provides men with ultimate authority, both within and outside the family unit. Economic conditions contribute to the dependency of women on men; in 1978 U.S. women earned, on the average, 58 percent of what men earned (U.S. Department of Labor, 1980). In sum, the position of women in U.S. society makes it extremely difficult for them to reject the authority of men and develop independent lives free of marital violence (Dobash and Dobash, 1979; Pagelow, 1981).

Material and cultural conditions are the background in which personal interpretations of events are developed. Women who depend on their husbands for practical support also depend on them as sources of self-esteem, emotional support, and continuity. This paper looks at how women make sense of their victimization within the context of these dependencies. Without dismissing the importance of the macro forces of gender politics, we focus on inter- and intrapersonal responses to violence. We first describe six techniques of rationalization used by women who are in relationships where battering has occurred. We then turn to catalysts which may serve as forces to reevaluate rationalizations and to initiate serious attempts at escape. Various physical and emotional responses to battering are described, and finally, we outline the consequences of leaving or attempting to leave a violent relationship.

THE DATA

The data for this study were drawn from diverse sources. From July, 1978 to September, 1979 we were participant observers at a shelter for battered women located in the southwestern United States. The shelter was located in a suburban city of a major urban center. The shelter served five cities as well as the downtown population, resulting in a service population of 170,000. It was funded primarily by the state through an umbrella agency concerned with drug, mental health, and alcoholism problems. It was initially staffed by paraprofessionals and volunteers, but since this research it has become professionalized and is run by several professional social workers.

During the time of the research, 120 women passed through the shelters; they brought with them 165 children. The women ranged in age from 17 to 68, generally had family incomes below $15,000, and did not work outside the home. The characteristics of shelter residents are summarized in Table 1.

We established personal relationships with each of these women, and kept records of their experiences and verbal accounts. We also tape-recorded informal conversations, staff meetings, and crisis phone conversations with battered women. This daily interaction with shelter residents and staff permitted first-hand observation of feelings and thoughts about the battering experience. Finally, we taped interviews with 10 residents and five battered women who had left their abusers without entering the shelter. All quotes in this paper are taken from our notes and tapes.

Table 1 / Demographic Characteristics of Shelter Residents During First Year of Operation (*N* = 120)

Age		*Education*	
−17	2%	Elementary school	2%
18–24	33%	Junior high	8%
25–34	43%	Some high school	28%
35–44	14%	High school graduate	43%
45–54	6%	Some college	14%
55+	1%	College graduate	2%
		Graduate school	1%
Ethnicity		*Number of Children*	
White	78%	0	19%
Black	3%	1	42%
Mexican-American	10%	2	21%
American Indian	8%	3	15%
Other	1%	4	2%
		5+	1%
		Pregnant	7%
Family Income		*Employment Status*	
−$ 5,000	27%	Full time	23%
$ 6,000–10,000	36%	Part time	8%
$11,000–15,000	10%	Housewife	54%
$16,000+	10%	Student	5%
No response*	17%	Not employed	8%
		Receiving welfare	2%

*Many women had no knowledge of their husbands' income.

In addition to this participant study, both authors have been involved with the problem of domestic violence for more than 10 years. In 1976–77, Ferraro worked as a volunteer at Rainbow Retreat, the oldest shelter still functioning in the United States. In 1977–78, we both helped to found a shelter for battered women in our community. This involvement has led to direct contact with hundreds of women who have experienced battering, and many informal talks with people involved in the shelter movement in the United States and Europe.

The term battered woman is used in this paper to describe women who are battered repeatedly by men with whom they live as lovers. Marriage is not a prerequisite for being a battered woman. Many of the women who entered the shelter we studied were living with, but were not legally married to, the men who abused them.

Rationalizing Violence

Marriages and their unofficial counterparts develop through the efforts of each partner to maintain feelings of love and intimacy. In modern, Western cultures, the value placed on marriage is high; individuals invest a great amount of emotion in their spouses, and expect a return on that investment. The majority of women who marry still adopt the roles of wives and mothers as primary identities, even when they work outside the home, and thus have a strong motivation to succeed in their domestic roles. Married women remain economically dependent on their husbands. In 1978, married men in the United States earned an average of $293 a week, while married women earned $167 a week (U.S. Department of Labor, 1980). Given these high expectations and dependencies, the costs of recognizing failures and dissolving marriages are significant. Divorce is an increasingly common phenomenon in the United States, but it is still labeled a social problem and is seldom undertaken without serious deliberations and emotional upheavals (Bohannan, 1971). Levels of commitment vary widely, but some degree of commitment is implicit in the marriage contract.

When marital conflicts emerge there is usually some effort to negotiate an agreement or bargain, to ensure the continuity of the relationship (Scanzoni, 1972). Couples employ a variety of strategies, depending on the nature and extent of resources available to them, to resolve conflicts without dissolving relationships. It is thus possible for marriages to continue for years, surviving the inevitable conflicts that occur (Sprey, 1971).

In describing conflict-management, Spiegel (1968) distinguishes between "role induction" and "role modification." Role induction refers to conflict in which "one or the other parties to the conflict agrees, submits, goes along with, becomes convinced, or is persuaded in some way" (1968:402). Role modification, on the other hand, involves adaptations by both partners. Role induction seems particularly applicable to battered women who accommodate their husbands' abuse. Rather than seeking help or escaping, as people typically do when attacked by strangers, battered women often rationalize violence from their husbands, at least initially. Although remaining with a violent man does not indicate that a woman views violence as an acceptable aspect of the relationship, the length of time that a woman stays in the marriage after abuse begins is a rough index of her efforts to accommodate the situation. In a U.S. study of 350 battered women, Pagelow (1981) found the median length of stay after violence began was four years; some left in less than one year, others stayed as long as 42 years.

Battered women have good reasons to rationalize violence. There are few institutional, legal, or cultural supports for women fleeing violent marriages. In Roy's (1977:32) survey of 150 battered women, 90 percent said they "thought of leaving and would have done so had the resources been available to them." Eighty percent of Pagelow's (1981) sample indicated previous, failed attempts to leave their husbands. Despite the development of the international shelter movement, changes in police practices, and legislation to protect battered women since 1975, it remains extraordinarily difficult for a battered woman to escape a violent husband determined to maintain his control. At least one woman, Mary Parziale, has been murdered by an abusive husband while residing in a shelter (Beverly, 1978); others have been murdered after leaving shelters to establish new, independent homes (Garcia, 1978). When these practical and social constraints are combined with love for and commitment to an abuser, it is obvious that there is a strong incentive—often a practical necessity—to rationalize violence.

Previous research on the rationalizations of deviant offenders has revealed a typology of "techniques of neutralization," which allow offenders to view their actions as normal, acceptable, or at least justifiable (Sykes and Matza, 1957). A similar typology can be constructed for victims. Extending the concepts developed by Sykes and Matza, we assigned the responses of battered women we interviewed to one of six categories of rationalization: (1) the appeal to the salvation ethic; (2) the denial of the victimizer; (3) the denial of injury; (4) the denial of victimization; (5) the denial of options; and (6) the appeal to higher loyalties. The women usually employed at least one of these techniques to make sense of their situations; often they employed two or more, simultaneously or over time.

1) *The appeal to the salvation ethic:* This rationalization is grounded in a woman's desire to be of service to others. Abusing husbands are viewed as deeply troubled, perhaps "sick," individuals, dependent on their wives' nurturance for survival. Battered women place their own safety and happiness below their commitment to "saving my man" from whatever malady they perceive as the source of their husbands' problems (Ferraro, 1979a). The appeal to the salvation ethic is a common response to an alcoholic or drug-dependent abuser. The battered partners of substance-abusers frequently describe the charming, charismatic personality of their sober mates, viewing this appealing personality as the "real man" being destroyed by disease. They then assume responsibility for helping their partners to overcome their problems, viewing the batterings they receive as an index of their part-

ners' pathology. Abuse must be endured while helping the man return to his "normal" self. One woman said:

> I thought I was going to be Florence Nightingale. He had so much potential; I could see how good he really was, and I was going to "save" him. I thought I was the only thing keeping him going, and that if I left he'd lose his job and wind up in jail. I'd make excuses to everybody for him. I'd call work and lie when he was drunk, saying he was sick. I never criticized him, because he needed my approval.

2) *The denial of the victimizer:* This technique is similar to the salvation ethic, except that victims do not assume responsibility for solving their abusers' problems. Women perceive battering as an event beyond the control of both spouses, and blame it on some external force. The violence is judged situational and temporary, because it is linked to unusual circumstances or a sickness which can be cured. Pressures at work, the loss of a job, or legal problems are all situations which battered women assume as the causes of their partners' violence. Mental illness, alcoholism, and drug addiction are also viewed as external, uncontrollable afflictions by many battered women who accept the medical perspective on such problems. By focusing on factors beyond the control of their abuser, women deny their husbands' intent to do them harm, and thus rationalize violent episodes.

> He's sick. He didn't used to be this way, but he can't handle alcohol. It's really like a disease, being an alcoholic. . . . I think too that this is what he saw at home, his father is a very violent man, and alcoholic too, so it's really not his fault, because this is all he has ever known.

3) *The denial of injury:* For some women, the experience of being battered by a spouse is so discordant with their expectations that they simply refuse to acknowledge it. When hospitalization is not required—and it seldom is for most cases of battering[1]—routines quickly return to normal. Meals are served, jobs and schools are attended, and daily chores completed. Even with lingering pain, bruises, and cuts, the normality of everyday life overrides the strange, confusing memory of the attack. When husbands refuse to discuss or acknowledge the event, in some cases even accusing their wives of insanity, women sometimes come to believe the violence never occurred. The denial of injury does not mean that women feel no pain. They know they are hurt, but define the hurt as tolerable or normal. Just as individuals tolerate a wide range of physical discomfort before seeking medical help, battered women tolerate a wide range of physical abuse before defining it as an injurious assault. One woman explained her disbelief at her first battering:

> I laid in bed and cried all night. I could not believe it had happened, and I didn't want to believe it. We had only been married a year, and I was pregnant and excited about starting a family. Then all of a sudden, this! The next morning he told me he was sorry and it wouldn't happen again, and I gladly kissed and made up. I wanted to forget the whole thing, and wouldn't let myself worry about what it meant for us.

4) *The denial of victimization:* Victims often blame themselves for the violence, thereby neutralizing the responsibility of the spouse. Pagelow (1981) found that 99.4 percent of battered women felt they did not deserve to be beaten, and 51 percent said they had done nothing to provoke an attack. The battered women in our sample did not believe violence against them was justified, but some felt it could have been avoided if they had been more passive and conciliatory. Both Pagelow's and our samples are biased in this area, because they were made up almost entirely of women who had already left their abusers, and thus would have been unlikely to feel major responsibility for the abuse they received. Retrospective accounts of victimization in our sample, however, did reveal evidence that some women believed their right to leave violent men was restricted by their participation in the conflicts. One subject said:

> Well, I couldn't really do anything about it, because I did ask for it. I knew how to get at him, and I'd keep after it and keep after it until he got fed up and knocked me right out. I can't say I like it, but I shouldn't have nagged him like I did.

As Pagelow (1981) noted, there is a difference between provocation and justification. A battered woman's belief that her actions angered her spouse to the point of violence is not synonymous with the belief that violence was therefore *justified.* But belief in provocation may diminish a woman's capacity for retaliation or self-defense, because it blurs her concept of responsibility. A woman's acceptance of responsibility for the violent incident is encouraged by an abuser who continually denigrates her and makes unrealistic demands. Depending on the social supports available, and the personality of the battered woman, the man's accusations of inadequacy may assume the status of truth. Such beliefs of inferiority inhibit the development of a notion of victimization.

5) *The denial of options:* This technique is composed of two elements: practical options and emotional options. Practical options, including alternative housing, source of income, and protection from an abuser, are clearly limited by the patriarchal structure of Western society. However, there are differences in the ways battered women respond to these obstacles, ranging from determined struggle to acquiescence. For a variety of reasons, some battered women do not take full advantage of the practical opportunities which are available to escape, and some return to abusers voluntarily even after establishing an independent lifestyle. Others ignore the most severe constraints in their efforts to escape their relationships. For example, one resident of the shelter we observed walked 30 miles in her bedroom slippers to get to the shelter, and required medical attention for blisters and cuts to her feet. On the other hand, a woman who had a full-time job, had rented an apartment, and had been given by the shelter all the clothes, furniture, and basics necessary to set up housekeeping, returned to her husband two weeks after leaving the shelter. Other women refused to go to job interviews, keep appointments

with social workers, or move out of the state for their own protection (Ferraro, 1981b). Such actions are frightening for women who have led relatively isolated or protected lives, but failure to take action leaves few alternatives to a violent marriage. The belief of battered women that they will not be able to make it on their own—a belief often fueled by years of abuse and oppression—is a major impediment to [acknowledgment] that one is a victim and taking action.

The denial of *emotional* options imposes still further restrictions. Battered women may feel that no one else can provide intimacy and companionship. While physical beating is painful and dangerous, the prospect of a lonely, celibate existence is often too frightening to risk. It is not uncommon for battered women to express the belief that their abuser is the only man they could love, thus severely limiting their opportunities to discover new, more supportive relationships. One woman said:

> He's all I've got. My dad's gone, and my mother disowned me when I married him. And he's really special. He understands me, and I understand him. Nobody could take his place.

6) *The appeal to higher loyalties:* This appeal involves enduring battering for the sake of some higher commitment, either religious or traditional. The Christian belief that women should serve their husbands as men serve God is invoked as a rationalization to endure a husband's violence for later rewards in the afterlife. Clergy may support this view by advising women to pray and try harder to please their husbands (Davidson, 1978; McGlinchey, 1981). Other women have a strong commitment to the nuclear family, and find divorce repugnant. They may believe that for their children's sake, any marriage is better than no marriage. One woman we interviewed divorced her husband of 35 years after her last child left home. More commonly women who have survived violent relationships for that long do not have the desire or strength to divorce and begin a new life. When the appeal to higher loyalties is employed as a strategy to cope with battering, commitment to and involvement with an ideal overshadows the mundane reality of violence.

CATALYSTS FOR CHANGE

Rationalization is a way of coping with a situation in which, for either practical or emotional reasons, or both, a battered woman is stuck. For some women, the situation and the beliefs that rationalize it, may continue for a lifetime. For others, changes may occur within the relationship, within individuals, or in available resources which serve as catalysts for redefining the violence. When battered women reject prior rationalizations and begin to view themselves as true victims of abuse, the victimization process begins.[2]

There are a variety of catalysts for redefining abuse; we discuss six: (1) a change in the level of violence; (2) a change in resources; (3) a change in the relationship; (4) despair; (5) a change in the visibility of violence; and (6) external definitions of the relationship.

1) *A change in the level of violence:* Although Gelles (1976) reports that the severity of abuse is an important factor in women's decisions to leave violent situations, Pagelow (1981) found no significant correlation between the number of years spent cohabiting with an abuser and the severity of abuse. On the contrary: the longer women lived with an abuser, the more severe the violence they endured, since violence increased in severity over time. What does seem to serve as a catalyst is a sudden change in the relative level of violence. Women who suddenly realize that battering may be fatal may reject rationalizations in order to save their lives. One woman who had been severely beaten by an alcoholic husband for many years explained her decision to leave on the basis of a direct threat to her life:

> It was like a pendulum. He'd swing to the extremes both ways. He'd get drunk and beat me up, then he'd get sober and treat me like a queen. One day he put a gun to my head and pulled the trigger. It wasn't loaded. But that's when I decided I'd had it. I sued for separation of property. I knew what was coming again, so I got out. I didn't want to. I still loved the guy, but I knew I had to for my own sanity.

There are, of course, many cases of homicide in which women did not escape soon enough. In 1979, 7.6 percent of all murders in the United States where the relationship between the victim and the offender was known were murders of wives by husbands (Flanagan *et al.*, 1982). Increases in severity do not guarantee a reinterpretation of the situation, but may play a part in the process.

2) *A change in resources:* Although some women rationalize cohabiting with an abuser by claiming they have no options, others begin reinterpreting violence when the resources necessary for escape become available. The emergence of safe homes or shelters since 1970 has produced a new resource for battered women. While not completely adequate or satisfactory, the mere existence of a place to go alters the situation in which battering is experienced (Johnson, 1981). Public support of shelters is a statement to battered women that abuse need not be tolerated. Conversely, political trends which limit resources available to women, such as cutbacks in government funding to social programs, increase fears that life outside a violent marriage is economically impossible. One 55-year-old woman discussed this catalyst:

> I stayed with him because I didn't want my kids to have the same life I did. My parents were divorced, and I was always so ashamed of that.... Yes, they're all on their own now, so there's no reason left to stay.

3) *A change in the relationship:* Walker (1979), in discussing the stages of a battering relationship, notes that violent incidents are usually followed

by periods of remorse and solicitude. Such phases deepen the emotional bonds, and make rejection of an abuser more difficult. But as battering progresses, periods of remorse may shorten, or disappear, eliminating the basis for maintaining a positive outlook on the marriage. After a number of episodes of violence, a man may realize that his victim will not retaliate or escape, and thus feel no need to express remorse. Extended periods devoid of kindness or love may alter a woman's feelings toward her partner so much so that she eventually begins to define herself as a victim of abuse. One woman recalled:

> At first, you know, we used to have so much fun together. He has kind've, you know, a magnetic personality; he can be really charming. But it isn't fun anymore. Since the baby came, it's changed completely. He just wants me to stay at home, while he goes out with his friends. He doesn't even talk to me, most of the time. . . . No, I don't really love him anymore, not like I did.

4) *Despair:* Changes in the relationship may result in a loss of hope that "things will get better." When hope is destroyed and replaced by despair, rationalizations of violence may give way to the recognition of victimization. Feelings of hopelessness or despair are the basis for some efforts to assist battered women, such as Al-Anon.[3] The director of an Al-Anon organized shelter explained the concept of "hitting bottom":

> Before the Al-Anon program can really be of benefit, a woman has to hit bottom. When you hit bottom, you realize that all of your own efforts to control the situation have failed; you feel helpless and lost and worthless and completely disenchanted with the world. Women can't really be helped unless they're ready for it and want it. Some women come here when things get bad, but they aren't really ready to be committed to Al-Anon. Things haven't gotten bad enough for them, and they go right back. We see this all the time.

5) *A change in the visibility of violence:* Creating a web of rationalizations to overlook violence is accomplished more easily if no intruders are present to question their validity. Since most violence between couples occurs in private, there are seldom conflicting interpretations of the event from outsiders. Only 7 percent of the respondents in Gelles' (1974) study who discussed spatial location of violence indicated events which took place outside the home, but all reported incidents within the home. Others report similar findings (Pittman and Handy, 1964; Pokorny, 1965; Wolfgang, 1958). If violence does occur in the presence of others, it may trigger a reinterpretation process. Battering in private is degrading, but battering in public is humiliating, for it is a statement of subordination and powerlessness. Having others witness abuse may create intolerable feelings of shame which undermine prior rationalizations.

> He never hit me in public before—it was always at home. But the Saturday I got back (returned to husband from shelter), we went Christmas shopping and he slapped me in the store because of some stupid joke I made. People saw it,

> I know, I felt so stupid, like, they must all think what a jerk I am, what a sick couple, and I thought, "God, I must be crazy to let him do this."

6) *External definitions of the relationship:* A change in visibility is usually accomplished by the interjection of external definitions of abuse. External definitions vary depending on their source and the situation; they either reinforce or undermine rationalizations. Battered women who request help frequently find others—and especially officials—don't believe their story or are unsympathetic (Pagelow, 1981; Pizzey, 1974). Experimental research by Shotland and Straw (1976) supports these reports. Observers usually fail to respond when a woman is attacked by a man, and justify nonintervention on the grounds that they assumed the victim and offender were married. One young woman discussed how lack of support from her family left her without hope:

> It wouldn't be so bad if my own family gave a damn about me.... Yeah, they know I'm here, and they don't care. They didn't care about me when I was a kid, so why should they care now? I got raped and beat as a kid, and now I get beat as an adult. Life is a big joke.

Clearly, such responses from family members contribute to the belief among battered women that there are no alternatives and that they must tolerate the abuse. However, when outsiders respond with unqualified support of the victim and condemnation of violent men, their definitions can be a potent catalyst toward victimization. Friends and relatives who show genuine concern for a woman's well-being may initiate an awareness of danger which contradicts previous rationalizations.

> My mother-in-law knew what was going on, but she wouldn't admit it.... I said, "Mom, what do you think these bruises are?" and she said "Well, some people just bruise easy. I do it all the time, bumping into things."... And he just denied it, pretended like nothing happened, and if I'd said I wanted to talk about it, he'd say, "life goes on, you can't just dwell on things."... But this time, my neighbor *knew* what happened, she saw it, and when he denied it, she said, "I can't believe it! You know that's not true!"... and I was so happy that finally, somebody else saw what was goin' on, and I just told him then that this time I wasn't gonna' come home!

Shelters for battered women serve not only as material resources, but as sources of external definitions which contribute to the victimization process. They offer refuge from a violent situation in which a woman may contemplate her circumstances and what she wants to do about them. Within a shelter, women meet counselors and other battered women who are familiar with rationalizations of violence and the reluctance to give up commitment to a spouse. In counseling sessions, and informal conversations with other residents, women hear horror stories from others who have already defined themselves as victims. They are supported for expressing anger and rejecting responsibility for their abuse (Ferraro,

1981a). The goal of many shelters is to overcome feelings of guilt and inadequacy so that women can make choices in their best interests. In this atmosphere, violent incidents are reexamined and redefined as assaults in which the woman was victimized.

How others respond to a battered woman's situation is critical. The closer the relationship of others, the more significant their response is to a woman's perception of the situation. Thus, children can either help or hinder the victim. Pizzey (1974) found adolescent boys at a shelter in Chiswick, England, often assumed the role of the abusing father and themselves abused their mothers, both verbally and physically. On the other hand, children at the shelter we observed often became extremely protective and nurturing toward their mothers. This phenomenon has been thoroughly described elsewhere (Ferraro, 1981a). Children who have been abused by fathers who also beat their mothers experience high levels of anxiety, and rarely want to be reunited with their fathers. A 13-year-old, abused daughter of a shelter resident wrote the following message to her stepfather:

> I am going to be honest and not lie. No, I don't want you to come back. It's not that I am jealous because mom loves you. It is [I] am afraid I won't live to see 18. I did care about you a long time ago, but now I can't care, for the simple reason you['re] always calling us names, even my friends. And another reason is, I am tired of seeing mom hurt. She has been hurt enough in her life, and I don't want her to be hurt any more.

No systematic research has been conducted on the influence children exert on their battered mothers, but it seems obvious that the willingness of children to leave a violent father would be an important factor in a woman's desire to leave.

The relevance of these catalysts to a woman's interpretation of violence vary with her own situation and personality. The process of rejecting rationalizations and becoming a victim is ambiguous, confusing, and emotional. We now turn to the feelings involved in a victimization.

THE EMOTIONAL CAREER OF VICTIMIZATION

As rationalizations give way to perceptions of victimization, a woman's feelings about herself, her spouse, and her situation change. These feelings are imbedded in a cultural, political, and interactional structure. Initially, abuse is contrary to a woman's cultural expectations of behavior between intimates, and therefore engenders feelings of betrayal. The husband has violated his wife's expectations of love and protection, and thus betrayed her confidence in him. The feeling of betrayal, however, is balanced by the husband's efforts to explain his behavior, and by the woman's reluctance to abandon faith. Additionally, the political dominance of men within and outside the family mediate women's ability to question the validity of their husband's actions.

At the interpersonal level, psychological abuse accompanying violence often invokes feelings of guilt and shame in the battered victim. Men define violence as a response to their wives' inadequacies or provocations, which leads battered women to feel that they have failed. Such character assaults are devastating, and create long-lasting feelings of inferiority (Ferraro, 1979b):

> I've been verbally abused as well. It takes you a long time to... you may say you feel good and you may... but inside, you know what's been said to you and it hurts for a long time. You need to build up your self-image and make yourself feel like you're a useful person, that you're valuable, and that you're a good parent. You might think these things, and you may say them.... I'm gonna prove it to myself.

Psychologists working with battered women consistently report that self-confidence wanes over years of ridicule and criticism (Hilberman and Munson, 1978; Walker, 1979).

Feelings of guilt and shame are also mixed with a hope that things will get better, at least in the early stages of battering. Even the most violent man is nonviolent much of the time, so there is always a basis for believing that violence is exceptional and the "real man" is not a threat. The vacillation between violence and fear on the one hand, and nonviolence and affection on the other was described by a shelter resident:

> First of all, the first beatings—you can't believe it yourself. I'd go to bed, and I'd cry, and I just couldn't believe this was happening. And I'd wake up the next morning thinking that couldn't of happened, or maybe it was my fault. It's so unbelievable that this person that you're married to and you love would do that to you but yet you can't leave either because, ya' know, for the other 29 days of the month that person loves you and is with you.

Hope wanes as periods of love and remorse dwindle. Feelings of love and intimacy are gradually replaced with loneliness and pessimism. Battered women who no longer feel love for their husbands but remain in their marriages enter a period of emotional dormancy. They survive each day, performing necessary tasks, with a dull depression and lack of enthusiasm. While some battered women live out their lives in this emotional desert, others are spurred by catalysts to feel either the total despair or mortal fear which leads them to seek help.

Battered women who perceive their husbands' actions as life-threatening experience a penetrating fear that consumes all their thoughts and energies. The awareness of murderous intent by a presumed ally who is a central figure in all aspects of her life destroys all bases for safety. There is a feeling that death is imminent, and that there is nowhere to hide. Prior rationalizations and beliefs about a "good marriage" are exploded, leaving the woman in a crisis of ambiguity (Ridington, 1978).

Feelings of fear are experienced physiologically as well as emotionally. Battered women experience aches and fatigue, stomach pains, diarrhea or constipation, tension headaches, shakes, chills, loss of appetite, and insomnia. Sometimes, fear is expressed as a numbed shock, similar to rape trauma syndrome (Burgess and Holmstrom, 1974), in which little is felt or communicated.

If attempts to seek help succeed, overwhelming feelings of fear subside, and a rush of new emotions are felt: the original sense of betrayal reemerges, creating strong feelings of anger. For women socialized to reject angry feelings as unfeminine, coping with anger is difficult. Unless the expression of anger is encouraged in a supportive environment, such women may suppress anger and feel only depression (Ball and Wyman, 1978). When anger is expressed, it often leads to feelings of strength and exhilaration. Freedom from threats of violence, the possibility of a new life, and the unburdening of anger create feelings of joy. The simple pleasures of going shopping, taking children to the park, or talking with other women without fear of criticism or punishment from a husband, constitute amazing freedoms. One middle-aged woman expressed her joy over her newly acquired freedom this way:

> Boy, tomorrow I'm goin' downtown, and I've got my whole day planned out, and I'm gonna' do what *I* wanna' do, and if somebody doesn't like it, to *hell* with them! You know, I'm having so much fun, I should've done this years ago!

Probably the most typical feeling expressed by women in shelters is confusion. They feel both sad and happy, excited and apprehensive, independent, yet in need of love. Most continue to feel attachment to their husbands, and feel ambivalent about divorce. There is grief over the loss of an intimate, which must be acknowledged and mourned. Although shelters usually discourage women from contacting their abusers while staying at the shelter, most women do communicate with their husbands—and most receive desperate pleas for forgiveness and reconciliation. If there is not strong emotional support and potential material support, such encourage ment by husbands often rekindles hope for the relationship. Some marriages can be revitalized through counseling, but most experts agree that long-term batterers are unlikely to change (Pagelow, 1981; Walker, 1979). Whether they seek refuge in shelters or with friends, battered women must decide relatively quickly what actions to take. Usually, a tentative commitment is made, either to independence or working on the relationship, but such commitments are usually ambivalent. As one woman wrote to her counselor:

> My feelings are so mixed up sometimes. Right now I feel my husband is really trying to change. But I know that takes time. I still feel for him some. I don't

know how much. My mind still doesn't know what it wants. I would really like when I leave here to see him once in a while, get my apartment, and sort of like start over with our relationship for me and my baby and him, to try and make it work. It might. It kind of scares me. I guess I am afraid it won't. . . . I can only hope this works out. There's no telling what could happen. No one knows.

The emotional career of battered women consists of movement from guilt, shame, and depression to fear and despair, to anger, exhilaration, and confusion. Women who escape violent relationships must deal with strong, sometimes conflicting, feelings in attempting to build new lives for themselves free of violence. The kind of response women receive when they seek help largely determines the effects these feelings have on subsequent decisions.

* * *

Notes

1. National crime survey data for 1973–76 show that 17 percent of persons who sought medical attention for injuries inflicted by an intimate were hospitalized. Eighty-seven percent of injuries inflicted by a spouse or ex-spouse were bruises, black eyes, cuts, scratches, or swelling (National Crime Survey Report, 1980).
2. Explanation of why and how some women arrive at these feelings is beyond the scope of this paper. Our goal is to describe feelings at various stages of the victimization process.
3. Al-Anon is the spouse's counterpart to Alcoholics Anonymous. It is based on the same self-help, 12-step program that A.A. is founded on.

References

Ball, Patricia G., and Elizabeth Wyman
1978 "Battered wives and powerlessness: What can counselors do?" Victimology 2(3–4):545–552.
Beverly
1978 "Shelter resident murdered by husband." Aegis, September/October:13.
Bohannan, Paul (ed.)
1971 Divorce and After. Garden City, New York: Anchor.
Burgess, Ann W., and Linda Lytle Holmstrom
1974 Rape: Victims of Crisis. Bowie, Maryland: Brady.
Colorado Association for Aid to Battered Women
1978 Services to Battered Women. Washington, D.C.: Office of Domestic Violence, Department of Health, Education and Welfare.
Davidson, Terry
1978 Conjugal Crime. New York: Hawthorn.
Dobash, R. Emerson, and Russell P. Dobash
1979 Violence Against Wives. New York: Free Press.
Ferraro, Kathleen J.
1979a "Hard love: Letting go of an abusive husband." Frontiers 4(2):16–18.
1979b "Physical and emotional battering: Aspects of managing hurt." California Sociologist 2(2):134–149.

1981a "Battered women and the shelter movement." Unpublished Ph.D. dissertation, Arizona State University.
1981b "Processing battered women." Journal of Family Issues 2(4):415–438.
Flanagan, Timothy J., David J. van Alstyne, and Michael R. Gottfredson (eds.)
1982 Sourcebook of Criminal Justice Statistics: 1981. U.S. Department of Justice, Bureau of Justice Statistics, Washington, D.C.: U.S. Government Printing Office.
Gacquin, Deidre A.
1978 "Spouse abuse: Data from the National Crime Survey." Victimology 2:632–643.
Garcia, Dick
1978 "Slain women 'lived in fear.' " The Times (Erie, Pa.) June 14:B1.
Gelles, Richard J.
1974 The Violent Home. Beverly Hills: Sage.
1976 "Abused wives: Why do they stay?" Journal of Marriage and the Family 38(4):659–668.
Hilberman, Elaine
1980 "Overview: The 'wife-beater's wife' reconsidered." American Journal of Psychiatry 137(11):1336–1347.
Hilberman, Elaine, and Kit Munson
1978 "Sixty battered women." Victimology 2(3–4):460–470.
Johnson, John M.
1981 "Program enterprise and official cooptation of the battered women's shelter movement." American Behavioral Scientist 24(6):827–842.
McGlinchey, Anne
1981 "Woman battering and the church's response." Pp. 133–140 in Albert R. Roberts (ed.), Sheltering Battered Women. New York: Springer.
Martin, Del
1976 Battered Wives. San Francisco: Glide.
National Crime Survey Report
1980 Intimate Victims. Washington, D.C.: U.S. Department of Justice.
O'Brien, John E.
1971 "Violence in divorce-prone families." Journal of Marriage and the Family 33(4):692–698.
Pagelow, Mildred Daley
1981 Woman-Battering. Beverly Hills: Sage.
Pittman, D. J. and W. Handy
1964 "Patterns in criminal aggravated assault." Journal of Criminal Law, Criminology, and Police Science 55(4):462–470.
Pizzey, Erin
1974 Scream Quietly or the Neighbors Will Hear. Baltimore: Penguin.
Pokorny, Alex D.
1965 "Human violence: A comparison of homicide, aggravated assault, suicide, and attempted suicide." Journal of Criminal Law, Criminology, and Police Science 56(December):488–497.
Ridington, Jillian
1978 "The transition process: A feminist environment as reconstitutive milieu." Victimology 2(3–4):563–576.
Roberts, Albert R.
1981 Sheltering Battered Women. New York: Springer.

Roy, Maria (ed.)
1977 Battered Women. New York: Van Nostrand.
Saul, Leon J.
1972 "Personal and social psychopathology and the primary prevention of violence." American Journal of Psychiatry 128(12):1578–1581.
Scanzoni, John
1972 Sexual Bargaining. Englewood Cliffs, N.J.: Prentice-Hall.
Shotland, R. Lance, and Margret K. Straw
1976 "Bystander response to an assault: When a man attacks a woman." Journal of Personality and Social Psychology 34(5):990–999.
Snell, John E., Richard Rosenwald, and Ames Robey
1964 "The wifebeater's wife: A study of family interaction." Archives of General Psychiatry 11(August):107–112.
Spiegel, John P.
1968 "The resolution of role conflict within the family." Pp. 391–411 in N. W. Bell and E. F. Vogel (eds.), A Modern Introduction to the Family. New York: Free Press.
Sprey, Jetse
1971 "On the management of conflict in families." Journal of Marriage and the Family 33(4):699–706.
Steinmetz, Suzanne K.
1978 "The battered husband syndrome." Victimology 2(3–4):499–509.
Steinmetz, Suzanne K., and Murray A. Straus (eds.)
1974 Violence in the Family. New York: Harper & Row.
Straus, Murray A.
1978 "Wife beating: How common and why?" Victimology 2(3–4):443–458.
1979 "Measuring intrafamily conflict and violence: The conflict tactics (CT) scales." Journal of Marriage and the Family 41(1):75–88.
Straus, Murray A., Richard J. Gelles, and Suzanne K. Steinmetz
1980 Behind Closed Doors: Violence in the American Family. Garden City: Doubleday.
Sykes, Gresham M., and David Matza
1957 "Techniques of neutralization: A theory of delinquency." American Sociological Review 22(6):667–670.
Tierney, Kathleen J.
1982 "The battered women movement and the creation of the wife beating problem." Social Problems 29(3):207–220.
U.S. Department of Labor
1980 Handbook of Labor Statistics. Washington, D.C.: U.S. Government Printing Office.
Walker, Lenore E.
1979 The Battered Woman. New York: Harper & Row.
Wolfgang, Marvin E.
1958 Patterns in Criminal Homicide. New York: John Wiley.
Women's Advocates
1980 Women's Advocates: The Story of a Shelter. St. Paul, Minnesota: Women's Advocates.

Part 4 / Institutional Deviance

In Part 3, I described how deviant behavior may initially be managed in a private setting. The material that was presented demonstrated how such behavior may become subject to regulation by a social-control agent or agency. When such regulation occurs, the actor's behavior is screened by the institution and its staff, and a label may be placed on him or her. The individual then becomes an institutional deviant, expected thereafter to conform to the institution's definition of the label. Some people will accept this labeling. In this event, the person's public identity (how others view him or her) meshes with personal identity (how the person views himself or herself), so that we can speak of the secondary, or career, deviant. Other deviants, however, will reject the label and attempt to structure and present to others a nondeviant image of self. The selections in this part explore such possibilities as these; they also illustrate clearly how institutional careers are initiated and perpetuated. Throughout the following discussion of the various articles, the "organizational paradigm," which was presented in the general introduction, is applied.

TYPING BY AGENTS OF SOCIAL CONTROL

I have argued previously that it is difficult to understand deviance unless we first analyze the institution or organization out of which a specific social-control agent operates. It is particularly important to know how the existing theory of the office (working ideology), existing deviant categories, and diagnostic stereotypes are applied to clients.

Once a person has been initially identified as a deviant or potential deviant, he or she frequently becomes subject to institutional control and scrutiny. The article by Thomas J. Scheff and Daniel M. Culver, "The Societal Reaction to Deviance: Ascriptive Elements in the Psychiatric Screening of Mental Patients in a Midwestern State," offers a vivid account of what may happen to those actors brought involuntarily before a psychiatric screening board.

Scheff and Culver note that most patients are incarcerated. Even though many patients did not meet the minimal criteria for admission, twenty-four out of the twenty-six cases examined were committed. Scheff and Culver explain this finding by arguing that the theory of the office is predicated solidly upon the "presumption of mental illness," at least as far as it relates to the involuntary patient. Thus, when such patients come before the board, they are almost invariably committed; this suggests that the commitment decision has already been made, with the psychiatrists seeming merely to go through the motions. This approach is apparent from the brief examinations given, the type of questions asked, and the comments offered by various psychiatric personnel. By committing a patient, Scheff and Culver reason, the psychiatrists are confirming the mental institution's expectations of how the involuntary actor should be typed. They are also able to deal with any ambiguity that may arise concerning a person's condition; they thereby remove the threat of negative public reaction that could result if such patients were released.

The selection by Roger Jeffery, "Normal Rubbish: Deviant Patients in Casualty Departments," presents a specific account of how medical patients are initially typed by physicians. His observations are based on data gathered at three Casualty departments in an English city. Jeffery finds that two major categories exist for the evaluation of potential patients: good or interesting, and bad or rubbish. Those patients who were classified as "good" usually met one of three criteria: (1) they offered doctors a chance to practice skills necessary for passing their examinations, (2) they allowed staff members to practice their skills, and (3) they tested the general competence of the staff. In effect, "good" patients fell within the realm of expectations associated with the medical profession and its practitioners. The "rubbish" did not fit these molds.

Of interest is Jeffery's statement that, unlike the category of "good patient," the category of "rubbish" was generated by the staff members themselves. Further, the workers possessed definite notions as to what "normal rubbish" looked like; they also felt that they could predict features related to a patient's past life, his or her behavior within the department, and his or her behavior outside the facility. These expected traits, Jeffery points out, were used to guide treatment, as well as to shunt patients into standard career lines. He then describes the various categories of "rubbish," particularly in terms of how the occupants are perceived, responded to, and treated by the medical personnel. Four major categories of "normal rubbish" are noted: trivia, drunks, those suffering form an overdose, and tramps. For example, it is believed that tramps can be recognized by their rotten clothing, bad smell, untrustworthiness, and abusive behavior. Jeffery offers some case material in support of such conceptions. He then outlines the various justifications that medical personnel use to legitimate their handling of the "rubbish," and ends by describing how the staff may punish people in this category (e.g., by delaying medical treatment).

SOCIAL-CONTROL AGENTS AND THE AMPLIFICATION OF DEVIANCE

As was noted in the general introduction, very little direct attention has been given to the decision makers who label behavior as deviant; as a result, most of them can operate with relative impunity. This is especially apparent in terms of how involuntary patients and those viewed as "rubbish" are frequently treated. Accordingly, a systematic and ongoing analysis is needed in order to clarify how social-control agents, both formal (e.g., police) and informal (e.g., teachers), conduct themselves, as well as how they arrive at their decisions. The evidence points to the need for a heightened degree of monitoring and accountability and indicates that some significant structural-organizational changes are in order (e.g., eradicating the involuntary career line and doing away with the "rubbish" career route). In studying the decision-making processes involved, one must also entertain the very real possibility that the decision makers themselves, as well as their organizations, may become involved in deviant pursuits. They may, additionally, contribute to rule-breaking on the part of social actors—an event that can lead to institutional typing, sanctioning, and treatment. The pieces in Part 4 explore possibilities such as these. Here, the primary concern is with those contingencies that may give rise to the *beginning* stages of a deviant career for actors, agents, and organizations.

Gary T. Marx, in "Ironies of Social Control: Authorities as Contributors to Deviance Through Escalation, Nonenforcement and Convert Facilitation," focuses on social-control apparatuses and their agents. His thesis is that social control can contribute to, or even generate, rule-breaking behavior. Marx then discusses three situations under which this can occur: escalation, nonenforfcement, and covert facilitation. Escalation, for example, refers to the situation where agents, in taking enforcement action, unintentionally encourage rule-breaking. As an illustration, police involvement in family disturbances can give rise to violations of the law where none was imminent and can lead to police and citizen injuries. Similarly, high-speed chases can produce tragic results. People may be injured, killed, or charged with manslaughter—persons who, in the absence of the chase, might not have been charged with any offense. Marx also comments on how post-apprehension escalation may work. Of interest here are the ways in which authorities may, because of their reactions, make additional violations of the law more likely. Nonenforcement, the second situation covered by Marx, occurs when authorities, by taking no enforcement action, intentionally permit rule-breaking. As an example, Marx describes how the police, in return for information, may treat an informant leniently or even let him or her go free. This interdependent or exchange system, Marx maintains, is very highly developed in the case of the drug scene. Covert facilitation, the third situation discussed by Marx, occurs when agents, by taking hidden or deceptive enforcement action, intentionally encourage rule-breaking. Marx offers many illustrations of this (e.g., using decoys, pursuing "dirty tricks" campaigns, planting "lost" wallets near selected police, offering bribes to police officers and other officials).

In "The Social Context of Police Lying," Jennifer Hunt and Peter K. Manning explore the subject of police lying. They use as their source data obtained from an eighteen-month field study of a large urban police force, and they operate on the assumption that police, like many situated in an official position, lie. Hunt and Manning analyze the types and ways in which police lie. They note initially that instructors in the police academy not only often encourage recruits to lie but tell the recruits that lying is an element of "good police work." During classes on the law and courts, however, recruits receive a different message; they are taught that the best way to win in court is by presenting a factual account of an event. Once the rookie is on the job the situation changes, and he or she is taught when it is appropriate to lie. In fact, learning to lie is a prerequisite to gaining membership on the force. This is particularly important in view of the observation that the police in Metro City routinely engage in a range of illicit activities such as drinking and sleeping on the job. And those rookies who show little skill in constructing or using lies are often subject to criticism. Associated with lies is a range of acceptable justifications and excuses of which the officers can avail themselves. Accounts, however, are often audience-specific. For example, a story directed at an "external" audience such as an attorney or the media is often viewed as more problematic than one directed at a supervisor. Hunt and Manning offer various illustrations of how case lies are used in court to obtain a conviction. For example, "probable cause" can be constructed in numerous ways (e.g., by adding to the facts). The researchers also report how the court can be manipulated to gain a conviction. The case of the boy who "hung out" with a corner group offers an excellent case in point. Throughout this specific analysis, the involved officer, who believes the boy is guilty, constructs and presents an account consisting of a combination of excuses and justifications. The researchers then describe cover stories, or those lies that officers tell in an attempt to shield themselves against disciplinary action. For example, one who does not respond to a radio call may claim that his or her radio was dead. Similarly, an officer who uses brutal force is often expected to lie to protect him- or herself. Hunt and Manning conclude by noting that the extent to which an organization uses lies varies across selected dimensions.

SANCTIONING AND TREATMENT

Once individuals have been typed and screened, they frequently become subject to institutional sanctioning and treatment. Such processing increases the probability that a person will eventually become a career deviant, particularly in the manner described by Lemert (Part 2).

"Accounts, Attitudes, and Solutions: Probation Officer-Defendant Negotiations of Subjective Orientations," by Jack W. Spencer, offers an account of the organizational processing of criminal defendants. He is specifically concerned with analyzing how probation officers arrive at their sentencing recommendations. Spencer's observations are based on data collected in a county probation department over a period of nine months. He begins by noting that most research has focused on the legal (e.g., nature of the offense) and extra-legal factors (e.g., sex, race, class) that may be used in the rendering of a sentence. He argues that such a two-pronged approach is insufficient because it fails to incorporate a central component that most probation officers view as being critical: an offender's subjective orientation to his or her criminal activity. Spencer locates four major subjective orientations: (1) accounts for offenses, (2) attitudes toward the offenses, (3) attitudes toward the consequences of the offenses, and (4) attitudes toward changing behavior. He then describes how probation officers, during their negotiations with defendants, used these criteria to initially label clients. Once a defendent was typed and cast into one of the niches of the threefold criminal typology that existed, the probation officer was free to render a sentence recommendation. Spencer concludes by commenting on a central feature of the organizational processing of criminal defendents—the agency did not process individuals; rather, it processed *types* of clients who had been labeled in selected ways. This "bureaucratic matching game" (i.e., using an agency's existing diagnostic stereotypes to initially classify clients for placement in career lines) is especially evident in the next piece.

Jacqueline P. Wiseman, in "Court Responses to Skid Row Alcoholics," describes the process of "platoon sentencing" whereby 50 to 250 men are sentenced within a very short period of time. Wiseman's classification of social types and probable sentences provides an excellent illustration of how institutional stereotypes relating to skid row alcoholics are actually applied. For example, the alcoholic who is gravely ill is frequently given a suspended sentence and taken to a hospital. Of interest, too, is the way corrupt personnel, many of whom are ex-alcoholics, attempt to present a specific image of the alcoholic to the judge. Wiseman further points out that if the alcoholic is slated for institutional treatment, his behavior becomes regulated by some "people-changing institution" (e.g., an alcoholic ward or hospital). Moreover, the alcoholic becomes subject to a different theory of the office (and associated institutional stereotypes) and a different set of institutional expectations. He or she is expected to act in accordance with a new status, and failure to do so may result in the application of various types of institutional sanctions.

EFFECTS OF INSTITUTIONAL PROCESSING

I have argued previously that the labeling ceremony or institutional processing can be viewed from two major perspectives: the institution's or the actor's. Thus far, not only have the selections dealt with processing from the institution's perspective, but very little direct focus has been given to the actor's perceptions and responses. If, however, we are to approach a more complete understanding of the effects of various types of processing, then we must try to assume the perspective of individuals who are affected. Erving Goffman's work "The Moral Career of the Mental Patient" represents what many consider to be a classic attempt to do so.

Goffman is concerned with analyzing the *moral career* of the mental patient, particularly in terms of how patients perceive and respond to their treatment. Of major concern, then, is the impact of the ward experience upon *self*. He points out initially, as indicated especially in the work of Scheff and Culver, that very few patients come willingly to the hospital. Rather, many arrive as a result of family or police action. (In this sense, then, the article further substantiates the discussion of the way in which behavior in private domains may become regulated by some institution.) Goffman argues that the prepatient career can be analyzed in terms of an "extrusory model." In essence, this means that the patient initially has certain relationships and rights; however, he or she is left with very few after admission. Throughout Goffman's insightful analysis, one can obtain an excellent understanding of how the actor's public identity becomes transformed into a "deviant" identity—in this case, that of a mental patient. Important to this process are such phenomena as the "alienative coalition" and the "betrayal funnel." Goffman argues further that "the last step in the prepatient career can involve his realization—justified or not—that he has been deserted by society and turned out of relationships by those closest to him." At this stage the patient may begin to orient himself to the "ward system." Some patients may, for example, accept the "sick role" and develop a set of rationalizations to "explain" their hospitalization. Such strategies enable the patient to regain and sustain a certain semblance of self—a self that has been subjected to a frontal assault from the institution, its personnel, family members and relatives, and, frequently, other patients. With his or her acceptance of this label, the individual begins to take on the identity of the secondary, or career, deviant.

Bradley J. Fisher, in "Illness Career Descent in Institutions for the Elderly," continues this theme. He is specifically concerned with examining how shifts in one's career can affect one's sense of self. He elects to focus on the elderly, and particularly on those social psychological consequences that may result from placement in specific illness career slots within retirement facilities. Fisher offers data obtained from initial interviews with 65 subjects over a two-year period. He also presents information gathered from a subsample of 35 residents, many of whom he interviewed once or twice a month over a one-year period. Fisher begins by describing the impact of the regimented nature of the retirement facility on the residents, and he notes that the "complainers" can suffer some serious consequences. Fisher offers some interesting observations on what happens to those who, because of illness, experience a downward shift in their position (e.g., from maintaining one's own "apartment" to placement in the intermediate care facility). As an illustration, most independent residents avoid contact with the less able, the reason being that contact might bring about their own downward slide or demise. This lack of contact, Fisher notes, helps to maintain and perpetuate a range of stereotypes. Interesting, too, is the way in which residents begin scrutinizing the behavior of those who have been "relocated." Comments may be made to the effect that "he's not as sharp," or "he seems more confused." Fisher continues by describing other ways in which a resident's self-image may become tarnished or damaged. He also outlines how, over time, a relocated resident's self-image can be enhanced (e.g., by developing new roles and associated obligations). Many of Fisher's observations on the identity transformation process have direct relevance to the prospects for change; these will be discussed in further detail in Part 6.

23 / The Societal Reaction to Deviance: Ascriptive Elements in the Psychiatric Screening of Mental Patients in a Midwestern State

THOMAS J. SCHEFF
DANIEL M. CULVER

The case for making the societal reaction to deviance a major independent variable in studies of deviant behavior has been succinctly stated by Kitsuse:

> A sociological theory of deviance must focus specifically upon the interactions which not only define behaviors as deviant but also organize and activate the application of sanctions by individuals, groups, or agencies. For in modern society, the socially significant differentiation of deviants from the non-deviant population is increasingly contingent upon circumstances of situation, place, social and personal biography, and the bureaucratically organized activities of agencies of control.[1]

In the case of mental disorder, psychiatric diagnosis is one of the crucial steps which "organizes and activates" the societal reaction, since the state is legally empowered to segregate and isolate those persons whom psychiatrists find to be committable because of mental illness.

Recently, however, it has been argued that mental illness may be more usefully considered to be a social status than a disease, since the symptoms of mental illness are vaguely defined and widely distributed, and the definition of behavior as symptomatic of mental illness is usually dependent upon social rather than medical contingencies.[2] Furthermore, the argument continues, the status of the mental patient is more often an ascribed status, with conditions for status entry external to the patient, than an achieved status with conditions for status entry dependent upon the patient's own behavior. According to this argument, the societal reaction is a fundamentally important variable in all stages of a deviant career.

The actual usefulness of a theory of mental disorder based on the societal reaction is largely an empirical question: to what extent is entry to the status of mental patient independent of the behavior or "condition" of the patient? The present paper will explore this question for one phase of the societal reaction: the legal screening of persons alleged to be mentally ill. This screening represents the official phase of the societal reaction, which occurs after the alleged deviance has been called to the attention of the community by a complainant. This report will make no reference to the initial deviance or other situation which resulted in the complaint, but will deal entirely with procedures used by the courts after the complaint has occurred.

The purpose of the description that follows is to determine the extent of uncertainty that exists concerning new patients' qualifications for involuntary confinement in a mental hospital, and the reactions of the courts to this type of uncertainty. The data presented here indicate that, in the face of uncertainty, there is a strong presumption of illness by the court and the court psychiatrists.[3] In the discussion that follows the presentation of findings, some of the causes, consequences and implications of the presumption of illness are suggested.

The data upon which this report is based were drawn from psychiatrists' ratings of a sample of patients newly admitted to the public mental hospitals in a Midwestern state, official court records, interviews with court officials and psychiatrists, and our observations of psychiatric examinations in four courts. The psychiatrists' ratings of new patients will be considered first.

In order to obtain a rough measure of the incoming patient's qualifications for involuntary confinement, a survey of newly admitted patients was conducted with the cooperation of the hospital psychiatrists. All psychiatrists who made admission examinations in the three large mental hospitals in the state filled out a questionnaire for the first ten consecutive patients they examined in the month of June, 1962. A total of 223 questionnaires were returned by the 25 admission psychiatrists. Although these returns do not constitute a probability sample of all new patients admitted during the year, there were no obvious biases in the drawing of the sample. For this reason, this group of patients will be taken to be typical of the newly admitted patients in Midwestern State.

The two principal legal grounds for involuntary confinement in the United States are the police power of the state (the state's right to protect itself from dangerous persons) and *parens patriae* (the state's right to assist those persons who, because of their own incapacity, may not be able to assist themselves).[4] As a measure of the first ground, the potential dangerousness of the patient, the questionnaire contained this item: "In your opinion, if this patient were released at the present time, is it likely he would harm himself or others?" The psychiatrists were given six options, ranging from Very Likely to Very Unlikely. Their responses were: Very Likely, 5%; Likely, 4%; Somewhat Likely, 14%; Somewhat Unlikely, 20%; Unlikely, 37%; Very Unlikely, 18%. (Three patients were not rated, 1%.)

As a measure of the second ground, *parens patriae*, the questionnaire contained the item:

Based on your observation of the patient's behavior, his degree of mental impairment is:
None ______ Minimal ______ Mild ______ Moderate ______ Severe ______

The psychiatrists' responses were: None, 2%; Minimal, 12%; Mild, 25%; Moderate, 42%; Severe, 17%. (Three patients were not rated, 1%.) To be clearly qualified for involuntary confinement, a patient should be rated as likely to harm self or others (Very Likely, Likely, or Somewhat Likely) and/or as Severely Mentally Impaired. However, voluntary patients should be excluded from this analysis, since the court is not required to assess their qualifications for confinement. Excluding the 59 voluntary admissions (26% of the sample), leaves a sample of 164 involuntary confined patients. Of these patients, 10 were rated as meeting both qualifications for involuntary confinement, 21 were rated as being severely mentally impaired, but not dangerous, 28 were rated as dangerous but not severely mentally impaired, and 102 were rated as not dangerous nor as severely mentally impaired. (Three patients were not rated.)

According to these ratings, there is considerable uncertainty connected with the screening of newly admitted involuntary patients in the state, since a substantial majority (63%) of the patients did not clearly meet the statutory requirements for involuntary confinement. How does the agency responsible for assessing the qualifications of confinement, the court, react in the large numbers of cases involving uncertainty?

On the one hand, the legal rulings on this point by higher courts are quite clear. They have repeatedly held that there should be a presumption of sanity. The burden of proof of insanity is to be on the petitioners, there must be a preponderance of evidence, and the evidence should be of a "clear and unexceptionable" nature.[5]

On the other hand, existing studies suggest that there is a presumption of illness by mental health officials. In a discussion of the "discrediting" of patients by the hospital staff, based on observations at St. Elizabeth's Hospital, Washington, D.C., Goffman states:

> [The patient's case record] is apparently not regularly used to record occasions when the patient showed capacity to cope honorably and effectively with difficult life situations. Nor is the case record typically used to provide a rough average or sampling of his past conduct. [Rather, it extracts] from his whole life course a list of those incidents that have or might have had "symptomatic" significance.... I think that most of the information gathered in case records is quite true, although it might seem also to be true that almost anyone's life course could yield up enough denigrating facts to provide grounds for the record's justification of commitments.[6]

Mechanic makes a similar statement in his discussion of two large mental hospitals located in an urban area in California:

> In the crowded state or county hospitals, which is the most typical situation, the psychiatrist does not have sufficient time to make a very complete psychiatric

> diagnosis, nor do his psychiatric tools provide him with the equipment for an expeditious screening of the patient....
>
> In the two mental hospitals studied over a period of three months, the investigator never observed a case where the psychiatrist advised the patient that he did not need treatment. Rather, all persons who appeared at the hospital were absorbed into the patient population regardless of their ability to function adequately outside the hospital.[7]

A comment by Brown suggests that it is a fairly general understanding among mental health workers that state mental hospitals in the U.S. accept all comers.[8]

Kutner, describing commitment procedures in Chicago in 1962, also reports a strong presumption of illness by the staff of the Cook County Mental Health Clinic:

> Certificates are signed as a matter of course by staff physicians after little or no examination....The so-called examinations are made on an assembly-line basis, often being completed in two or three minutes, and never taking more than ten minutes. Although psychiatrists agree that it is practically impossible to determine a person's sanity on the basis of such a short and hurried interview, the doctors recommend confinement in 77% of the cases. It appears in practice that the alleged-mentally-ill is presumed to be insane and bears the burden of proving his sanity in the few minutes allotted to him....[9]

These citations suggest that mental health officials handle uncertainty by presuming illness. To ascertain if the presumption of illness occurred in Midwestern State, intensive observations of screening procedures were conducted in the four courts with the largest volume of mental cases in the state. These courts were located in the two most populous cities in the state. Before giving the results of these observations, it is necessary to describe the steps in the legal procedures for hospitalization and commitment.

STEPS IN THE SCREENING OF PERSONS ALLEGED TO BE MENTALLY ILL

The process of screening can be visualized as containing five steps in Midwestern State:

1. The application for judicial inquiry, made by three citizens. This application is heard by deputy clerks in two of the courts (C and D), by a court reporter in the third court, and by a court commissioner in the fourth court.
2. The intake examination, conducted by a hospital psychiatrist.
3. The psychiatric examination, conducted by two psychiatrists appointed by the court.

4. The interview of the patient by the guardian *ad litem*, a lawyer appointed in three of the courts to represent the patient. (Court A did not use guardians *ad litem.*)
5. The judicial hearing, conducted by a judge.

These five steps take place roughly in the order listed, although in many cases (those cases designated as emergencies) step No. 2, the intake examination, may occur before step No. 1. Steps No. 1 and No. 2 usually take place on the same day or the day after hospitalization. Steps No. 3, No. 4, and No. 5 usually take place within a week of hospitalization. (In courts C and D, however, the judicial hearing is held only once a month.)

This series of steps would seem to provide ample opportunity for the presumption of health, and a thorough assessment, therefore, of the patient's qualifications for involuntary confinement, since there are five separate points at which discharge could occur. According to our findings, however, these procedures usually do not serve the function of screening out persons who do not meet statutory requirements. At most of these decision points, in most of the courts, retention of the patient in the hospital was virtually automatic. A notable exception to this pattern was found in one of the three state hospitals; this hospital attempted to use step No. 2, the intake examination, as a screening point to discharge patients that the superintendent described as "illegitimate," i.e., patients who do not qualify for involuntary confinement.[10] In the other two hospitals, however, this examination was perfunctory and virtually never resulted in a finding of health and a recommendation of discharge. In a similar manner, the other steps were largely ceremonial in character. For example, in court B, we observed twenty-two judicial hearings, all of which were conducted perfunctorily and with lightning rapidity. (The mean time of these hearings was 1.6 minutes.) The judge asked each patient two or three routine questions. Whatever the patient answered, however, the judge always ended the hearings and retained the patient in the hospital.

What appeared to be the key role in justifying these procedures was played by step No. 3, the examination by the court-appointed psychiatrists. In our informal discussions of screening with the judges and other court officials, these officials made it clear that although the statutes give the court the responsibility for the decision to confine or release persons alleged to be mentally ill, they would rarely if ever take the responsibility for releasing a mental patient without a medical recommendation to that effect. The question which is crucial, therefore, for the entire screening process is whether or not the court-appointed psychiatric examiners presume illness. The remainder of the paper will consider this question.

Our observations of 116 judicial hearings raised the question of the adequacy of the psychiatric examination. Eighty-six of the hearings failed to establish that the patients were "mentally ill" (according to the criteria stated by the judges in interviews).[11] Indeed, the behavior and responses of

48 of the patients at the hearings seemed completely unexceptionable. Yet the psychiatric examiners had not recommended the release of a single one of these patients. Examining the court records of 80 additional cases, there was still not a single recommendation for release.

Although the recommendation for treatment of 196 out of 196 consecutive cases strongly suggests that the psychiatric examiners were presuming illness, particularly when we observed 48 of these patients to be responding appropriately, it is conceivable that this is not the case. The observer for this study was not a psychiatrist (he was a first year graduate student in social work) and it is possible that he could have missed evidence of disorder which a psychiatrist might have seen. It was therefore arranged for the observer to be present at a series of psychiatric examinations, in order to determine whether the examinations appeared to be merely formalities or whether, on the other hand, through careful examination and interrogation, the psychiatrists were able to establish illness even in patients whose appearance and responses were not obviously disordered. The observer was instructed to note the examiners' procedures, the criteria they appeared to use in arriving at their decision, and their reaction to uncertainty.

Each of the courts discussed here employs the services of a panel of physicians as medical examiners. The physicians are paid a flat fee of ten dollars per examination, and are usually assigned from three to five patients for each trip to the hospital. In court A, most of the examinations are performed by two psychiatrists, who went to the hospital once a week, seeing from five to ten patients a trip. In court B, C and D, a panel of local physicians was used. These courts seek to arrange the examinations so that one of the examiners is a psychiatrist, the other a general practitioner. Court B has a list of four such pairs, and appoints each pair for a month at a time. Courts C and D have a similar list, apparently with some of the same names as court B.

To obtain physicians who were representative of the panel used in these courts, we arranged to observe the examinations of the two psychiatrists employed by court A, and one of the four pairs of physicians used in court B, one a psychiatrist, the other a general practitioner. We observed 13 examinations in court A and 13 examinations in court B. The judges in courts C and D refused to give us the names of the physicians on their panels, and we were unable to observe examinations in these courts. (The judge in court D stated that he did not want these physicians harassed in their work, since it was difficult to obtain their services even under the best of circumstances.) In addition to observing the examinations by four psychiatrists, three other psychiatrists used by these courts were interviewed.

The medical examiners followed two lines of questioning. One line was to inquire about the circumstances which led to the patient's hospitalization, the other was to ask standard questions to test the patient's orientation and his capacity for abstract thinking by asking him the date, the President, Governor, proverbs, and problems requiring arithmetic calculation. These questions were often asked very rapidly, and the patient was usually allowed only a very brief time to answer.

It should be noted that the psychiatrists in these courts had access to the patient's record (which usually contained the Application for Judicial Inquiry and the hospital chart notes on the patient's behavior), and that several of the psychiatrists stated that they almost always familiarized themselves with this record before making the examination. To the extent that they were familiar with the patient's circumstances from such outside information, it is possible that the psychiatrists were basing their diagnoses of illness less on the rapid and peremptory examination than on this other information. Although this was true to some extent, the importance of the record can easily be exaggerated, both because of the deficiencies in the typical record, and because of the way it is usually utilized by the examiners.

The deficiencies of the typical record were easily discerned in the approximately one hundred applications and hospital charts which the author read. Both the applications and charts were extremely brief and sometimes garbled. Moreover, in some of the cases where the author and interviewer were familiar with the circumstances involved in the hospitalization, it was not clear that the complainant's testimony was any more accurate than the version presented by the patient. Often the original complaint was so paraphrased and condensed that the application seemed to have little meaning.

The attitude of the examiners toward the record was such that even in those cases where the record was ample, it often did not figure prominently in their decision. Disparaging remarks about the quality and usefulness of the record were made by several of the psychiatrists. One of the examiners was apologetic about his use of the record, giving us the impression that he thought that a good psychiatrist would not need to resort to any information outside his own personal examination of the patient. A casual attitude toward the record was openly displayed in 6 of the 26 examinations we observed. In these 6 examinations, the psychiatrist could not (or in 3 cases, did not bother to) locate the record and conducted the examination without it, with one psychiatrist making it a point of pride that he could easily diagnose most cases "blind."

In his observations of the examinations, the interviewer was instructed to rate how well the patient responded by noting his behavior during the interview, whether he answered the orientation and concept questions correctly, and whether he denied and explained the allegations which resulted in his hospitalization. If the patient's behavior during the interview obviously departed from conventional social standards (e.g., in one case the patient refused to speak), if he answered the orientation questions incorrectly, or if he did not deny and explain the petitioners' allegations, the case was rated as meeting the statutory requirements for hospitalization. Of the 26 examinations observed, eight were rated as Criteria Met.

If, on the other hand, the patient's behavior was appropriate, his answers correct, and he denied and explained the petitioners' allegations, the interviewer rated the case as not meeting the statutory criteria. Of the 26 cases, seven were rated as Criteria Not Met. Finally, if the examination was inconclusive, but the interviewer felt that more extensive investigation might have established that the criteria were met, he rated the cases as Criteria Possibly Met. Of the 26 examined, 11 were rated in this way. The interviewer's instructions were that whenever he was in doubt he should avoid using the rating Criteria Not Met.

Even giving the examiners the benefit of the doubt, the interviewer's ratings were that in a substantial majority of the cases he observed, the examination failed to establish that the statutory criteria were met. The relationship between the examiners' recommendations and the interviewer's ratings are shown in the following table. The interviewer's ratings suggest that the examinations established that the statutory criteria were met in only eight cases, but the examiners recommended that the patient be retained in the hospital in 24 cases, leaving 16 cases which the interviewer rated as uncertain, and in which retention was recommended by the examiners. The observer also rated the patient's expressed desires regarding staying in the hospital, and the time taken by the examination. The ratings of the patient's desire concerning staying or leaving the hospital were: Leave, 14 cases; Indifferent, 1 case; Stay, 9 cases; and Not Ascertained, 2 cases. In only one of the 14 cases in which the patient wished to leave was the interviewer's rating Criteria Met. [Table 1 shows the ratings and recommendations.]

The interviews ranged in length from five minutes to 17 minutes, with the mean time being 10.2 minutes. Most of the interviews were hurried, with the questions of the examiners coming so rapidly that the examiner often interrupted the patient, or one examiner interrupted the other. All of the examiners seemed quite hurried. One psychiatrist, after stating in an interview (before we observed his examinations) that he usually took about thirty minutes, stated:

> It's not remunerative. I'm taking a hell of a cut. I can't spend 45 minutes with a patient. I don't have the time, it doesn't pay.

Table 1 / Observer's Ratings and Examiners' Recommendations

Observer's Ratings		CRITERIA MET	CRITERIA POSSIBLY MET	CRITERIA NOT MET	TOTAL
Examiners' Recommendations	Commitment	7	9	2	18
	30-Day Observation	1	2	3	6
	Release	0	0	2	2
	Total	8	11	7	26

In the examinations that we observed, this physician actually spent 8, 10, 5, 8, 8, 7, 17, and 11 minutes with the patients, or an average of 9.2 minutes.

In these short time periods, it is virtually impossible for the examiner to extend his investigation beyond the standard orientation questions, and a short discussion of the circumstances which brought the patient to the hospital. In those cases where the patient answered the orientation questions correctly, behaved appropriately, and explained his presence at the hospital satisfactorily, the examiners did not attempt to assess the reliability of the petitioner's complaints, or to probe further into the patient's answers. Given the fact that in most of these instances the examiners were faced with borderline cases, that they took little time in the examinations, and that they usually recommended commitment, we can only conclude that their decisions were based largely on a presumption of illness. Supplementary observations reported by the interviewer support this conclusion.

After each examination, the observer asked the examiner to explain the criteria he used in arriving at his decision. The observer also had access to the examiner's official report, so that he could compare what the examiner said about the case with the record of what actually occurred during the interview. This supplementary information supports the conclusion that the examiner's decisions are based on the presumption of illness, and sheds light on the manner in which these decisions are reached:

1. The "evidence" upon which the examiners based their decision to retain often seemed arbitrary.
2. In some cases, the decision to retain was made even when no evidence could be found.
3. Some of the psychiatrists' remarks suggest prejudgment of the cases.
4. Many of the examinations were characterized by carelessness and haste.

The first question, concerning the arbitrariness of the psychiatric evidence, will now be considered.

In the weighing of the patient's responses during the interview, the physician appeared not to give the patient credit for the large number of correct answers he gave. In the typical interview, the examiner might ask the patient fifteen or twenty questions: the date, time, place, who is President, Governor, etc., what is 11 × 10, 11 × 11, etc., explain "Don't put all your eggs in one basket," "A rolling stone gathers no moss," etc. The examiners appeared to feel that a wrong answer established lack of orientation, even when it was preceded by a series of correct answers. In other words, the examiners do not establish any standard score on the orientation questions, which would give an objective picture of the degree to which the patient answered the questions correctly, but seem at times to search until they find an incorrect answer.

For those questions which were answered incorrectly, it was not always clear whether the incorrect answers were due to the patient's "mental illness," or to the time pressure in the interview, the patient's lack of education, or other causes. Some of the questions used to establish orientation were sufficiently difficult that persons not mentally ill might have difficulty with them. Thus one of the examiners always asked, in a rapid-fire manner: "What year is it? What year was it seven years ago? Seventeen years before that?" etc. Only two of the five patients who were asked this series of questions were able to answer it correctly. However, it is a moot question whether a higher percentage of persons in a household survey would be able to do any better. To my knowledge, none of the orientation questions that are used have been checked in a normal population.

Finally, the interpretations of some of the evidence as showing mental illness seemed capricious. Thus one of the patients, when asked, "In what way are a banana, an orange, and an apple alike?" answered, "They are all something to eat." This answer was used by the examiner in explaining his recommendation to commit. The observer had noted that the patient's behavior and responses seemed appropriate and asked why the recommendation to commit had been made. The doctor stated that her behavior had been bizarre (possibly referring to her alleged promiscuity), her affect inappropriate ("When she talked about being pregnant, it was without feeling"), and with regard to the question above:

> She wasn't able to say a banana and an orange were fruit. She couldn't take it one step further, she had to say it was something to eat.

In other words, this psychiatrist was suggesting that the patient manifested concreteness in her thinking, which is held to be a symptom of mental illness. Yet in her other answers to classification questions, and to proverb interpretations, concreteness was not apparent, suggesting that the examiner's application of this test was arbitrary. In another case, the physician stated that he thought the patient was suspicious and distrustful, because he had asked about the possibility of being represented by counsel at the judicial hearing. The observer felt that these and other similar interpretations might possibly be correct, but that further investigation of the supposedly incorrect responses would be needed to establish that they were manifestations of disorientation.

In several cases where even this type of evidence was not available, the examiners still recommended retention in the hospital. Thus, one examiner, employed by court A stated that he had recommended 30-day observation for a patient whom he had thought *not* to be mentally ill, on the grounds that the patient, a young man, could not get along with his parents, and "might get into trouble." This examiner went on to say:

> We always take the conservative side. [Commitment or observation] Suppose a patient should commit suicide. We always make the conservative decision. I had rather play it safe. There's no harm in doing it that way.

It appeared to the observer that "playing safe" meant that even in those cases where the examination established nothing, the psychiatrists did not consider recommending release. Thus in one case the examination had established that the patient had a very good memory, was oriented and spoke quietly and seriously. The observer recorded his discussion with the physician after the examination as follows:

> When the doctor told me he was recommending commitment for this patient too (he had also recommended commitment in the two examinations held earlier that day) he laughed because he could see what my next question was going to be. He said, "I already recommended the release of two patients this month." This sounded like it was the maximum amount the way he said it.

Apparently this examiner felt that he had a very limited quota on the number of patients he could recommend for release (less than two percent of those examined).

The language used by these physicians tends to intimate that mental illness was found, even when reporting the opposite. Thus in one case the recommendation stated: "No gross evidence of delusions or hallucinations." This statement is misleading, since not only was there no gross evidence, there was not any evidence, not even the slightest suggestion of delusions or hallucinations, brought out by the interview.

These remarks suggest that the examiners prejudge the cases they examine. Several further comments indicate prejudgment. One physician stated that he thought that most crimes of violence were committed by patients released too early from mental hospitals. (This is an erroneous belief.)[12] He went on to say that he thought that all mental patients should be kept in the hospital at least three months, indicating prejudgment concerning his examinations. Another physician, after a very short interview (8 minutes), told the observer:

> On the schizophrenics, I don't bother asking them more questions when I can see they're schizophrenic because *I know what they are going to say.* You could talk to them another half hour and not learn any more.

Another physician, finally, contrasted cases in which the patient's family or others initiated hospitalization ("petition cases," the great majority of cases) with those cases initiated by the court:

> The petition cases are pretty *automatic.* If the patient's own family wants to get rid of him you know there is something wrong.

The lack of care which characterized the examinations is evident in the forms on which the examiners make their recommendations. On most of these forms, whole sections have been left unanswered. Others are answered in a peremptory and uninformative way. For example, in the section entitled Physical Examination, the question is asked: "Have you made a physical examination of the patient? State fully what is the present physical condition," a typical answer is "Yes. Fair," or, "Is apparently in good health." Since in none of the examinations we observed was the patient actually physically examined, these answers appear to be mere guesses. One of the examiners used regularly in court B, to the question "On what subject or in what way is derangement now manifested?" always wrote in "Is mentally ill." The omissions, and the almost flippant brevity of these forms, together with the arbitrariness, lack of evidence, and prejudicial character of the examinations, discussed above, all support the observer's conclusion that, except in very unusual cases, the psychiatric examiner's recommendation to retain the patient is virtually automatic.

Lest it be thought that these results are unique to a particularly backward Midwestern State, it should be pointed out that this state is noted for its progressive psychiatric practices. It will be recalled that a number of the psychiatrists employed by the court as examiners had finished their psychiatric residencies, which is not always the case in many other states. A still common practice in other states is to employ, as members of the "Lunacy Panel," partially retired physicians with no psychiatric training whatever. This was the case in Stockton, California, in 1959, where the author observed hundreds of hearings at which these physicians were present. It may be indicative of some of the larger issues underlying the questions of civil commitment that, in these hearings, the physicians played very little part; the judge controlled the questioning of the relatives and patients, and the hearings were often a model of impartial and thorough investigation.

DISCUSSION

Ratings of the qualifications for involuntary confinement of patients newly admitted to the public mental hospitals in a Midwestern state, together with observations of judicial hearings and psychiatric examinations by the observer connected with the present study, both suggest that the decision as to the mental condition of a majority of the patients is an uncertain one. The fact that the courts seldom release patients, and the perfunctory manner in which the legal and medical procedures are carried out, suggest that the judicial decision to retain patients in the hospital for treatment is routine and largely based on the presumption of illness. Three reasons for this presumption will be discussed: financial, ideological, and political.

Our discussions with the examiners indicated that one reason that they perform biased "examinations" is that their rate of pay is determined by the length of time spent with the patient. In recommending retention, the examiners are refraining from interrupting the hospitalization and commitment procedures already in progress, and thereby allowing someone else, usually the hospital, to make the effective decision to release or commit. In order to recommend release, however, they would have to build a case showing why these procedures should be interrupted. Building such a case would take much more time than is presently expended by the examiners, thereby reducing their rate of pay.

A more fundamental reason for the presumption of illness by the examiners, and perhaps the reason why this practice is allowed by the courts, is the interpretation of current psychiatric doctrine by the examiners and court officials. These officials make a number of assumptions, which are now thought to be of doubtful validity:

1. The condition of mentally ill persons deteriorates rapidly without psychiatric assistance.
2. Effective psychiatric treatments exist for most mental illnesses.
3. Unlike surgery, there are no risks involved in involuntary psychiatric treatment: it either helps or is neutral, it can't hurt.
4. Exposing a prospective mental patient to questioning, cross-examination, and other screening procedures exposes him to the unnecessary stigma of trial-like procedures, and may do further damage to his mental condition.
5. There is an element of danger to self or others in most mental illness. It is better to risk unnecessary hospitalization than the harm the patient might do himself or others.

Many psychiatrists and others now argue that none of these assumptions are necessarily correct.

1. The assumption that psychiatric disorders usually get worse without treatment rests on very little other than evidence of an anecdotal character. There is just as much evidence that most acute psychological and emotional upsets are self-terminating.[13]
2. It is still not clear, according to systematic studies evaluating psychotherapy, drugs, etc., that most psychiatric interventions are any more effective, on the average, than no treatment at all.[14]
3. There is very good evidence that involuntary hospitalization and social isolation may affect the patient's life: his job, his family affairs, etc. There is some evidence that too hasty exposure to psychiatric treatment may convince the patient that he is "sick," prolonging what might have been an otherwise transitory episode.[15]
4. This assumption is correct, as far as it goes. But it is misleading because it fails to consider what occurs when the patient who does not wish to be hospitalized is forcibly treated. Such patients often become extremely indignant and angry, particularly in the case, as often happens, when they are deceived into coming to the hospital on some pretext.

5. The element of danger is usually exaggerated both in amount and degree. In the psychiatric survey of new patients in state mental hospitals, danger to self or others was mentioned in about a fourth of the cases. Furthermore, in those cases where danger is mentioned, it is not always clear that the risks involved are greater than those encountered in ordinary social life. This issue has been discussed by Ross, an attorney:

> A truck driver with a mild neurosis who is "accident prone" is probably a greater danger to society than most psychotics; yet, he will not be committed for treatment, even if he would be benefited. The community expects a certain amount of dangerous activity. I suspect that as a class, drinking drivers are a greater danger than the mentally ill, and yet the drivers are tolerated or punished with small fines rather than indeterminate imprisonment.[16]

From our observations of the medical examinations and other commitment procedures, we formed a very strong impression that the doctrines of danger to self or others, early treatment, and the avoidance of stigma were invoked partly because the officials believed them to be true, and partly because they provided convenient justification for a pre-existing policy of summary action, minimal investigation, avoidance of responsibility and, after the patient is in the hospital, indecisiveness and delay.

The policy of presuming illness is probably both cause and effect of political pressure on the court from the community. The judge, an elected official, runs the risk of being more heavily penalized for erroneously releasing than for erroneously retaining patients. Since the judge personally appointed the panel of psychiatrists to serve as examiners, he can easily transmit the community pressure to them, by failing to reappoint a psychiatrist whose examinations were inconveniently thorough.

Some of the implications of these findings for the sociology of deviant behavior will be briefly summarized. The discussion above, of the reasons that the psychiatrists tend to presume illness, suggests that the motivations of the key decision-makers in the screening process may be significant in determining the extent and direction of the societal reaction. In the case of psychiatric screening of persons alleged to be mentally ill, the social differentiation of the deviant from the non-deviant population appears to be materially affected by the financial, ideological, and political position of the psychiatrists, who are in this instance the key agents of social control.

Under these circumstances, the character of the societal reaction appears to undergo a marked change from the pattern of denial which occurs in the community. The official societal reaction appears to reverse the presumption of normality reported by the Cummings as a characteristic of informal societal reaction, and instead exaggerates both the amount and degree of deviance.[17] Thus, one extremely important contingency influencing the severity of the societal reaction may be whether or not the original deviance comes to official notice. This paper suggests that in the area of mental disorder, perhaps in contrast to other areas of deviant behavior, if the official societal reaction is invoked, for whatever reason, social differentiation of the deviant from the non-deviant population will usually occur.

CONCLUSION

This paper has described the screening of patients who were admitted to public mental hospitals in early June, 1962, in a Midwestern state. The data presented here suggest that the screening is usually perfunctory, and that in the crucial screening examination by the court-appointed psychiatrists, there is a presumption of illness. Since most court decisions appear to hinge on the recommendation of these psychiatrists, there appears to be a large element of status ascription in the official societal reaction to persons alleged to be mentally ill, as exemplified by the court's actions. This finding points to the importance of lay definitions of mental illness in the community, since the "diagnosis" of mental illness by laymen in the community initiates the official societal reaction, and to the necessity of analyzing social processes connected with the recognition and reaction to the deviant behavior that is called mental illness in our society.

Notes

1. John K. Kitsuse, "Societal Reaction to Deviant Behavior: Problems of Theory and Method," *Social Problems*, 9 (Winter, 1962), pp. 247–257.
2. Edwin M. Lemert, *Social Pathology*, New York: McGraw-Hill, 1951; Erving Goffman, *Asylums*, Chicago: Aldine, 1962.
3. For a more general discussion of the presumption of illness in medicine, and some of its possible causes and consequences, see the author's "Decision Rules, Types of Error and Their Consequences in Medical Diagnosis," *Behavioral Science*, 8 (April, 1963), pp. 97–107.
4. Hugh Allen Ross, "Commitment of the Mentally Ill: Problems of Law and Policy," *Michigan Law Review*, 57 (May, 1959), pp. 945–1018.
5. This is the typical phrasing in cases in the *Dicennial Legal Digest*, found under the heading "Mental Illness."
6. Goffman, *op. cit.*, pp. 155, 159.
7. David Mechanic, "Some Factors in Identifying and Defining Mental Illness," *Mental Hygiene*, 46 (January, 1962), pp. 66–75.
8. Esther Lucile Brown, *Newer Dimensions of Patient Care*, Part I, New York: Russell Sage, 1961, p. 60, fn.
9. Luis Kutner, "The Illusion of Due Process in Commitment Proceedings," *Northwestern University Law Review*, 57 (Sept. 1962), pp. 383–399.
10. Other exceptions occurred as follows: the deputy clerks in courts C and D appeared to exercise some discretion in turning away applications they considered improper or incomplete, at step No. 1; the judge in Court D appeared also to perform some screening at step No. 5. For further description of these exceptions see "Rural-Urban Differences in the Judicial Screening of the Mentally Ill in a Midwestern State." (In press)
11. In interviews with the judges, the following criteria were named: Appropriateness of behavior and speech, understanding of the situation, and orientation.
12. The rate of crimes of violence, or any crime, appears to be less among ex-mental patients than in the general population. Henry Brill and Benjamin Maltzberg, "Statistical Report Based on the Arrest Record of 5354 Ex-patients Released from New York State Mental Hospitals During the Period 1946–48." Mimeo available from the authors; Louis H. Cohen and Henry

Freeman, "How Dangerous to the Community Are State Hospital Patients?" *Connecticut State Medical Journal*, 9 (Sept. 1945), pp. 697–700; Donald W. Hastings, "Follow-up Results in Psychiatric Illness," *Amer. Journal of Psychiatry*, 118 (June 1962), pp. 1078–1086.

13. For a review of epidemiological studies of mental disorder see Richard J. Plunkett and John E. Gordon, *Epidemiology and Mental Illness*, New York: Basic Books, 1960. Most of these studies suggest that at any given point in time, psychiatrists find a substantial proportion of persons in normal populations to be "mentally ill." One interpretation of this finding is that much of the deviance detected in these studies is self-limiting.

14. For an assessment of the evidence regarding the effectiveness of electroshock, drugs, psychotherapy, and other psychiatric treatments, see H. J. Eysenck, *Handbook of Abnormal Psychology*, New York: Basic Books, 1961, Part III.

15. For examples from military psychiatry, see Albert J. Glass, "Psychotherapy in the Combat Zone," in *Symposium on Stress*, Washington, D.C., Army Medical Service Graduate School, 1953, and B. L. Bushard, "The U.S. Army's Mental Hygiene Consultation Service," in *Symposium on Preventive and Social Psychiatry*, 15–17 (April 1957), Washington, D.C.: Walter Reed Army Institute of Research, pp. 431–43. For a discussion of essentially the same problem in the context of a civilian mental hospital, cf. Kai T. Erikson, "Patient Role and Social Uncertainty—A Dilemma of the Mentally Ill," *Psychiatry*, 20 (August 1957), pp. 263–275.

16. Ross, *op. cit.*, p. 962.

17. Elaine Cumming and John Cumming, *Closed Ranks*, Cambridge, Mass.: Harvard University Press, 1957, 102; for further discussion of the bipolarization of the societal reaction into denial and labeling, see the author's "The Role of the Mentally Ill and the Dynamics of Mental Disorder: A Research Framework," *Sociometry*, 26 (December, 1963), pp. 436–453.

24 / Normal Rubbish: Deviant Patients in Casualty Departments

ROGER JEFFERY

ENGLISH CASUALTY DEPARTMENTS

Casualty departments have been recognized as one of the most problematic areas of the NHS since about 1958, and several official and semi-official reports were published in the following years, the most recent being a House of Commons Expenditure Committee Report.[1] The greatest public concern is voiced when departments are closed permanently, or over holiday weekends, because of shortages of staff.[2] The major criticisms have been that Casualty departments have to operate in old, crowded, and ill-equipped surroundings, and that their unpopularity with doctors has meant that the doctors employed as Casualty Officers are either overworked or of poor quality. "Poor quality" in this context seems to mean either doctors in their pre-registration year, or doctors from abroad. The normal appointment to the post of Casualty Officer (CO) is for six months, and many doctors work this period only because it is required for those who wish to sit the final examinations for FRCS. Although consultants have in general played very little part in the running of casualty departments (which is one reason for their poor facilities) there has been dispute over whether they should be the responsibility of orthopaedic or general surgeons: some hospitals have appointed physicians as consultants-in-charge.[3] These problems with the doctors have apparently not affected the nursing staff and in general Casualty seems to be able to attract and keep enough nurses.

The reasons for the unpopularity of Casualty work amongst doctors have usually been couched either in terms of the poor working conditions, or in terms of the absence of a career structure within Casualty work. Most Casualty staff are junior doctors; very rarely are appointments made above the level of Senior House Officer, and there are very few full-time consultant appointments. Other reasons which are less frequently put forward, but seem to underlie these objections relate more to the nature of the work, and in particular to the notion that the Casualty department is an interface between hospital and community. Prestige amongst doctors is, at least in part, related to the distance a doctor can get from the undifferentiated mass of patients, so that teaching hospital consultancies are valued because they are at the end of a series of screening mechanisms.[4] Casualty is one of these screening mechanisms, rather like general practitioners in this respect. However, they are unusual in the hospital setting in the freedom of patients to gain entrance without having seen a GP first; another low prestige area similar in this respect is the VD clinic. One of the complaints of the staff is that they are obliged, under a Ministry of Health circular, to see every patient who presents himself; and having been seen, the chances are high that the patient will then be treated. The effect of this openness is that there is a great variety of patients who present themselves, and this has hindered the development of a specialty in Casualty work. There is a Casualty Surgeons' Association, and some appointments include "Traumatic Surgery," but it is obvious that these cover only a small selection of the patients seen in casualty, as has been recognized by the employment of physicians as well. Casualty has been unsuited to the processes of differentiation and specialization which have characterized the recent history of the medical profession, and this helps to explain the low prestige of the work, and the low priority it has received in hospital expenditure.

The material on which this paper is based was gathered at three Casualty departments in an English City. The largest was in the city centre, the other two were suburban; of the seven months of field work, $4\frac{1}{2}$ were in the city centre. These departments would appear to be above average in terms of the criteria discussed above: all were fully staffed; only two of the seventeen doctors employed during the fieldwork period were immigrant; all were senior house officers, and one department had a registrar as well; and the working conditions were reasonable. The data presented came from either fieldwork notes or tape-recorded, open-ended interviews with the doctors.

TYPIFICATIONS OF PATIENTS

As Roth[5] and Strong and Davis[6] have argued, moral evaluation of patients seems to be a regular feature of medical settings, not merely amongst medical students or in mental hospitals. As Gibson[7] and Godse[8] have both pointed out, social and moral evaluations are important for the treatment given to patients defined as "overdoses" and those defined as drunk or drug-dependent, and in the English Casualty departments I studied these categories were of considerable salience to the staff. In general, two broad categories were used to evaluate patients good or interesting, and bad or rubbish. They were sometimes used as if they were an exhaustive dichotomy, but more generally appeared as opposite ends of a continuum.

> (CO to medical students) If there's anything interesting we'll stop, but there's a lot of rubbish this morning.

> We have the usual rubbish, but also a subdural haemorrhage.
>
> On nights you get some drunken dross in, but also some good cases.

In most of this paper I shall be discussing the category of rubbish, but I shall first deal with the valued category, the good patients.

GOOD PATIENTS

Good patients were described almost entirely in terms of their medical characteristics, either in terms of the symptoms or the causes of the injury. Good cases were head injuries, or cardiac arrests, or a stove-in chest; or they were RTA's (Road Traffic Accidents). There were three broad criteria by which patients were seen to be good, and each related to medical considerations.

(i) If they allowed the CO to practice skills necessary for passing professional examinations. In order to pass the FRCS examinations doctors need to be able to diagnose and describe unusual conditions and symptoms. Casualty was not a good place to discover these sorts of cases, and if they did turn up a great fuss was made of them. As one CO said, the way to get excellent treatment was to turn up at a slack period with an unusual condition. The most extreme example of this I witnessed was a young man with a severe head injury from a car accident. A major symptom of his head injury was the condition of his eyes, and by the time he was transferred to another hospital for neurological treatment, twelve medical personnel had looked into his eyes with an ophthalmoscope, and an *ad hoc* teaching session was held on him. The case was a talking point for several days, and the second hospital was phoned several times for a progress report.[9] Similar interest was shown in a man with gout, and in a woman with an abnormally slow heart beat. The general response to cases like this can be summed up in the comments of a CO on a patient with bilateral bruising of the abdomen:

> This is fascinating. It's really great. I've never seen this before.

(ii) If they allowed staff to practice their chosen specialty. For the doctors, the specific characteristics of good patients of this sort were fairly closely defined, because most doctors saw themselves as future specialists—predominantly surgeons. They tended to accept, or conform to, the model of the surgeon as a man of action who can achieve fairly rapid results. Patients who provided the opportunity to use and act out this model were welcomed. One CO gave a particularly graphic description of this:

> But I like doing surgical procedures. These are great fun. It just lets your imagination run riot really (laughs) you know, you forget for a moment you are just a very small cog incising a very small abscess, and you pick up your scalpel like anyone else (laughs). It's quite mad when you think about it but it's very

> satisfying. And you can see the glee with which most people leap on patients with abscesses because you know that here's an opportunity to do something.

Another one put it like this:

> Anything which involves, sort of, a bit of action. . . . I enjoy anything which involves bone-setting, plastering, stitching, draining pus.

For some CO's, Casualty work had some advantages over other jobs because the clientele was basically healthy, and it was possible to carry out procedures which showed quick success in terms of returning people to a healthy state.

In two of the hospitals much of this practical action was carried out by the senior nurses, and the doctors left them the more minor surgical work. These nurses too were very pleased to be able to fulfil, even if in only a minor way, the role of surgeon, and found it very rewarding.

(iii) If they tested the general competence and maturity of the staff. The patients who were most prized were those who stretched the resources of the department in doing the task they saw themselves designed to carry out—the rapid early treatment of acutely ill patients. Many of the CO's saw their Casualty job as the first in which they were expected to make decisions without the safety net of ready advice from more senior staff. The ability to cope, the ability to make the decisions which might have a crucial bearing on whether a patient lived or died, this was something which most staff were worried about in advance. However, they were very pleased with patients who gave them this experience. The most articulate expression of this was from a CO who said:

> I really do enjoy doing anything where I am a little out of my depth, where I really have to think about what I am doing. Something like a bad road traffic accident, where they ring up and give you a few minutes warning and perhaps give you an idea of what's happening. . . . And when the guy finally does arrive you've got a rough idea of what you are going to do, and sorting it all out and getting him into the right specialty, this kind of thing is very satisfying, even though you don't do very much except perhaps put up a drip, but you've managed it well. And I find that very pleasing. It might be a bit sordid, the fact that I like mangled up bodies and things like this, but the job satisfaction is good.

Good patients, then, make demands which fall squarely within the boundaries of what the staff define as appropriate to their job. It is the medical characteristics of these patients which are most predominant in the discussions, and the typifications are not very well developed. Indeed, unpredictability was often stressed as one of the very few virtues of the Casualty job, and this covered not only the variability in pressure—sometimes rushed off their feet, sometimes lounging around—but also the variability between patients, even if they had superficial similarities. This is in marked contrast to "rubbish."

RUBBISH

While the category of the good patient is one I have in part constructed from comments about "patients I like dealing with" or "the sort of work I like to do," "rubbish" is a category generated by the staff themselves. It was commonly used in discussions of the work, as in the following quotes:

> It's a thankless task, seeing all the rubbish, as we call it, coming through.
>
> We get our share of rubbish, in inverted commas, but I think compared with other Casualty departments you might find we get less rubbish.
>
> I wouldn't be making the same fuss in another job—it's only because it's mostly bloody crumble like women with insect bites.
>
> I think the (city centre hospital) gets more of the rubbish—the drunks and that.
>
> He'll be tied up with bloody dross down there.

Rubbish appeared to be a mutually comprehensible term, even though some staff members used other words, like dross, dregs, crumble or grot. There appeared to be some variation in the sorts of cases included under these terms, but I shall argue later that these differences related to the differential application of common criteria, rather than any substantive disagreement.

In an attempt to get a better idea of what patients would be included in the category of rubbish I asked staff what sorts of patients they did not like having to deal with, which sorts of patients made them annoyed, and why. The answers they gave suggested that staff had developed characteristics of "normal" rubbish—the normal suicide attempt, the normal drunk, and so on—which they were thinking of when they talked about rubbish.[10] In other words, staff felt able to predict a whole range of features related not only to his medical condition but also to his past life, to his likely behaviour inside the Casualty department, and to his future behaviour. These expected features of the patient could thus be used to guide the treatment (both socially and medically) that the staff decided to give the patient. Thus patients placed in these categories would tend to follow standard careers, as far as the staff were concerned, in part because of their common characteristics and in part because they were treated as if they had such common characteristics. The following were the major categories of rubbish mentioned by staff.

(i) Trivia. The recurring problem of Casualty departments, in the eyes of the doctors, has been the "casual" attender. In the 19th century the infirmaries welcomed casual attenders as a way of avoiding the control of the subscribers, but since before the inauguration of the NHS there have been frequent complaints about the patients who arrive without a letter from their GP and with a condition which is neither due to trauma nor urgent.[11]

For the staff of the Casualty departments I studied, normal trivia banged their heads, their hands or their ankles, carried on working as usual, and several days later looked into Casualty to see if it was all right. Normal trivia drops in when it is passing, or if it happens to be visiting a relative in the hospital. Trivia "didn't want to bother my doctor." Normal trivia treats Casualty like a perfunctory service,[12] on a par with a garage, rather than as an expert emergency service, which is how the staff like to see themselves.

> They come in and say "I did an injury half an hour ago, or half a day ago, or two days ago. I'm perfectly all right, I've just come for a check-up."

> (Trivia) comes up with a pain that he's had for three weeks, and gets you out of bed at 3 in the morning.

Trivia stretches the boundaries of reasonable behaviour too far, by bringing for advice something which a reasonable person could make up his own mind about. Trivia must find Casualty a nice place to be in, else why would they come? For trivia, Casualty is a bit of a social centre: they think "It's a nice day, I might as well go down to Casualty." By bringing to Casualty conditions which should be taken to the GP, trivial trivialises the service Casualty is offering, and lowers its status to that of the GP.

(ii) Drunks.[13] Normal drunks are abusive and threatening. They come in shouting and singing after a fight and they are sick all over the place, or they are brought in unconscious, having been found in the street. They come in the small hours of the night, and they often have to be kept in until morning because you never know if they have been knocked out in a fight (with the possibility of a head injury) or whether they were just sleeping it off. They come in weekend after weekend with the same injuries, and they are always unpleasant and awkward.

> They keep you up all hours of the night, and you see them the next day, or in out-patients, and they complain bitterly that "the scar doesn't look nice" and they don't realize that under there you've sewn tendons and nerves, that they're bloody lucky to have a hand at all.

> The person who comes along seeking admission to a hospital bed at 2 o'clock in the morning and he's rolling around and is incomprehensible, and one's got other much more serious cases to deal with but they make such a row you've got to go to them.

(iii) Overdoses.[14] The normal overdose is female, and is seen as a case of self-injury rather than of attempted suicide. She comes because her boyfriend/husband/parents have been unkind, and she is likely to be a regular visitor. She only wants attention, she was not seriously trying to kill herself, but she uses the overdose as moral blackmail. She makes sure she does not succeed by taking a less-than-lethal dose, or by ensuring that she is discovered fairly rapidly.

> In the majority of overdoses, you know, these symbolic overdoses, the sort of "5 aspirins and 5 valiums and I'm ill doctor, I've taken an overdose."

> By and large they are people who have done it time and time again, who are up, who have had treatment, who haven't responded to treatment.

> Lots of the attempts are very half-hearted. They don't really mean it, they just want to make a bit of a fuss, so that husband starts loving them again and stops going drinking.

> Most of the people I've met, they've either told someone or they have done it in such a way that someone has found them. I think there's very few that really wanted to, you know.

(iv) Tramps. Normal tramps can be recognized by the many layers of rotten clothing they wear, and by their smell. They are a feature of the cold winter nights and they only come to Casualty to try to wheedle a bed in the warm for the night. Tramps can never be trusted: they will usually sham their symptoms. New CO's and young staff nurses should be warned, for if one is let in one night then dozens will turn up the next night. They are abusive if they don't get their way: they should be shouted at to make sure they understand, or left in the hope that they will go away.

> (Tramps are) nuisance visitors, frequent visitors, who won't go, who refuse to leave when you want them to.

> (Tramps are) just trying to get a bed for the night.

These four types covered most of the patients included in rubbish, or described as unpleasant or annoying. There were some other characterizations mentioned less frequently, or which seemed to be generated by individual patients, or which seemed to be specific to particular members of staff. "Nutcases" were in this uncertain position: there were few "typical" features of psychiatric patients, and these were very diffuse. Nutcases might be drug addicts trying to blackmail the CO into prescribing more of their drug by threatening to attempt suicide if they do not get what they want; but in general they are just 'irrational' and present everyone with insoluble problems. Since Casualty staff tended to be primarily surgical in orientation they had little faith in the ability of the psychiatrists to achieve anything except to remove a problem from the hands of Casualty. "Smelly," "dirty," and "obese" patients were also in this limbo. Patients with these characteristics were objected to, but there was no typical career expected for these patients: apart from the one common characteristic they were expected to be different.

As Sudnow[15] suggests, staff found it easier to create typical descriptions if they had to deal with many cases of that sort. However, it was not necessary for any one member of staff to have dealt with these cases, since the experiences of others would be shared. "Rubbish" was a common topic of general conversations, and in this way staff could find out not only about patients who had come in while they were off duty, but also about notable cases in the past history of the department. The register of patients would also contain clues about the classification of patients this way—staff frequently vented their feelings by sarcastic comments both on the patient's record card and on the register. Again, the receptionists tended to be a repository for information of this kind, partly because they and the senior nurses had worked longest in the departments. In the departments I studied this common fund of knowledge about patients was sufficient to recognize regular visitors and tramps: other departments were reputed to keep "black books" to achieve the same purpose.

The departments thus varied in the categories of patients typified under rubbish. The city centre hospital had all types, but only one of the suburban hospitals had tramps in any number, and neither of them had many drunks. Overdoses and trivia were, it seems, unavoidable. Comments on drunks and tramps in the suburban hospitals tended to stress their infrequency and staff had difficulty in typing them. As one CO at a suburban hospital said about drunks,

> Some are dirty, but so are some ordinary people. Some are clean. Some are aggressive, some are quiet. Some are obnoxious. It's the same with ordinary people.

The features of rubbish which are attended to are not the strictly medical ones—they are left as understood. These non-medical features were not essential parts of any diagnosis, since it is not necessary to know that a man is a drunk or a tramp to see that he has cut his head. Similarly, the medical treatment of an overdose does not depend on the intentions of the patient, nor on the number of previous occasions when an overdose has been taken. The features which were attended to were more concerned with the ascription of responsibility or reasonableness. However, the staff could find out these features of patients in the course of the routine questions asked in order to establish a diagnosis.[16] Thus the questions "when did this happen?" and "how did this happen?" provide information not only relevant to the physical signs and symptoms which can be expected, but also to the possibility that this is trivia. "How many pills did you take?" establishes not only the medical diagnosis but also the typicality of the overdose. Similarly, questions designed to find out whether or not the patient will follow the doctor's orders (to change the dressing, or to return to the outpatients clinic) will affect not only the orders the doctor will give but will also provide evidence about the typicality of the tramp or drunk.

RULES BROKEN BY RUBBISH

In their elaboration of *why* certain sorts of patients were rubbish, staff organized their answers in terms of a number of unwritten rules which they said rubbish had broken. These rules were in part concensual, and in part ideological. Thus some patients negotiated their status with staff in terms of these rules, while other patients rejected these rules and argued for rights even though in the eyes of the staff, they might not deserve them. In so far as they were ideological, these rules can be seen as attempts by medical staff to increase their control over their clientele, so that they could spend more time on "good" patients. The rules which the staff were trying to enforce can be seen as the obverse of professionalisation, in two senses. First, they are the obverse of attempts to specialize and to build up specialized knowledge, which implies that some areas will be excluded. Secondly, they are the obverse of attempts to increase control over the clientele, which implies that those who cannot be controlled should be excluded.[17] These rules, then, can be seen as the criteria by which staff judged the legitimacy of claims made by patients for entry into the sick role, or for medical care. I have organized them on lines similar to the classic discussion by Parsons of the sick role.[18]

These rules can also be seen as specifications of "conventionality" and "theoreticity," to use McHugh's terms,[19] which help to underline the continuity between his work and Parsons's. For McHugh, conventionality is an assessment that a given act "might have been otherwise"—someone has failed to follow a rule in a situation when the normal grounds for failure (accident, coercion, miracle) are absent. Theoreticity refers to the assessment that an actor "knows what he is doing."

These, then, are rules inductively generalised from accounts given by staff.

a) Patients must not be responsible, either for their illness or for getting better: medical staff can only be held responsible if, in addition, they are able to treat the illness.

The first half of this rule was broken by all normal rubbish. Drunks and tramps were responsible for their illnesses, either directly or indirectly. Drunks will continue to fall over or be involved in fights because they are drunk, and they are responsible for their drunkenness. Tramps are responsible for the illnesses like bronchitis which are a direct result of the life the tramp has chosen to lead. Normal overdoses knew what they were doing, and chose to take an overdose for their own purposes. Trivia *chose* to come to Casualty, and could be expected to deal with their illnesses themselves. All normal rubbish had within their own hands the ability to affect a complete cure, and since there was little the Casualty staff could do about it, they could not be held responsible to treat the illnesses of normal rubbish. Comments which reflected this rule included,

> I don't like having to deal with drunks in particular. I find that usually they're quite aggressive. I don't like aggressive people. And I feel that, you know, they've got themselves into this state entirely through their own follies, why the hell should I have to deal with them on the NHS? So I don't like drunks, I think they are a bloody nuisance. I don't like overdoses, because I've got very little sympathy with them on the whole, I'm afraid.

(Q: Why not?)
mm well you see most of them don't mean it, it's just to draw attention to themselves, you see I mean they take a non-lethal dose and they know it's not lethal.

I do feel that tramps could have been helped, and have been helped and have rejected it. So often I feel this is brought on by themselves.

People who create a lot of trouble because of their own folly.

If patients can be held responsible, then the staff feel they have no moral obligation to treat them, though the legal obligation may remain. However, responsibility is not easily assigned. Thus some staff find it very difficult to decide about responsibility in psychiatric cases, and they express ambivalence over whether or not tramps, drunks and overdoses are "really ill" in their underlying state. As one CO said, he did not mind treating

Anyone who is genuinely ill—I'm not talking about the psychiatric types I suppose, they're genuinely ill but the thing is I don't really understand psychiatric illness.

The staff normally felt uncertain about the existence of an illness if there was no therapy that they, or anyone else, could provide to correct the state, and it would seem that this uncertainty fostered frustration which was vented as hostility towards these patients. One example of this was in the comments on overdoses, and the distinctions made between those who really tried to commit suicide (for whom there is some respect) and the rest (viewed as immature calls for attention). This seems to be behind the following comments:

And I mean, certainly with overdoses, and sometimes you feel, if they are that determined, why not let them put themselves out of their misery.

I think it's all so unnecessary, you know, if you are going to do the job, do it properly, don't bother us!

It's the same I'm sure in any sphere, that if you're doing something and you're treating it and—say you're a plumber and the thing keeps going wrong because you haven't got the right thing to put it right, you get fed up with it, and in the end you'd much rather hit the thing over the . . . hit the thing with your hammer. Or in this case, to give up rather than go on, you know, making repeated efforts.

Similar feelings were expressed about drunks:[20]

They're jolly difficult people to deal with, there's no easy answer. Unlike someone who's got something you can put right. With them, the thing that's wrong is much more difficult to put right.

You know that whatever you do for them is only 5% of their problem, and you're not really approaching the other 95% or touching it.

b) Patients should be restricted in their reasonable activities by the illnesses they report with.

This rule has particular point in a Casualty department, and trivia who have been able to delay coming to the department most obviously break this rule. This is implicit in the comments already reported about trivia. However, there is another aspect to this rule, which refers to the discussion of the relationship between deviance and illness, which I shall return to later. This is the requirement that the activities being followed should be reasonable, and the obvious offenders against this rule are the tramps. It applies also to other sorts of patients, who may be attributed one deviant trait ("hippy type") which then places them in the position of being an "illegitimate aspirer to the sick role" as a generalization from one deviant trait to a deviant character. Comments which applied [to] this role included:

> I also like some patient relationships, providing the patient is a co-operative, pleasant, useful human being. I am afraid I get very short, very annoyed, with neurotic patients and with patients who I think are just dropouts from society really—it's a horrible thing to say—not worth helping.

> If a man has led a full productive life, he's entitled to good medical attention, because he's put a lot into society.

> (Tramps) put nothing in, and are always trying to get something out.

Obviously the Protestant Ethic of work is alive and well in Casualty departments.

c) Patients should see illness as an undesirable state.

The patients who most obviously offend against this rule are the overdoses and the tramps. The overdoses are seen to want to be ill in order to put moral pressure on someone, or to get attention. Tramps want to be ill in order to get the benefits of being a patient—a warm bed and warm meals. Trivia are also suspected of being neurotic or malingering, in order to explain why they come, as in the following comments:

> In fact you get entirely indifferent, you think that everyone's neurotic, you just don't care. You just say "you haven't got a fracture mate, you can't sue me, I haven't missed anything." And that's all you think about, getting them out.

d) Patients should co-operate with the competent agencies in trying to get well.

The major non-co-operative patients were the drunks and the overdoses. Drunks fail to be co-operative by refusing to stay still while being sutured or examined, and overdoses fight back when a rubber tube is being forced down their throats so that their stomachs can be washed out. These are both cases where patients *refuse* to co-operate, rather than being unable to co-operate, as would be the case for patients in epileptic or diabetic fits. Similarly, they refuse to co-operate in getting "well" because they cannot be trusted to live their lives in [the] future in such a way that they would avoid the same injuries. The normal overdose, after all, is one who has been in time and time again, as is the normal drunk. Other patients may also offend against this rule, like skinheads who were hurt in a fight and said they were going to get their own back on their enemies:

> We're wasting everybody's time by X-raying that bloke because he's only going to do it again.

However, it was noticeable that if recurrent injuries were a result of what the staff regarded as reasonable activities (such as playing rugby) similar hostility was not provoked. In general, then, patients had a duty to live their lives in order to avoid injury, to remain well, and patients who did not do this were not worth helping.

These four rules, then, seemed to cover the criteria by which normal rubbish was faulted. It can be seen that each of them required quite fine judgement about, for example, whether a patient was unco-operative by choice or because of some underlying illness. Discussions of dirty patients included an attempt to find out if they were ill and could not clean themselves, and an abusive tramp had his behaviour reinterpreted when he later had a fit—his abuse was put down to the effects of the tension preceding the fit. In other cases there was evidence of negotiation between patients and staff over how the patient was to be classified. Patients would provide evidence which did not match the normal pattern for rubbish. Certainly the staff treated differently patients who demonstrated they were abnormal overdoses or tramps. For example, respect was shown to the man who took an overdose, then slashed his wrists when he came into Casualty and finally drowned himself in the bathroom of the Casualty ward. Lesser respect was accorded to others who also made serious attempts to kill themselves. Overdoses who demonstrated that they were unlikely to repeat the behaviour were also treated better, like a thirty-year old social worker who brought himself in and then actively assisted with the washout proceedings. Again, the clean, well-spoken tramp who had diabetes which he kept under control was helped to get somewhere other than the Salvation Army hotel to sleep for the night. Though I did not interview patients about this, there is impressionistic evidence that patients were aware of the rules which staff tried to impose, and attempted to organize their interactions with staff in order to put up a good front in terms of those rules. This was certainly the case with patients who negotiated for abnormal status, and was perhaps true for other patients. Patients with relatively minor ailments would frequently stress the accidental nature of the injury, their reasons for assessing it as serious, the reasonableness for their activities at the time of the accident, and their desire to get back to work.

PUNISHMENT

Rubbish could be punished by the staff in various ways, the most important being to increase the amount of time that rubbish had to spend in Casualty before completing treatment. In each hospital there were ways of advancing and retarding patients so that they were not seen strictly in the order in which they arrived. Good patients, in general being the more serious, could be seen immediately by being taken directly to the treatment area, either by the receptionist or by the ambulanceman. Less serious cases, including the trivia, would go first to a general waiting area. Patients there were normally left until all serious cases had been dealt with. However, during relatively busy periods these arrangements only permitted rather gross division of cases, so that the general area would also include many patients who were not regarded as trivia, and would usually contain some "good" patients as well. In slack periods this technique was more finely used, so that if the nurse or receptionist was sure that the patient was rubbish she could delay calling the doctor.

However, the staff could also delay treatment for overdoses, tramps and drunks in a more selective fashion. Patients in these categories could be taken to relative backwaters and shut into rooms so that they could be ignored until the staff were prepared to deal with them. Sometimes staff employed a deliberate policy of leaving drunks and tramps in the hope that they would get annoyed at the delay and take their own discharge.

The other forms of punishment used were verbal hostility or the vigorous restraint of unco-operative patients. Verbal hostility was in general fairly restrained, at least in my presence, and was usually less forthright than the written comments made in the "medical" notes, or the comments made in discussions with other staff. Vigorous treatment of patients was most noticeable in the case of overdoses, who would be held down or sat upon while the patient was forced to swallow the rubber tube used. Staff recognized that this procedure had an element of punishment in it, but defended themselves by saying that it was necessary. However, they showed no sympathy for the victim, unlike cases of accidental self-poisoning by children. Drunks and tramps who were unco-operative could be threatened with the police, who were called on a couple of occasions to undress a drunk or to stand around while a tramp was treated.

Punishment was rarely extended to a refusal to see or to treat patients, except for a few tramps who came to the department but never got themselves registered, merely sitting in the warm for a while, and for some patients who arrived in the middle of the night and were persuaded by the staff nurse to come back later. The staff were very conscious of the adverse publicity raised whenever patients were refused treatment in Casualty departments, and they were also worried by the medico-legal complications to which Casualty departments are prone, and this restrained their hostility and the extent of the delay they were prepared to put patients to. A cautionary tale was told to emphasize the dangers of not treating rubbish properly, concerning a tramp who was seen in a Casualty department and discharged. A little later the porter came in and told the CO that the tramp had collapsed and died outside on the pavement. The porter then calmed the worries of the CO by saying "It's all right sir, I've turned him round so that it looks as though he was on his way *to* Casualty."

DEVIANCE AND ILLNESS

What I have argued so far is that Casualty staff classify patients broadly into good and rubbish patients. The features of good patients which are attended to are medical in character, whereas rubbish is described in predominantly social terms. In addition, there are typical sorts of rubbish which are picked out for particular comment, the normal trivia, normal overdoses, normal tramps and normal drunks. Staff justify their hostile typifications of those patients by arguing that they have broken most of the rules which should govern who is a legitimate aspirant for entry into patienthood. Other patients who break one or more of these rules also evoke hostile responses in staff, but are not typified in the same way. Patients who break these rules are likely to be penalised, if possible by being kept waiting longer than necessary, but the threat of legal problems ensures that they will get some diagnosis and treatment. On these grounds it seems clear to me that these patients are seen as deviant, in that they are given an unflattering label, are seen to break rules, and are liable to punishment. While I would be happy to leave the matter there, in one respect at least the discussion so far is inadequate. This results from the attempt by several sociologists of medicine to treat illness, and the sick role, as themselves deviant, whereas I have implied that illness is not deviant, only those who make illegitimate claims to be allowed entry to the sick role or to patienthood are deviant. Therefore it is necessary to consider the debate about the relationship between illness and deviance, though I cannot in the space available give full justice to it.

There are two alternative ways of dealing with my material which leave no contradiction between my discussion and that of those who see the sick role as deviance. The first is that of Bagley, who would regard rubbish as "counter-deviance," that is, deviance from the deviant role of sickness.[21] This seems to me to be an unnecessary creation of a new term, one which seems to have few if any uses outside medical sociology and which begs the original question of why sickness should be seen as deviance at all. The second way of avoiding contradictions might be to argue that doctors do not regard sickness as deviance because they are largely cut off from the rest of society—they share a sub-universe of meanings which is separate from those of the rest of society.[22] This would allow for sickness in the wider society to be seen as deviance, and for the attitudes and behavior of doctors to be irrelevant to this question. *A priori* it seems implausible that the extent of separation between the world of the medical staff could be so divorced from that of the rest of society, or that the attitudes of those staff could be reasonably regarded as irrelevant, though this seems to be the position which Freidson holds.[23] Neither of these solutions, then, seem adequate enough to allow me to avoid looking more closely at the prior argument about sickness and deviance.

Rather than recapitulate all contributions to this debate I shall relate my material to the position recently taken by Dingwall.[24] He uses McHugh's analysis to argue that illness makes an actor vulnerable to *prima facie* charges of conventionality, because it involved the breaking of rules which are applied to all competent members of a society. However, any specific illness may or may not make an actor vulnerable to a charge of theoreticity, depending on whether or not he is able to deny any charges that he is willfully ill, or responsible in other ways for his condition. Illness is thus "clearly deviance" by the first criterion, but a matter of negotiation by the second criterion. Dingwall's attempt to separate the two criteria in this way seems rather misleading, since it is the application of both criteria together which will lead actors to level charges of deviance (or not); but in general, this argument takes us much further than earlier discussions, focussed at different levels.

If, then, we accept Dingwall's argument that the study of the moral status of illness should start with the study of its ascription in everyday settings, the evidence I have presented suggests that illness is a morally ambiguous condition. It makes actors vulnerable to charges of deviant behaviour, but the resolution of those charges depends on negotiation, and is contextually specific. Part of the work done by Casualty staff is the production of deviance as the obverse of the production of legitimate illness. The special characteristics of Casualty departments perhaps make these processes more obvious than elsewhere, but they are probably a general feature of medical encounters.

Notes

1. See for example, the British Orthopedic Association, "Memorandum on Accident Services," Journal of Bone and Joint Surgery, Vol. 41B, No. 3, 1959, pp. 457–63; Nuffield Provincial Hospitals Trust, *Casualty Services and their Setting*, London, O.U.P., 1960; and House of Commons Expenditure Committee, 4th Report, *Accident and Emergency Services*, London H.M.S.O. 1974. A fuller survey of this literature can be found in H. Gibson, *Rules, Routines and Records*, Ph.D. thesis, Aberdeen University, 1977.

2. See e.g., the summary in *World Medicine*, February 1972, p. 11.

3. Reported in the Expenditure Committee Report, op. cit, pp. xii–xiii.

4. This is similar to Freidson's distinction between client control and colleague control: see E. Freidson, *Patients' Views of Medical Practice*, New York, Russell Sage Foundation, 1961.

5. J. Roth, "Some Contingencies of the Moral Evaluation and Control of Clientele: The case of the Hospital Emergency Service," *A.J.S.* Vol. 77, No. 5, March 1972. The studies of medical students which are relevant are: H. Becker *et al., Boys in White*, Chicago, University of Chicago Press, 1961; and R. K. Merton *et al.* (eds), *The Student Physician*, Cambridge, Harvard University Press, 1957.

6. P. Strong and A. Davis, "Who's Who in Paediatric Encounters: Morality, Expertise and the Generation of Identity and Action in Medical Settings," in A. Davis (ed), *Relationships between Doctors and Patients*, Westmead, Teakfield, 1978, pp. 51–2.

7. H. Gibson, op. cit., chapter 9.

8. A. H. Godse, "The Attitudes of Casualty Staff and Ambulancemen towards Patients Who Take Drug Overdoses," *Social Science and Medicine*, Vol. 12, 5A, September 1978, pp. 341–6.

9. This case, while not as spectacular as one reported by Sudnow, does suggest a general level of depersonalization in British teaching hospitals rather higher than in American hospitals. See D. Sudnow, *Passing On*, New York, Prentice-Hall 1968.

10. I am using normal in the sense that Sudnow uses, in D. Sudnow, "Normal Crimes," *Social Problems*, Vol. 12, Winter 1965.

11. This topic recurs in the reports referenced in note 1 above, and in most of the research reports on casualty case-loads in the medical press. In an attempt to discourage casual attenders the Ministry of Health changed the title of the departments from "Casualty" to "Accident and Emergency" during the 1960s. However, most of the staff continued to call it Casualty (and I have followed their usage) and there is no evidence that the change of name has altered the nature of the case-load.

12. See E. Goffman, *Asylums*, Harmondsworth, Penguin, 1968, especially the section "Notes on the Vicissitudes of the Tinkering Trades."

13. Gibson (op. cit. pp. 164–86) discusses the ways in which "drunk" fails as a medical category since a wide variety of careers and treatments are associated with drunk patients, which tends to support the argument that this is essentially a moral category.

14. Godse (op. cit.) suggests that there is generalised hostility towards all drug overdoses, but he elaborates his discussion with respect to three types. One of these—deliberate suicide attempts or gestures—fails to distinguish between what I call "normal" overdoses and those believed by the staff to be serious suicide attempts. Gibson (op. cit. pp. 186–94) also reports that staff presumed that most, if not all, cases of self-poisoning were seen as acts of self-injury, willfully and directly caused, rather than as attempts to commit suicide.

15. Sudnow, "Normal Crimes," op. cit.

16. P. Strong and A. Davis, op. cit., p. 52.

17. In the research of a similar kind carried out by the author in Pakistan, doctors were both less interested in good patients and less bothered by rubbish; similarly, they had less autonomy over their working conditions.

18. T. Parsons, *The Social System*, New York, The Free Press, 1951. Although Parsons never says where he developed the sick role model from, it is plausible that it comes from his discussions with doctors in his Boston study, and from his course in psychotherapy (see his footnote, 2, pp. 428–9). If so, and if we reformulate the sick role in the way that I have, this may overcome some of the problems which have been pointed out by other writers: for example, the inapplicability of the sick role to chronic illness. That is, there is indeed a preference by doctors for an illness which is temporary, transitory and curable, and part of the reason for the low prestige of work with geriatric or chronic patients is that doctors are uneasy dealing with patients who do not conform to this pattern.

19. P. McHugh, "A Commonsense Conception of Deviance," in H. P. Drietzel (ed.), *Recent Sociology No. 2*, New York, Crowell Collier Macmillan, 1968.

20. Similar uncertainty has been reported from America amongst a general population and amongst social workers. See H. A. Mulford and D. E. Miller, "Measuring Community Acceptance of the Alcoholic as a Sick Person," *Quarterly Journal of Studies in Alcoholism*, Vol. 25, June 1964; and H. P. Chalfont and R. A. Kurtz, "Alcoholics and the Sick Role: Assessments by Social Workers," *Journal of Health and Social Behaviour*, Vol. 12, March 1971.

21. C. Bagley, "The Sick Role, Deviance and Medical Care," *Social and Economic Administration*, Vol. 4, 1971.

22. This is the sort of argument made by Becker *et al.*, op. cit., in discussing the sources of negative evaluations by medical students.

23. E. Freidson, *Profession of Medicine*, New York, Dodd Mead, 1970. He advances similar arguments in "Disability and Deviance," in M. B. Sussman, (ed), *Sociology and Rehabilitation*, Washington DC, ASA 1966.

24. R. Dingwall, *Aspects of Illness*, London, Martin Robertson, 1976.

25 / Ironies of Social Control: Authorities as Contributors to Deviance through Escalation, Nonenforcement, and Covert Facilitation

GARY T. MARX

Many current theoretical approaches to deviance causation tend to neglect a crucial level of analysis: the specific interactive context within which rule breaking occurs. Anomie (Merton, 1957) and subcultural theorists (Sutherland and Cressey, 1974) and combinations of these approaches (Cloward and Ohlin, 1960) tend to focus on rather abstract initial group properties such as opportunity structures and norms, rather than on the interactive group processes out of which behavior emerges. Those questioning the mechanistic force of such variables nevertheless stress the independence of the deviant as a maker of choices (Matza, 1966).

Even when attention is given to situational aspects of rule breaking, as with some functionalists, the focus tends to be too mechanistic. In what can be called the trampoline model of social control (Homans, 1950; Parsons, 1951), norm violations lead to reparative social control responses. Social controllers are thought to be in a relentless struggle with autonomous criminals, who freely choose to violate the law, and who always do what they are charged with having done. The systemic and reciprocal effects become most apparent *after* the deviance appears. In contrast (and closer to the perspective to be developed here), theorists such as Reiss (1951) and Hirschi (1969) see social control as an important variable in the production of deviance. However, they argue that it is the absence of social control that helps to explain deviance. I shall argue that its *presence* does too.

Whatever merit the above approaches have for dealing with various aspects of deviance, they must be supplemented by a theoretical perspective which focuses on the immediate context of the rule infraction. Such a perspective must at least take as an empirical question the degree of autonomy in the actions of the rule violator, and whether people actually do what they are charged with having done.

In current theories the deviant is seen either as autonomous or as a pawn of broad social and cultural forces. Most interpretations tend to reify the categories of authority and "criminal" and to draw the line between them too sharply. They miss the interdependence that may exist between these groups and the extent to which authorities may induce or help others to break the law, be involved in law breaking themselves, or create false records about others' supposed law breaking. Conversely, the extent to which those engaged in illegal activities may be contributing to social order is also ignored. Here I focus on some neglected aspects of the role of authorities in law violations.

The idea that authorities may play a role in generating deviance is not new. Clearly, the labeling perspective has focused attention on the role of authorities—for example, the work of Tannenbaum (1938), Kitsuse (1962), Becker (1963), Wilkins (1965), Scheff (1966), Lemert (1951, 1972) and Hawkins and Tiedeman (1975). In such work, authorities have been seen to "create" deviance by defining some of a wide range of behavior as illegal, using their discretion about which laws will then be most actively enforced, and singling out some of those who violate these laws for processing by the criminal justice system. Subsequent restrictions on the behavior of those processed as deviants, such as their being singled out for special attention by authorities, and subsequent changes in their self-images, are thought to result in their becoming even more involved in deviant activities.

These are not, however, the roles that authorities play in creating deviance on which I wish to focus. Much of the labeling argument is true by definition; that which isn't seems plausible enough and has the easy virtue of overlapping with the underdog world view of many who hold it, though systematic research in its support cannot be said to be overwhelming (Manning, 1973; Wellford, 1975; Gove, 1980). Yet if subsequent evidence suggests that labeling as such does not, on balance, amplify deviance and even deters it, I think a strong case can still be made for the important role of authorities.

I do begin at an abstract level with what I see to be a fundamental insight of the labeling perspective: the possible irony of social controllers creating what they set out to control. But then I emphasize a different set of factors. In spite of its calling attention to the role of authorities, the emphasis in the labeling approach is usually placed on what authorities do to others already known or thought to be deviant. Its main concern is with the secondary rather than primary deviance. Its usual focus is not on the behavior of control agents before or during the rule breaking, nor on the degree of autonomy in the actions of the rule breaker. Nor is its usual focus even on whether the deviance actually occurred, preferring instead, in Rains' (1975:10) words, "to describe the full process of imputation without regard for warrant." But here I will deliberately focus on infraction—on some of the ways in which it is shaped or induced by prior or concomitant actions of authorities, and on some of the causes involved.[1]

Situations where social control contributes to, or even generates, rule-breaking behavior include these three ideal types:

1. Escalation (by taking enforcement action, authorities unintentionally encourage rule breaking).
2. Nonenforcement (by strategically taking *no enforcement action*, authorities intentionally permit rule breaking).
3. Covert facilitation (by taking *hidden or deceptive enforcement action*, authorities intentionally encourage rule breaking).

These are analytic distinctions. In a given empirical instance all may be present.

In much of the rest of the paper I discuss these types of social control. I use examples from criminal justice situations primarily, but believe the processes are also evident in other social settings, such as the school, family and work.

Documents and published accounts are major sources. However, I have also drawn on interviews and observations made over a seven-year period in 18 U.S. police departments while studying community police patrols, community service officers, civilian police planners, and performance measures, plus those made during a year spent studying English and French police. My initial interest in the topic grew out of work done for the Kerner Commission in 1968 on police behavior in civil disorders.

ESCALATION

The clearest cases of authorities contributing to rule breaking involve escalation. As with facilitation, authorities' intervention is conducive to deviance. However, secrecy need not be involved (the facilitation can be overt), and the final consequence is generally not consciously, or at best publicly, sought by controllers when they initially enter the situation.[2] It is not simply that social control has no effect, rather that it can amplify. (In the language of cybernetics, this is a case of deviation amplifying feedback [Cf. Maruyama, 1963]—in everyday language, snowballing or mushrooming.) In escalation the very process of social control directly triggers violations. In urging that attention be focused on the deviant act as such, Cohen has written:

> The history of a deviant act is a history of an interaction process. The antecedents of the act are an unfolding sequence of acts contributed by a set of actors (1965:9).

Nowhere is this logic clearer than in the case of escalation. Five major analytic elements of escalation are:

1. An increase in the *frequency* of the original violations.
2. An increase in the *seriousness* of violations, including the greater use of violence.
3. The appearance of *new* categories of violators and/or victims (without a net diminution of those previously present).
4. An increase in the commitment, and/or skill and effectiveness of those engaged in the violation.
5. The appearance of violations whose very definition is tied to social control intervention.

Escalation may stem from initial or postapprehension enforcement efforts.

Police involvement in family conflict, crowd, and automobile chase situations can contribute to violations when none were imminent, or it can increase the seriousness of these situations. In responding to challenges to their authority or to interpersonal conflict situations, preemptive police actions (euphemistically called by some with a sardonic smile, "constructive coercion" and "preventive violence") may lead to further violence.

A three-year study of police-citizen incidents in New York City notes "the extent to which the handling of relatively minor incidents such as traffic violations or disorderly disputes between husbands and wives seemed to create a more serious situation than existed prior to the police attempt to control the situation" (McNamara, 1967). Family disturbance calls are an important source of police injuries to citizens and vice versa. Bard has similarly observed that "there is more than ample evidence that insensitive, untrained, and inept police management of human problems is a significant breeding ground for violence" (1971:3). Certain styles of intervention are likely to provoke aggressive responses.

An English policeman characterized the 1960s' riot control behavior of American police in some cities as "oilin' the fire." Police responses to crowd situations offer many examples of escalation (Marx, 1970; Stark, 1972). Provocative overreaction (referred to by another English policeman as "cracking a nut with a sledgehammer") can turn a peaceful crowd into a disorderly one. In the 1967 riot in New Haven, for example, a small group of angry but as yet law-abiding blacks marched in the street—to be met by police tear gas; this then provoked a small riot. Or in Detroit a small riot emerged during the Poor People's March when, during a meeting in a large hall, police inside the building tried to push people outside, at the same time that mounted police outside were trying to push people back inside. Such police reactions and subsequent arrests may occur in the most benign of circumstances, such as at sporting events or concerts.

High-speed chases offer another all too tragic example. They result in injuries, in death, and often in manslaughter charges against persons who, in the absence of the chase, might have faced minimal or no charges. For example, in a Boston suburb, a car being chased by two police cruisers at speeds of 95 miles an hour killed a footpatrolman. The young driver of the car was subsequently charged not only with speeding but with manslaughter. The same day a 15-year-old youth facing manslaughter charges hung himself in a jail in a nearby town. He was arrested the week before, following a high-speed chase in which his car killed two people (*Boston Globe*, November 21, 1975). The high-speed chase, perhaps because of the risks and emotions involved and the denial of police authority, also figures disproportionately in situations where prisoners are abused. The escalation here has second-order effects, coming to involve new offenders (police themselves) as well as new offenses (e.g., assault and denial of civil rights).

One consequence of strong enforcement actions can be to change the personnel and social organization of those involved in illegal activities. For example, stepped-up enforcement efforts with respect to heroin and cocaine appear to have moved the drug traffic away from less sophisticated and skilled local, often amateur, groups to more highly skilled, centralized, better organized criminal groups (Young, 1971; Sabbag, 1976; Adler *et al.*, forthcoming). The greater skill and sophistication of those now drawn into the activity may mean the development of new markets. Increased risks may mean greater profits, as well as incentives to develop new consumers and markets. The more professional criminals are more likely to be able to avoid prosecution and are in a better position to induce police corruption.

Increased corruption, a frequent escalatory consequence of stepped-up enforcement efforts, is one of a number of second-order forms of illegality which may indirectly appear. Even attacking corruption may generate other problems. Thus, following reform efforts in one city (Sherman, 1978:257), police morale declined and citizen complaints went up sharply, as did police use of firearms. In Boston a recent increase in high-speed chases and attendant offenses and injuries is directly traceable to an order to enforce traffic laws more stringently. Another second-order effect can be seen in the monopoly profits which may accrue to those who provide vice in a context of strong enforcement pressures. These profits can be invested in still other illegal activities. Thus, some of the tremendous profits earned by organized crime groups that emerged during prohibition, and the skills developed then, went into gambling, labor racketeering and narcotics. Violence may increase among criminal groups contending for new monopoly profits. Their monopoly may also have been aided by informing on competitors. The increased cost of the product they provide may mean increased illegality on the part of customers facing higher prices (Schur, 1965). A link between drug addiction and street crime, for example, has often been argued.

Authorities may directly provide new resources which have unintended effects. Part of the increased homicide rates in the 1970s, for example, particularly among minority youths, has been attributed to vastly augmented amounts of federal "buy" money for drugs. This increased the opportunity for youths to become informers, and some of them were subsequently killed. The drugs, stolen goods, money, weapons, and tips sometimes given to informers and others who aid police may be used in subsequent crimes. A more benign resource may be the youth workers sent to work with gangs in their environment. Some of the detached street-worker programs, aimed at reducing gang delinquency, may have actually increased it: by strengthening identification with the gang, they made it more cohesive and encouraged new recruits (Klein, 1969). Klein observes that the assumed advantages of group work with gangs are "mythical," and he advocates abandoning standard detached worker programs. In Chicago, antipoverty funds for self-help programs among gangs offered resources, opportunities and incentives which created a context for fraud, extortion and violence (Short, 1974).

Contemporary American law has evolved an increasing number of crimes which emerge solely as an artifact of social control intervention. These emerge incidentally to efforts to enforce other laws. If authorities had not taken action, the offense would not have been committed. Resisting arrest or assaulting an officer are familiar examples. The prosecution of white-collar crimes offers a different example.

Prosecutors who initially set out to make cases of corruption, fraud, or food and drug violations may be unable to prove the targeted crime, yet still be able to prosecute for perjury or obstruction of justice. The latter violations become possible only after an investigation begins, and can exist regardless of the quality of evidence for the case the prosecutor originally hoped to make.

More routine are white-collar offenses involving the violation of requirements imposed on citizens to aid in the investigation of still other crimes. In and of themselves the violations need not produce social harm. In the effort to detect and sanction infractions the criminal justice system can promote crimes because of its own need for information. Failing to file reports or filing a false statement to the U.S. government are examples. Failure to file an income tax form is a crime even if one owes no taxes.[3]

Most of the escalation examples considered here have involved the initial enforcement effort and one point in time. The work of Wilkins (1965) and that of Lemert (1951, 1972) call attention to postapprehension escalation and a person's "career" as a deviant. Wilkins sees a spiraling interactive process whereby rule breaking leads to sanctioning, which then leads to more serious rule breaking, which in turn leads to more serious sanctioning and so on. Lemert focuses on how people may change their lives and self-conceptions in response to being formally processed, punished, stigmatized, segregated or isolated. To the extent that their lives and identities come to be organized around the facts of their publicly labeled deviance, they are secondary deviants.

However, postapprehension escalation can occur without an accelerating spiral or changes in self-image. Having been apprehended for one offense, or identified as a rule violator, can set in motion actions by authorities that make additional violations more likely. For one thing, contact with the criminal justice system may alter one's status (e.g., to probationer, inmate or parolee) so that one is guilty of a misdemeanor or felony for acts that would be legally inoffensive if committed by others. In addition, being placed in such statuses may provide actors with inducements to the commission of a crime, either by way of opportunity or pressure, to which others are not exposed.

Among the most poignant and tragic examples of escalation are those that emerge from the application of the initial sanction. Prisoners, such as George Jackson, who are sent up at a young age for a short term, then who find their sentences continually lengthened because of their behavior in prison, are clear examples. According to one study, only 6 of 40 offenses punishable in one state prison would be misdemeanors or felonies if done outside (Barnes and Teeters, 1959, as cited in Lemert, 1972:81). Similarly, violation of some of the regulations faced by those on parole or probation can send them to prison, but the same acts are not illegal when done by others.

For those not yet in prison, the need to meet bail and expensive legal fees can exert pressure to obtain such funds illegally. Clarence Darrow reported the case of a young thief who wanted the famous lawyer to defend him. Darrow asked if he had any money. The young man said, "No," and then with a smile said he thought he could raise some by that evening. An undercover narcotics detective (more taken by the seeming stupidity of those he arrests than of the system that generates their behavior) reports, "I even make buys again from guys who I've arrested and come right back out to make some fast bread for their expenses in court" (Schiano and Burton, 1974:93). There seems to be the possibility of infinite regress here.

Escalation is of course only one form that the interdependence and reciprocal influences among rule breakers and enforcers can take. It is treated here because of its irony. A more common form is probably displacement (without a significant increase or decrease in infractions). Displacement may occur with respect to other types of rule breaking, rule breakers, victims, place and procedure (Reppetto, 1976a).

Social control actions may unintentionally generate functional alternatives. The relationship between controllers and controlled may often be characterized as a movable equilibrium. As in sports or any competitive endeavor, new strategies, techniques and resources may give one side a temporary advantage, but the other side tends to find ways to neutralize, avoid or counter them. The action may become more sophisticated, practitioners more skilled, and the nature of the game may be altered—but the game does not stop. A saying among Hong Kong drug dealers in response to periodic clampdowns captures this nicely: "Shooting the singer is no way to stop the opera."

NONENFORCEMENT

In nonenforcement, the contribution of authorities to deviance is more indirect than with escalation or covert facilitation. Rule breaking does not expand unintentionally and authorities do not set people up and covertly facilitate it. Instead, those involved in nonenforcement relationships (e.g., with police) may break rules partly because they believe they will not be appropriately sanctioned. Here we have an exchange relationship between police and offenders. Offenders perform services for police; in return they are allowed to break rules and may receive other benefits.

When it is organized and specialized, nonenforcement is the most difficult of the three forms of interdependence to identify empirically. As a strategy it is often illegal and is more likely to be hidden. One does not find conditions for its use spelled out in policy manuals. Indeed the opposite is more apt to be true. In prohibiting nonenforcement, training and policy guidelines often go to great lengths to point out its dangers. Police are sworn to uphold the law: not to do so may involve them in malfeasance, aiding and abetting a felon, compounding a felony, perjury, and a host of other violations. Some anticorruption policies are from one perspective antinonenforcement policies. They seek to create conditions that will work against collusive nonenforcement relations; at the same time the realities of the police job are such that it emerges as a major fact of police life.

Obtaining reliable information on this process is difficult. Police sometimes deny its existence, and almost always deny its possible criminogenic implications, while their critics may exaggerate them. The existence of nonenforcement cannot be denied, although given the absence of systematic research, there is much room for disagreement about its extensiveness and its net consequences.[4] My purpose here is to analyze it as an ideal-typical category which sometimes has crime-generative effects.

Nonenforcement may literally involve taking no enforcement action, passing on information regarding police and criminal activities (including tips on raids), using improper procedures that will not stand up in court, offering ineffective testimony, helping a person facing charges to obtain leniency, giving gifts of contraband, and taking enforcement action against competitors. While there is sometimes overlap, we can differentiate "self-interested nonenforcement" involving traditional police corruption from "principled nonenforcement"—of most interest here—where police actions are thought to serve broader organizational goals.[5] Nonenforcement or leniency can be an important resource that authorities offer to those engaged in rule breaking whose cooperation they need. It is protected by the legitimate discretion in the police role and the United States' comparatively high standards of proof and rules of evidence required for conviction.

Police may adopt a policy of nonenforcement with respect to 1) informants who give them information about the law breaking of others and/or help in facilitating the controlled commission of a crime; 2) vice entrepreneurs who agree to keep their own illegal behavior within agreed upon bounds; 3) individuals who either directly regulate the behavior of others using resources police lack or means they are denied, or who take actions desired by authorities but considered too politically risky for them to undertake.

A former director of the FBI states, "Without informants we're nothing" (*New York Times*, April 16, 1974). The informant system, central to many types of law enforcement, is a major source of nonenforcement. Informants can offer police a means of getting information and making arrests that cannot come from other sources, given strictures against electronic surveillance, search and seizure, coercion, and the difficulty of infiltration. In return the system can work to the advantage of rule breakers. In the words of an FBI agent known for his ability to cultivate informants among those in organized crime:

> They [informants] worked with agents because it was profitable for them: They avoided prison, got reduced sentences or parole for friends and relatives, maybe enjoyed some revenge against guys who had betrayed them, and picked up informer fees and some very substantial sums in the way of rewards paid by insurance companies delighted to refund five percent in return for saving the ninety-five percent liability (Villano, 1977:103).

The system can be used by both police and informants as a form of institutionalized blackmail. Potentially damaging action such as arrest or denouncement of someone as an informant or offender is withheld as long as the cooperation sought is forthcoming.

The tables can also get turned, as the informant manipulates the control agent into corrupt activities (or merely acquiesces in the agent's desire for these). For example, in the case of drugs, the exchange of immunity or drugs for information can, in a series of incremental changes, lead to joint marketing and other criminal ventures (Commission, 1972). The nonenforcement may become mutual and the balance of power shift. The informant not only controls the flow of information but could even threaten exposure, which may entail greater risk for the police officer than for the drug dealer (Moore, 1977; Karchmer, 1979).

Where the informant is involved in the controlled commission of a crime, social control actions may generate rule breaking in two ways. Criminogenic effects may be present because police ignore illegal activities of the informant. But they may also be present because informants covertly facilitate the rule breaking of others. Informants facing charges or desiring drugs, for example, may have strong incentives to facilitate others' deviance.[6]

Louis Tackwood, an informant for the Los Angeles Police Department for ten years, worked first in traditional crime and later in radical politics. He appears to have committed numerous crimes, yet never to have been sentenced. He recalls:

> I never worried about getting caught. It was the idea of the money, the free crime. Here's a cat, a person, who like me has been successful in forming several organizations for crime. Here are the police officers telling me, hey, we want you to work for us. Two things went through my mind then—money and I got a free hand to do anything I want to do (Citizens Committee and Tackwood, 1973:24).

In more muted terms, a former commander of detectives in Chicago hints at how the informant system in a context of secrecy and specialization may work at cross-purposes:

> The burglary detectives may be inclined to "pass" a junkie with a small amount of drugs if he can turn up stolen property, while the narco squad will forget a few nickel and dime burglaries in return for cooperation in apprehending a major peddler. Homicide investigators looking for information on a murder will view a busy prostitute only as a source of information (Reppetto, 1976b).

People often become informants while in jail, or facing arrest. Sentencing may be deferred for a period of time while the informant "works off" the charges (for example, see Cloyd, 1979). In some police circles this is known as "flipping" or "turning" a man. With respect to drug enforcement, in some cities a point system is used whereby the informant receives one point for each marijuana purchase and two points for the purchase of harder drugs. If the informant earns a fixed number of points, such as ten, charges will be dropped. There is no doubt considerable variation *among* departments and *within*. Accounts such as that offered by Tackwood are perhaps best treated as ideal-typical illustrations.

The practice of police foregoing prosecution in return for information is more common than granting the informant a wild license to burglarize. Even here, the prior knowledge that one may be able to trade information for leniency can be conducive to law violations. Individuals sometimes manage to avoid arrest by falsely claiming that they are informants.

The exchange system is most highly developed for drugs. Something of a *de facto* license to deal may be offered ("you don't look too close at him"). To be useful the informant must be close to or involved in capering. In commenting on large transactions a detective observes, "Any junk dealer that you work with as an informant is moving junk when you're working with him. It has to be. You can't waste time chasing after some churchgoing Mary. If he's selling onions, what's he gonna tell you? The only way he can know what's coming down is if he's doing business." In this case the arrangement was "one for three." "For every load he gives you, he moves three." The rationale is clearly stated (Grosso and Rosenberg, 1979:55): "If he gives us one, it's one we wouldn't have had otherwise, right?"

The system occasionally is reproduced as a means of internal control. The Knapp Commission (1972) in New York offered leniency to corrupt police in return for their cooperation in catching other police. See Shecter and Phillips (1974), Daley (1978), and Grosso and Rosenberg (1979) for some of the ambiguities surrounding this procedure.

Certain occupational categories such as the fence have historically involved the informant's role (Klockars, 1974). The fence may offer information to the police, can return stolen goods—and in the case of thief takers, such as Jonathan Wild, even directly apprehend thieves, while receiving a degree of immunity and police help in regulating their clientele and employees.

The major vice control strategy at the turn of the century was one of containment, and it is still important. In what would only seem a contradiction to the outside observer, late nineteenth century police in many cities had written rules governing how houses of prostitution and gambling were to be run, though these were clearly illegal. Some vice entrepreneurs took pride in the honest quality of the services they provided. The very extensive Lexow hearings (Senate Committee, 1895) on the New York police show how they systematically licensed gambling, prostitution and police activities (Steffens, 1957, offers a classic discussion).

In return for noninterference from police (often further bought by the payment of bribes), vice entrepreneurs may agree to engage in self-policing and operate with relative honesty (i.e., run orderly disorderly houses), restrict their activities to one type of vice, stay in a given geographical area, and run low-visibility operations. By favoring certain vice operators and cooperating with them to keep others out, police may introduce a degree of control and stability into what would otherwise be a chaotic cutthroat situation. Establishing a peaceful racket organization may also be seen as a way of not alienating a local community that demands vice activities (Whyte, 1967). The goal becomes compromises reached through negotiation and regulation, rather than elimination of the activity.

Instead of being offered as a reward for self-regulation, nonenforcement may also be extended for regulating others. The literature on prisons gives many examples of the role selected prisoners play in maintaining order. Concessions, some clearly illegal, may be given to key prisoners in return for their regulating the behavior of others through questionable means (Sykes, 1958; Cloward *et al.*, 1960).

These represent cases where full control is technically impossible. Authorities need the continuing support of at least some of those they wish to control, and they are willing to pay a price for it. In other cases authorities may be capable of repressive action but prefer to delegate it because it is seen as too risky for them to undertake directly. For example, in 1963 the FBI experienced strong pressure to find the killer of civil rights leader Medgar Evers. They had learned the names of some of those involved and had the murder weapon, but could not obtain evidence on who fired the shot. Under FBI direction, an active burglar and fence kidnapped and threatened to kill a key figure in the plot, and was able to obtain a signed statement identifying the murderer. In return, the cooperative burglar was "the beneficiary of the best the Bureau could do for him"—he avoided a long prison sentence for armed robbery and kept $800 in cash stolen from the man's wallet (Villano, 1977).

Vigilante-type groups offer another example. Police may look the other way and essentially delegate certain enforcement rights to a group that wishes to take action that police might like to take but are unwilling to. The summary justice of the southern lynch mob, and group violence against blacks, were often conspicuous because of the lack of a restraining police presence. Until recently in many areas of the South, police (when not themselves members) ignored or gave encouragement to the Klan. The weak, if not openly supportive, attitude of many southern leaders in the face of discrimination and white violence significantly encouraged the Klan. This greatly hampered the federal effort to enforce civil rights laws and protect civil rights workers. With respect to traditional offenses, it has been claimed that in some urban minority areas police have been less than diligent in investigating the murders of drug pushers supposedly carried out by vigilantes seeking to rid their communities of pushers.

Still another type of nonenforcement can originate in some criminals' possession of unique skills, or even in their having the same enemies as authorities do. The fact that organized crime and the United States government have had some common enemies (Mussolini in Italy, and Castro in Cuba) has sometimes led to cooperation between them. In Italy local mafiosi were active in the underground and provided the Allies with intelligence for the invasion of Sicily. As the Allies then moved on to the Italian mainland, anti-Fascist mafia were appointed to important positions in many towns and villages. The French liner *Normandie* was burned in New York, just before it was to become an Allied troop ship. Following this incident, the government sought the aid of mob-controlled longshoremen, truckers and guards as help against waterfront sabotage and infiltration during World War II.[7] Help was received from Joe (Socks) Lanza on the East Side and Lucky Luciano on the West Side. Just what the government offered in return is less clear, although Luciano's cooperation won him, at least, a transfer to more comfortable prison quarters near Albany (Talese, 1972:206).

Recent reports of connections between the CIA and the underworld may simply be the continuation of an old American tradition. The CIA with its "executive action program" designed to "eliminate the effectiveness of foreign leaders" also delegated some of its dirty work (such as assassination efforts directed against Castro and Lumumba) to underworld figures. In Castro's case organized crime figures were thought to have "expertise and contacts not available to law-abiding citizens." They also had a motive which it was thought would take attention away from sponsorship of the U.S. government. According to one estimate (Schlesinger, 1978), Castro's coming to power cost organized crime $100 million a year. Outsiders were used by the CIA to avoid having "an Agency person or government person get caught" (Select Committee, 1975:74).

A former bank robber and forger involved in the unsuccessful plot to assassinate Lumumba was given plastic surgery and a toupee by the CIA before being sent to the Congo. This man was recommended by the Chief of the CIA's Africa Division as a "field operative" because "if he is given an assignment which may be morally wrong in the eyes of the world, but necessary because his case officer ordered him to carry it out, then it is right, and he will dutifully undertake appropriate action for its execution without pangs of conscience. In a word, he can rationalize all actions" (Select Committee, 1975:46). It appears that in extreme cases one crucial element which agents of social control may obtain in such exchange relationships is a psychopathic personality not inhibited by conventional moral restraints.

In a related example in Indochina, the U.S. took over the French policy of ignoring (or even encouraging) the growing of and trafficking in opium, in return for anticommunist activities. According to McCoy (1972), the CIA provided planes and military equipment used by Laotian Hill tribes to ship opium to Saigon, where it was then processed into heroin (see also Chambliss, 1977).

Still another type of strategic nonenforcement, one not involving exchanges, happens when authorities fail to take action about a violation they know is planned, or in progress, until the violation is carried out. This permits arrest quotas to be met and can lead to heavier charges, greater leverage in negotiations, better evidence, and a higher level of offender arrest. For example, an experienced cocaine smuggler, who could easily identify "amateurs" in the business, argues that federal agents always waited for such persons to be arrested before talking to them. He notes:

> Rather than walk up to someone obviously headed for trouble—where they might flash a badge and say, "Get smart, kid, it's not going to work"—they will, as a matter of policy, allow him to risk his life with the local heavies, get a few snorts of pure, and walk into jail at the airport back home. Why prevent smuggling when you can punish it—isn't that what jails are for? (Sabbag, 1976:120)

COVERT FACILITATION

The passive nonenforcement involving exchange relationships described above can be differentiated from a more active surreptitious role authorities may play as they (or their agents) directly enter into situations in order to facilitate rule breaking by others. The rule breaking that emerges from nonenforcement may be seen by authorities as an undesirable if perhaps necessary side effect. In the case of covert facilitation, authorities consciously seek to encourage rule breaking: getting someone to break the rule is the major goal. Both law and internal policy are often favorable to police facilitation of crime. This is a very old phenomenon. Eve, after all, was set up by the serpent. In the Bible she says, "The serpent beguiled me and I did eat." Indicating awareness of the paradoxical (provocative yet lawful) nature of the tactic, some police describe it as *lawful* entrapment. A not atypical policy manual of one police department contains a section on "permissible tactics for arranging the controlled commission of an offense." Police are told that they or their agents under appropriate conditions may:

A. affirmatively suggest the commission of the offense to the subject;

B. attempt to form a relationship with the subject of sufficient closeness to overcome the subject's possible apprehension over his trustworthiness;

C. offer the subject more than one opportunity to commit the offense;

D. create a continuing opportunity for the subject to commit the offense;

E. minimize the possibility of being apprehended for committing the offense.

For the purposes of this paper we identify at least three types of covert facilitation:

1. disguised police or their agents cooperating with others in illegal actions;
2. police secretly generating opportunities for rule breaking without being coconspirators;
3. police secretly generating motives for rule breaking without being coconspirators.

With respect to the "controlled commission of an offense," police or their agents may enter into relationships with those who don't know that they are police, to buy or sell illegal goods and services or to victimize others. The former is the most common. Agents of social control may purchase or sell drugs, pose as tourists seeking prostitutes, as prostitutes seeking customers, or as homosexuals seeking partners. They may pose as fences buying or selling stolen goods, as hit men taking a contract, as criminals trying to bribe prosecutors, and as entrepreneurs running pornographic bookstores. They may join groups that are (or become) involved in car theft, burglary or robbery. They may infiltrate political groups thought to be dangerous. The last decade reveals many examples of covert facilitation as authorities responded to widespread protest (Marx, 1974).

Both of the two other types of covert facilitation (deceptively creating opportunity structures or motives but without collusion) have a "give-them-enough-rope" quality. Police activity here is more passive and the deception is of a greater order from that involved in the "controlled commission of an offense." Police do not directly enter into criminal conspiracies with their targets, and charges of entrapment would not be supported—but they do attempt to structure the world in such a way that violations are made more likely.

The use of decoys to draw street crime is a major form of police creation of opportunity structures. Police anticrime squads, increasingly in vogue, may disguise their members as old women, clerics, derelicts, tennis players and bike riders; they may use attractive police women in civilian clothes to induce robbery and assault, with other police watching from close by (Halper and Ku, 1976). Private guards posing as inattentive customers paying for small purchases with large bills routinely test cashier honesty. Plainclothed "security inspectors" may test employee vigilance by seeing if they can get away with shoplifting. There is almost no limit to the variety of attractive opportunities for property theft that can be generated. Other examples include leaving packages in a watched unmarked decoy car with its windows open, leaving expensive skis (which, when moved, emit an electronic signal audible only to guards) in a conspicuous place at ski resorts, and opening crates of expensive merchandise at airport storage terminals and dusting them with an invisible powder than can be seen only by an ultraviolet light machine that employees pass as they leave work (Marx, 1980).

Covert facilitation involving the creation of motives can be seen in many counterintelligence activities. Here the goal may be disruption and subversion (rather than strictly law enforcement). In "dirty tricks" campaigns, police may take clandestine actions in the hope of provoking factionalism and violence. In one extreme example, an FBI agent in Tucson, Arizona, instigated a series of bombings of a Mafia home and a business to encourage fighting among rival organized crime groups (Talese, 1972). In one of the more bizarre cases of the last decade, the FBI, in "Operation Hoodwink," sought to encourage conflict between the Communist Party and elements in organized crime (Donner, 1976). The FBI was also responsible for burning cars of leftist activists so that it appeared to be done by rival political groups (*New York Times*, July 11, 1976). Undercover agents operating on opposing sides apparently played an important role in the violent split that occurred between the Huey Newton and Eldridge Cleaver factions of the Black Panthers. Perhaps more common are efforts to make it appear that an individual involved in criminal or radical politics is an informant, by planting information or contriving leaks. The "informant" may then be subject to possible retaliatory violence. This may be done by a genuine informant as part of a strategy of subversion or to cast blame elsewhere if arrests are to be made where it will be obvious that an informant was present (Schiano and Burton, 1974; Villano, 1977).

Some of the trickery of uniformed police might also be classified here. In the following extreme example from Wambaugh (1975:47), the power of the police office is used to generate a motive. A black bar known for heavy-drinking patrons is staked out. The plan is:

> ... to find a drunk sleeping in his car in the parking lot at the rear and wake him gently telling him that he had better go home and sleep it off. Then they would wait down the street in the darkness and arrest the grateful motorist for drunk driving as he passed by.[8]

In a version of turnabout as fair play (at least to reform police executives), covert facilitation may also be turned inward in efforts to deal with corrupt police and assess police honesty. Tactics recently used by the New York City police include: planting illegally parked cars with money in them to see if police tow truck operators would steal it; planting "lost" wallets near randomly selected police to see if they would be turned in intact; offering bribes to arresting officers; putting through a contrived "open door" call to an apartment where marked money was prominently displayed to see if two officers under suspicion would steal it (they did); establishing phoney gambling operations to see if police sought protection money; and having an undercover officer pose as a pusher to see if other undercover narcotics agents paid out the full amount of "buy" money they claimed (*New York Times*, November 29, 1972 and December 28, 1973; Sherman, 1978).

Government lawyers, judges and congressmen may also be targets of such tactics. Thus Sante A. Bario, a federal drug agent, posed as Salvatore Barone, a Las Vegas underworld figure, and was "arrested" in a Queens bar for carrying two loaded pistols. He then offered an assistant district attorney under suspicion $15,000 and the "charges" were dismissed (as was the assistant D.A.; Lardner, 1977); Operation Abscam, part of a federal bribery investigation, involved undercover agents posing as Arab sheiks who offered money to congressmen in return for favors (*New York Times*, Feb. 4, 1980).

For convenience we have thus far treated three types of interdependence as if they were distinct empirically as well as analytically. However, there are deviance and social control situations in which each or several are present—or where they merge or may be temporally linked. One of the things rule breakers may offer to police in return for nonenforcement is aid in covertly facilitating someone else's rule breaking. The arrest that emerges out of this can involve escalation. For example, a drug informant's petty theft may be ignored (nonenforcement) in return for his making controlled buys (covert facilitation). The arrest growing out of this may lead to additional charges if the suspect is involved in a high-speed chase and fights with the arresting officers after they call him a name. Escalation may lead to a later policy of nonenforcement in those situations where authorities perceive that their intervention would in fact only make matters worse.[9] Stepped-up enforcement may also lead to nonenforcement by increasing opportunities for police corruption.

* * *

Notes

1. Other forms of interdependence treated in the larger work from which this article is drawn, but ignored here, include: 1) "cops as robbers," where authorities are self-interested rule breakers; 2) the falsely accused; 3) the efforts of citizens to provoke, bribe, or otherwise implicate police in their rule breaking.

2. Because of their intentionality, nonenforcement and covert facilitation are social control strategies; this cannot be said of escalation which is defined by its unintended consequences, though these may be present with the former as well. Sometimes, of course, police may follow a policy of deliberate provocation in the hope of encouraging escalation so that they can legally use force, bring heavier charges, or dispense "alley justice."

3. As Jack Katz has pointed out in a private communication, "Such laws reflect the fact that in a way large sections of our society are always under investigation for a crime."

4. Estimates of how widespread this is vary. A knowledgeable crime reporter (Plate, 1975:103) observes, "the number of criminals actually licensed by police to make a living in this way is quite extraordinary." According to one estimate, 50 percent of those arrested by the old Federal Bureau of Narcotics were converted into "specialized employees" (McIntyre, 1967:10–13).

5. Here we ignore the many other sources of nonenforcement such as lack of resources, intimidation, bureaucratic timidity, lack of belief in the rule, or compassion, as well as the suspension of law enforcement in order to have something to hold over a person should the need arise later.

6. A narcotics agent critical of this practice notes: They put such pressure on the informant that, in effect, you've got him by the nuts. That's even what they call it, "the nut," working off the nut, or the violation. The pressure [on the informant] is so great he'll manufacture information, make up some to get off the hook. It's just a perfect example of how law enforcement is maintaining the problem (Browning, 1976).

7. A more cynical interpretation is that Luciano actually arranged for the destruction of the *Normandie* as the prelude for his subsequently exchanging mob protection against future "foreign" sabotage (Gosch and Hammer, 1975).

8. This is mentioned because of its analytic significance. Far more common is the reverse: monitoring bars as they close and encouraging drunks not to drive, or even arranging transportation for them.

9. In the case of civil disorders, however, underreaction as part of a policy of nonenforcement can have the unintended consequence of encouraging the spread of disorder. The three largest civil disorders of the 1960s (Watts, Newark and Detroit) were all characterized by an initial period of police underreaction. Given the infraction-generating potential of both over- and underreaction, police often find themselves criticized no matter how they respond, and policies are cyclical.

References

Adler, P. A., P. Adler and J. Douglas
Forthcoming "Organized crime: Drug dealing for pleasure and profit." In J. Douglas, Observations of Deviance, second edition. New York: Random House.

Bard, M.
1971 "Iatrogenic violence." The Police Chief (January):16–17.

Barnes, H. and N. Teeters
1959 New Horizons in Criminology. Englewood Cliffs, N.J.: Prentice-Hall.

Becker, H.
1963 Outsiders. Glencoe, Ill.: Free Press.

Browning, F.
1976 "An American gestapo." Playboy, February.

Chambliss, W.
1977 "Markets, profits, labor and smack." Contemporary Crises I:53–76.

Citizens Research and Investigation Committee and Louis F. Tackwood
1973 The Glass House Tapes. New York: Avon Books.
Cloward, R. and L. Ohlin
1960 Delinquency and Opportunity: A Theory of Delinquent Groups. Glencoe, Ill.: Free Press.
Cloward, R. *et al.*
1960 Theoretical Studies in Social Organization of the Prison. New York: Social Science Research Council.
Cloyd, J.
1979 "Prosecution's power, procedural rights, and pleading guilty: The problem of coercion in plea bargaining cases." Social Problems 26 (4):452–466.
Commission to Investigate Allegations of Police Corruption and the City's Anti-Corruption Procedures
1972 The Knapp Commission Report on Police Corruption. New York: Braziller.
Cohen, A.
1965 "The sociology of the deviant act." American Sociological Review 30: 5–14.
Daley, R.
1978 The Prince of the City. Boston: Houghton Mifflin.
Donner, F.
1976 "Let him wear a wolf's head: What the FBI did to William Albertson." Civil Liberties Review 3 (April–May):12–22.
Gosch, M. and R. Hammer
1975 The Last Testament of Lucky Luciano. Boston: Little, Brown.
Gove, W. R. (ed.)
1980 The Labeling of Deviance. Beverly Hills, Calif.: Sage.
Grosso, S. and P. Rosenberg
1979 Point Blank. New York: Avon Books.
Halper, A. and R. Ku
1976 New York City Police Department Street Crime Unit. Washington, D.C.: U.S. Government Printing Office.
Hawkins, R. and G. Tiedeman
1975 The Creation of Deviance. Columbus, Ohio: C. Merrill.
Hirschi, T.
1969 Causes of Delinquency. Berkeley: University of California Press.
Homans, G.
1950 The Human Group. New York: Harcourt, Brace and World.
Karchmer, C.
1979 "Corruption towards performance: Goals and operations in proactive law enforcement." Paper presented to Western Political Science Association, Portland, Oregon.
Kitsuse, J.
1962 "Societal reactions to deviant behavior: Problems of theory and method." Social Problems 9 (Spring):247–256.
Klein, M.
1969 "Gang cohesiveness, delinquency and a street work program." Journal of Research in Crime and Delinquency 6 (1):135–166.
Klockars, C.
1974 The Professional Fence. New York: Free Press.

Lardner, J.
1977 "How prosecutors get nabbed." New Republic, January 29:22–25.
Lemert, E.
1951 Social Pathology. New York: McGraw-Hill.
1972 Human Deviance, Social Problems and Social Control. Englewood Cliffs, N.J.: Prentice-Hall.
McCoy, A.
1972 The Politics of Heroin in Southeast Asia. New York: Harper and Row.
McIntyre, D., Jr.
1967 Law Enforcement in the Metropolis. Chicago: American Bar Foundation.
McNamara, J. H.
1967 "Uncertainty in police work: The relevance of police recruits' background and training." Pp. 163–252 in D. Bordua (ed.). The Police. New York: Wiley.
Manning, P.
1973 "On deviance." Contemporary Sociology: A Journal of Reviews 2: 123–128.
Maruyama, M.
1963 "The second cybernetics: Deviation-amplifying mutual causative processes." American Scientist 51:164–179.
Marx, G.
1970 "Civil disorder and the agents of social control." Journal of Social Issues 26 (1):19–57.
1974 "Thoughts on a neglected category of social movement participant: Agents provocateurs and informants." American Journal of Sociology 80 (2):402–442.
1980 "The new police undercover work." Journal of Urban Life 8 (4): 400–446.
Matza, D.
1966 Delinquency and Drift. New York: Wiley.
Merton, R.
1957 Social Theory and Social Structure. Glencoe, Ill.: Free Press.
Moore, M.
1977 Buy and Bust. Lexington, Mass.: Lexington Press.
Parsons, T.
1951 The Social System. New York: Free Press.
Plate, N.
1975 Crime Pays: The Theory and Practice of Professional Crime in the United States. New York: Simon and Schuster.
Rains, P.
1975 "Imputations of deviance: A retrospective essay on the labeling perspective." Social Problems 23 (1):1–11.
Reiss, A.
1951 "Delinquency as the failure of personal and social control." American Sociological Review 16 (April):196–207.
Reppetto, T. A.
1976a "Crime prevention and the displacement phenomenon." Crime and Delinquency (April):166–177.
1976b "The uneasy milieu of the detective." Pp. 130–136 in A. Niederhoffer and A. Blumberg (eds.), The Ambivalent Force, 2nd edition. Hindsdale, Ill.: Dryden.
Sabbag, R.
1976 Snow Blind. New York: Avon.

Scheff, T.
1966 Being Mentally Ill: A Sociological Theory. Chicago: Aldine.
Schiano, A. and A. Burton
1974 Solo. New York: Warner.
Schlesinger, A.
1978 Robert Kennedy and His Times. Boston: Houghton Mifflin.
Schur, E.
1965 Crimes Without Victims. Englewood Cliffs, N.J.: Prentice-Hall.
Select Committee to Study Governmental Operations With Respect to Intelligence Activities
1975 Alleged Assassination Plots Involving Foreign Leaders. Washington, D.C.: U.S. Government Printing Office.
Senate Committee Appointed to Investigate the Police Dept. of New York City
1895 Report and Proceedings. Albany, New York.
Shecter, L. and W. Phillips
1974 On the Pad. New York: G. P. Putnam.
Sherman, L.
1978 Scandal and Reform. Berkeley: University of California Press.
Short, J. F.
1974 "Youth, gangs, and society: Micro- and macrosociological processes." Sociological Quarterly 15 (Winter):3–19.
Stark, R.
1972 Police Riots: Collective Violence and Law Enforcement. Belmont, Calif.: Wadsworth.
Steffens, L.
1957 Shame of the Cities. New York: Hill and Wang.
Sutherland, E. H. and D. Cressey
1974 Criminology. Philadelphia: Lippincott.
Sykes, G.
1958 The Society of Captives. Princeton, N.J.: Princeton University Press.
Talese, G.
1972 Honor Thy Father. Greenwich, Conn.: Fawcett Crest.
Tannenbaum, F.
1938 Crime and the Community. Boston: Ginn.
Villano, A. with G. Astor
1977 Brick Agent. New York: Quadrangle.
Wambaugh, J.
1975 The Choirboys. New York: Dell.
Wellford, C.
1975 "Labeling theory and criminology: An assessment." Social Problems 22 (3):332–345.
Whyte, W. F.
1967 Street Corner Society. Chicago: University of Chicago Press.
Wilkins, L.
1965 Social Deviance. Englewood Cliffs, N.J.: Prentice-Hall.
Young, J.
1971 "The roles of the police as amplifiers of deviancy." Pp. 27–61 in S. Cohen (ed.), Images of Deviance. London: Penguin Books.

26 / The Social Context of Police Lying

JENNIFER HUNT
PETER K. MANNING

INTRODUCTION

Police, like many people in official capacities, lie. We intend here to examine the culturally grounded bases for police lying using ethnographic materials.[1] Following the earlier work of Manning (1974), we define lies as speech acts which the speaker knows are misleading or false, and are intended to deceive. Evidence that proves the contrary must be known to the observer.[2] Lying is not an obvious matter: it is always socially and contextually defined with reference to what an audience will credit; thus, its meaning changes and its effects are often ambiguous (Goffman 1959, pp. 58–66). The moral context of lying is very important insofar as its definition may be relative to membership status. The outsider may not appreciate distinctions held scrupulously within a group; indeed, differences between what is and is said may constitute a lie to an outsider, but these distinctions may not be so easily made by an insider. In a sense, lies do not exist in the abstract; rather they are objects within a negotiated occupational order (Maines 1982). In analytic terms, acceptable or normal lies become one criteria for membership within a group, and inappropriate lying, contextually defined, sets a person on the margins of that order.

The structural sources of police lying are several. Lying is a useful way to manipulate the public when the applying of the law and other threats are of little use (see Bittner 1970; Muir 1977; Westley 1970; Skolnick 1966; Klockars 1983, 1984; Wilson 1968; Stinchombe 1964). The police serve as gatherers and screeners of facts, shaping them within the legal realities and routines of court settings (Buckner 1978). The risks involved in establishing often problematic facts and the adversarial context of court narratives increases the value of secrecy and of concealing and controlling information generally (Reiss 1974). Police are protected for their lies by law under stipulated circumstances (see McBarnett 1981; Ericson and Shearing 1986).[3] The internal organization of policing as well as the occupational culture emphasize control, punishment, and secrecy (Westley 1970; Manning 1977).

Some police tasks, especially those in specialized police units such as vice, narcotics and internal affairs, clearly require and reward lying skills more than others, and such units may be subject to periodic scandals and public outcry (Manning 1980). The unfilled and perhaps impossible expectations in drug enforcement may escalate the use of lies in the "war on drugs," further reducing public trust when officers' lies are exposed. Most police officers in large forces at one time or another participate in some form of illicit or illegal activity, from the violation of departmental morals codes to the use of extra-legal force. Perhaps more importantly, there is an accepted view that it is impossible to "police by the book;" that any good officer, in the course of a given day, will violate at least one of the myriad rules and regulations governing police conduct. This is certain; what is seen as contingent is when, how and where detection by whom will take place.

Lying is a sanctioned practice, differentially rewarded and performed, judged by local occupationally-grounded standards of competence.[4] However, it is likely that these standards are changing; as police claims to professional competence and capacity to control crime and incivilities in cities are validated, and absent any changes in internal or external sources of control and accountability (Cf. Reiss 1974), police may encounter less external pressure and public support in routine tasks and are less likely to be called into account. Policing has emerged as a more "professional" occupation and may be less at risk generally to public outcry. One inference of this line of conjecture is that lying is perceived as less risky by police. The occupational culture in departments studied by researchers contains a rich set of stories told to both colleagues and criminals. However, like the routinely required application of violence, some lies are "normal," and acceptable to audiences, especially colleagues, whereas others are not.

Given the pervasiveness of police lies, it is surprising that no research has identified and provided examples of types of lies viewed from the officers' perspective. We focus here on patrol officers' lies and note the skill with which they cope with situations in which lies are produced. Some officers are more frequently in trouble than others, and some more inclined to lie. We suggest a distinction between lies that excuse from those that justify an action, between troublesome and non-troublesome lies, and between case and cover lies. Lies are troublesome when they arise in a context such as a courtroom or a report in which the individual is sworn to uphold the truth. In such a context, lying may risk legal and/or moral sanctions, resulting in punishment and a loss in status. *Case lies* and *cover stories* are routinely told types of troublesome lies. Case lies are stories an officer utilizes systematically in a courtroom or on paper to facilitate the conviction of a suspect. Cover stories are lies an officer tells in court, to supervisors, and to colleagues in order to provide a verbal shield or mitigation in the event of anticipated discipline.

METHODOLOGY

The senior author was funded to study police training in a large Metropolitan police department ("Metro City"). Continuous fieldwork, undertaken as a known observer-participant for eighteen months, focused on the differences and similarities in the socialization experiences of young female and male officers.[5] The fieldwork included observation, participation in training with an incoming class in the policy academy, tape-recording interviews in relaxing informal settings with key informants selected for their verbal skills and willingness to give lengthy interviews. The social milieu encouraged them to provide detailed and detached stories. The observer had access to the personnel files of the two hundred officers who entered the force during the research period. She attended a variety of off-duty events and activities ranging from meetings of the Fraternal Order of the Police, sporting events, parties, and funerals (for further details see Hunt 1984). The data presented here are drawn primarily from tape recorded interviews.

LEARNING TO LIE

In the police academy, instructors encouraged recruits to lie in some situations, while strongly discouraging it in others. Officers are told it is "good police work," and encouraged to lie, to substitute guile for force, in situations of crisis intervention, investigation and interrogation, and especially with the mentally ill (Harris 1973).[6] During classes on law and court testimony, on the other hand, students were taught that the use of deception in court was illegal, morally wrong, and unacceptable and would subject the officer to legal and departmental sanctions. Through films and discussions, recruits learned that the only appropriate means to win court cases was to undertake and complete a "solid," "by the books" investigation including displaying a professional demeanor while delivering a succinct but "factual" narrative in court testimony.

Job experience changes the rookies' beliefs about the circumstances under which it is appropriate to lie. Learning to lie is a key to membership. Rookies in Metro City learn on the job, for example, that police routinely participate in a variety of illicit activities which reduce the discomfort of the job such as drinking, sleeping on duty, and staying inside during inclement weather. As these patterns of work avoidance may result in discovery, they demand the learning of explanatory stories which rationalize informal behavior in ways that jeopardize neither colleagues nor supervisors (Cain 1973; Chatterton 1975). Rookies and veteran police who demonstrate little skill in constructing these routine lies were informally criticized. For example, veteran officers in Metro City commented sympathetically about rookies who froze on footbeats because they were too green to know that "a good cop never gets cold or wet..." and too new to have attained expertise in explaining their whereabouts if they were to leave their beats. After a few months in the district, several veteran officers approvingly noted that most of the rookies had learned not only where to hide but what to say if questioned by supervisors.

Rookies also learn the situational utility of lying when they observe detectives changing reports to avoid unnecessary paperwork and maintain the clearance rate. In the Metro City police department, some cases defined initially as robberies, assaults, and burglaries were later reduced to less serious offenses (Cf. Sudnow 1965). Police argued that this practice reduced the time and effort spent on "bullshit jobs" little likely to be cleared. Rookies who opposed this practice and insisted on filing cases as they saw fit were ridiculed and labeled troublemakers. As a result, most division detectives provided minimal cooperation to these "troublemakers." This added the task of reworking already time-consuming and tedious reports to the workload of young officers who were already given little prospective guidance and routine assistance in completing their paperwork.

Young police also observe veterans lying in court testimony regarding, for example, the presence of probable cause in situations of search, seizure and arrest (see, for example, McClure 1986, pp. 230–232).

There are also counter-pressures. While learning to lie, rookies also recognize that the public and court officials disapprove of lying, and that if caught in a serious lie, they may be subject to either legal sanctioning and/or departmental punishment. But recognizing external standards and their relevance does not exhaust the learning required. There are also relevant tacit rules within the occupational culture about what constitutes a normal lie. Complexity and guile, and agile verbal constructions are appreciated, while lying that enmeshes or makes colleagues vulnerable or is "sloppy" is condemned. Lying is judged largely in pragmatic terms otherwise. Soon, some rookies are as skillful as veterans at lying.[7]

POLICE ACCOUNTS OF LYING

Lies are made normal or acceptable by means of socially approved vocabularies for relieving responsibility or neutralizing the consequences of an event. These accounts are provided *after* an act if and when conduct is called into question (see the classic, Mills 1940; Sykes and Matza 1957; Scott and Lyman 1968). Police routinely normalize lying by two types of accounts, excuses and justifications (Van Maanen 1980; Hunt 1985; Waegel 1984). These accounts are not mutually exclusive, and a combination is typically employed in practice. The greater the number of excuses and justifications condensed in a given account, the more the police officer is able to reduce personal and peer related conflicts. These accounts are typically tailored to an audience. A cover story directed to an "external" audience such as the district attorneys, courts, or the media is considered more problematic than a lie directed to supervisors or peers (Manning 1974). Lies are more troublesome also when the audience is perceived as less trustworthy (Goffman 1959, p. 58).

Excuses deny full responsibility for an act of lying but acknowledge its inappropriateness. Police distinguish passive lies which involve omission, or covering oneself, from active lies such as a "frame," of a person for a crime by, for example, planting a gun, or the construction of a sophisticated story. The latter are more often viewed as morally problematic.

Justifications accept responsibility for the illegal lie in question but deny that the act is wrongful or blameworthy. They socially construct a set of justifications, used with both public and other police, according to a number of principles (These are analogous to the neutralizations found by Sykes and Matza 1957 in another context). When lying, police may appeal to "higher" loyalties that justify the means used, deny that anyone is truly hurt or a victim of the lies. Police may also deny injury by claiming that court testimony has little consequence as it is merely an extension of the "cops and robbers" game. It is simply a tool in one's repertoire that requires a modicum of verbal skill (see Sudnow 1965; Blumberg 1967). Finally, as seen in "cover stories," officers justify lies instrumentally and pragmatically (see Van Maanen 1980; Waegel 1984).

LYING IN ACTION

Case Stories and the Construction of Probable Cause

The most common form of case lying, used to gain a conviction in court, involves the construction of probable cause for arrest, or search and seizure in situations where the legally required basis in the street encounter is weak or absent.[8] Probable cause can be constructed by reorganizing the sequence of events, "shading" or adding to the facts, omitting embarrassing facts, or entering facts into a testimony that were not considered at the time of arrest or while writing the report.

The following is a typical case story-account chosen from a taped interview in which probable cause was socially constructed. The officer was called to a "burglary in progress" with no further details included and found a door forced open at the back of the factory.

> So I arrive at the scene, and I say, I know: I do have an open property and I'm going in to search it. And I'm looking around, and I hear noise. Then, I hear glass break. And I run to the window, and obviously something just jumped out the window and is running and I hear skirmishing. So I run, and I still don't see anyone yet. I just hear something. I still haven't seen anyone. You hear a window, you see a window and you hear footsteps running. Then you don't hear

it anymore. I don't find anybody. So I say to myself "whoever it is is around here somewhere." So, fifteen minutes go by, twenty go by. The job resumes.

One cop stays in the front and about a half an hour or forty-five minutes later, low and behold, I see someone half a block away coming out of a field. Now, the field is on the other side of the factory. It's the same field that I chased this noise into. So a half hour later I see this guy at quarter to four in the morning just happened to be walking out of this field. So I grab him. "Who are you? What are you doing?" Bla bla bla.... And I see that he has flour on him, like flour which is what's inside of this factory. So I say to myself, "you're the suspect under arrest for burglary." Well, I really, at this point it was iffy if I had probable cause or not.... A very conservative judge would say that that was enough.... But probably not, because the courts are so jammed that that weak probable cause would be enough to have it thrown out. So in order to make it stick, what I said was "As I went to the factory and I noticed the door open and I entered the factory to search to see if there was anybody inside. Inside, by the other side of the wall, I see a young black male, approximately twenty two years old, wearing a blue shirt and khaki pants, jump out of the window, and I chase him and I lost him in the bushes. An hour later I saw this very same black male walking out of the field and I arrested him. He was the same one I saw inside." O.K.?...

What I did was to construct probable cause that would definitely stick in court and I knew he was guilty. So in order to make it stick.... That's the kind of lies that happen all the time. I would defend that.[9]

The officer's account of his activity during the arrest of a suspect and subsequent testimony in court reveals a combination of excuses and justifications which rationalize perjury. He clearly distinguishes the story he tells the interviewer from the lie he told in court. Near the end of the vignette, by saying "O.K.?," he seeks to emphasize phatic contact as well to establish whether the interviewer understood how and why he lied and how he justified it. Within the account, he excuses his lies with reference to organizational factors ("conservative judges"—those who adhere to procedural guarantees—and "overcrowded courts"), and implies that these are responsible for releasing guilty suspects who should be jailed. These factors force the officer to lie in court in order to sustain an ambiguous and weak probable cause. The officer further justifies his lies by claiming that he believes the suspect to be guilty and responsible for perpetrating crime more serious than the lie used to convict him. He ends by claiming that such lies are acceptable to his peers—they "happen all the time"—and implicitly appeals to the higher goal of justice. As in this case, officers can shape and combine observed and invented facts to form a complex, elaborate yet coherent, picture which may help solve a crime, clear a case, or convict a criminal.

Case Stories and the Manipulation of the Court as an Informal Entity

As a result of community pressure in Metro City, a specialized unit was created to arrest juveniles who "hung out" on street corners and disturbed neighborhoods. The unit was considered a desirable assignment because officers worked steady shifts and were paid overtime for court appearances. They were to be judged by convictions obtained, not solely upon their arrests. An officer in this unit explains some of the enforcement constraints produced by the law and how they can be circumvented:

> Legally . . . when there's any amount of kids over five there is noise, but it's not really defined legally being unruly even though the community complains that they are drunk and noisy. Anyway, you get there, you see five kids and there's noise. It's not really criminal, but you gotta lock them up, particularly if someone had called and complained. So you lock them up for disorderly conduct and you tell your story. If they plead not guilty then you have to actually tell a story.
>
> . . . It's almost like a game. The kids know that they can plead guilty and get a $12.50 fine or a harder judge will give them a $30.50 fine or they can plead not guilty and have the officer tell their story of what occurred which lead to the arrest.
>
> . . . The game is who manipulates better, the kid or the cop? The one who lies better wins.
>
> Well, the kids are really cocky. I had arrested this group of kids, and when we went to court the defense attorney for the kids was arguing that all of the kids, who I claimed were there the first time that I warned them to get offa the corner, weren't there at all. Now, you don't really have to warn them to get offa the corner before you arrest them, but the judge likes it if you warn them once.
>
> Meanwhile, one of the kids is laughing in the courtroom, and the judge asks why he's laughing in her courtroom and showing disrespect.
>
> At this point, the kid's attorney asks me what the kid was wearing when I arrested him. I couldn't remember exactly what he had on so I just gave the standard uniform; dungarees, shirt, sneakers. . . . Then, the defense attorney turns around and asks the kid what he was wearing and he gives this description of white pants with a white sports jacket. Now, you just know the kid is lying because there ain't a kid in that neighborhood who dresses like that. But, anyway, I figure they got me on this one.
>
> But then I signal the District Attorney to ask me how I remembered this kid outta the whole bunch who was on the corner. So the District Attorney asks me, "Officer, what was it that made you remember this male the first time?" And I said, "Well, your honor, I referred this one here because the first time that I warned the group to get off the corner, this male was the one that laughed the hardest." I know this would get the Judge because the kid has pissed her off in the first place by laughing in the courtroom. Well, the judge's eyes lit up like she knew what I was talking about.
>
> "Found guilty. . . . 60 dollars." (The Judge ruled).

In this case, the officer believed the boy was guilty because he "hung out" regularly with the juvenile corner group. Although the officer forgot the boy's dress on the day he was arrested, he testifies in court that it was the "standard [juvenile] uniform." The boy, however, claims he wore pants and a sports jacket. The officer was in a potentially embarrassing and awkward spot. In order to affirm the identification of the suspect and win the case, the officer constructs another lie using the District Attorney's question. He manipulates the emotions of the judge whose authority was previously threatened by the boy's disrespectful courtroom demeanor. He claims that he knows this was the boy because he displayed arrogance by laughing when arrested just as he had in court.

The officer's account of the unit's organization, the arrest, and his courtroom testimony reveals a combination of excuses and justifications. He justifies his lie to make the arrest without probable cause and to gain a conviction citing the organizational and community pressures. He also justifies perjury by denying the reality and potential injury to the suspect caused by his actions. He sees courtroom communications as a game, and argues that the penalty is minor in view of the offense and the age of the suspect. The officer argues instrumentally that the lie was a means to gain or regain control as well as a means to punish an offender who has not accepted the police definition of the situation. The latter is evident in the officer's assertion that the boys are "really cocky." Their attempts to question the police version of the story by presenting themselves as clean cut children with good families is apparently viewed as a demonstration of deliberate arrogance deserving of retaliation in the form of a lie which facilitates their conviction.

Another officer from the same unit describes a similar example of case construction to gain a conviction. The clumsy character of the lie suggests that the officer believes he is at little risk of perjury. According to a colleague's account:

> We arrested a group of kids in a park right across from the hospital. They all know us and we know them, so they are getting as good as we are at knowing which stories go over better on the judge. So the kids in this instance plead not guilty which is a real slap in the face because you know that they are going to come up with a story that you are going to have to top [That is, the case will go to court and require testimony].
>
> So, the kids' story was that they were just sitting in the park and waiting for someone and that they were only having a conversation. [The police officer's testimony was]: "The kids were making so much noise, the kids were so loud.... They had this enormous radio blasting and the people in the hospital were so disturbed that they were just hanging outta the windows. And some nuns, some of the nuns that work in the hospital, they were coming outside because it was so loud." And the thing that appalled the officer the most was that this was going on right in front of the entrance to the hospital. The kids were acting in such a manner that the officer immediately arrested them without even a warning.
>
> Well, the kid, when he hears this, likely drops dead. He kept saying "what radio, what radio?" The funny part of it was that the other police officers who were in the back of the courtroom watching the cop testify kept rolling their eyes at him. First of all, because when he said that the people were hanging outta the hospital windows, the windows in the hospital don't open. They're sealed. Another thing was that the cop said this occurred at the entrance of the hospital.

> Two years ago this was the entrance to the hospital. But it's not the entrance now. Another thing was that there never was a radio. But when the officer testified regarding the radio, he got confused. He actually did think there was one but in fact, the radio blasting was from another job. The cop realized after he testified that the kid didn't have a radio blasting.

The lies are described as instrumental: they are designed to regain control in court and to punish the offender for violating the officer's authority by verbally "slapping him in the face." In addition, the court-as-a-game-metaphor is evident in the notion that each participant must top the other's story in court. The amused reaction evidenced by peers listening to what they viewed as absurd testimony, rolling their eyes, also suggests their bemused approval. The informant's ironic identification of his colleague's factual errors points out the recognized and displayed limits and constraints upon lying. The officers recognized the difference between a rather sloppy or merely effective lie and an admired lie that artfully combines facts, observations, and subtle inferences. Perhaps it is not unimportant to note that the police engaged in the first instance in a kind of social construction of the required social order. The police lied in virtually every key facet of this situation because they believed that the juveniles should be controlled. What might be called the police ordering of a situation was the precondition for both of these court lies. Such decisions are potentially a factor in community policing when police define and then defend in court with lies their notions of public order (see Wilson and Kelling 1982).

Cover Stories

A cover story is the second kind of legal lie that police routinely tell on paper, in court, and to colleagues. Like most case stories, cover stories are constructed using sub-cultural nuances to make retelling the dynamics of encounters legally rational. Maintaining the capacity to produce a cover story is viewed as an essential skill required to protect against disciplinary action.

A cover story may involve the manipulation of legal and departmental rules, or taken-for-granted-knowledge regarding a neighborhood, actions of people and things. A common cover story involves failure to respond to a radio call. Every officer knows, for example, that some districts have radio "dead spots" where radio transmissions do not reach. If "radio" (central communications) calls an officer who doesn't respond or accept, "pick up the job," radio will usually recall. If he still doesn't respond, another officer typically takes the job to cover for him, or a friendly dispatcher may assign the job to another unit. However, if radio assigns the same job to the same car a third time and the unit still doesn't accept the job, the officer may be subject to formal disciplinary action. One acceptable account for temporary unavailability (for whatever reason) is to claim that one's radio malfunctioned or that one was in a "dead spot" (see Rubinstein 1973; Manning 1988).

The most common cover stories involving criminal matters are constructed to protect the officer against charges of brutality or homicide. Such cover stories serve to bridge the gap between the normal use of force which characterizes the informal world of the street and its legal use as defined by the court.

Self-protection is the presumed justification for cover stories. Since officers often equate verbal challenges with actual physical violence, both of which are grounds for retaliatory violence, either may underlie a story.[10] Threats of harm to self, partner, or citizens, are especially powerful bases for rationalizations. Even an officer who is believed by colleagues to use brutal force and seen as a poor partner as a result, is expected to lie to protect himself (see Hunt 1985; Waegel 1984). He or she would be considered odd, or even untrustworthy, if he or she did not. There is an interaction between violence and lying understood by police standards.

In the following account, the officer who fired his weapon exceeded "normal" force and committed a "bad shooting" (see Van Maanen 1980). Few officers would condone the shooting of an unarmed boy who they did not see commit a crime. Nevertheless, the officers participate in the construction of a cover story to protect their colleague against disciplinary action and justify it on the basis of self-defense and loyalty. Officers arrived at a scene that had been described mistakenly in a radio call as a "burglary in progress" (in fact, boys were stripping a previously stolen car). Since this is a call with arrest potential, it drew several police vehicles and officers soon began to chase the suspect(s):

> Then they get into a back yard chasing one kid. The kid starts running up a rain spout like he's a spider man, and one of the cops took a shot at him. So now they're all panicky because the kid made it to the roof and he let out a scream and the cops thought that they hit him. And that was a bad shooting! What would you think if you was that kid's mother? Not only did they not have an open property, but they don't know if it's a stolen car at all. Well, when they shot the kid I gave them an excuse by mistake, inadvertently. I was on the other side of the place with my partner when I heard the one shot. [The officer telling the story is on one side of an iron gate, and another officer J.J. was on the other side. He kicks open the gate, thinking it is locked. It is not locked and swings wildly open, striking J.J. in the head]...
>
> J.J. keeps stepping backward like he wanted to cry... like he was in a daze. "It's all right, it's not bleeding." I says to him... like he was stunned.
>
> So then the Sergeant gets to the scene and asks what happened, cause this shot has been fired, and the kid screamed, and you figure some kid's been hit and he's up on the roof.
>
> They gotta explain this dead kid and the shot to the sergeant when he gets there. So J.J. and Eddy discuss this. Eddy was the cop who'd fired the shot at the kid climbing up the rain spout, and all of a sudden they decide to claim he got hit with something in the head, and J.J. yells, "I'm hit, I'm hit." Then Eddy,

> thinking his partner's been shot, fires a shot at the kid. So they reported this all to the Captain and J.J. gets reprimanded for yelling "I'm shot" when he said, "I'm hit."
>
> J.J. was never involved at all, but he just says this to cover for Eddy.
>
> Meanwhile, the fire department is out there looking on the roof for the kid and they never found him so you figure he never got hit.

Here, the officer telling the story demonstrates his solidarity with colleagues by passively validating (refusing to discredit) the construction of an episode created by collusion between two other officers. The moral ambiguity of participation in such a troublesome lie is recognized and indicated by the interviewed officer. He disclaims responsibility for his involvement in the lie by insisting that he was not at the scene of the shooting and only "by mistake... inadvertently... gave them [the other officers] an excuse" used to create the cover story. In such morally ambiguous situations, individual officers remain in some moral tension. Note the officers' role-taking capacity, empathy, and concern for the generalized other when he asks in the vignette what the interviewer's thoughts would be if "...you was that kid's mother?" Such views may conflict with those of peers and supervisors. Moral tensions also arise in situations producing case stories.

The Morally Ambiguous Lie in a Case Story

Occasionally, officers cannot fully neutralize their sense of self-responsibility in the context of the police role. Their lies remain troubling in a moral sense. Such lies suggest the moral limits of pragmatism within the police, but in this case, the lie may be also a sign of the youth and gender of the officer involved. In the following example, a five-year veteran police officer experiences a profound moral dilemma as a result of pressures to frame a boy for a burglary she did not see him commit and did not believe he had committed. She refuses, even under peer and supervisory officers' pressure to do so, to produce a case story lie. Refusing to lie in this instance does not constitute a violation of police officers' sense of mutual obligation since she does not jeopardize peers. She sets the scene by noting that she and her partner are talking to John near his butcher shop when Frankie, a powerful and well-connected community member, approaches her and wants her to watch his shop. He claims a guy is trying to pass a bad check. She continues:

> Well, Frankie's a close friend of the Police Commissioner and his sister's married to the owner of a drug manufacturing company. He donated a lot of money to the mayor's political campaign.... The police commissioner vacations at Frankie's sister's summer home in [an elite resort location].... Frankie has "a lot of pull" and we [the police] sometimes call ourselves "Frankie's private little army."
>
> Anyway, I tell Frankie, "O.K. I'll watch the store." But I don't think anything's really gonna happen. Frankie's just jealous because I'm spending more time with John than with him. Anyway, I go in the butcher shop and talk to John and

when I come out, I hear Frankie screaming, "Stop him, stop him!" I respond, "Stop who?" Frankie says, "Stop the guy walking with the bag." I see a black kid walking away from the store with a bag in his hand and I call him over. I ask Frankie "What's going on?" He responds, "Something's fishy, something fishy's going on." At this point, the kid opens the bag in front of me and there's nothing in it and I search the kid.... The so called bad check that the kid was trying to cash at Frankie's store turned out to be a valid money order. I ask the kid to come over to the car and make out a ped stop. Thank God, I made up a good ped stop.... I got all the information on the kid.

At this point a "man with a gun" [call] comes over the radio. As no one else picks up the job, we take it. It was unfounded and I tell my partner that we'd better go back and check on Frankie because there might be trouble. When we return I ask Frankie, "Is everything all right?" He responds, "No it isn't." I say, "What's wrong?" Frankie says, "I told you he took something." I say, "That's not good enough, you have to tell me what he took... not that 'something's fishy and he must have taken something.'... Did you see him take anything?" Frankie responds, "Three radios."

I go inside the appliance store to see the missing radios and there are a number of radios on a shelf way above the counter where it would be difficult for anyone to reach them, particularly a kid. I ask Frankie if he wants me to take the report or if he would prefer a regular district car to do it. He tells me, "You take it!" I take a report and right away call a 43rd district car to take it into the detectives.

An hour later, I got a call to go to the district. The captain asks me again, "What did you do to Frankie?" I tell him, "nothing." The captain asks me again, "What did you do to Frankie?" I say "nothing," and tell him exactly what had occurred at the incident. The captain says, "Did you run him [the suspect] through the computer?" I say, "No, I didn't... because he had legitimate identification." The captain then tells me, "Well, you better get your story together because Frankie's going before the Board of Inquiry. You fucked up. Now, tomorrow you're gonna apologize!" I say, "But if I apologize, it makes it seem like I did something wrong. I did nothing wrong." The captain adds, "Don't argue with me, I told you what you're gonna do."

An hour later, I receive a call from the Division detective and he wants to know my side of the story. I tell him what happened. The detective says, "Well, we have to put out a warrant for the kid's arrest." I say, "For what?" The detective explains, "Believe me, the only reason this kid is getting locked up is because it's Frankie.... Have you ever been burnt by Frankie? Do you know who Frankie is?"

The detective then asks, "Will you go to court?" I say, "why should I go to court, I didn't make the arrest." The detective says, "Well, you're the key to the identification of the kid." I respond, "O.K. you send me to court and I'll make the asshole out of him that he is." The detective then says, "O.K. if I'm not man enough to stand this up in court, then I won't ask you to do it.... Let the old bastard do it himself."

Later, I'm called back into the Captain's office... and he tells me that "You're in for it now... the detectives have put out a warrant for the kid's arrest and that makes you look foolish...." He then orders me to tell my story again. I tell it again. Finally, I say, "I didn't lock the kid up because I had no probable cause and to this day, I have no probable cause." The Captain warns me, "Well,

> you're going to the Board of Inquiry and there's nothing you can say that will get you out of this one.... I hope your partner's a good front man." I told him, "My partner don't need to lie."

In this incident, the officer is unwilling, in spite of quite direct threats and pressures, to neutralize her felt responsibility by constructing a case story lie. She believed that the boy was innocent and did not believe that "higher truth" was served by participating in a lie that would have framed the boy and saved Frankie's face. She also thought her lie would facilitate the conviction of the boy for burglary, an offense that was so serious that injury to him could not be denied. The officer not only refused to lie but agreed to testify for the boy if subpoened to appear in court.

This ambiguous lie highlights several important subpoints. The officer clung to a version of the situation that denied the relevance of lying, and featured her view of the facts, her duty and her distrust of Frankie. The pressure to lie illustrated here makes evident some divergence of opinions about what is acceptable practice by rank and function. She refuses to lie in part because neither she nor her partner were at fault in her eyes (in contrast to the other examples in this article in which officers understood that both the public and themselves viewed a story as a lie), and her refusal does not jeopardize other officers. The officer first is confronted by her Captain who tells her she "fucked up" and should apologize. He implies that she should agree with Frankie's view (which she, in turn, views as a lie), be prepared to apologize, and to go before a Board of Inquiry. The division detective is ambivalent and unsure of what to do, and passes responsibility on to her. He asks her if she will go to court. The Captain again calls her in and by telling her that a warrant has been issued by detectives, i.e., that there is probable cause in the case, and that she will look foolish for persisting in her story. He does not go into the details of the case with her, just listens to her story and then implies that she is lying and that her partner will have to lie for her before the Board of Inquiry.

While officers are oriented to peers and their sergeants and are sensitive to those loyalties (Cain 1973), administrative officers may justify their actions with regard to higher political obligations, organizational pressures or even loyalty to the Police Commissioner or the Mayor (even though such politicians may have no direct involvement in the case). If a case involves for an officer such higher loyalties and patronage as well as political corruption, there is more to be lost by *not* lying.[11] Detectives are more cynical and view their role as mediating between the street realities and those of the courtroom. Their standards for judging normal lies differ from those of uniformed officers. This patrol officer, however, defined her loyalties in terms of her immediate peers and the public rather than officials whom she viewed as corrupt. Rank, age, and other factors not explored here may mediate an officer's relationship with the community, his/her allegiance to the police department, and sense of right and wrong.

CONCLUSION

This ethnographic analysis relies principally upon the perspective of the officers observed and interviewed. It draws, however, on broad ethnographic accounts or general formulations of the police mandate and tasks. We attempt to integrate the pressures inherent in the inevitable negotiation within hierarchical systems between official expectations and roles, and one's individual sense of self. Officers learn how to define and control the public and other officers, and to negotiate meanings. The social constructions or lies which arise result from situational integration of organizational, political and moral pressures. These are not easily captured in rules, norms, or values. Repeatedly, officers must negotiate organizational realities *and* maintain self-worth. Police lies, serving in part to maintain a viable self, are surrounded by cultural assumptions and designations, a social context which defines normal or acceptable lies and distinguishes them from those deviant or marginal to good practice. The meanings imputed to the concepts "lie," "lying," and "truth" are negotiated and indicate or connote subtle intergroup relationships. In a crisis, ability to display solidarity by telling a proper and effective lie is highly valued and rewarded. The ironic epithet "police liar" is neutralized. Subtle redefinition of truth includes forms of group-based honesty that are unrecognized by legal standards or by the standards of outsiders. These findings have implications that might be further researched.

Lying is a feature of everyday life found in a variety of personal, occupational and political interactions. Although telling the full truth may be formally encouraged throughout life, it is not always admired or rewarded. Neither truth nor lies are simple and uniform; cultural variation exists in the idea of normal lying and its contrast conception. Those who continue to tell the truth and do not understand communications as complex negotiations of formal and informal behavioral norms, find themselves in social dilemmas, and are vulnerable to the variety of labels used in everyday life like "tactless," "undersocialized," "deviant," or "mentally ill." The application of the label is contingent upon taken-for-granted modes of deception that structure interpersonal relations. As the last few years have shown, given the impossible mandate of the police, certain police tasks are more highly visible, e.g., drug enforcement, and even greater pressure to lie may emerge. Thus, the mandate is shaped and patterned by tasks as well as general social expectations, the sources of lying may differ as well.

The cultural grounds explored here are features of any organization which lies as a part of its routine activities, such as government agencies carrying out domestic intelligence operations and covert foreign activities. Standards of truth and falsehood drawn from everyday life do not hold here, and this shifting ground of fact and reality is often difficult to grasp and hold for both insiders and outsiders. As a result, organization members, like the police, develop sophisticated and culturally sanctioned mechanisms for neutralizing the guilt and responsibility that troublesome and even morally ambiguous lying may often entail. In time, accounts which retrospectively justify and excuse a lie may become techniques of neutralization which prospectively facilitate the construction of new lies with ready-made justifications. When grounds for lying are well-known in advance, it takes a self-reflective act to tell the truth, rather than to passively accept and use lies when they are taken-for-granted and expected. Police, like politicians, look to "internal standards" and practices to pin down the meaning of events that resonate with questions of public morality and propriety (Katz 1977). When closely examined in a public inquiry, the foreground of everyday internal standards may become merely the background for a public scandal. Normal lies, when revealed and subjected to public standards, can become the basis for scandals. This may be the first occasion on which members of the organization recognize their potential to be seen in such a fashion.

Finally, the extent to which an organization utilizing lies or heavily dependent upon them perceives that it is "under seige" varies. In attempts to shore up their mandate, organizations may tacitly justify lying. As a result, the organization may increase its isolation, lose public trust and credibility, and begin to believe its own lies. This differentially occurs within policing, across departments, and in agencies of control generally. Such dynamics are suggested by this analysis.

Acknowledgment

20 June 89. Revision of a paper presented by the senior author to The Society for the Study of Social Problems, New York, 1986. We acknowledge the very useful comments from this journal's reviewers as well as from Betsy Cullum-Swan, Peter and Patti Adler.

Notes

1. The many social functions of lying, a necessary correlate of trust and symbolic communication generally, are noted elsewhere (Ekman 1985; Simmel 1954; Manning 1977). Our focus is restricted. We do not discuss varieties of concealment, falsification and leakage (Ekman 1985, pp. 28–29), nor interpersonal dynamics, such as the consequence of a sequence of lies and cover lies that often occur. We omit the case in which the target, such as a theater audience or someone conned, is prepared in advance to accept lies (Ekman 1984, p. 28). Nor do we discuss in detail horizontal or vertical collusions within organizations that generate and sustain lying (e.g., Honeycombe 1974).

2. We do not distinguish "the lie" from the original event, since we are concerned with verbal rationalizations in the sense employed by Mills (1940), Lindesmith and Strauss (1956) and Scott and Lyman (1968). We cluster what might be called accounts for lies (lies about lies found in the interview material included here) with lies, and argue that the complexity of the formulations, and their embeddedness in any instance (the fact that a story may include several excuses, and justifications, and may include how these, in turn, were presented to a judge) makes it misleading to adhere to a strict typology of lies such as routine vs. non-routine, case lies (both justifications and excuses) vs. cover stories (both justifications and excuses), and troublesome vs. not troublesome lies. If each distinction were worked out in a table, as one reader noted, omitting ambiguous lies, at least 16 categories of lies would result. After

considering internal distinctions among lies in policing, we concluded that a typology would suggest a misleading degree of certainty and clarity. More ethnographic material is required to refine the categories outlined here.

3. Police organization, courts, and the law permit sanctioned freedom to redefine the facts of a case, the origins of the case, the bases of the arrest and the charge, the number of offenders and the number of violations. Like many public officials, they are allowed to lie when public well-being is at issue (for example, posing as drug dealers, buying and selling drugs, lying about their personal biographies and so on. See Manning 1980; Hellman 1975). Officers are protected if they lie in order to enter homes, to encourage people to confess, and to facilitate people who would otherwise be committing crimes to commit them. They have warrant to misrepresent, dissemble, conceal, and reveal as routine aspects of an investigation.

4. Evidence further suggests, in a point we do not examine here, that departments differ in the support given for lies. This may be related to legalistic aspects of the social organization of police departments (Cf. Wilson 1968, Ch. 6). Ironically, for members of specialized units like "sting operations" or narcotics, the line between truth and lies becomes so blurred that according to Ekman's definition (the liar must know the truth and intend to lie), they are virtually always "telling the truth." Furthermore, as noted above, such units are more vulnerable to public criticism because they are held to unrealistic standards, and feel greater pressure to achieve illegally what cannot be accomplished legally. Marx (1988) argues that increased use of covert deceptive operations leads to further penetration of private life, confusion of public standards, and reduced expectations of police morality.

5. She spent some 12 weeks in recruit classes at the academy. For fifteen months, she rode as a non-uniformed research observer, usually in the front seat of a one officer car, from 4–midnight and occasionally on midnight to eight shifts. Although she rode with veteran officers for the first few weeks in order to learn official procedures, the remainder of the time was spent with rookie officers. Follow-up interviews were conducted several years after the completion of the initial 18 months of observation.

6. Typically, recruits were successful in calming the "psychotic" actor when they demonstrated convincingly that they shared the psychotic's delusion and would rescue him/her from his/her persecutors by, for instance, threatening to shoot them. Such techniques were justified scientifically by trained psychologists who also stressed their practical use to avoid violence in potentially volatile situations.

7. Previous research has shown how detailed the knowledge is of officers of how and why to lie, and it demonstrates that trainees are taught to lie by specific instructions and examples (see Harris 1973; McClure 1984; Fielding 1988).

8. Technically, adding facts one recalls later, even in court, are not the basis for lies. Lies, in our view, must be intended.

9. This is taken verbatim from an interview, and thus several rather interesting linguistic turns (especially changes in perspective) are evidenced. Analysis of this sociolinguistically might suggest how this quote replicates in microcosm the problem officers have in maintaining a moral self. They dance repeatedly along the edges of at least two versions of the truth.

10. Waegel (1984) explores the retrospective and prospective accounts police use to excuse and justify the use of force. However, he does not distinguish accounts told by colleagues which are viewed as true by the speaker and those told to representatives of the legal order which are viewed as lies and fit the description of a cover story. For example, the account of accidental discharge which Waegel perceives as a denial of responsibility may also be a cover story which itself is justified as "self defense" against formal reprimand. In contrast, other police excuses and justifications invoked to account for the use of force are often renditions of events that present the officer in the morally favorable light rather than actual lies (see Van Maanen 1980; Hunt 1985; Waegel 1984). Whether the police categorize their use of force as "normal" or "brutal" (Hunt 1985) also structures the moral assessment of a lie, a point which Waegel also overlooks. Thus, acts of normal force which can be excused or justified with reference to routine accounting practices may necessitate the construction of cover stories which became morally neutral by virtue of the act they disguise. Other acts of violence viewed as demonstrating incompetence or brutality may not be excused or justified according to routine accounting practices. Although cover stories in such cases are perceived as rational, they may not provide moral protection for the officer because the lie takes on aspects of moral stigma associated with the act of violence which it conceals.

11. Supervisors and higher administrators, of course, collude in maintaining the viability of lies because they *share* the beliefs of officers that it is not possible to police by the book, and

that one should not rock the boat and should keep your head down (Van Maanen 1975). It is viewed as impossible to manage routine tasks without lying both to colleagues and supervisors (Punch 1985). The working bases of corruption are thus laid, as well as the potential seen in so many corruption scandals of cover-ups, lies about lies, and vertical and horizontal collusion in lying as seen in both the Watergate and the Iran-Contra affairs.

References

Bittner, E. 1970. *Functions of the Police in an Urban Society.* Bethesda: NIMH.

——. 1974. "A Theory of Police: Florence Nightingale in Pursuit of Willie Sutton." in *The Potential for Reform of Criminal Justice,* edited by H. Jacob. Beverly Hills: Sage.

Blumberg, A. 1967. *Criminal Justice.* Chicago: Quadrangle Books.

Buckner, H. T. 1978. "Transformations of Reality in the Legal Process," *Social Research* 37:88–101.

Cain, M. 1973. *Society and the Policeman's Role.* London: Routledge, Kegan Paul.

Chatterton, M. 1975. "Organizational Relationships and Processes in Police Work: A Case Study of Urban Policing." Unpublished Ph.D. thesis, University of Manchester.

——. 1979. "The Supervision of Patrol Work Under the Fixed Points System." in *The British Police,* edited by S. Holdaway. London: Edward Arnold.

Ekman, P. 1985. *Telling Lies.* New York: W.W. Norton.

Ericson, R. and C. Shearing. 1986. "The Scientification of the Police." in *The Knowledge Society,* edited by G. Bohme and N. Stehr. Dordrecht and Boston: D. Reidel.

Fielding, N. 1988. *Joining Forces.* London: Tavistock.

Goffman, E. 1959. *The Presentation of Self in Everyday Life.* New York: Doubleday Anchor Books.

Harris, R. 1973. *The Police Academy.* New York: Wiley.

Honeycombe, G. 1974. *Adam's Tale.* London: Arrow Books.

Hunt, J. C. 1985. "Police Accounts of Normal Force." *Urban Life* 13:315–342.

——. 1984. "The Development of Rapport Through the Negotiation of Gender in Fieldwork among the Police." *Human Organization.*

Katz, J. 1977. "Cover-up and Collective Integrity: on the Natural Antagonisms of Authority Internal and External to Organizations." *Social Problems* 25:3–17.

Klockars, C. 1983. "The Dirty Harry Problem." *Annals of the American Academy of Political and Social Science* 452 (November):33–47.

——. 1984. "Blue Lies and Police Placebos." *American Behavioral Scientist* 27:529–544.

Lindesmith, A. and A. Strauss. 1956. *Social Psychology.* New York: Holt, Dryden.

McBarnett, D. 1981. *Conviction.* London: MacMillan.

McClure, J. 1986. *Cop World.* New York: Laurel/Dell.

Maines, D. 1982. "In Search of Mesostructure: Studies in the Negotiated Order." *Urban Life* 11:267–279.

Manning, P. K. 1974. "Police Lying." *Urban Life* 3:283–306.

——. 1977. *Police Work.* Cambridge: MA: M.I.T. Press.

——. 1980. *Narc's Game.* Cambridge: MA: M.I.T. Press.

——. 1988. *Symbolic Communication: Signifying Calls and the Police Response.* Cambridge, MA: M.I.T. Press.

Marx, G. 1988. *Undercover. Policework in America: Problems and Paradoxes of a Necessary Evil.* Berkeley: University of California Press.

Mills, C. W. 1940. "Situated Actions and Vocabularies of Motive." *ASR* 6 (December): 904–913.

Punch, M. 1985. *Conduct Unbecoming.* London: Tavistock.

Reiss, A. J., Jr. 1971. *The Police and the Public.* New Haven: Yale University Press.

——. 1974. "Discretionary Justice." Pp. 679–699 in *The Handbook of Criminal Justice,* edited by Daniel Glaser. Chicago: Rand-McNally.

Rubinstein, J. 1973. *City Police.* New York: Farrar, Straus and Giroux.

Scott, M. B. and S. Lyman. 1968. "Accounts." *American Sociological Review* 33:46–62.

Simmel, G. 1954. *The Society of Georg Simmel,* edited by Kurt Wolff. Glencoe: Free Press.

Skolnick, J. 1966. *Justice Without Trial.* New York: Wiley.

Stinchcombe, A. 1964. "Institutions of Privacy in the Determination of Police Administrative Practice." *American Journal of Sociology* 69:150–160.

Sykes, G. M. and D. Matza. 1957. "Techniques of Neutralization: A Theory of Delinquency." *American Sociological Review* 22:664–670.

Van Maanen, J. 1974. "Working the Street . . . " in *Prospects for Reform in Criminal Justice,* edited by H. Jacob. Newbury Park, CA: Sage.

——. 1975. "Police Socialization: A Longitudinal Examination of Job Attitudes in an Urban Police Department." *Administrative Science Quarterly* 20 (June): 207–228.

——. 1978. "The Asshole." in *Policing: A View from the Street,* edited by P. K. Manning and J. Van Maanen. New York: Random House.

——. 1980. "Beyond Account: The Personal Impact of Police Shootings." *Annals of the American Academy of Political and Science* 342: 145–156.

Waegel, W. 1984. "How Police Justify the Use of Deadly Force." *Social Problems* 32: 144–155.

Westley, W. 1970. *Violence and the Police.* Cambridge: MA: M.I.T. Press.

Wilson, J. Q. 1968. *Varieties of Police Behavior.* Cambridge: Harvard University Press.

Wilson, J. Q. and G. Kelling. 1982. "The Police and Neighborhood Safety: Broken Windows." *Atlantic* 127 (March): 29–38.

27 / Accounts, Attitudes, and Solutions: Probation Officer–Defendant Negotiations of Subjective Orientations

JACK W. SPENCER

One of the principal concerns of sociologists and criminologists has been how criminal defendants are sentenced for their crimes. Probation officers (POs) play a significant role in the sentencing process because they make sentencing recommendations to the courts. Therefore, an examination of how POs make their recommendations is crucial for a full understanding of this sentencing process. Previous research has failed to examine important aspects of the processes whereby POs arrive at these recommendations.

Historically, the dominant approach to the study of criminal behavior has been deterministic. Thus, most of the researchers and theorists in this area have been concerned with delineating the causal factors associated with the occurrence of crime (Bonger, 1916; Cloward and Ohlin, 1960; Merton, 1957; Sellin, 1938). Since the 1930s, other sociologists and criminologists have reacted to this deterministic approach by stressing the importance of examining the processes of formal social reaction to criminal behavior (Becker, 1963; Cicourel, 1968; Lemert, 1951; Schur, 1971; Tannenbaum, 1938). These theorists have argued that it is the operation of the criminal justice system which defines or labels criminal behavior. In the mid-1970s, research on the criminal justice system began to take a deterministic approach. That is, this research examined the causal factors associated with criminal justice outcomes. Much of this research was concerned with the influence of legal vs. extra-legal variables on sentencing decisions (Bernstein *et al.*, 1977; Burke and Turk, 1975; Chiricos and Waldo, 1975).

This same approach has dominated research on decision-making by POs. That is, researchers have examined the variables which determine the decision which POs make (Carter, 1967; Dembo, 1972; Hagan, 1977; Reed and King, 1966).[1] One of these decisions is the sentence recommendation that POs make to the courts. While this approach has led to important insights it has left an important gap in our understanding of how POs arrive at these recommendations.

What has been left relatively unexamined are the *processes* whereby POs first interview defendants and then make recommendations. Previous research has found that a defendant's attitude is an important factor in these recommendations (Carter, 1967; Gross, 1967). However, we know little about the presentencing interview within which POs assess defendants' attitudes, nor how POs link this information with other factors in deciding what recommendation to make.

This paper is intended to bridge this gap. First, I discuss a set of factors—defendant's subjective orientations to criminal behavior—which includes defendants' attitudes. Next, I examine how POs assess these subjective orientations during presentence interviews. Finally, I discuss how these assessments affect the ways POs label defendants for the purpose of making sentence recommendations.

METHOD

In 1981, I spent nine months collecting data on the organizational processing of criminal defendants at a county probation department in the midwestern United States. This project was part of my dissertation research. The present study is based on part of that data, and consists of: (1) field notes of observations; (2) interviews with POs; and (3) tape recordings of presentencing interviews.

The probation department I studied comprised four divisions: felony, misdemeanor, juvenile, and substance-abuse. The staff consisted of a chief PO, three division heads, six POs, two substance-abuse counselors, and various support staff. I excluded the juvenile and substance-abuse division from the study early in the research.[2] The chief and all the POs in the felony and misdemeanor divisions agreed to participate in the research. Before each presentencing interview I identified myself, explained the nature of my research to the defendant involved, and obtained his or her written consent to record the interaction. No defendants refused to be included in the study.

The POs were extremely helpful, allowing me access to most sources of information that I needed, offering important ethnographic data during informal conversations, and discussing particular cases which I included in the study. After a short time my presence in the department became taken for granted: I was allowed to occupy a desk while not observing presentencing interviews and, when needed, would answer the telephones and run errands.

I collected data on 23 presentencing interviews in the following manner. After obtaining written consent from the defendant, I went to a corner of the room and started the tape recorder. During the interview I noted characteristics of the defendant and salient aspects of the interaction not captured by the tape recorder, such as nonverbal behavior. After the interview was completed and the defendant had left the room, I interviewed the POs about their perception of the interaction, the defendant, and the offense.

The method I used to analyze the data closely resembles Glaser and Strauss's (1967) grounded theory approach. Thus, I formulated theoretical propositions and constructs from the data, modifying these by comparing them with subsequent data, and developing hypotheses which accounted for the relationships between these constructs. I also used Cicourel's (1975, 1978, 1980) model of discourse processes which stresses the relationship between these processes, various predicates of knowledge which participants possess, and how the participants articulate or link that knowledge with information which emerges in the interactive setting.

DEFENDANTS' SUBJECTIVE ORIENTATIONS

Most previous research on sentencing recommendations has divided input factors into legal and extra-legal categories, in the process either ignoring such factors as attitudes or categorizing them as extra-legal. The POs I studied considered attitudes and other related factors in making sentencing recommendations. However, such factors were relatively distinct from those traditionally designated extra-legal (e.g., race, age, employment stability) both in how they were elicited in presentencing interviews and how they affected sentencing recommendations. This finding led me to formulate a third category of factors, which I call defendant's subjective orientations to their criminal behavior. I found four subjective orientations to be relevant: (1) accounts for the offenses; (2) attitudes toward the offenses; (3) attitudes toward the consequences of the offenses; and (4) attitudes toward changing their behavior. I discuss each of these in turn.

1) Accounts for the Offenses

According to Scott and Lyman (1968:46) an account is "a statement made by a social actor to explain unanticipated or untoward behavior." In my data the defendants' accounts consisted of two elements: the factors involved in the commission of the offense and the degree of intent involved.

There were generally two types of *factors*: motivating and causal. Motivating factors involved problematic situations in which the defendants sought to accomplish some particular goal and to which the commission of the offenses presented a solution. Causal factors, on the other hand, led to the commission of the offenses, in spite of the conscious intentions of the defendants. The degree of responsibility the defendants claimed decided the type of factor.

The amount of prior planning by the defendant determined the *degree of intent*. Relevant components of this element included the point at which defendants had decided to commit the offense and whether they had considered the method by which it would be committed. Of primary importance to the POs was whether the offense was spontaneous or calculated. Combining these two elements—the factors and the degree of intent—results in a four-fold typology of accounts, of which only two will concern us here: rational and non-rational accounts.[3]

Rational accounts were ones in which defendants claimed some degree of prior planning and in which they had been in control of their actions. For example, one rational account for shoplifting involved a defendant who claimed to have desired an item yet, lacking sufficient money, decided to steal it. *Non-rational* accounts were those in which defendants claimed they committed the offense relatively spontaneously and because of some identifiable factor which was beyond their immediate control. For example, one defendant claimed he had assaulted someone because he had been drunk and their argument had gotten "out of hand."

Defendants' accounts were important for sentencing recommendations for four reasons: (1) The POs believed planned offenses deserved more severe sanctions than those which were more spontaneous. (2) POs sometimes regarded a causal factor as a mitigating circumstance deserving a more lenient recommendation. (3) The type of account could affect the type of recommendation. For example, in some cases a claim that alcohol or drugs led to the commission of an offense encouraged the PO to recommend counseling rather than incarceration. (4) In lieu of information to the contrary, POs did not usually accept non-rational accounts since they mitigate some of the defendant's responsibility. Thus, defendants who offered rational accounts were generally viewed as cooperative and responsible; those who made (unwarranted) claims to non-rational accounts were seen as presenting a "line."

2) Attitudes toward the Offense

POs generally viewed any offense which resulted in a conviction as a serious affair. For example, POs viewed with concern the theft of even a few inexpensive items from a store because such losses to stores create higher prices for customers. Similarly, pranks were defined as serious since they usually involved theft or property damage, or both.

POs regarded as relevant two basic components of defendants' attitudes toward their offense—their attitude toward the wrongfulness of the act and toward the seriousness of the act. Defendants who accepted that their behavior was wrong or illegal, and who shared the PO's definition that their behavior was serious, were viewed as holding an acceptable attitude.

In addition, POs regarded defendants' attitudes as indicators of underlying character or behavior traits. Thus, defendants who exhibited acceptable attitudes were viewed as possessing some generally redeeming traits which made them less likely to commit subsequent offenses. POs viewed unacceptable attitudes, however, as cause for more severe sanctions, since they believed that such defendants were more likely to become recidivists.[4] In addition, defendants who did not even pay lip service to acceptable attitudes in presenting interviews were seen as not taking the proceedings seriously—in effect, an improper demeanor.

3) Attitudes toward the Consequences

POs expected defendants to anticipate the effects of their behavior. That is, if a certain behavioral option was expected to have negative consequences, this was supposed to act as at least a partial deterrent to that behavior. Thus, POs regarded defendants' attitudes toward the consequences of their behavior as related to their likelihood of recidivism. Two sets of consequences are relevant: (1) the possible legal sanctions; and (2) the non-legal, negative effects of a criminal record on current or future endeavors. In both instances, POs considered an acceptable attitude one in which the defendant expressed concern about these consequences. This concern included both an awareness of the likelihood of the consequences and of their adverse nature.

4) Attitudes toward Changing Their Behavior

POs believed that people do not engage in serious violations of the law under normal circumstances. The corollary of this maxim was that serious violations were the result or manifestation of some problem, to which there was an identifiable solution. In this regard, POs viewed as relevant non-legal solutions which defendants could pursue. In an important sense, POs viewed how defendants felt about these solutions as an indication of their attitudes toward changing their criminal behavior. When defendants offered non-rational accounts for their offenses, solutions were sought for the particular causal factor. For example, if an offense was caused by a defendant's alcoholism, the PO addressed solutions which the defendant could pursue and which would alleviate the problem, such as counseling. However, when rational accounts were offered, the POs located the problem in the defendant's choices of behaviors, and attention was focused on identifying more appropriate (legal) alternatives. For example, one defendant accounted for his theft of food by saying he was out of money and hadn't eaten in two days. The PO tried to point out to the defendant that there were legal alternatives available, such as welfare, which would have solved his problem. In either case, if defendants expressed a willingness to pursue a solution, they were viewed as possessing acceptable attitudes toward changing their behavior.

POs viewed as acceptable three attitudes by defendants toward changing their behavior: (1) Defendants were expected to express concern about the particular factor (causal or motivating) which had been identified. (2) They were expected to express an awareness of an appropriate solution. (3) They were expected to express a willingness to pursue these solutions—that is, demonstrate that these solutions were viewed as both feasible and desirable. POs viewed defendants who expressed these acceptable attitudes as less likely to commit further offenses, since they were more likely to solve the problem and thus change their behavior. In these cases, sentence recommendations were less severe, since legal sanctions were less necessary as a deterrent.

NEGOTIATIONS BETWEEN PROBATION OFFICERS AND DEFENDANTS

In addition to legal and extra-legal factors, POs took into account defendants' subjective orientations to criminal behavior in deciding what sentence to recommend. POs elicited most information about legal and extra-legal factors by asking defendants simple questions. However, POs elicited information about subjective orientations in a more complex way. They engaged defendants in a process of negotiation aimed at reaching a shared agreement which at least approximated the POs' notions of propriety or acceptability. In conducting these negotiations, POs used a variety of interactional strategies to seek desired responses in each of the four subjective orientations.[5]

1) Accounts for the Offenses

The POs generally viewed rational accounts as more reasonable and acceptable than non-rational accounts. Therefore, when they requested accounts from defendants, their questions implied or assumed a request for a rational account. The POs used two strategies in requesting such accounts.

1) They asked a question which implied a decision-making process on the part of the defendant (D).

PO: Why'dja decide to take the motorcycle?

2) They asked a series of indirect questions in an attempt to establish the conditions for a rational account.

PO: You knew you were on probation when you did this.
D: Uh huh.
PO: Did that concern you at all? Did you think about that?

Through either of these strategies, the POs attempted to elicit a rational account from the defendants. If the defendants' responses confirmed the

POs' assumptions about such an account, the negotiation was concluded. However, when responses did not confirm that assumption, the negotiation took a different format.

The defendants were viewed by POs as more likely to offer a non-rational account, in the hope of mitigating some responsibility on their part. Due to this, the POs responded to such accounts with an additional request to establish specific conditions for a rational account.

PO: Why'dja decide to take the motorcycle?
D: Uh, its stupidity. We were messing around and then—and we didn't have no reason.
PO: What were you gonna do with it?

If the response to this request still contained a claim to a non-rational account, the PO turned to a series of questions in an attempt to establish conditions for that type of account.

PO: What were you gonna do with [the motorcycle]?
D: I don't know.
PO: How drunk or high were ya?
D: I was still aware of what was goin on.
PO: What did you have to drink or smoke that night?
D: Uhm, we'd been drinking beer and smoking marijuana; and going around to different parties all that night.

Only when such conditions were established did the PO accept a non-rational account.

While the POs accepted claims to rational accounts unconditionally, claims to non-rational accounts were not so readily accepted. Further, while they made direct requests for rational accounts, requests for non-rational accounts were only approached in a piecemeal fashion which did not allow the defendant to make a singular, direct claim to that type of account.

2) Attitudes toward the Offenses

While the POs defined defendants' offenses as wrong and serious enough to be concerned about, defendants did not always share this definition. The POs used four strategies in trying to obtain defendants' agreement with their definition of criminal offenses.

1) The POs would request examples of behaviors which defendants felt were subsumed under the latters' definition. The PO would then show the defendants that these behaviors were actually examples of the POs definition of the offense.

D: I realize there's a difference between stealing and a college prank.
PO: Give me another example of a college prank—a legitimate college prank.
D: Another thing [people on] my [dormitory] floor have done, which I think is worse than the thing that I did, and that's paintin' a bridge outside of the

front of the dorm, which is not the dorm's property. It's university property. That's permanently defacing it. I would say [this] is a college prank that was worse than the one I did.

PO: So there's somethin' you would call a prank that you admitted was wrong. It's probably a criminal offense, yet you think they're mainly college pranks.

The effectiveness of this strategy lay in the POs ability to convince the defendants that, since these examples can be subsumed under the POs definition, so could the defendants' current offenses.

2) The POs pointed out the seriousness of the offenses' potential or actual harm to others. For example, one defendant was convicted of shoplifting after eating candy while shopping and not paying for it.

PO: Why didn't you pay for [the candy]?

D: Where I come from, people do this all the time—"try it before you buy it." I've always done it. Everyone does it where I come from. No one considers it a crime. It's like spitting or littering; there's some obscure law against it.

PO: Ya know, if everybody did that the store is out a lot of money and they're gonna pass that loss on to the customers. I'm not real happy about the prospects of paying higher prices so you can eat the candy.

This strategy pointed out to defendants that their behaviors were not isolated events, but rather had consequences for other people. In this way, the POs attempted to validate their claim to the definition of offenses as serious and wrong.

3) The POs argued that other aspects of the defendants' behaviors associated with the commission of the offenses were wrong and, in some cases, could also have been charged as criminal offenses. They did this in the hope of convincing the defendants that the acts they had been charged with were wrong and worthy of concern. For example, a teenage university student and his friends were drinking late one night. They decided to climb over the fence surrounding the university football stadium and "play some football." To prove they had been there, they decided to take a soft drink canister back to the dormitory. The defendant was subsequently arrested and convicted of theft. Throughout the presentencing interview, the defendant steadfastly denied that what he had done was wrong or should have been charged as a criminal offense.

PO: Did ya know that you were also doing what's known as criminal trespass? What'd you do, climb over the fence?

D: Yeah. I considered that a college prank, too.

PO: Ya know that's another Class A misdemeanor. That's another year in jail if they charge you with that. You were committing a crime just by being there. Then you chose to steal something. You were drinking beer—that's another offense [since you were underage]. I mean you were doing a whole series of things here which resulted in your getting arrested.

4) The POs pointed out the potential legal consequences of a conviction. For example, one defendant presented a particularly cavalier attitude

toward both his current and previous offenses. The PO seemed to think that this attitude was bolstered by the fact that the defendant had reached a plea agreement with the prosecutor. According to the agreement, in exchange for the defendant's guilty plea, the prosecutor would not argue for a severe sentence at the sentencing hearing. In addition, the PO thought the defendant "was high on something" during the interview.

PO: Do you have any prior criminal record as a juvenile?
D: Yes. I don't know what it all is. It's not very much, probably four charges—stupid charges like common nuisance, vandalism, vehicle theft, and I don't know what. Probably one or two more after that.
PO: Do you know that with a [class] C Felony you can get eight years?
D: I know.
PO: You realize if you get probation, which [there] is no guarantee you will, that plea agreement don't mean nothin' till it's accepted, alright?
D: Uh huh.
PO: Only thing this plea agreement does.... Look, you're looking at two-to-eight [years], OK? All this plea agreement's gonna do—instead of the prosecutor getting up there and wanting your ass for eight years he's gonna stand mute. He's not gonna argue anything one way or another, but you can still be given the full amount. Do you understand that?
D: Yes, sir.
PO: Where they'll send ya ain't like boy's school. You're an adult now and you're gonna be treated as such.

The POs generally felt that this strategy was effective, even when other strategies had failed, since the prospects of incarceration and/or a substantial fine was enough "to get the attention of most of the people."

3) Attitudes toward Consequences

Often the defendants had not considered the specific consequences of their convictions. The strategies the POs used in negotiating these attitudes were indirect and based on a lay version of cognitive dissonance theory (Festinger, 1957). The POs believed that if the defendants came to express acceptable attitudes "on their own, it [would] mean more to them," and they would be more inclined to act according to these acceptable attitudes than if the POs had directly presented these attitudes for their consideration. To this end the POs used two strategies.

1) The POs used defendants' expressions of an appropriate orientation to address another orientation.

D: So, I mean, I'm really scared this is on my record, 'cause I want to go to law school, ya know, like my old man, and I've heard that you can't get into law school if you have a criminal record.
PO: Does the possible sentence worry you any?
D: I couldn't care less about the sentence.
PO: Could you care less about a year of your life in jail?

D: I would be concerned about that, yes.
PO: So you are concerned about the sentence?
D: Yeah, I'm concerned about the sentence. I wanna go to school, ya know, and I don't want my dad to know.

The POs used this strategy to indicate to defendants that the attitude they expressed toward the first topic was also appropriate for the second one.

2) The POs linked background information about the defendants to the topic currently under negotiation.

PO: Have you thought about what [your conviction] is gonna do to your chances of getting into med school?
D: From the second I got out of the [store].
PO: And?
D: It's, it's gonna hurt me bad. There's a real good possibility they'd kick me out.

In this example, the defendant had been convicted of shoplifting. The PO had learned in a previous part of the interview that the defendant planned to go to medical school and used this information in negotiating his attitudes toward the consequences of his offense. This strategy was particularly effective; it pointed out to defendants that the things they valued had been placed in jeopardy by their behavior.

4) Attitudes toward Changing Their Behavior

The POs used three indirect strategies in trying to get defendants to change their behavior. Which strategy the POs used was determined by the outcome of the negotiations over accounts.

1) When the POs and the defendants had reached agreement on a rational account, the POs used strategies which addressed alternative courses of action, ones which would have allowed the defendants to achieve their goal without breaking the law. In other words, the POs tried to make the defendants aware of legal (and, therefore, more desirable) alternatives to the particular courses of action they had chosen. The goal was to find solutions to the problem of the defendant's criminal behavior. A typical question in this strategy was:

PO: Think there might've been a way to avoid this?

2) When a non-rational account had been agreed upon, the POs used a strategy which allowed the defendants to consider courses of action which would alleviate or overcome the causal factor responsible for the offense. In addition, since a non-rational account mitigated some of the defendant's responsibility, the POs attempted to get the defendants to take some responsibility in solving the problem itself.

PO: Do you think alcohol is the root of your problems?
D: Yeah. I think its got a lot to do with it because I don't have no juvenile record at all or nothin'. It's only been while I've been drinking.
PO: What have you done to work on your drinking problem?
D: I tried to get away from it but I can't. It's just like on Sunday night. [The bar] opens up about noon and I can't wait to go up there and start drinkin'.
PO: If you knew this was a problem, why didn't you go get some help?

3) When no mutually satisfactory account had been agreed upon, the POs addressed this orientation in a different way. Since no problem had been identified, rather than addressing solutions, the POs addressed the defendant's risk of recidivism. They challenged the defendants to offer reasons why they would not be likely to commit a crime in the future. In this way, the defendants were asked to provide prospective accounts for their behavior.

PO: Why don't you tell me what you would like the judge to know about you; why you did these [crimes]; and what's to convince us you're not gonna keep stealing. Sounds to me like you've got sticky fingers.
D: Uhm, I know I won't do it again.
PO: Why not?
D: 'Cause ya know, I'm doin' too much for myself now, lots of things that I wouldn't want to lose. I have a full time job and friends that I admire are trying to teach me to stay out of trouble.

NEGOTIATING LABELS

> [Accounts] presuppose an identifiable speaker and audience. The particular identities of the interactants must often be established as part of the encounter in which the account is presented. In other words, people generate role identities for one another in social situations.... Every account is a manifestation of underlying negotiation of identities (Scott and Lyman, 1968:58).

I have argued that defendants' accounts of their offenses, as well as other subjective orientations, are subject to negotiation during presentencing interviews. Analysis revealed that these subjective orientations are one of the central components of a typology of defendants which POs possessed and used in making sentence recommendations. I posit, therefore, that *in the process of negotiating subjective orientations, the PO and the defendant were simultaneously negotiating the particular defendant type that the former would use to define the latter.*

In the bureaucratic processing of defendants this type can be conceptualized as a *label* which POs attached to defendants for the purpose of making sentence recommendations. Thus, the POs did not so much process individuals as they *processed types of individuals who had been labeled in particular ways.* The particular label attached to an individual defendant depended on the POs' linking of characteristics of the individuals with characteristics of the general category or type.[6]

Ethnographic data revealed that, in making sentence recommendations, POs used a three-fold typology of criminal defendants which was based on the defendants' risk of recidivism.

1) Low-risk defendants were usually in trouble with the criminal justice system for the first time, were between the ages of 18 and 25, and were either attending university or had a steady job. These defendants, therefore, had much to lose by possessing a criminal record and they took their current involvement with the courts seriously. As one PO put it, "These people have made one screwy mistake and it's shaken them up so much we'll probably never see them again." For example, one defendant had been convicted of attempted theft after he had altered a sales receipt to obtain items he hadn't paid for. This defendant was unusually cooperative during the interview and expressed concern about the fact that business associates and local bankers would find out about the criminal record he now possessed. His PO told me, "I don't think we'll see him come through here again. This was his first offense and I think it really made an impression on him."

2) High-risk defendants usually had at least two prior arrests and convictions, little formal education, and were seen as unwilling or unable to hold a steady job. Often, they were perceived as not taking their involvement with the courts seriously. For these reasons, POs saw these defendants as likely to be in and out of trouble for much of their adult lives. For example, a defendant had been convicted of burglary and had several other theft-related convictions. In addition, he had never held a job for more than three months at a time. The PO who handled the case told me:

   > This [defendant] is just too lazy to work.... He commits these burglaries because of that. I'll bet ya we see this guy again. He's definitely [high-risk] material.

3) The final category of defendants consisted of individuals whose risk of recidivism was neither definitely high nor low, but was seen as problematic. Some of these defendants had been in trouble with the law before, generally involving minor offenses such as shoplifting. Others possessed characteristics such as alcoholism or a "bad attitude" which POs considered likely to be related to future criminal behavior. While there was no specific set of characteristics which defined this category of defendants, POs pointed out that what they did share was the potential for "heading for trouble." For example, a defendant had been convicted of theft and had two prior theft-related offenses. However, he also was working two jobs to pay off a student loan and return to

the university. The PO described the defendant's risk of recidivism in the following way:

> It's hard to tell with him. He's got these [prior offenses], but he's got these things [two jobs, a car] going for him. If he was in a situation where he could steal, I don't know.

What was important for POs was that, whatever the problem, these defendants were "workable." As one PO put it:

> I spend the most time with these [defendants]. I try to make them aware of alternatives . . . or refer them for heavy-duty counseling, or do some things myself so hopefully they won't get in trouble again.

By the time POs began negotiations with defendants, they already possessed information about their criminal records and background. Thus, they had already formed initial impressions of the defendants, and had attached to them a provisional label on the basis of available information. What remained to be accomplished in the interview was to attach an unambiguous label upon which a sentence recommendation could be based.

The initial label was provisional for three reasons: (1) POs only possessed partial information about defendants. (2) Labels based on prior information could be misleading. Thus, some defendants had all the "objective" indicators of a low-risk defendant, yet may have exhibited unacceptable attitudes associated with problematic or high-risk defendants. The converse was also true. (3) In some cases the background information may have been too ambiguous to allow even a provisional labeling. For example, a defendant may have had the criminal record of a high-risk defendant, yet also have had low-risk characteristics such as a steady job or a college degree. In these cases, the determining characteristics may have been the defendants' subjective orientations.

POs used various strategies in negotiating reasonable or acceptable responses with defendants for each subjective orientation. At the aggregate level of types, however, with each verbal expression of an orientation, defendants were making claim to a certain defendant type. Thus, expressing concern about the consequences of the offense functioned as a claim to a low-risk defendant, while an unwillingness to accept the POs' definition of the offense as serious and wrong served as a claim to a high-risk defendant. These claims to defendant types were always relative to the initial impression the PO had of a defendant. A defendant initially labeled as high-risk who expressed consistently acceptable orientations was (in the eyes of the PO) making claim to a type of defendant whose risk was problematic (a change in label from high-risk to low-risk being unlikely). On the other hand, a defendant initially labeled low-risk who offered unacceptable orientations was seen as jeopardizing that label in favor of one of the others. For example, a defendant with various characteristics of a low-risk defendant (university student, relatively wealthy background, no prior record) presented consistently unacceptable orientations. After the negotiations, the PO labeled the defendant as one whose risk of recidivism was problematic, based largely on his "bad attitude."

While POs and defendants negotiated the labels that the former attached to the latter, this was not accomplished directly. Rather, it was accomplished piecemeal by negotiating the individual components of that label. Consider the following example.

PO: Didn't the time that you spent a day in jail over the [shoplifting] thing have any impact on you when you decided to steal the motorcycle? Didn't you think about that at all? Did you think about what might happen if you got caught?
D: To be truthful, as far as I remember, I didn't even think about that.
PO: You didn't even consider it. Did you realize you can go to prison for four years?
D: I do now, yes.
PO: How does that feel?
D: I wouldn't want that to happen.
PO: Do you realize that's a possibility?
D: Yes.
PO: Was it worth it?
D: No, not at all.

On the surface level, the PO and the defendant were negotiating the latter's attitude toward the consequences of his offense. However, at the aggregate level of types of defendants, the PO's strategies functioned to say, "By saying this, you are claiming to be a high-risk defendant; if you are that type, how do you feel about this?" In most cases, POs closed the negotiations when they reached a point where they could accomplish an unambiguous labeling of the defendants which made sense, given their linking of the defendant's characteristics with those characteristics of the more general type which was being assigned to the case. As Cicourel (1978:28) argues, this linking or articulation is accomplished by using abductive reasoning, that is, the "... inferential step that occurs in first stating and then reflecting upon a hypothesis that would choose among several possible explanations of some set of facts."

CONCLUSIONS

My findings suggest three implications for future research on POs. First, I have argued that research on POs has failed to recognize the existence of a third set of factors—defendants' subjective orientations—in sentencing recommendations. My findings suggest that POs treat the components of this set of factors in ways qualitatively different from other sets of factors. They elicited these factors in different ways. These factors affected the impression the PO formed of the defendant. They also affected the particular sentencing recommendation made by the PO. A consideration of this set of factors is important for a full explanation of the outcome of this particular aspect of the criminal justice system.

Second, my findings point to the need for research on the interaction between POs and defendants. I believe that one of the reasons subjective orientations have been largely ignored in the past is that they are only directly accessible through a detailed analysis of this discourse between POs and defendants. When such factors as attitudes have been considered in previous research, they have been treated as stable entities rather than as entities subject to manipulation, as I have found. More generally, a lack of understanding about these negotiations leaves us with a lack of understanding about one of the crucial aspects of the *processes* involved in presentencing interviews.

Finally, my findings point to the need to include ethnographic data in studies of criminal justice processes. In this paper, I focused on both actual discourse processes as well as background ethnographic data. Much of my analysis would have been speculative had it not been for the insights I gained from detailed ethnographic information.[7] Knowledge of the categories POs use is crucial for understanding their actions and decisions concerning defendants and probationers, since these categories are involved in a process of typing in which POs subsume individual cases under more general categories.

Notes

1. There are, of course, exceptions. For example, Cicourel (1968) empirically examined the routine practices of police and POs in the processing of juvenile cases. Prus and Stratton (1976) delineate a process model of how parole officers move from individual definitions to official action.

2. I excluded the juvenile division because of the high degree of confidentiality surrounding juvenile cases in the county. I would not have been allowed access to certain data, and POs anticipated some difficulty in obtaining consent from the juveniles' parents. Substance-abuse was excluded because its goals and focus (clinical evaluation and counseling) were distinct from the rest of the divisions' goals of sentencing recommendations and supervision. While this data would have been valuable for comparative analysis, the lack of sufficient time and other resources precluded such an expansion of the present study.

3. These two types of accounts, and two others (opportunistic and pathological), form a typology of accounts obtained by intersecting the types of factors with degree of intent. Thus, an opportunistic account involved motivating factors and no prior planning, while a pathological account was one in which defendants claimed the offense was due to causal factors but in which they engaged in prior planning. While these latter two types of accounts are logical possibilities, they rarely occurred in the data and, thus, were not particularly important for this study.

4. I am not aware of any research which addresses this issue. However, the POs held this view because unacceptable attitudes were common among defendants who were, or became, recidivists.

5. It should be noted that these negotiations were primarily invoked by POs when defendants expressed unreasonable or unacceptable orientations. When a defendant expressed an acceptable or reasonable orientation the need for negotiation on that point was precluded and the POs introduced another topic. The majority of strategies discussed below were used by

POs in attempting to change (or assess the possibility of changing) defendants' orientations when they were deemed unacceptable.

6. Sudnow (1965) makes the same argument regarding public defenders and their processing of clients. He argues that the goal of their interactions with clients is an assessment of the applicability of characteristics of "normal crimes" with an instant case.

7. See Corsaro (1982) for a detailed discussion of the importance of ethnography in the analysis of discourse processes.

References

Becker, Howard

1963 Outsiders: Studies in the Sociology of Deviance. New York: Free Press.

Bernstein, Ilene, William Kelly, and Patricia Doyle

1977 "Social reactions to deviants: The case of criminal defendants." American Sociological Review 42(5):743–755.

Bonger, Willem

1916 Criminality and Economic Conditions. Translated by Henry P. Horton. Boston: Little, Brown.

Burke, Peter, and Austin Turk

1975 "Factors affecting post-arrest dispositions: A model for analysis." Social Problems 22(3):313–332.

Carter, Robert

1967 "The presentence report and the decision-making process." Journal of Research in Crime and Delinquency 4(2):203–211.

Chiricos, Theodore, and Gordon Waldo

1975 "Socioeconomic status and criminal sentencing: An empirical assessment of a conflict proposition." American Sociological Review 40(6):753–772.

Cicourel, Aaron

1968 The Social Organization of Juvenile Justice. New York: Wiley and Sons.

1975 "Discourse and text: Cognitive, and linguistic processes in studies of social structure." Versus: Quaderni di studi Semiotica, September–December: 33–84.

1978 "Language and society: Cognitive, cultural, and linguistic aspects of language use." Social wissenschaftliche Annalen Band 2, Seite B25–B58. Physica–Verlag, Wien.

1980 "Three models of discourse analysis: The role of social structure." Discourse Processes 3(2): 102–132.

Cloward, Richard, and Lloyd Ohlin

1960 Delinquency and Opportunity: A Theory of Delinquent Gangs. Glencoe, Ill.: Free Press.

Corsaro, William

1982 "Something old and something new: The importance of prior ethnography in the collection and analysis of audiovisual data." Sociological Methods and Research 11(2):145–166.

Dembo, Richard

1972 "Orientations and activities of parole officers." Criminology 10(4): 193–215.

Festinger, Leon

1957 A Theory of Cognitive Dissonance. Evanston, Ill.: Row, Peterson.

Glaser, Barney, and Anselm Strauss

1967 The Discovery of Grounded Theory. Chicago: Aldine.

Gross, Seymour
1967 "The prehearing juvenile report: Probation officers' conceptions." Journal of Research in Crime and Delinquency 4(2):212–217.
Hagan, John
1977 "Criminal justice in rural and urban communities: A study of the bureaucratization of justice." Social Forces 55(3):597–612.
Lemert, Edwin
1951 Social Pathology. New York: McGraw-Hill.
Merton, Robert
1957 Social Theory and Social Structure. Glencoe, Ill.: Free Press.
Prus, Robert, and John Stratton
1976 "Parole revocation decision-making: Private typings and official designations." Federal Probation 40(1):48–53.
Reed, John, and Charles King
1966 "Factors in the decision-making of North Carolina probation officers." Journal of Research in Crime and Delinquency 3(2):120–128.
Schur, Edwin
1971 Labeling Deviant Behavior. New York: Harper and Row.
Scott, Marvin, and Stanford Lyman
1968 "Accounts." American Sociological Review 33(1):46–62.
Sellin, Thorsten
1938 Culture, Conflict, and Crime. New York: Social Science Research Council.
Sudnow, David
1965 "Normal crimes: Sociological features of the penal code." Social Problems 12(3):255–276.
Tannenbaum, Frank
1938 Crime and the Community. Boston: Ginn.

28 / Court Responses to Skid Row Alcoholics

JACQUELINE P. WISEMAN

* * *

Matching sentences with men who plead guilty is thus the judge's true concern. This task must be handled within the pressures created by restricting drunk court to a morning session in one courtroom, regardless of the number of men scheduled to be seen that day.

Up until last year (when drunk arrests were temporarily reduced because of the large number of hippies and civil rights demonstrators in jail), 50 to 250 men were often sentenced within a few hours. Appearance before the judge was handled in platoons of five to 50. This meant the judge decided the fate of each defendant within a few short minutes. Thus judicial compassion attained assembly-line organization and speed.

As a court observer noted:

> The Court generally disposes of between 50 and 100 cases per day, but on any Monday there are 200 to 250 and on Monday mornings after holiday weekends the Court may handle as many as 350 cases. I would estimate that, on the average, cases take between 45 seconds and one minute to dispose of.[1]

Later, with drunk arrests drastically curtailed, the court handled no more than 50 cases in an average morning, and perhaps 125 on the weekends, according to the observer.[2] Right after a civil rights demonstration that resulted in many arrests, only 33 persons were observed in drunk court. This reduction in the quantity of defendants, however, did not appear to increase the length of time spent on each person. Rather, it seemed to reduce it. The observer noted the average length of time per person was 30 seconds, although the size of platoons was reduced from 50 to 15 or 20.

SENTENCING CRITERIA

How is the judge able to classify and sentence a large, unwieldy group of defendants so quickly? The answer is he utilizes social characteristics as indicators to signify drinking status—just as in an arrest situation the policeman looked for social characteristics to identify alcoholic trouble-making potential, combined with the arrestee's legal impotence. The effect is essentially the same: the men are objectified into social types for easy classification. In the case of the judge, the legal decision process must be more refined than for a policeman's arrest, no-arrest decision. Therefore, the judge's sentencing criteria are more complex, as they must include all possible decision combinations.

From court observations, plus interviews with court officers and judges, three primary criteria for typing defendants in drunk court emerge:

The General Physical Appearance of the Man

Is he shaky and obviously in need of drying out? Here, some of the judges ask the men to extend their hands before sentencing and decide the sentence on the degree of trembling.

Physical appearance may actually be the most potent deciding factor. As one court officer put it, when asked how the judges decide on a sentence:

> Primarily by appearance. You can tell what kind of shape they're in. If they're shaking and obviously need drying out, you know some are on the verge of the DT's so these get 10 to 15 days [in jail] to dry out....

One of the seasoned judges said that his criteria were as follows:

> I rely on his record and also his "looks." Their "looks" are very important. I make them put their hands out—see if they are dirty and bloody in appearance.[3]

Past Performance

How many times have they been up before the court on a drunk charge before? A record of past arrests is considered to be indicative of the defendant's general attitude toward drinking. The longer and more recent the record, the greater the need for a sentence to aid the defendant to improve his outlook on excessive liquor consumption. (This is in some contradiction to the presumed greater need the man must have for drying out, since previous recent jailings mean that he could not have been drinking for long.)

The previous comment, plus the answer by a court officer to the question, "Who gets dismissed?" illustrates this criteria for sentencing:

> A person with no previous arrests [gets dismissed]. If they have had no arrests, then the judge hates for them to have a conviction on their record. *The more arrests they've had and the more recently they've had them, the more likely they are to get another sentence.* (Emphasis mine.)...

The Man's Social Position

Does he have a job he could go to? Is he married? Does he have a permanent address, or will he literally be on the streets if he receives a dismissal?

For these data, dress is an all-important clue, age a secondary one. A man who looks down-and-out is more likely to receive a sentence than the well-dressed man. According to a court officer:

> If they look pretty beat—clothes dirty and in rags, then you figure that they need some help to stop drinking before they kill themselves....
>
> If they're under 21 we usually given them a kick-out. If they are a business man or a lawyer we have them sign a civil release so they can't sue and let them go....

An observer reports that a judge freed a young man with the following remarks:

> I am going to give you a suspended sentence and hope that this experience will be a warning to you. I don't want you to get caught up in this cycle....

Transients form a category of their own and get a special package deal—if they will promise to leave town, they draw a suspended sentence or probation. The parallel between this practice and the police policy of telling some Skid Row drunks to "take a walk" need only be mentioned. The following interchanges are illustrative:

Judge: I thought you told me the last time you were in here that you were going to leave Pacific City.
Defendant: I was supposed to have left town yesterday. I just got through doing time.
Judge: Go back to Woodland. Don't let me see you in here again or we are going to put you away. Thirty days suspended....
Defendant: I am supposed to leave with the circus tomorrow. If I don't go, I will be out of work for the whole season.
Judge: You promised to leave three times before. Thirty days in the County Jail....

By combining the variables of physical appearance, past performance, and social position, a rough description of social types expected in drunk court, and matching sentences for each type is shown in Table 1.

OTHER SENTENCING ASSISTANCE

Even with the aid of a simplified mental guide, the judge cannot be expected to assemble and assimilate sufficient material on each man, review it, mentally type the man, and then make a sentencing decision in less than a minute. Thus, it is not surprising that almost all drunk court judges employ the aid of one assistant and sometimes two court attachés who are familiar with the Row and its inhabitants. These men are known as court liaison officers. Because of personal familiarity with chronic drunkenness offenders, the liaison officers are able to answer questions about each accused person quickly and to recommend a case disposition. Such persons obviously operate as an informal screening board.

Table 1 / Paradigm of Social Types and Sentences in Drunk Court

Social Type	*Probable Sentence*
A young man who drank too much: a man under 40, with a job, and perhaps a wife, who has not appeared in court before.	A kick-out or a suspended sentence.
The young repeater: same as above, but has been before judge several times (may be on way to being an alcoholic).	Suspended sentence or short sentence (five–ten days) to scare him, or possible attendance at Alcoholism School.
The repeater who still looks fairly respectable. (Image vacillating between an alcholic and a drunk.)	30-day suspended sentence, with possible attendance at Alcoholism School.
Out-of-towner (social characteristics not important as they have nonlocal roots). Therefore not important as to whether overindulged, a chronic drunk, or an alcoholic.	Suspended sentence on condition he leave town. Purpose is to discourage him from getting on local loop and adding to taxpayer's load.
The middle-aged repeater who has not been up for some time. (May be an alcoholic who has relapsed.)	Suspended sentence with required attendance at Alcoholism School or given to custody of Christian Missionaries.
The derelict-drunk who looks "rough," i.e., suffering withdrawal, a hangover, has cuts and bruises, may have malnutrition or some diseases connected with heavy drinking and little eating; a chronic drunk; seedy clothing, stubble beard, etc.	30–60–90 day sentence depending on number of prior arrests and physical condition at time of arrest. (Has probably attended Alcoholism School already.)
The man who looks gravely ill (probably a chronic alcoholic).	County hospital under suspended sentence.

The most important court helper in Pacific City is a man who knows most of the Row men by sight and claims also to know their general outlook on alcohol and life. Known to the defendants as "the Rapper," this man often sits behind the judge and suggests informally who would benefit most from probation and assignment to Alcoholism School, who might need the "shaking-up" that jail provides, and who ought to be sent to alcoholic screening at City Hospital and perhaps on to State Mental Hospital. As each man is named, the Rapper whispers to the judge, who then passes sentence.[4]

In Pacific City, the man who was the Rapper for a period of time was an ex-alcoholic who could claim intimate knowledge of the chronic drunkenness offender because he had drunk with them. A relative of the Rapper was highly placed in city politics, and the Rapper made no secret of the fact that his appointment was politically engineered.[5] During the course of the study (several times in fact), the Rapper himself "fell off the wagon" and underwent treatment at Northern State Mental Hospital, one of the stations on the loop. While there, the Rapper told about his recent job with the court and how he helped the judge:

> Each man arrested has a card with the whole record on it. We would go over the cards before the case came up. We see how many times he's been arrested. I could advise the judge to give them probation or a sentence. Many times, the family would call and request a sentence. I would often arrange for them to get probation plus clothes and a place to stay at one of the halfway houses. Oh, I'll help and help, but when they keep falling off—I get disgusted.[6]

The Christian Missionaries also send a liaison man to the drunk court sessions. He acts as Rapper at special times and thereby also serves in an informal screening capacity. Sponsorship by this organization appears to guarantee that the defendant will get a suspended sentence. For instance, this interchange was observed in court several times:

Judge: turning to Missionary representative: "Do you want him [this defendant]?" (Meaning, "Will you take him at one of your facilities?")
Missionary: (Nods "Yes.")
Judge: "Suspended sentence." . . .

Another observer discussed this arrangement with a veteran judge:

Interviewer: *Isn't there any attempt made to consider the men for rehabilitation?* The men are screened by the Christian Missionaries usually. The Christian Missionaries send someone down to the jail who tries to help them. They talk with the men and screen them. Nobody does the job that the Christian Missionaries do in the jails.
Interviewer: *The Court abdicates the screening of defendants to the Christian Missionaries, then?* Not completely. We try to keep a record. Some of these men we can help but most we can't. I know by heart all of their alibis and stories.[7]

Another important informal court post is filled by an employee who is known to some of the men as "the Knocker." The job of the Knocker is to maintain the personal records of the men who appear before drunk court and to supply the judge with this information. A court observer reported the following:

> The Knocker spoke to the judge in just about every case. However, I do not know what he said. He may just be reading to the judge the official records, or he may be giving his personal judgment about the possibility of the defendant being picked up again in the near future. One thing seems clear: the judge receives his information from the Knocker just before he hands out the sentence.

Sometimes it is difficult to distinguish the Knocker (who merely gives information to the judge) from the Rapper (who "suggests" the proper sentence). In 1963, two of these court liaison officers worked together. An interview with one partner is quoted below:

Interviewer: *What do you do?*

Up here we act as a *combination district attorney and public defender.* We are more familiar with these guys than the judges are. The judges alternate. We have the previous arrest records. A lot of times, guys will give phony names. It may take us a while to catch up with them. We try to remember if we have seen a guy before. (Emphasis mine.)

Interviewer: *How does a judge decide whether to sentence the men and if so, for how long?*

We help him out on that. If a guy has been in three times in four weeks, they should get a minimum of 30 days. They need to dry out. You know, if a man has been arrested three times in four weeks, you ask yourself the question: "How many times has he been drunk that he wasn't arrested?" Also, you look at the condition of a man—he may even need hospitalization.

Interviewer: *You mean you can tell whether a man ought to be sent to jail by looking at him?*

Some of them look a lot more rough looking than others. You can tell they have been on a drunk for more than one day. They are heavily bearded. They have probably been sleeping in doorways or on the street. You can tell they have been on a long drunk....

Thus perhaps the most revealing aspect of the sentencing procedure is the virtual absence of interest in the *charge* and the judge's role as spokesman for the court officer's decision. This may account for the fact the judge seldom discusses the case with the defendant, except in a jocular, disparaging way.... The following interchanges, which illustrate this attitude, were witnessed by observers:

Defendant: I was sleeping in a basement when a man attacked me with a can opener.
Judge: Did you also see elephants?...
Judge: What is your story this time?
Defendant: (As he begins to speak, Judge interrupts.)
Judge: You gave me that line yesterday; 30 days in the County Jail....

JUSTIFYING THE SENTENCING PROCESS

How does the municipal court judge, serving in drunk court sessions, allow himself to be a party to such extra-legal activities as platoon sentencing, the heavy reliance on advice from "friends of the court," and the utilization of extraneous social characteristics in setting the sentence? Why is there not a conflict with his self-image of judicial compassion for the individual and scrupulous attention to legal niceties?

For some judges, this conflict is resolved by falling back on the alcoholism-as-an-illness view of drunkenness, and by redefining many of the men who appear before him as *patients* rather than defendants. Thus, when asked to describe their duties, drunk court judges often sound like physicians dealing with troublesome patients for whom they must prescribe unpleasant but necessary medicine, rather than judges punishing men for being a public annoyance. As an example of this:

> I know that jail isn't the best place for these men, but we have to do something for them. We need to put them someplace where they can dry out. You can't just let a man go out and kill himself. . . .

> This is a grave and almost hopeless problem. But you have to try some kind of treatment. Often they are better off in jail than out on the street. . . .

The drunk court judges sometimes add the wish that the city provided a more palatable alternative to the County Jail, but then reiterate the view that it is better than no help at all.

Court attachés have essentially the same attitude:

> Some of these guys are so loaded that they will fall and break their skull if you don't lock them up. Half of these guys have no place to stay anyway except a dingy heap. They are better off in jail. . . .

> The whole purpose of the law is to try to help them. It's for the protection of themselves and for others, that's the way the law reads. For example, say you're driving through here [Skid Row] and you hit a drunk. He could get killed and if you don't stop and render aid, you could become a criminal. . . .

> Giving them 30 days in County Jail is sometimes a kindness. *You are doing them a favor, like a diabetic who won't take his insulin.* Sometimes you must hurt him to help him. (Emphasis mine.) . . .

Like the Skid Row police, the officers, the judge and his coterie are reinforced in their definition of the situation as clinical, and of themselves as diagnosticians and social internists, by the fact that relatives often call the court and ask that a man be given time in jail for his own good. The judge usually complies. Furthermore, as has been mentioned, there is at the jail a branch of the Out-Patient Therapy Center that was originally established to work for the rehabilitation of alcoholics. . . . Having this jail clinic allows the drunk court judge to say:

> I sentence you to 30 days and I will get in touch with the social worker at the County Jail and she will help you.[8]

> I sentence you to therapy with the psychologists at the County Jail. (Also reported by court observers.)

Creation of the Pacific City Alcoholism School also allows the judge to feel that he is fulfilling both judicial and therapeutic duties, giving the defendant a suspended sentence on the condition that he will attend the lecture sessions.

Where the name of the social worker or psychologist of Alcoholism School is not invoked as part of the sentence, an awareness of alcoholism as an illness is frequently used as an introductory statement to indicate the reasoning of the courts for giving a jail sentence.

> We realize that you men are sick and need help. Any action I might take, therefore, should not in any sense be construed as punishment. Jail in this case is not a punitive measure, but to help you with your alcoholism problem.

However, the uneasiness of the judge with the jailing of alcoholics has other indicators. The captain of the County Jail, for instance, reports that inmates serving time for public drunkenness have only to write a letter requesting modification and it is almost automatically forthcoming, something not true for modification requests of prisoners convicted of other misdemeanors.[9]

That drunk court's methods and procedures of handling the Row men go against the judicial grain also seems to be indicated by the fact court officers claim a new judge must be "broken in" to drunk court before he operates efficiently. When the judge first arrives, he will sentence differently from an experienced judge and in the direction of greater leniency. This upsets the established pattern.

The result is he is taken in hand and guided to do "the right thing" by the veteran court aids. As one court aid put it:

> Most of the judges are pretty good—they rely on us. Sometimes you get a new judge who wants to do things his way. We have to break them in, train them. This court is very different. We have to break new judges in. It takes some of them some time to get adjusted to the way we do things.[10]

The high rate of recidivism of chronic drunkenness offenders leads some experts to question the value of jail as a cure for alcoholism or chronic drunkenness.[11] Publicly, at least, the judges appear to hold to the view that the current arrest and incarceration process *can* be helpful, but that often the alcoholic simply does not respond to "treatment" permanently and needs periodic "doses" of jail-therapy. As one judge put it:

> Some men have simply gone so far that you can't do anything for them. They are hopeless. All we can do is send them to jail to dry out from time to time.[12]

* * *

Notes

1. Frederic S. LeClercq, "Field Observations in Drunk Court of the Pacific City Municipal Court" (unpublished memorandum, 1966), p. 1.
2. These observations were made almost two years after LeClercq made his.
3. LeClercq, "Field Observations in Drunk Court," p. 12.
4. The use of a "Rapper" is apparently not a local phenomenon. Bogue notes it also in his study of the Chicago Skid Row. See Donald J. Bogue, *Skid Row in American Cities* (Chicago: University of Chicago, 1963), p. 414.

5. When the Rapper started drinking again, he was not replaced; rather, court officers and an official of the Christian Missionaries fulfilled his duties.

6. The Rapper was under treatment again for alcoholism at State Mental Hospital when he made this statement.... Kurt Lewin discusses this phenomenon of rejection of one's own (if they are a minority group of some type) in "Self-Hatred Among Jews," Chap. 12 of *Resolving Social Conflict* (New York: Harper Publishing Company, 1945).

7. LeClercq, "Field Observations in Drunk Court," p. 11.

8. Reported by inmate in County Jail on public drunkenness charge.

9. Source: Captain, County Jail.

10. LeClercq, "Field Observations in Drunk Court," p. 7.

11. As previously mentioned, the chief deputy of County Jail puts the number of recidivists at 85 percent of the total admissions in any one year. A small "loop," made by a chronic drunkenness offender who goes between municipal jail and Skid Row, has been well chronicled by D. J. Pittman and C. W. Gordon in *The Revolving Door* (Glencoe, Ill.: The Free Press, 1958).

12. Statement made by Municipal Judge from city near Pacific City.

29 / The Moral Career of the Mental Patient

ERVING GOFFMAN

Traditionally the term *career* has been reserved for those who expect to enjoy the rises laid out within a respectable profession. The term is coming to be used, however, in a broadened sense to refer to any social strand of any person's course through life. The perspective of natural history is taken: unique outcomes are neglected in favor of such changes over time as are basic and common to the members of a social category, although occurring independently to each of them. Such a career is not a thing that can be brilliant or disappointing; it can no more be a success than a failure. In this light, I want to consider the mental patient, drawing mainly upon data collected during a year's participant observation of patient social life in a public mental hospital,[1] wherein an attempt was made to take the patient's point of view.

One value of the concept of career is its two-sidedness. One side is linked to internal matters held dearly and closely, such as image of self and felt identity; the other side concerns official position, jural relations, and style of life, and is part of a publicly accessible institutional complex. The concept of career, then, allows one to move back and forth between the personal and the public, between the self and its significant society, without having overly to rely for data upon what the person says he thinks he imagines himself to be.

This paper, then, is an exercise in the institutional approach to the study of self. The main concern will be with the *moral* aspects of career—that is, the regular sequence of changes that career entails in the person's self and in his framework of imagery for judging himself and others.[2]

The category "mental patient" itself will be understood in one strictly sociological sense. In this perspective, the psychiatric view of a person becomes significant only in so far as this view itself alters his social fate—an alteration which seems to become fundamental in our society when, and only when, the person is put through the process of hospitalization.[3] I therefore exclude certain neighboring categories: the undiscovered candidates who would be judged "sick" by psychiatric standards but who never come to be viewed as such by themselves or others, although they may cause everyone a great deal of trouble;[4] the office patient whom a psychiatrist feels he can handle with drugs or shock on the outside; the mental client who engages in psychotherapeutic relationships. And I include anyone, however robust in temperament, who somehow gets caught up in the heavy machinery of mental hospital servicing. In this way the effects of being treated as a mental patient can be kept quite distinct from the effects upon a person's life of traits a clinician would view as psychopathological.[5] Persons who become mental hospital patients vary widely in the kind and degree of illness that a psychiatrist would impute to them, and in the attributes by which laymen would describe them. But once started on the way, they are confronted by some importantly similar circumstances and respond to these in some importantly similar ways. Since these similarities do not come from mental illness, they would seem to occur in spite of it. It is thus a tribute to the power of social forces that the uniform status of mental patient cannot only assure an aggregate of persons a common fate and eventually, because of this, a common character, but that this social reworking can be done upon what is perhaps the most obstinate diversity of human materials that can be brought together by society. Here there lacks only the frequent forming of a protective group-life by ex-patients to illustrate in full the classic cycle of response by which deviant subgroupings are psychodynamically formed in society.

This general sociological perspective is heavily reinforced by one key finding of sociologically oriented students in mental hospital research. As has been repeatedly shown in the study of nonliterate societies, the awesomeness, distastefulness, and barbarity of a foreign culture can decrease in the degree that the student becomes familiar with the point of view to life that is taken by his subjects. Similarly, the student of mental hospitals can discover that the craziness or "sick behavior" claimed for the mental patient is by and large a product of the claimant's social distance from the situation that the patient is in, and is not primarily a product of mental illness. Whatever the refinements of the various patients' psychiatric diagnoses, and whatever the special ways in which social life on the "inside" is unique, the researcher can find that he is participating in a community not significantly different from any other he has studied.[6] Of course, while restricting himself to the off-ward grounds community of paroled patients, he may feel, as some patients do, that life in the locked wards is bizarre; and while on a locked admissions or convalescent ward, he may feel that chronic "back" wards are socially crazy places. But he need only move his sphere of sympathetic participation to the "worst" ward in the hospital, and this too can come into social focus as a place with a livable and continuously meaningful social world. This in no way denies that he will find a minority in any ward or patient group that continues to seem quite beyond the capacity to follow rules of social organization, or that the orderly fulfillment of normative expectations in patient society is partly made possible by strategic measures that have somehow come to be institutionalized in mental hospitals.

The career of the mental patient falls popularly and naturalistically into three main phases: the period prior to entering the hospital, which I shall call the *prepatient phase*; the period in the hospital, the *inpatient phase*; the period after discharge from the hospital, should this occur, namely, the *ex-patient phase*.[7] This paper will deal only with the first two phases.

THE PREPATIENT PHASE

A relatively small group of prepatients come into the mental hospital willingly, because of their own idea of what will be good for them, or because of wholehearted agreement with the relevant members of their family. Presumably these recruits have found themselves acting in a way which is evidence to them that they are losing their minds or losing control of themselves. This view of oneself would seem to be one of the most pervasively threatening things that can happen to the self in our society, especially since it is likely to occur at a time when the person is in any case sufficiently troubled to exhibit the kind of symptom which he himself can see. As Sullivan described it,

> What we discover in the self-system of a person undergoing schizophrenic changes or schizophrenic processes, is then, in its simplest form, an extremely fear-marked puzzlement, consisting of the use of rather generalized and anything but exquisitely refined referential processes in an attempt to cope with what is essentially a failure at being human—a failure at being anything that one could respect as worth being.[8]

Coupled with the person's disintegrative re-evaluation of himself will be the new, almost equally pervasive circumstance of attempting to conceal from others what he takes to be the new fundamental facts about himself, and attempting to discover whether others too have discovered them.[9] Here I want to stress that perception of losing one's mind is based on culturally derived and socially engrained stereotypes as to the significance of symptoms such as hearing voices, losing temporal and spatial orientation, and sensing that one is being followed, and that many of the most spectacular and convincing of these symptoms in some instances psychiatrically signify merely a temporary emotional upset in a stressful situation, however terrifying to the person at the time. Similarly, the anxiety consequent upon this perception of oneself, and the strategies devised to reduce this anxiety, are not a product of abnormal psychology, but would be exhibited by any person socialized into our culture who came to conceive of himself as someone losing his mind. Interestingly, subcultures in American society apparently differ in the amount of ready imagery and encouragement they supply for such self-views, leading to differential rates of *self*-referral; the capacity to take this disintegrative view of oneself without psychiatric prompting seems to be one of the questionable cultural privileges of the upper classes.[10]

For the person who has come to see himself—with whatever justification—as mentally unbalanced, entrance to the mental hospital can sometimes bring relief, perhaps in part because of the sudden transformation in the structure of his basic social situations; instead of being to himself a questionable person trying to maintain a role as a full one, he can become an officially questioned person known to himself to be not so questionable as that. In other cases, hospitalization can make matters worse for the willing patient, confirming by the objective situation what has theretofore been a matter of the private experience of self.

Once the willing prepatient enters the hospital, he may go through the same routine of experiences as do those who enter unwillingly. In any case, it is the latter that I mainly want to consider, since in America at present these are by far the more numerous kind.[11] Their approach to the institution takes one of three classic forms: they come because they have been implored by their family or threatened with the abrogation of family ties unless they go "willingly"; they come by force under police escort; they come under misapprehension purposely induced by others, this last restricted mainly to youthful prepatients.

The prepatient's career may be seen in terms of an extrusory model; he starts out with relationships and rights, and ends up, at the beginning of his hospital stay, with hardly any of either. The moral aspects of this career, then, typically begin with the experience of abandonment, disloyalty, and embitterment. This is the case even though to others it may be obvious that he was in need of treatment, and even though in the hospital he may soon come to agree.

The case histories of most mental patients document offense against some arrangement for face-to-face living—a domestic establishment, a work place, a semipublic organization such as a church or store, a public region such as a street or park. Often there is also a record of some *complainant*, some figure who takes that action against the offender which eventually leads to his hospitalization. This may not be the person who makes the first move, but it is the person who makes what turns out to be the first effective move. Here is the *social* beginning of the patient's career, regardless of where one might locate the psychological beginning of his mental illness.

The kinds of offenses which lead to hospitalization are felt to differ in nature from those which lead to other extrusory consequences—to imprisonment, divorce, loss of job, disownment, regional exile, noninstitutional psychiatric treatment, and so forth. But little seems known about these differentiating factors; and when one studies actual commitments, alternate outcomes frequently appear to have been possible. It seems true, moreover, that for every offense that leads to an effective complaint, there are many psychiatrically similar ones that never do. No action is taken; or action is taken which leads to other extrusory outcomes; or ineffective action is taken, leading to the mere pacifying or putting off of the person who complains. Thus, as Clausen and Yarrow have nicely shown, even offenders who are eventually hospitalized are likely to have had a long series of ineffective actions taken against them.[12]

Separating those offenses which could have been used as grounds for hospitalizing the offender from those that are so used, one finds a vast number of what students of occupation call career contingencies.[13] Some of these contingencies in the mental patient's career have been suggested, if not explored, such as socio-economic status, visibility of the offense, proximity to a mental hospital, amount of treatment facilities available, community regard for the type of treatment given in available hospitals, and so on.[14] For information about other contingencies one must rely on atrocity tales: a psychotic man is tolerated by his wife until she finds herself a boyfriend, or by his adult children until they move from a house to an apartment; an alcoholic is sent to a mental hospital because the jail is full, and a drug addict because he declines to avail himself of psychiatric treatment on the outside; a rebellious adolescent daughter can no longer be managed at home because she now threatens to have an open affair with an unsuitable companion; and so on. Correspondingly there is an equally important set of contingencies causing the person to bypass this fate. And should the person enter the hospital, still another set of contingencies will help determine when he is to obtain a discharge—such as the desire of his family for his return, the availability of a "manageable" job, and so on. The society's official view is that inmates of mental hospitals are there primarily because they are suffering from mental illness. However, in the degree that the "mentally ill" outside hospitals numerically approach or surpass those inside hospitals, one could say that mental patients *distinctively* suffer not from mental illness, but from contingencies.

Career contingencies occur in conjunction with a second feature of the prepatient's career—the *circuit of agents*—and agencies—that participate fatefully in his passage from civilian to patient status.[15] Here is an instance of that increasingly important class of social system whose elements are agents and agencies, which are brought into systemic connection through having to take up and send on the same persons. Some of these agent-roles will be cited now, with the understanding that in any concrete circuit a role may be filled more than once, and a single person may fill more than one of them.

First is the *next-of-relation*—the person whom the prepatient sees as the most available of those upon whom he should be able to most depend in times of trouble; in this instance the last to doubt his sanity and the first to have done everything to save him from the fate which, it transpires, he has been approaching. The patient's next-of-relation is usually his next of kin; the special term is introduced because he need not be. Second is the *complainant*, the person who retrospectively appears to have started the person on his way to the hospital. Third are the *mediators*—the sequence of agents and agencies to which the prepatient is referred and through which he is relayed and processed on his way to the hospital. Here are included police, clergy, general medical practitioners, office psychiatrists, personnel in public clinics, lawyers, social service workers, school teachers, and so on. One of these agents will have the legal mandate to sanction commitment and will exercise it, and so those agents who precede him in the process will be involved in something whose outcome is not yet settled. When the mediators retire from the scene, the prepatient has become an inpatient, and the significant agent has become the hospital administrator.

While the complainant usually takes action in a lay capacity as a citizen, an employer, a neighbor, or a kinsman, mediators tend to be specialists and differ from those they serve in significant ways. They have experience in handling trouble, and some professional distance from what they handle. Except in the case of policemen, and perhaps some clergy, they tend to be more psychiatrically oriented than the lay public, and will see the need for treatment at times when the public does not.[16]

An interesting feature of these roles is the functional effects of their interdigitation. For example, the feelings of the patient will be influenced by whether or not the person who fills the role of complainant also has the role of next-of-relation—an embarrassing combination more prevalent, apparently, in the higher classes than in the lower.[17] Some of these emergent effects will be considered now.[18]

In the prepatient's progress from home to the hospital he may participate as a third person in what he may come to experience as a kind of *alienative coalition*. His next-of-relation presses him into coming to "talk things over" with a medical practitioner, an office psychiatrist, or some other counselor. Disinclination on his part may be met by threatening him with desertion, disownment, or other legal action, or by stressing the joint and explorative nature of the interview. But typically the next-of-relation will have set the interview up, in the sense of selecting the professional, arranging for time, telling the professional something about the case, and so on. This move effectively tends to establish the next-of-relation as the responsible person to whom pertinent findings can be divulged, while effectively establishing the other as the patient. The prepatient often goes to the interview with the understanding that he is going as an equal of someone who is so bound together with him that a third person could not come between them in fundamental matters; this, after all, is one way in which close relationships are defined in our society. Upon arrival at the office the prepatient suddenly finds that he and his next-of-relation have not been accorded the same roles, and apparently that a prior understanding between the professional and the next-of-relation has been put in operation against him. In the extreme but common case the professional first sees the prepatient alone, in the role of examiner and diagnostician, and then sees the next-of-relation alone, in the role of advisor, while carefully avoiding talking things over seriously with them both together.[19] And even in those nonconsultative cases where public officials must forcibly extract a person from a family that wants to tolerate him, the next-of-relation is likely to be induced to "go along" with the official action, so that even here the prepatient may feel that an alienative coalition has been formed against him.

The moral experience of being third man in such a coalition is likely to embitter the prepatient, especially since his troubles have already probably led to some estrangement from his next-of-relation. After he enters the hospital, continued visits by his next-of-relation can give the patient the "insight" that his own best interests were being served. But the initial visits may temporarily strengthen his feeling of abandonment; he is likely to beg his visitor to get him out or at least to get him more privileges and to sympathize with the monstrousness of his plight—to which the visitor ordinarily can respond only by trying to maintain a hopeful note, by not "hearing" the requests, or by assuring the patient that the medical authorities know about these things and are doing what is medically best. The visitor then nonchalantly goes back into a world that the patient has learned is incredibly thick with freedom and privileges, causing the patient to feel that his next-of-relation is merely adding a pious gloss to a clear case of traitorous desertion.

The depth to which the patient may feel betrayed by his next-of-relation seems to be increased by the fact that another witnesses his betrayal—a factor which is apparently significant in many three-party situations. An offended person may well act forbearantly and accommodatively toward an offender when the two are alone, choosing peace ahead of justice. The presence of a witness, however, seems to add something to the implications of the offense. For then it is beyond the power of the offended and offender to forget about, erase, or suppress what has happened; the offense has become a public social fact.[20] When the witness is a mental health commission, as is sometimes the case, the witnessed betrayal can verge on a "degradation ceremony."[21] In such circumstances, the offended patient may feel that some kind of extensive reparative action is required before witnesses, if his honor and social weight are to be restored.

Two other aspects of sensed betrayal should be mentioned. First, those who suggest the possibility of another's entering a mental hospital are not likely to provide a realistic picture of how in fact it may strike him when he arrives. Often he is told that he will get required medical treatment and a rest, and may well be out in a few months or so. In some cases they may thus be concealing what they know, but I think, in general, they will be telling what they see as the truth. For here there is a quite relevant difference between patients and mediating professionals; mediators, more so than the public at large, may conceive of mental hospitals as short-term medical establishments where required rest and attention can be voluntarily obtained, and not as places of coerced exile. When the prepatient finally arrives he is likely to learn quite quickly, quite differently. He then finds that the information given him about life in the hospital has had the effect of his having put up less resistance to entering than he now sees he would have put up had he known the facts. Whatever the intentions of those who participated in his transition from person to patient, he may sense they have in effect "conned" him into his present predicament.

I am suggesting that the prepatient starts out with at least a portion of the rights, liberties, and satisfactions of the civilian and ends up on a psychiatric ward stripped of almost everything. The question here is *how* this stripping is managed. This is the second aspect of betrayal I want to consider.

As the prepatient may see it, the circuit of significant figures can function as a kind of *betrayal funnel.* Passage from person to patient may be effected through a series of linked stages, each managed by a different agent. While each stage tends to bring a sharp decrease in adult free status, each agent may try to maintain the fiction that no further decrease will occur. He may even manage to turn the prepatient over to the next agent while sustaining this note. Further, through words, cues, and gestures, the prepatient is implicitly asked by the current agent to join with him in sustaining a running line of polite small talk that tactfully avoids the administrative facts of the situation, becoming, with each stage, progressively more at odds with these facts. The spouse would rather not have to cry to get the prepatient to visit a psychiatrist; psychiatrists would rather not have a scene when the prepatient learns that he and his spouse are being seen separately and in different ways; the police infrequently bring a prepatient to the hospital in a strait jacket, finding it much easier all around to give him a cigarette, some kindly words, and freedom to relax in the back seat of the patrol car; and finally, the admitting psychiatrist finds he can do his work better in the relative quiet and luxury of the "admission suite" where, as an incidental consequence, the notion can survive that a mental hospital is indeed a comforting place. If the prepatient heeds all of these implied requests and is reasonably decent about the whole thing, he can travel the whole circuit from home to hospital without forcing anyone to look directly at what is happening or to deal with the raw emotion that his situation might well cause him to express. His showing consideration for those who are moving him toward the hospital allows them to show consideration for him, with the joint result that these interactions can be sustained with some of the protective harmony characteristic of ordinary face-to-face dealings. But should the new patient cast his mind back over the sequence of steps leading to hospitalization, he may feel that everyone's *current* comfort was being busily sustained while his long-range welfare was being undermined. This realization may constitute a moral experience that further separates him for the time from the people on the outside.[22]

I would now like to look at the circuit of career agents from the point of view of the agents themselves. Mediators in the person's transition from civil to patient status—as well as his keepers, once he is in the hospital—have an interest in establishing a responsible next-of-relation as the patient's deputy or *guardian*; should there be no obvious candidate for the role, someone may be sought out and pressed into it. Thus while a person is gradually being transformed into a patient, a next-of-relation is gradually being transformed into a guardian. With a guardian on the scene, the whole transition process can be kept tidy. He is likely to be familiar with the prepatient's civil involvements and business, and can tie up loose ends that might otherwise be left to entangle the hospital. Some of the prepatient's abrogated civil rights can be transferred to him, thus helping to sustain the legal fiction that while the prepatient does not actually have his rights he somehow actually has not lost them.

Inpatients commonly sense, at least for a time, that hospitalization is a massive unjust deprivation, and sometimes succeed in convincing a few persons on the outside that this is the case. It often turns out to be useful, then, for those identified with inflicting these deprivations, however justifiably, to be able to point to the cooperation and agreement of someone whose relationship to the patient places him above suspicion, firmly defining him as the person most likely to have the patient's personal interest at heart. If the guardian is satisfied with what is happening to the new inpatient, the world ought to be.[23]

Now it would seem that the greater the legitimate personal stake one party has in another, the better he can take the role of guardian to the other. But the structural arrangements in society which lead to the acknowledged merging of two persons' interests lead to additional consequences. For the person to whom the patient turns for help—for protection against such threats as involuntary commitment—is just the person to whom the mediators and hospital administrators logically turn for authorization. It is understandable, then, that some patients will come to sense, at least for a time, that the closeness of a relationship tells nothing of its trustworthiness.

There are still other functional effects emerging from this complement of roles. If and when the next-of-relation appeals to mediators for help in the trouble he is having with the prepatient, hospitalization may not, in fact, be in his mind. He may not even perceive the prepatient as mentally sick, or, if he does, he may not consistently hold to this view.[24] It is the circuit of mediators, with their greater psychiatric sophistication and their belief in the medical character of mental hospitals, that will often define the situation for the next-of-relation, assuring him that hospitalization is a possible solution and a good one, that it involves no betrayal, but is rather a medical action taken in the best interests of the prepatient. Here the next-of-relation may learn that doing his duty to the prepatient may cause the prepatient to distrust and even hate him for the time. But the fact that this course of action may have had to be pointed out and prescribed by professionals, and be defined by them as a moral duty, relieves the next-of-relation of some of the guilt he may feel.[25] It is a poignant fact that an adult son or daughter may be pressed into the role of mediator, so that the hostility that might otherwise be directed against the spouse is passed on to the child.[26]

Once the prepatient is in the hospital, the same guilt-carrying function may become a significant part of the staff's job in regard to the next-of-relation.[27] These reasons for feeling that he himself has not betrayed the patient, even though the patient may then think so, can later provide the next-of-relation with a defensible line to take when visiting the patient in the hospital and a basis for hoping that the relationship can be re-established after its hospital moratorium. And of course this position, when sensed by the patient, can provide him with excuses for the next-of-relation, when and if he comes to look for them.[28]

Thus while the next-of-relation can perform important functions for the mediators and hospital administrators, they in turn can perform important functions for him. One finds, then, an emergent unintended exchange or reciprocation of functions, these functions themselves being often unintended.

The final point I want to consider about the prepatient's moral career is its peculiarly *retroactive* character. Until a person actually arrives at the hospital there usually seems no way of knowing for sure that he is destined to do so, given the determinative role of career contingencies. And until the point of hospitalization is reached, he or others may not conceive of him as a person who is becoming a mental patient. However, since he will be held against his will in the hospital, his next-of-relation and the hospital staff will be in great need of a rationale for the hardships they are sponsoring. The medical elements of the staff will also need evidence that they are still in the trade they were trained for. These problems are eased, no doubt unintentionally, by the case-history construction that is placed on the patient's past life, this having the effect of demonstrating that all along he had been becoming sick, that he finally became very sick, and that if he had not been hospitalized much worse things would have happened to him—all of which, of course, may be true. Incidentally, if the patient wants to make sense out of his stay in the hospital, and, as already suggested, keep alive the possibility of once again conceiving of his next-of-relation as a decent, well-meaning person, then he too will have reason to believe some of this psychiatric work-up of his past.

Here is a very ticklish point for the sociology of careers. An important aspect of every career is the view the person constructs when he looks backward over his progress; in a sense, however, the whole of the prepatient career derives from this reconstruction. The fact of having had a prepatient career, starting with an effective complaint, becomes an important part of the mental patient's orientation, but this part can begin to be played only after hospitalization proves that what he had been having, but no longer has, is a career as a prepatient.

THE INPATIENT PHASE

The last step in the prepatient's career can involve his realization—justified or not—that he has been deserted by society and turned out of relationships by those closest to him. Interestingly enough, the patient, especially a first admission, may manage to keep himself from coming to the end of this trail, even though in fact he is now in a locked mental hospital ward. On entering the hospital, he may very strongly feel the desire not to be known to anyone as a person who could possibly be reduced to these present circumstances, or as a person who conducted himself in the way he did prior to commitment. Consequently, he may avoid talking to anyone, may stay by himself when possible, and may even be "out of contact" or "manic" so as to avoid ratifying any interaction that presses a politely reciprocal role upon him and opens him up to what he has become in the eyes of others. When the next-of-relation makes an effort to visit, he may be rejected by mutism, or by the patient's refusal to enter the visiting room, these strategies sometimes suggesting that the patient still clings to a remnant of relatedness to those who made up his past, and is protecting this remnant from the final destructiveness of dealing with the new people that they have become.[29]

Usually the patient comes to give up this taxing effort at anonymity, at not-hereness, and begins to present himself for conventional social interaction to the hospital community. Thereafter he withdraws only in special ways—by always using his nickname, by signing his contribution to the patient weekly with his initial only, or by using the innocuous "cover" address tactfully provided by some hospitals; or he withdraws only at special times, when, say, a flock of nursing students makes a passing tour of the ward, or when, paroled to the hospital grounds, he suddenly sees he is about to cross the path of a civilian he happens to know from home. Sometimes this making of oneself available is called "settling down" by the attendants. It marks a new stand openly taken and supported by the patient, and resembles the "coming out" process that occurs in other groupings.[30]

Once the prepatient begins to settle down, the main outlines of his fate tend to follow those of a whole class of segregated establishments—jails, concentration camps, monasteries, work camps, and so on—in which the inmate spends the whole round of life on the grounds, and marches through his regimented day in the immediate company of a group of persons of his own institutional status.[31]

Like the neophyte in many of these "total institutions," the new inpatient finds himself cleanly stripped of many of his accustomed affirmations, satisfactions, and defenses, and is subjected to a rather full set of mortifying experiences: restriction of free movement; communal living; diffuse authority of a whole echelon of people; and so on. Here one begins to learn about the limited extent to which a conception of oneself can be sustained when the usual setting of supports for it are suddenly removed.

While undergoing these humbling moral experiences, the inpatient learns to orient himself in terms of the "ward system."[32] In public mental hospitals this usually consists of a series of graded living arrangements built around wards, administrative units called services, and parole statuses. The "worst" level involves often nothing but wooden benches to sit on, some quite indifferent food, and a small piece of room to sleep in. The "best" level may involve a room of one's own, ground and town privileges, contacts with staff that are relatively undamaging, and what is seen as good food and ample recreational facilities. For disobeying the pervasive house rules, the inmate will receive stringent punishments expressed in terms of loss of privileges; for obedience he will eventually be allowed to reacquire some of the minor satisfactions he took for granted on the outside.

The institutionalization of these radically different levels of living throws light on the implications for self of social settings. And this in turn affirms that the self arises not merely out of its possessor's interactions with significant others, but also out of the arrangements that are evolved in an organization for its members.

There are some settings which the person easily discounts as an expression or extension of him. When a tourist goes slumming, he may take pleasure in the situation not because it is a reflection of him but because it so assuredly is not. There are other settings, such as living rooms, which the person manages on his own and employs to influence in a favorable direction other persons' views of him. And there are still other settings, such as a work place, which express the employee's occupational status, but over which he has no final control, this being exerted, however tactfully, by his employer. Mental hospitals provide an extreme instance of this latter possibility. And this is due not merely to their uniquely degraded living levels, but also to the unique way in which significance for self is made explicit to the patient, piercingly, persistently, and thoroughly. Once lodged on a given ward, the patient is firmly instructed that the restrictions and deprivations he encounters are not due to such things as tradition or economy—and hence dissociable from self—but are intentional parts of his treatment, part of his need at the time, and therefore an expression of the state that his self has fallen to. Having every reason to initiate requests for better conditions, he is told that when the staff feels he is "able to manage" or will be "comfortable with" a higher ward level, then appropriate action will be taken. In short, assignment to a given ward is presented not as a reward or punishment, but as an expression of his general level of social functioning, his status as a person. Given the fact that the worst ward levels provide a round of life that inpatients with organic brain damage can easily manage, and that these quite limited human beings are present to prove it, one can appreciate some of the mirroring effects of the hospital.[33]

The ward system, then, is an extreme instance of how the physical facts of an establishment can be explicitly employed to frame the conception a person takes of himself. In addition, the official psychiatric mandate of mental hospitals gives rise to even more direct, even more blatant, attacks upon the inmate's view of himself. The more "medical" and the more progressive a mental hospital is—the more it attempts to be therapeutic and not merely custodial—the more he may be confronted by high-ranking staff arguing that his past has been a failure, that the cause of this has been within himself, that his attitude to life is wrong, and that if he wants to be a person he will have to change his way of dealing with people and his conceptions of himself. Often the moral value of these verbal assaults will be brought home to him by requiring him to practice taking this psychiatric view of himself in arranged confessional periods, whether in private sessions or group psychotherapy.

Now a general point may be made about the moral career of inpatients which has bearing on many moral careers. Given the stage that any person has reached in a career, one typically finds that he constructs an image of his life course—past, present, and future—which selects, abstracts, and distorts in such a way as to provide him with a view of himself that he can usefully expound in current situations. Quite generally, the person's line concerning self defensively brings him into appropriate alignment with the basic values of his society, and so may be called an *apologia*. If the person can manage to present a view of his current situation which shows the operation of favorable personal qualities in the past and a favorable destiny awaiting him, it may be called a *success story*. If the facts of a person's past and present are extremely dismal, then about the best he can do is to show that he is not responsible for what has become of him, and the term *sad tale* is appropriate. Interestingly enough, the more the person's past forces him out of apparent alignment with central moral values, the more often he seems compelled to tell his sad tale in any company in which he finds himself. Perhaps he partly responds to the need he feels in others of not having their sense of proper life courses affronted. In any case, it is among convicts, "wino's," and prostitutes that one seems to obtain sad tales the most readily.[34] It is the vicissitudes of the mental patient's sad tale that I want to consider now.

In the mental hospital, the setting and the house rules press home to the patient that he is, after all, a mental case who has suffered some kind of social collapse on the outside, having failed in some over-all way, and that here he is of little social weight, being hardly capable of acting like a full-fledged person at all. These humiliations are likely to be most keenly felt by middle-class patients, since their previous condition of life little immunizes them against such affronts; but all patients feel some downgrading. Just as any normal member of his outside subculture would do, the patient often responds to this situation by attempting to assert a sad tale proving that he is not "sick," that the "little trouble" he did get into was really somebody else's fault, that his past life course had some honor and rectitude, and that the hospital is therefore unjust in forcing the status of mental patient upon him. This self-respecting tendency is heavily institutionalized within the patient society where opening social contacts typically involve the participants' volunteering information about their current ward location and length of stay so far, but not the reasons for their stay—such interaction being conducted in the manner of small talk on the outside.[35] With greater familiarity, each patient usually volunteers relatively acceptable reasons for his hospitalization, at the same time accepting without open immediate question the lines offered by other patients. Such stories as the following are given and overtly accepted.

> I was going to night school to get a M.A. degree, and holding down a job in addition, and the load got too much for me.
>
> The others here are sick mentally but I'm suffering from a bad nervous system and that is what is giving me these phobias.
>
> I got here by mistake because of a diabetes diagnosis, and I'll leave in a couple of days. [The patient had been in seven weeks.]
>
> I failed as a child, and later with my wife I reached out for dependency.
>
> My trouble is that I can't work. That's what I'm in for. I had two jobs with a good home and all the money I wanted.[36]

The patient sometimes reinforces these stories by an optimistic definition of his occupational status: A man who managed to obtain an audition as a radio announcer styles himself a radio announcer; another who worked for some months as a copy boy and was then given a job as a reporter on a large trade journal, but fired after three weeks, defines himself as a reporter.

A whole social role in the patient community may be constructed on the basis of these reciprocally sustained fictions. For these face-to-face niceties tend to be qualified by behind-the-back gossip that comes only a degree closer to the "objective" facts. Here, of course, one can see a classic social function of informal networks of equals: they serve as one another's audience for self-supporting tales—tales that are somewhat more solid than pure fantasy and somewhat thinner than the facts.

But the patient's *apologia* is called forth in a unique setting, for few settings could be so destructive of self-stories except, of course, those stories already constructed along psychiatric lines. And this destructiveness rests on more than the official sheet of paper which attests that the patient is of unsound mind, a danger to himself and others—an attestation, incidentally, which seems to cut deeply into the patient's pride, and into the possibility of his having any.

Certainly the degrading conditions of the hospital setting belie many of the self-stories that are presented by patients; and the very fact of being in the mental hospital is evidence against these tales. And of course, there is not always sufficient patient solidarity to prevent patient discrediting patient, just as there is not always a sufficient number of "professionalized" attendants to prevent attendant discrediting patient. As one patient informant repeatedly suggested to a fellow patient:

> If you're so smart, how come you got your ass in here?

The mental hospital setting, however, is more treacherous still. Staff has much to gain through discreditings of the patient's story—whatever the felt reason for such discreditings. If the custodial faction in the hospital is to succeed in managing his daily round without complaint or trouble from him, then it will prove useful to be able to point out to him that the claims about himself upon which he rationalizes his demands are false, that he is not what he is claiming to be, and that in fact he is a failure as a person. If the psychiatric faction is to impress upon him its views about his personal make-up, then they must be able to show in detail how their version of his past and their version of his character hold up much better than his own.[37] If both the custodial and psychiatric factions are to get him to cooperate in the various psychiatric treatments, then it will prove useful to disabuse him of *his* view of their purposes, and cause him to appreciate that they know what they are doing, and are doing what is best for him. In brief, the difficulties caused by a patient are closely tied to his version of what has been happening to him, and if cooperation is to be secured, it helps if this version is discredited. The patient must "insightfully" come to take, or affect to take, the hospital's view of himself.

Notes

1. The study was conducted during 1955–56 under the auspices of the Laboratory of Socil-environmental Studies of the National Institute of Mental Health. I am grateful to the Laboratory Chief, John A. Clausen, and to Dr. Winfred Overholser, Superintendent, and the late Dr. Jay Hoffman, then First Assistant Physician of Saint Elizabeths Hospital, Washington, D.C., for the ideal cooperation they freely provided. A preliminary report is contained in Goffman, "Interpersonal Persuasion," pp. 117–193; in *Group Processes: Transactions of the Third Conference*, edited by Bertram Schaffner: New York, Josiah Macy, Jr. Foundation, 1957. A shorter version of this paper was presented at the Annual Meeting of the American Sociological Society, Washington, D.C., August 1957.

2. Material on moral career can be found in early social anthropological work on ceremonies of status transition, and in classic social psychological descriptions of those spectacular changes in one's view of self that can accompany participation in social movements and sects. Recently new kinds of relevant data have been suggested by psychiatric interest in the problem of "identity" and sociological studies of work careers and "adult socialization."

3. This point has recently been made by Elaine and John Cumming, *Closed Ranks;* Cambridge, Commonwealth Fund, Harvard Univ. Press, 1957; pp. 101–102. "Clinical experience supports the impression that many people define mental illness as 'That condition for which a person is treated in a mental hospital.'...Mental illness, it seems, is a condition which afflicts people who must go to a mental institution, but until they do almost anything they do is normal." Leila Deasy has pointed out to me the correspondence here with the situation in white collar crime. Of those who are detected in this activity, only the ones who do not manage to avoid going to prison find themselves accorded the social role of the criminal.

4. Case records in mental hospitals are just now coming to be exploited to show the incredible amount of trouble a person may cause for himself and others before anyone begins to think about him psychiatrically, let alone take psychiatric action against him. See John A. Clausen and Marian Radke Yarrow, "Paths to the Mental Hospital," *J. Social Issues* (1955) 11:25–32; August B. Hollingshead and Fredrick C. Redlich, *Social Class and Mental Illness;* New York, Wiley, 1958: pp. 173–174.

5. An illustration of how this perspective may be taken to all forms of deviancy may be found in Edwin Lemert, *Social Pathology;* New York, McGraw-Hill, 1951; see especially pp. 74–76. A specific application to mental defectives may be found in Stewart E. Perry, "Some Theoretic Problems of Mental Deficiency and Their Action Implications," *Psychiatry* (1954) 17:45–73; see especially p. 68.

6. Conscientious objectors who voluntarily went to jail sometimes arrived at the same conclusion regarding criminal inmates. See, for example, Alfred Hassler, *Diary of a Self-made Convict;* Chicago, Regnery, 1954; p. 74.

7. This simple picture is complicated by the somewhat special experience of roughly a third of ex-patients—namely, readmission to the hospital, this being the recidivist or "repatient" phase.

8. Harry Stack Sullivan, *Clinical Studies in Psychiatry;* edited by Helen Swick Perry, Mary Ladd Gawel, and Martha Gibbon; New York, Norton, 1956; pp. 184–185.

9. This moral experience can be contrasted with that of a person learning to become a marihuana addict, whose discovery that he can be "high" and still "op" effectively without being detected apparently leads to a new level of use. See Howard S. Becker, "Marihuana Use and Social Control," *Social Problems* (1955) 3:35–44; see especially pp. 40–41.

10. See footnote 4: Hollingshead and Redlich, p. 187, Table 6, where relative frequency is given of self-referral by social class grouping.

11. The distinction employed here between willing and unwilling patients cuts across the legal one, of voluntary and committed, since some persons who are glad to come to the mental hospital may be legally committed, and of those who come only because of strong familial pressure, some may sign themselves in as voluntary patients.

12. Clausen and Yarrow; see footnote 4.

13. An explicit application of this notion to the field of mental health may be found in Edwin M. Lemert, "Legal Commitment and Social Control," *Sociology and Social Research* (1946) 30:370–378.

14. For example, Jerome K. Meyers and Leslie Schaffer, "Social Stratification and Psychiatric Practice: A Study of an Outpatient Clinic," *Amer. Sociological Rev.* (1954) 19: 307–310, Lemert, see footnote 5; pp. 402–403. *Patients in Mental Institutions*, 1941; Washington, D.C., Department of Commerce, Bureau of Census, 1941; p. 2.

15. For one circuit of agents and its bearing on career contingencies, see Oswald Hall, "The Stages of a Medical Career," *Amer. J. Sociology* (1948) 53:227–336.

16. See Cumming, footnote 3; p. 92.

17. Hollingshead and Redlich, footnote 4; p. 187.

18. For an analysis of some of these circuit implications for the inpatient, see Leila C. Deasy and Olive W. Quinn, "The Wife of the Mental Patient and the Hospital Psychiatrist," *J. Social Issues* (1955) 11:49–60. An interesting illustration of this kind of analysis may also be found in Alan G. Gowman, "Blindness and the Role of Companion," *Social Problems* (1956) 4:68–75. A general statement may be found in Robert Merton, "The Role Set: Problems in Sociological Theory," *British J. Sociology* (1957) 8:106–120.

19. I have one case record of a man who claims he thought *he* was taking his wife to see the psychiatrist, not realizing until too late that his wife had made the arrangements.

20. A paraphrase from Kurt Riezler, "The Social Psychology of Shame," *Amer. J. Sociology* (1943) 48:458.

21. See Harold Garfinkel, "Conditions of Successful Degradation Ceremonies," *Amer. J. Sociology* (1956) 61:420–424.

22. Concentration camp practices provide a good example of the function of the betrayal funnel in inducing cooperation and reducing struggle and fuss, although here the mediators could not be said to be acting in the best interests of the inmates. Police picking up persons from their homes would sometimes joke good-naturedly and offer to wait while coffee was being served. Gas chambers were fitted out like delousing rooms, and victims taking off their clothes were told to note where they were leaving them. The sick, aged, weak, or insane who were selected for extermination were sometimes driven away in Red Cross ambulances to camps referred to by terms such as "observation hospital." See David Boder, *I Did Not Interview the Dead;* Urbana, Univ. of Illinois Press, 1949; p. 81; and Elie A. Cohen, *Human Behavior in the Concentration Camp;* London, Cape, 1954; pp. 32, 37, 107.

23. Interviews collected by the Clausen group at NIMH suggest that when a wife comes to be a guardian, the responsibility may disrupt previous distance from in-laws, leading either to a new supportive coalition with them or to a marked withdrawal from them.

24. For an analysis of these nonpsychiatric kinds of perception, see Marian Radke Yarrow, Charlotte Green Schwartz, Harriet S. Murphy, and Leila Calhoun Deasy, "The Psychological Meaning of Mental Illness in the Family," *J. Social Issues* (1955) 11:12–24; Charlotte Green Schwartz, "Perspectives on Deviance: Wives' Definitions of their Husbands' Mental Illness," *Psychiatry* (1957) 20:275–291.

25. This guilt-carrying function is found, of course, in other role-complexes. Thus, when a middle-class couple engages in the process of legal separation or divorce, each of their lawyers

usually takes the position that his job is to acquaint his client with all of the potential claims and rights, pressing his client into demanding these, in spite of any nicety of feelings about the rights and honorableness of the ex-partner. The client, in all good faith, can then say to self and to the ex-partner that the demands are being made only because the lawyer insists it is best to do so.

26. Recorded in the Clausen data.

27. This point is made by Cumming, see footnote 3; p. 129.

28. There is an interesting contrast here with the moral career of the tuberculosis patient. I am told by Julius Roth that tuberculosis patients are likely to come to the hospital willingly, agreeing with their next-of-relation about treatment. Later in their hospital career, when they learn how long they yet have to stay and how depriving and irrational some of the hospital rulings are, they may seek to leave, be advised against this by the staff and by relatives, and only then begin to feel betrayed.

29. The inmate's initial strategy of holding himself aloof from ratifying contact may partly account for the relative lack of group-formation among inmates in public mental hospitals, a connection that has been suggested to me by William R. Smith. The desire to avoid personal bonds that would give license to the asking of biographical questions could also be a factor. In mental hospitals, of course, as in prisoner camps, the staff may consciously break up incipient group-formation in order to avoid collective rebellious action and other ward disturbances.

30. A comparable coming out occurs in the homosexual world, when a person finally comes frankly to present himself to a "gay" gathering not as a tourist but as someone who is "available." See Evelyn Hooker, "A Preliminary Examination of Group Behavior of Homosexuals," *J. Psychology* (1956) 42:217–225; especially p. 221. A good fictionalized treatment may be found in James Baldwin's *Giovanni's Room;* New York, Dial, 1956; pp. 41–63. A familiar instance of the coming out process is no doubt to be found among prepubertal children at the moment one of these actors sidles *back* into a room that had been left in an angered huff and injured *amour-propre*. The phrase itself presumably derives from a *rite-de-passage* ceremony once arranged by upper-class mothers for their daughters. Interestingly enough, in large mental hospitals the patient sometimes symbolizes a complete coming out by his first active participation in the hospital wide patient dance.

31. See Goffman, "Characteristics of Total Institutions," pp. 43–84; in *Proceedings of the Symposium of Preventive and Social Psychiatry;* Washington, D.C., Walter Reed Army Institute of Research, 1958.

32. A good description of the ward system may be found in Ivan Belknap, *Human Problems of a State Mental Hospital;* New York, McGraw-Hill, 1956; see especially p. 164.

33. Here is one way in which mental hospitals can be worse than concentration camps and prisons as places in which to "do" time; in the latter, self-insulation from the symbolic implications of the settings may be easier. In fact, self-insulation from hospital settings may be so difficult that patients have to employ devices for this which staff interpret as psychotic symptoms.

34. In regard to convicts, see Anthony Heckstall-Smith, *Eighteen Months;* London, Wingate, 1954; pp. 52–53. For "wino's" see the discussion in Howard G. Bain, "A Sociological Analysis of the Chicago Skid-Row Lifeway;" unpublished M.A. thesis, Dept. of Sociology, pp. 141–146. Bain's neglected thesis is useful source of material on moral careers.

Apparently one of the occupational hazards of prostitution is that clients and other professional contacts sometimes persist in expressing sympathy by asking for a defensible dramatic explanation for the fall from grace. In having to bother to have a sad tale ready, perhaps the prostitute is more to be pitied than damned. Good examples of prostitute sad tales may be found in Sir Henry Mayhew, "Those that Will Not Work," pp. 210–272; in his *London Labour and the London Poor,* Vol. 4; London, Griffin, Bohn, and Cox, 1862. For a contemporary source, see *Women of the Streets,* edited by C. H. Rolph; London, Zecker and Warburg, 1955; especially p. 6. "Almost always, however, after a few comments on the police, the girl would begin to explain how it was that she was in the life, usually in terms of self-justification." Lately, of course, the psychological expert has helped out the profession in the construction of wholly remarkable sad tales. See, for example, Hardld Greenwald, *Call Girl;* New York, Ballantine, 1958.

35. A similar self-protecting rule has been observed in prisons. Thus, Hassler, see footnote 6, in describing a conversation with a fellow-prisoner; "He didn't say much about why he

was sentenced, and I didn't ask him, that being the accepted behavior in prison" (p. 76). A novelistic version for the mental hospital may be found in J. Kerkhoff, *How Thin the Veil: A Newspaperman's Story of His Own Mental Crack-up and Recovery;* New York, Greenberg, 1952; p. 27.

36. From the writer's field notes of informal interaction with patients, transcribed as near verbatim as he was able.

37. The process of examining a person psychiatrically and then altering or reducing his status in consequence is known in hospital and prison paralance as *bugging,* the assumption being that once you come to the attention of the testers you either will automatically be labeled crazy or the process of testing itself will make you crazy. Thus psychiatric staff are sometimes seen not as *discovering* whether you are sick, but as *making* you sick; and "Don't bug me, man," can mean, "Don't pester me to the point where I'll get upset." Sheldom Messenger has suggested to me that this meaning of bugging is related to the other colloquial meaning, of wiring a room with a secret microphone to collect information usuable for discrediting the speaker.

30 / Illness Career Descent in Institutions for the Elderly

BRADLEY J. FISHER

Declining health affects the lives of older individuals in a variety of ways: undermining previously established supports of their positive self-image; reversing the generational role as the reins of authority are transferred from the aging parent to his or her children; threatening the degree of control over major life decisions (Aizenberg and Treas, 1985; Troll and Bengston, 1982) and increasing the risk of institutionalization.

Although research has shown that institutions for the aged can have positive consequences such as improved relations with family members (Smith and Bengston, 1979) and opportunities for new friendships and social interactions (Tesch et al., 1981), they also threaten the self-concept and self-worth of older individuals (Hunter et al., 1982; Lieberman, 1969; Pollack et al., 1962; Tobin and Lieberman, 1976). Institutionalization entails a loss of privacy and control so that individuals have difficulty maintaining their idealized self-image (Goffman, 1959). Institutionalization also renders one vulnerable to negative labels imposed by others (Goffman, 1961). To cope with these social processes, people develop cognitive strategies, the subject matter of this paper.

In my research, I have found it helpful to view this combined social and cognitive process as "illness career descent." It involves the relationship between the downward trajectory of chronic illness (Strauss, 1973) and the individual's downward trajectory through a health-care facility (Morgan, 1982). Illness can be viewed as a career or a process with a beginning, intervening stages, and an end. Illness trajectory refers to the organization of work done over the course of the illness and the impact on those involved in this work (Strauss, 1985). Illness career descent includes additional features of the illness career and its trajectory such as relocation, environmental regimentation, changes in control, and "...other symbolically altered interactional sequences that indicate that the sick person's identity has been individuated and differentiated in the social setting" (Manning and Zucker, 1976, p. 102). Throughout the process of illness career descent, the individual is confronted with the task of renegotiating an image of self in the face of an uncertain future.

This paper examines life at a retirement facility, Rolling Meadows,[1] and some of the ways that residency affects the self-image of those who live there. More specifically, it employs a social psychological perspective to clarify the social and cognitive aspects of illness career descent and how these impact on the self-image of residents moved from one classification to another, i.e., from independent living to the intermediate care floor.

METHODS

For two years, I investigated social and cultural factors affecting elderly people's ability to adjust to life in a retirement facility. Qualitative data on resident and staff perceptions of the adjustment process were gathered through participant observation and interviews. One-shot open-ended interviews with 65 residents at the retirement facility provided information concerning residents' perceptions of declining health, their placement in the retirement facility, and their attitudes toward self. Open-ended interviews with the full range of staff members as well as executive staff provided information concerning the formal structure of the facility, procedures for relocating residents, and staff perceptions of the facility and of residents' behavior. Finally, interviews were conducted with a subsample of 35 residents on the average of once or twice a month over a one-year period. These interviews, lasting between 30 to 60 minutes, focused on the resident's response to declining health of self and others, finding friends within the facility, interactions with residents and staff, grief over the loss of a spouse or friend, loss of control over life activities, and the advantages and disadvantages of living within the multi-level care facility.

Description of the Setting

Rolling Meadows is a modern retirement complex located in a metropolitan area of 1.5 million people. It offers multi-level care by combining a residential (230 units) and a nursing home (70 beds) facility. At full capacity, Rolling Meadows can house 300 individuals. In the residential section, residents rent their apartments rather than "buying in" with a lump sum as required by continuing care contracts at other facilities. Everything within the retirement complex is geared to the health condition of the people served there. Currently, the average age is 84.

The residency structure has been designed to accommodate older people as their health deteriorates. There are three distinct types of residency: independent living for those who can maintain their own "apartments"[2] with minimal supervision; intermediate care for those requiring moderate supervision and 24-hour nursing service availability; and health care for those persons requiring skilled nursing care. The various residency classifications are separated spatially: independent living is available on floors 1, 2, 3, and 5; intermediate care (ICF) is on the fourth floor; and the health care facility is a separate building attached to the back of the residential section.

There is very little interaction among residents of differing classifications. In part, residential segregation is formally reinforced by separate dining rooms for each classification of individuals. In addition, since activities are geared to the general capabilities of residents in each classification, most activities are attended only by those residents of a similar classification. Thus, residency classifications separate the residents spatially as well as socially (Fischer, 1985; Morgan, 1982).

When people enter the retirement complex their ability to manage daily responsibilities is assessed and then used to determine their initial placement within the institution. It is the responsibility of staff members to monitor residents' general health while providing supportive services. Staff observations and evaluations, taken collectively, form the rationale for moving a resident from one classification to the next. Staff members act as in-house experts, i.e., highly credible sources of information about the residents' ability to function within each residency classification. As a result, the residents' interactions with staff members take on added significance.

Change in the residents' health condition is discussed by the Resident Care committee composed of various department heads. Depending on the availability of apartments or beds, residents may be moved from one residency level to the next. While there have been two occasions where a resident was moved from a lower to a higher residency classification (i.e., from the nursing home to the ICF), the movement of residents is almost exclusively downward. Just as the chronically ill patient will never fully return to the pre-illness state of health (DiMatteo and Friedman, 1982), similarly, the resident who is moved to a new classification rarely returns to his or her prior residency classification. A resident who is moved "down" is located in a new (and segregated) location affecting all other aspects of his or her social existence at the facility.

FINDINGS

The Negative Impact of Loss of Control

Living in the retirement facility requires that people live in a more regimented social environment as the following quotes from independent residents illustrate: "Here we're bound by rules and regulations." "This is institutional living. You can't get around that. Institutional life is very different from private life." "My life has become more regimented. That's what most people have a problem with here. Can't always do what we want to." Brody (1977) notes that residents who try to exert control over their lives within the retirement facility get labeled by staff as "bad residents." Compliant residents make it easier for staff to run the facility in a smooth and efficient manner. Becoming a "complainer" results in undesirable consequences for the residents' relationships with staff and other residents as the following quotes illustrate:

> They removed the chairs that were here in the lobby just outside the dining area. They told us that it was a fire hazard but I think they thought it looked bad for people to be sitting around up here. I wanted to say something but I've learned to be careful. The nurses don't come around as quickly when you need them if you complain a lot. [ICF resident]

> She's a new resident and is always complaining about everything. She's a real bitch. Everyone hates her and picks on her all the time. No one wants to be near her. I don't blame them. [Independent resident]

> If they [the staff] do something I don't like, I don't say anything. They're my lifeline. I depend on them for almost everything. They're awfully good to me around here and I don't want that to change. [Independent resident]

In Rolling Meadows, when residents are relocated downward, they have less control over their own lives and are increasingly subject to supervision by nursing personnel as well as being at the mercy of staff schedules and convenience. A few comments by ICF residents illustrate this loss of control:

> They tell you when to eat and how you're supposed to dress. I like to think I can decide those things for myself. It's no fun having to depend on others to do things for you.

> When you want them to do something for you, you wait until they find the time, but when they want you to do something they want it done right now.

> They treat me like a child up here. Like I can't do anything for myself. I know my health isn't as good as it once was. I'm beginning to feel like I'm no good for anything anymore.

Residents are sensitized to their loss of control by such incidents as the removal of chairs in the lobby. They begin to believe they are helpless and no longer attempt to shape their social environment.

Resident Placement as a Source of Stigmatization

Another major threat to the resident's self-image is the stigma associated with the various residency levels. Residents make attributions about the characteristics of other residents based on their floor location. Independent residents refer to those on the ICF as "those less fortunate people," "those confused people who make no sense," and "those with their minds all gone." Those in the nursing home facility are referred to as "the slowly dying," "the living dead," "the crazies," or the "feeble-minded" (Fisher, 1984).

There is, in fact, great variation of residents' abilities in all three locations. Degree of ambulation ranges from those who need no supportive devices to those who use canes, walkers, or wheel chairs. Similarly, the residents' level of confusion varies in all three groups. Despite these wide variations, independent residents continue to view the other two residency groups as less physically able and less competent. These insidious stereotypes persist even though some of the ICF residents are very articulate.

Being relocated to the ICF or health care facility threatens the self-image of the individual since membership in a given residency category has negative connotations. Residents who are moved to the ICF have less opportunities to interact with their prior friendship group. This increases their vulnerability to the labeling of others since they will frequently be absent at interactions where they might otherwise defend their reputations. Opportunity for contact between members of all three residency groups usually occurs at general facility activities (e.g., general resident meetings, music recitals, talent shows, etc.). Independent residents frequently avoid interacting with residents from the ICF or health center by changing seats or turning away.

Most independent residents avoid the ICF unless they need to go to the nurses' station which is located on that floor. As one independent resident stated: "It's too depressing to see all the sick and confused people up there." Residents fear that association with the less able will contribute to their own demise (Gubrium, 1975). Infrequent contact between residents of differing classifications maintains stereotypic views since independent residents will seldom be confronted with direct experiences which challenge their prejudicial attitudes.

When independent residents do have contact with an ICF resident who does not fit the "ideal prototype" such a person is viewed as an exception. This leaves the perceiver's stereotypic view intact to influence future social behavior (Lord et al., 1984). Some independent residents maintain that their friends, who have been moved to the ICF, are the exceptions among the "confused and incompetent."

> Mildred was moved to that floor a few weeks ago. She's not like the others up there. She's still got most of her marbles. Most of them up there you can't even talk to.

While belonging to a social network allows a resident some protection from this stereotyping process, the segregation of the residency groups puts a strain on friendships. Residents begin scrutinizing the behavior of "relocated" friends for further signs of deterioration. Mr. Hill, recently moved to the ICF because of increasing heart problems, became the subject of his friends' whisperings: "he doesn't look as fit as he used to," "he's not as sharp," and "he seems more confused." Contrary to these comments, there was no observable change in either Mr. Hill's appearance or his mental clarity. Such gossip serves to support the residents' general attitude about those on the ICF by implying that relocated friends may initially be atypical, but over time will begin displaying the characteristics more commonly associated with ICF residents.

Evaluation and Resistance: The Cognitive Phase

It has been argued that residency classification becomes a salient aspect of each resident's self-identity at the institution. The discussion has centered on how the social environment and interactions with other residents can act as threats to the relocated resident's self-image. In addition to these symbolic interactions, there are cognitive processes going on within the resident who has been told that he or she is to be relocated.

The staff's evaluation of and decision to relocate a resident is usually communicated to residents approximately two weeks before the move. Residents have usually been approached by staff prior to this time on specific behavioral or physical problems so residents are aware they are being observed and evaluated.

> They've talked to me before so I try and keep active and do a lot of things. I'm hoping that they'll see that as a sign that I'm OK. I just don't want to be moved to that floor. I couldn't stand it. I'd go crazy for sure. [Independent resident]

Knowing that one is at risk of relocation and being told one is to be relocated create very different responses. Residents at risk attempt to postpone the move by changing or hiding undesirable behavior. Those who are being relocated confront the task of resolving the inconsistency between their self-perception and what is being communicated to them by the staff's decision to move them to the ICF. Unless the resident is willing to accept the label of an ICF resident (and all the associated stereotypes) as reflecting an accurate self-conception, then cognitive inconsistency will result. This will vary depending on the individual's level of cognitive functioning. Those who are mentally confused may show little or no concern for the evaluations of others and may experience no threat to their self-image.

When informed of the staff's decision, most residents attempt to resist the move in several ways: derogation of the source of the communication, changing the opinion of the communicator, or seeking others who share one's opinion (Aronson et al., 1963). While these strategies might postpone the move and reduce cognitive dissonance, they are not equally plausible options for the residents to employ.

It is unlikely that the resident will derogate the source of the communication since most residents believe that the staff are highly reliable care providers. While some residents do occasionally accuse the staff of incompetency, such claims are rarely sustained over extended periods of time. Credibility may vary from one staff member to the next, however, staff members are generally recognized as legitimate and credible sources of evaluation and information.[3]

Some residents try to change the opinion of staff members by convincing them that certain incidents (e.g., incontinence, forgetfulness) are not representative of their true state of health. This is unlikely to succeed since these are collective decisions supported by all or a majority of the staff members on the Resident Care committee.

The third possibility is that residents may seek out others who will support their opinion that a move to the ICF is unnecessary. Residents frequently enlist family members to prevent the move. This is rarely successful since family members can usually be convinced of the appropriateness of the move and join with the staff to persuade the resident to comply with the move.

When an apartment is available, staff members seldom postpone moving a resident to the ICF. Resistance is sometimes countered by threatening to evict the resident usually resulting in the resident's compliance. If the resident's resistance efforts are successful, the delay is only a temporary solution since those who have gotten to the point of marginality are likely to continue experiencing a decline in health eventually mandating the postponed move.

The resistance phase typically lasts from four to six seeks depending on the length of time prior to actual relocation. While most of the resistance takes place prior to the move, it often continues for a few weeks after a resident's relocation. Very few residents protest beyond this point as it is physically and mentally taxing and receives little social support from staff or other residents.

Acceptance and Tarnished Self-Image: The Cognitive Consonance Phase

Even though the resident has been moved, he or she still suffers from cognitive dissonance by holding a view of self that is sharply discrepant from the view held by the staff. The only way for residents to reduce cognitive dissonance is by changing their own opinion and accept their move to the ICF as justified.[4] This will result in a tarnished self-image as residents accept that the stereotypes previously held about those on the ICF now describe themselves as well. Residents relocated to the ICF initially come to see themselves as somehow changed and less competent as the following quotes illustrate:

> When I was a resident on the 2nd floor, everyone thought I was so sweet. But now that I'm living here it seems that my friends aren't so sweet on me anymore. They never come up to visit me. That hurts a lot. It's as if I'm not worth having as a friend anymore.

> I used to be involved in all these committees they have here and got quite a few things done. I was fairly well respected. After I moved to this floor I tried to stay with the Activity committee, but people don't seem to listen to me like they used to. I guess my ideas aren't as good as they once were.

The residents change their own opinion to initially reduce cognitive disonance and this has a negative impact on their self-image.

The duration of the second phase varies widely among individuals and may be a matter of weeks or months. Most residents begin to move out of this phase within four to eight weeks. The length of this phase appears to depend on the extent of residents' contact with staff, their ability to develop new friendships, and the opportunity for residents to develop and maintain new social roles.

Revised Opinion and Adjustment: The Enhanced Self-Image Phase

While residents who are relocated experience a negative shift in self-image, they also show a remarkable ability to adjust. Relocated residents enhance their self-image by developing new roles for themselves as the following excerpt from field notes illustrates:

> Mr. Hill was moved to the ICF after a brief hospitalization. He seemed to have a changed opinion of himself. "There's really no one up here I want to talk to. My old friends don't seem to want to bother and come up and see me. Maybe they don't think I'm as with it anymore. Maybe I'm not. Now that I'm here I guess I have to admit I'm not the person I used to be."
>
> After the first month, Mr. Hill volunteered to collect donations for the ICF Christmas party and was highly praised by the staff for how well he handled the job. Since then, he has adopted the role of advocate for the rights of ICF residents. As he put it: "I like to think of myself as the person who keeps their interests at heart, sort of a guardian."

Mr. Hill is an example of a resident who actively sought out ways to enhance his self-image. Mr. Hill's self-image is not as positive as it was prior to his move to the ICF since he still feels he is being treated like a "second-class citizen," but he does have a better opinion of himself than he did just after the move.

Another example of this process of enhanced self-image is Mrs. Dowling who became the flower arranger on the ICF:

> I used to do all the flower arrangements downstairs, but when they moved me up here they said it was too much for me. I really missed that a lot. When I can get the flowers I do up some arrangements. It makes me feel good and it cheers up the other people here to see them.

Some older people enhance their self-image by comparing themselves to others who are worse off, i.e., a "poor dear" (Hochschild, 1973). Independent residents reassure themselves of their good fortune by comparing themselves to "those unfortunate people" on the ICF. Residents who have moved to the ICF often enhance their self-image by finding a "poor dear" within their new residency category or in the next lower category.

> When I first met Mitch he was in awful shape. He could hardly do anything for himself. He's come a long way since I've been working with him. It really makes me feel good knowing I could help someone. Keeps me on my toes. [ICF]

> What I've seen in the health center is absolutely pathetic. Of course, the people I go see there are pathetic. [ICF]

> I think of those in the nursing home with no freedom at all. Those poor things. They can't go anywhere by themselves. [ICF]

By working with those who are less able or comparing themselves to a "poor dear," residents reassure themselves that while they have lost some privileges and personal autonomy, compared to those worse off, they don't have it so bad!

As residents adjust to the ICF by developing new roles for themselves, this behavioral adjustment also involves a shift in their view about what it means to be an ICF resident. Earlier it was argued that residents achieve cognitive consistency by changing their opinions of themselves, but at a cost to their self-image. Thoughts which are initially consistent, however, may not remain so with exposure to new information. Staff members are a main source of new information and provide opportunities for residents to get to know others residing on the ICF. By continually presenting the positive side of living on the ICF, the staff encourage residents to adopt a more positive attitude.

Research has shown that direct experience with an attitude object helps the individual to more clearly identify their feelings toward the object (Fazio and Zanna, 1980; Hamilton, 1979). Residents who are moved to the ICF now have more direct experience with life and people on the ICF. Residents use this information to attack previously held stereotypes and to see the ICF in a more positive light.

> When they first moved me here I didn't like it at all. But the staff up here are so good to me. They come around and check on me and talk to me. I would still prefer to be in my old apartment but it's not so bad up here.

> I used to think that all the people on this floor were crazy. Now that I've been here awhile I can see there are people up here that have it more on the ball than some of those downstairs [in independent living].

But why should residents be inclined to change their attitudes about the ICF in a positive rather than in a negative direction? First, the residents experience growing cognitive inconsistency if they continue to hold both their prior negative thoughts about the ICF along with the influx of positive information resulting from direct experience with residents and staff. Also, they will still be suffering from a negative shift in self-image after being moved to the ICF against their will. If people seek to maintain and enhance their self-image and to avoid cognitive inconsistency, then residents will think positively about the ICF thus resolving their cognitive inconsistency and, at the same time, enhance their self-image.

By re-evaluating the thoughts which supported their previously held stereotypes, the relocated residents find that some of these perceptions were incorrect or exaggerated. The residents enhance their self-image by altering "... the various ideas, beliefs, images, and other elements associated with the attitude object or issue" (Petty and Cacioppo, 1981, p. 110). By changing their attitude about the ICF and those who live there in a positive direction, they correspondingly change what residence on the ICF reflects about their own capabilities.

Along with re-evaluating prior stereotypes, residents attempt to enhance their self-image through post-decisional dissonance reduction. Even though the residents have been strongly encouraged to make the move, they have also been forced to choose between two somewhat equally unattractive alternatives, i.e. move to the ICF or move out of the retirement complex. Residents feel better about their relocation by reflecting on the appropriateness of the move. Residents often state that it was a difficult decision to make but was ultimately the best choice as far as their health needs were concerned. Residents justify the move for reasons other than medical concerns as the following comments illustrate: "The food up here is better." "It's less crowded in the dining room." "We get so much more personal attention from the staff." These perceptions support the residents' compliance with the move and also reinforce a positive attitude about their location and, consequently, about themselves.

Summary and Recommendations

This study suggests that declining health has a negative impact on the residents' self-image due to the formal and informal structure of the retirement facility. The process of illness career descent refers to the downward movement of residents through the facility resulting in a loss of control, stigmatization, and the disruption of social support networks. In addition to these social consequences, residents experience a three stage process as they negotiate a new image of self. While the downward trajectory of chronic illness is unavoidable, illness career descent is a socially constructed reality.

Further research is needed to increase our understanding of the way older people adjust to life disruptions accompanying illness career descent and how this impacts upon their self-image. These are mentally competent individuals who are quite aware of changes in their health, but it is their relocation which so dramatically changes the way they feel about themselves. Some key questions remain unanswered: What is the extent of illness career descent in other multi-level care facilities? What is the full range of illness career descent including relocation from one's homes to a retirement facility and from the ICF to the skilled nursing facility? Do these two groups also experience the same three-stage cognitive process? Would negative stereotyping be lessened or heightened if residents lived in more heterogeneous groups rather than being formally segregated on the basis of capabilities? How does the structure of the facility encourage or inhibit opportunities for residents to develop new roles for themselves? Does the retirement facility's need for efficiency necessarily conflict with the residents' maintaining a sense of control? Answers to these questions become increasingly important with current projections of a growing population of frail elderly. If multi-level care facilities are a trend of the future, then we must strive to understand the social and structural processes that affect those who live within their walls.

Acknowledgments

The author wishes to express his deepest appreciation to Jacob Climo, Peter Conrad, Stan Kaplowitz, and Shulamit Reinharz for their encouragement and their suggestions on earlier drafts of this paper. Address correspondence to: Department of Sociology, Michigan State University, East Lansing, MI 48824.

Notes

1. The term retirement facility is used to denote any living arrangement for elderly people ranging from congregate housing to institutionalization in a nursing home. The name of this retirement facility as well as the names of residents used in this paper are fictitious.

2. While the living units are referred to as apartments they do not have cooking facilities. Residents are discouraged from doing any cooking in their rooms. Hot plates are explicitly prohibited.

3. Residents who have been moved to the retirement complex against their will may not operate with these same assumptions. They have not chosen to move in and may not hold the belief that the staff are competent in dealing with the concerns of the aged.

4. Residents could choose to leave the retirement complex, but this rarely occurs since they would have to find another place which would accommodate their special health-care needs. When such departures do occur they generally involve issues unrelated to a move to the ICF.

References

Aizenberg, Rhonda and Judith Treas
1985 "The family in late life: Psychosocial and demographic considerations." Pp. 169–189 in J. E. Birren and K. W. Schaie (eds.), *Handbook of the Psychology of Aging*. New York: Van Nostrand Reinhold.

Aronson, Elliott, Judith A. Turner, and J. Merrill Carlsmith
1963 "Communicator credibility and communicator discrepancy as determinants of opinion change." *Journal of Abnormal and Social Psychology* 67:31–36.

Brody, Elaine
1977 *Long-Term Care of Older People*. New York: Human Sciences Press.

DiMatteo, M. Robin, and Howard S. Friedman
1982 *Social Psychology and Medicine*. Massachusetts: Olgeschlager, Gunn, and Hain.

Fazio, Russell H. and Mark P. Zanna
1980 "Direct experience and attitude-behavior consistency." Pp. 162–203 in L. Berkowitz (ed.), *Advances in Experimental Social Psychology* Vol 14. New York: Academic Press.

Fisher, Bradley J., 1984
"Rolling Meadows—It's not quite like home: Further reflections on life at a retirement facility." Unpublished Manuscript, Michigan State University.
1985 "Living in the gray zone: The problem with current definitions of congregate housing." Paper presented at the meetings of the Michigan Sociological Society, Holland, Michigan.

Goffman, Erving R.
1959 *The Presentation of Self in Everyday Life*. New York: Doubleday Anchor.
1961 *Asylums*. New York: Doubleday Anchor.
Gubrium, Jaber F.
1975 *Living and Dying at Murray Manor*. New York: St. Martin's Press.
Hamilton, David L.
1979 "A cognitive attributional analysis of stereotyping." Pp. 53–84 in L. Berkowitz (ed.), *Advances in Experimental Social Psychology* Vol. 12. New York: Academic Press.
Hochschild, Arlie R.
1973 *The Unexpected Community*. New Jersey: Prentice-Hall.
Hunter, Kathleen, Margaret W. Linn, and Rachel Harris
1981 "Characteristics of high and low self-esteem in the elderly." *The International Journal on Aging and Human Development* 14:117–126.
Lieberman, Morton A.
1969 "Institutionalization of the aged: Effects on behavior." *Journal of Gerontology* 24: 330–339.
Lord, Charles G., Mark R. Lepper, and Diane Mackie
1984 "Attitude prototypes as determinants of attitude behavior consistency." *Journal of Personality and Social Psychology* 46: 1254–1266.
Manning, Peter K. and Martine Zucker
1976 *The Sociology of Mental Health and Illness*. Indianapolis: Bobbs-Merrill.
Morgan, David L.
1982 "Failing health and the desire for independence: Two conflicting aspects of health care in old age." *Social Problems* 30:40–50.
Petty, Richard E. and John T. Cacioppo
1981 *Attitudes and Persuasion: Classic and Contemporary Approaches*. Iowa: Wm. C. Brown.
Pollack, Max, Eric Karp, Robert L. Kahn, and Alvin I. Goldfarb
1962 "Perception of self in institutionalized aged subjects." *Journal of Gerontology* 17: 405–408.
Smith, Kristen F., and Vern L. Bengston
1979 "Positive consequences of institutionalization: Solidarity between elderly parents and their middle aged children." *The Gerontologist* 19: 438–447.
Strauss, Anselm
1973 "America: In Sickness And In Health–Chronic Illness" *Society*. Pp. 33–39.
Strauss, Anselm, Shizuko Fagerhaugh, Barbara Suczek, and Carolyn Wiener
1985 *Social Organization of Medical Work*. Chicago IL: University of Chicago Press.
Tesch, Stephanie, Susan K. Whitbourne, and Milton F. Nehrke
1981 "Friendship, social interaction, and subjective well-being of older men in an institutional setting." *International Journal of Aging and Human Development* 13:317–327.
Tobin, Sheldon S., and Morton A. Lieberman
1976 *Last Home For The Aged*. San Francisco: Jossey-Bass.
Troll, Lillian E. and Vern L. Bengston
1982 "Intergenerational relations throughout the life span." Pp. 890–911 in B. B. Wolman (ed.), *Handbook of Developmental Psychology*. Englewood Cliffs, NJ: Prentice-Hall.

Part 5 / Noninstitutional Deviance

In Part 4, I described how institutional careers may be initiated and perpetuated. The material in that section examined how various types of institutional processing may affect people. An equally important concern is the way in which noninstitutional careers may evolve. As noted earlier, such careers or activities generally arise as a result of the actor's own desires and needs; this means that frequently the actor plays an assertive role in moving into a particular type of activity, consciously structuring and presenting a specific image of self to others. Often, too, as indicated in the general introduction, there may be a degree of overlap between institutional and noninstitutional careers. For instance, prostitutes, skid row alcoholics, homosexuals, and thieves may be arrested and thus pulled into, rather than intentionally entering, an institutional career. The selections in this part describe events such as these.

STRUCTURES AND ORGANIZATIONAL COMPONENTS

"The Social Organization of Deviants," by Joel Best and David F. Luckenbill, provides an excellent framework for understanding the social organizations in which deviants become involved. The authors make an initial distinction between the social organization of *deviants* and the social organization of *deviance*. The former refers to the "patterns of relationships between deviant actors," whereas the latter refers to the "patterns of relationships between the various roles performed in deviant transactions." Best and Luckenbill elect to focus on the social organization of deviants. Deviant organizations, they reason, can vary along certain dimensions, most notably in terms of their sophistication (i.e., complexity, degree of coordination, and purposiveness). For example, with regard to complexity, organizations can have varying divisions of labor, degrees of stratification, and degrees of role specialization. Best and Luckenbill note that in terms of sophistication, deviants organize in identifiable ways. They discuss five organizational forms: loners, colleagues, peers, mobs, and formal organizations. Each of these forms can be analyzed relative to four variables (i.e., whether the deviants associate with each other, whether they engage in deviance together, whether there is an elaborate division of labor, and whether activities extend over time and space). The authors describe various types of each organizational form. They then examine the consequences of organizing as loners, colleagues, peers, mobs, or formal organizations. Best and Luckenbill argue that the degree of sophistication of a deviant organization has consequences for deviants and social-control agents. Five propositions are advanced in support of this argument. The authors' second hypothesis is especially relevant for the next section on entering and learning about deviant cultures. Specifically, they hypothesize that "the more sophisticated the form of deviant organization, the more elaborate the socialization of its members." The underlying assumption here is that "neophyte deviants" not only must learn how to perform deviant acts and attain the appropriate skills and techniques, but they must also develop a *cognitive perspective* (e.g., learn the relevant rationalizations and language). As an illustration, loners do not depend on others for instruction, but pool hustlers do.

David F. Luckenbill, in "Deviant Career Mobility: The Case of Male Prostitutes," contends that, even though the topic of deviant career has been given substantial focus, research on involvement (i.e., the stage between entry into a deviant world and departure from it) has been limited. Similarly, little evidence exists with respect to deviant career mobility or the changes in rank or position that the occupant of a deviant world may experience during his or her involvement. Luckenbill raises some interesting questions. Do deviants maintain their initial positions, or do they move between or among ranks? Further, what contingencies might shape patterns of mobility? Inquiries such as these are examined through the use of interview data gathered on twenty-eight male prostitutes or "hustlers" over a period of twenty-eight months. Luckenbill's data indicate that the world of male prostitution is, like the world of drugs and gambling, stratified along certain dimensions. With respect to the vertical or hierarchical dimension, the male prostitutes described three tiers: street hustling, bar hustling, and escort prostitution. Frequently their explanations of these rankings were based on observed differences in lifestyle, with most respondents believing that escorts enjoy a better lifestyle than bar and street hustlers. Further analyses established three patterns of career mobility: stability, minimum ascent, and maximum ascent. Seven subjects, for example, remained in the same rank during their career, whereas fifteen moved from street hustling to bar hustling. Luckenbill continues by describing those subjective and objective contingencies that prompted career shifts among the prostitutes. As an illustration, some street hustlers who had initially defined the street as exciting ultimately became fearful of it. Through involvement with friends, the disenchanted learned about the location of hustler bars, as well as the advantages and requirements associated with bar hustling. Before the street hustler could make the shift in rank, however, three basic occupational requirements had to be satisfied: he had to be at least twenty-one years of age, honest, and attractive in appearance.

ENTERING AND LEARNING DEVIANT CULTURES

The statements by Best and Luckenbill and by Luckenbill indicate that deviant organizations can be characterized in terms of their relative degree of sophistication. Best and Luckenbill also highlight the fact that a person can gain initial entry to organizations through various channels. Once individuals gain entry, however, they must, if they elect to stay, learn the existing culture and traditions. A similar requirement exists with respect to the institutional deviant. Failure to meet expectations may result in such penalties as ostracism or exclusion from the group. (The general social-psychological processes involved in learning deviant cultures were highlighted in my discussion of the cultural transmission model in Part 2.) The selections in this section deal primarily with entry routes and offer specific illustrations of how actors become socialized into deviant or semideviant careers. In this respect, Heyl's research on the training of house prostitutes is especially insightful.

In "Drifting into Dealing: Becoming a Cocaine Seller," Sheigla Murphy, Dan Waldorf, and Craig Reinarman outline the various modes and levels of entry into the world of cocaine sales. Their observations are based on interviews with eighty ex-cocaine sellers. All had sold cocaine for at least a year; however, none had done so for a period of six months prior to the interviews. Actual entry into the world of cocaine sales is, according to the researchers, a fluid process, with most sellers drifting into their dealing career. The authors go on to describe five basic ways that people begin to sell cocaine. The first mode of entry is the *go-between,* in which a person who initially buys for his or her friends begins to envision the profits that may result from selling. The second avenue is the *stash dealer,* in which a user sells small amounts to support his or her own cocaine needs. The *connoisseur,* the third mode of entry, includes those who seek to buy high-quality drugs through wholesale purchases, and the fourth entry route entails the *apprenticeship,* a trainee-style of connection. In this situation, the novice takes over all aspects of an established dealer's business after learning the ropes. The fifth and final entry route described involves what is termed the *product line expansion.* Here dealers start selling other drugs (e.g., marijuana) and then move into cocaine sales when a supply becomes available. Of importance, too, is the authors' analysis of how a seller may exhibit a subtle transformation of his or her identity. Once situated in the role of the dealer, selling often becomes viewed as a job or career. Significant, too, is the observation that the "dealer identity" did not seem to replace former "legitimate" identities but was, instead, added to a subject's other conventional identities. Thus, sellers would, and depending upon the situation, emphasize different aspects of their identities. The researchers end by describing some of the values and expectations that characterize the business relationships existing between sellers and customers.

Barbara Sherman Heyl, in "The Madam as Teacher: The Training of House Prostitutes," describes the socialization of house prostitutes. Heyl primarily focuses on the "female trainer-trainee relationship" that exists at the house level. Once a novice enters the house she becomes trained by the "madam." A major portion of the training involves instruction in the appropriate sexual techniques—fellatio, coitus, and "half and half." The newcomer is also taught the house rules (such as the amount of time to be spent with a customer and the specific sums of money to be charged for various types of sexual services), client management, and how to "hustle." Throughout this training, an attempt is made to effectively isolate the novice from her prior lifestyle and associations. This specific process is important in structuring an occupational identity as a "professional" (i.e., a view of self as a career prostitute). Heyl goes on to note that the house prostitute, unlike the call girl, must go through considerable training; this is primarily due to the structure of the profession. Specifically, established houses require close interaction among their participants and thus they hire only the trained prostitute. Like the Murphy *et al.* study, Heyl's offers an excellent application of the cultural transmission model discussed in Part 2. The research also graphically illustrates how the existing theory of the office and associated stereotypes become inculcated within the house prostitute—a process that may produce a career, or secondary, deviant.

PATTERNS AND VARIATIONS

As is apparent from the preceding statements, deviant or semideviant occupations vary in terms of their sophistication and corresponding organizational structure. Quite clearly, the house prostitute, given the particular nature of the profession, is subjected to a more elaborate and intense degree of socialization than is the case with the call girl. This observation highlights the fact that deviance and the deviant career can exhibit a variety of patterns, each with its own recruiting offices, entry routes, career lines, socialization mechanisms, and career shifts. Deviant pursuits can also exhibit, in accordance with Best and Luckenbill's concern with the social organization of deviance, a range of mutually beneficial relationships; this is especially evident in the next two selections.

In "State-Organized Crime," William J. Chambliss presents a description of selected types of crimes committed by state officials. State-organized crime, according to his definition, consists of those "acts defined by law as criminal and committed by state officials in the pursuit of their jobs as representatives of the state." He cites various examples of state complicity in criminal activities and then offers some specific accounts. He initially describes instances of government involvement in smuggling. His analysis of the role that narcotics played in the Vietnam War is insightful, particularly in terms of the CIA's involvement. For example, the CIA and its Air America not only offered a convenient source of transportation to the opium-growing lords, but the Agency also played a major role in establishing the solvency of Nugan Hand Bank; this bank benefited from large deposits made by both the drug lords and the CIA. The bank's connection to the CIA is, according to Chambliss, evident and becomes especially so when the composition of the bank's directors and officers is examined. Chambliss offers additional accounts linking the CIA to drug trafficking and arms smuggling. In terms of arms smuggling, the author describes what some have referred to as the "secret government within our government." Here a group of state officials sold weapons to Iran and then diverted the funds to the Contras. Why would government agents become involved in such criminal activities? Chambliss argues in part that, although the government seemed committed to fighting "communism," the funding and required support were often lacking. Hence, alternative sources of funding were sometimes sought. And as noted by Chambliss, obliging connections and sources were often in place. Chambliss concludes with a description of the state's involvement in selected assassinations and murders.

Andrew Szasz, in "Corporations, Organized Crime, and The Disposal of Hazardous Waste: An Examination of the Making of a Criminogenic Regulatory Structure," offers another interesting account of the types of relationships that can exist between or among legitimate and illegitimate enterprises or entrepreneurs. He focuses on the disposal of toxic waste, particularly the way in which organized crime became involved in its disposal. A basic thesis is Szasz's argument that corporate generators of hazardous waste products helped to create a regulatory structure that was accessible and attractive to organized crime. Szasz begins by describing how attempts were made to regulate the disposal of hazardous waste—efforts that resulted in the creation of the federal Resource Conservation and Recovery Act (RCRA). RCRA established procedures for the safe disposal of hazardous substances and authorized states to register the corporate generators of the waste. RCRA also mandated the licensing of hauling and disposal firms. Given organized crime's traditionally heavy involvement in garbage hauling and landfilling, extension of their influence to the illegal disposal of hazardous wastes was relatively straightforward. For example, when RCRA mandated the licensing of firms, mob-connected haulers acquired state permits and called themselves hazardous waste haulers. Organized crime also controlled some final disposal sites; hence, it was easy to have the manifest signed and then state that the waste had been disposed of properly. Other organized crime figures seized control of phony disposal sites and treatment facilities. Szasz continues by describing those political and social-structural factors that enabled organized crime to "'colonize' the hazardous waste disposal industry." Specifically, lax implementation and incompetent enforcement of the provisions of RCRA allowed organized crime to gain a strong foothold in the hazardous waste business. Interim licenses were granted and the manifest system was monitored loosely. Szasz also points to the role of generators of waste. For example, corporate generators lobbied for narrow definitions of hazardous waste as well as less stringent rules for disposal.

THE EFFECTS OF DEVIANT CAREERS

Involvement in activities, careers, and professions that are commonly viewed as deviant by others is not without its personal and social costs. If, for example, deviance becomes known, the actor may become stigmatized and subsequently discredited. Thus, those who engage in potentially discrediting behavior must manage their "front" in such a way as to avoid detection by socially significant "straights." The articles in this section focus directly on the social actor, particularly on the management strategies that may be invoked to protect a person's identity and self-image from erosion, damage, or outright destruction.

William E. Thompson, in "Handling the Stigma of Handling the Dead: Morticians and Funeral Directors," presents an account of how people attempt to manage the stigma associated with their occupation. His observations are based on two years of field work entailing interviews with nineteen morticians and funeral directors. Some interesting results emerge. He notes initially that the morticians and funeral directors are painfully aware of the stigma associated with their occupation; this stigmatization seems to flow not only from the fact that they handle the dead but also from the view that they profit from death and grief. Thompson then outlines the strategies that are employed in an effort to neutralize and assuage the stigma encountered. One strategy involves avoiding the terms "dead" and "death" and substituting other words (e.g., "time of sorrow" or "hour of sadness"). "Coffins" become "caskets" and "burial" becomes "interment." Selected funeral directors may shift the focus of their work away from the dead and redefine themselves as "grief therapists" and "bereavement counselors." Maintaining role distance is another strategy employed to protect one's sense of self; this can entail emotional detachment, such as the situation where the mortician or funeral director may, instead of focusing on the person, emphasize the technical aspects involved in embalming. Other tactics of neutralization and stigma management and reduction include using humor, countering the stereotypes, appealing to professionalism, and stressing service. Thompson concludes by noting that, even though morticians and funeral directors appear to suffer from a lack of occupational prestige, they do, as a group, seem to do well, socioeconomically, in terms of material gains and pleasures. The next selection by Davis echoes many of these same concerns.

David S. Davis, in "Good People Doing Dirty Work: A Study of Social Isolation," argues, like Thompson, that individuals who are engaged in activities or occupations viewed unfavorably by others may experience damage to their identity and self-image. He initiates his analysis by offering a useful distinction between "unrespectable" and "disrespectable" people. The unrespectable may, for example, accept an audience's view of them as lacking in merit, whereas the disrespectable may reject such an evaluation. A tendency also exists whereby the disrespectable may become socially isolated. Davis examines notions such as these through a combination of interview, observational, and reputational data obtained on twenty-five bailbondsmen who are engaged in what is often viewed by society as "dirty work" (i.e., in this case, for a fee, obtaining the pretrial release of defendants). These observations are supplemented with data gathered from a national survey. Davis notes that, like other low-status occupations, the bailbonds profession suffers from a lack of respect on many fronts. He presents case materials in support of this assessment. The occupants of this status are not only aware of the stigmatized nature of their activity but some, in a conscious effort to reject such a notion, utter protestations to the effect that they have been falsely accused. These feelings of being rejected by members of conventional society are not without their structural and personal consequences, with a major outcome being that the falsely accused tend to gravitate to a life of social isolation; this often means, moreover, that their primary reference groups become the professional and petty criminals. Davis concludes with a discussion of the marginal man—a conception that appears to apply rather nicely to selected categories of bailbondsmen studied by the researcher.

31 / The Social Organization of Deviants

JOEL BEST
DAVID F. LUCKENBILL

Ethnographic research on particular social scenes provides data for general, grounded theories (Glaser and Strauss, 1967). For the study of deviance, field studies have supplied the basis for the development of general theories of the social psychology of deviance (Goffman, 1963; Lofland, 1969; Matza, 1969). However, while several reports about specific forms of deviance focus on social organization (Einstader, 1969; McIntosh, 1971; Mileski and Black, 1972; Shover, 1977; Zimmerman and Wieder, 1977), there is no satisfactory general theory of the social organization of deviance.

Sociologists of varying perspectives have debated the nature of social organization among juvenile delinquents, professional criminals, organized criminals and white-collar criminals. Others have developed typologies of deviants that include social organizational features (Clinard and Quinney, 1973; Gibbons, 1965, 1977; Miller, 1978). However, these treatments of social organization suffer from several flaws. First, they are often too narrow, focusing on a single type of deviance, such as burglary or, more broadly, crime. Second, they usually are content with describing the organizational forms of different types of deviance. They fail to locate such forms along a dimension of organization or examine the consequences of organizational differences for deviants and social control agents. Third, they typically confuse two different bases for analyzing social organization: a general theory must distinguish between the social organization of *deviants* (the patterns of relationships between deviant actors) and the social organization of *deviance* (the patterns of relationships between the various roles performed in deviant transactions).

In this paper, we present a framework for understanding the social organization of deviants.[1] By examining reports of field research, several forms of social organization are identified and located along a dimension of organizational sophistication. Then some propositions are developed regarding the consequences of organizational variation for deviants and social control agents. Finally, some implications for the study of social organization are considered.

FORMS OF DEVIANT ORGANIZATION

The social organization of deviants refers to the structure or patterns of relationships among deviant actors in the context of deviant pursuits. The social organization of deviants varies along a dimension of sophistication. Organizational sophistication involves the elements of complexity, coordination and purposiveness (cf. Cressey, 1972). Organizations vary in the complexity of their division of labor including the size of membership, degree of stratification, and degree of specialization of organizational roles. Organizations also vary in their coordination among roles including the degree to which rules, agreements, and codes regulating relationships are formalized and enforced. Finally, organizations vary in the purposiveness with which they specify, strive toward, and achieve their objectives. Forms of organization which display high levels of complexity, coordination, and purposiveness are more sophisticated than those forms with lower levels.

Research reports suggest that deviants organize in several identifiable ways along the dimension of sophistication. Beginning with the least sophisticated, we will discuss five forms: loners, colleagues, peers, mobs and formal organizations. These organizational forms can be defined in terms of four variables: (1) whether the deviants associate with one another; (2) whether they participate in deviance together; (3) whether their deviance requires an elaborate division of labor; and (4) whether their organization's activities extend over time and space (see Table 1). *Loners* do not associate with other deviants, participate in shared deviance, have a division of labor, or maintain their deviance over extended time and space. *Colleagues* differ from loners because they associate with fellow deviants. *Peers* not only associate with one another, but also participate in deviance together. In *mobs*, the shared participation requires an elaborate division of labor. Finally, *formal organizations* involve mutual association and participation, an elaborate division of labor, and deviant undertakings extended over time and space.

Table 1 / Characteristics of Different Forms of the Social Organization of Deviants

	Type of Organization				
Variable	LONERS	COLLEAGUES	PEERS	MOBS	FORMAL ORGANIZATIONS
Mutual association	−	+	+	+	+
Mutual participation	−	−	+	+	+
Division of labor	−	−	−	+	+
Extended organization	−	−	−	−	+

The descriptions of these forms of organization must be qualified in two ways. First, the forms are presented as ideal types. There is variation among the types of deviants within each form, as well as between one form and another. The intent is to sketch out the typical features of each form, recognizing that particular types of deviants may not share all of the features of their form to the same degree. Organizational sophistication can be viewed as a continuum, with deviants located between, as well as on, the five points. Describing a number of forms along this continuum inevitably understates the complexities of social life. Second, the descriptions of these forms draw largely from field studies of deviance in the contemporary United States, and attempt to locate the deviants studied along the dimension of organizational sophistication. A particular type of deviant can be organized in various ways in different societies and at different times. The references to specific field studies are intended to place familiar pieces of research within this framework; they are not claims that particular types of deviants invariably organize in a given way.

Loners

Some deviants operate as individuals. These loners do not associate with other deviants for purposes of sociability, the performance of deviant activities, or the exchange of supplies and information. Rather, they must supply themselves with whatever knowledge, skill, equipment and ideology their deviance requires. Loners lack deviant associations, so they cannot receive such crucial forms of feedback as moral support or information about their performance, new opportunities, or changes in social control strategies. They often enter deviance as a defensive response to private troubles (Lofland, 1969). Because their entry does not require contact with other deviants, as long as they can socialize themselves, loners frequently come from segments of the population which are less likely to be involved in the more sophisticated forms of deviance; it is not uncommon for loners to be middle-aged, middle-class or female. Because their deviance often is defensive, and because they lack the support of other deviants, loners' careers typically are short-lived. Examples of loners include murderers (Luckenbill, 1977), rapists (Amir, 1971), embezzlers (Cressey, 1953), check forgers (Lemert, 1967:99–134; Klein and Montague, 1977), physician narcotic addicts (Winick, 1961), compulsive criminals (Cressey, 1962), heterosexual transvestites (Buckner, 1970), amateur shoplifters (Cameron, 1964), some gamblers (Lesieur,1977), and many computer criminals (Parker, 1976).[2]

Colleagues

Like loners, colleagues perform as individuals. Unlike loners, however, colleagues associate with others involved in the same kind of deviance. Colleagues thus form a simple group which provides important services for members. First, colleagues often socialize newcomers, providing training in deviant skills as well as an ideology which accounts for and justifies their deviance. Association also offers sociability among members with whom one's deviant identity need not be concealed: an actor can take down his or her guard without fear of discovery by agents of social control (Goffman, 1959, 1963). Also, association provides a source of information about ways to obtain deviant equipment, new techniques, new opportunities for engaging in deviance, and strategies for avoiding sanctioning. Colleagues learn and are held to a loose set of norms which direct conduct in both deviant and respectable activities. "Don't inform on a colleague" and "Never cut in on a colleague's score" exemplify such norms. The moral climate established by these expectations increases the stability of colleagues' social scene. At the same time, only some deviant activities and some people are suited for such a loose form of organization. A successful career as a colleague depends ultimately on the individual's performance when operating alone. As a result, newcomers often sample the scene and, when they encounter difficulties, drift away. Only the more successful colleagues maintain extended deviant careers. Some examples of colleagues include most prostitutes (Hirschi, 1962; Bryan, 1965, 1966), pimps (Milner and Milner, 1972), and pool hustlers (Polsky, 1967).

Peers

Like colleagues, peers associate with one another and benefit from services provided by their fellows. Peers are involved in the socialization of novices, considerable sociable interaction, and the maintenance of a loose, unwritten code of conduct to be followed by individuals who wish to remain in the peer group. Unlike colleagues, peers participate in deviant acts together; they are involved in deviant transactions at the same time and in the same place. In some cases, such mutual participation is required by the nature of the deviant activity. This is exemplified in the performance of homosexual acts, or in the "task force raids" where a collection of young men engages in simple acts of violence such as gang fighting or rolling drunks (Cressey, 1972). In other cases, mutual participation is required because peers form a network for supplying one another with essential goods and services, as found in the distribution of illicit drugs. In either event, peers interact basically as equals; there is a minimal division of labor and specialized roles are uncommon. Although individuals pass through these social scenes, peer groups often are quite stable, perhaps because peer groups solve structural problems within society for their members. Two common varieties of deviant peers are young people who have not yet entered integrated adult work roles, and those who frequent a deviant marketplace and depend on their contacts with one another for the satisfaction of illicit needs. Examples of peers include hobos (Anderson,

1923), homosexuals (Humphreys, 1970; Mileski and Black, 1972; Warren, 1974), group-oriented gamblers (Lesieur, 1977), swingers (Bartell, 1971), gang delinquents (Shaw, 1930; Matza, 1964; Rosenberg and Silverstein, 1969), motorcycle outlaws (Thompson, 1966), skid row tramps (Wiseman, 1970; Rubington, 1978), and illicit drug users (Blumer, 1967; Carey, 1968; Feldman, 1968; Stoddart, 1974).

Mobs

Mobs are small groups of professional or career deviants organized to pursue specific, profitable goals.[3] Their deviance requires the coordinated actions of members performing specialized roles—a more sophisticated division of labor than that found among peers. Thus, work is divided among confidence artists (the inside man and the outside man), pickpockets (the tool and the stall), or card and dice hustlers (the mechanic and the shootup man; Maurer, 1962, 1964; Prus and Sharper, 1977). Ordinarily, at least one of the roles in the mob is highly skilled, requiring considerable practice and training to perfect. This training (normally via apprenticeship), the need for on-the-job coordination, and the common practice of traveling from city to city as a mob lead to intensive interaction between mobsters. Elaborate technical argots develop, as well as elaborate codes specifying mobsters' obligations to each other.

Mobs have complex links to outsiders. They are organized to accomplish profitable yet safe crimes. McIntosh (1971) describes the historical shift from craft thieving, where mobs develop routine procedures for stealing relatively small sums from individuals, to project thieving, where larger amounts are taken from corporate targets using procedures specifically tailored to the particular crime. In either case, mob operations are planned and staged with an eye toward avoiding arrest. Also, mobs may attempt to neutralize the criminal justice system by bribing social control agents not to make arrests, "fixing" those cases where arrests take place, or making restitution to victims in return for dropped charges. Mobs also have ties to others who purchase stolen goods, provide legal services, and supply information and deviant equipment. Finally, a network of sociable and business contacts ties mobs to one another, enabling strategic information to spread quickly. These arrangements ensure that mobs can operate at a consistently profitable level with minimal interference. Consequently, the careers of individual mobsters, as well as those of specific mobs, seem to be more stable than those of deviants organized in less sophisticated ways.[4] Examples of mobs are the groups of professional criminals specializing in confidence games (Sutherland, 1937; Maurer, 1962), picking pockets (Maurer, 1964), shoplifting (Cameron, 1964), armed robbery (Einstader, 1969; Letkemann, 1973), burglary (Shover, 1977), and card and dice hustling (Prus and Sharper, 1977).

Formal Organizations

Formal organizations of deviants differ from mobs in the scope of their actions.[5] Normally they involve more people, but, more importantly, their actions are coordinated to efficiently handle deviant tasks on a routine basis over considerable time and space. While mobsters work as a group in a series of episodic attacks, formal organizations are characterized by delegated responsibility and by routine and steady levels of productivity. In many ways, formal organizations of deviants share the features which characterize such respectable bureaucracies as military organizations, churches, and business firms. They have a hierarchal division of labor, including both vertical and horizontal differentiation of positions and roles and established channels for vertical and horizontal communication. A deviant formal organization may contain departments for planning, processing goods, public relations and rule enforcement, with positions for strategists, coordinators, accountants, lawyers, enforcers, and dealers in illicit goods. There may be recruitment policies for filling these diversified positions, and entry into the organization may be marked by a ritual ceremony of passage. Formal organizations usually have binding, but normally unwritten, rules and codes for guiding members in organizational action, and these rules are actively enforced.

Formal organizations of deviants can make large profits by operating efficiently. At the same time, they must protect themselves from harm or destruction. As in less sophisticated forms of organization, loyal members are expected to maintain the group's secrets. In addition, deviant formal organizations attempt to locate power in the office, rather than in an individual charismatic leader. Although charismatic leadership obviously plays a part in some deviant formal organizations, the successful organization is able to continue operations when a leader dies or is arrested. Finally, deviant formal organizations typically invest considerable energy in neutralizing the criminal justice system by corrupting both high- and low-level officials. The scope and efficiency of their operations, their organizational flexibility, and their ties to agencies of social control make formal organizations of deviants extremely stable. Examples of such deviant formal organizations include very large urban street gangs (Keiser, 1969; Dawley, 1973), smuggling rings (Green, 1969), and organized crime "families" (Cressey, 1969; Ianni, 1972).

THE SIGNIFICANCE OF THE SOCIAL ORGANIZATION OF DEVIANTS

The identification and description of these different organizational forms permit a comparative analysis. What are the consequences of organizing as loners, colleagues, peers, mobs, or formal organizations? A comparison suggests that the sophistication of a form of deviant social organization has several consequences for both deviants and social control agents. Five propositions can be advanced.

I. *The more sophisticated the form of deviant organization, the greater its members' capability for complex deviant operations.* Deviant activities, like conventional activities, vary in their complexity. The complexity of a deviant operation refers to the number of elements required to carry it through; the more component parts to an activity, the more complex it is.[6] Compared to simple activities, complex lines of action demand more careful preparation and execution and take longer to complete. The complexity of a deviant activity depends upon two identifiable types of elements. First, there are the *resources* which the actors must be able to draw upon. Some activities require that the deviant utilize special knowledge, skill, equipment, or social status in order to complete the operation successfully, while simple acts can be carried out without such resources. Second, the *organization of the deviant transaction* affects an activity's complexity.[7] Some deviant acts can be accomplished with a single actor, while others require two or more people. The actors in a transaction can share a common role, as in a skid row bottle gang, or the transaction may demand different roles, such as offender and victim or buyer and seller. Furthermore, the degree to which these roles must be coordinated, ranging from the minimal coordination of juvenile vandals to the precision routines performed by mobs of pickpockets, varies among situations. The more people involved, the more roles they perform; and the more coordination between those roles, the more complex the deviant transaction's organization. The more resources and organization involved in a deviant operation, the more complex the operation is.

In general, deviants in more sophisticated forms of organization commit more complex acts.[8] The deviant acts of loners tend to be simple, requiring little in the way of resources or organization. Although colleagues work apart from one another, they generally share certain resources, such as shared areas. The hustlers' pool hall and the prostitutes' red light district contain the elements needed to carry out deviant operations, including victims and clients. Peers may interact in situations where they are the only ones present, performing complementary or comparable roles, as when two people engage in homosexual intercourse or a group of motorcycle outlaws makes a "run." Peers also may undertake activities which involve nonmembers, as when members of a delinquent gang rob a passerby. The activities carried out by mobs involve substantially more coordination among the members' roles. In an armed robbery, for instance, one member may be assigned to take the money, while a second provides "cover" and a third waits for the others in the car, ready to drive away on their return. Finally, the activities of formal organizations tend to be particularly complex, requiring substantial resources and elaborate organization. Major off-track betting operations, with staff members at local, district and regional offices who carry out a variety of clerical and supervisory tasks on a daily basis, represent an exceedingly complex form of deviance.

The relationship between the sophistication of organization and the complexity of deviant activities is not perfect. Loners can engage in acts of considerable complexity, for example. The computer criminal who single-handedly devises a complicated method of breaking into and stealing from computerized records, the embezzler who carries through an elaborate series of illicit financial manipulations, and the physician who juggles drug records in order to maintain his or her addiction to narcotics are engaged in complex offenses requiring substantial resources. However, these offenses cannot be committed by everyone. These loners draw upon resources which they command through their conventional positions, turning them to deviant uses. The computer criminal typically is an experienced programmer, the embezzler must occupy a position of financial trust, and the physician has been trained in the use of drugs. Possessing these resources makes the loner's deviance possible. Thus, the more concentrated the resources necessary for a deviant operation, the less sophisticated the form of organization required. However, when resources are not concentrated, then more sophisticated forms of organization are necessary to undertake more complex deviant operations.

Sophisticated forms of deviant organization have advantages beyond being able to undertake complex operations by pooling resources distributed among their members. Some deviant activities require a minimal level of organization; for example, homosexual intercourse demands the participation of two parties. In many other cases, it may be possible to carry out a deviant line of action using a relatively unsophisticated form of organization, but the task is considerably easier if a sophisticated form of organization can be employed. This is so because more sophisticated forms of deviant organization enjoy several advantages: they are capable of conducting a larger number of deviant operations; the operations can occur with greater frequency and over a broader range of territory; and, as discussed below, the members are better protected from the actions of social control agents. Of course, sophisticated organizations may engage in relatively simple forms of deviance, but the deviant act is often only one component in a larger organizational context. Taking a particular bet in the policy racket is a simple act, but the racket itself, handling thousands of bets, is complex indeed. Similarly, a murder which terminates a barroom dispute between two casual acquaintances is very different from an execution which is ordered and carried out by members of a formal organization, even though the two acts may appear equally simple. In the latter case, the killing may be intended as a means of maintaining discipline by demonstrating the organization's ability to levy sanctions against wayward members.

II. *The more sophisticated the form of deviant organization, the more elaborate the socialization of its members.* Neophyte deviants need to acquire two types of knowledge: 1) they must learn how to perform deviant acts, and how to gain appropriate *skills and techniques*; 2) they must develop a *cognitive perspective*, a distinctive way of making sense of their new, deviant world (cf. Shibutani, 1961:118–127). Such a perspective includes an ideology which accounts for the deviance, the individual's participation in deviance, and the organizational form, as well as a distinctive language for speaking about these and other matters.

As forms of deviant organization increase in sophistication, socialization becomes more elaborate. Loners do not depend upon other deviants for instruction in deviant skills or for a special cognitive perspective; they learn through their participation in conventional social scenes. Murderers, for instance, learn from their involvement in conventional life how to respond in situations of interpersonal conflict, and they employ culturally widespread justifications for killing people (Bohannon, 1960; Wolfgang and Ferracuti, 1967). Embezzlers learn the technique for converting a financial trust in the course of respectable vocational training, adapting justifications such as "borrowing" from conventional business ideology (Cressey, 1953). In contrast, colleagues teach one another a great deal. Although pool hustlers usually know how to shoot pool before they enter hustling, their colleagues provide a rich cognitive perspective, including a sense of "we-ness," some norms of behavior, a system for stratifying the hustling world, and an extensive argot (Polsky, 1967).[9] Peers receive similar training or, in some cases, teach one another through a process of emerging norms (Turner, 1964). Juvenile vandals, for example, can devise new offenses through their mutually constructed interpretation of what is appropriate to a particular situation (Wade, 1967). Sometimes, the knowledge peers acquire has largely symbolic functions that affirm the group's solidarity, as when a club of motorcycle outlaws devises a written constitution governing its members (Reynolds, 1967:134–136). In mobs and formal organizations, the cognitive perspective focuses on more practical matters; their codes of conduct specify the responsibilities members have in their dealings with one another, social control agents and others. Greater emphasis is also placed on the acquisition of specialized skills, with an experienced deviant coaching an apprentice, frequently over an extended period of time.

Two circumstances affect the socialization process in different forms of deviant organization. First, the sophistication of the organization affects the scope and style of the training process. The amount of training tends to increase with the sophistication of the organization. The skills required to perform deviant roles vary, but there is a tendency for more sophisticated forms of organization to incorporate highly skilled roles. Further, the more sophisticated forms of organization often embody cognitive perspectives of such breadth that the deviant must acquire a large body of specialized knowledge. In addition, the socialization process tends to be organized differently in different forms of deviant organization. While loners serve as their own agents of socialization, and colleagues and peers may socialize one another, mobs and formal organizations almost always teach newcomers through apprenticeship to an experienced deviant. Second, the socialization process is affected by the newcomer's motivation for entering deviance. Loners, of course, choose deviance on their own. In the more sophisticated forms, newcomers may ask for admission, but they often are recruited by experienced deviants. While peers may recruit widely, as when a delinquent gang tries to enlist all of the neighborhood boys of a given age, mobs and formal organizations recruit selectively, judging the character and commitment of prospective members and sometimes demanding evidence of skill or prior experience. For loners, entry into deviance frequently is a defensive act, intended to ward off some immediate threat. Peers, on the other hand, often are using deviance to experience stimulation; their deviance has an adventurous quality (Lofland, 1969). In contrast, mobs and formal organizations adopt a more professional approach: deviance is instrumental, a calculated means of acquiring economic profits.[10] These differences in the scope of socialization, the way the process is organized, and the neophyte's motivation account for the relationship between sophistication of organization and the elaborateness of the socialization.

III. *The more sophisticated the form of deviant organization, the more elaborate the services provided its members.* Every social role poses practical problems for its performers. In some cases these problems can be solved by providing the actors with supplies of various sorts. Actors may require certain *equipment* to perform a role. They may also need *information* about their situation in order to coordinate their behavior with the ongoing action and successfully accomplish their part in an operation. One function of deviant social organization is to solve such practical problems by supplying members with needed equipment and information. More sophisticated forms of social organization are capable of providing more of these services.

Deviants differ in their requirements for equipment. Some need little in the way of equipment; a mugger may be able to get by with a piece of pipe. In other cases, deviants make use of specialized items which have few, if any, respectable uses (e.g., heroin or the booster boxes used in shoplifting).[11] Most loners require little equipment. When specialized needs exist, they are met through conventional channels accessible to the deviants, as when a physician narcotic addict obtains illicit drugs from hospital or clinic supplies. Colleagues also supply their own equipment, for the most part, although they may receive some assistance; pool hustlers, for example, provide their own cues, but they may rely on financial backers for funding. Peers adopt various patterns toward equipment. In some cases, peer groups develop to facilitate the distribution and consumption of deviant goods, such as illicit drugs. In other instances, peers use equipment as a symbol of their deviant status, as when gang members wear special costumes. The equipment used by mobsters is more utilitarian; many of their trades demand specialized tools, for safecracking, shoplifting and so forth. In addition to a craftsman's personal equipment, the mob may require special materials for a specific project. Norms often exist that specify the manner in which these equipment purchases will be financed. In still other instances, some mobsters with expensive pieces of equipment may cooperate with several different mobs who wish to make use of them (such as the "big store" which is centrally located for the use of several confidence mobs). Formal organizations also have extensive equipment requirements. Because their operations extend over considerable time, formal organizations may find it expedient to invest in an elaborate array of fixed equipment. Off-track bookmaking, for example, may involve the purchase or rental of offices, desks, calculators, computer lines, special telephone lines, office supplies and automobiles. Special staff members may have the responsibility for maintaining this equipment (Bell, 1962:134). In addition, some formal organizations are involved in producing or distributing deviant equipment for the consumption of other deviants; drug smuggling offers the best example.

Deviants need information in order to determine their courses of action. To operate efficiently, they need to know about new opportunities for deviant action; to operate safely, they need to know about the movements of social control agents. The more sophisticated forms of organization have definite advantages in acquiring and processing information. Loners, of course, depend upon themselves for information; opportunities or threats outside their notice cannot be taken into account. Colleagues and peers can learn more by virtue of their contacts with the deviant "grapevine," and they may have norms regarding a member's responsibility to share relevant information. In mobs, information is sought in more systematic ways. In the course of their careers, mobsters develop perceptual skills, enabling them to "case" possible targets (Letkemann, 1973). In addition, some mobs rely on outsiders for information; spotters may be paid a commission for pointing out opportunities for theft. A formal organization can rely upon its widely distributed membership for information and its contacts with corrupted social control agents.

The degree to which deviants need special supplies varies with the requirements of their operations, the frequency with which they interact with victims or other nondeviants, and their visibility to social control agents. Supplies other than equipment and information may be required in some instances. However, for most supply problems, sophisticated forms of social organization enjoy a comparative advantage.

IV. *The more sophisticated the form of deviant organization, the greater its members' involvement in deviance.* Complex deviant operations require planning and coordinated action during the deviant act. Socialization and supply also involve interaction among an organization's members. More sophisticated forms of deviant organization, featuring complex operations and elaborate socialization and supply, are therefore more likely to involve intensive social contact with one's fellow deviants. Furthermore, because deviants face sanctions from social control agents and respectable people, their contacts with other deviants are an important source of social support. The differences in the ability of forms and social organization to provide support for their members have important social psychological consequences for deviants' careers and identities.

The dimensions of deviant careers vary from the form of deviant organization. Longer deviant careers tend to occur in more sophisticated forms of organization. For naive loners, deviance can comprise a single episode, a defensive act to ward off an immediate threat. For systematic loners, and many colleagues and peers, involvement in deviance is limited to one period in their life. Prostitutes grow too old to compete in the sexual marketplace, delinquents move into respectable adult work roles, and so forth. Members of mobs and formal organizations are more likely to have extended careers. Where the roles are not too physically demanding, deviance can continue until the individual is ready to retire from the work force (Inciardi, 1977). Deviant careers also vary in the amount of time they demand while the individual is active; some kinds of deviance take up only a small portion of the person's hours, but other deviant roles are equivalent to full-time, conventional jobs. Although the relationship is not perfect, part-time deviance is associated with less sophisticated forms of deviant organization.[12]

Social organization is also related to the relative prominence of the deviant identity in the individual's self-concept. Individuals may view their deviance as tangential to the major themes in their lives, or as a central focus, an identity around which much of one's life is arranged. The latter pattern is more likely to develop in sophisticated forms of deviant organization, for, as Lofland (1969) points out, several factors associated with deviant social organization facilitate the assumption of deviant identity, including frequenting places populated by deviants, obtaining deviant equipment, and receiving instruction in deviant skills and ideology. These factors also would appear to be associated with the maintenance of deviance as a central identity. Loners seem especially adept at isolating their deviance, viewing it as an exception to the generally conventional pattern their lives take. This is particularly true when the deviance was initially undertaken to defend that conventional life style from some threat. Even when an individual is relatively committed to deviance, normal identities can serve as an important resource. In his discussion of the World War II underground, Aubert (1965) notes that normal identities served to protect its members. In the same way, an established normal status shields the deviant from the suspicion of social control agents and, if the members refrain from revealing their conventional identities to one another, against discovery brought about by deviant associates who invade their respectable lives. Such considerations seem to be most important in middle-class peer groups organized around occasional leisure-time participation in a deviant marketplace, such as homosexuality and swinging.[13] Other deviants, particularly members of mobs and formal organizations, may associate with their fellows away from deviant operations, so that both their work and their sociable interaction take place among deviants. This is also true for peer groups that expand into "communities" and offer a wide range of services to members. Active members of urban gay communities can largely restrict their contacts to other homosexuals (Harry and Devall, 1978; Wolf, 1979). In these cases there is little need to perform conventional roles, aside from their obvious uses as concealment, and the deviant identity is likely to be central for the individual.

The degree to which an individual finds a deviant career and a deviant identity satisfying depends, in part, on the form of deviant organization of which he or she is a part. As in any activity, persons continue to engage in deviance only as long as the rewards it offers are greater than the rewards which could be obtained through alternative activities. The relevant rewards vary from one person to the next and from one type of deviance to another; a partial list includes money, physical and emotional satisfaction, valued social contacts, and prestige. Because the relative importance of these rewards varies with the individual, it is impossible to measure the differences in rewards between forms of deviant organization. There is some evidence that monetary profits are generally higher in more sophisticated forms of deviant organization. While an occasional loner can steal a very large sum through an embezzlement or a computer crime, most mobs can earn a reasonably steady income, and rackets run by formal organizations consistently bring in high profits. A more revealing measure of satisfaction is career stability; members of more sophisticated forms of deviant organization are more likely to remain in deviance. Loners' careers are short-lived, even when they are involved in systematic deviance. Lemert's (1967) account of the failure of professional forgers to remain at large suggests that the lack of social support is critical. As noted above, persons frequently drift out of their roles as colleagues and peers when other options become more attractive. The long-term careers of members of mobs and formal organizations suggest that these forms are more likely to satisfy the deviant.[14]

V. *The more sophisticated the form of deviant organization, the more secure its members' deviant operations.* The social organization of deviants affects the interaction between deviants and social control agents. This relationship is complicated because increased sophistication has consequences which would seem to make social control effects both easier and more difficult. On the one hand, the more sophisticated the deviant organization, the greater its public visibility and its chances of being subject to social control actions. Because more sophisticated forms of organization have more complex deviant operations, there are more people involved with the organization as members, victims, customers and bystanders. Therefore, there are more people capable of supplying the authorities with information about the identities, operations, and locations of organizational members. On the other hand, more sophisticated forms of organization are more likely to have codes of conduct requiring their members to be loyal to the organization and to maintain its secrets. Further, more sophisticated forms of organization command resources which can be used to protect the organization and its members from social control agents. While highly sophisticated organizations find it more difficult to conceal the fact that deviance is taking place, they often are more successful at shielding their members from severe sanctions.

Notes

1. A second paper, in preparation, will discuss the social organization of deviance.

2. Following Lemert (1967), loners can be subdivided into naive loners, for whom deviance is an exceptional, one-time experience, and systematic loners, whose deviance forms a repeated pattern. Lemert's analysis of the problems confronting systematic check forgers, who have trouble maintaining a deviant identity with little social support, suggests that systematic loners may have particularly instable careers.

3. The term "mob," as it is used here, is drawn from the glossary in Sutherland: "A group of thieves who work together; same as 'troupe' and 'outfit' " (1937:239; cf. Maurer, 1962, 1964). A more recent study uses the term "crew" (Prus and Sharper, 1977).

4. Although the mob is able to accomplish its ends more efficiently, the same tasks are sometimes handled by loners. For example, see Maurer (1964:166–168) and Prus and Sharper (1977:22).

5. Our use of the term "formal organization" is not meant to imply that these organizations have all of the characteristics of an established bureaucracy. Rather, "formal" points to the deliberately designed structure of the organization—a usage consistent with Blau and Scott (1962:5).

6. The complexity of a deviant activity must be distinguished from two other types of complexity. First, the definition of organizational sophistication, given above, included the complexity of the division of labor among the deviants in a given organizational form as one criterion of sophistication. Second, the complexity of an activity should not be confused with the complexity of its explanation. A suicide, for example, can be easily accomplished, even though a complex social-psychological analysis may be required to explain the act.

7. This point illustrates the distinction, made earlier, between the social organization of deviance (the pattern of relationships between the roles performed in a deviant transaction) and the social organization of deviants (the pattern of relationships between deviant actors). The former, not the latter, affects an activity's complexity.

8. In most cases, loners do not possess the resources required for more than one type of complex deviance; physicians, for instance, are unable to commit computer thefts. In contrast, members of more sophisticated forms of organization may be able to manage several types of operations, as when a mob's members shift from picking pockets to shoplifting in order to avoid the police, or when an organized crime family is involved in several different rackets simultaneously (Maurer, 1964; Ianni, 1972:87–106).

9. Within a given form of organization, some cognitive perspectives may be more elaborate than others. While pool hustlers have a strong oral tradition, founded on the many hours they share together in pool halls, prostitutes have a relatively limited argot. Maurer (1939) argues that this is due to the restricted contact they have with one another during their work.

10. Here and elsewhere, colleagues represent a partial exception to the pattern. Colleagues resemble members of mobs and formal organizations in that they adopt an instrumental perspective, view deviance as a career, are socialized through apprenticeship to an experienced deviant, and accept deviance as a central identity. While peers have a more sophisticated form of organization, their mutual participation in deviance is based on their shared involvement in an illicit marketplace or leisure-time activity. In contrast, colleagues usually are committed to deviance as means of earning a living.

Yet, because colleagues share a relatively unsophisticated form of organization, they labor under restrictions greater than those faced by mobs and formal organizations. Socialization is of limited scope; call girls learn about handling money and difficult clients, but little about sexual skills (Bryan, 1965). The code of conduct governing colleagues is less encompassing and less binding than those for more sophisticated forms, and the deviance of colleagues is usually less profitable. The absence of the advantages associated with organizational sophistication leads colleagues, despite their similarities to mobs and formal organizations, into an unstable situation where many individuals drift away from deviance.

11. Sometimes such equipment is defined as illicit, and its possession constitutes a crime.

12. Two reasons can be offered to explain this relationship. If a type of deviance is not profitable enough to support the individual, it may be necessary to take other work, as when a pool hustler moonlights (Polsky, 1967). Also, many loners have only a marginal commitment to deviance and choose to allocate most of their time to their respectable roles. This is particularly easy if the form of deviance requires little time for preparation and commission.

13. Swingers meeting new couples avoid giving names or information which could be used to identify them (Bartell, 1971:92–95); and Humphreys (1970) emphasizes that many tearoom participants are attracted by the setting's assurance of anonymity.

14. During their careers, deviants may shift from one organizational form or one type of offense to another. The habitual felons interviewed by Petersilia *et al.* (1978) reported that, while many of their offenses as juveniles involved more than one partner (presumably members of a peer group), they preferred to work alone or with a single partner on the crimes they committed as adults. The most common pattern was for juveniles who specialized in burglaries to turn to robbery when they became adults.

References

Amir, Menachem
1971 Patterns in Forcible Rape. Chicago: University of Chicago Press.

Anderson, Nels
1923 The Hobo. Chicago: University of Chicago Press.

Aubert, Vilhelm
1965 The Hidden Society. Totowa, N.J.: Bedminster.

Bartell, Gilbert
1971 Group Sex. New York: New American.

Bell, Daniel
1962 The End of Ideology. Revised edition. New York: Collier.

Blau, Peter M. and W. Richard Scott
1962 Formal Organizations. San Francisco: Chandler.

Blumer, Herbert
1967 The World of Youthful Drug Use. Berkeley: University of California Press.

Bohannon, Paul
1960 African Homicide and Suicide. Princeton: Princeton University Press.

Bryan, James H.
1965 "Apprenticeships in prostitution." Social Problems 12:287–297.
1966 "Occupational ideologies and individual attitudes of call girls." Social Problems 13:441–450.

Buckner, H. Taylor
1970 "The transvestic career path." Psychiatry 33:381–389.

Cameron, Mary Owen
1964 The Booster and the Snitch. New York: Free Press.

Carey, James T.
1968 The College Drug Scene. Englewood Cliffs, N.J.: Prentice-Hall.

Clinard, Marshall B. and Richard Quinney
1973 Criminal Behavior Systems: A Typology. Second edition. New York: Holt, Rinehart and Winston.

Cressey, Donald R.
1953 Other People's Money. New York: Free Press.
1962 "Role theory, differential association, and compulsive crimes." Pp. 443–467 in Arnold M. Rose (ed.), Human Behavior and Social Processes. Boston: Houston Mifflin.

1969 Theft of the Nation. New York: Harper & Row.
1972 Criminal Organization. New York: Harper & Row.
Dawley, David
1973 A Nation of Lords. Garden City, N.Y.: Anchor.
Einstader, Werner J.
1969 "The social organization of armed robbery." Social Problems 17:64–83.
Feldman, Harvey W.
1968 "Ideological supports to becoming and remaining a heroin addict." Journal of Health and Social Behavior 9:131–139.
Gibbons, Don C.
1965 Changing the Lawbreaker. Englewood Cliffs, N.J.: Prentice-Hall.
1977 Society, Crime, and Criminal Careers. Third edition. Englewood Cliffs, N.J.: Prentice-Hall.
Glaser, Barney G. and Anselm L. Strauss
1967 The Discovery of Grounded Theory. Chicago: Aldine.
Goffman, Erving
1959 The Presentation of Self in Everyday Life. Garden City, N.Y.: Anchor.
1963 Stigma. Englewood Cliffs, N.J.: Prentice-Hall.
Green, Timothy
1969 The Smugglers. New York: Walker.
Harry, Joseph and William B. Devall
1978 The Social Organization of Gay Males. New York: Praeger.
Hirschi, Travis
1962 "The professional prostitute." Berkeley Journal of Sociology 7:33–49.
Humphreys, Laud
1970 Tearoom Trade. Chicago: Aldine.
Ianni, Francis A. J.
1972 A Family Business. New York: Sage.
Inciardi, James A.
1977 "In search of the class cannon." Pp. 55–77 in Robert S. Weppner (ed.), Street Ethnography. Beverly Hills, Calif.: Sage.
Keiser, R. Lincoln
1969 The Vice Lords. New York: Holt, Rinehart and Winston
Klein, John F. and Arthur Montague
1977 Check Forgers. Lexington, Mass.: Lexington.
Lemert, Edwin M.
1967 Human Deviance, Social Problems, and Social Control. Englewood Cliffs, N.J.: Prentice-Hall.
Lesieur, Henry R.
1977 The Chase. Garden City, N.Y.: Anchor.
Letkemann, Peter
1973 Crime as Work. Englewood Cliffs, N.J.: Prentice-Hall.
Lofland, John
1969 Deviance and Identity. Englewood Cliffs, N.J.: Prentice-Hall.
Luckenbill, David F.
1977 "Criminal homicide as a situated transaction." Social Problems 25: 176–186.
Matza, David
1964 Delinquency and Drift. New York: Wiley.
1969 Becoming Deviant. Englewood Cliffs, N.J.: Prentice-Hall.

Maurer, David W.
1939 "Prostitutes and criminal argots." American Journal of Sociology 44: 346–350.
1964 The Big Con. New York: New American.
1964 Whiz Mob. New Haven, Conn.: College and University Press.
McIntosh, Mary
1971 "Changes in the organization of thieving." Pp. 98–133 in Stanley Cohen (ed.), Images of Deviance. Baltimore, Maryland: Penguin.
Mileski, Maureen and Donald J. Black
1972 "The social organization of homosexuality." Urban Life and Culture 1: 131–166.
Miller, Gale
1978 Odd Jobs: The World of Deviant Work. Englewood Cliffs, N.J.: Prentice-Hall.
Milner, Christina and Richard Milner
1972 Black Players. Boston: Little, Brown.
Parker, Donn B.
1976 Crime by Computer. New York: Scribner's.
Petersilia, Joan, Peter W. Greenwood and Marvin Lavin
1978 Criminal Careers of Habitual Felons. Santa Monica, Calif.: Rand.
Polsky, Ned
1967 Hustlers, Beats, and Others. Chicago: Aldine.
Prus, Robert C. and C. R. D. Sharper
1977 Road Hustler. Lexington, Mass.: Lexington.
Reynolds, Frank
1967 Freewheelin' Frank. New York: Grove.
Rosenberg, Bernard and Harry Silverstein
1969 Varieties of Delinquent Experience. Waltham, Mass.: Blaisdell.
Rubington, Earl
1978 "Variations in bottle-gang controls." Pp. 383–391 in Earl Rubington and Martin S. Weinberg (eds.), Deviance: The Interactionist Perspective. Third edition. New York: Macmillan.
Shaw, Clifford R.
1930 The Jack-Roller. Chicago: University of Chicago Press.
Shibutani, Tamotsu
1961 Society and Personality. Englewood Cliffs, N.J.: Prentice-Hall.
Shover, Neal
1977 "The social organization of burglary." Social Problems 20:499–514.
Stoddart, Kenneth
1974 "The facts of life about dope." Urban Life and Culture 3:179–204.
Sutherland, Edwin H.
1937 The Professional Thief. Chicago: University of Chicago Press.
Thompson, Hunter S.
1966 Hell's Angels. New York: Ballantine.
Turner, Ralph H.
1964 "Collective behavior." Pp. 382–425 in Robert E. L. Faris (ed.), Handbook of Modern Sociology. Chicago: Rand McNally.
Wade, Andrew L.
1967 "Social processes in the act of juvenile vandalism." Pp. 94–109 in Marshall B. Clinard and Richard Quinney (eds.), Criminal Behavior Systems: A

Typology. New York: Holt, Rinehart and Winston.
Warren, Carol A. B.
1974 Identity and Community in the Gay World. New York: Wiley.
Winick, Charles
1961 "Physician narcotic addicts." Social Problems 9:174–186.
Wiseman, Jacqueline P.
1970 Stations of the Lost. Englewood Cliffs, N.J.: Prentice-Hall.
Wolf, Deborah G.
1979 The Lesbian Community. Berkeley: University of California Press.
Wolfgang, Marvin E. and Franco Ferracuti
1967 The Subculture of Violence. London: Tavistock.
Zimmerman, Don H. and D. Lawrence Wieder
1977 "You can't help but get stoned." Social Problems 25:198–207.

32 / Deviant Career Mobility: The Case of Male Prostitutes

DAVID F. LUCKENBILL

An important topic in the study of deviance is the deviant career, the individual's movement through the deviant experience. However, sociological knowledge about different phases of the career is uneven (see Luckenbill and Best, 1981; Rains, 1982). There has been a good deal of research on entry—the process of moving from respectability into deviance—and a fair amount on departure—the process of moving from deviance into respectability. But research on involvement—the intermediate stage between entry and departure—has been rather limited. In the 1960s and early 1970s researchers examined the subjective career, looking at changes in the deviant's identity, motivation, and commitment over the course of involvement (Becker, 1963; Goffman, 1961; Lofland, 1969; Stebbins, 1971). More recently, a number of researchers have turned their attention to the objective career. Focusing on the "habitual deviant," they examined, among other things, the range, seriousness, sophistication, and rate of unlawful behavior during involvement (Blumstein et al., 1978; Chaiken and Chaiken, 1982; Petersilia et al., 1978; Peterson et al., 1980; Wolfgang et al., 1972). Yet, there has been relatively little research on mobility, on changes in the deviant's position or rank within a deviant world over the course of involvement.[1]

Research demonstrates that some deviant worlds, particularly deviant occupational worlds, such as drug dealing and gambling, are stratified (see Bales, 1984). This invites a number of questions about vertical mobility, the process of moving through a stratification system. Given a stratified world, do deviants generally maintain their standings during involvement, or do they move between ranks? If they are mobile, in what direction do they move? And what contingencies shape their patterns of mobility? There are few, if any, definitive answers to these questions. Researchers addressing such problems use different theoretical perspectives and present different images of career mobility. Those adopting a sociological approach generally indicate that advancement is a likely mode of involvement given relevant knowledge, career orientations, and relationships. But those adopting an economic approach generally indicate that advancement is an unlikely mode of involvement given particular obstacles to the acquisition of vital resources and connections. These alternative positions can be found, for example, in the scholarly literature on careers in drug dealing (Adler and Adler, 1983b; Blum, 1972:31–58; Carey, 1968:68–117; Hellman, 1980:148–58; Moore, 1977:51–61) and gambling (Bales, 1984; Hayano, 1982:129–34; Lesieur, 1977:109–43; Reuter, 1983:26–37), worlds that are organized around the distribution of illicit commodities.

This paper examines career mobility in male prostitution, a world that is organized around the distribution of an illicit service. First, I identify the stratification system in male prostitution and describe its three principal tiers, those of street hustling, bar hustling, and escort prostitution. Second, I describe how 28 male prostitutes moved through this system over the course of their careers and identify the subjective and objective contingencies shaping their patterns of mobility. Finally, I draw on these findings to discuss more broadly the properties of a deviant world that make mobility possible and the properties that affect mobility where it is possible.

SAMPLE AND METHOD

The data derive from in-depth interviews with 28 male prostitutes, or "hustlers," in Chicago.[2] The respondents ranged from 18 to 34 years of age. Three were black, two were Hispanic, and the remainder were white. Seven had fathers who held white-collar jobs, five had fathers who were unemployed or absent from the home, and the rest had fathers who held blue-collar jobs. Whereas 18 respondents did not complete high school, 10 finished high school and four of them finished at least two years of college. Nine were raised in the Chicago area; the remainder grew up elsewhere. Importantly, prostitutes from all three tiers of the stratification system were sampled. Twenty-six respondents had experience as street hustlers, the lowest echelon; 21 had experience as bar hustlers, the middle echelon; and eight had experience as escorts, the highest echelon. An effort also was made to select veteran prostitutes. At the time of interviewing, three respondents had been involved in prostitution for less than two years, 17 had been involved for more than two years, and eight had been retired for less than two years, after careers ranging from four to eleven years.

The respondents were not incarcerated at the time of interviewing; most were actively involved in vice. As a consequence, finding and interviewing them was difficult. They were leery of outsiders and did not like to spend time talking when they could be hustling. The respondents were contacted through a graduate research assistant whose research ties with Chicago's gay community earned him a reputation as a trustworthy person. He located the respondents, beginning with those who worked the streets and the bars, and ending with those who worked for agencies. We interviewed the respondents in settings which they found convenient, including their residences, the offices in two bars, and the graduate assistant's apartment. The interviews lasted from 45 to 90 minutes, and four respondents were interviewed on two or three occasions. All of the interviews were recorded on tape. The process of contacting and interviewing the respondents spanned 28 months.

Each interview covered a wide variety of matters relating to careers in prostitution. Two sets of open-ended questions focused on stratification and mobility. To determine the stratification system in male prostitution, we asked the respondents to identify, describe, and assess the different kinds of male prostitutes. They indicated that prostitutes differ on a number of dimensions, one of which may be regarded as vertical. We also asked the respondents to describe their careers from entry to departure or to their current state of involvement. This line of questioning tapped mobility, revealing changes in rank over their careers. And, as they described their careers, the respondents were asked to explain their career shifts or failures to shift.

STRATIFICATION OF MALE PROSTITUTION

To study mobility in the respondents' careers, it is first necessary to determine whether the world of male prostitution is stratified and, if so, on what dimension(s) it is stratified. I do not use "stratification" to refer strictly to a dimension involving differences in prestige. Any dimension on which the respondents consistently differentiated prostitutes in terms of the degree to which they possess things that are valued, whether or not these involve prestige, may be regarded as a stratification system. To determine if and how the world is stratified, the respondents were questioned along a couple of lines. They were asked to identify the different kinds of male prostitutes and describe the differences between them, and they were asked to evaluate these differences and explain the basis of their evaluations.

The respondents identified and discussed several kinds of prostitutes, and these can be differentiated along four dimensions. Three may be regarded as lateral dimensions: (1) sex identification (heterosexual and homosexual hustlers); (2) sex role (masculine and feminine hustlers); and (3) sexual services (specialists, who engage in sadomasochism, straight hustlers, who limit themselves to fellatio, and generalists, who engage in most any sexual activity). I treat these as lateral dimensions because the respondents did not rank prostitutes arrayed along them. That is, one kind of prostitute was seen as no more likely to possess things that are valued than another; they were simply different.

The fourth dimension may be regarded as vertical because the respondents arranged prostitutes in a hierarchial order. The respondents ranked prostitutes by mode of operation, and their rankings were generally consistent. Beginning with the lowest tier, the respondents identified three ranks: street hustling, bar hustling, and escort prostitution. The street hustler stands around particular avenues, parks, bus stations, or bookstore entrances, attracts a customer from the passers-by, quickly arranges a sexual sale with him, and then moves to a private setting to perform a brief sexual exchange. The bar hustler frequents particular gay bars or discos, attracts a customer from the patrons, socializes with him for a time, arranges a sale, and moves to a private place for sex. The escort operates through an escort or modeling agency; a customer contacts the agency and requests a "date," the agency operator and customer agree on the terms of the date, and the escort takes the job, contacting the customer at his residence and engaging in sex and other agreed upon activities, such as having dinner.

When they were asked to explain the basis of their rankings, most of the respondents promptly spoke of differences in lifestyle—fashionable dress and appearance, comfortable and secure living arrangements, considerable leisure time, and so on. Twenty-two respondents claimed that escorts enjoy a better lifestyle than bar hustlers, and 23 claimed that bar hustlers enjoy a better lifestyle than street hustlers.[3] However, when asked to elaborate upon the reasons for their evaluations, these respondents revealed that their rankings also reflected differences in income and safety (which affect lifestyle). Income consists of fees times volume of business. The respondents indicated that the higher the rank, the larger the fee per "trick." Estimates varied, but they were consistent with the scale described by John:[4]

> Street hustlers, that hang around on corners, make $10, maybe $15, per trick, at the least; the most, $20, $25. Bar hustlers can go up to $50, $60, $70. Escort services, $150, $200, with the hustler getting 60% plus tips.

They also indicated that the higher the rank, the greater or more stable the volume of sales. They said that the bar hustler can get as many, if not more, tricks as a street hustler, and an escort can get as many dates as he wants. With respect to safety, the respondents insisted that freedom from arrest and other risks is greater in bar hustling than in street hustling. Whereas the street hustler operates in a public setting that is visible to the police, the bar hustler operates in a secluded setting that shields illicit arrangements. The street hustler keeps his initial contact with customers brief, so as to avoid police observation, and this hinders his screening of undercover police officers. But the bar hustler socializes with prospective customers, and this gives him time to screen undercover officers. The respondents maintained that escort prostitution is even safer than bar hustling. While street and bar hustlers perform their own, sometimes limited screening of customers, the escort can rely on the agency operator to screen police officers.

In sum, male prostitution is stratified by mode of operation, and this scheme corresponds to the schemes described in other research reports (Allen, 1980; Hoffman, 1972; Reiss, 1961; Ross, 1959).[5] Two comments are in order. First, this scheme is not a prestige hierarchy. In describing and assessing the three modes of operation, 19 respondents indicated that bar hustlers are no more respected than street hustlers and escorts are no more respected than bar hustlers. Still, almost 80 percent of the respondents, representing all modes of operation, maintained that street hustlers, bar hustlers, and escorts enjoy different levels of income and safety. Thus, a prostitute in one tier is no "better" than a prostitute in another tier. Rather, each tier involves a distinctive relational system carrying distinctive advantages in acquiring things that are valued: the higher the echelon, the more likely a prostitute can attract high-paying customers and the greater the resources upon which he can draw to reduce his risks of operation. Second, this scheme is subjective, based on the respondents' beliefs that different modes of operation feature differences in income and safety.

PATTERNS OF MOBILITY

Analysis of the respondents' careers reveals three patterns of mobility in male prostitution. The first is stability. Seven hustlers maintained throughout their careers the same ranks as the ones at which they entered. The second pattern is minimum ascent. Fifteen hustlers began as street hustlers and then moved into bar hustling, the rank at which they worked when they quit or expected to quit prostitution. The third pattern is maximum ascent. Six hustlers began as street hustlers, moved into bar hustling, and then turned to escort prostitution. However, all six eventually returned to bar hustling, the rank at which they operated when they quit or expected to quit. This section first looks at stability and then ascent. Instead of analyzing the two patterns of ascent separately, maximum ascent is examined as an extension of minimum ascent.

Stability

Seven hustlers maintained their standings over the course of their careers. Five worked as street hustlers, and two operated as escorts. These men provided different reasons for their particular points of entry. The street hustlers started on the street for the same reasons that all of the upwardly mobile hustlers started on the street: their youth, experience with the street scene, and ignorance of the hustler bars limited them to street hustling. The escorts started in the agencies because their early understanding of hustling was confined to escort prostitution. They knew little or nothing about street and bar hustling but learned about escort prostitution from friends or lovers. They subsequently applied for positions in known agencies. Lloyd pursued escort prostitution in order to augment his legitimate income. Paul pursued it out of curiosity: "I wanted to know if I could do it. I didn't know if I could be sexually active with somebody just for money." They were interviewed by the agency operators and, because they were at least 18 years of age, sexually versatile, and relatively attractive, were offered jobs.

The hustlers maintained their respective positions. The escorts learned about street and bar hustling, but they never worked the street or bars and had no intention of doing so. They enjoyed escort prostitution—the extra money, the ease of operation, and the freedom to construct their own schedules. Furthermore, they regarded street and bar hustling as personally degrading and unnecessary. Unlike the street hustlers, who used prostitution as their principal source of income, the escorts did not consider prostitution vital to their lives; if dismissed from an agency (a common event), they would rely on their respectable jobs to make ends meet. In contrast, the street hustlers learned about and dabbled in bar hustling. Yet they found it unsatisfying. As Jerry argued:

> I didn't like working the bars because you got to bullshit around too much. When you work in the street, you know what the guy's looking for and he knows what you're there for. It's so much easier.

Consequently, they resumed street hustling, regarding it as easier or more exciting, and they expressed little desire to move.

Ascent

While seven hustlers developed relatively stable careers, 21 developed ascending careers. These hustlers started on the street and turned to the bars, and some turned later to the escort agencies. The concept of "career contingencies" is useful in explaining their ascent. Career contingencies refer to "those factors on which mobility from one position to another depends," and they include both objective facts of social structure and changes in the orientations and desires of the individual (Becker, 1963:24). As we will see, a number of contingencies worked together to produce career shifts.

Street Hustling. All of the mobile hustlers began their careers on the street. They gave several reasons for this point of departure. They were too young to enter the bars. As Dennis observed:

> Everybody starts on the street. [Why's that?] Age. Most hustlers that I know started early. And they were young, very young—13, 14, 15, 16, pre-high school.

When the hustlers began to work regularly, they ranged from 13 to 18 years of age. But youth alone did not limit them to street hustling, for 16 of them moved into bar hustling long before they reached the legal drinking age (generally by using fake identification). Why, then, did they start on the street instead of in the bars?

The answer resides in the hustlers' familiarity with and access to the street and ignorance of the hustler bars. As novices, they were familiar with the street. Familiarity developed in either of two ways. The newcomer may have been introduced to the street by an experienced person. Rick began working particular avenues in Detroit because his lover (a street hustler) recommended them, and Jim's "sugardaddy" showed him New York's street scene:

> He showed me everything. He said that if you see something different you want, or you want to do this or you want to do that, you want to learn about the hustlers, I'll show you. And he showed me bookstores, showed me the streets, the corners, the hustlers, the johns. He just showed me everything.

Or the newcomer may have had some experience with the street. Before they turned to prostitution, some of the hustlers had "cruised" particular streets and parks for partners for sexual trades. In these ventures, they learned that such settings contained men willing to pay for sex. When they started to hustle, they worked these settings to tap this pool of customers. In addition to familiarity, the hustlers had access to the street. Unlike the bar and escort agencies, the street was open to anyone; entry required neither special attributes, such as being over a specific age, nor financial investment, such as buying drinks. Thus, Bob began on the street "because I couldn't afford to go to the bars." Finally, five of the hustlers started on the street because they were ignorant of the other scenes. Gordon began on the street "because I didn't know about the bars." Actually, they knew about gay bars, but they did not know that some were "hustler bars," where patrons regularly arranged sexual sales.

Bar Hustling. After working the street from six months to five years, the hustlers moved into bar hustling. Their move can be explained in terms of the interplay of several contingencies: changed definitions of the street led to their disenchantment with street hustling; an appreciation of the bars led to their closure on bar hustling; and the satisfaction of several basic requirements enabled them to conclude the shift.

When they entered prostitution, the hustlers defined the street as an exciting and gainful setting in which to work. Over time, however, they grew fearful of it. Due to a variety of perilous events experienced personally or by colleagues, they came to regard the setting as dangerous. In particular, they realized that the street carried substantial risks of arrest and harassment. Randy recalled:

> It was getting so bad I was going to jail for disorderly conduct almost every night. And it was physical harassment, too. Quite a few times [officers] would come by and take their flashlight and give you a kick in the stomach with it and tell you to keep walking.

They also found that the street was infested with predatory colleagues and exploitative customers. As Marty observed:

> Hustling Bughouse Square [a notorious Chicago park], you're going to have problems. You got a lot of different kinds of assholes out there. When someone pulls up and says "Get in," you get in. And you can look at their eyes, and they can be throwing fire out of their eyes, and have a knife under the seat. You're just in a bad situation. I avoid it by not hustling in the street. I hustle in the bars now.

Seven of the hustlers also grew uncomfortable with the street. They came to regard it as an embarrassing setting in which to ply their trade. Rick commented, "I didn't like sitting out there, having people driving by, like tourists driving by and looking at you, pointing at you." Definitions of the street as dangerous or embarrassing led to their disenchantment with street hustling and receptiveness to bar hustling.

At some point in their street involvement, the hustlers learned from friends or colleagues about the existence and location of particular hustler bars and the basic advantages of and requirements for entering them. After learning about the bars, or after experiencing or hearing about an especially dangerous or embarrassing incident on the street, they decided to try their luck in the bars. With two or three visits, they determined that the bars offered more than the street and, in light of this assessment, closed on bar hustling. In observing and associating with those who frequented the bars, the hustlers came to define the bars as a safe setting in which to operate. They learned that the bars were not open to anyone, as was the street. Bartenders operated as gatekeepers, screening those persons suspected of being "rip-off" hustlers, exploitative customers, and undercover officers. Though screening may have been oriented toward keeping peace and ensuring a steady level of business, it was believed to make the bars reasonably safe. In addition, the hustlers recognized that they could probably earn more money by working the bars, as men drawn from the bars would spend more for sex than those who patronized the street. Eddie turned to the bars not only to reduce his risks but also to make more money:

> I figured I could probably make more in a bar. . . . Guys that pull up in a car, they're out for a quick $20 trick and it's over with. Guys that come to the bars, they're going to have to pay the hustler's price. The hustler's already socializing with this [customer] and that one. In order for [a customer] to get him away from everybody else, he's going to have to top these other people's offers.

Jim added that "you also stand a chance of running across that one big buck in a bar, whereas you don't on the street." Finally, the hustlers found the bars a more comfortable setting in which to work. In addition to protecting them from inclement weather and providing them with a source of recreation, the bars allowed them to relax, socialize, and arrange sales in privacy.

Disenchantment with street hustling and an appreciation of bar hustling do not sufficiently account for the career shift. In describing their move, the hustlers identified three requirements they had to satisfy in order to enter and work successfully in the bars. They had to be at least 21 years of age or be able to pass as an adult by using fake identification. They also had to be "good"—honest, pleasant, and the like. As Marty pointed out, "You can't be a bad hustler. You can't be a rip-off and go into the bars. Well, you can, but not for any period of time." Mike argued that bartenders would permit a hustler to work the bar "as long as he's cool and doesn't start no trouble." They claimed that hustlers who had a reputation for exploiting others would be barred from entry, while those who were boisterous or belligerent would be thrown out. Finally, unlike hustlers who worked the street, they had to have an attractive appearance, coming across as an appealing and desirable partner. Dennis observed:

> You have to have a *savoir faire,* a character that is appealing, that is irresistible, that you can't find on the street. An aura about yourself that you are unattainable, so that tricks can take you out and show you off to all these people, their friends.

The hustlers maintained that bar hustlers differed from street hustlers in appearance. They claimed that, compared with street hustlers, bar hustlers associated with a more demanding and liberal clientele and engaged in more extensive interaction with customers. Therefore, to attract customers, bar hustlers had to present themselves as men who were more tasteful and restrained than those who could be found on the street. Such a presentation required cleanliness, fashionable clothes, an ability to carry on a simple conversation, and an appealing front, such as that of a dancer.

Fifteen of the 21 hustlers who moved from street to bar hustling did not turn to escort prostitution. Their reasons for not making the move differed. Three hustlers never heard about escort prostitution. Three others heard about it and wanted to join an agency, but they were not sure how to do so. As John pointed out, "If I'm going to continue in this profession, then I'd like to go up to the male escort." However,

> to get into a male escort service, you would have to know people and set yourself up for it. Personally, I don't know who to contact yet. I'm trying to find out now so I can get out of the bar scene.

Nine bar hustlers knew about escort prostitution but had no desire to enter it. They liked the bars, regarding them as a source of pleasure, and they liked bar hustling, considering it an easy and profitable enterprise. They also disliked the notion of splitting fees with an escort agency. They believed that escorts made good money with little risk, but they wanted to keep all of their earnings. As Ray argued, "I never made no money for nobody else. Whatever I do, it goes in my pocket, every fucking penny."

Escort Prostitution. After working the bars from eight months to two years, six hustlers turned to escort prostitution. As with their previous move into bar hustling, their decision was contingent on changing definitions of these respective forms of prostitution.

When they moved into bar hustling, the hustlers defined the bars as a safe, comfortable, and profitable place to work. However, with increasing involvement, they began to question the value of the bars. They came to view the bars as somewhat dangerous. Although the bar scene presented fewer problems than the street, bar hustling still carried some risk of arrest and exploitation. Bartenders sometimes failed to screen patrons and eject those who were troublesome. As Jaime pointed out, "the bartenders will try and help you out. They'll pass the word. But sometimes they fuck up."

More subjectively, the hustlers grew weary of bar life and bar hustling. Voicing the sentiments of others, Don argued that he had grown tired of the hangovers, the shallow relationships, and the dejected persons who populated the bars. He also had grown tired of "hustling," of contacting customers, haggling over money, and settling on places for having sex. The perceived dangerousness of the bars paired with a weariness of working them engendered a disenchantment with bar hustling and an openness to escort prostitution.

The hustlers varied in the way they managed their dissatisfaction with bar hustling. Although they knew about the agencies—having learned of their existence and desirability from friends and colleagues—only three of the six sought out escort prostitution. Don, Jaime, and Dennis attempted to join an agency after a distressing incident in the bars, such as losing a prospective customer to an unscrupulous hustler. Looking through gay periodicals, they came across agency want-ads for "escorts" or "models." Understanding that these titles were euphemisms for prostitutes, they phoned the agencies in hope of landing jobs. They were subsequently interviewed by the operators and offered positions. By contrast, Eddie, George, and Marty were recruited into escort prostitution.They were working the bars when agency operators spotted them. Posing as normal customers, the operators arranged sexual sales with them and, finding their performances satisfactory, offered them jobs.

On the basis of their initial conversations with the agency operators, the hustlers decided that the agencies were more desirable than the bars and, as a result, accepted offers of employment. From these conversations, they believed that working through an agency would be safer. They were informed that the operators carefully screened police officers and troublemakers and arranged the activities and fees for dates with suitable customers so that escorts and customers would not argue about these matters. They also were told that the operators would provide bail and legal aid in case of arrest. In addition, the hustlers believed that working through an agency would make their lives easier because the operators would perform the troublesome tasks of making contact with customers and arranging the terms of dates. Finally, the hustlers believed that they could make more money by joining an agency. They were told that escorts, even though they split fees with their agencies, earned more in a sexual sale than bar hustlers. When Jaime worked the bars, his "going rate" was about $30 per trick. When he interviewed for an escort position, he was informed that his dates would bring fees for $60 to $200 and that he was entitled to 60 percent of them plus all of the gratuities he received. Most of them also were told that escorts enjoyed a steady flow of business. Dennis learned that he could have as many dates as he wanted, since the agency had a large clientele. This stood in sharp contrast to bar hustling, where trade fluctuated considerably.

Changed definitions of bar hustling and escort prostitution do not fully explain the career shift. In discussing their move, the hustlers identified several requirements they had to meet in order to enter and operate in an agency. To gain entry, they had to be at least 18 years of age, for the law required that an "escort" or "model" be an adult. They also had to have an attractive appearance. Such an appearance, they maintained, involved the presentation of self as tasteful and polished. This called for cleanliness, stylish dress, an appealing front, and social skills beyond an ability to carry on a simple conversation in a bar. Dennis observed, "You have to be somewhat of a philosopher, a psychiatrist, a physical therapist, and an entertainer. You have to be able to go anyplace and fit." When asked what he looked for in an escort, Lonnie, a former escort agency operator, responded:

> Clean, well kept, well dressed, as opposed to the average hustler. Looks are not the most important thing as far as I'm concerned.... Someone you could use in operating an agency has to be able to dress and go out to dinner. A lot of customers want to take their dates out to dinner and get to know them a little bit before they go to bed with them. So they got to be able to dress, to go to dinner.

To maintain their positions, the hustlers had to satisfy three performance standards. They had to be obedient, abiding by whatever terms the operators and customers agreed upon and delivering the appropriate share of all fees to the operators. They had to be proficient in the sexual activities requested by customers. And they had to treat customers honestly; they could not harm or steal from customers or even pressure customers into providing gratuities. From the operators' standpoint, attractiveness, obedience, proficiency, and honesty were important qualities for escorts because they helped to ensure profits, forestall complaints, and generate return business.

The hustlers' satisfaction of these requirements was determined by the operators. They judged the hustlers' attractiveness and proficiency through an interview and possibly a trial. Consider, for example, Dennis' entry:

> I called the man and we talked. He wanted to know if I knew what was going on, if I was a cop, what experience I had had, this and that, kind of schooling, the whole shot. Then, he arranged for an appointment at his office. I went to the office and filled out a questionnaire, basically an application. What kind of dates would you like? Interested in modeling, traveling? Can you give massages? And then, how many dates can you handle? What days? The whole shot. That's just the beginning. I had to go to the casting couch. Before I got the job, the man tried me himself, to make sure I could perform whatever.

The operators judged the hustlers' obedience and honesty through inservice contact and feedback from customers. Lonnie argued:

> You know how good a boy is after you send him out one or two times. That's one thing about an agency, a customer will call and complain. If there's a problem, if a boy is not going to work out, you're going to know because the customer will call back.

The six hustlers who moved into escort prostitution did not remain at that level. They left the agencies anywhere from three weeks to six months after entering them. Two hustlers were released by their agencies. George and Don were told that they were being discharged in order to make way for "new faces." And four hustlers quit their agencies. Dennis left because he wanted to return home; he did not join another agency "because there was no such thing as an escort service in Ft. Wayne, Indiana." But the others quit because they found escort prostitution troublesome. Marty departed when he discovered that his agency failed to screen customers adequately and would not help him in case of arrest:

> I wasn't with them very long. It was three weeks when I caught my first bust, and after that, I got out of it. They didn't screen him [the undercover officer] properly. They must not have. The [operator] promised me that if I ever took a fall, he would be there to bail me out. And when I took the fall, he wasn't there.

Jaime quit because he had no choice over his customers or what he did with them. Eddie agreed, adding that he was exploited by his agency.

Rather than quit prostitution altogether, the hustlers returned to bar hustling. Three made the move grudgingly. Don, George, and Dennis enjoyed escort prostitution but figured they had little chance of entering another agency. Opposed to working the street, they resumed bar hustling, viewing it as a decent way to make ends meet. But Marty, Jaime, and Eddie made the move eagerly. They believed that, under the auspices of a first-class agency, escort prostitution could be better than bar hustling. Yet, given their unpleasant experiences with the agencies, they preferred bar hustling. They reasoned that they could screen customers more effectively in the bars and refuse to engage in unacceptable activities, thus avoiding the kinds of trouble they had in the agencies.

DISCUSSION

This analysis suggests that deviant career advancement is rather easy. Given some knowledge of the world and a little initiative, practically anyone who wants to move up can do so. This may seem reasonable from the standpoint of some deviants, but it glosses over the complexities of the various worlds in which deviants operate. Indeed, a body of literature adopting an economic approach to deviance suggests that mobility is possible only in a particular kind of deviant world and that advancement is possible only for a small portion of those who participate in such a world. I will conclude by considering the properties of a deviant world that make mobility possible and the conditions that affect career advancement where it is possible.

By definition, vertical mobility is only possible in a world that is hierarchically organized. Research suggests that hierarchical organization is more characteristic of deviant occupational worlds, such as prostitution and drug dealing, than of deviant recreational worlds, such as adolescent drinking and drug use (Bales, 1984; Luckenbill and Best, 1981). Most of the hustlers recognized different modes of operation in their world and ranked street hustlers, bar hustlers, and escorts on the basis of perceived differences in level of income and risk of arrest. Similarly, drug dealers identify different types of dealers and rank them by level of profit (Adler and Adler, 1983b). However, while drug users recognize different types of users, they do not appear to arrange them in a hierarchical order (see Rubington, 1967).

Given hierarchical organization, two properties of a deviant would make mobility possible. First, mobility calls for dissemination of information about the stratification system. Such information includes knowledge of the hierarchy, knowledge that mobility is possible, and knowledge of how to move through the hierarchy. Without such information, members may assume that the positions at which they entered the world are the only positions, and they may resign themselves to those positions. This, in fact, was the case for a few of the hustlers we interviewed. The extent to which information about the system is distributed depends on the degree to which members associate with one another. The greater their association—due to the cooperative nature of their deviance (as in gambling) or to the shared site of operation (as in prostitution)—the greater the dissemination of information. Those hustlers who were able to describe the stratification system socialized regularly with colleagues, while those few who were ignorant of it characterized themselves as loners.

Second, mobility calls for an open system. The system must be open in two respects. It must be open in the sense that rank is based, at least in part, on achievement. Male prostitution is open because hustlers can move between ranks through personal effort. To be sure, there is variation in the requirements for operating at a given rank and thus in the effort needed to enter it. In male prostitution, and some other deviant worlds, gatekeepers decide whether hustlers can enter one or more ranks, and gatekeepers and customers decide whether hustlers who have gained admission can continue to operate there. These persons vary in the standards they use to assess hustlers and in the degree to which they adhere to their standards. The less demanding their standards or the more loosely they apply them, the less effort hustlers need to meet them and make the shift. The system also must be open in the sense that positions are available at one or more ranks. Openings exist when there is sufficient turnover of members or when the market can support more individuals at a given rank. Male prostitution is open because it has a high rate of turnover owing to the brevity of the typical career as well as to the mobility of hustlers (Luckenbill, 1985). Drug dealing is open both because of high turnover among lower- and middle-level dealers (Lieb and Olson, 1976) and because the market can support more middle- and upper-level dealers (Moore, 1977:67–115).

Although mobility should be possible in a world that is open and whose stratification system is known, involvement in such a world does not guarantee advancement. A number of scholars adopting an economic approach in the study of deviant occupational worlds indicate that advancement is difficult and therefore limited to small proportions of individuals involved in such worlds (Bales, 1984; Moore, 1977; Reuter, 1983; Rubin, 1973).[6] These scholars assume that members of these worlds want to advance. This is so because deviants are regarded as rational and self-interested. If deviants pursue those activities which are most profitable, which maximize their benefits and minimize their costs, then it follows that, in a stratified world, all deviants would want to advance. At the same time, these scholars indicate that relatively few members can advance. This is so because of the economic organization of these deviant worlds. Two conditions pivotal to career advancement are resources (capital and manpower) and connections (suppliers and customers), and the illegality of a world's activity severly limits their acquisition and maintenance, making advancement difficult (Hellman, 1980:148–49, 172–74; Luksetich and White, 1982:234–67; Moore, 1977:54–56; Reuter, 1983:109–50).

This economic view is valuable, for it offers important insights into a number of objective career contingencies which sociologists generally ignore. However, given the findings of this and other sociological investigations, it suffers from several shortcomings. First, the economic view overstates the degree to which members of deviant occupational worlds want to advance. Those who adopt an economic approach assume that deviants want to advance so as to maximize profits. Yet, research shows that deviants adopt different orientations toward involvement. Some want to move up. After visiting the bars and finding them safe, lucrative, and comfortable, many of the street hustlers turned to bar hustling. But others do not want to move up. After dabbling with bar hustling, some of the street hustlers decided that street hustling was easier or more exciting, and they continued to work the street. As this suggests, career orientations develop and change with involvement, and they are influenced by social relationships, which, parenthetically, mediate what are taken as objective features of the world. Many lower-level drug dealers enter dealing given the possibility of acquiring free drugs and making a few dollars with minimal effort. Yet, as Lieb and Olson (1976:361) found, early dealing is more a matter of friendship than of making a profit. Through participation with suppliers, customers, and colleagues, lower-level dealers come to realize that dealing is a serious business with significant benefits and costs. At this point, some reorient themselves toward earning more money and enduring the risks, while others reorient themselves toward quitting (Lieb and Olson, 1976:362–63).

Second, the economic view exaggerates the extent to which advancement is difficult and thus limited. It claims that advancement is difficult because the illegality of a world's principal activity impedes the acquisition and maintenance of critical resources and connections. Yet, the significance of resources and connections to advancement, hence the difficulty of advancement, depends on the nature of the illicit enterprise. In a world that is organized around the distribution of an illicit commodity, such as drugs, advancement calls for substantial resources and diverse connections, and there are serious obstacles to the acquisition of capital and the cultivation of suppliers, making advancement difficult (Moore, 1977:49–50, 54–57; but see Adler and Adler, 1980). But in a world that is organized around the distribution of an illicit service, such as sex, advancement calls for little capital and no suppliers. Accordingly, advancement is less difficult. Hustlers can move from the street to the bars with relative ease, and many do so. Similarly, it has been observed that female prostitutes can move among certain modes of operation with ease (Prus and Irini, 1980:69–70).

Third, the economic view oversimplifies the nature of connections. In general, it treats a connection as a business relationship with a supplier or customer that is actively established by an individual trying to advance. From a sociological perspective, however, a connection may be defined as any social relationship that facilitates or supports an individual's role performance. Accordingly, to make a career shift, an individual may need to develop and sustain a wide variety of connections. Obviously, an individual involved in the distribution of an illicit commodity requires relationships with suppliers and customers. But an individual also may require satisfying relationships with gatekeepers and colleagues, for they not only decide who can enter and operate at a given rank but they also provide encouragement and various forms of assistance (Adler and Adler, 1983a; Prus and Irini, 1980:249–55). Also, a connection can be established in different ways. An individual can actively cultivate a connection, as when a bar hustler spots a want-ad for escorts, phones the agency operator, and applies for a job. An individual can be recruited from a lower echelon, as when an agency operator, posing as an ordinary customer, offers a bar hustler a job. Or an individual can establish a connection from a friendship. Adler and Adler (1983b:198) found that for many middle-level drug dealers, entry followed the development of friendships with other dealers, who introduced them to important members of the dealing world. Further, as a relationship, a connection has social as well as business dimensions. Consequently, the maintenance of a connection typically involves more than making the relationship economically profitable. To maintain his regular customers, a hustler should not only satisfy them but also spend time socializing with them outside the context of carrying out sales. To maintain his colleagues, a hustler should refrain from "stealing" their customers and should share their "fast life," which is organized around drug use and promiscuous sex.

Finally, the economic view overlooks some additional consequences of connections for advancement. Although this view suggests that connections at one level can facilitate the development of connections to the next level, it ignores the possibility that connections can provide the knowledge and skill for advancement. Through association with suppliers, gatekeepers, customers, and colleagues, an individual learns how to be competent at a given rank, and such competence may be vital to advancement. After moving into bar hustling, a hustler learns how to socialize with customers and how to behave in public establishments—skills which are needed to move into escort prostitution. Given the importance of connections at the middle level, it is not surprising that none of the street hustlers moved directly into the escort agencies.

Deviant career mobility may be possible only in particular occupational worlds, but the idea that all members of such worlds want to advance and that economic properties of such worlds severly constrain advancement is dubious. The difficulty of advancement depends on the nature of the world's principal activity. Furthermore, while advancement may well be affected by economic properties, such as limited access to capital, the desire and the capacity to advance are fundamentally affected by such noneconomic conditions as individuals' career orientations and social relationships.

Notes

1. Much the same observation has been made about sociological research on career mobility in respectable occupational worlds (Spilerman, 1977). A social world refers to an "internally recognizable constellation of actors, organizations, events, and practices which have coalesced into a perceived sphere of interest and involvement for participants" (Unruh, 1979:115). In a deviant world, the participants' interest and involvement focus on a form of deviant behavior.

2. One respondent was omitted when it was determined through a follow-up interview that he had not worked as an escort but helped an agency operator run the service. In addition, one former owner-operator of a Chicago escort agency was interviewed. He was asked about the structure and operation of his agency, the kind of men he hired, their length of stay, and so on.

3. Three bar hustlers and one street hustler were not familiar with escorts, and two bar hustlers, who knew about escorts, did not believe that they enjoy a better lifestyle than bar hustlers. Further, two escorts, two bar hustlers, and one street hustler did not think that bar hustlers enjoy a better lifestyle than street hustlers.

4. All names are pseudonyms.

5. While my description is consistent with the schemes described in other reports, the hustlers did not identify certain modes of operation discussed in other reports. In particular, they did not mention brothel or call-boy prostitution (Pittman, 1971; Ross, 1959). When asked about these modes, the hustlers said they were equivalent to escort prostitution. In addition, five hustlers identified the "kept boy" as the highest echelon. A kept boy has an exclusive relationship with one man who supports him in exchange for companionship and sex. That the kept boy is a prostitute is questionable. When asked about kept boys; some of the hustlers said that being kept is outside their occupational world because it is a lawful way to make ends meet. Thus, the kept boy is excluded from the stratification system.

6. These scholars differ in the way they portray deviant occupational worlds. For example, Moore (1977) and Rubin (1973) depict the worlds of drug dealing and gambling as highly-structured, well-integrated, and monopolistic, owing to domination by particular groups. Reuter (1983) and, to some extent, Bales (1984) depict such worlds as poorly structured, loosely integrated, and competitive, flowing from the surreptitious feature of the operations. Still, these scholars share certain ideas about deviant career mobility.

References

Adler, Patricia A. and Peter Adler

1980 "The irony of secrecy in the drug world." Urban Life 8:447–65.

1983a "Relations between dealers: the social organization of illicit drug transactions." Sociology and Social Research 67:260–78.

1983b "Shifts and oscillations in deviant careers: the case of upper-level drug dealers and smugglers." Social Problems 31:195–207.

Allen, Donald M.
1980 "Young male prostitutes: a psychosocial study." Archives of Sexual Behavior 9:399–426.
Bales, Kevin B.
1984 "The dual labor market of the criminal economy." Pp. 140–64 in Randall Collins (ed.), Sociological Theory—1984. San Francisco: Jossey-Bass.
Becker, Howard S.
1963 Outsiders. New York: Free Press.
Blum, Richard H.
1972 The Dream Sellers. San Francisco: Jossey-Bass.
Blumstein, Alfred, Jacqueline Cohen, and Daniel Nagin (eds.)
1978 Deterrence and Incapacitation: Estimating the Effects of Criminal Sanctions on Crime Rates. Washington, DC: National Academy of Sciences.
Carey, James T.
1968 The College Drug Scene. Englewood Cliffs, NJ: Prentice-Hall.
Chaiken, Jan and Marcia Chaiken
1982 Varieties of Criminal Behavior. Santa Monica, CA: Rand Corporation.
Goffman, Erving
1961 Asylums. Garden City, NY: Anchor.
Hayano, David M.
1982 Poker Faces: The Life and Work of Professional Card Players. Berkeley, CA: University of California Press.
Hellman, Daryl A.
1980 The Economics of Crime. New York: St. Martin's Press.
Hoffman, Martin
1972 "The male prostitute." Sexual Behavior 2:19–21.
Lesieur, Henry R.
1977 The Chase. Garden City, NY: Anchor.
Lieb, John and Sheldon Olson
1976 "Prestige, paranoia and profit: on becoming a dealer of illicit drugs in a university community." Journal of Drug Issues 6:356–67.
Lofland, John
1969 Deviance and Identity. Englewood Cliffs, NJ: Prentice-Hall.
Luckenbill, David F.
1985 "Entering male prostitution." Urban Life 14:131–53.
Luckenbill, David F. and Joel Best
1981 "Careers in deviance and respectability: the analogy's limitations." Social Problems 29:197–206.
Luksetich, William A. and Michael D. White
1982 Crime and Public Policy. Boston: Little, Brown.
Moore, Mark Harrison
1977 Buy and Bust. Lexington, MA: Lexington Books.
Petersilia, Joan, Peter W. Greenwood, and Marvin Lavin
1978 Criminal Careers of Habitual Offenders. Washington, DC: U.S. Government Printing Office.
Peterson, Mark, Harriet Braiker, and Sue Polich
1980 Doing Crime: A Survey of California Inmates. Santa Monica, CA: Rand Corporation.
Pittman, David J.
1971 "The male house of prostitution." Transaction 8:21–27.

Prus, Robert and Styllianoss Irini
1980 Hookers, Rounders and Desk Clerks. Toronto: Gage.
Rains, Prue
1982 "Deviant careers." Pp. 21–41 in M. Michael Rosenberg, Robert A. Stebbins, and Allen Turowetz (eds.), The Sociology of Deviance. New York: St. Martin's Press.
Reiss, Albert J.
1961 "The social integration of queers and peers." Social Problems 9:102–20.
Reuter, Peter
1983 Disorganized Crime: The Economics of the Visible Hand. Cambridge, MA: MIT Press.
Ross, H. Laurence
1959 "The 'hustler' in Chicago." Journal of Student Research 1:13–19.
Rubin, Paul H.
1973 "The economic theory of the criminal firm." Pp. 155–66 in Simon Rottenberg (ed.), The Economics of Crime and Punishment. Washington, DC: American Enterprise Institute for Public Policy Research.
Rubington, Earl
1967 "Drug addiction as a deviant career." International Journal of the Addictions 2:3–20.
Spilerman, Seymour
1977 "Careers, labor market structure, and socioeconomic achievement." American Journal of Sociology 83:551–93.
Stebbins, Robert A.
1971 Commitment to Deviance. Westport, CT: Greenwood.
Unruh, David R.
1979 "Characteristics and types of participation in social worlds." Symbolic Interaction 2:115–29.
Wolfgang, Marvin E., Robert M. Figlio, and Thorsten Sellin
1972 Delinquency in a Birth Cohort. Chicago: University of Chicago Press.

33 / Drifting into Dealing: Becoming a Cocaine Seller

SHEIGLA MURPHY
DAN WALDORF
CRAIG REINARMAN

INTRODUCTION

No American who watched television news in the 1980s could have avoided images of violent drug dealers who brandished bullets while driving BMW's before being hauled off in handcuffs. This new stereotype of a drug dealer has become a staple of popular culture, the very embodiment of evil. He works for the still more vile villains of the "Columbian cartel," who make billions on the suffering of millions. Such men are portrayed as driven by greed and utterly indifferent to the pain from which they profit.

We have no doubt that some such characters exist. Nor do we doubt that there may be a new viciousness among some of the crack cocaine dealers who have emerged in ghettos and barrios already savaged by rising social problems and falling social programs. We have grave doubts, however, that such characterizations tell us anything about cocaine sellers more generally. If our interviews are any guide, beneath every big-time dealer who may approximate the stereotype there are hundreds of smaller sellers who do not.

This paper describes such sellers, not so much as a way of debunking a new devil but rather as a way of illuminating how deviant careers develop and how the identities of the individuals who move into this work are transformed. Along with the many routine normative strictures against drug use in our culture, there has been a mobilization in recent years for a "war on drugs" which targets cocaine dealers in particular. Many armaments in the arsenal of social control from propaganda to prisons have been employed in efforts to dissuade people from using/selling such substances. In such a context it is curious that ostensibly ordinary people not only continue to use illicit drugs but also take the significant additional step of becoming drug sellers. To explore how this happens, we offer an analysis of eighty depth interviews with former cocaine sellers. We sought to learn something about how it is that otherwise conventional people—some legally employed, many well educated—end up engaging in a sustained pattern of behavior that their neighbors might think of as very deviant indeed.

DEVIANT CAREERS AND DRIFT

Our reading of this data was informed by two classic theoretical works in the deviance literature. First, in *Outsiders,* Howard Becker observed that, "The career lines characteristic of an occupation take their shape from the problems peculiar to that occupation. These, in turn, are a function of the occupation's position vis-a-vis other groups in society" (1963:102). He illustrated the point with the dance musician, caught between the jazz artist's desire to maintain creative control and a structure of opportunities for earning a living that demanded the subordination of this desire to mainstream musical tastes. Musicians' careers were largely a function of how they managed this problem. When the need to make a living predominated, the basis of their self conceptions shifted from art to craft.

Of course, Becker applied the same proposition to more deviant occupations. In the next section, we describe five discrete modes of becoming a cocaine seller which center on "the problems peculiar to" the world of illicit drug use and which entail a similar shift in self conception. For example, when a drug such as cocaine is criminalized, its cost is often greatly increased while its availability and quality are somewhat limited. Users are thus faced with the problems of avoiding detection, reducing costs, and improving availability and quality. By becoming involved in sales, users solve many of these problems and may also find that they can make some money in the bargain. As we will show, the type of entree and the level at which it occurs are functions of the individual's relationship to networks of other users and suppliers. At the point where one has moved from being a person who *has* a good connection for cocaine to a person who *is* a good connection for cocaine, a subtle shift in self conception and identity occurs.

Becker's model of deviant careers entails four basic steps, three of which our cocaine sellers took. First, the deviant must somehow avoid the impact of conventional commitments that keep most people away from intentional non-conformity. Our cocaine sellers passed this stage by ingesting illegal substances with enough regularity that the practice became normalized in their social world. Second, deviant motives and interests must develop. These are usually learned in the process of the deviant activity and from interaction with other deviants. Here too our cocaine sellers had learned the pleasures of cocaine by using it, and typically were moved toward involvement in distribution to solve one or more problems entailed in such use. Once involved, they discovered additional motivations which we will describe in detail below.

Becker's third step in the development of deviant careers entails public labeling. The person is caught, the rule is enforced, and his or her public identity is transformed. The new master status of "deviant," Becker argues, can be self fulfilling when it shapes others' perceptions of the person and limits his or her possibilities for resuming conventional roles and activities. Few of our respondents had been publicly labeled deviant, but they did describe a gradual change in identity that may be likened to self-labeling. This typically occurred when they deepened their deviance by dealing on top of using cocaine. This shift in self conception for our subjects was more closely linked to Becker's fourth step—movement into an organized deviant group in which people with a common fate and similar problems form subcultures. There they learn more about solving problems and ideologies which provide rationales for continuing the behavior, thus further weakening the hold of conventional norms and institutions and solidifying deviant identities. In the case of our subjects, becoming sellers further immersed them into deviant groups and practices to the point where many came to face the problems of, and to see themselves as, "dealers."

The fact that these processes of deeper immersion into deviant worlds and shifts in self conception were typically gradual and subtle brought us to a second set of theoretical reference points in the work of David Matza (1964; 1969).[1] In his research on delinquency, Matza discovered that most so-called delinquents were not self-consciously committed to deviant values or lifestyles, but on the contrary continued to hold conventional beliefs. Most of the time they were law abiding, but because the situation of "youth" left them free from various restraints, they often *drifted* in and out of deviance. Matza found that even when caught being delinquent, young people tended to justify or rationalize their acts through "techniques of neutralization" (Sykes and Matza, 1957) rooted in conventional codes of morality. Although we focus on *entering* selling careers, we found that Matza's concept of drift (1964) provided us with a useful sensibility for making sense of our respondents' accounts. The modes of entree they described were as fluid and non-committal as the drift into and out of delinquency that he described.

None of the career paths recounted by our subjects bear much resemblance to stereotypes of "drug dealers."[2] For decades the predominant image of the illicit drug dealer was an older male reprobate sporting a long, shabby overcoat within which he had secreted a cornucopia of dangerous consciousness-altering substances. This proverbial "pusher" worked school yards, targeting innocent children who would soon be chemically enslaved repeat customers. The newer villains have been depicted as equally vile but more violent. Old or new, the ideal-typical "drug dealer" is motivated by perverse greed and/or his own addiction, and has crossed a clearly marked moral boundary, severing most ties to the conventional world.

The cocaine sellers we interviewed, on the other hand, had more varied and complex motives for selling cocaine. Moreover at least within their subcultures, the moral boundaries were both rather blurry and as often wandered along as actually crossed. Their life histories reminded us of Matza's later but related discussion of the *overlap* between deviance and conventionality:

> Overlap refers to... the marginal rather than gross differentiation between deviant and conventional folk and the considerable though variable interpenetration of deviant and conventional culture. Both themes sensitize us to the regular exchange, traffic, and flow—of persons as well as styles and precepts—that occur among deviant and conventional worlds. (1969:68)

Our subjects were already seasoned users of illicit drugs. For years their drug use coexisted comfortably with their conventional roles and activities; having a deviant dimension to their identities appeared to cause them little strain. In fact, because their use of illicit drugs had gone on for so long, was so common in their social worlds, and had not significantly affected their otherwise normal lives, they hardly considered it deviant at all.

Thus, when they began to sell cocaine as well as use it, they did not consider it a major leap down an unknown road but rather a series of short steps down a familiar path. It was not as if ministers had become mobsters; no sharp break in values, motives, world views, or identities was required. Indeed, few woke up one morning and made a conscious decision to become sellers. They did not break sharply with the conventional world and actively choose a deviant career path; most simply drifted into dealing by virtue of their strategies for solving the problems entailed in using a criminalized substance, and only then developed additional deviant motives centering on money.

To judge from our respondents, then, dealers are not from a different gene pool. Since the substances they enjoy are illegal, most regular users of such drugs become involved in some aspect of distribution. There is also a growing body of research on cocaine selling and distribution that has replaced the simplistic stereotype of the pusher with complex empirical evidence about underground economies and deviant careers (e.g., Langer, 1977; Waldorf *et al.*, 1977, 1991; Adler, 1985; Plasket and Quillen, 1985; Morales, 1986a, 1986b; Sanchez and Johnson, 1987; Sanabria, 1988; and Williams, 1989). Several features of underground economies or black markets in drugs contribute to widespread user participation in distribution. For example, some users who could obtain cocaine had other user-friends who wanted it. Moreover, the idea of keeping such traffic among friends offered both sociability and safety. For others, cocaine's high cost inspired many users to become involved in purchasing larger amounts to take advantage of volume discounts. They then sold part of their supply to friends in order to reduce the cost of personal use. The limited supply of cocaine in the late seventies and early eighties made for a sellers' market, providing possibilities for profits along with steady supplies. For most of our subjects, it was not so much that they learned they could make money and thus decided to become dealers but rather, being involved in distribution anyway, they learned they could make money from it. As Becker's model suggests, deviant motives are learned in the course of deviant activities; motivation follows behavior, not the other way around.

After summarizing our sampling and interviewing procedures, we describe in more detail: 1) the various modes and levels of entree into cocaine sales; 2) some of the practices, rights and responsibilities entailed in dealing; and 3) the subtle transformation of identity that occurred when people who consider themselves rather conventional moved into careers considered rather deviant.

SAMPLE AND METHODS

The sample consists of 80 ex-sellers who sold cocaine in the San Francisco Bay Area. We interviewed them in 1987 and 1988. Most had stopped selling before crack sales peaked in this area. Only five of the eighty had sold crack or rock. Of these five, two had sold on the street and two had sold in "rock party houses"[3] as early as 1978. It is important to note, therefore, that the sellers we describe are very likely to be different from street crack dealers in terms of the product type, selling styles, visibility, and thus the risks of arrest and attendant violence.

The modes and levels of entree we describe should not be considered exhaustive. They are likely to vary by region, subculture, and level of dealing. For example, our sample and focus differed from those of Adler (1985), who studied one community of *professional* cocaine dealers at the *highest levels* of the distribution system. Her ethnographic account is rich in insights about the lifestyles and career contingencies of such high-level dealers and smugglers. These subjects decided to enter into importing and or dealing and to move up the ranks in this deviant occupation in order to obtain wealth and to live the sorts of lives that such wealth made possible. Adler's dealers were torn, however, between the lures of fast money and the good life and the stress and paranoia inherent in the scene. Thus, she reported "oscillations" wherein her dealers moved in and out of the business, usually to be lured back in by the possibility of high profits. Our dealers tended to have different motivations, career trajectories, and occupational exigencies. Most were lower in the hierarchy and non-professional (some maintained "straight" jobs); few set out to achieve success in an explicitly deviant career, to amass wealth, or to live as "high rollers." Moreover, our study was cross-sectional rather than longitudinal, so our focus was on how a wide variety of cocaine sellers entered careers rather than on the full career trajectories of a network of smugglers and sellers.

To be eligible for the study our respondents had to have sold cocaine steadily for at least a year and to have stopped selling for at least 6 months. We designed the study to include only *former* sellers so that respondents would feel free to describe all their activities in detail without fear that their accounts could somehow be utilized by law enforcement authorities.

They spoke of six different levels or types of sellers: smugglers, big dealers, dealers, sellers (unspecified), bar dealers, and street dealers. The social organization of cocaine sales probably varies in other areas. We located and interviewed ex-sellers from the full range of these dealer-identified sales levels, but we have added two categories in order to provide a more detailed typology. Our eight levels of sales were defined according to the units sold rather than the units bought. So, for example, if a seller bought quarters or eighths of ounces and regularly sold grams, we categorized him or her as a gram dealer rather than a part-ounce dealer.

Levels of Sales	Number of Interviews
Smugglers	2
Kilograms/pounds	13
Parts of kilos and pounds	6
Ounce dealers	18
Part-ounce dealers	13
Gram dealers	12
Part-gram dealers	11
Crack dealers	5
Total	80

Unlike most other studies of dealing and the now infamous street crack dealers, the majority of our respondents sold cocaine hydrochloride (powder) in private places. There are a number of styles of selling drugs—selling out of homes, selling out of rock houses and shooting galleries, selling out of party houses, selling out of rented "safe houses" and apartments, delivery services (using telephone answering, answering machines, voice mail and telephone beepers), car meets,[4] selling in bars, selling in parks, and selling in the street. Within each type there are various styles. For example, in some African-American communities in San Francisco a number of sellers set up business on a street and respond to customers who come by on foot and in automobiles. Very often a number of sellers will approach a car that slows down or stops to solicit customers; drugs and money are exchanged then and there. Such sales activities are obvious to the most casual observers; even television camera crews often capture such transactions for the nightly news. On certain streets in the Mission District, a Latino community in San Francisco, street drug sales are less blatant. Buyers usually walk up to sellers who stand on the street among numerous other people who are neither buyers nor sellers. There, specific transactions rarely take place on the street itself; the participants generally retreat to a variety of shops and restaurants. Buyers seldom use cars for transactions and sellers tend not to approach a car to solicit customers.

Despite the ubiquity of street sales in media accounts and the preponderance of street sellers in arrest records, we set out to sample the more hidden and more numerous sellers who operate in private. Most users of cocaine hydrochloride are working- or middle-class. They generally avoid street sellers both because they want to avoid being observed and because they believe that most street sellers sell inferior quality drugs (Waldorf *et al.*, 1991). Further, we found that people engaged in such illegal and furtive transactions tend to prefer dealing with people like themselves, people they know.

We located our respondents by means of chain referral sampling techniques (Biernacki and Waldorf, 1981; Watters and Biernacki, 1989). This is a method commonly used by sociologists and ethnographers to locate hard-to-find groups and has been used extensively in qualitative research on drug use (Lindesmith, 1947; Becker, 1953; Feldman, 1968; Preble and Casey, 1969; Rosenbaum, 1981; Biernacki, 1986). We initiated the first of our location chains in 1974–75 in the course of a short-term ethnography of cocaine use and sales among a small friendship network (Waldorf *et al.*, 1977). Other chains were developed during a second study of cocaine cessation conducted during 1986–1987 (Reinarman *et al.*, 1988; Macdonald *et al.*, 1988; Murphy *et al.*, 1989; Waldorf *et al.*, 1991). Another three chains were developed during the present study. We located the majority of our respondents via referral chains developed by former sellers among their previous customers and suppliers. Initial interviewees referred us to other potential respondents whom we had not previously known. In this way we were able to direct our chains into groups of ex-sellers from a variety of backgrounds.

We employed two interview instruments: an open-ended, exploratory interview guide designed to maximize discovery of new and unique types of data, and a more structured survey designed to gather basic quantifiable data on all respondents. The open-ended interviews were tape-recorded, transcribed, and content-analyzed. These interviews usually took from 2 to 4 hours to complete, but when necessary we conducted longer and/or follow-up interviews (e.g., one woman was interviewed for 10 hours over three sessions). The data analyzed for this paper was drawn primarily from the tape-recorded depth interviews.

There is no way to ascertain if this (or any similar) sample is representative of all cocaine sellers. Because the parameters of the population are unknowable, random samples on which systematic generalizations might be based cannot be drawn. We do know that, unlike other studies of drug sellers, we placed less emphasis on street sellers and included dealers at all levels. We also attempted to get a better gender and ethnic mix than studies based on captive samples from jails or treatment programs. Roughly one in three (32.5%) of our dealers are female and two of five (41.2%) are persons of color.

Table 1 / Demographics (N=80)

Age: Range = 18–60 years
Mean 37.1
Median = 35.4

	Number	Percent
Sex:		
Male	54	67.5
Female	26	32.5
Ethnicity:		
African-American	28	35.0
White	44	58.8
Latino(a)	4	5.0
Asian	1	1.2
Education:		
Less than high school grad	11	13.8
High school graduate	18	22.5
Some college	31	38.8
B.A. or B.S. degree	12	15.0
Some graduate	3	3.8
Graduate degree	5	6.3

[Percentages may not equal 100% due to rounding]

Our respondents ranged in age from 18 to 60, with a mean age of 37.1 years. Their education level was generally high, presumably an indication of the relatively large numbers of middle-class people in the sample.

DEALERS

Dealers are people who are "fronted" (given drugs on consignment to be paid for upon sale) and/or who buy quantities of drugs for sale. Further, in order to be considered a dealer by users or other sellers a person must: 1) have one or more reliable connections (suppliers); 2) make regular cocaine purchases in amounts greater than a single gram (usually an eighth of an ounce or greater) to be sold in smaller units; 3) maintain some consistent supplies for sale; and 4) have a network of customers who make purchases on a regular basis. Although the stereotype of a dealer holds that illicit drug sales are a full-time occupation, many dealers, including members of our sample, operate part-time and supplement income from a legal job.

As we noted in the introduction, the rather average, ordinary character of the respondents who fit this definition was striking. In general, without prior knowledge or direct observation of drug sales, one would be unable to distinguish our respondents from other, non-dealer citizens. When telling their career histories, many of our respondents invoked very conventional, middle-class American values to explain their involvement in dealing (e.g., having children to support, mortgages or rent to pay in a high-cost urban area, difficulty finding jobs which paid enough to support a family). Similarly, their profits from drug sales were used in "normal" ways—to buy children's clothes, to make house or car payments, to remodel a room. Moreover, like Matza's delinquents, most of our respondents were quite law-abiding, with the obvious exception of their use and sales of an illicit substance.

When they were not dealing, our respondents engaged in activities that can only be described as mainstream American. For example, one of our dealers, a single mother of two, found herself with a number of friends who used cocaine and a good connection. She needed extra income to pay her mortgage and to support her children, so she sold small amounts of cocaine within her friendship network. Yet while she sold cocaine, she worked at a full-time job, led a Girl Scout troop, volunteered as a teacher of cardio-pulmonary resuscitation (CPR) classes for young people, and went to Jazzercize classes. Although she may have been a bit more civic-minded than many others, her case served to remind us that cocaine sellers do not come from another planet.

MODES OF ENTREE INTO DEALING

Once they began selling cocaine, many of our respondents moved back and forth between levels in the distribution hierarchy. Some people dealt for short periods of time and then quit, only to return several months later at another level of sales.[5] The same person may act as a broker on one deal, sell a quarter gram at a profit to a friend on another, and then pick up an ounce from an associate and pass it on to another dealer in return for some marijuana in a third transaction. In a few instances each of these roles were played by the same person within the same twenty-four hour period.

But whether or not a dealer/respondent moved back and forth in this way, s/he usually began selling in one of five distinct ways. All five of these modes of entree pre-suppose an existing demand for cocaine from people known to the potential dealers. A person selling any line of products needs two things, a group of customers and a product these customers are interested in purchasing. Cocaine sellers are no different. In addition to being able and willing to pay, however, cocaine customers must also be trustworthy because these transactions are illegal.

The first mode of entree, *the go-between,* is fairly straightforward. The potential seller has a good cocaine connection and a group of friends who place orders for cocaine with him/her. If the go-between's friends use cocaine regularly enough and do not develop their own connections, then a period of months or even years might go by when the go-between begins to spend more and more time and energy purchasing for them. Such sellers generally do not make formal decisions to begin dealing; rather, opportunities regularly present themselves and go-betweens gradually take advantage of them. For example, one 30 year-old African-American who became a gram dealer offered this simple account of his passage from go-between to seller:

> Basically, I first started because friends pressured me to get the good coke I could get. I wasn't even making any money off of it. They'd come to me and I'd call up my friend who had gotten pretty big selling a lot of coke. (Case # E-5)

This went on for six months before he began to charge his friends money for it. Then his connection started fronting him eighths of ounces at a time, and he gradually became an official dealer, regularly selling drugs for a profit. Others who began in this way often took only commissions-in-kind (a free snort) for some months before beginning to charge customers a cash mark-up.

Another African-American male began selling powdered cocaine to snorters in 1978 and by the mid-eighties had begun selling rock cocaine (crack) to smokers. He described his move from go-between to dealer as follows:

> Around the time I started indulging [in cocaine] myself, people would come up and say, "God, do you know where I can get some myself?" I would just say, "Sure, just give me your money," I would come back and either indulge with them or just give it to them depending on my mood. I think that's how I originally set up my clientele. I just had a certain group of people who would come to me because they felt that I knew the type of people who could get them a real quality product.
>
> And pretty soon I just got tired of, you know, being taken out of situations or being imposed upon. . . . I said that it would be a lot easier to just do it myself. And one time in particular, and I didn't consider myself a dealer or anything, but I had a situation one night where 5 different people called me to try to get cocaine . . . not from me but it was like, "Do you know where I can get some good cocaine from?" (Case # E-11)

Not all go-betweens-cum-dealers start out so altruistically. Some astute businessmen and women spot the profit potential early on and immediately realize a profit, either in-kind (a share of the drugs purchased) or by tacking on a surcharge to the purchase price. The following respondent, a 39 year-old African-American male, described this more profit-motivated move from go-between to formal seller:

> Well, the first time that I started it was like I knew where to get good stuff . . . and I had friends that didn't know where to get good stuff. And I knew where to get them really good stuff and so I would always put a couple of dollars on it, you know, if I got it for $20 I would sell it to them for $25 or $30 or whatever.

> It got to be where more and more people were coming to me and I was going to my man more and I would be there 5 or 6 times a day, you know. So he would tell me, "Here, why don't you take this, you know, and bring me x-amount of dollars for it." So that's how it really started. I got fronted and I was doing all the business instead of going to his house all the time, because he had other people that were coming to his house and he didn't want the traffic. (Case # E-13)

The second mode of entree is the *stash dealer,* or a person who becomes involved in distribution and/or sales simply to support or subsidize personal use. The name is taken from the term "stash," meaning a personal supply of marijuana (see Fields, 1985, on stash dealers in the marijuana trade). This forty-one year-old white woman who sold along with her husband described her start as a stash dealer this way:

Q: So what was your motivation for the sales?

A: To help pay for my use, because the stuff wasn't cheap and I had the means and the money at the time in order to purchase it, where our friends didn't have that amount of money without having to sell something.... Yeah, friendship, it wasn't anything to make money off of, I mean we made a few dollars.... (Case # E-7)

The respondents who entered the dealing world as stash dealers typically started out small (selling quarter and half grams) and taking their profits in product. However, this motivation contributed to the undoing of some stash dealers in that it led to greater use, which led to the need for greater selling, and so on. Unless they then developed a high-volume business that allowed them to escalate their cocaine use and still make profits, the reinforcing nature of cocaine tempted many of them to use more product than was good for business.

Many stash dealers were forced out of business fairly early on in their careers because they spent so much money on their own use they were financially unable to "re-cop" (buy new supplies). Stash dealers often want to keep only a small number of customers in order to minimize both the "hassle" of late-night phone calls and the risk of police detection, and they do not need many customers since they only want to sell enough to earn free cocaine. Problems arise, however, when their small group of customers do not buy the product promptly. The longer stash dealers had cocaine in their possession, the more opportunities they had for their own use (i.e., for profits to "go up your nose"). One stash dealer had an axiom about avoiding this: "It ain't good to get high on your own supply" (Case # E-57). The predicament of using rather than selling their product often afflicts high-level "weight dealers" as well, but they are better able to manage for longer periods of time due to larger volumes and profit margins.

The third mode of entry into cocaine selling had to do with users' desire for high-quality, unadulterated cocaine. We call this type the *connoisseur.* Ironically, the motivation for moving toward dealing in this way is often health-related. People who described this mode of entree described their concerns, as users, about the possible dangers of ingesting the various adulterants or "cuts" commonly used by dealers to increase profits. User folklore holds that the larger the quantity purchased, the purer the product. This has been substantiated by laboratory analysis of the quality of small amounts of street drugs (typically lower) as opposed to larger police seizures (typically higher).

The connoisseur type of entry, then, begins with the purchase of larger quantities of cocaine than they intend to use in order to maximize purity. Then they give portions of the cocaine to close friends at a good price. If the members of the network start to use more cocaine, the connoisseurs begin to make bigger purchases with greater regularity. At some point they begin to feel that all this takes effort and that it makes sense to buy large quantities not only to get purer cocaine but to make some money for their efforts. The following 51 year-old, white business executive illustrated the connoisseur route as follows:

> I think the first reason I started to sell was not to make money or even to pay for my coke, because I could afford it. It was to get good coke and not to be snorting a lot of impurities and junk that people were putting into it by cutting it so much. So I really think that I started to sell it or to get it wholesale so that I would get the good stuff. And I guess my first, . . . what I did with it in the beginning, because I couldn't use all that I had to buy to get good stuff, I sold it to some of my friends for them to sell it, retail it. (Case # E-16)

Connoisseurs, who begin by selling unneeded quantities, often found they unlearned certain attitudes when they moved from being volume buyers looking for quality toward becoming dealers looking for profit. It was often a subtle shift, but once their primary motivation gradually changed from buying-for-purity to buying-to-sell they found themselves beginning to think and act like dealers. The shift usually occurred when connoisseurs realized that the friends with whom they had shared were in fact customers who were eager for their high quality cocaine and who often made demands on their time (e.g., friends seeking supplies not merely for themselves, but for other friends a step or two removed from the original connoisseur). Some connoisseurs also became aware of the amount of money that could be made by becoming business-like about what had been formally friendly favors. At such points in the process they began to buy-to-sell, for a profit, as well as for the purpose of obtaining high-quality cocaine for personal use. This often meant that, rather than buying sporadically, they had to make more regular buys; for a successful businessperson must have supplies when customers want to buy or they will seek another supplier.

The fourth mode of entree into cocaine selling is an *apprenticeship*. Like the other types, apprentices typically were users who already had loosened conventional normative strictures and learned deviant motives by interacting with other users and with dealers; and they, too, drifted into dealing. However, in contrast to the first three types, apprentices moved toward dealing less to solve problems inherent in using a criminalized substance than to solve the problems of the master dealer. Apprenticeships begin in a personal relationship where, for example, the potential seller is the lover or intimate of a dealer. This mode was most often the route of entry for women, although one young man we interviewed learned to deal from his father. Couples often start out with the man doing the dealing—picking up the product, handling the money, weighing and packaging, etc. The woman gradually finds herself acting as an unofficial assistant—taking telephone messages, sometimes giving people prepackaged cocaine and collecting money. Apprentices frequently benefit from being involved with the experienced dealer in that they enjoy both supplies of high-quality cocaine and indirect financial rewards of dealing.

Some of our apprentices moved into official roles or deepened their involvement when the experienced dealer began to use too much cocaine to function effectively as a seller. In some such cases the abuse of the product led to an end of the relationship. Some apprentices then left dealing altogether while others began dealing on their own. One 32 year-old African-American woman lived with a pound dealer in Los Angeles in 1982. Both were freebasers (cocaine smokers) who sold to other basers. She described her evolution from apprentice to dealer this way:

> I was helping him with like weighing stuff and packaging it and I sort of got to know some of the people that were buying because his own use kept going up. He was getting more out of it, so I just fell into taking care of it partly because I like having the money and it also gave me more control over the situation, too, for awhile, you know, until we both got too out of it. (Case # E-54)

The fifth mode of entree into cocaine selling entailed the *expansion of an existing product line*. A number of the sellers we interviewed started out as marijuana salespersons and learned many aspects of the dealers' craft before they ever moved to cocaine. Unlike in the other modes, in this one an existing marijuana seller already had developed selling skills and established a network of active customers for illicit drugs. Expansion of product line (in business jargon, horizontal integration) was the route of entry for many of the multiple-ounce and kilo cocaine dealers we interviewed. The combination of the availability of cocaine through their marijuana connection and their marijuana customers' interest in purchasing cocaine, led many marijuana sellers to add cocaine to their product line.

Others who entered dealing this way also found that expanding from marijuana to cocaine solved some problems inherent in marijuana dealing. For example, cocaine is far less bulky and odoriferous than marijuana and thus did not present the risky and costly shipping and storage problems of multiple pounds of marijuana. Those who entered cocaine selling via this product line expansion route also recognized, of course, that there was the potential for higher profits with cocaine. They seemed to suggest that as long as they were already taking the risk, why shouldn't they maximize the reward? Some such dealers discontinued marijuana sales altogether and others merely added cocaine to their line. One white, 47 year-old mother of three grown children described how she came to expand her product line:

Q: How did you folks [she and her husband] get started dealing?
A: The opportunity just fell into our lap. We were already dealing weed and one of our customers got this great coke connection and started us onto dealing his product. We were selling him marijuana and he was selling us cocaine.
Q: So you had a network of weed buyers, right? So you could sell to those...?
A: There was a shift in the market. Yeah, because weed was becoming harder [to find] and more expensive and a bulkier product. The economics of doing a smaller, less bulkier product and more financially rewarding product like cocaine had a certain financial appeal to the merchant mentality. (Case # E-1)

CONSCIOUS DECISION TO SELL

As noted earlier, the majority of our sample were middle class wholesalers who, in the various ways just described, drifted into dealing careers. The few street sellers we interviewed did not drift into sales in the same way. We are obliged to note again that the five modes of entry into cocaine selling we have identified should not be taken as exhaustive. We have every reason to believe that for groups and settings other than those we have studied there are other types of entree and career trajectories. The five cases of street sellers we did examine suggest that entree into street-level sales was more of a conscious decision of a poor person who decided to enter an underground economy, not an effort to solve a user's problems. Our interviews with street sellers suggest that they choose to participate in an illicit profit-generating activity largely because licit economic opportunities were scarce or nonexistent. Unlike our other types, such sellers sold to strangers as well as friends, and their place of business was more likely to be the street corner rather than homes, bars, or nightclubs. For example, one 30 year-old Native American ex-prostitute described how she became a street crack dealer this way:

> I had seen in the past friends that were selling and stuff and I needed extra money so I just one day told one of my friends, you know, if he could help me, you know, show me more or less how it goes. So I just went by what I seen. So I just started selling it. (Case # E-AC 1)

A few higher-level dealers also made conscious decisions to sell (see Adler, 1985), particularly when faced with limited opportunity structures. Cocaine selling, as an occupation, offers the promise of lavish lifestyles otherwise unattainable to most ghetto youth and other impoverished groups. Dealing also provides an alternative to the low-paying, dead-end jobs typically available to those with little education and few skills. A 55 year-old African-American man who made his way up from grams to ounce sales described his motivation succinctly: "The chance presented itself to avoid the 9 to 5" (Case # E-22).

Street sellers and even some higher-level dealers are often already participating in quasi-criminal lifestyles; drug sales are simply added to their repertoire of illicit activities. The perceived opportunity to earn enormous profits, live "the good life," and set your own work schedule are powerful enticements to sell. From the perspective of people with few life chances, dealing cocaine may be seen as their only real chance to achieve the "American Dream" (i.e., financial security and disposable income). Most of our sample were not ghetto dwellers and/or economically disadvantaged. But for those who were, there were different motivations and conscious decisions regarding beginning sales. Popular press descriptions of cocaine sellers predominantly portray just such street sellers. Although street sellers are the most visible, our data suggest that they represent what might be called the tip of the cocaine dealing iceberg.

LEVELS OF ENTRY

The levels at which a potential dealer's friends/connections were selling helped determine the level at which the new dealer entered the business. If the novitiate was moving in social scenes where "big dealers" are found, then s/he is likely to begin by selling grams and parts of grams. When supplies were not fronted, new dealers' personal finances, i.e., available capital, also influenced how much they could buy at one time.

Sellers move up and down the cocaine sales ladder as well as in and out of the occupation (see Adler, 1985). Some of our sellers were content to remain part-ounce dealers selling between a quarter and a half an ounce a week. Other sellers were more ambitious and eventually sought to become bigger dealers in order to increase profits. One interviewee reported that her unusually well organized suppliers had sales quotas, price fixing, and minimum purchase expectations which pushed her toward expansion. The levels of sales and selling styles of the new dealer's suppliers, then, interacted with personal ambitions to influence eventual sales careers.

Another important aspect of beginning to sell cocaine is whether the connection is willing to "front" the cocaine (risk a consignment arrangement) rather than requiring the beginner to pay in full. Having to pay "up front" for one's inventory sometimes slowed sales by tying up capital, or even deterred some potential dealers from entering the business. Fronted cocaine allowed people with limited resources to enter the occupation. Decisions to front or not to front were based primarily on the connection's evaluation of the new seller's ability to "move" the product. This was seen as a function of the potential volume of business the beginning seller could generate among his/her networks of friends and/or customers. The connection/fronter also evaluates the trustworthiness of the potential dealer, as well as their own capability of absorbing the loss should the deal "go bad" and the frontee be unable to pay. The judgement of the fronter is crucial, for a mistake can be very costly and there is no legal recourse.

LEARNING TO DEAL

In the go-between, stash and connoisseur modes of entree, novices gradually learn the tricks of the trade by observing the selling styles of active dealers, and ultimately by doing. Weighing, packaging, and pricing the product are basic techniques. A scale, preferably a triple-beam type... accurate to the tenth of a gram, is a necessary tool. In the last ten years answering machines, beepers, and even cellular phones have become important tools as well. Learning how to manage customers and to establish selling routines and rules of procedure are all essential skills that successful dealers must master.

The dealers who enter sales through the apprenticeship and product line expansion modes have the advantage of their own or their partner/seller's experience. Active marijuana sellers already have a network of customers, scales, familiarity with metric measures, and, most important, a connection to help them move into a new product line. Apprentices have lived with and/or observed the selling styles of their dealer/mentors and have access to their equipment, connections and customers. Both apprentices and marijuana dealers who have expanded into cocaine also know how to "maintain a low profile" and avoid any kind of attention that might culminate in arrest. In this way they were able to reduce or manage the paranoia that often inheres in drug dealing circles.

Many sellers learn by making mistakes, often expensive mistakes. These include: using too much cocaine themselves, fronting drugs to people who do not pay for them, and adding too much "cut" (usually an inactive adulterant such as vitamin B) to their product so they develop a reputation for selling inferior cocaine and sometimes have difficulty selling the diluted product. One 32 year-old African American male made one such error in judgment by fronting to too many people who did not "come through." It ended up costing him $15,000:

> It was because of my own recklessness that I allowed myself to get into that position. There was a period where I had a lot of weight that I just took it and just shipped it out to people I shouldn't have shipped it out to.... I did this with 10 people and a lot of them were women to be exact. I had a lot of women coming over to my house and I just gave them an ounce apiece one time.... So when maybe 6 of those people didn't come through... there was a severe cramp in my cash flow. This made me go to one of the family members to get the money to re-cop. (Case # E-11)

Business Sense/People Sense

Many people have a connection, the money to make the initial buy, a reputation for being reliable, and a group of friends interested in buying drugs, but still lack the business sense to be a successful dealer. Just because a person drifts into dealing does not mean that he or she will prosper and stay in dealing. We found a variety of ways in which people initially became dealers, few of which hinged on profits. But what determined whether they continued dealing was their business sense. Thus even though a profit orientation had little to do with becoming a dealer, the ability to consistently realize profits had a major influence over who remained a dealer. In this sense, cocaine selling was like any other capitalist endeavor.

According to our respondents, one's ability to be a competent dealer depended on being able to separate business from pleasure. Success or failure at making this separation over time determined whether a profit was realized. Certain business practices were adopted by prosperous dealers to assist them in making this important distinction. For example, prepackaging both improves quality control and helps keep inventory straight; establishing rules for customers concerning when they can purchase and at what prices reduces the level of hassle; limiting the amount of fronting can reduce gross sales volume, but it also reduces financial risk and minimizes the amount of debt collection work; and limiting their own personal use keeps profits from disappearing up one's nose or in one's pipe.

Being a keen judge of character was seen as another important component of being a skilled dealer. Having the "people skills" to judge whether a person could be trusted to return with the money for fronted supplies, to convince people to pay debts that the dealer had no legal mechanisms for collecting, and to engender the trust of a connection when considerable amounts of money were at stake, are just a few of the sophisticated interpersonal skills required of a competent dealer.

Adler also discusses the importance of a "good personal reputation" among upper level dealers and smugglers:

> One of the first requirements for success, whether in drug trafficking, business enterprise broadly, or any life undertaking, is the establishment of a good personal reputation. To make it in the drug world, dealers and smugglers had to generate trust and likability. (1985:100)

Adler's general point applies to our respondents as well, although the experiences of some of our middle and lower level dealers suggested a slight amendment: A likable person with a good reputation could sell a less than high quality product, but an unlikable person, even one with a bad reputation, could still do a considerable amount of business if s/he had an excellent product. One 47 year-old white woman described her "difficult" husband/partner, "powder keg Paul":

> He would be so difficult, you couldn't believe it. Somebody [this difficult] better have a super primo product to make all this worthwhile.... He's the kind of guy you don't mind buying from because you know you'll get a good product, but he's the kind of guy you never want to sell to... he was that difficult. (Case # E-1)

High quality cocaine, in other words, is always at a premium in this subculture, so even without good people skills a dealer or connection with "good product" was tolerated.

FROM USER TO DEALER: THE TRANSFORMATION OF IDENTITY

In each of our respondents' deviant careers there occurred what Becker referred to as a change in self conception. Among our respondents, this took the form of a subtle shift in identity from a person who *has* a good connection for cocaine to a person who *is* a good connection for cocaine. There is a corresponding change in the meaning of, and the motives for, selling. The relationship between the seller and the customer undergoes a related transformation, from "picking up something for a friend" to conducting a commercial transaction. In essence, dealing becomes a business quite like most others, and the dealer gradually takes on the professional identity of a business person. Everett Hughes, writing on the sociology of work, urged social scientists to remember that when we look at work,

> We need to rid ourselves of any concepts which keep us for seeing that the essential problems of men at work are the same whether they do their work in the laboratories of some famous institution or in the messiest vat of a pickle factory. (1951:313)

When they had fully entered the dealer role, our respondents came to see selling cocaine as a job—work, just like other kinds of work save for its illegality. For most, selling cocaine did not mean throwing out conventional values and norms. In fact, many of our respondents actively maintained their conventional identities (see Broadhead, 1983). Such identities included those of parents, legally employed workers, neighbors, church-goers and softball players, to list just a few. Dealer identities tended not to replace former, "legitimate" identities but were added to a person's repertoire of more conventional identities.

Like everyone else in modern life, sellers emphasized one or another dimension of their identities as appropriate to the situation. In his study of heroin addicts Biernacki notes that, "The arrangement of identities must continuously be managed in such a way as to stress some identities at certain points in particular social worlds and situations, and at the same time to de-emphasize others" (1986:23). Our sellers, too, had to become adept at articulating the proper identity at the proper time. By day, one woman dealer was a concerned mother at her daughter's kindergarten field trip, and that same evening she was an astute judge of cocaine quality when picking up an ounce from her connection. At least for our interviewees, selling cocaine rarely entailed entirely terminating other social roles and obligations.

Yet, at some point in all of our sellers' careers, they found themselves transformed from someone who has a good connection to someone who is a good connection, and they gradually came to accept the identity of dealer as a part of their selves. Customers began to treat them like a salesperson, expecting them to be available to take calls and do business and even for services such as special off-hour pick-ups and deliveries or reduced rates for volume purchases. When dealers found themselves faced with such demands, they typically began to feel *entitled* to receive profits from selling. They came to be seen as dealers by others, and in part for this reason, came to see themselves as dealers. As Becker's (1963) model suggests, selling *behavior* usually preceded not only motivation but also changes in attitude and identity. As one 38 year-old white woman put it,

> I took over the business and paid all my husband's debts and started to make some money. One day I realized I was a coke dealer.... It was scary, but the money was good. (Case # E-75)

Acceptance of the dealer identity brings with it some expectations and values shared by dealers and customers alike. Customers have the expectation that the dealer will have a consistent supply of cocaine for sale. Customers also expect that the dealer will report in a fairly accurate manner the quality of his/her present batch of drugs within the confines of the *caveat emptor* philosophy that informs virtually all commercial activities in market societies. Buyers do not expect sellers to denigrate their product, but they do not expect the dealer to claim that their product is "excellent" if it is merely "good." Customers assume the dealer will make a profit, but dealers should not be "too greedy." A greedy dealer is one who makes what is estimated by the buyer to be excessive profits. Such estimations of excessiveness vary widely among customers and between sellers and buyers. But the fact that virtually all respondents spoke of some unwritten code of fairness suggests that there is, in E. P. Thompson's (1971) phrase, a "moral economy" of drug dealing that constrains the drive for profit maximization even within an illicit market.[6]

For their part, dealers expect that customers will act in a fashion that will minimize their changes of being arrested by being circumspect about revealing their dealer status. One simply did not, for example, bring to a dealer's house friends whom the dealer had not met. Dealers want customers to appreciate the risks undertaken to provide them with cocaine. And dealers come to feel that such risks deserve profits. After all, the seller is the one who takes the greatest risks; s/he could conceivably receive a stiff jail sentence for a sales conviction. While drifting into dealing and selling mostly to friends and acquaintances mitigated the risks of arrest and reduced their paranoia, such risks remained omnipresent.

In fact, the growing realization of such risks—and the rationalization it provided for dealing on a for-profit basis—was an integral part of becoming a cocaine seller. As our 38 year-old white woman dealer put it, "When it's all said and done, I'm the one behind bars, and I had better have made some money while I was selling or why in the hell take the risk?" (Case # E-75)

Acknowledgment

The research reported herein was funded by a grant from the National Institute of Justice (#7-0363-9-CA-IJ), Bernard A. Gropper, Ph.D., Program Manager, Drugs, Alcohol and Crime Programs, Center for Crime Control Research. The views expressed herein are those of the authors alone. The authors are grateful to the anonymous reviewers of *Qualitative Sociology* for helpful comments.

Address correspondence to Sheigla Murphy, Institute for Scientific Analysis, 2235 Lombard Street, San Francisco, CA, 94123.

Notes

1. Adler also refers briefly to Matza's formulations within her discussion of becoming a dealer (pp. 127–128, 1985).

2. It must be noted at the outset that the predominately white, working and middle class cocaine sellers we interviewed are very likely to differ from inner-city crack dealers depicted in the media. While there is now good reason to believe that both the profits and the violence reported to be endemic in the crack trade have been exaggerated (e.g., Reuter, 1990, and Goldstein *et al.*, 1989, respectively), our data are drawn from a different population, selling a different form of the drug, who were typically drawn to selling for different reasons. Thus the exigencies they faced and their responses to them are also likely to differ from those of inner-city crack sellers.

3. Rock party houses are distinct from "rock houses" or "crack houses." In the former, sellers invite only selected customers to their homes to smoke rock and "party." Unlike crack houses, where crack is sold to all comers, outsiders are never invited to rock party houses, and the arrangement is social and informal. Proprietors of both types, however, charge participants for the cocaine.

4. Car meets are transactions that take place in cars. Arrangements are made over the telephone in advance and both buyer and seller arrange to meet at parking lots, usually at busy shopping centers, and exchange drugs and money. Each arrives in his or her own car and leaves separately.

5. These movements back and forth among different levels of involvement in dealing were different from the "shifts and oscillations" found among the cocaine dealers studied by Adler (1985:133–141). She studied a circle of high-level dealers over an extended period of field work and found that the stresses and strains of dealing at the top of the pyramid often led her participants to attempt to get out of the business. While many of our interviewees felt similar pressures later in their careers and subsequently quit, our focus here is on becoming a cocaine seller.

6. In addition to lore about "righteous" and "rip off" dealers, there were present other norms that suggested the existence of such an unwritten code or moral economy, e.g., refusing to sell to children or to adults who "couldn't handle it" (i.e., had physical, financial, familial, or work-related problems because of cocaine use).

References

Adler, P. (1985). *Wheeling and Dealing: An Ethnography of an Upper-Level Drug Dealing Community*. New York: Columbia University Press.

Becker, H. S. (1953). "Becoming a marijuana user." *American Journal of Sociology* 59:235–242.

Becker, H. S. (1986). *Pathways from Heroin Addiction*. Philadelphia: Temple University Press.

Biernacki, P., & Waldorf, D. (1981). "Snowball sampling: problems and techniques of chain referral sampling." *Sociological Methods and Research* 10:141–163.

Broadhead, R. (1983). *The Private Lives and Professional Identity of Medical Students.* New Brunswick, NJ: Transaction Books.

Feldman, H. W. (1968). "Ideological supports to becoming and remaining a heroin addict." *Journal of Health and Social Behavior* 9:131–139.

Fields, A. (1985). "Weedslingers: a study of young black marijuana dealers." *Urban Life* 13:247–270.

Goldstein, P., Brownstein, H., Ryan, P., & Belucci, P. (1989). "Crack and homicide in New York City, 1988." *Contemporary Drug Problems* 16:651–687.

Grinspoon, L., & Bakalar, J. (1976). *Cocaine: A Drug and Its Social Evolution.* New York: Basic Books.

Hughes, E. (1951). "Work and the self." In John Rohrer and Muzafer Sherif (eds.), *Social Work at the Crossroads.* New York: Harper and Brothers, 313–323.

Langer, J. (1977)."Drug entrepreneurs and dealing culture." *Social Problems* 24:377–386.

Lindesmith, A. (1947). *Addiction and Opiates.* Chicago: Aldine Press.

Macdonald, P., Waldorf, D., Reinarman, C., & Murphy, S. (1988). "Heavy cocaine use and sexual behavior." *Journal of Drug Issues* 18:437–455.

Murphy, S., Reinarman, C., & Waldorf, D. (1989). "An eleven year follow-up of a network of cocaine users." *British Journal of the Addictions* 84:427–436.

Matza, D. (1964). *Delinquency and Drift.* New York: Wiley.

Matza, D. (1969). *Becoming Deviant.* Englewood Cliffs, NJ: Prentice-Hall.

Morales, E. (1986a). "Coca culture: the white gold of Peru." *Graduate School Magazine of City University of New York* 1:4–11.

Morales, E. (1986b). "Coca and cocaine economy and social change in the Andes in Peru." *Economic Development and Social Change* 35:143–161.

Morales, E. (1988). *Cocaine: The White Gold Rush in Peru.* Tucson, AZ: University of Arizona Press.

Plasket, B., & Quillen, E. (1985). *The White Stuff.* New York: Dell Publishing Company.

Preble, E., & Casey, J. H., Jr. (1969). "Taking care of business: the heroin user's life on the streets." *The International Journal of the Addictions* 4:1–24.

Reinarman, C., Waldorf, D., & Murphy, S. (1988). "Scapegoating and social control in the construction of a public problem: empirical and critical findings on cocaine and work." *Research in Law, Deviance and Social Control* 9:37–62.

Reuter, P. (1990). *Money from Crime: The Economics of Drug Dealing.* Santa Monica, CA: Rand Corporation.

Rosenbaum, M. (1981). *Women on Heroin.* New Brunswick, NJ: Rutgers University Press.

Sanabria, H. (1988). *Coca, Migration and Socio-Economic Change in a Bolivian Highland Peasant Community.* Ph.D. thesis, University of Wisconsin.

Sanchez, J., & Johnson, B. (1987). "Women and the drug crime connection: crime rates among drug abusing women at Riker's Island." *Journal of Psychoactive Drugs* 19:205–215.

Sykes, G., & Matza, D. (1957). "Techniques of neutralization." *American Sociological Review* 22:664–670.

Thompson, E. P. (1971). "The moral economy of the English crowd in the eighteenth century." *Past and Present* 50:76–136.

Waldorf, D., Reinarman, C., Murphy, S., & Joyce, B. (1977). *Doing Coke: An Ethnography of Cocaine Snorters and Sellers.* Washington, DC: Drug Abuse Council.

Waldorf, D., Reinarman, C., & Murphy, S. (1991). *Cocaine Changes.* Philadelphia: Temple University Press.

Watters, J. K., & Biernacki, P. (1989). "Targeted sampling: options for the study of hidden populations." *Social Problems* 36:416–430.

Williams, T. (1989). *The Cocaine Kids.* New York: Addison-Wesley.

34 / The Madam as Teacher: The Training of House Prostitutes

BARBARA SHERMAN HEYL

Although the day of the elaborate and conspicuous high-class house of prostitution is gone, houses still operate throughout the United States in a variety of altered forms. The business may be run out of trailers and motels along major highways, luxury apartments in the center of a metropolis or run-down houses in smaller, industrialized cities. (Recent discussions of various aspects of house prostitution include: Gagnon and Simon, 1973:226–7; Hall, 1973:115–95; Heyl, 1974; Jackson, 1969:185–92; Sheehy, 1974:185–204; Stewart, 1972; and Voglotti, 1975:25–80.) Madams sometimes find themselves teaching young women how to become professional prostitutes. This paper focuses on one madam who trains novices to work at the house level. I compare the training to Bryan's (1965) account of the apprenticeship of call girls and relate the madam's role to the social organization of house prostitution.

Bryan's study of thirty-three Los Angeles call girls is one of the earliest interactionist treatments of prostitution. His data focus on the process of entry into the occupation of the call girl and permit an analysis of the structure and content of a woman's apprenticeship. He concluded that the apprenticeship of call girls is mainly directed toward developing a clientele, rather than sexual skills (1965:288, 296–7). But while Bryan notes that pimps seldom train women directly, approximately half of his field evidence in fact derives from pimp-call girl apprenticeships. Thus, in Bryan's study (as well as in subsequent work on entry into prostitution as an occupation) there was a missing set of data on the more typical female trainer-trainee relationship and on the content and the process of training at other levels of the business in nonmetropolitan settings. This paper attempts to fill this gap.

I. ANN'S TURN-OUT ESTABLISHMENT

A professional prostitute, whether she works as a streetwalker, house prostitute, or call girl, can usually pick out one person in her past who "turned her out," that is, who taught her the basic techniques and rules of the prostitute's occupation.[1] For women who begin working at the house level, that person may be a pimp, another "working girl," or a madam. Most madams and managers of prostitution establishments, however, prefer not to take on novice prostitutes, and they may even have a specific policy against hiring turn-outs [see Erwin (1960:204–5) and Lewis (1942:222)]. The turn-out inexperience may cost the madam clients and money; to train the novice, on the other hand, costs her time and energy. Most madams and managers simply do not want the additional burden.

It was precisely the madam's typical disdain for turn-outs that led to the emergence of the house discussed in this paper—a house specifically devoted to training new prostitutes. The madam of this operation, whom we shall call Ann, is forty-one years old and has been in the prostitution world twenty-three years, working primarily at the house level. Ann knew that pimps who manage women at this level have difficulty placing novices in houses. After operating several houses staffed by professional prostitutes, she decided to run a school for turn-outs partly as a strategy for acquiring a continually changing staff of young women for her house. Pimps are the active recruiters of new prostitutes, and Ann found that, upon demonstrating that she could transform the pimps' new, square women into trained prostitutes easily placed in professional houses, pimps would help keep her business staffed.[2] Ann's house is a small operation in a middle-sized industrial city (population 300,000), with a limited clientele of primarily working-class men retained as customers for ten to fifteen years and offered low rates to maintain their patronage.

Although Ann insists that every turn-out is different, her group of novices is remarkably homogeneous in some ways. Ann has turned out approximately twenty women a year over the six years while she has operated the training school. Except for one Chicano, one black and one American Indian, the women were all white. They ranged in age from eighteen to twenty-seven. Until three years ago, all the women she hired had pimps. Since then, more women are independent (so-called "outlaws"), although many come to Ann sponsored by a pimp. That is, in return for being placed with Ann, a turn-out gives the pimp a percentage of her earnings for a specific length of time. At present eighty percent of the turn-outs come to Ann without a long-term commitment to a pimp. The turn-outs stay at Ann's on the average of two to three months. This is the same average length of time Bryan (1965:290) finds for the apprenticeship in his call-girl study. Ann seldom has more than two or three women in training at any one time. Most turn-outs live at the house, often just a large apartment near the older business section of the city.

II. THE CONTENT OF THE TRAINING

The data for the following analysis are of three kinds. First, tape recordings from actual training sessions with fourteen novices helped specify the structure and content of the training provided. Second, lengthy interviews with three of the novices and multiple interviews with Ann were conducted to obtain data on the training during the novice's first few days at the house before the first group training sessions were conducted and recorded by Ann. And third, visits to the house on ten occasions and observations of Ann's interaction with the novices during teaching periods extended the data on training techniques used and the relationship between madam and novice. In additon, weekly contact with Ann over a four-year period allowed repeated review of current problems and strategies in training turn-outs.

Ann's training of the novice begins soon after the woman arrives at the house. The woman first chooses an alias. Ann then asks her whether she has ever "Frenched a guy all the way," that is, whether she has brought a man to orgasm during the act of fellatio. Few of the women say they have. By admitting her lack of competence in a specialized area, the novice has permitted Ann to assume the role of teacher. Ann then launches into instruction on performing fellatio. Such instruction is important to her business. Approximately eighty percent of her customers are what Ann calls "French tricks." Many men visit prostitutes to receive sexual services, including fellatio, their wives or lovers seldom perform. This may be particularly true of the lower- and working-class clientele of the houses and hotels of prostitution (Gagnon and Simon, 1973:230). Yet the request for fellatio may come from clients at all social levels; consequently, it is a sexual skill today's prostitute must possess and one she may not have prior to entry into the business (Bryan, 1965:293; Winick and Kinsie, 1971:180, 207; Gray, 1973:413).

Although Ann devotes much more time to teaching the physical and psychological techniques of performing fellatio than she does to any other sexual skill, she also provides strategies for coitus and giving a "half and half"—fellatio followed by coitus. The sexual strategies taught are frequently a mixture of ways for stimulating the client sexually and techniques of self-protection during the sexual acts. For example, during coitus, the woman is to move her hips "like a go-go dancer's" while keeping her feet on the bed and tightening her inner thigh muscles to protect herself from the customer's thrust and full penetration. Ann allows turn-outs to perform coitus on their backs only, and the woman is taught to keep one of her arms across her chest as a measure of self-defense in this vulnerable position.

After Ann has described the rudimentary techniques for the three basic sexual acts—fellatio, coitus, and "half and half"—she begins to explain the rules of the house operation. The first set of rules concerns what acts the client may receive for specific sums of money. Time limits are imposed on the clients, roughly at the rate of $1 per minute; the minimum rate in this house is $15 for any of the three basic positions. Ann describes in detail what will occur when the first client arrives: he will be admitted by either Ann or the maid; the women are to stand and smile at him, but not speak at him (considered "dirty hustling"); he will choose one of the women and go to the bedroom with her. Ann accompanies the turn-out and the client to the bedroom and begins teaching the woman how to check the man for any cuts or open sores on the genitals and for any signs of old or active venereal disease. Ann usually rechecks each client herself during the turn-out's first two weeks of work. For the first few days Ann remains in the room while the turn-out and client negotiate the sexual contract. In ensuing days Ann spends time helping the woman develop verbal skills to "hustle" the customer for more expensive sexual activities.

The following analysis of the instruction Ann provides is based on tape recordings made by Ann during actual training sessions in 1971 and 1975. These sessions took place after the turn-outs had worked several days but usually during their first two weeks of work. The tapes contain ten hours of group discussion with fourteen different novices. The teaching tapes were analyzed according to topics covered in the discussions, using the method outlined in Barker (1963) for making such divisions in the flow of conversation and using Bryan's analysis of the call girl's apprenticeship as a guide in grouping the topics. Bryan divides the content of the training of call girls into two broad dimensions, one philosophical and one interpersonal (1965:291–4). The first emphasizes a subcultural value system and sets down guidelines for how the novice *should* treat her clients and her colleagues in the business. The second dimension follows from the first but emphasizes actual behavioral techniques and skills.

The content analysis of the taped training sessions produced three major topics of discussion and revealed the relative amount of time Ann devoted to each. The first two most frequently discussed topics can be categorized under Bryan's dimension of interpersonal skills; they were devoted to teaching situational strategies for managing clients. The third topic resembles Bryan's value dimension (1965:291–2).

The first topic stressed physical skills and strategies. Included in this category were instruction on how to perform certain sexual acts and specification of their prices, discussion of particular clients, and instruction in techniques for dealing with certain categories of clients, such as "older men" or "kinky" tricks. This topic of physical skills also included discussion of, and Ann's demonstration of, positions designed to provide the woman maximum comfort and protection from the man during different sexual acts. Defense tactics, such as ways to get out of a sexual position and out of the bedroom quickly, were practiced by the novices. Much time was devoted to analyzing past encounters with particular clients. Bryan finds similar discussions of individual tricks among novice call girls and their trainers (1965:293). In the case of Ann's turn-outs these discussions were often initiated by a novice's complaint or question about a certain client and his requests or behavior in the bedroom. The novice always received tips and advice from Ann and the other women present on how to manage that type of bedroom encounter. Such sharing of tactics allows the turnout to learn what Gagnon and Simon call "patterns of client management" (1973:231).

Ann typically used these discussions of bedroom difficulties to further the training in specific sexual skills she had begun during the turn-out's first few days at work. It is possible that the addition of such follow-up sexual training to that provided during the turn-out's first days at the house results in a more extensive teaching of actual sexual skills than that obtained either by call girls or streetwalkers. Bryan finds that in the call-girl training—except for fellatio—"There seems to be little instruction concerning sexual techniques as such, even though the previous sexual experience of the trainee may have been quite limited" (1965:293). Gray (1973:413) notes that her sample of streetwalker turn-outs were rarely taught specific work strategies:

> They learned these things by trial and error on the job. Nor were they schooled in specific sexual techniques: usually they were taught by customers who made the specific requests.

House prostitution may require more extensive sexual instruction than other forms of the business. The dissatisfied customer of a house may mean loss of business and therefore loss of income to the madam and the prostitutes who work there. The sexually inept streetwalker or call girl does not hurt business for anyone but herself; she may actually increase business for those women in the area should dissatisfied clients choose to avoid her. But the house depends on a stable clientele of satisfied customers.

The second most frequently discussed topic could be labeled: client management—verbal skills. Ann's primary concern was teaching what she calls "hustling." "Hustling" is similar to what Bryan terms a "sales pitch" for call girls (1965:292), but in the house setting it takes place in the bedroom while the client is deciding how much to spend and what sexual acts he wishes performed. "Hustling" is designed to encourage the client to spend more than the minimum rate.[3] The prominence on the teaching tapes of instruction in this verbal skill shows its importance in Ann's training of novices.

On one of the tapes Ann uses her own turning-out experience to explain to two novices (both with pimps) why she always teaches hustling skills as an integral part of working in a house.

Ann as a Turn-out[4]

Ann: Of course, I can remember a time when I didn't know that I was supposed to hustle. So that's why I understand that it's difficult to *learn* to hustle. When I turned out it was $2 a throw. They came in. They gave me their $2. They got a hell of a fuck. And that was it. Then one Saturday night I turned *forty-four* tricks! And Penny [the madam] used to put the number of tricks at the top of the page and the amount of money at the bottom of the page—she used these big ledger books. Lloyd [Ann's pimp] came in at six o'clock and he looked at that book and he just *knew* I had made all kinds of money. Would you believe I had turned forty-two $2 tricks and

> two $3 tricks—because two of 'em got generous and gave me an extra buck! [Laughs] I got my ass whipped. And I was so tired—I thought I was going to die—I was 15 years old. And I got my ass whipped for it. [Ann imitates an angry Lloyd:] "Don't you know you're supposed to ask for more money?!" No, I didn't. Nobody told me that. All they told me was it was $2. So that is learning it the *hard* way. I'm trying to help you learn it the *easy* way, if there is an easy way to do it.

In the same session Ann asks one of the turn-outs (Linda, age eighteen) to practice her hustling rap.

Learning the Hustling Rap

Ann: I'm going to be a trick. You've checked me. I want you to carry it from there. [Ann begins role-playing: she plays the client; Linda, the hustler.]

Linda: [mechanically] What kind of party would you like to have?

Ann: That had all the enthusiasm of a wet noodle. I really wouldn't *want* any party with that because you evidently don't want to give me one.

Linda: What kind of party would you *like* to have?

Ann: I usually take a half and half.

Linda: Uh, the money?

Ann: What money?

Linda: The money you're supposed to have! [loudly] 'Cause you ain't gettin' it for free!

Ann: [Upset] Linda, if you *ever*, ever say that in my joint.... Because that's fine for street hustling. In street hustling, you're going to *have* to hard–hustle those guys or they're not going to come up with anything. Because they are going to *try* and get it for free. But when they walk in here, they *know* they're not going to get it for free to begin with. So try another tack—just a little more friendly, not quite so hard-nosed. [Returning to role-playing:] I just take a half and half.

Linda: How about fifteen [dollars]?

Ann: You're leading into the money too fast, honey. Try: "What are you going to spend?" or "How much money are you going to spend?" or something like that.

Linda: How much would you like to spend?

Ann: No! Not "like." 'Cause they don't *like* to spend anything.

Linda: How much *would* you like to spend?

Ann: Make it a very definite, positive statement: "How much are you going to spend?"

Ann considers teaching hustling skills her most difficult and important task. In spite of her lengthy discussion on the tapes of the rules and techniques for dealing with her customer sexually, Ann states that it may take only a few minutes to "show a girl how to turn a trick." A substantially longer period is required, however, to teach her to hustle. To be adept at hustling, the woman must be mentally alert and sensitive to the client's response to what she is saying and doing and be able to act on those perceptions of his reactions. The hustler must maintain a steady patter of verbal coaxing, during which her tone of voice may be more important than her actual words.

In Ann's framework, then, hustling is a form of verbal sexual aggression. Referring to the problems in teaching novices to hustle, Ann notes that "taking the aggressive part is something women are not used to doing; particularly young women." No doubt, hustling is difficult to teach partly because the woman must learn to discuss sexual acts, whereas in her previous experience, sexual behavior and preferences had been negotiated nonverbally (see Gagnon and Simon, 1973:228). Ann feels that to be effective, each woman's "hustling rap" must be her own—one that comes naturally and will strike the clients as sincere. All of that takes practice. But Ann is aware that the difficulty in learning to hustle stems more from the fact that it involved inappropriate sex-role behavior. Bryan concludes that it is precisely this aspect of soliciting men on the telephone that causes the greatest distress to the novice call girl (1965:293). Thus, the call girl's income is affected by how much business she can bring in by her calls, that is, by how well she can learn to be socially aggressive on the telephone. The income of the house prostitute, in turn, depends heavily on her hustling skills in the bedroom. Ann's task, then, is to train the novice, who has recently come from a culture where young women are not expected to be sexually aggressive, to assume that role with a persuasive naturalness.

Following the first two major topics—client management through physical and verbal skills—the teaching of "racket" (prostitution world) values was the third-ranking topic of training and discussion on the teaching tapes. Bryan notes that the major value taught to call girls is "that of maximizing gains and minimizing effort, even if this requires transgressions of either a legal or moral nature" (1965:291). In her training, however, Ann avoids communicating the notion that the novices may exploit the customers in any way they can. For example, stealing or cheating clients is grounds for dismissal from the house. Ann cannot afford the reputation among her tricks that they risk being robbed when they visit her. Moreover, being honest with clients is extolled as a virtue. Thus, Ann urges the novices to tell the trick if she is nervous or unsure, to let him know she is new to the business. This is in direct contradiction to the advice pimps usually give their new women to hide their inexperience from the trick. Ann asserts that honesty in this case means that the client will be more tolerant of mistakes in sexual technique, be less likely to interpret hesitancy as coldness, and be generally more helpful and sympathetic. Putting her "basic principle" in the form of a simple directive, Ann declares: "Please the trick, but at the same time get as much money for pleasing him as you possibly can." Ann does not consider hustling to be client exploitation. It is simply the attempt to sell the customer the product with the highest profit margin. That is, she would defend hustling in terms familiar to the businessman or sales manager.

That Ann teaches hustling as a value is revealed in the following discussion between Ann and Sandy—a former hustler and long-time friend of Ann. Sandy, who married a former trick and still lives in town, has come over to the house to help instruct several novices in the hustling business.

Whores, Prostitutes and Hustlers

Ann: [To the turn-outs:] Don't get up-tight that you're hesitating or you're fumbling, within the first week or even the first five years. Because it takes that long to become a good hustler. I mean you can be a whore in one night. There's nothing to that. The first time you take money you're a whore.

Sandy: This girl in Midtown [a small, Midwestern city] informed me—I had been working there awhile—that I was a "whore" and she was a "prostitute." And I said: "Now what the hell does that mean?" Well the difference was that a prostitute could pick her customer and a whore had to take anybody. I said: "Well honey, I want to tell you something. I'm neither one." She said: "Well, you *work*." I said: "I know, but I'm a *hustler*. I make *money* for what I do."

Ann: And this is what I turn out—or try to turn out—hustlers. Not prostitutes. Not whores. But hustlers.

For Ann and Sandy the hustler deserves high status in the prostitution business because she has mastered a specific set of skills that, even with many repeat clients, earn her premiums above the going rate for sexual acts.

In the ideological training of call girls Bryan finds that "values such as fairness with other working girls, or fidelity to a pimp, may occasionally be taught" (1965:291–2); the teaching tapes revealed Ann's affirmation of both these virtues. When a pimp brings a woman to Ann, she supports his control over that woman. For example, if during her stay at the house, the novices break any of the basic rules—by using drugs, holding back money (from either Ann or the pimp), lying or seeing another man—Ann will report the infractions to the woman's pimp. Ann notes: "If I don't do that and the pimp finds out, he knows I'm not training her right, and he won't bring his future ladies to me for training." Ann knows she is dependent on the pimps to help supply her with turn-outs. Bryan, likewise, finds a willingness among call girls' trainers to defer to the pimps' wishes during the apprenticeship period (1965:290).

Teaching fairness to other prostitutes is particularly relevant to the madam who daily faces the problem of maintaining peace among competing women at work under one roof. If two streetwalkers or two call girls find that they cannot get along, they need not work near one another. But if a woman leaves a house because of personal conflicts, the madam loses a source of income. To minimize potential negative feelings among novices, Ann stresses mutual support, prohibits "criticizing another girl," and denigrates the "prima donna"—the prostitute who flaunts her financial success before the other women.

In still another strategy to encourage fair treatment of one's colleagues in the establishment, Ann emphasizes a set of rules prohibiting "dirty hustling"—behavior engaged in by one prostitute that would undercut the business of other women in the house. Tabooed under the label of "dirty hustling" are the following: appearing in the line-up partially unclothed; performing certain disapproved sexual positions, such as anal intercourse; and allowing approved sexual extras without charging additional fees. The norms governing acceptable behavior vary from house to house and region to region, and Ann warns the turn-outs to ask about such rules when they begin work in a new establishment. The woman who breaks the work norms in a house, either knowingly or unknowingly, will draw the anger of the other women and can be fired by a madam eager to restore peace and order in the house.

Other topics considered on the tapes—in addition to physical skills, "hustling" and work values—were instruction on personal hygiene and grooming, role-playing of conversational skills with tricks on topics not related to sex or hustling ("living room talk"), house rules not related to hustling (such as punctuality, no perfume, no drugs), and guidelines for what to do during an arrest. There were specific suggestions on how to handle personal criticism, questions and insults from clients. In addition, the discussions on the tapes provided the novices with many general strategies for becoming "professionals" at their work, for example, the importance of personal style, enthusiasm ("the customer is always right"), and a sense of humor. In some ways these guidelines resemble a beginning course in salesmanship. But they also provide clues, particularly in combination with the topics on handling client insults and the emphasis on hustling, on how the house prostitute learns to manage a stable and limited clientele and cope psychologically with the repetition of the clients and the sheer tedium of the physical work (Hughes, 1971:342–5).

III. TRAINING HOUSE PROSTITUTES—A PROCESS OF PROFESSIONAL SOCIALIZATION

Observing how Ann trains turn-outs is a study in techniques to facilitate identity change (see also Davis, 1971 and Heyl, 1975, Chapter 2). Ann uses a variety of persuasive strategies to help give the turn-outs a new occupational identity as a "professional." One strategy is to rely heavily on the new values taught the novice to isolate her from her previous life style and acquaintances. Bryan finds that "the value structure [taught to novice call girls] serves, in general, to create in-group solidarity and to alienate the girl from 'square' society" (1965:292). Whereas alienation from conventional society may be an indirect effect of values taught to call girls, in Ann's training of house prostitutes the expectation that the novice will immerse herself in the prostitution world ("racket life") is made dramatically explicit.

In the following transcription from one of the teaching tapes, the participants are Ann (age thirty-six at the time the tape was made), Bonnie (an experienced turn-out, age twenty-five) and Kristy (a new turn-out, age eighteen). Kristy has recently linked up with a pimp for the first time and volunteers to Ann and Bonnie her difficulty in adjusting to the racket rule of minimal contact with the square world—a rule her pimp is enforcing by not allowing Kristy to meet and talk with her old friends. Ann (A) and Bonnie (B) have listened to Kristy's (K) complaints and are making suggestions. (The notation "B-K" indicates that Bonnie is addressing Kristy.)

Kristy's Isolation from the Square World

B-K: What you gotta do is sit down and talk to him and weed out your friends and find the ones he thinks are suitable companions for you—in your new type of life.
K-B: None of them.
A-K: What about *his* friends?
K-A: I haven't met many of his friends. I don't like any of 'em so far.
A-K: You are making the same mistake that makes me so goddamned irritated with square broads! You're taking a man and trying to train *him*, instead of letting the man train you.
K-A: What?! I'm not trying to train him, I'm just....
A-K: All right, you're trying to force him to accept your friends.
K-A: I don't care whether he accepts them or not. I just can't go around not talking to anybody.
A-K: "Anybody" is your old man! He is your world. And the people he says you can talk to are the people that are your world. But what you're trying to do is force your square world on a racket guy. It's like oil and water. There's just no way a square and a racket person can get together. That's why when you turn out you've got to change your mind completely from square to racket. And you're still trying to hang with squares. You can't do it.

Strauss' (1969) concept of "coaching" illuminates a more subtle technique Ann employs as she helps the novice along, step by step, from "square" to "racket" values and lifestyle. She observes carefully how the novice progresses, elicits responses from her about what she is experiencing, and then interprets those responses for her. In the following excerpt from one of the teaching tapes, Ann prepares two novices for feelings of depression over their newly-made decisions to become prostitutes.

Turn-out Blues

Ann: And while I'm on the subject—depression. You know they've got a word for it when you have a baby—it's called "postpartum blues." Now, I call it "turn-out blues." Every girl that ever turns out has 'em. And, depending on the girl, it comes about the third or fourth day. You'll go into a depression for no apparent reason. You'll wake up one morning and say: "Why in

> the hell am I doing this? Why am I here? I wanna go home!" And I can't do a thing to help you. The only thing I can do is to leave you alone and hope that you'll fight the battle yourself. But knowing that it will come and knowing that everybody else goes through it too, does help. Just pray it's a busy night! So if you get blue and you get down, remember: "turn-out blues"—everybody gets it. Here's when you'll decide whether you're going to stay or you're gonna quit.

Ann's description of "turn-out blues" is a good example of Strauss' account (1969:111–2) of how coaches will use prophecy to increase their persuasive power over their novices. In the case of "turn-out blues," the novice, if she becomes depressed about her decision to enter prostitution, will recall Ann's prediction that this would happen and that it happens to all turn-outs. This recollection may or may not end the woman's misgivings about her decision, but it will surely enhance the turn-out's impression of Ann's competence. Ann's use of her past experience to make such predictions is a form of positive leverage; it increases the probability that what she says will be respected and followed in the future.

In Bryan's study the call girls reported that their training was more a matter of observation than direct instruction from their trainer (1965:294). Ann, on the other hand, relies on a variety of teaching techniques, including lecturing and discussion involving other turn-outs who are further along in the training process and can reinforce Ann's views. Ann even brings in guest speakers, such as Sandy, the former hustler, who participates in the discussion with the novices in the role of the experienced resource person. "Learning the Hustling Rap," above, offers an example of role-playing—another teaching technique Ann frequently employs to help the turn-outs develop verbal skills. Ann may have to rely on more varied teaching approaches than the call-girl trainer because: (1) Ann herself is not working, thus her novices have fewer opportunities to watch their trainer interact with clients than do the call-girl novices; and (2) Ann's livelihood depends more directly on the success of her teaching efforts than does that of the call-girl trainer. Ann feels that if a woman under her direction does not "turn out well," not only will the woman earn less money while she is at her house (affecting Ann's own income), but Ann could also lose clients and future turn-outs from her teaching "failure."[5]

The dissolution of the training relationship marks the end of the course. Bryan claims that the sharp break between trainer and trainee shows that the training process itself is largely unrelated to the acquisition of a skill. But one would scarcely have expected the trainee to report "that the final disruption of the apprenticeship was the result of the completion of adequate training" (1965:296). Such establishments do not offer diplomas and terminal degrees. The present study, too, indicates that abrupt breaks in the training relationship are quite common. But what is significant is that the break is precipitated by personal conflicts exacerbated by both the narrowing of the skill-gap between trainer and trainee and the consequent increase in the novice's confidence that she can make it on her own. Thus, skill acquisition counts in such an equation, not in a formal sense ("completion of adequate training"), but rather in so far as it works to break down the earlier bonds of dependence between trainer and trainee.

IV. THE FUNCTION OF TRAINING AT THE HOUSE LEVEL OF PROSTITUTION

Bryan concludes that the training is necessitated by the novice's need for a list of clients in order to work at the call-girl level and not because the actual training is required to prepare her for such work. But turn-outs at the house level of prostitution do not acquire a clientele. The clients are customers of the house. In fact, the madam usually makes sure that only she has the names or phone numbers of her tricks in order to keep control over her business. If Ann's turn-outs (unlike call girls) do not acquire a clientele in the course of their training, why is the training period necessary?

Although Ann feels strongly that training is required to become a successful hustler at the house level, the function served by the training can be seen more as a spin-off of the structure of the occupation at that level: madams of establishments will often hire only trained prostitutes. Novices who pose as experienced hustlers are fairly easily detected by those proficient in the business working in the same house; to be found out all she need do is violate any of the expected norms of behavior: wear perfume, repeatedly fail to hustle any "over-money" or engage in dirty hustling. The exposure to racket values, which the training provides, may be more critical to the house prostitute than to the call girl. She must live and work in close contact with others in the business. Participants in house prostitution are more integrated into the prostitution world than are call girls, who can be and frequently are "independent"—working without close ties to pimps or other prostitutes. Becoming skilled in hustling is also less important for the call girl, as her minimum fee is usually high, making hustling for small increments less necessary. The house prostitute who does not know how to ask for more money, however, lowers the madam's income as well—another reason why madams prefer professional prostitutes.

The training of house prostitutes, then, reflects two problems in the social organization of house prostitution: (1) most madams will not hire untrained prostitutes; and (2) the close interaction of prostitutes operating within the confines of a house requires a common set of work standards and practices. These two factors differentiate house prostitution from call-girl and streetwalking operations and facilitate this madam's task of turning novices into professional prostitutes. The teaching madam employs a variety of coaching techniques to train turn-outs in sexual and hustling skills and to expose them to a set of occupational rules and values. Hers is an effort to prepare women with conventional backgrounds for work in the social environment of a house of prostitution where those skills and values are expected and necessary.

Notes

1. This situation-specific induction into prostitution may be castrated with the "smooth and almost imperceptible" transition to the status of poolroom "hustler" noted by Polsky (1969:80–1).

2. In the wider context of the national prostitution scene, Ann's situation reflects the "minor league" status of her geographical location. In fact, she trains women from other communities who move on to more lucrative opportunities in the big city. See the stimulating applications of the concept of "minor league" to the study of occupations in Faulkner (1974).

3. The term "hustling" has been used to describe a wide range of small-time criminal activities. Even within the world of prostitution, "hustling" can refer to different occupational styles; see Ross' description of the "hustler" who "is distinguished from ordinary prostitutes in frequently engaging in accessory crimes of exploitation," such as extortion or robbery (1959:16). The use of the term here is thus highly specific, reflecting its meaning in Ann's world.

4. The indented sections (for example, "Ann as a Turn-out" and "Learning the Hustling Rap") are transcriptions from the teaching tapes. Redundant expressions have been omitted, and the author's comments on the speech tone or delivery are bracketed. Italic words indicate emphasis by the speaker.

5. These data bear only on the skills and values to which Ann *exposes* the turn-outs; confirmation of the effects of such exposure awaits further analysis and is a study in its own right. See Bryan's (1966) study of the impact of the occupational perspective taught by call-girl trainers on the individual attitudes of call-girls. See Davis (1971:315) for a description of what constitutes successful "in-service training" for streetwalkers.

References

Barker, Roger G. (ed.)
1963 The Stream of Behavior: Explorations of its Structure and Content. New York: Appleton-Century-Crofts.

Bryan, James H.
1965 "Apprenticeships in prostitution." Social Problems 12 (Winter):287–97.
1966 "Occupational ideologies and individual attitudes of call girls." Social Problems 13 (Spring):441–50.

Davis, Nanette J.
1971 "The prostitute: Developing a deviant identity." Pp. 297–332 in James M. Henslin (ed.), Studies in the Sociology of Sex. New York: Appleton-Century-Crofts.

Erwin, Carol
1960 The Orderly Disorderly House. Garden City, N.Y.: Doubleday.

Faulkner, Robert R.
1974 "Coming of age in organizations: A comparative study of career contingencies and adult socialization." Sociology of Work and Occupations 1 (May): 131–73.

Gagnon, John H. and William Simon
1973 Sexual Conduct: The Social Sources of Human Sexuality. Chicago: Aldine.

Gray, Diana
1973 "Turning-out: A study of teenage prostitution." Urban Life and Culture 1 (January):401–25.
Hall, Susan
1973 Ladies of the Night. New York: Trident Press.
Heyl, Barbara S.
1974 "The madam as entrepreneur." Sociological Symposium 11 (Spring): 61–82.
1975 "The house prostitute: A case study." Unpublished Ph.D. dissertation, Department of Sociology, University of Illinois-Urbana.
Hughes, Everett C.
1971 "Work and self." Pp. 338–47 in The Sociological Eye: Selected Papers. Chicago: Aldine-Atherton.
Jackson, Bruce
1969 A Thief's Primer. Toronto, Ontario: Macmillan.
Lewis, Gladys Adelina (ed.)
1942 Call House Madam: The Story of the Career of Beverly Davis. San Francisco: Martin Tudordale.
Polsky, Ned.
1969 Hustlers, Beats and Others. Garden City, N.Y.: Doubleday.
Ross, H. Laurence
1959 "The 'Hustler' in Chicago." Journal of Student Research 1:13–19.
Sheehy, Gail
1974 Hustling: Prostitution in Our Wide-Open Society. New York: Dell.
Stewart, George I.
1972 "On first being a john." Urban Life and Culture 1 (October):255–74.
Strauss, Anselm L.
1969 Mirrors and Masks: The Search for Identity. San Francisco: Sociology Press.
Vogliotti, Gabriel R.
1975 The Girls of Nevada. Secaucus, N.J.: Citadel Press.
Winick, Charles and Paul M. Kinsie
1971 The Lively Commerce: Prostitution in the United States. Chicago: Quadrangle Books.

35 / State-Organized Crime

WILLIAM J. CHAMBLISS

STATE-ORGANIZED CRIME DEFINED

The most important type of criminality organized by the state consists of acts defined by law as criminal and committed by state officials in the pursuit of their job as representatives of the state. Examples include a state's complicity in piracy, smuggling, assasinations, criminal conspiracies, acting as an accessory before or after the fact, and violating laws that limit their activities. In the latter category would be included the use of illegal methods of spying on citizens, diverting funds in ways prohibited by law (e.g., illegal campaign contributions, selling arms to countries prohibited by law, and supporting terrorist activities).

State-organized crime does not include criminal acts that benefit only individual officeholders, such as the acceptance of bribes or the illegal use of violence by the police against individuals, unless such acts violate existing criminal law and are official policy. For example, the current policies of torture and random violence by the police in South Africa are incorporated under the category of state-organized crime because, apparently, those practices are both state policy and in violation of existing South African law. On the other hand, the excessive use of violence by the police in urban ghettoes is not state-organized crime for it lacks the necessary institutionalized policy of the state.

PIRACY

In the history of criminality, the state-supported piracy that occurred between the sixteenth and nineteenth centuries is an outstanding example of state-organized crime (Andrews, 1959, 1971).

When Christopher Columbus came to the Americas in search of wealth and spices in 1492, he sailed under the flag of Spain although he himself was from Genoa. Vasco da Gama followed Columbus 6 years later, sailing under the Portuguese flag. Between Spain and Portugal, a vast new world was conquered and quickly colonized. The wealth of silver and gold was beyond their wildest dreams. A large, poorly armed native American population made the creation of a slave labor force for mining and transporting the precious metals an easy task for the better armed Spanish and Portuguese settlers willing to sacrifice human life for wealth. Buttressed by the unflagging belief that they were not only enriching their motherland and themselves but also converting the heathens to Christianity, Spanish and Portuguese colonists seized the opportunity to denude the newly found lands of their wealth and their people (Lane-Poole, 1890). Portugal, as a result of Vasco da Gama's voyages, also established trade routes with India that gave it a franchise on spices and tea. Portuguese kings thus became the "royal grocers of Europe" (Howes, 1615; Collins, 1955).

In Europe during the sixteenth and seventeenth centuries, nation-states were embroiled in intense competition for control of territory and resources. Then, as now, military power was the basis for expansion and the means by which nation-states protected their borders. Military might, in turn, depended on labor and mineral resources, especially gold and silver. The wealthier nations could afford to invest in more powerful military weapons, especially larger and faster ships, and to hire mercenaries for the army and navy. Explorations cost money as well. When Spain and Portugal laid claim to the Americas, they also refused other nations the right to trade with their colonies (Mainwaring, 1616). Almost immediately, conflict developed between Spain and Portugal, but the pope intervened and drew a line dividing the New World into Spanish and Portuguese sectors, thereby ameliorating the conflict. But the British, French, and Dutch were not included in the pope's peace. They were forced to settle for less desirable lands or areas not yet claimed by the Spanish and Portuguese.

Although they lacked the vision to finance explorers such as Christopher Columbus and Vasco da Gama, France, England, and Holland nonetheless possessed powerful navies. They were also the home of some of the world's more adventurous pirates, who heretofore had limited their escapades to the European and African coasts.

With the advent of Spain and Portugal's discovery of vast new sources of wealth, other European nations were faced with a dilemma: They could sit idly by and watch the center of power tip inexorably toward the Iberian Peninsula, or they could seek ways to interfere with the growing wealth of their neighbors to the south. One alternative, of course, was to go to war. Another, less risky for the moment but promising some of the same results, was to enter into an alliance with pirates. France, England, and Holland chose the less risky course.

To transport the gold and silver from the Spanish Main (the Caribbean coast of South America) to Bilbao and from Brazil to Lisbon required masterful navigational feats. A ship laden with gold and silver could not travel fast and was easy prey for marauders (Exquemling, 1670). To complicate matters, ships were forced by the prevailing winds and currents to travel in a predictable direction. These conditions provided an open invitation for pirates to exploit the weaknesses of the transporting ships to their advantage. Poverty and a lack of alternatives drove many young men to sea in search of a better life. Some came to the New World as convicts or indentured slaves. The lure of the pirate's life was an alternative that for all its hardships was more appealing than the conditions of serfdom and indentured servitude.

The French government was the first to seize the opportunity offered by engaging in piracy (Ritchie, 1986). It saw in piracy a source of wealth and a way of neutralizing some of the power of Spain and Portugal. Although piracy was an act second to none in seriousness in French law (summary execution was the punishment), the French government nonetheless instructed the governors of its islands to allow pirate ships safe portage in exchange for a share of the stolen merchandise. Thus, the state became complicitous in the most horrific sprees of criminality in history.

The pirate culture condoned violence on a scale seldom seen. There was no mercy for the victims of the pirates' attacks. Borgnefesse, a French pirate who wrote his memoirs after retiring to a gentleman's life in rural France, was an articulate chronicler of these traits. He wrote, for example, of how he once saved a young girl "not yet into puberty" from being raped by two "beastly filibusters" who were chasing her out of a house in a village that he and his men had attacked (LeGolif, 1680). Borgnefesse wrote of being embarrassed that on that occasion he felt "pity" for the young girl and violated one of the ironclad laws of the pirate's world: that women were prizes for whoever found them in the course of a raid. The would-be rapists resisted his effort to save the girl and "told me I was interfering in a matter which was none of my business, that pillage was permitted in the forcing of the women as well as the coffers."

It was commonplace among pirates to "take no prisoners" unless, of course, they could be useful to the victors. Borgnefesse described how he cut off the heads of everyone on board a Spanish "prize" because the enemy angered him by injuring his arm during the battle. Another time he and his men took all the people on a captured ship, tied them up in the mainsail, threw them in the water, and then drank rum while listening to the screams of the slowly drowning men. For all his criminal exploits, however, Borgnefesse was well protected by French ships and French colonies.

England and Holland were quick to join the French. Sir Richard Hawkins and his apprentice, Francis Drake, were issued "letters of marque" from the Admiralty directing governors of British colonies and captains of British warships to give safe passage and every possible assistance to Hawkins and Drake as they were acting "under order of the Crown" (British Museum, 1977). Their "orders" were to engage in piracy against Spanish and Portuguese ships. Thus, the state specifically instructed selected individuals to engage in criminal acts. The law, it must be emphasized, did not change. Piracy remained a crime punishable by death but some pirates were given license to murder, rape, plunder, destroy, and steal.

The state's complicity in piracy was more successful, one suspects, than even the most avaricious monarchs expected. On one voyage (between 1572 and 1573), Drake returned to England with enough gold and silver to support the government and all its expenses for a period of 7 years (Corbett, 1898a, 1898b). Most of this wealth came from Drake's attack on the town of Nombre de Dios, which was a storage depot for Spanish gold and silver. In this venture Drake joined forces with some French pirates and ambushed a treasure train.

Drake was knighted for his efforts, but the Spanish were not silent. They formally challenged Britain's policies, but the queen of England denied that Drake was operating with her blessing (after, of course, taking the gold and silver that he brought home) and Drake was tried as a criminal. He was publicly exiled, but privately he was sent to Ireland, where he reemerged several years later (in 1575) serving under the first Earl of Essex in Ireland.

Borgnefesse and Sir Francis Drake are only two of hundreds of pirates who plied their trade between 1400 and 1800 (Senior, 1976). Their crimes were supported by, and their proceeds shared with, whatever nation-state offered them protection and supplies. In theory, each nation-state only protected its own pirates, but in practice, they all protected any pirates willing to share their gains.

To rationalise the fundamental contradiction between the law and the interests of the state, European nations created a legal fiction. Issued either directly from the monarch or the Admiralty, the letters of marque gave pirates a sort of license, but with specific limitations on the kinds of acts that were permissible. One restriction was that the pirates were not to (a) attack ships of the country issuing the letter, (b) plunder villages or towns, or (c) open the captured cargo until they returned to port.

The reality of piracy was quite at odds with all of these limitations. Much of the success of piracy depended on attacking towns and villages, during which raping, plundering, and razing the town were accepted practices. Pirates sometimes kept one or more officers from captured shops along with their letters of marque and identifying flags in order to show them in case of attack by a ship from another country. This also enabled a pirate ship from France, say, to raise an English flag and attack a French ship. For the pirates loyalty to the nation came second to the search for gold.

At one time or another virtually every European nation, and the United States as well, between 1500 and 1800 was complicitous in piracy. In the United States, Charleston, South Carolina, several New England towns, and New York were safe harbors for pirates. In return for sharing in the prize, these towns provided safety from capture by foreign authorities and a safe place for pirates to celebrate their victories.

John Paul Jones became an American hero through his success as a pirate and was even given a commission in the navy (de la Croix, 1962; MacIntyre, 1975). Jean and Pierre Lafitte were the toast of New Orleans society while they enriched themselves by organizing and aiding pirates and smugglers at the mouth of the Mississippi River. Their status was considerably enhanced when the federal government enlisted their aid in the war against England

and made Jean an officer of the U.S. Navy in return for helping to defeat the British Navy that was gathering its forces for an attack on New Orleans (Verrill, 1924). In time of war, nations enlisted pirates to serve in their navy. In time of peace, they shared in the profits.

During the period of 1600 to 1900, capitalism was becoming firmly established as the dominant economic system of the world. The essential determinant of a nation's ability to industrialize and to protect its borders was the accumulation of capital. Not only was another nation's wealth a threat to the autonomy of neighboring states, one nation's gain was invariably another's loss. Piracy helped to equalize the balance and reduce the tendency toward the monopolization of capital accumulation. The need for capital accumulation does not end with the emergence of capitalism; it continues so long as the economy and a nation's military and economic strength depend on it. When piracy ceased to be a viable method for accumulating capital, other forms of illegality were employed. In today's world, there is evidence that some small city-states in the Far East (especially in Indonesia) still pursue a policy of supporting pirates and sharing in their profits. But piracy no longer plays a major role in state-organized crime; today, the role is filled by smuggling.

SMUGGLING

Smuggling occurs when a government has successfully cornered the market on some commodity or when it seeks to keep a commodity of another nation from crossing its borders. In the annals of crime, everything from sheep to people, wool to wine, gold to drugs, and even ideas, have been prohibited for either export or import. Paradoxically, whatever is prohibited, it is at the expense of one group of people for the benefit of another. Thus, the laws that prohibit the import or export of a commodity inevitably face a built-in resistance. Some part of the population will always want to either possess or to distribute the prohibited goods. At times, the state finds itself in the position of having its own interests served by violating precisely the same laws passed to prohibit the export or import of the goods it has defined as illegal.

Narcotics and the Vietnam War

Sometime around the eighth century, Turkish traders discovered a market for opium in Southeast Asia (Chambliss, 1977; McCoy, 1973). Portuguese traders several centuries later found a thriving business in opium trafficking conducted by small ships sailing between trading ports in the area. One of the prizes of Portuguese piracy was the opium that was taken from local traders and exchanged for tea, spices, and pottery. Several centuries later, when the French colonized Indochina, the traffic in opium was a thriving business. The French joined the drug traffickers and licensed opium dens throughout Indochina. With the profits from those licenses, the French supported 50% of the cost of their colonial government (McCoy, 1973: 27).

When the Communists began threatening French rule in Indochina, the French government used the opium profits to finance the war. It also used cooperation with the hill tribes who controlled opium production as a means of ensuring the allegiance of the hill tribes in the war against the Communists (McCoy, 1973).

The French were defeated in Vietnam and withdrew, only to be replaced by the United States. The United States inherited the dependence on opium profits and the cooperation of the hill tribes, who in turn depended on being allowed to continue growing and shipping opium. The CIA went a step further than the French and provided the opium-growing feudal lords in the mountains of Vietnam, Laos, Cambodia, and Thailand with transportation for their opium via Air America, the CIA airline in Vietnam.

Air America regularly transported bundles of opium from airstrips in Laos, Cambodia, and Burma to Saigon and Hong Kong (Chambliss, 1977: 56). An American stationed at Long Cheng, the secret CIA military base in northern Laos during the war, observed:

> ... so long as the Meo leadership could keep their wards in the boondocks fighting and dying in the name of, for these unfortunates anyway, some nebulous cause... the Meo leadership [was paid off] in the form of a carte-blanch to exploit U.S.-supplied airplanes and communication gear to the end of greatly streamlining the opium operations.... (Chambliss, 1977: 56).

This report was confirmed by Laotian army General Ouane Rattikone, who told me in an interview in 1974 that he was the principal overseer of the shipment of opium out of the Golden Triangle via Air America. U.S. law did not permit the CIA or any of its agents to engage in the smuggling of opium.

After France withdrew from Vietnam and left the protection of democracy to the United States, the French intelligence service that preceded the CIA in managing the opium smuggling in Asia continued to support part of its clandestine operations through drug trafficking (Kruger, 1980). Although those operations are shrouded in secrecy, the evidence is very strong that the French intelligence agencies helped to organize the movement of opium through the Middle East (especially Morocco) after their revenue from opium from Southeast Asia was cut off.

In 1969 Michael Hand, a former Green Beret and one of the CIA agents stationed at Long Cheng when Air America was shipping opium, moved to Australia, ostensibly as a private citizen. On arriving in Australia, Hand entered into a business partnership with an Australian national, Frank Nugan. In 1976 they established the Nugan Hand Bank in Sydney (Commonwealth of New South Wales, 1982a, 1982b). The Nugan Hand Bank began as a storefront operation with minimal capital investment, but almost immediately it boasted deposits of over $25 million. The rapid growth of the bank resulted from large deposits of secret funds made by narcotics and arms smugglers and large deposits from the CIA (Nihill, 1982).

In addition to the records from the bank that suggest the CIA was using the bank as a conduit for its funds, the bank's connection to the CIA and other U.S. intelligence agencies is evidenced by the people who formed the directors and principal officers of the bank, including the following:

- Admiral Earl F. Yates, president of the Nugan Hand Bank was, during the Vietnam War, chief of staff for strategic planning of U.S. forces in Asia and the Pacific.
- General Edwin F. Black, president of Nugan Hand's Hawaii branch, was commander of U.S. troops in Thailand during the Vietnam War and, after the war, assistant army chief of staff for the Pacific.
- General Erle Cocke, Jr., head of the Nugan Hand Washington, D.C., office.
- George Farris, worked in the Nugan Hand Hong Kong and Washington, D.C. offices. Farris was a military intelligence specialist who worked in a special forces training base in the Pacific.
- Bernie Houghton, Nugan Hand's representative in Saudi Arabia. Houghton was also a U.S. naval intelligence undercover agent.
- Thomas Clines, director of training in the CIA's clandestine service, was a London operative for Nugan Hand who helped in the takeover of a London-based bank and was stationed at Long Cheng with Michael Hand and Theodore S. Shackley during the Vietnam War.
- Dale Holmgreen, former flight service manager in Vietnam for Civil Air Transport, which became Air America. He was on the board of directors of Nugan Hand and ran the bank's Taiwan office.
- Walter McDonald, an economist and former deputy director of CIA for economic research, was a specialist in petroleum. He became a consultant to Nugan Hand and served as head of its Annapolis, Maryland, branch.
- General Roy Manor, who ran the Nugan Hand Philippine office, was a Vietnam veteran who helped coordinate the aborted attempt to rescue the Iranian hostages, chief of staff for the U.S. Pacific command, and the U.S. government's liaison officer to Philippine President Ferdinand Marcos.

On the board of directors of the parent company formed by Michael Hand that preceded the Nugan Hand Bank were Grant Walters, Robert Peterson, David M. Houton, and Spencer Smith, all of whom listed their address as c/o Air America, Army Post Office, San Francisco, California.

Also working through the Nugan Hand Bank was Edwin F. Wilson, a CIA agent involved in smuggling arms to the Middle East and later sentenced to prison by a U.S. court for smuggling illegal arms to Libya. Edwin Wilson's associate in Mideast arms shipments was Theordore Shackley, head of the Miami, Florida, CIA station.[1] In 1973, when William Colby was made director of Central Intelligence, Shackley replaced him as head of covert operations for the Far East; on his retirement from the CIA William Colby became Nugan Hand's lawyer.

In the late 1970s the bank experienced financial difficulties, which led to the death of Frank Nugan. He was found dead of a shotgun blast in his Mercedes Benz on a remote road outside Sydney. The official explanation was suicide, but some investigators speculated that he might have been murdered. In any event, Nugan's death created a major banking scandal and culminated in a government investigation. The investigation revealed that millions of dollars were unaccounted for in the bank's records and that the bank was serving as a money-laundering operation for narcotics smugglers and as a conduit through which the CIA was financing gun smuggling and other illegal operations throughout the world. These operations included illegally smuggling arms to South Africa and the Middle East. There was also evidence that the CIA used the Nugan Hand Bank to pay for political campaigns that slandered politicians, including Australia's Prime Minister Witham (Kwitny, 1977).

Michael Hand tried desperately to cover up the operations of the bank. Hundreds of documents were destroyed before investigators could get into the bank. Despite Hand's efforts, the scandal mushroomed and eventually Hand was forced to flee Australia. He managed this, while under indictment for a rash of felonies, with the aid of a CIA official who flew to Australia with a false passport and accompained him out of the country. Hand's father, who lives in New York, denies knowing anything about his son's whereabouts.

Thus, the evidence uncovered by the government investigation in Australia linked high-level CIA officials to a bank in Sydney that was responsible for financing and laundering money for a significant part of the narcotics trafficking originating in Southeast Asia (Commonwealth of New South Wales, 1982b; Owen, 1983). It also linked the CIA to arms smuggling and illegal involvement in the democratic processes of a friendly nation. Other investigations reveal that the events in Australia were but part of a worldwide involvement in narcotics and arms smuggling by the CIA and French intelligence (Hougan, 1978; Kruger, 1980; Owen, 1983).

Arms Smuggling

One of the most important forms of state-organized crime today is arms smuggling. To a significant extent, U.S. involvement in narcotics smuggling after the Vietnam War can be understood as a means of funding the purchase of military weapons for nations and insurgent groups that could not be funded legally through congressional allocations or for which U.S. law prohibited support (NARMIC, 1984).

In violation of U.S. law, members of the National Security Council (NSC), the Department of Defense, and the CIA carried out a plan to sell millions of dollars worth of arms to Iran and use profits from those sales to support the Contras in Nicaragua (Senate Hearings, 1986). The Boland amendment, effective in 1985, prohibited any U.S. official from directly or indirectly assisting the Contras. To circumvent the law, a group of intelligence and military officials established a "secret team" of U.S. operatives, including Lt. Colonel Oliver North, Theodore Shackley, Thomas Clines, and Maj. General Richard Secord, among others (testimony before U.S. Senate, 1986). Shackley and Clines, as noted, were CIA agents in Long Cheng; along with Michael Hand they ran the secret war in Laos, which was financed in part from profits from opium smuggling. Shackley and Clines had also been involved in the 1961 invasion of Cuba and were instrumental in hiring organized-crime figures in an attempt to assassinate Fidel Castro.

Senator Daniel Inouye of Hawaii claims that this "secret government within our government" waging war in Third World countries was part of the Reagan doctrine (the *Guardian,* July 29, 1987). Whether President Reagan or then Vice President Bush were aware of the operations is yet to be established. What cannot be doubted in the face of overwhelming evidence in testimony before the Senate and from court documents is that this group of officials of the state oversaw and coordinated the distribution and sale of weapons to Iran and to the Contras in Nicaragua. These acts were in direct violation of the Illegal Arms Export Control Act, which made the sale of arms to Iran unlawful, and the Boland amendment, which made it a criminal act to supply the Contras with arms or funds.

The weapons that were sold to Iran were obtained by the CIA through the Pentagon. Secretary of Defense Caspar Weinberger ordered the transfer of weapons from Army stocks to the CIA without the knowledge of Congress four times in 1986. The arms were then transferred to middlemen, such as Iranian arms dealer Yaacov Nimrodi, exiled Iranian arms dealer Manucher Ghorbanifar, and Saudi Arabian businessman Adman Khashoggi. Weapons were also flown directly to the Contras, and funds from the sale of weapons were diverted to support Contra warfare. There is also considerable evidence that this "secret team," along with other military and CIA officials, cooperated with narcotics smuggling in Latin American in order to fund the Contras in Nicaragua.

In 1986, the Reagan administration admitted that Adolfo Chamorro's Contra group, which was supported by the CIA, was helping a Colombian drug trafficker transport drugs into the United States. Chamorro was arrested in April 1986 for his involvement (Potter and Bullington, 1987: 54). Testimony in several trials of major drug traffickers in the past 5 years has revealed innumerable instances in which drugs were flown from Central

America into the United States with the cooperation of military and CIA personnel. These reports have also been confirmed by military personnel and private citizens who testified that they saw drugs being loaded on planes in Central America and unloaded at military bases in the United States. Pilots who flew planes with arms to the Contras report returning with planes carrying drugs.

At the same time that the United States was illegally supplying the Nicaraguan Contras with arms purchased, at least in part, with profits from the sale of illegal drugs, the administration launched a campaign against the Sandanistas for their alleged involvement in drug trafficking. Twice during his weekly radio shows in 1986, President Reagan accused the Sandanistas of smuggling drugs. Barry Seal, an informant and pilot for the Drug Enforcement Administration (DEA) was ordered by members of the CIA and DEA to photograph the Sandanistas loading a plane. During a televised speech in March 1986, Reagan showed the picture that Seal took and said that is showed Sandinista officials loading a plane with drugs for shipment to the United States. After the photo was displayed, Congress appropriated $100 million in aid for the Contras. Seal later admitted to reporters that the photograph he took was a plane being loaded with crates that did not contain drugs. He also told reporters that he was aware of the drug smuggling activities of the Contra network and a Colombian cocaine syndicate. For his candor, Seal was murdered in February 1987. Shortly after his murder, the DEA issued a "low key clarification" regarding the validity of the photograph, admitting that there was no evidence that the plane was being loaded with drugs.

Other testimony linking the CIA and U.S. military officials to complicity in drug trafficking includes the testimony of John Stockwell, a former high-ranking CIA official, who claims that drug smuggling and the CIA were essential components in the private campaign for the Contras. Corroboration for these assertions comes also from George Morales, one of the largest drug traffickers in South America, who testified that he was approached by the CIA in 1984 to fly weapons into Nicaragua. Morales claims that the CIA opened up an airstrip in Costa Rica and gave the pilots information on how to avoid radar traps. According to Morales, he flew 20 shipments of weapons into Costa Rica in 1984 and 1985. In return, the CIA helped him to smuggle thousands of kilos of cocaine into the United States. Morales alone channeled $250,000 quarterly to Contra leader Adolfo Chamorro from his trafficking activity. A pilot for Morales, Gary Betzner, substantiated Morales's claims and admitted flying 4,000 pounds of arms into Costa Rica and 500 kilos of cocaine to Lakeland, Florida, on his return trips. From 1985 to 1987, the CIA arranged 50 to 100 flights using U.S. airports that did not undergo inspection.

The destination of the flights by Morales and Betzner was a hidden airstrip on the ranch of John Hull. Hull, an admitted CIA agent, was a primary player in Oliver North's plan to aid the Contras. Hull's activities were closely monitored by Robert Owen, a key player in the Contra Supply network. Owen established the Institute for Democracy, Education, and Assistance, which raised money to buy arms for the Contras and which, in October 1985, was asked by Congress to distribute $50,000 in "humanitarian aid" to the Contras. Owen worked for Oliver North in coordinating illegal aid to the Contras and setting up the airstrip on the ranch of John Hull.

According to an article in the *Nation,* Oliver North's network of operatives and mercenaries had been linked to the largest drug cartel in South America since 1983. The DEA estimates that Colombian Jorge Ochoa Vasquez, the "kingpin" of the Medellin drug empire, is responsible for supplying 70% to 80% of the cocaine that enters the United States every year. Ochoa was taken into custody by Spanish police in October 1984 when a verbal order was sent by the U.S. Embassy in Madrid for his arrest. The embassy specified that Officer Cos–Gayon, who had undergone training with the DEA, should make the arrest. Other members of the Madrid Judicial Police were connected to the DEA and North's arms smuggling network. Ochoa's lawyers informed him that the United States would alter his extradition if he agreed to implicate the Sandanista government in drug trafficking. Ochoa refused and spent 20 months in jail before returning to Colombia. The Spanish courts ruled that the United States was trying to use Ochoa to discredit Nicaragua and released him. (The *Nation,* September 5, 1987.)

There are other links between the U.S. government and the Medellin cartel. Jose Blandon, General Noreiga's former chief advisor, claims that DEA operations have protected the drug empire in the past and that the DEA paid Noriega $4.7 million for his silence. Blandon also testified in Senate committee hearings that Panama's bases were used as training camps for the Contras in exchange for "economic" support from the United States. Finally, Blandon contends that the CIA gave Panamanian leaders intelligence documents about U.S. senators and aides; the CIA denies these charges. (The *Christian Science Monitor,* February 11, 1988: 3.)

Other evidence of the interrelationship among drug trafficking, the CIA, the NSC, and aid to the Contras includes the following:

- In January 1983, two Contra leaders in Costa Rica persuaded the Justice Department to return over $36,000 in drug profits to drug dealers Julio Zavala and Carlos Cabezas for aid to the Contras (Potter and Bullington, 1987: 22).
- Michael Palmer, a drug dealer in Miami, testified that the State Department's Nicaraguan humanitarian assistance office contracted with his company, Vortex Sales and Leasing, to take humanitarian aid to the Contras. Palmer claims that he smuggled $40 million in marijuana to the United States between 1977 and 1985 (The *Guardian,* March 20, 1988: 3).
- During House and Senate hearings in 1986, it was revealed that a major DEA investigation of the Medellin drug cartel of Colombia, which was

expected to culminate in the arrest of several leaders of the cartel, was compromised when someone in the White House leaked the story of the investigation to the *Washington Times* (a conservative newspaper in Washington, D.C.), which published the story on July 17, 1984. According to DEA Administrator John Lawn, the leak destroyed what was "probably one of the most significant operations in DEA history" (Sharkey, 1988: 24).

- When Honduran General Jose Buseo, who was described by the Justice Department as an "international terrorist," was indicted for conspiring to murder the president of Honduras in a plot financed by profits from cocaine smuggling, Oliver North and officials from the Department of Defense and the CIA pressured the Justice Department to be lenient with General Buseo. In a memo disclosed by the Iran-Contra committee, North stated that if Buseo was not protected "he will break his longstanding silence about the Nic[araguan] resistance and other sensitive operations" (Sharkey, 1988: 27).

On first blush, it seems odd that government agencies and officials would engage in such wholesale disregard of the law. As a first step in building an explanation for these and other forms of state-organized crime, let us try to understand why officials of the CIA, the NSC, and the Department of Defense would be willing to commit criminal acts in pursuit of other goals.

WHY?

Why would government officials from the NSC, the Defense Department, the State Department, and the CIA become involved in smuggling arms and narcotics, money laundering, assassinations, and other criminal activities? The answer lies in the structural contradictions that inhere in nation-states (Chambliss, 1980).

As Weber, Marx, and Gramsci pointed out, no state can survive without establishing legitimacy. The law is a fundamental cornerstone in creating legitimacy and an illusion (at least) of social order. It claims universal principles that demand some behaviors and prohibit others. The protection of property and personal security are obligations assumed by states everywhere both as a means of legitimizing the state's franchise on violence and as a means of protecting commercial interests (Chambliss and Seidman, 1982).

The threat posed by smuggling to both personal security and property interests makes laws prohibiting smuggling essential. Under some circumstances, however, such laws contradict other interests of the state. This contradiction prepares the ground for state-organized crime as a solution to the conflicts and dilemmas posed by the simultaneous existence of contradictory "legitimate" goals.

The military-intelligence establishment in the United States is resolutely committed to fighting the spread of "communism" throughout the world. This mission is not new but has prevailed since the 1800s. Congress and the presidency are not consistent in their support for the money and policies thought by the frontline warriors to be necessary to accomplish their lofty goals. As a result, programs under way are sometimes undermined by a lack of funding and even by laws that prohibit their continuation (such as the passage of laws prohibiting support for the Contras). Officials of government agencies adversely affected by political changes are thus placed squarely in a dilemma: If they comply with the legal limitations on their activities they sacrifice their mission. The dilemma is heightened by the fact that they can anticipate future policy changes that will reinstate their resources and their freedom. When that time comes, however, programs adversely affected will be difficult if not impossible to re-create.

A number of events that occurred between 1960 and 1980 left the military and the CIA with badly tarnished images. Those events and political changes underscored their vulnerability. The CIA lost considerable political clout with elected officials when its planned invasion of Cuba (the infamous Bay of Pigs invasion) was a complete disaster. Perhaps as never before in its history, the United States showed itself vulnerable to the resistance of a small nation. The CIA was blamed for this fiasco even though it was President Kennedy's decision to go ahead with the plans that he inherited from the previous administration. To add to the agency's problems, the complicity between it and ITT to invade Chile and overthrow the Allende government was yet another scar (see below), as was the involvement of the CIA in narcotics smuggling in Vietnam.

These and other political realities led to a serious breach between Presidents Kennedy, Johnson, Nixon, and Carter and the CIA. During President Nixon's tenure in the White House, one of the CIA's top men, James Angleton, referred to Nixon's national security advisor, Henry Kissinger (who became secretary of state) as "objectively, a Soviet Agent" (Hougan, 1984: 75). Another top agent of the CIA, James McCord (later implicated in the Watergate burglary) wrote a secret letter to his superior, General Paul Gaynor, in January 1973 in which he said:

> When the hundreds of dedicated fine men and women of the CIA no longer write intelligence summaries and reports with integrity, without fear of political recrimination—when their fine Director [Richard Helms] is being summarily discharged in order to make way for a politician who will write or rewrite intelligence the way the politicians want them written, instead of the way truth and best judgment dictates, our nation is in the deepest of trouble and freedom itself was never so imperiled. Nazi Germany rose and fell under exactly the same philosophy of governmental operation. (Hougan, 1984: 26–27)

McCord (1974: 60) spoke for many of the top military and intelligence officers in the United States when he wrote in his autobiography: "I believed that the whole future of the nation was at stake." These views show the depth of feeling toward the dangers of political "interference" with what is generally accepted in the military-intelligence establishment as their mission (Goulden, 1984).

When Jimmy Carter was elected president, he appointed Admiral Stansfield Turner as director of Central Intelligence. At the outset, Turner made it clear that he and the president did not share the agency's view that they were conducting their mission properly (Goulden, 1984; Turner, 1985). Turner insisted on centralizing power in the director's office and on overseeing clandestine and covert operations. He met with a great deal of resistance. Against considerable opposition from within the agency, he reduced the size of the covert operation section from 1,200 to 400 agents. Agency people still refer to this as the "Halloween massacre."

Old hands at the CIA do not think their work is dispensable. They believe zealously, protectively, and one is tempted to say, with religious fervor, that the work they are doing is essential for the salvation of humankind. With threats from both Republican and Democratic administrations, the agency sought alternative sources of revenue to carry out its mission. The alternative was already in place with the connections to the international narcotics traffic, arms smuggling, the existence of secret corporations incorporated in foreign countries (such as Panama), and the established links to banks for the laundering of money for covert operations.

STATE-ORGANIZED ASSASSINATIONS AND MURDER

Assassination plots and political murders are usually associated in people's minds with military dictatorships and European monarchies. The practice of assassination, however, is not limited to unique historical events but has become a tool of international politics that involves modern nation-states of many different types.

In the 1960s a French intelligence agency hired Christian David to assassinate the Moroccan leader Ben Barka (Hougan, 1978: 204–207). Christian David was one of those international "spooks" with connections to the DEA, the CIA, and international arms smugglers, such as Robert Vesco.

In 1953 the CIA organized and supervised a coup d'etat in Iran that overthrew the democratically elected government of Mohammed Mossadegh, who had become unpopular with the United States when he nationalized foreign-owned oil companies. The CIA's coup replaced Mossadegh with Reza Shah Pahlevi, who denationalized the oil companies and with CIA guidance established one of the most vicious secret intelligence organizations in the world: SAVAK. In the years to follow, the shah and CIA-trained agents of SAVAK murdered thousands of Iranian citizens. They arrested almost 1,500 people monthly, most of whom were subjected to inhuman torture and punishments without trial. Not only were SAVAK agents trained by the CIA, but there is evidence that they were instructed in techniques of torture (Hersh, 1979: 13).

In 1970 the CIA repeated the practice of overthrowing democratically elected governments that were not completely favorable to U.S. investments. When Salvador Allende was elected president of Chile, the CIA organized a coup that overthrew Allende, during which he was murdered, along with the head of the military, General Rene Schneider. Following Allende's overthrow, the CIA trained agents for the Chilean secret service (DINA). DINA set up a team of assassins who could "travel anywhere in the world... to carry out sanctions including assassinations" (Dinges and Landau, 1980: 239). One of the assassinations carried out by DINA was the murder of Orlando Letellier, Allende's ambassador to the United States and his former minister of defense. Letellier was killed when a car bomb blew up his car on Embassy Row in Washington, D.C. (Dinges and Landau, 1982).

Other bloody coups known to have been planned, organized, and executed by U.S. agents include coups in Guatemala, Nicaragua, the Dominican Republic, and Vietnam. American involvement in those coups was never legally authorized. The murders, assassinations, and terrorist acts that accompany coups are criminal acts by law, both in the United States and in the country in which they take place.

More recent examples of murder and assassination for which government officials are responsible include the death of 80 people in Beirut, Lebanon, when a car bomb exploded on May 8, 1985. The bomb was set by a Lebanese counterterrorist unit working with the CIA. Senator Daniel Moynihan has said that when he was vice president of the Senate Intelligence Committee, President Reagan ordered the CIA to form a small antiterrorist effort in the Mideast. Two sources said that the CIA was working with the group that planted the bomb to kill the Shiite leader Hussein Fadallah (the *New York Times,* May 13, 1985).

A host of terrorist plans and activities connected with the attempt to overthrow the Nicaraguan government, including several murders and assassinations, were exposed in an affidavit filed by free-lance reporters Tony Avirgan and Martha Honey. They began investigating Contra activities after Avirgan was injured in an attempt on the life of Contra leader Eden Pastora. In 1986, Honey and Avirgan filed a complaint with the U.S. District Court in Miami charging John Hull, Robert Owen, Theodore Shackley, Thomas Clines, Chi Chi Quintero, Maj. General Richard Secord, and others working for the CIA in Central America of criminal conspiracy and the smuggling of cocaine to aid the Nicaraguan rebels.

A criminal conspiracy in which the CIA admits participating is the publication of a manual, *Psychological Operation in Guerrilla Warfare,* which was distributed to the people of Nicaragua. The manual describes how the people should proceed to commit murder, sabotage, vandalism, and violent acts in order to undermine the government. Encouraging or instigating such crimes is not only a violation of U.S. law, it was also prohibited by Reagan's executive order in 1981, which forbade any U.S. participation in foreign assassinations.

The CIA is not alone in hatching criminal conspiracies. The DEA organized a "Special Operations Group," which was responsible for working out plans to assassinate political and business leaders in foreign countries who were involved in drug trafficking. The head of this group was a former CIA agent, Lou Conein (also known as "Black Luigi"). George Crile wrote in the *Washington Post* (June 13, 1976):

> When you get down to it, Conein was organizing an assassination program. He was frustrated by the big-time operators who were just too insulated to get to.... Meetings were held to decide whom to target and what method of assassination to employ.

Crile's findings were also supported by the investigative journalist Jim Hougan (1978: 132).

It is a crime to conspire to commit murder. The official record, including testimony by participants in three conspiracies before the U.S. Congress and in court, makes it abundantly clear that the crime of conspiring to commit murder is not infrequent in the intelligence agencies of the United States and other countries.

It is also a crime to cover up criminal acts, but there are innumerable examples of instances in which the CIA and the FBI conspired to interfere with the criminal prosecution of drug dealers, murderers, and assassins. In the death of Letellier, mentioned earlier, the FBI and the CIA refused to cooperate with the prosecution of the DINA agents who murdered Letellier (Dinges and Landau, 1980: 208–209). Those agencies were also involved in the cover-up of the criminal activities of a Cuban exile, Ricardo (Monkey) Morales. While an employee of the FBI and the CIA, Morales planted a bomb on an Air Cuba flight from Venezuela, which killed 73 people. The Miami police confirmed Morales's claim that he was acting under orders from the CIA (Lernoux, 1984: 188). In fact, Morales, who was arrested for overseeing the shipment of 10 tons of marijuana, admitted to being a CIA contract agent who conducted bombings, murders, and assassinations. He was himself killed in a bar after he made public his work with the CIA and the FBI.

Colonel Muammar Qaddafi, like Fidel Castro, has been the target of a number of assassination attempts and conspiracies by the U.S. government. One plot, the *Washington Post* reported, included an effort to "lure [Qaddafi] into some foreign adventure of terrorist exploit that would give a growing number of Qaddafi opponents in the Libyan military a chance to seize power, or such a foreign adventure that might give one of Qaddafi's neighbors, such as Algeria or Egypt, a justification for responding to Qaddafi militarily" (the *Washington Post*, April 14, 1986). The CIA recommended "stimulating" Qaddafi's fall "by encouraging disaffected elements in the Libyan army who could be spurred to assassination attempts" (the *Guardian*, November 20, 1985: 6).

Opposition to government policies can be a very risky business, as the ecology group Greenpeace discovered when it opposed French nuclear testing in the Pacific. In the fall of 1985 the French government planned a series of atomic tests in the South Pacific. Greenpeace sent its flagship to New Zealand with instructions to sail into the area where the atomic testing was scheduled to occur. Before the ship could arrive at the scene, however, the French secret service located the ship in the harbor and blew it up. The blast from the bomb killed one of the crew.

Note

1. It was Shackley who, along with Rafael "Chi Chi" Quintero, a Cuban-American, forged the plot to assassinate Fidel Castro by using organized-crime figures Santo Trafficante, Jr., John Roselli, and Sam Giancana.

Author's Note

Portions of this paper are based on William J. Chambliss, *Exploring Criminology* (New York: Macmillan, 1988).

The historical documents used for the research on piracy were provided by the British Museum Library, the Franklin D. Roosevelt Library in New York, Columbia University Library, and the Naval Archives. For the more recent happenings and machinations of the CIA, DEA, and other government agencies, the primary data bases are confidential interviews with people involved in the events described, or people closely associated with the events, and information obtained through Freedom of Information requests. Attribution to people who generously gave their time and in some cases took risks for the sake of providing a better understanding of the world we live in is, of course, impossible. Where possible the information forthcoming from the interviews has been supplemented by reference to published government documents, newspaper reports, and verifiable research.

Acknowledgments

This research owes a debt to so many people it is impossible to acknowledge them all. The many informants and officials who cooperated with various parts of the research and the librarians who helped uncover essential historical documents must come first. I am also deeply indebted to Raquel Kennedy, Pernille Baadsager, Richard Appelbaum, Marjorie Zatz, Alan Block, Jim Petras, Ray Michalowski, Stan Cohen, Hi Schwendinger, Tony Platt, and Martha Huggins for their insights and help at many stages in the development of the research. I am also indebted to a confidential donor who helped support the research effort in Thailand during 1974.

References

Anderson, Jack, and Lee Whitten
1976 The CIA's "sex squad." The Washington Post, June 22:B13.
Andrews, K.R.
1959 English Privateering Voyages to the West Indies 1598–1695. Ser. 11, vol. 111. London: Hakluyt Society.

1971 The Last Voyage of Drake and Hawkins. New York: Cambridge University Press.
Block, Alan A., and William J. Chambliss
1981 Organizing Crime. New Yorker: Elsevier.
British Museum
1977 Sir Francis Drake. London: British Museum Publications.
Chambliss, William J.
1968 The tolerance policy: An invitation to organized crime. Seattle October: 23–31.
1971 Vice, corruption, bureaucracy and power. Wisconsin Law Review 4: 1,150–1,173.
1975a On the paucity of original research on organized crime: A footnote to Galliher and Cain. The American Sociologist 10:36–39.
1975b Toward a political economy of crime. Theory and Society 2:149–170.
1977 Markets, profits, labor and smack. Contemporary Crises 1:53–57.
1980 On lawmaking. British Journal of Law and Society 6:149–172.
1988a Exploring Criminology. New York: Macmillan.
1988b On the Take: From Petty Crooks to Presidents. Revised ed. Bloomington: Indiana University Press.
Chambliss, William J., and Robert B. Seidman
1982 Law, Order and Power. Rev. ed. Reading, Mass.: Addison-Wesley.
Church Committee
1976 Intelligence Activities and the Rights of Americans. Washington, D.C.: Government Printing Office.
Commonwealth of New South Wales
1982a New South Wales Joint Task Force on Drug Trafficking. Federal Parliament Report. Sydney: Government of New South Wales.
1982b Preliminary Report of the Royal Commission to Investigate the Nugan Hand Bank Failure. Federal Parliament Report. Sydney: Government of New South Wales.
Corbett, Julian S.
1898a Drake and the Tudor Army. 2 vols. London: Longmans, Green.
1898b Paper Relating to the Navy during the Spanish War, 1585–1587. Vol. 11. London: Navy Records Society.
Crewdson, John M., and Jo Thomas
1977 Abuses in testing of drugs by CIA to be panel focus. The New York Times, September 20.
de La Croix, Robert
1962 John Paul Jones. London: Frederik Muller.
Dinges, John, and Saul Landau
1980 Assassination on Embassy Row. New York: McGraw-Hill.
1982 The CIA's link to Chile's plot. The Nation, June 12:712–713.
Exquemling, A. O.
1670 De Americanaenshe Zee-Roovers. MS. 301. London, British Museum.
Goulden, Joseph C.
1984 Death Merchant: The Brutal True Story of Edwin P. Wilson. New York: Simon and Schuster.
Hersh, Seymour
1979 Ex-analyst says CIA rejected warning on Shah. The New York Times,

January 7:A10. Cited in Piers Beirne and James Messerschmidt, Criminology. New York: Harcourt Brace Jovanovich, forthcoming.
Hougan, Jim
1978 Spooks: The Haunting of America—The Private Use of Secret Agents. New York: William Morrow.
1984 Secret Agenda: Watergate, Deep Throat, and the CIA. New York: Random House.
Jacobs, John
1977a The diaries of a CIA operative. The Washington Post, September 5:1.
1977b Turner cites 149 drug-test projects. The Washington Post, August 4:1.
Klein, Lloyd
1988 Big Brother Is Still Watching You. Paper presented at the annual meetings of the American Society of Criminology, Chicago, November 12.
Kruger, Henrik
1980 The Great Heroin Coup. Boston: South End Press.
Kwitny, Jonathan
1987 The Crimes of Patriots. New York: W. W. Norton.
Lane-Poole
1890 The Barbary Corsairs. London: T. Fisher Unwin.
LeGolif, Louis
1680 Manuscripts of Louis LeGolif alias Borgnefesse. London, British Museum.
Lernoux, Penny
1984 The Miami connection. The Nation, February 18:186–198.
MacIntyre, Donald
1975 The Privateers. London: Paul Elek.
Mainwaring, Henry
1616 Of the Beginnings, Practices, and Suppression of Pirates. No publisher acknowledged.
McCord, James W., Jr.
1974 A Piece of Tape. Rockville, Md.: Washington Media Services.
McCoy, Alfred W.
1973 The Politics of Heroin in Southeast Asia. New York: Harper & Row.
NARMIC
1984 Military Exports to South Africa: A Research Report on the Arms Embargo. Philadelphia: American Friends Service Committee.
Nihill, Grant
1982 Bank links to spies, drugs. The Advertiser, November 10:1.
Owen, John
1983 Sleight of Hand: The $25 Million Nugan Hand Bank Scandal. Sydney: Calporteur Press.
Parenti, Michael
1983 Democracy for the Few. New York: St. Martin's.
Petras, James
1977 Chile: Crime, class consciousness and the bourgeoisie. Crime and Social Justice 7:14–22.
Potter, Gary W., and Bruce Bullington
1987 Drug Trafficking and the Contras: A Case Study of State-Organized Crime. Paper presented at annual meeting of the American Society of Criminology, Montreal.

Ritchie, Robert C.
1986 Captain Kidd and the War Against the Pirates. Cambridge, Mass.: Harvard University Press.
Rockefeller Report
1975 Report to the President by the Commission on CIA Activities within the United States. Washington, D.C.: Government Printing Office.
Schwendinger, Herman, and Julia Schwendinger
1975 Defenders of order or guardians of human rights. Issue in Criminology 7:72–81.
Senate Hearings
1986 Senate Select Committee on Assassination, Alleged Assassination Plots Involving Foreign Leaders. Interim Report of the Senate Select Committee to Study Governmental Operations with Respect to Intelligence Activities. 94th Cong., 1st sess., November 20. Washington D.C.: Government Printing Office.
Senior, C. M.
1976 A Nation of Pirates: English Piracy in its Heyday. London: David and Charles Newton Abbot.
Sharkey, Jacqueline
1988 The Contra-drug tradeoff. Common Cause Magazine, September-October: 23–33.
Tilly, Charles
1985 War making and state making as organized crime. In P. Evans, D. Rueschemeyer, and T. Skocpol (eds.), Bringing the State Back In. Cambridge: Cambridge University Press.
Turner, Stansfield
1985 Secrecy and Democracy: The CIA in Transition. New York: Houghton Miflin.
U.S. Department of State
1985 Revolution Beyond Our Border: Information on Central America. State Department Report N 132. Washington, D.C.: U.S. Department of State.
Verrill, A. Hyatt
1924 Smugglers and Smuggling. New York: Duffield.

36 / Corporations, Organized Crime, and the Disposal of Hazardous Waste: An Examination of the Making of a Criminogenic Regulatory Structure

ANDREW SZASZ

The generation of hazardous waste is a necessary side effect of modern industrial production. Factories must cope daily with large accumulations of unrecyclable chemical byproducts generated by normal production techniques. The processing or disposal of these byproducts is a significant cost of production, a cost that, like all other costs of production, the prudent owner or manager minimizes.

Until recently, industrial hazardous waste was not legally distinguished from municipal garbage and other solid wastes. It was disposed of with ordinary garbage, at very low cost to the generator, mostly in coastal waters or in landfills unfit to adequately contain it. However, concern grew during the 1970s that improper disposal of hazardous waste was creating an environmental and public health burden of unknown but potentially massive scale. This concern finally moved some states and eventually the federal government to begin to legislate new regulations. The centerpiece of this regulatory effort was the federal Resource Conservation and Recovery Act (RCRA) of 1976. On paper, RCRA mandated comprehensive mechanisms to guarantee the safe disposal of hazardous waste. It established standards and procedures for classifying substances as hazardous. It authorized the states to register corporate generators of hazardous waste and license hauling and disposal firms. It mandated the creation of a manifest system that would document the movement of hazardous waste "from cradle to grave," from the generator, through the hands of the transporter, to the shipment's final destination at a licensed disposal site.

By legally distinguishing hazardous waste from other wastes and by directing that such wastes be treated differently than municipal solid waste, the new regulations dramatically increased, almost overnight, the demand for hazardous waste hauling and disposal services. Unhappily, recent state and federal investigations have documented both that illegal waste disposal is widespread (U.S. General Accounting Office, 1985; U.S. House of

Representatives, 1980) and that organized crime elements traditionally active in garbage hauling and landfilling have entered this burgeoning and potentially profitable new market (Block and Scarpitti, 1985; U.S. House of Representatives, 1980, 1981a). Although the exact extent of organized crime involvement in hazardous waste hauling and disposal is uncertain,[1] the fact of that involvement is beyond question. A situation exists, then, in which corporations, some at the heart of the American economy, discharge their regulatory obligations under RCRA by entering into direct contractual relationships with firms dominated by organized crime. The goal in this paper is to analyze in detail the complex nature of this relationship between corporate generators of hazardous waste and elements of organized crime that are active in industrial waste disposal. This goal will be approached by analyzing the formation and implementation of RCRA legislation.

The subject of this paper speaks to two distinct criminological literatures: works that examine the relationship between legitimate and illicit enterprise and works that examine crimogenic market structures. Recent scholarship has challenged the commonsense distinction between legitimate business and organized crime. Schelling (1967), Smith and Alba (1979), Smith (1980), and Albanese (1982) all argue that the most fundamental aspect of organized crime is that it is a form of entrepreneurial activity and that its ethnic or conspiratorial nature is of secondary importance. Recent scholarship also challenges the equally widely held belief that the relationship between the underworld and legitimate business consists solely of the former exploiting the latter through extortion, racketeering, and so on (Drucker, 1981). At minimum, it is argued that the relationship is one of mutually beneficial interdependence (Martens and Miller-Longfellow, 1982). This is clearly supported by excellent case studies of labor racketeering (Block and Chambliss, 1981), organized crime on the waterfront (Block, 1982), and arson (Brady, 1983). Chambliss (1978: 181–182) argues the even stronger view that organized crime can exist only because the structure of the legitimate economy and its accompanying political organization make its emergence possible and even inevitable. In a similar vein, Smith (1980) and Smith and Alba (1979) challenge the very distinction between business and organized crime and begin to dissolve that distinction in the common dynamic of a market economy. The study of organized crime participation in hazardous waste disposal presents an opportunity to once again examine this relationship between legitimate and illegitimate entrepreneurship.

The story of RCRA may also have links to the concept of crimogenic market processes. Farberman's (1975) and Leonard and Weber's (1977) studies of auto retailing and Denzin's (1977) study of the liquor industry showed that the normal operating logic of an industry may force some sectors of that industry into illegal activity in order to survive, much less thrive, in doing their part of the business. Needleman and Needleman (1979) subsequently expanded the concept by describing a second type of crim-inogenesis in which the criminal activity is not forced. It is, instead, an unwelcome drain on business, but it is unavoidable because the conditions that make it possible are necessary to the overall functioning of that industry and could not be altered without fundamentally affecting how business is conducted in that industry. Needleman and Needleman discussed securities fraud as an example of what they call a "crime-facilitative," as opposed to a "crime-coercive" market sector. The fact that RCRA not only cannot prevent illegal hazardous waste dumping but has also attracted organized crime participation in illegal hazardous waste activity suggests that the concept of criminogenesis may be fruitfully extended to regulatory processes as well.

In the first sections of this paper, some background is presented on hazardous waste as a social issue and the nature and extent of organized crime involvement in hazardous waste hauling and disposal is summarized. At the core of the paper, the conditions that made this involvement possible are analyzed. It is shown that the most common explanations—lax implementation and enforcement by state and local officials—are incomplete. Analysis of the formation of RCRA legislation shows that corporate generators of hazardous waste were instrumental in securing a regulatory structure that would prove highly attractive to and well suited for organized crime participation. In other words, generators are deeply implicated in the creation of conditions that have their relationship to organized crime possible. This finding is used to critique two explanations of this relationship suggested during Congressional hearings, generator "ignorance" and generator "powerlessness." It is then argued that the relationship has two other important aspects: generators did not consciously desire or intend this outcome, but they nonetheless benefitted from it once it occurred. The paper concludes with a discussion of the relevance of the findings to the two areas of criminological research mentioned above.

THE ISSUE BACKGROUND: HAZARDOUS WASTE FACTS

The Environmental Protection Agency (EPA) defines waste products as "hazardous" if they are flammable, explosive, corrosive, or toxic. Major industries central to the modern national economy, such as the petroleum, chemical, electronic, and pharmaceutical industries, generate copious amounts of hazardous waste. Although there is still great uncertainty about the exact effect of industrial hazardous waste on public health (Greenberg and Anderson, 1984: 84–105), improper management may result in explosions, fires, pollution of water resources, and other uncontrolled releases that put surrounding communities at risk and may result in physical harm ranging from skin irritation to increased incidence of cancer, lung disease, birth defects, and other serious illnesses.

How much hazardous waste has accumulated? How much is currently generated? Neither question can be answered confidently at this time. The generation and disposal of hazardous waste was completely unregulated until the late 1970s. In the absence of regulation, there was no systematic data-gathering effort. Consequently, there is great uncertainty about the magnitude and composition of hazardous waste accumulated up to the passage of the RCRA. Estimates have risen regularly as more sites are located and assessed. The EPA's most recent estimate is that there are 25,000 sites nationally that contain some hazardous waste. Of these, about 2,500 are priority sites judged by the EPA to be imminently hazardous to public health. More recent research by the General Accounting Office (GAO) and the Office of Technology Assessment (OTA) suggests that there may be 378,000 total sites nationally, perhaps 10,000 of them requiring priority attention (Shabecoff, 1985).

In theory, at least, the availability of data should have improved greatly following passage of the RCRA. Generators of hazardous waste were now required to create written documentation—the manifest—of the amount and content of every shipment of hazardous waste signed over to outside haulers and disposers. This documentation would be forwarded to state agencies following final disposition of each waste shipment. However, the actual quality of the data produced was compromised by several factors. First, there was little agreement over what substances should be defined as hazardous. Congressional and EPA testimony (U.S. Environmental Protection Agency, 1976, 1979; U.S. House of Representatives, 1975, 1976; U.S. Senate, 1974, 1979) shows that industrial spokesmen argued that too many substances had been unjustifiably included, while environmentalists argued that some materials had been improperly excluded. Second, firms generating less than one metric ton (2,200 lbs.) of hazardous waste per month are exempt from RCRA regulation (U.S. House of Representatives, 1983: 56, 60). There are over four million privately owned industrial sites in the nation. The "small generator" exemption leaves all but a few tens of thousands of these sites out of RCRA's registration and manifest system. Third, some firms that generate significant amounts of hazardous waste have either failed to cooperate with EPA requests for data (Williams and Matheny, 1984: 436–437) or have failed to identify themselves to the EPA as regulable generators (U.S. General Accounting Office, 1985: 14–20). Fourth, even those firms that appear to comply with reporting requirements may not be reporting accurately the types and quantities of hazardous waste they generate (U.S. GAO, 1985: 20–23). Consequently, knowledge of the amount and content of current hazardous waste generation is still imprecise. Estimates, like estimates of historical accumulation, have been rising. In 1974, the EPA was estimating hazardous waste generation at 10 million metric tons per year (U.S. Senate, 1974: 70). In 1980, the EPA estimate had risen to 40 million metric tons. In 1983, new research led the EPA to nearly quadruple its estimate to 150 million metric tons (Block and Scarpitti, 1985: 46), while the OTA was estimating 250 million metric tons per year (U.S. House of Representatives, 1983: 1).[2]

Where does hazardous waste end up? In response to EPA inquiries in 1981, 16% of generating firms reported treating their wastes completely on site and another 22% reported treating part of their wastes on site. The remaining 62% contracted with other parties to handle all of their wastes (Block and Scarpitti, 1985: 48–49). Where do transported wastes actually end up? The exemptions and noncooperation cited above leave an unknown fraction of total hazardous waste movement out of the paperwork of the manifest system (U.S. GAO, 1985: 3–4, 14–24). The manifests that are filed are poorly monitored and vulnerable to undetected falsification (Greenberg and Anderson, 1984: 242; U.S. GAO, 1985: 25–31; U.S. House of Representatives, 1980: 140, 1981b: 124). Consequently, this question also cannot be answered with great certainty. On the basis of admittedly poor and incomplete data, the OTA estimates that no more than 10% to 20% of all hazardous waste is rendered harmless by incineration or by chemical or biological treatment. There are few facilities that can treat wastes in these ways and the price of treatment is much higher than the price of other means of disposal (U.S. House of Representatives, 1983: 2, 5–6). The remaining 80% to 90% is either landfilled or disposed of illegally. Only a small proportion of hazardous waste goes into landfills that have the siting studies, proper containment practices, and continuous monitoring to be fully licensed by the EPA, since there are only about 200 such landfills in the nation (Block and Scarpitti, 1985: 49; U.S. House of Representatives, 1981b: 187). Even these top landfills are only required by the EPA to keep wastes contained for 30 years (U.S. House of Representatives, 1983: 2).[3] Most hazardous waste goes to landfills that have only interim license to operate, landfills that are of much poorer quality and are likely to pollute the surrounding land and water within a few years.

Illegal hazardous waste dumping is even more likely to have adverse short-term environmental and public health consequences. The full extent of illegal hazardous waste disposal is not known. State officials interviewed by the GAO agreed that illegal disposal was occurring, but had no firm information on the scope of this activity (U.S. GAO, 1985: 10). One study done for the EPA surveyed hazardous waste generators in 41 cities and estimated that one in seven generators had illegally disposed some of their wastes during the two years preceding the study (U.S. GAO, 1985: 10). A wide array of illegal disposal practices have been documented. Waste shipments may end up commingled with ordinary garbage. A 20 cubic yard "dumpster" full of dry garbage can be made to absorb up to sixty 55 gallon drums of liquid hazardous waste (U.S. House of Representatives, 1980: 63) and then be deposited in unlicensed municipal landfills never designed to contain hazardous waste. Liquid hazardous waste may be released along a roadway. An 8,000 gallon truck can be emptied in 8 minutes (U.S. House of Representatives, 1980: 101). Shipments may simply be stockpiled at sites awaiting alleged transfer that never happens or at disposal facilities that have no real disposal capability (U.S. House of Representatives, 1980: 10). Wastes may be drained into local city sewer systems, rivers, and oceans, or dumped in out-of-the-way rural spots (U.S. House of Representatives, 1980: 93). Flammable hazardous waste may be commingled with fuel oil and sold as pure heating oil (U.S. House of Representatives, 1980: 63–64) or sprayed on unsuspecting communities' roads for dust control (U.S. House of Representatives, 1980: 151).

ORGANIZED CRIME PARTICIPATION IN THE HAZARDOUS WASTE DISPOSAL INDUSTRY

> Congressman Albert Gore: "At what point did companies picking up garbage begin to get into the toxic waste disposal business?"
>
> Harold Kaufman: "To my knowledge, it's when the manifest system came out is when they found out the profit motive" (U.S. House of Representatives, 1980: 8).

New Jersey Attorney General John J. Degnan pointed out to a Congressional audience that organized crime activity accounts for only a fraction of the illegal dumping taking place in the United States (U.S. House of Representatives, 1980: 87). Nonetheless, organized crime was ideally suited to develop the methodology of illegal hazardous waste practices to the fullest. In those parts of the nation where garbage hauling and landfilling was historically controlled by organized crime, their movement into the newly created hazardous waste market was an obvious extension of current activity. In New Jersey, for example, organized crime had controlled the garbage industry through ownership of garbage hauling firms, through ownership of or control of landfills, and through labor racketeering (U.S. House of Representatives, 1981: 1–45). The new regulations governing hazardous waste would have had to have been carefully written and tenaciously enforced were organized crime to be kept from applying this highly developed infrastructure to the new market. In fact, as will be shown below, the opposite happened and organized crime easily entered both the hauling and the disposal phases of the hazardous waste handling industry.

Hauling. Organized crime had dominated traditional garbage hauling in states like New York and New Jersey for decades. Once associates of organized crime owned a number of hauling firms in any geographical area, they established an organizational infrastructure that governed their relationships and ensured high profits. Threats and violence persuaded other firms to join that infrastructure and abide by its rules or to sell and get out. The keystone of this infrastructure was the concept of "property rights" or "respect." Municipal solid waste hauling contracts were illegally apportioned among haulers. Having a property right meant that a hauler held rights to continue picking up the contract at sites he currently serviced without competition from others. Other firms would submit artificially high bids or would not bid at all when a contract came up for renewal, thereby assuring that the contractor kept his traditional site. This system of *de facto* territorial monopolies permitted noncompetitive pricing and made the lowly business of garbage hauling a very lucrative activity. Property rights were recognized and enforced by organized crime authorities. Conflicts were adjudicated in meetings of the Municipal Contractors Association. Decisions of the MCA were enforced by threats and, if necessary, violence (U.S. House of Representatives, 1981a: 1–42).[4] As is shown below, when the RCRA mandated the licensing of firms deemed fit to transport hazardous waste, mob-connected garbage haulers found it easy to acquire state permits and declare themselves to be hazardous waste haulers. Quite naturally, they brought their traditional forms of social organization with them. Individual haulers holding established property rights assumed that they would transfer those property rights to a new type of waste (U.S. House of Representatives, 1980: 22). They also met as a group to set up a Trade Waste Association modeled after the Municipal Contractors Association to apportion and enforce property rights in the new market (U.S. House of Representatives, 1980: 9–10, 1981a: 1–12, 212).

Disposal. The manifest system requires that someone will be willing to sign off on the manifest and declare that a waste shipment has been properly disposed of. This means, as Congressman Florio (Democrat, New Jersey) pointed out (U.S. House of Representatives, 1980: 30), that mob control over hauling is not enough: organized crime figures had to have ownership of, or at least influence over, final disposal sites. This requirement did not prove to be a serious stumbling block, however. Many landfills were already owned wholly or in part by organized crime figures, a legacy of past mob involvement in the garbage business. These sites readily accepted dubious shipments of hazardous waste thinly disguised as ordinary municipal waste (U.S. House of Representatives 1981a: 228, 1981b). Landfill owners not directly associated with organized crime could be bribed to sign manifests for shipments never received or to accept hazardous waste that was manifested elsewhere (U.S. House of Representatives, 1980: 70, 90). In addition, known organized crime figures started or seized control of a network of phony disposal and "treatment" facilities such as Chemical Control Corporation, Elizabeth, New Jersey; Modern Transportation, Kearny, New Jersey; and Duane Marine, Perth Amboy, New Jersey.[5] Licensed by the state, these outfits could legally receive hazardous waste and sign off on the manifest. They would then either stockpile it on site (where it would stay until it exploded, burned, or otherwise came to the attention of authorities) or dump it along roadways, down municipal sewers, into the ocean, or elsewhere (Block and Scarpitti, 1985: 145, 158, 298; U.S. House of Representatives, 1980: 25). In the extreme, actual ownership of or access to disposal sites was unnecessary for those willing to file totally fanciful manifests. Congressman Gore cited one case in which several major corporations signed over their wastes to an out-of-state facility that subsequently was shown to simply not exist (U.S. House of Representatives, 1980: 70, 135).[6]

ENABLING CAUSES: THE MAKING OF A VULNERABLE REGULATORY STRUCTURE

In retrospect, it is hardly surprising that, given the opportunity, organized crime would enter the newly created market for hazardous waste handling. It was an extension of their current business activity. They had the equipment and organization. They had both the know-how and the will to corrupt the manifest system. It was an attractive prospect. Both the potential size of the market and the potential profits were enormous. Even if they charged only a fraction of the true price of legitimate disposal, that price would be much higher than the price they charged to move the same stuff when it was legally just garbage, but their operating expenses would stay the same (if they commingled hazardous waste with ordinary garbage) or decrease (if they simply dumped). Why organized crime would want to enter into relationship with corporate generators when the opportunity presented itself needs no subtle unraveling. The more complex task is to determine what political and social-structural conditions made it possible for them to "colonize" the hazardous waste disposal industry.

Lax Implementation, Incompetent and/or Corrupt Enforcement

Explanations of organized crime presence in hazardous waste handling focused on lax implementation and improper enforcement. Congressional hearings produced dramatic evidence that, at least in New Jersey, the state where organized crime intrusion into hazardous waste is most thoroughly documented, the major provisions of the RCRA were poorly implemented and enforced. Interim hauling and disposal licenses were freely granted. The manifest system was not sufficiently monitored.

Interim Licensing. Congress had mandated an extended transition period during which both transporters and disposal firms would operate under temporary permits until an adequate national hazardous waste industry developed. Generators lobbied quite heavily on this point (U.S. EPA, 1976: 238, 1979: 153, 307; Gansberg, 1979) and Congress had to agree to this provision because the shortage of adequate hazardous waste facilities was so severe. American industry would have choked in its own accumulating wastes had it not been permitted to continue to use less-than-adequate means of disposal. A reasonable concession to economic realities, implementation of interim licensing was poorly managed. House of Representatives testimony shows that New Jersey issued hauling permits to any applicant who paid a nominal $50 fee (U.S. House of Representatives, 1980: 14–15). Existing landfills and even totally bogus firms with no real disposal facilities found it equally easy to get interim disposal permits (U.S. House of Representatives, 1980: 10).

Harold Kaufman (key FBI informant on mob involvement in hazardous waste disposal, testifying about his old firm, Duane Marine): "The State licensed us. We were the first ones licensed. . . . "

Gore: "And this was a chemical waste disposal facility, is that right?"

Kaufman: "Well, that is what it was called. It never disposed of anything, but you can call it that."

Manifest Oversight. Once a license was obtained, lax supervision of the manifest system made illegal and unsafe disposal of hazardous waste a relatively straightforward, low-risk activity (U.S. House of Representatives, 1980: 140).

Gore: "What enforcement efforts are you making to prevent the abuse of the manifest system?"

Edwin Stier (New Jersey Division of Criminal Justice): "The only way the manifest system is going to be properly, effectively enforced is through the proper analysis of the information that comes from the manifest. . . . Anyone who assumes that a manifest system which looks good on paper can control the flow and disposition of toxic waste without the kind of support both technical and manpower support that is necessary to make it effective, I think, is deluding himself. [However] . . . we aren't looking specifically for manifest case violations. We aren't pulling every manifest in that is filed with the department of environmental protection and looking for falsification of manifests specifically because we don't have the time, the resources, or the specific lead information to do that."

Congressional testimony revealed that until 1980 New Jersey did not have a single person assigned to monitor the manifests being filed in Trenton (U.S. House. of Representatives, 1981b: 124). A recent study by the General Accounting Office (U.S. GAO, 1985: 25–31) found that the manifest system does not detect illegal disposal, in part because of inadequate monitoring.

Congressional hearings also produced evidence suggesting that the relevant New Jersey agencies—the Interagency Hazardous Waste Strike Force, the Division of Criminal Justice, and the Division of Environmental Protection—were incapable of producing effective enforcement even when tipped off to specific instances of hazardous waste dumping (U.S. House of Representatives, 1980: 144–146, 1981b: 110–124). Block and Scarpitti (1985) present many other examples that appear to show corruption or, at best, ineptitude on the part of state officials responsible for investigation and prosecution of illegal hazardous waste practices.

Lax implementation and enforcement undoubtedly played a big role in facilitating organized crime entry into the hazardous waste disposal industry. There are, however, more fundamental conditioning factors that logically and temporally preceded these causes. RCRA is a regulatory structure ripe with potential for subversion. Why did Congress create a regulatory structure so vulnerable to lax enforcement? A review of RCRA's legislative history shows quite clearly that corporate generators moved decisively to shape the emerging federal intervention to their liking. They determinedly fought for and achieved a regulatory form that would demand of them the least real change and a form that would minimize their liability for potential violations of the new regulations.

GENERATORS' STRATEGIC INTERVENTION IN THE LEGISLATIVE DEBATE OVER THE FORM OF POLICY

Compared to the regulatory mechanism written into the final language of the RCRA, some potential alternative forms that were proposed and then rejected would have proved much less hospitable to noncompliance in general and to the entry of organized crime in particular. The federal government could have mandated specific treatment and disposal practices, or directed generators to treat all of their wastes themselves, or legislated that generators retain full responsibility for their wastes even if they assign them to other parties for shipping and disposal. Generators, led by representatives of major oil and chemical corporations, explicitly and vigorously opposed any such language. They hammered away with striking unanimity at two fundamental points: that the government should in no way interfere in firms' production decisions, and that generators should not be held responsible for the ultimate fate of their hazardous wastes.

Generators repeatedly warned Congress neither to appropriate to itself the power to intervene in production processes nor to require generators to follow specific waste treatment practices. They stressed, instead, that regulatory controls are more properly imposed at the stage of final disposition. Here are some representative statements:

> We believe that the disposal of wastes ought to be regulated instead of regulating the nature and use of the product or the type of manufacturing process used (E.I. DuPont de Nemours and Co., U.S. Senate, 1974: 454).

> Authority to control production, composition, and distribution of products... would be devastating to free enterprise commerce (Dow Chemical, U.S. Senate, 1974: 1,478).

> [Stauffer Chemical opposes generator permits which] would place controls on raw materials, manufacturing processes, products and distribution (Stauffer, U.S. Senate, 1974: 1,745).

> ...legislation should not impede the natural interaction of raw materials, market and other forces that ultimately control the nature, quality, price, and success of products developed in our free enterprise system (Union Carbide, U.S. Senate, 1974: 1,748).

> No specific requirements or prohibitions should be set governing the recovery, reuse or disposal of industrial wastes.... Generators should be free to increase or decrease waste production rates, terminate waste production, treat their own

wastes, and negotiate treatment or disposal service contracts in a free and competitive market (American Petroleum Institute, U.S. EPA, 1976: 1,406, 1,410).

...the generator should be free to decide whether to treat or dispose of wastes (Manufacturing Chemists Association, U.S. EPA, 1976: 565).

...economic incentive alone should determine the degree of waste recycle and recovery.... We are opposed to regulations specifying the kind and amount of processing and recycle of wastes [by the generator]. [The] greatest emphasis should be placed on establishing standards which assure that the ultimate disposal method is satisfactory (DuPont, U.S. EPA, 1976: 72–73).[7]

Generator unanimity was equally impressive on the second issue of responsibility. They were willing to have limited responsibility, to label their wastes, and make sure they contracted only with firms approved by state authorities, but they vehemently opposed the idea that generators should bear legal responsibility for their wastes from cradle to grave. They argued that responsibility should pass to the party in physical possession of the hazardous waste. Under such a system, they further pointed out, only the hauler and disposer need to be licensed and the government should not license generators. Here are some representative statements:

We agree that the generator has some responsibility in the area,... [i.e.] make some determination that the disposer is competent and has the proper permits for disposal.... However, the waste hauler and disposer have responsibility to assure, respectively, that the wastes are delivered for disposal at the proper location and are properly disposed. Irresponsible action is invited if the person holding the waste has no responsibility for it (DuPont, U.S. EPA, 1976: 73–74).

[The generator should] confirm the competence and reliability of transporters, treaters and processors to whom the waste may be transferred.... Each transporter, treater and disposer should be responsible for his individual activities while the waste is in his possession (Monsanto, U.S. EPA, 1976: 410–411).

MCA recommends that the responsibility for the waste should be associated with physical possession of the waste, so that the generator should not be held liable for negligence of the transporter and the disposer of the waste. (Manufacturing Chemists Association, U.S. EPA, 1976: 565).

We feel that permits should only be required of the disposal site operator (B.F. Goodrich, U.S. Senate, 1974: 1,441).

...permits for both generation and disposal of hazardous waste is doubly redundant.... A permit system for generators of wastes is unneeded and would tend to stagnate technology at the level prevailing at the time the permit was issued (Dow Chemical, U.S. Senate, 1974: 1,478–1,479).

...we consider permits for the generation of hazardous wastes to be unneeded, and could result in unnecessary restriction of manufacturing operations (Union Carbide, U.S. Senate, 1974: 464).[8]

The generators also lobbied for the other provisions to their liking—a narrow definition of what substances should be regulated as hazardous, flexible time frames for implementation, and less stringent rules for on-site disposal[9]—but the two points above were the heart of their legislative intervention. In the end, they didn't get everything they wanted. The government would make generators register with the EPA. On-site, generator self-disposal would be subject to the same rules that governed off-site disposal firms. However, the overall forms of RCRA passed by Congress embodied both of their major demands.

THE LEGACY OF GENERATOR INATTENTION AND INACTION

The generators also contributed indirectly to the shaping of RCRA legislation through their historical lack of attention to proper hazardous waste disposal. The EPA estimated in 1974 that ocean dumping and improper landfilling cost about 5% of the price of environmentally adequate disposal and it reported that

> Given this permissive legislative climate, generators of waste are under little or no pressure to expend resources for adequate management of their hazardous wastes. (U.S. Senate, 1974: 71)

Lack of generator demand for adequate disposal facilities discouraged the inflow of investment capital, and an adequate waste disposal industry had failed to develop by the time RCRA legislation was being debated. Had legislators ignored this situation and required an immediate shift to proper disposal, a production crisis could have been triggered as wastes accumulated and firms found few legal outlets for them. Industrial spokesmen predicted dire consequences. In a representative statement, a Union Carbide spokesman warned legislators:

> Those wastes which are non-incinerable and have no commercial value must be disposed of. To deny opportunity for disposal would effectively eliminate much of the chemical process industry. Disposal in or on the land or disposal in the oceans are the only viable alternatives available. (U.S. Senate, 1974: 461)

Neither individual officeholders nor whole governments stay in office long if they pass legislation which, even for the best and most popular of reasons, brings to a halt industrial sectors central to the national economy. Congressmen had to be realistic and mandate years of transition during which hazardous waste would be hauled and disposed by operators having only interim licenses. This reasonable concession to the reality of the situation, a legacy of generator inattention, created a loophole through which many less-than-qualified parties could legally participate as providers in the hazardous waste market.[10]

Notes

I wish to gratefully acknowledge that this paper has benefited from comments by Frank Henry, Judith Gerson, Wendy Strimling, Vern Baxter, John Campbell, Carroll Estes, members of the Pew Writing Seminar, and several anonymous reviewers.

1. The extent of involvement is unclear for two reasons:

First, investigation has focused on the New York, Connecticut, and New Jersey region. This is a strategic site for investigation because so much hazardous waste is produced in the Tri-State area (for example, New Jersey ranks number one in the nation in annual hazardous waste generation) and because mob involvement in garbage in this region has been thoroughly documented. But, for the same reasons, this region may not be typical of the rest of the nation. Recent investigatory reporting concerning environmental pollution and political corruption in Louisiana (Getschow and Petzinger, 1984; Petzinger and Getschow, 1984a, 1984b; Snyder, 1985a, 1985b, 1985c, 1985d, 1985e, 1985f) shows that waste disposal is a corrupt business there as well, but that corruption grows out of the specific history of oil industry domination of that state's economy and its politics and appears to be quite different from patterns of corruption in the Northeast. This suggests that the post-RCRA relationship between corporate generators and waste disposers may be heavily influenced by variations in regional history predating RCRA.

Second, on a more theoretical level, the boundary between organized crime and legitimate business is, at points, somewhat ambiguous. Take, for example, SCA, the nation's third largest hazardous waste company. SCA undertook a vigorous acquisition program in New Jersey and quickly bought up about 20 garbage hauling and landfill companies. Some of these were formerly owned by organized crime figures. SCA is a corporation whose stock is traded on the New York Stock Exchange and its corporate board boasts outside directors associated with IBM, Houghton-Mifflin Co., MIT, and the Boston Co. (U.S. House of Representative, 1980, 1981a), but Congressional testimony indicates that when SCA bought mob-owned firms, it hired the former owners as managers and appears to have allowed them free hand to run their business as they had before acquisition.

2. Methods of estimation are discussed in depth by Greenberg and Anderson (1984).

3. It is generally admitted that even the best landfill is only temporary and inadequate: "No landfill can be made safe from all substances"—Albert Gore (U.S. House of Representatives, 1983: 2). George J. Tyler, Assistant Commissioner of the New Jersey Department of Environmental Protection, speaking about the Lone Pine landfill in Freehold, New Jersey (U.S. House of Representatives, 1981b: 188): "The landfill is leaking into the water, but so does every landfill in the country." The landfill at Wilsonville, Illinois, owned and operated by SCA (see Note 1), is, according to Dr. Raymond D. Harbison, a toxicologist, EPA consultant, and professor of pharmacology at Vanderbilt University, "the most scientific landfill in this country" (U.S. House of Representatives, 1981a: 267). Geological and soil permeability feasibility tests were conducted before construction was begun. Trenches were carefully dug. Arriving waste is sampled and tested, then buried in either nonleaking 55 gallon drums or double-walled paper bags. Monitoring wells surround the site. Yet subsequent studies show that the soil is more porous than originally thought and water is seeping in at rates greater than predicted. Furthermore, the landfill is built over an abandoned coal mine and feasibility tests underestimated the likelihood of "subsidence," land sinkage that may compromise the site's ability to keep substances safety contained. If this is the best site in the nation, the Office of Technology Assessment is right to worry that current efforts to clean up the worst abandoned sites under the Superfund program only transfer the problem to other places and future times (Shabecoff, 1985: 31).

4. Of parenthetical interest here is the methodological similarity between organized crime's property rights system in garbage and price-fixing by Westinghouse, General Electric, and other firms in the famous heavy electrical equipment price fixing scandal of 1961 (Geis, 1977).

5. Modern Transportation, a firm that would ultimately receive half the manifested hazardous waste originating in northern New Jersey, was incorporated in 1972 by Richard Miele, co-owner with known organized crime figures of numerous garbage-related firms and landfills (Block and Scarpitti, 1985: 297). Chemical Control Corporation was taken over by Johnny Albert, one of the organizers of the New Jersey Trade Waste Association (Block and Scarpitti, 1985: 256–260; U.S. House of Representatives, 1980: 10). Duane Marine was so enmeshed in organized crime networks and activities that its former employee, Harold Kaufman, became the central federal informant on these activities.

6. Albert Gore in the case of Capital Recovery: "The subcommittee's investigation has uncovered evidence that since August, 1976, major industrial companies, such as Koppers, Inc., in one case Exxon, Union Chemical Company in the state of New Jersey certified that over 270,000 gallons of chemical waste were delivered to an out-of-state facility in Wilmington, Delaware, named Capital Recovery. From all the available evidence, Capital Recovery is nothing more than a paper corporation. It has no offices or any site in Wilmington. There is no phone listing, no city or State real estate tax or business tax information no annual report has been filed..." (U.S. House of Representatives, 1980: 135–136).

7. Other companies and associations making the same argument during these hearings included Monsanto, Exxon, B.F. Goodrich, Alcoa, the Texas Chemical Council, and the Western Oil and Gas Association.

8. The same point was also raised by Stauffer Chemicals, Marathon Oil, American Cyanamid, Berylco, Shell, Alcoa, the Texas Chemical Council, the Western Oil and Gas Association, the American Petroleum Institute, and the New Jersey Manufacturers Association.

9. The issue of flexible time frames was raised by the National Association of Manufacturers (U.S. House of Representatives, 1976: 190) and Exxon (U.S. EPA, 1976: 940). Arguing for a restricted definition of what is regulable hazardous waste were DuPont (U.S. EPA, 1976: 69), the American Iron and Steel Institute (U.S. EPA, 1976: 100), American Cyanamid (U.S. EPA, 1976: 1,550), B.F. Goodrich (U.S. Senate, 1974: 1,440), Stauffer (U.S. Senate, 1974: 1,746). Monsanto (U.S. EPA, 1976: 406–407), and Dow (U.S. EPA, 1976: 956), argued for fewer restrictions for on-site disposal.

10. It should be noted that generators intervened not only in policy formation but also engaged in ongoing efforts to weaken regulatory impact during implementation. They appeared at EPA implementation hearings to emphasize that the criteria for declaring substances hazardous were still too broad, that proposed disposal requirements were too stringent, that interim standards were burdensome and inflexible, and that recordkeeping and reporting requirements were onerous. Especially active in this period were trade associations such as the Manufacturing Chemists Association, the Synthetic Organic Chemists Manufacturing Association, the American Petroleum Institute, and the National Paint and Coatings Association, as well as large individual corporations such as Dow and DuPont (U.S. EPA, 1979; U.S. Senate, 1979). EPA officials complained privately that "the millions of pages of testimony filed by representatives of industry on virtually each clause of every implementation proposal" created "a major obstacle" to timely implementation of RCRA (Shabecoff, 1979: 1).

References

Albanese, Jay S.
1982 What Lockheed and La Cosa Nostra have in common: The effect of ideology on criminal justice policy. Crime and Delinquency 28: 211–232.

Barnett, Harold C.
1981 Corporate capitalism, corporate crime. Crime and Delinquency 27: 4–23.

Block, Alan A.
1982 "On the Waterfront" revisited: The criminology of waterfront organized crime. Contemporary Crisis 6: 373–396.

Block, Alan A. and William J. Chambliss
1981 Organizing Crime. New York: Elsevier.

Block, Alan A. and Frank R. Scarpitti
1985 Poisoning for Profit: The Mafia and Toxic Waste in America. New York: William Morrow.

Brady, James
1983 Arson, urban economy and organized crime: The case of Boston. Social Problems 31: 1–27.

Chambliss, William J.
1978 On the Take: From Petty Crooks to Presidents. Bloomington: Indiana University Press.

Clinard, Marshall B., Peter C. Yeager, Jeanne M. Brissette, David Petrashek, and Elizabeth Harries
1979 Illegal Corporate Behavior. Washington, D.C.: U.S. Government Printing Office.
Clinard, Marshall B. and Peter C. Yeager
1980 Corporate Crime. New York: The Free Press.
Crenson, Matthew A.
1971 The Un-Politics of Air Pollution: A Study of Non-Decisionmaking in the Cities. Baltimore: Johns Hopkins University Press.
Denzin, Norman K.
1977 Notes on the crimogenic hypothesis: A case study of the American liquor industry. American Sociological Review 42: 905–920.
Drucker, Peter P.
1981 What is business ethics? The Public Interest 63: 18–36.
Etzioni, Amitai
1985 Shady corporate practices. New York Times. November 15.
Farberman, Harvey A.
1975 A crimogenic market structure: The automobile industry. Sociological Quarterly 16: 438–457.
Gansberg, Martin
1979 New Jersey Journal. New York Times. January 21.
Geis, Gilbert
1977 The heavy electrical equipment antitrust cases of 1961. In Gilbert Geis and Robert F. Meier (eds.), White-Collar Crime: Offenses in Business, Politics, and the Professions (rev. ed.). New York: Free Press.
Getschow, George and Thomas Petzinger, Jr.
1984 Oil's legacy: Louisiana marshlands, laced with oil canals, are rapidly vanishing. The Wall Street Journal. October 24.
Governor's Commission on Science and Technology for the State of New Jersey
1983 Report of the Governor's Commission on Science and Technology.
Greenberg, Michael R. and Richard F. Anderson
1984 Hazardous Waste Sites: The Credibility Gap. Piscataway, NJ: Center for Urban Policy Research.
Leonard, William N. and Marvin G. Weber
1977 Automakers and dealers: A study of crimogenic market forces. In Gilbert Geis and Robert F. Meier (eds.), White-Collar Crime: Offenses in Business, Politics, and the Professions (rev. ed.). New York: Free Press.
Martens, Frederick T. and Colleen Miller-Longfellow
1982 Shadows of substance: Organized crime reconsidered. Federal Probation 46: 3–9.
Marx, Karl
1967 Capital: A Critique of Political Economy, Vol. 1. New York: International Publishers.
Needleman, Martin L. and Carolyn Needleman
1979 Organizational crime: Two models of crimogenesis. Sociological Quarterly 20: 517–528.
Petzinger, Thomas, Jr. and George Getschow
1984a Oil's legacy: In Louisiana, big oil is cozy with officials and benefit is mutual. The Wall Street Journal. October 22.

1984b Oil's legacy: In Louisiana, pollution and cancer are rife in the petroleum area. The Wall Street Journal. October 23.
Shabecoff, Philip
1979 House unit attacks lags on toxic waste. New York Times. October 14.
1985 Toxic waste threat termed far greater than U.S. estimates. New York Times. March 10.
Schelling, Thomas C.
1967 Economics and criminal enterprise. The Public Interest 7: 61–78.
Smith, Dwight C., Jr.
1980 Paragons, pariahs, and pirates: A spectrum-based theory of enterprise. Crime and Delinquency 26: 358–386.
Smith, Dwight C., Jr., and Richard D. Alba
1979 Organized crime and American life. Society 3: 32–38.
Snyder, David
1985a Toxic scars crisscross Louisiana. The New Orleans Times-Picayune. September 8.
1985b Early action was met with disbelief. The New Orleans Times-Picayune. September 8.
1985c Wastes choke scenic bayous of St. Charles. The New Orleans Times-Picayune. September 10.
1985d Chemical specter fills Cajun paradise with sense of fear. The New Orleans Times-Picayune. September 11.
1985e He won't be stopped, landfill operator warns. The New Orleans Times-Picayune. September 11.
1985f 10-year struggle to shut down waste site stymied by state. The New Orleans Times-Picayune. September 12.
Szasz, Andrew
1982 The dynamics of social regulation: A study of the formation and evolution of the Occupational Safety and Health Administration. Unpublished doctoral dissertation. Madison: University of Wisconsin.
1984 Industrial resistance to occupational safety and health legislation: 1971–1981. Social Problems 32: 103–116.
U.S. Environmental Protection Agency
1976 Hazardous Waste Management: Public Meetings. December 2–11.
1979 Public Hearings on the Proposed Regulations Implementing Sections 3001 to 3004 of the Resource Conservation and Recovery Act. February 22–23.
U.S. General Accounting Office
1985 Illegal Disposal of Hazardous Waste: Difficult to Detect or Deter. Comptroller General's Report to the Subcommittee on Investigations and Oversight, Committee on Public Works and Transportation, House of Representatives.
U.S. House of Representatives
1975 Waste Control Act of 1975. Hearings held by the Subcommittee on Transportation and Commerce, Committee on Interstate and Foreign Commerce. April 8–11, 14–17.
1976 Resource Conservation and Recovery Act of 1976. Hearings held by the Subcommittee on Transportation and Commerce, Committee on Interstate and Foreign Commerce. June 29–30.
1980 Organized Crime and Hazardous Waste Disposal. Hearings held by Subcommittee on Oversight and Investigations, Committee on Interstate and Foreign Commerce. December 16.

1981a Organized Crime Links to the Waste Disposal Industry. Hearings held by Subcommittee on Oversight and Investigations, Committee on Energy and Commerce. May 28.
1981b Hazardous Waste Matters: A Case Study of Landfill Sites. Hearings held by Subcommittee on Oversight and Investigations, Committee on Energy and Commerce. June 9.
1982 Hazardous Waste Enforcement. Hearings held by Subcommittee on Oversight and Investigations, Committee on Energy and Commerce. December.
1983 Hazardous Waste Disposal. Hearings held by Subcommittee on Oversight and Investigations. Committee on Science and Technology. March 30 and May 4.

U.S. Senate
1974 The Need for a National Materials Policy. Hearings held by the Subcommittee on Environmental Pollution, Committee on Public Works. June 11–13, July 9–11, 15–18.
1979 Oversight of RCRA Implementation. Hearings held by the Subcommittee on Environmental Pollution and Resource Protection, Committee on Environmental and Public Works. March 28–29.

Williams, Bruce A. and Albert R. Matheny
1984 Testing theories of social regulation: Hazardous waste regulation in the American states. Journal of Politics 46: 428–458.

37 / Handling the Stigma of Handling the Dead: Morticians and Funeral Directors

WILLIAM E. THOMPSON

In a complex, industrialized society a person's occupation or profession is central to his or her personal and social identity. As Pavalko (1988) pointed out, two strangers are quite "... likely to 'break the ice' by indicating the kind of work they do." As a result, individuals often make a number of initial judgments about others based on preconceived notions about particular occupations.

This study examines how morticians and funeral directors handle the stigma associated with their work. Historically, stigma has been attached to those responsible for caring for the dead, and the job typically was assigned to the lower classes (e.g., the Eta of Japan and the Untouchables in India), and in some cases, those who handled the dead were forbidden from touching the living (Bendann, 1930; Murray, 1964; Kearl, 1989). Today, the stigma has grown to new and potentially more threatening proportions for those engaged in the profession, for during the twentieth century Americans have become preoccupied with the denial of death (Sudnow, 1967; Becker, 1973; Charmaz, 1980; Jackson, 1980; Fulton, 1988; Momeyer, 1988; Kearl, 1989).[1] As Stephenson (1985, p. 223) noted, "In a society which seeks to deny the reality of death, the funeral director is a living symbol of this dreaded subject."

Two major problems faced by members of the funeral industry are that they make their living by doing work considered taboo by most Americans and that they are viewed as profiting from death and grief—a fact from which they must continually attempt to divert public attention. The "7-billion-dollar-a-year American funeral industry" has received much criticism over the past 2 decades, and widespread complaints have led to "congressional hearings, new trade practices rules from the Federal Trade Commission, and undercover sting operations by various consumer groups" (Kearl, 1989, p. 271). Those in the funeral business were further stigmatized when it was revealed that 58% of the funeral homes studied by the FTC had committed at least one billing abuse against their bereaved clients, and public testimony revealed "horror stories" of inflated charges for funeral services neither required nor requested (Kearl, 1989, p. 278).

Morticians and funeral directors are fully aware of the stigma associated with their work, so they continually strive to enhance their public image and promote their social credibility. They must work to shift the emphasis of their work from the dead to the living, and away from sales and toward service. As Aries (1976, p. 99) noted:

> In order to sell death, it had to be made friendly... since 1885... [funeral directors have] presented themselves not as simple sellers of services, but as "doctors of grief" who have a mission... [which] consists in aiding the mourning survivors to return to normalcy.

Couched within the general theoretical framework of symbolic interactionism, there are a variety of symbolic and dramaturgical methods whereby morticians and funeral directors attempt to redefine their occupations and minimize and/or neutralize negative attitudes toward them and what they do.

METHOD

This study reflects over 2 years of qualitative fieldwork as outlined by Schatzman and Strauss (1973), Spradley (1979), and Berg (1989). Extensive ethnographic interviews were conducted during 1987–1989 with 19 morticians and funeral directors in four states: Kansas, Missouri, Oklahoma, and Texas. The funeral homes included both privately owned businesses and branches of large franchise operations. They were located in communities ranging from less than 1,000 population to cities of over 1 million people.

First contacts were made by telephone, and appointments were made to tour the funeral homes and meet with the directors and morticians. Initial taped interviews ranged from $1\frac{1}{2}$ to a little over 4 hours in duration. In all but two cases, follow-up interviews were used to obtain additional information about the individuals and their work.

Rather than limiting questions to a standardized interview schedule, the researcher soon discovered that, as with most ethnographic fieldwork (Spradley, 1979; Berg, 1989), interviewees were much more comfortable and provided more information during casual conversation. Consequently, the structured portion of the interview focused primarily on demographic data, educational credentials, how they decided to enter the profession, how they felt about their jobs, and how they handled the stigma associated with their work. The questions were open-ended, and answers to one question invariably led to a variety of spontaneous follow-up questions.

RESPONDENTS

Interviewees included people from different age groups, both sexes, and both whites and nonwhites. There were 16 males and 3 females interviewed for this study, ranging in age from 26 to 64 years. Most of the respondents were between their late 30s and early 50s. Fourteen of the males were both morticians (licensed embalmers) and licensed funeral directors. The other two males were licensed embalmers who were employed in funeral homes, but were not licensed funeral directors. None of the females had been trained or licensed to embalm. Two of the females were licensed funeral directors, and the other woman was neither licensed as an embalmer nor funeral director. She was married to a man who was licensed to do both, and she simply helped out around the funeral home—usually answering the phone and helping with bookkeeping. All the women admitted, however, that they often helped out in the embalming room and in making funeral arrangements.

Seventeen of the people interviewed were white. The other two were African-American brothers who jointly owned and operated a funeral home located in a city of approximately 150 thousand people. Only one was a licensed funeral director and licensed embalmer. They candidly admitted, however, that they both worked in the embalming room and arranged funeral services.

With only one exception, all of the morticians and funeral directors interviewed were more than willing to talk about their occupations. They were aware that the author was conducting research, and several of them commented that the funeral industry was much maligned and stigmatized, and they were anxious to get an opportunity to "set the record straight," or "tell their side of the story" about their jobs. As the interviews progressed, however, the author was struck by the candor with which most of the interviewees responded to questions and provided additional information. Only one of the funeral directors, a single 50-year-old white male, was reluctant to talk about his work, refused to be taped, and was extremely guarded throughout the interview. He attempted to answer as many questions as possible with short, cryptic responses, and on several occasions became quite defensive and asked: "Why did you ask that?" and "What are you going to do with this information?" Despite his defensiveness, his answers indicated that his experiences as a mortician and funeral director were very similar to the others interviewed. In fact, his reticence about answering some of the questions served to underscore the fact that he believed there was a great deal of stigma attached to his work and he wanted to be careful not to add to it (a point he made verbally during the interview).

OCCUPATIONAL STIGMA

Erving Goffman (1963) defined *stigma* as any attribute that sets people apart and discredits them or disqualifies them for full social acceptance. This paper explores what happens when people are discredited (stigmatized) because of the work they perform, and how they attempt to reduce or eliminate the stigma.

People are most likely to be stigmatized because of their work if it is viewed as deviant by other members of society. George Ritzer (1977) cited three criteria, any one of which can cause an occupation to be considered deviant: (a) if it is illegal, (b) if it is considered immoral, and (c) if it is considered improper.

The first category of occupations, those that are illegal, has been widely studied by sociologists. Even a cursory list of studies on organized crime, prostitution, shoplifting, counterfeiting, confidence swindling, professional thievery, and other illegal occupations would be voluminous. The second category of deviant occupations is less straightforward than the first. Although many occupations that are considered immoral also have been made illegal (e.g., prostitution), there is much less agreement on the morality of occupations than on their legality.

The final category is a fascinating one, and perhaps the most ripe for sociological investigation. It includes those jobs that may not be considered "a proper or fitting occupation by society" (Polsky, 1969, p. 32). In any society there are certain jobs that most people prefer not to do. These jobs often require little or no training, pay very little, rank low in occupational prestige, and involve "dirty work" (Hughes, 1971; Garson, 1975). As Hughes (1971, p. 344) pointed out:

> ...the delegation of dirty work to someone else is common among humans. Many cleanliness taboos...depend for their practice upon success in delegating the tabooed activity to someone else.

Although the occupations of mortician and funeral director do not fit neatly into any of Ritzer's three categories, preparing the dead for funerals, burial, and/or cremation can be characterized as "dirty work." The stigma associated with these occupations is not so much that they are literally unclean, although embalming can be rather messy. It is, however, no more so than surgery—a highly prestigious profession. Rather, they are figuratively unclean because they violate social taboos against handling the dead.

The Stigma of Handling the Dead

Ritualistic disposal of dead human bodies is a cultural universal (Bendann, 1930; Habenstein & Lamers, 1960; Huntington & Metcalf, 1979). These ceremonies "...manifest the collective image of death—what the larger society thinks and feels about death" (Stephenson, 1985). In American society, death is surrounded by mystery and taboos. David Sudnow (1967) pointed out that Americans shun the idea that death is a natural process begun at birth; instead, they view death as a very brief process or an act.

Until the turn of the century, in this country, people died at home and friends and family members prepared the bodies for burial (Lesy, 1987). As medical knowledge and technology progressed and became more specialized, more and more deaths occurred outside the home—usually in hospitals. Death became something to be handled by a select group of highly trained professionals—doctors, nurses, and hospital staff. As fewer people witnessed death firsthand, it became surrounded with more mystery, and physically handling the dead became the domain of only a few.

Members or friends of the family relinquished their role in preparing bodies for disposal to an *undertaker,* "... a special person who would 'undertake' responsibility for the care and burial of the dead" (Amos, 1983, p. 2). From the beginning stigma was associated with funerary occupations because they were "linked to the American death orientation whereby the industry is the cultural scapegoat for failed immortality" (Kearl, 1989, p. 278).

To counter this stigma, undertakers (later to be called morticians) initially emphasized the scientific aspects of their work. Embalming and preparation for burial were presented as highly technical skills that required scientific knowledge and sophisticated training. Most states began licensing embalmers around the end of the nineteenth century (Amos, 1983). These licensed embalmers did not enjoy the prestige accorded to the medical profession, however, and almost immediately were surrounded by mystery and viewed as unusual, if not downright weird. They were not family members or friends of the deceased faced with the unsavory but necessary responsibility for disposing of a loved one's body, but strangers who *chose* to work with dead bodies—for compensation. Although most welcomed the opportunity to relinquish this chore, they also viewed those who willingly assumed it with some skepticism and even disdain. Having failed to gain the desired prestige associated with the scientific aspects of embalming, and realizing that emphasizing embalming only served to increase what was perhaps the most stigmatizing aspect of their work (handling the dead), morticians shifted the focus away from their working on the dead body to their work with the living by emphasizing their roles as funeral directors and bereavement counselors.

In contemporary American society, those who routinely handle the dead have entered what Michael Lesy calls the "forbidden zone." Lesy (1987, p. 5) points out:

> In some cultures, the dead are ritually unclean and those who touch them must be ritually cleansed. In America, those who deal with the dead have social identities that shift back and forth like stationary objects that seem to move from left to right and back again as one eye is opened and the other is closed. Sometimes they look like pariahs and deviants, sometimes like charlatans. Other times they look like heroes or even adepts, initiates, and priests. Those who deal with death work at an intersection of opposites, tainted by the suffering and decay of the body, transfigured by the plight of the self and the destiny of the soul. The world never considers anyone who routinely deals with death to be "pure"....

Sudnow (1967, pp. 51–64) underscored the negative attitudes toward people who work with the dead in describing how those who work in a morgue, for example, are "death-tainted" and work very hard to rid themselves of the social stigma associated with their jobs. Morticians and funeral directors cannot escape from this "taint of death" and they must constantly work to "counteract the stigma" directed at them and their occupations (Charmaz, 1980, p. 182). Warner (1959, p. 315) described the funeral director as "a private enterpriser who will do the ritually unclean and physically distasteful work of disposing of the dead in a manner satisfying to the living, at a price which they can pay." Fulton (1961) echoed this definition when he wrote, "In a word, the funeral director, by virtue of his close association with death, and by the 'relative' attitude he takes toward all funerals is, in a religious sense, 'unclean' " (p. 322).

Are morticians and funeral directors really that stigmatized? After all, they generally are well-known and respected members of their communities. In small communities and even many large cities, local funeral homes have been owned and operated by the same family for several generations. These people usually are members of civic organizations, have substantial incomes, and live in nice homes and drive nice automobiles. Most often they are viewed as successful business people. On the other hand, their work is surrounded by mystery, taboos, and stigma, and they often are viewed as cold, detached, and downright morbid for doing it. All the respondents in this study openly acknowledged that stigma was associated with their work. Some indicated that they thought the stigma primarily came from the "misconception" that they were "getting rich" off other people's grief; others believed it simply came from working with the dead. Clearly these two aspects of their work—handling the dead and profiting from death and grief—emerged as the two most stigmatizing features of the funeral industry according to respondents. Pine (1975) noted that funeral directors cannot escape the "contamination by death," and contended:

> ...people view individuals in such work as different...because they feel that they themselves could never do it and that there must be something "strange" about those who voluntarily choose to do it. (p. 38)

Kathy Charmaz (1980, pp. 174–206) discussed the stigma experienced by morticians, funeral directors, and others involved in "death work," and the negative impact that working with the dead can have on self-image. It is important from their perspective, she notes, that "who they are should not be defined by what they do" (p. 174). This idea was confirmed by all the respondents in this study in one way or another. As one funeral director/embalmer noted, "I don't want to be thought of as somebody who likes working with the *dead*—that's morbid—I enjoy what I do because I like working with the *living*."

MANAGING STIGMA

Erving Goffman wrote the most systematic analysis of how individuals manage a "spoiled" social identity in his classic work, *Stigma* (1963). He described several techniques, such as "passing," "dividing the social world," "mutual aid," "physical distance," "disclosure," and "covering," employed by the *discredited* and *discreditable* to manage information and conceal their stigmatizing attributes (pp. 41–104). Although these techniques work well for the physically scarred, blind, stammerers, bald, drug addicted, ex-convicts, and many other stigmatized categories of people, they are less likely to be used by morticians and funeral directors.

Except perhaps when on vacation, it is important for funeral directors to be known and recognized in their communities and to be associated with their work. Consequently, most of the morticians and funeral directors studied relied on other strategies for reducing the stigma associated with their work. Paramount among these strategies were: symbolic redefinition of their work, role distance, professionalism, emphasizing service, and enjoying socioeconomic status over occupational prestige. This was much less true for licensed embalmers who worked for funeral directors, especially in chain-owned funeral homes in large cities. In those cases the author found that many embalmers concealed their occupation from their neighbors and others with whom they were not intimately acquainted, by using the techniques of information control discussed by Goffman (1963).

Symbolic Redefinition

A rose by any other name may smell as sweet, but death work by almost any other name does not sound quite as harsh. One of the ways in which morticians and funeral directors handle the stigma of their occupations is through symbolically negating as much of it as possible. Language is the most important symbol used by human beings, and Woods and Delisle (1978, p. 98) revealed how sympathy cards avoid the use of the terms "dead" and "death" by substituting less harsh words such as "loss," "time of sorrow," and "hour of sadness." This technique is also used by morticians and funeral directors to reduce the stigma associated with their work.

Words that are most closely associated with death are rarely used, and the most harsh terms are replaced with less ominous ones. The term *death* is almost never used by funeral directors; rather they talk of "passing on," "meeting an untimely end," or "eternal slumber." There are no *corpses* or *dead bodies;* they are referred to as "remains," "the deceased," "loved one," or more frequently, by name (e.g., "Mr. Jones"). Use of the term *body* is almost uniformly avoided around the family. Viewing rooms (where the embalmed body is displayed in the casket) usually are given serene names such as "the sunset room," "the eternal slumber room," or, in one case, "the guest room."[2] Thus, when friends or family arrive to view the body, they are likely to be told that "Mr. Jones is lying in repose in the eternal slumber room." This language contrasts sharply with that used by morticians and funeral directors in "backstage" areas (Goffman, 1959, p. 112) such as the embalming room where drowning victims often are called "floaters," burn victims are called "crispy critters," and others are simply referred to as "bodies" (Turner & Edgley, 1976).

All the respondents indicated that there was less stigma attached to the term *funeral director* than *mortician* or *embalmer,* underscoring the notion that much of the stigma they experienced was attached to physically handling the dead. Consequently, when asked what they do for a living, those who acknowledge that they are in the funeral business (several indicated that they often do not) referred to themselves as "funeral directors" even if all they did was the embalming. *Embalming* is referred to as "preservation" or "restoration," and in order to be licensed, one must have studied "mortuary arts" or "mortuary science." Embalming no longer takes place in an *embalming room,* but in a "preparation room," or in some cases the "operating room."

Coffins are now "caskets," which are transported in "funeral coaches" (not *hearses*) to their "final resting place" rather than to the *cemetery* or worse yet, *graveyard,* for their "interment" rather than *burial.* Thus linguistically, the symbolic redefinition is complete, with death verbally redefined during every phase, and the stigma associated with it markedly reduced.

All the morticians and funeral directors in this study emphasized the importance of using the "appropriate" terms in referring to their work. Knowledge of the stigma attached to certain words was readily acknowledged, and all indicated that the earlier terminology was stigma-laden, especially the term "undertaker," which they believed conjured up negative images in the mind of the public. For example, a 29-year-old male funeral director indicated that his father still insisted on calling himself an "undertaker." "He just hasn't caught up with the twentieth century," the son remarked. Interestingly, when asked why he did not refer to himself as an undertaker, he replied, "It just sounds so old-fashioned [pause] plus, it sounds so morbid." As Pine (1975) noted, the special argot of the funeral industry performs an important function in reducing the stigma associated with the work and allows funeral directors to achieve role distance.

In addition to using language to symbolically redefine their occupations, funeral directors carefully attempt to shift the focus of their work away from the care of the dead (especially handling the body), and redefine it primarily in terms of caring for the living. The dead are de-emphasized as most of the funeral ritual is orchestrated for the benefit of the friends and family of the deceased (Turner & Edgley, 1976). By redefining themselves as "grief therapists," or "bereavement counselors" their primary duties are associated with making funeral arrangements, directing the services, and consoling the family in their time of need.

ROLE DISTANCE

Because a person's sense of self is so strongly linked to occupation, it is common practice for people in undesirable or stigmatized occupations to practice role distance (e.g., Garson, 1975; Terkel, 1974; Ritzer, 1977; Pavalko, 1988; Thompson, 1983). Although the specific role-distancing techniques vary across different occupations and among different individuals within an occupation, they share the common function of allowing individuals to violate some of the role expectations associated with the occupation, and to express their individuality within the confines of the occupational role. Although the funeral directors and morticians in this study used a variety of role distancing techniques, three common patterns emerged: emotional detachment, humor, and countering the stereotype.

Emotional Detachment

One of the ways that morticians and funeral directors overcome their socialization regarding death taboos and the stigma associated with handling the dead is to detach themselves from the body work. Charmaz (1980) pointed out that a common technique used by coroners and funeral directors to minimize the stigma associated with death work is to routinize the work as much as possible. When embalming, morticians focus on the technical aspects of the job rather than thinking about the person they are working on. One mortician explained:

> When I'm in the preparation room I never think about *who* I'm working on, I only think about what has to be done next. When I picked up the body, it was a person. When I get done, clean and dress the body, and place it in the casket, it becomes a person again. But in here it's just something to be worked on. I treat it like a mechanic treats an automobile engine—with respect, but there's no emotion involved. It's just a job that has to be done.

Another mortician described his emotional detachment in the embalming room:

> You can't think too much about this process (embalming), or it'll really get to you, For example, one time we brought in this little girl. She was about four years old—the same age as my youngest daughter at the time. She had been killed in a wreck; had gone through the windshield; was really a mess. At first, I wasn't sure I could do that one—all I could think of was my little girl. But when I got her in the prep room, my whole attitude changed. I know this probably sounds cold, and hard I guess, but suddenly I began to think of the challenge involved. This was gonna be an open-casket service, and while the body was in pretty good shape, the head and face were practically gone. This was gonna take a lot of reconstruction. Also, the veins are so small on children that you have to be a lot more careful. Anyway, I got so caught up in the job, that I totally forgot about working on a little girl. I was in the room with her about six hours when ______ [his wife] came in and reminded me that we had dinner plans that night. I washed up and went out to dinner and had a great time. Later that night, I went right back to work on her without even thinking about it. It wasn't until the next day when my wife was dressing the body, and I came in, and she was crying, that it hit me. I looked at the little girl, and I began crying. We both just stood there crying and hugging. My wife kept saying "I know this was tough for you," and "yesterday must have been tough." I felt sorta guilty, because I knew what she meant, and it should've been tough for me, real tough, emotionally,

but it wasn't. The only "tough" part had been the actual work, especially the reconstruction—I had totally cut off the emotional part. It sometimes makes you wonder. Am I really just good at this, or am I losing something. I don't know. All I know is, if I'd thought about the little girl the way I did that next day, I never could have done her. It's just part of this job—you gotta just do what has to be done. If you think about it much, you'll never make it in this business.

Humor

Many funeral directors and morticians use humor to detach themselves emotionally from their work.[3] The humor, of course, must be carefully hidden from friends and relatives of the deceased, and takes place in back-stage areas such as the embalming room, or in professional group settings such as at funeral directors' conventions.

The humor varies from impromptu comments while working on the body to standard jokes[4] told over and over again. Not unexpectedly, all the respondents indicated a strong distaste for necrophilia jokes. One respondent commented, "I can think of nothing less funny—the jokes are sick, and have done a lot of damage to the image of our profession."

Humor is an effective technique of diffusing the stigma associated with handling a dead body, however, and when more than one person is present in the embalming room, it is common for a certain amount of banter to take place, and jokes or comments are often made about the amount of body fat or the overendowment, or lack thereof, of certain body parts. For example, one mortician indicated that a common remark made about males with small genitalia is, "Well, at least he won't be missed."

As with any occupation, levels of humor varied among the respondents. During an interview one of the funeral directors spoke of some of the difficulties in advertising the business, indicating that because of attitudes toward death and the funeral business, he had to be sure that his newspaper advertisements did not offend anyone. He reached into his desk drawer and pulled out a pad with several "fake ads" written on it. They included:

"Shake and Bake Special—Cremation with no embalming"

"Business is Slow, Somebody's Gotta Go"

"Try our Layaway Plan—Best in the Business"

"Count on Us, We'll be the Last to Let You Down"

"People are Dying to Use our Services"

"Pay Now, Die Later"

"The Buck Really Does Stop Here"

He indicated that he and one of his friends had started making up these fake ads and slogans when they were doing their mortuary internships. Over the years, they occasionally corresponded by mail and saw each other at conventions, and they would always try to be one up on the other with the best ad. He said, "Hey, in this business, you have to look for your laughs where you can find them." Garson (1975, p. 210) refers to a line from a song from *Mary Poppins,* "In every job that must be done, there is an element of fun."

Countering the Stereotype

Morticians and funeral directors are painfully aware of the common negative stereotype of people in their occupations. The women in this study were much less concerned about the stereotype, perhaps because simply being female shattered the stereotype anyway. The men, however, not only acknowledged that they were well aware of the public's stereotypical image of them, but also indicated that they made every effort *not* to conform to it.

One funeral director, for instance, said:

> People think we're cold, unfriendly, and unfeeling. I always make it a point to be just the opposite. Naturally, when I'm dealing with a family I must be reserved and show the proper decorum, but when I am out socially, I always try to be very upbeat—very alive. No matter how tired I am, I try not to show it.

Another indicated that he absolutely never wore gray or black suits. Instead, he wore navy blue and usually with a small pinstripe. "I might be mistaken for the minister or a lawyer," he said, "but rarely for an undertaker."

The word "cold," which often is associated with death, came up in a number of interviews. One funeral director was so concerned about the stereotype of being "cold," that he kept a handwarmer in the drawer of his desk. He said, "My hands tend to be cold and clammy. It's just a physical trait of mine, but there's no way that I'm going to shake someone's hand and let them walk away thinking how cold it was." Even on the warmest of days, he indicated that during services, he carried the handwarmer in his right-hand coat pocket so that he could warm his hand before shaking hands with or touching someone.

Although everyone interviewed indicated that he or she violated the public stereotype, each one expressed a feeling of being atypical. In other words, although they believed that they did not conform to the stereotype, they felt that many of their colleagues did. One funeral director was wearing jeans, a short-sleeved sweatshirt and a pair of running shoes during the interview. He had just finished mowing the lawn at the funeral home. "Look at me," he said, "Do I look like a funeral director? Hell, ____ [the funeral director across the street] wears a suit and tie to mow his grass—or, at least he would if he didn't hire it done."[5]

Others insisted that very few funeral directors conform to the public stereotype when out of public view, but feel compelled to conform to it when handling funeral arrangements, because it is an occupational role requirement. "I always try to be warm and upbeat," one remarked, "But, let's face it, when I'm working with a family, they're experiencing a lot of grief—I have to respect that, and act accordingly." Another indicated that he always lowered his voice when talking with family and friends of the deceased, and that it had become such a habit, that he found himself speaking softly almost all the time. "One of the occupational hazards, I guess," he remarked.

The importance of countering the negative stereotype was evident, when time after time, persons being interviewed would pause and say "I'm not what you expected, am I?" or something similar. It seemed very important for them to be reassured that they did not fit the stereotype of funeral director or mortician.

PROFESSIONALISM

Another method used by morticians and funeral directors to reduce occupational stigma is to emphasize professionalism. Amos (1983, p. 3) described embalming as:

> ...an example of a vocation in transition from an occupation to a profession. Until mid-nineteenth century, embalming was not considered a profession and this is still an issue debated in some circles today.

Most morticians readily admit that embalming is a very simple process and can be learned very easily. In all but two of the funeral homes studied, the interviewees admitted that people who were not licensed embalmers often helped with the embalming process. In one case, in which the funeral home was owned and operated by two brothers, one of the brothers was a licensed funeral director and licensed embalmer. The other brother had dropped out of high school and helped their father with the funeral business while his brother went to school to meet the educational requirements for licensure. The licensed brother said:

> By the time I got out of school and finished my apprenticeship, ____ [his brother] had been helping Dad embalm for over three years—and he was damned good at it. So when I joined the business, Dad thought it was best if I concentrated on handling the funeral arrangements and pre-service needs. After Dad died, I was the only licensed embalmer, so, "officially" I do it all—all the embalming and the funeral arrangements. But, to tell you the truth, I only embalm every now and then when we have several to do, 'cause ____ usually handles most of it. He's one of the best—I'd match him against any in the business.

Despite the relative simplicity of the embalming process and the open admission by morticians and funeral directors that "almost anyone could do it with a little practice," most states require licensure and certification for embalming. The four states represented in this study (Kansas, Oklahoma, Missouri, and Texas) have similar requirements for becoming a licensed certified embalmer. They include a minimum of 60 college hours with a core of general college courses (English, mathematics, social studies, etc.) plus 1 year of courses in the "mortuary sciences," or "mortuary arts." These consist of several courses in physiology and biology, and a 1-year apprenticeship under a licensed embalmer. To become a licensed funeral director requires the passing of a state board examination, which primarily requires a knowledge of state laws related to burial, cremation, disposal of the body, and insurance.

All the respondents in this study who were licensed and certified embalmers and funeral directors exceeded the minimum educational requirements. In fact, all but one of them had a college degree, and three had advanced degrees. The most common degree held was a Bachelor of Science in mortuary sciences. Two of the males had degrees in business (one held the MBA degree), one male had a Bachelor's degree with a major in biology and had attended one year of medical school, one male had a degree in geology, and one had a degree in music. One of the women had a Bachelor's degree in English; another held a degree in business; and one woman had a degree in nursing. Although the general consensus among them was that an individual did not need a college education to become a good embalmer, they all stressed the importance of a college education for being a successful funeral director. Most thought that some basic courses in business, psychology, death and dying, and "bereavement counseling" were valuable preparation for the field. Also, most of the funeral directors were licensed insurance agents, which allowed them to sell burial policies.

Other evidence of the professionalization of the funeral industry include state, regional, and national professional organizations that hold annual conventions and sponsor other professional activities; professional journals; state, regional, and national governing and regulating boards; and a professional code of ethics. Although the funeral industry is highly competitive, like most other professions, its members demonstrate a strong sense of cohesiveness and in-group identification.

Reduction of stigma is not the sole purpose for professionalization among funeral directors and morticians, as other benefits are reaped from the process. Nevertheless, as Charmaz (1980, p. 1982) noted, membership in the professional organizations of coroners and funeral directors is one of the most effective ways to "counteract the stigma conferred upon them." One of the married couples in this study indicated that it was reassuring to attend national conventions where they met and interacted with other people in the funeral industry because it helps to "reassure us that we're not weird." The wife went on to say:

> A lot of people ask us how we can stand to be in this business—especially ______ because he does all of the embalming. They act like we must be strange or something. When we go to the conventions and meet with all of the other people there who are just like us—people who like helping other people—I feel *normal* again.

All these elements of professionalization—educational requirements, exams, boards, organizations, codes of ethics, and the rest—lend an air of credibility and dignity to the funeral business while diminishing the stigma associated with it. Although the requirements for licensure and certification are not highly exclusive, they still represent forms of boundary maintenance, and demand a certain level of commitment from those who enter the field. Thus, professionalization helped in the transition of the funeral business from a vocation that can be pursued by virtually anyone to a profession that can be entered only by those with the appropriate qualifications. As Pine (1975, p. 28) indicated:

> Because professionalization is highly respected in American society, the word "profession" tends to be used as a symbol by occupations seeking to improve or enhance the lay public's conception of that occupation, and funeral directing is no exception. To some extent, this appears to be because the funeral director hopes to overcome the stigma of "doing death work."

"By claiming professional status, funeral directors claim prestige and simultaneously seek to minimize the stigma they experience for being death workers involved in 'dirty work' " (Charmaz, 1980, p. 192).

THE SHROUD OF SERVICE

One of the most obvious ways in which morticians and funeral directors neutralize the stigma associated with their work is to wrap themselves in a "shroud of service." All the respondents emphasized their service role over all other aspects of their jobs. Although their services were not legally required in any of the four states included in this study, all the respondents insisted that people desperately *needed* them.[6] As one funeral director summarized, "Service, that's what we're all about—we're there when people need us the most."

Unlike the humorous fantasy ads mentioned earlier, actual advertisements in the funeral industry focus on service. Typical ads for the companies in this study read:

"Our Family Serving Yours for over 60 Years"

"Serving the Community for Four Generations"

"Thoughtful Service in Your Time of Need"

The emphasis on service, especially on "grief counseling" and "bereavement therapy" shifts the focus away from the two most stigmatizing elements of funeral work: the handling and preparation of the body, which already has been discussed at length; and retail sales, which are widely interpreted as profiting from other people's grief. Many of the funeral directors indicated that they believed the major reason for negative public feelings toward their occupation was not only that they handled dead bodies, but the fact that they made their living off the dead, or at least, off the grief of the living.[7]

All admitted that much of their profit came from the sale of caskets and vaults, where markup is usually a minimum of 100%, and often 400–500%, but all played down this aspect of their work. The Federal Trade Commission requires that funeral directors provide their customers with itemized lists of all charges. The author was provided with price lists for all merchandise and services by all the funeral directors in this study. When asked to estimate the "average price" of one of their funerals, respondents' answers ranged from $3,000 to $4,000. Typically, the casket accounted for approximately half of the total expense. Respondents indicated that less than 5% of their business involved cremations, but that even then they often encouraged the purchase of the casket. One said, "A lot of people ask about cremation, because they think it's cheaper, but I usually sell them caskets even for cremation; then, if you add the cost of cremation and urn, cremation becomes more profitable than burial."

Despite this denial of the retail aspects of the job, trade journals provide numerous helpful hints on the best techniques for displaying and selling caskets, and great care is given to this process. In all the funeral homes visited, one person was charged with the primary responsibility for helping with "casket selection." In smaller family-operated funeral homes, this person usually was the funeral director's wife. In the large chain-owned companies, it was one of the "associate funeral directors." In either case, the person was a skilled salesperson.

Nevertheless, the sales pitch is wrapped in the shroud of service. During each interview, the author asked to be shown the "selection room," and to be treated as if he were there to select a casket for a loved one. All the funeral directors willingly complied, and most treated the author as if he actually were there to select a casket. Interestingly, most perceived this as an actual sales opportunity, and mentioned their "pre-need selection service" and said that if the author had not already made such arrangements, they would gladly assist him with the process. The words "sell," "sales," "buy," and "purchase" were carefully avoided. Also, although by law the price for each casket must be displayed separately, most funeral homes also displayed a "package price" that included the casket and "full services." If purchased separately, the casket was always more expensive than if it was included in the package of services. This gave the impression that a much more expensive casket could be purchased for less money if bought as part of a service package. It also implied that the services provided by the firm were of more value than the merchandise.

The funeral directors rationalized the high costs of merchandise and funerals by emphasizing that they were a small price to pay for the services performed. One insisted, "We don't sell merchandise, we sell service!" Another asked, "What is peace of mind worth?" and another, "How do you put a price on relieving grief?"

Another rationalization for the high prices was the amount of work involved in arranging and conducting funeral services. When asked about the negative aspects of their jobs, most emphasized the hard work and long hours involved.[8] In fact, all but two of the interviewees said that they did not want their children to follow in their footsteps, because the work was largely misunderstood (stigmatized), too hard, the hours too long, and "the income not nearly as high as most people think."

In addition to emphasizing the service aspect of their work, funeral directors also tend to join a number of local philanthropic and service organizations (Pine, 1975, p. 40). Although many businessmen find that joining such organizations is advantageous for making contacts, Stephenson (1985, p. 223) contended that the small-town funeral director "may be able to counter the stigma of his or her occupation by being active in the community, thereby counteracting some of the negative images associated with the job of funeral directing."

Socioeconomic Status versus Occupational Prestige

Ritzer (1977, p. 9) pointed out that some jobs suffer from "occupational status insecurity." This clearly is the case with morticians and funeral directors. They are members of an occupation wrought with "social stigma... an occupational group which is extremely sensitive to public criticism, and which works hard to enhance its position in society" (Stephenson, 1985, p. 225).

It seems that what funeral directors lack in occupational prestige, they make up for in socioeconomic status. Although interviewees were very candid about the number of funerals they performed every year and the average costs per funeral, most were reluctant to disclose their annual incomes. One exception was a 37-year-old funeral home owner, funeral director, and licensed embalmer in a community of approximately 25,000 who indicated that in the previous year he had handled 211 funerals and had a gross income of just under $750,000. After deducting overhead (three licensed embalmers on staff, a receptionist, a gardener, a student employee, insurance, costs, etc.), he estimated his net income to have been "close to $250,000." He quickly added, however, that he worked long hours, had his 5-day vacation cut to two (because of a "funeral call that he had to handle personally") and, despite his relatively high income (probably one of the two or three highest incomes in the community), he felt morally, socially, and professionally obligated to hide his wealth in the community. "I have to walk a fine line," he said, "I can live in a nice home, drive a nice car, and wear nice suits, because people know that I am a successful businessman—but, I have to be careful not to flaunt it."

One of the ways he reconciles this dilemma was by enjoying "the finer things in life" outside the community. He owned a condominium in Vail where he took ski trips and kept his sports car. He also said that none of his friends or neighbors there knew that he was in the funeral business. In fact, when they inquired about his occupation, he told them he was in insurance (which technically was true because he also was a licensed insurance agent who sold burial policies). When asked why he did not disclose his true occupational identity, he responded:

> When I tell people what I really do, they initially seem "put off," even repulsed. I have literally had people jerk their hands back during a handshake when somebody introduces me and then tells them what I do for a living. Later, many of them become very curious and ask a lot of questions. If you tell people you sell insurance, they usually let the subject drop.

Although almost all the funeral directors in this study lived what they characterized as fairly "conservative lifestyles," most also indicated that they enjoyed many of the material things that their jobs afforded them. One couple rationalized their recent purchase of a very expensive sailboat (which both contended they "really couldn't afford") by saying, "Hey, if anybody knows that you can't take it with you, it's us—we figured we might as well enjoy it while we can." Another commented, "Most of the people in this community would never want to do what I do, but most of them would like to have my income."

SUMMARY AND CONCLUSION

A person's occupation is an integral component of his or her personal and social identity. This study describes and analyzes how people in the funeral industry attempt to reduce and neutralize the stigma associated with their occupations. Morticians and funeral directors are particularly stigmatized, not only because they perform work that few others would be willing to do (preparing dead bodies for burial), but also because they profit from death. Consequently, members of the funeral industry consciously work at stigma reduction.

Paramount among their strategies are symbolically redefining their work. This especially involves avoiding all language that reminds their customers of death, the body, and retail sales; morticians and funeral directors emphasize the need for their professional services of relieving family grief and bereavement counseling. They also practice role distance, emphasize their professionalism, wrap themselves in a "shroud of service," and enjoy their relatively high socioeconomic status rather than lament their lower occupational prestige.

Stephenson (1985; p. 231) pointed out an interesting paradox:

> In spite of our current preoccupation with death, we have given it a taboo status that implies a great deal of underlying fear and anxiety. Anything that will ease our fears is used to protect us from death. We give millions of dollars to fight disease, we occupy our spare time with staying physically fit, and we blunt death's awful impact with the use of the skills of the funeral director. While critics may consider such activities as barbaric or in bad taste, they are certainly in harmony with the basic values of American society.

Morticians and funeral directors are in a precarious social situation. They perform work that the majority of society believes is needed (Kastenbaum & Aisenberg, 1973), and although their services are not legally required, they are socially demanded. Yet, their occupations place them in a paradoxical position of performing duties deemed by larger society as "necessary," but "undesirable." Try as they may, they cannot fully escape the stigma associated with their work.

All but two of the people in this study indicated that if they had it all to do over again, they would choose the same occupation. Yet, only one indicated that he hoped his children pursued the funeral business. And, even he commented, "...but, they need to understand that it's hard work, and largely unappreciated." All agreed that one of their major tasks was handling the stigma of handling the dead.

Handling the dead will not become any more glamorous in the future, and that aspect of the mortician's work probably will continue to be stigmatized. However, if Americans become more comfortable with death and their own mortality, it also is likely that emphasizing morticians' roles as bereavement counselors will no longer be sufficient to redefine their work. If that is indeed the case, how will morticians and funeral directors symbolically redefine their work in the future to neutralize the stigma associated with handling the dead and profiting from grief? This research suggests that there is a growing tendency for funeral directors to emphasize their roles as "pre-need counselors." Since death is inevitable, and an aged population is more likely to recognize that, funeral directors may even more prominently tout themselves as akin to financial planners who can help in the advance planning and preparation of funeral arrangements. This could be important in neutralizing the two most stigmatizing attributes of their work. First, like previous strategies, it de-emphasizes the body work; secondly, and perhaps more importantly, it may alleviate some of the stigma associated with profiting from death and grief because they would be viewed as helping people to prepare for funeral needs in advance so that they might create a "hedge" against inflation and make important financial decisions at a time when they are not grief-stricken. Future research on the funeral industry should focus on this emerging role.

Notes

An earlier version of this paper was presented at the Southwestern Sociological Association meetings in Fort Worth, TX, March 28–31, 1990.

1. The wholesale denial of death in contemporary American society has been seriously questioned by some. For example, Parsons and Lidz (1967) eloquently refuted the "denial of death" thesis, indicating that "American society has institutionalized a broadly stable, though flexible and changing, orientation to death that is fundamentally not a 'denial' but a mode of acceptance appropriate to our primary cultural patterns of activism" (p. 134). In a later article Parsons, Fox, & Lidz (1972, p. 368) argued that "what is often interpreted as 'denial' is in reality a kind of 'apathy'...." They insist that, in a religious sense, death must be viewed as "a reciprocal gift to God, the consummatory reciprocation of the gift of life" (p. 415). Others counter, however, that death and funerals have become increasingly secularized and

that although constantly confronted with the realities of death, most Americans choose to ignore and deny it as much as possible (see references cited).

2. In this case the denial of death was symbolically enhanced by having the embalmed body lying in bed, as if asleep. The funeral director indicated that this room was used when families had not yet decided on a casket, thus allowing for viewing of the body in what he called a "natural, peaceful surrounding."

3. This is a common practice among medical students who are notorious for using "cadaver jokes" and pranks to help overcome the taboos associated with death and to ease the tension experienced when dissecting cadavers (Hafferty, 1986, 1988; Knight, 1973).

4. The author asked each respondent to tell his/her favorite joke about the occupation. One respondent was very indignant and said he hated all the jokes about the profession. All the others, however, quickly launched into what amounted to almost an amateur comedy routine. The author routinely heard several of the same jokes time and time again. Clearly, the most popular was several variations on the theme of burying someone in a rented tuxedo.

5. In many communities (especially small towns) rival funeral homes are located in close proximity, often across the street, or within a block of one another. A colleague, Michael Stein at the University of Missouri, St. Louis, suggests this is not unlike the clustering of other "stigmatized places," such as adult bookstores or adult movie theaters.

6. In Kansas, Missouri, Oklahoma, and Texas, as in most states, bodies do not have to be embalmed or cremated if a legal death certificate is obtained and the body is disposed of within 24 hours.

7. Several studies have focused on how unscrupulous members of the funeral industry capitalize on the grief of their customers to reap enormous profits from the sales of caskets, vaults, burial clothing, grave markers, and a variety of unnecessary and often unwanted "services" (e.g., see Consumers' Union, 1977; Harmer, 1963, Mitford, 1963, Fulton, 1988).

8. One funeral director estimated that he spent approximately 125 hours on each funeral, and performed on the average of 100 funerals a year. By his estimate, if he worked 24 hours per day, he would have to work 561 days a year!

References

Amos, E. P. (1983). *Kansas funeral profession through the years.* Topeka: Kansas Funeral Directors' Association.

Aries, P. (1976). *Western attitudes toward death: From the Middle Ages to the present.* (P. M. Ranum, Trans.), p. 99. Baltimore: Johns Hopkins University Press.

Becker, E. (1973). *The denial of death.* New York: The Free Press.

Bendann, E. (1930). *Death customs: An analytical study of burial rites.* New York: Alfred A. Knopf.

Berg, B. L. (1989). *Qualitative research methods for the social sciences.* Boston: Allyn and Bacon.

Charmaz, K. (1980). *The social reality of death: Death in contemporary America.* Reading, MA: Addison-Wesley.

Consumers' Union. (1977). *Funerals: Consumers' last rights.* New York: W. W. Norton and Company.

Fulton, R. (1961). The clergyman and the funeral director: A study in role conflict. *Social Forces,* 39, 317–323.

Garson, B. (1975). *All the livelong day: The meaning and demeaning of routine work.* Garden City, New York: Doubleday.

Goffman, E. (1959). *The presentation of self in everyday life.* Garden City, New York: Anchor Doubleday.

Goffman, E. (1963). *Stigma: Notes on the management of spoiled identity.* Englewood Cliffs, NJ: Prentice-Hall.

Habenstein, R. W., & Lamers, W. M. (1960). *Funeral customs the world over.* Milwaukee: Bulfin Printers.

Hafferty, F. W. (1986, March). Cadaver story humor. Paper presented at the annual meeting of the Midwest Sociological Society, Des Moines, IA.
Hafferty, F. W. (1988). Cadaver stories and the emotional socialization of medical students. *Journal of Health and Social Behavior,* 29, 344–356.
Harmer, R. M. (1963). *The high cost of dying.* New York: Collier.
Hodge, R. W., Siegal, P. M., & Rossi, P. H. (1964). Occupational prestige in the United States, 1925–63. *American Journal of Sociology,* 70, 290–292.
Hughes, E. C. (1958). *Men and their work.* Glencoe, IL: The Free Press.
Hughes, E. C. (1971). *The sociological eye: Selected papers.* Chicago: Aldine-Atherton.
Huntington, R., & Metcalf, P. (1979). *Celebrations of death.* Cambridge: Cambridge University Press.
Jackson, C. O. (1980). Death shall have no dominion: The passing of the world of the dead in America. In R. A. Kalish (Ed.), *Death and dying: views from many cultures* (pp. 47–55). Farmingdale, NY: Baywood.
Kastenbaum, R. & Aisenberg, R. (1972). *The psychology of death.* New York: Springer.
Kearl, M. C. (1989). *Endings; A sociology of death and dying.* New York: Oxford University Press.
Knight, J. A. (1973). *Doctor to be: Coping with the trials and triumphs of medical school.* New York: Appleton-Century-Crofts.
Lesy, M. (1987). *The forbidden zone.* New York: Farrar, Straus & Giroux.
Mitford, J. (1963). *The American way of death.* New York: Simon & Schuster.
Momeyer, R. W. (1988). *Confronting death.* Bloomington: Indiana University Press.
Murray, M. A. (1969). *The splendor that was Egypt* (rev. ed.). New York: Praeger.
Parsons, T. & Lidz, V. M. (1967). Death in American society. In E. Shneidman (Ed.), *Essays in self-destruction* (pp. 133–170). New York: Science House.
Parsons, T., Fox, R. C., & Lidz, V. M. (1972). The "gift of life" and its reciprocation. *Social Research,* 39, 367–415.
Pavalko, R. M. (1988). *Sociology of occupations and professions* (2nd ed.). Itasca, IL: F. E. Peacock.
Pine, V. R. (1975). *Caretaker of the dead: The American funeral director.* New York: Irvington.
Polsky, N. (1969). *Hustlers, beats and others.* Garden City, NY: Anchor.
Ritzer, G. (1977). *Working: Conflict and change* (2nd ed.). Englewood Cliffs, NJ: Prentice-Hall.
Salomone, J. J. (1972). The funeral home as a work system: A sociological analysis. In C. D. Bryant (Ed.), *The social dimensions of work* (pp. 164–177). Englewood Cliffs, NJ: Prentice-Hall.
Schatzman, L., & Strauss, A. L. (1973). *Field research: Strategies for a natural sociology.* Englewood Cliffs, NJ: Prentice-Hall.
Spradley, J. P. (1979). *The ethnographic interview.* New York: Holt, Rinehart & Winston.
Stephenson, J. S. (1985). *Death, grief, and mourning: Individual and social realities.* New York: The Free Press.
Sudnow, D. (1967). *Passing on: The social organization of dying.* Englewood Cliffs, NJ: Prentice-Hall.
Terkel, S. (1974). *Working: People talk about what they do all day and how they feel about what they do.* New York: Pantheon.

Thompson, W. E. (1983). Hanging tongues: A sociological encounter with the assembly line. *Qualitative Sociology,* 6 (Fall): 215–237.

Turner, R. E. & Edgley, D. (1976). Death as theater: A dramaturgical analysis of the American funeral. *Sociology and Social Research,* 60 (July): 377–392.

Warner, W. L. (1959). *The living and the dead.* New Haven: Yale University Press.

Wass, H., Berardo, F. M., & Neimeyer, R. A. (1988). The funeral in contemporary society. In H. Wass, F. M. Berardo, & R. A. Neimeyer (Eds.), *Dying: Facing the facts* (2nd ed.). New York: Hemisphere.

Woods, A. S. & Delisle, R. G. (1978). The treatment of death in sympathy cards. In C. Winick (Ed.), *Deviance and mass media* (pp. 95–103). Beverly Hills: Sage.

38 / Good People Doing Dirty Work: A Study of Social Isolation

DAVID S. DAVIS

INTRODUCTION

Everett Hughes in his essay "Good People and Dirty Work" writes of how the extermination of Jews in Nazi Germany was dirty work carried out by a small group of individuals so that the rest of German society, most of whom supported this activity, could remain distant from it and maintain a conception of themselves as good. Hughes implies the pathological and defective may be found among those who do the dirty work in society. Hughes (1964:34) writes, "that we have a sufficient pool or fund of personalities warped toward perverse punishment and cruelty to do any amount of dirty work that the good people may be inclined to countenance." Others have argued that stigmatized occupations attract certain kinds of individuals who, because of their psychological or social characteristics contribute to the occupation's reputation (see Saunders [1981] for discussion of this point). However, given that there is an "unwillingness to think about the dirty work done [and] complicated mechanisms by which the individual mind keeps unpleasant or intolerable knowledge from consciousness" (Hughes, 1964:27) it could be argued that the definition of dirty workers as warped and perverse serves as a further distancing mechanism for the "good." Instead, perhaps, we should consider the possibility that many dirty workers are really no different from the good people; that they are good people *doing* dirty work. To strip them of their respectability by defining them as disrespectable (Ball, 1970) strengthens the respectability of others.

The theme of "dirty work" has been picked up by those who study occupations (Blau, 1982; Goldman, 1981; Killian; 1981, Saunders, 1981; Simoni and Ball, 1977; Jabobs and Retsky, 1975). In particular, some sociologists have been interested in the "manner in which the socially deviant do the 'necessary' but unacknowledged 'dirty work' for the 'good people' whose respectability must keep them above such things" (Simoni and Ball, 1977:361). The performance of what is perceived as dirty work plays a crucial part in an individual's self identity, since occupation has become the main determinant of status and prestige (Goldschalk, 1979; Hughes, 1951). Being a dirty worker can make claims to self worth difficult.

Ball (1970:329) notes that "respectability is a central concern of actors in the problematic dramas of mundane life." Respectability is not a generic characteristic of an individual or group, but is a product of social relationships. Ball distinguishes between the "*unrespectable*" who agree with the audience's perception of them as not meriting respect, and the "*disrespectable*" who reject the way in which they are perceived. In this paper we examine a group of dirty workers, some of whom are *unrespectable* and some of whom are *disrespectable.* We show how these different perceptions of self result in different social consequences. In particular, there is a tendency for the *disrespectable* to become socially isolated.

There have been only a few sociologists who have examined social isolation. Lemert (1953), for instance, in his discussion of solitary check forgers finds that their lack of integration, "is reflected in self-attitudes in which many refer to themselves as 'black-sheep' or as a kind of Dr. Jeckyll-Mr. Hyde person" (p. 148). In prison, the check forger is marginal to and is isolated from the other prisoners. Similarly, Wulbert (1965) accounts for the lack of organized collective behavior in mental hospitals and the opposite in prisons by an absence of inmate pride in the former and its presence in the latter. Inmate pride for mental patients would require an acceptance of their inmate status. If, by attitude, we mean "a process of individual consciousness which determines activity" (Thomas and Znaniecki, 1918: 21–22) for both systematic check forgers and institutionalized mental patients the reason for their social isolation must be sought, in part, in their *self attitudes.*

Schneider and Conrad (1980) in their study of epileptics present their subjects as being isolated from one another. The authors state that the "very desire to lead conventional and stigma-free lives further separates and isolates them from each other" (p. 42). Here the authors intimate that the reason for their isolation must be sought in the epileptic's *attitude toward conventional society.*

Goffman (1963:107–108) devotes a short discussion to the actor who finds it difficult to affiliate with like others:

> Whether closely aligned with his own kind or not, the stigmatized individual may exhibit identity ambivalence when he attains a close sight of his own kind behaving in a stereotyped way, flamboyantly or pitifully acting out the negative attributes imputed to them. The sight may repel him, since after all he supports the norms of the wider society, but his social and psychological identification with these offenders holds him to what repels him, transforming repulsion into shame, and then transforming ashamedness itself into something of which he is ashamed. In brief, he can neither embrace his group nor let it go.

While not socially isolated, this actor is somehow stuck between his tainted fellows and conventional society. He embraces the values and norms of conventional society, recognizes he violates them, but is repelled by his fellows. Part of the source of this ambivalence, for Goffman, is found in the actor's *attitude to like others.*

Faced with an inability to pass amidst conventional society and rejected by it, it would, from this work, appear that social isolation could result from a combination of three attitudes held by the discredited actor. First, a self attitude that the perception of himself as lacking in moral worth is unjustified; that he is not what he is said to be. Second, an attitude to like others that, to some extent, the attribution of stigma to the members of the group to which he belongs has at least some justification. Third, an attitude of acceptance toward conventional society's values and norms. Faced by rejection by members of conventional society, yet believing that he rightly belongs to it, it would make sense for the actor to reject affiliation with like others or other discredited actors when he believes them to lack respect. To associate with them would undermine his attempt to be seen as respectable. The crucial variable here is the actor's belief that he is unjustifiably being defined as a dirty worker, that he is being falsely accused. While this belief would not seem to necessarily result in social isolation, its presence would appear to increase the probability that social isolation will occur.

The following study examines a set of socially isolated stigmatized individuals and traces that adaptation to their consciousness of self as falsely accused. These individuals are bailbondsmen (also called bondsmen): those who work for a living by charging fees to get defendants out of jail prior to trial. They are contrasted with avowedly dishonest bailbondsmen (the unrespected), and compared as well with members of several other discredited occupations and statuses.

METHODS

Twenty-five bailbondsmen (one of whom was female), in and surrounding a county in a Northeastern state, were given unstructured interviews in sessions totalling from one to six hours. Two additional bondsmen in this area were intensively interviewed. One set of these interviews lasted 26 hours over ten sessions and the other lasted 18 hours over seven sessions. In addition to the interviews, over 100 hours were spent in participant observation and observing bondsmen as they worked in their offices, court rooms, and work related travel.

Using interview data, observations, and reputational data, bondsmen were classified as considering themselves "honest," meaning that engaging in dishonest, illegal, or unethical behavior as part of their routine work activities was seen by them to be rare and "dishonest," meaning that engaging in dishonest, illegal, or unethical behavior was seen by them to be part of and common to their work routine. For the latter, to have not engaged in those activities would have meant radically changing that routine.

Among the dishonest activities observed and self reported by bondsmen were: the bribing of lawyers, judges and policemen; recommending lawyers to defendants; soliciting cases from lawyers; withholding security deposits from defendants; having foreknowledge of crimes; and failing to report cash receipts as income. As part of this classification procedure most of the bondsmen were asked the following question about each of the bondsmen interviewed: "Do you consider [name of bondsman] to be honest or dishonest?" Bailbondsmen also rated themselves as either honest or dishonest. There was a high degree of agreement between ratings based on interviews and observations, and the bondsmen's ratings of themselves and others (Davis, 1982). Twenty-one bondsmen were classified as "honest" and six bondsmen were classified as "dishonest." To obtain additional information about bondsmen, the author attended a state regulated bailbondsman course, became a bondsman and conducted a national mail survey of bondsmen.

The survey consisted of a random sample of 307 bailbondsmen in 48 communities around the United States. The sample was stratified by the number of bailbondsmen per community. The sampling frame was bailbondsmen advertisements in the telephone yellow pages, which yielded names of 3120 bailbondsmen. Thirty-seven questionnaires were returned as "addressee unknown" and "not deliverable as addressed." Eighty-one bondsmen responded for a 33 percent response rate. There was no follow up.

This survey should not be taken to constitute a reliable random sample of bailbondsmen. For one thing, the universe of bailbondsmen may be quite different from those who advertise in the yellow pages, although from this study it appears that most bailbondsmen do advertise in the yellow pages. The most systematic bias may arise from the low response rate. The survey was a source of data that supplemented the other data collected.

THE BAILBONDSMAN

The bailbondsman is an individual who, for a fee, will post bail for an accused defendant and thereby achieve that defendant's release from custody. In return the bailbondsman assumes the risk of forfeiting the entire bail amount should the defendant fail to appear for trial. There are approximately 4200 bailbondsmen in the United States (DeRhoda, 1979; Lazar Institute, 1981). The results of the mail survey indicate 82 percent of bondsmen are male (n = 66) and 87 percent are white (n = 70). The mean age of the respondents was 47.8. Bondsmen are most likely to work alone. Thirty-three (89 percent, missing data = 44) of the respondents worked in low prestige jobs prior to becoming bondsmen, jobs only slightly higher in prestige than their fathers'. However, 22 percent (n = 8, missing data = 45) of the respondents had fathers who were bailbondsmen (Davis, 1982).

Bailbondsmen as Disrespected

Like many other occupations of low status in the occupational systems of which they are a part, the occupation of bailbondsmen lacks respect. An advocate of pawnbrokers describes the general problem of these low status occupations in the following passage (Levine, 1913:14; see also, Hartnett, 1981):

> In every trade there are practitioners whose business methods react unfavorably upon their fellow tradesmen. Public opinion is very prone to condemn all in the trade as equally delinquent, making little discrimination between the honest and the dishonest. This attitude is one from which the pawnbroker has most unjustly suffered.... Experience has taught them that the innocent as well as the guilty will suffer at the hands of an unthinking public.

The image of the "heavy-set, cigar chomping, sinister" (Wice, 1974:50) bailbondsman has never been a good one. In 1905 a former Police Chief of New York, William McAdoo (1905:80–81) wrote about them:

> They threaten the destruction of honest police captains... they hound and prosecute an officer who interferes with their schemes or lessens their profits; they drive good and honest policemen into being bad ones; they have a price for every man on the force.... The sergeant at the desk is often only their tool; and the Captain and his plainsclothesmen and other officers have in many cases made arrests only to furnish victims and money for these unspeakable scoundrels. There should be a law against the professional bondsman.

Most of what has been written about bondsmen emerges from both a reform minded perspective and the journalistic muckraking tradition. These approaches seek to present the occupation as dysfunctional for the criminal justice system and the bailbondsman as corrupt and criminal. Goldfarb (1965:101–102), for instance, pictures bondsmen as:

> ...undesirable persons, former felons, and generally repugnant characters. Some bondsmen are colorful Runyonesque characters. Some are legitimate businessmen. But too many are "low-lifes" whose very presence contaminates the business profession.... (V)ery frequently, if not generally, the bailbondsman is an unappealing and useless member of society. He lives on the law's inadequacy and his fellowmen's troubles. He gives nothing in return, or so little as to serve no overriding utilitarian purposes.

The bailbond system is seen to be corrupted by the individuals who become bailbondsmen. This corruption then spreads to other parts of the criminal justice system. Similar views have been echoed by investigatory committees (for instance, see U.S. Task Force on Law and Law Enforcement, 1970), newspapers, and magazines (for instance, see the recent expose in *Cleveland Plain Dealer* [1980] and other authors: see Roth, 1962; Breslin, 1963; Freed and Wald, 1964; Foote, 1966; Barnes, 1969; Smith and Ehrmann, 1974; Thomas, 1976). Bailbondsmen have been the constant object of vilifying attacks and moral crusades. Smith and Ehrmann (1974:36) wrote that, "the real evil in the [bail] situation is not the matter of easy bail, but the disreputable bondsman... so far as it may be impossible to eliminate the professional bondsman, his business should be regulated like that of the 'Loan Sharks' in many jurisdictions." The *Cleveland Plain Dealer* (1980) presented bailbondsmen as "parasites who feed off the misfortunes of others." They "feed on legal system, get fat on misery."

Bailbondsmen possess what Saunders (1981:43) has defined as occupational stigma.

> Occupational stigma is a discrediting attribute accorded to individuals or groups who are performing certain occupationally identifiable roles... by other individuals or groups within a community, representing an actual threat to full social acceptance for the socially disgraced (by reason of their work function) who are perceived as negatively departing from the work norm of those engaged in "respectable" occupational activities.

Awareness of Stigma

Bailbondsmen believe that conventional society perceives them as odious and they believe conventional society rejects association with them as a consequence of that perception. Both bailbondsmen who considered themselves to be respectable businessmen and those who consider themselves justly accused evinced this belief.[1] As one bondsman who considered himself to be falsely accused responded to the mail survey:

> Bailbondsmen, unlike other professionals, must start out with the opinion that they are crooks. It is a near impossibility for a bondsman, no matter how honest he is, to prove he is an honest businessman.

Another bondsman responded in an interview saying, "When people know you are a bondsman they don't want you in their house."

Workers in other dirty work occupations reveal a similar awareness. A garbageman interviewed in Perry's (1978:108) study of his occupation reported the following:

> People don't want to have anything to do with you. They ask you what you do. You tell them, and they right away think you make so much money. It's... okay, but it's not more than they get.... Maybe it is all in my head, but it seems like they go to the other side of the street if they see you coming.

In another study of garbagemen, Saunders (1981:32) reports one as saying, "I know chaps who change their clothes because they do not want their neighbors to know what work they do." And Bleackley (1929:xviii) describes the particular stigma of the hangman:

> (T)he necessity to perform unpleasant duties in other walks of life does not involve a social stigma. The occupations of the dentist and the dustman, the butcher, the sanitary inspector and the man midwife are frequently of an unsavoury description and yet we do not ostracise these persons in consequence. The surgeon

kills many more people every year than "Jack Ketch," but the reason we refrain from placing him beyond the pale is not because, unlike the hangman's work, it is not done on purpose. He happens to belong to a trade that is not taboo, whereas "Jack Ketch" does not.

Attitude to and Association with Like Others

Structurally, the relationship between bondsmen is primarily a competitive one, as they compete for a limited number of bailbonds within a geographically defined area. This may account, in part, for the antipathy between them. However, this antipathy is not universal. It is manifested, for the most part, by those bondsmen who consider themselves to be respectable and honest. As two of these bondsmen said:

> Ali Baba and his forty thieves would rank second to other bondsmen.

> Most bondsmen are shit. They have no morals. They are not stand up straight guys. Half of them aren't worth a damn.

Interaction between these bondsmen was limited to the requirements of their work. Indicative, was the comment of one in an interview:

> Look, I don't like to have too much to do with them [bondsmen]. I like to be around a better class of people if they'll let me.

This contrasted with the six bailbondsmen classified as "dishonest" who were interviewed and observed. They did not show antipathy to like others. Two of these six bailbondsmen were good friends. They each spoke about seeing each other socially outside the work setting. They also, upon occasion, participated in illegal activities together. An additional two of these bondsmen spoke of being friendly with other bondsmen (in other counties). None of the six bondsmen was averse to associating with other bondsmen.

Although bondsmen represent a discredited group which is the frequent object of attack by respectable society, organizations of bondsmen to counter these attacks appear to be rare, have low membership, and little commitment from most members (Davis, 1982). None of the bondsmen interviewed were members of such an organization.

The falsely accused bondsman, while recognizing individual bondsmen as respectable, attempts to separate himself from bondsmen as a whole. He sees himself as a particularly respectable businessman. Dishonest bondsmen on the other hand, tend to see themselves and other bondsmen as quite alike. One said, "We are in this boat together—all part of the swill."

Browne (1973:58) found a similar response among used car salesmen who "are quick to point out the difference between themselves and their kind of operation as contrasted with other used car salesmen and their less scrupulous, less honest kind of operation." This is despite the fact that Browne (p. 58) finds that "(t)hey are almost always operating well within the law. . . . " Similarly, an 18th century writer (Anonymous, 1745:4) describes pawnbrokers as rejecting association with others. They are "a Sett of Men that never associated with any other tradesmen.... "

Bailbondsmen have the opportunity to affiliate with discredited individuals apart from other bondsmen; clients of bondsmen and their acquaintances. However the falsely accused bondsmen interviewed and observed distanced themselves from their clients and their world. As one of these bondsmen said:

> To me it's strictly business. I don't want to be bothered by people like that. I wouldn't want them in my home either. It happens to be a lousy business I am in.

And another remarked:

> They're [clients] the lowest of the low. I wouldn't go near them except to get their money or help them.

By contrast, five of the six avowedly dishonest bondsmen were firmly enmeshed in a social network consisting of individuals who engaged in criminal activity on a frequent basis. Their relationships with them were both of a business and social nature.

Gold (1964:27) describes attitudes among janitors that are very similar to those of "disrespectable" bondsmen:

> Janitors are keenly aware of their occupation's lowly reputation in the community. Yet, as individuals, they develop self-conceptions of the sort that ordinarily would be found in members of established middle-class occupations. How, then, does the janitor reconcile his self-conceptions with corresponding social conceptions of janitors? He uses a simple, clear-cut device. After comparing himself with occupational associates, he tends to agree that the community is right in its evaluation of *them,* but that *he* is "different." He agrees that other janitors are unprincipled, disorderly, and irresponsible. However, he, the individual janitor, belongs to the category of practitioners who are morally sound, capable, and responsible.

Attitude to and Association with Conventional Society

Bailbondsmen routinely encounter rejection from respectable society. Bailbondsmen have described how this rejection may occur in the workplace:

> Judges think bondsmen are lower than whale shit. They think we socialize with criminals. A judge would never lower himself to talk to a bondsman.

And outside the workplace:

> When people know you are a bondsman they don't want you in their house.

Pine (1977:38), in his study of funeral directors, has found a similar tendency for them to be rejected:

> Another problem for funeral directors is the occasional banning of funeral homes from certain community areas. Even in the absence of zoning regulations, funeral

homes have been closed or forced to move when they were offensive to neighbors in residential areas. Also troublesome is that the funeral home ban may extend to the funeral director himself.... (F)uneral directors have been denied membership in organizations solely because of their occupation.

The falsely accused bailbondsman is aware of how he is perceived by respectable society. Respectable society forms, in a sense, the bailbondsman's "looking glass self" (Cooley, 1964:183–184). He believes respectable society both perceives him and judges him as dishonest and sleazy. But respectable society also forms his normative reference group. It is with them that he identifies and aspires to belong. To condemn conventional society as being as evil as the bailbondsman would be to corrupt his own aspiration to be accepted as respectable; it would bring him closer to the world of the stigmatized which he shuns. Rather he aligns himself with respectable society. The falsely accused sees respectable society as no better than he is and at the same time compares himself favorably to it. Thus, he not only points to the illegal activities of respectable people, but, in addition, sees his normal work activities on an equal footing with high status occupations. As one respondent wrote to illustrate the first point that dirty workers are to be found in all occupations:

I would suggest there are so many bad apples in other professions except a couple of educators used federal money to lobby and defame the profession (of bondsmen) because of some unethical men. There are many excellent men in the field. There are many excellent men in the field that are outstanding citizens. There are bad insurance agents, bad salesmen, bad students, just bad plain citizens, and bad politicians.... There are many corrupt police, courts, and other enforcement people, and the percentage is fairly high from what I see.

And in demonstrating the second point, that bailbonding is not dirty work, another respondent wrote:

It must be remembered that we are normally well educated and well versed in many professions. We, to operate successfully, must have in many respects the knowledge of attorneys, police officers, investigators, collection agencies, car salesmen, court clerks, judges and loan officers and bankers.

The falsely accused bailbondsman justifies his work as socially valuable. He sees himself as a good person *doing* dirty work. A bailbondsman said:

I feel that having bailbondsmen are a service to the community because all persons that are locked up cannot make a bond. And we try to be selective, but be kind where there is reason, even though persons may be involved with drugs, alcohol, and other habits. We also save the taxpayer money when he does not show in court. We stand the loss and have to find the missing person, and keep a record of those that do not show, and will see that other bondsmen will not take the same person out.

The falsely accused bailbondsman embraces conventional values of honesty, compassion, monetary success, professionalism. In interviews falsely accused bondsmen remarked:

> I treat my business as a career and handle it with care, compassion and brains. The reason I became a bondsman was there wasn't any here. Lots of blacks were getting arrested and nobody seemed to care. I got into it as a civil thing. This was a good will thing. I made money too. We all know that it's for the dollars.... You must be honest with the person, go according with the law, be honest with yourself.

Like the janitors described in Gold's (1964) study, the bailbondsman's "conceptions of himself are thoroughly wrapped up in his work. He is aware that society judges him, and that he judges himself, largely by the work he does. He is consciously trying to achieve higher status through public recognition of higher work status" (p. 21).

Social Isolation

The falsely accused bondsmen tend to lead lives of social isolation. Following Seeman's (1972) definition of social isolation, these bondsmen have a "low expectancy for inclusion and social acceptance, expressed typically in feelings of loneliness or feelings of rejection and repudiation."

These feelings have been detailed earlier in the paper. But there are other indicators of social isolation that we can point to. Only five of the twenty-one falsely accused bondsmen said they were members of community organizations, although, only two were active members. When I asked a bondsman why he was not a member of any organization he said:

> First of all, I haven't got the time for such stuff. Then I tried joining one once but they didn't like the idea of a bondsman being a member, I guess.

We find that for the falsely accused bondsman work activities are structured so that very little time is available for non-work activity:

> What social contact do you make? A college professor meets people that is his equal or better than you. You don't have to worry about your social life. If a bailbondsman wants to live a clean life and not associate with these people, he's limited. And then your time, you're working so many hours that you don't have time to go out and socialize. Your life passes you by and what do you end up with?

The twenty-one falsely accused bailbondsmen studied worked a mean of 76 hours a week. The six dishonest bailbondsmen worked, as bailbondsmen, a mean of 36 hours a week.

Many of the avowedly dishonest bondsmen saw their work as bondsmen as less central to their overall activities. One individual, for instance, could be said to have become a bondsman because of his involvement with others in criminal activity. He was active in many illegal activities prior to becoming a bondsman (fencing cars, running numbers, and gambling). Many of his friends and associates were also engaged in these and other illegal activities. He saw becoming a bondsman as an opportunity to make money regardless of whether it was done legally. His contact with criminals, he believed would be useful to him. Three of these bondsmen professed to have grown up with others who routinely engaged in criminal activity. The first job of one of these individuals prior to becoming a bondsman was to pay off bondsmen and lawyers for professional criminals who wanted cases fixed and for other services. Another commented, "The only people I knew were criminals."[2] As bondsmen, except for social isolation, immersion in a stigmatized subculture remained their most viable option. As one of these bondsmen commented during an interview:

> You know, I got my friends: car thieves, robbers, bad guys. But that's all I got. I'm stuck with them and they're stuck with me.

Unlike the falsely accused bondsmen, it is not respectable society that is their reference group, but the world peopled by professional and petty criminals. The falsely accused bondsman finds it difficult to join or embrace the straight world because it often will not have him. Yet to embrace the world of the stigmatized is not a solution either. To associate with his fellow bondsmen (some of whom are dishonest and all of whom are generally believed to be dishonest) would be to confirm and strengthen, in the eyes of his audience, their original evaluation of him, thus furthering the difficulty of becoming respectable. The falsely accused bondsman does not feel he is doing anything wrong. Rather, he feels wronged. The image he presents of himself as respectable clashes with the way he believes he is viewed by respectable society. Rather than immersing himself in a stigmatized subculture or forming, with other bondsmen, a subculture of the stigmatized or an organization of the stigmatized (solutions that would belie his self image of respectability) he often chooses social isolation.

Occupants of similarly disparaged work roles also report feelings of social isolation. Sanson the executioner (1881:xii, 19) describes his life in Paris:

> I have lived for twelve years under a name which is not mine, reaping with something like shame the friendship and good will which I constantly fear to be dispelled by the discovery of my former avocations.... A glance at (my ancestor) was sufficient to identify him as the executioner; men, women, and children recoiled from him.

In an 1824 pamphlet an anonymous writer describes the plight of the pawnbroker (Anonymous, 1824):

> Perhaps no class of men ever were greater sufferers from this cause (that honorable people dislike them) than the persons I am advocating. Owing to it, their personal intercourse, and friendly communication with society have been interrupted; clouds of suspicion have been raised without any cause, and evils believed which never existed.
>
> Their profession has been deemed dishonourable—their hearts callous—their sentiments illiberal; and, though I may be bold to say, many of them, in their walk of life, have been and are, considered persons of the most irreproachable

> character, yet the excellency of their conduct scarcely ever did more than remove the odium from themselves in the general circle to which they are confined, while the general prejudice has grown stronger from age, and more inveterate by repetition.

Similarly, Saunders (1981) in his study of lower grade workers in service organizations found that janitors and nightwatchmen are often isolates.

There were good reasons why many of the falsely accused bondsmen became socially isolated. Some of these reasons arise from the structure of the occupation itself which limits available options. Because bondsmen constantly have clients "out on the street" it is difficult to stop being a bondsman once one has become established in the occupation. Thus, it is difficult to resume or assume the role of the conformist.[3] At the same time, to pursue a livelihood as a bondsman, the individual must make it known that he is one; to advertise himself. This makes "passing" a difficult option to pursue. In addition, although there is some degree of cooperation between bondsmen, it is essentially a highly competitive business. Often resources are scarce and demand is low. Bondsmen also often work alone or in small partnerships. This may be less a result of animosity than economic rationality. As Robinson (1935:50) has argued, in conditions where there is a high degree of uncertainty, small firms are likely to be more successful than large ones. Organizational alliances become difficult to forge under these circumstances. However, these structural reasons cannot be seen as sufficient explanations for the social isolation of the falsely accused bondsman. As we pointed out, there are good reasons why we should expect organizations of bondsmen to form. In addition, we have seen that their dishonest counterparts are not socially isolated. The social isolation of the falsely accused is an adaptation to their dilemma of believing themselves to be respectable, desiring to be perceived and accepted as respectable, and encountering rejection from respectable society.

CONCLUSION

The social categories to which bailbondsmen, janitors, garbagemen, the mentally ill, and others belong are stigmatized. That is, these individuals by virtue of their membership in these social categories are perceived as blemished and defective. Further, as a result of this perception, they encounter rejection by conventional society. Rather than accept this view of themselves some of them attempt to be and define themselves as respectable and conformist. The falsely accused's knowledge and perception that like others may be engaged in discrediting behavior may make him wary of association with other members he believes may bring ill repute upon him in his quest for respectability. Given structural conditions that make other forms of adaptation (neutralization, passing, and "rehabilitation") difficult, this may result in his social isolation between conventional and stigmatized worlds.

Stonequist (1942:297), in his discussion of the marginal man, alludes to a similar phenomenon:

> The marginal man is the individual who lives in, or has ties of kinship with, two or more interacting societies between which there exists sufficient incompatibility to render his own adjustment to them difficult or impossible.

The social isolate is this marginal man. His isolation is made possible by three elements: 1) rejection or hostility from conventional society; 2) a belief on the part of the actor that he is being unjustly excluded from that society; and 3) an attitude toward like others and other stigmatized individuals that sees them as rightfully rejected.

We can see that if the actor can see like others as sharing in what he sees as his injustice that he may likely affiliate with them. One has only to point to the many organizations of discredited groups. But for each of these groups there are probably individuals who lie outside and isolated from them. While among Jews there are countless organizations and subcultural supports there is still the Wandering Jew (Stonequist, 1942:307):

> They (the individual marginal Jew) . . . are divided in their social allegiance, drawn forward by the Gentile world but uncertain of its hospitality, restrained by sentiments of loyalty to the Jewish world but repelled by its restrictions. They are self-conscious and feel inferior because their social status is in question. They are the partly assimilated, the partly accepted, the real Wandering Jews, at home neither in the ghetto nor in the world outside the ghetto.

Believing oneself to be falsely accused and isolating oneself from like others and discredited others results in a paradoxical and ironic situation. If being truly accused is likely to result in affiliation with stigmatized others in a situation where one is provided with social support, believing oneself to be falsely accused may result in a social role that lacks social support. The actor who considers himself "innocent" may suffer isolation as a result. The actor who considers himself correctly stigmatized may find himself in a more positive social position. Further, this social isolation makes it more difficult to neutralize the stigma and, at the same time, makes it easier to stigmatize the actor. The inability of the falsely accused bailbondsmen to organize and protest the attributions made against them, in turn, made it easier for the attributions to be made regardless of their validity.

This conception of self and its relationship to others can be seen to have a direct bearing on the very creation of stigma; who, how, and why some individuals and groups are successfully discredited. Under some circumstances (for instance, when members of a group are competing with one another) it may be easier to discredit certain groups of individuals when those individuals *deny* the validity of that definition. Denial of stigma may then result in increased difficulty in neutralizing the stigma.

Notes

1. While most members of the public may have only a superficial knowledge of bailbondsmen, the bailbondsman is in daily association with those individuals in part responsible for creating their disparaged image.

2. These bondsmen can be seen in one way as the archetypal deviant who is immersed in a subculture. However, they also illustrate the problem with that literature: the difficulty in determining whether their immersion in a deviant subculture was an adaptation to social reaction or a factor in producing their initial rule breaking.

3. Gold (1964:43) found that for similar reasons janitors who see retirement "as the termination of distasteful work . . . rarely reach their goal."

References

Anonymous
1745 A Plain Answer to a Late Pamphlet. Entitled The Business of Pawnbroking Stated and Defended. London: George Woodfall.

Anonymous
1824 An Apology for the Pawnbrokers Most Respectfully Addressed to the Members of Both Houses of Parliament, the Judges of the Land and the Justices of the Peace throughout the Kingdom, Leadenhall Street: S. McDowell.

Ball, Donald W.
1970 "The problematics of respectability." Pp. 326–371 in Jack D. Douglas (ed.), Deviance and Respectability: The Social Construction of Moral Meanings. New York: Basic.

Barnes, Fred
1969 "The professional bondsman: life isn't what it used to be." Sunday Magazine, Washington Star, August 17.

Blau, Judith
1982 "Prominence in a network of communication: work relations in a children's psychiatric hospital." Sociological Quarterly 23:235–251.

Bleackley, Horace
1929 The Hangmen of England. London: Chapman and Hall.

Breslin, Jimmy
1963 "Best bet for bail: a good crook." Life (March 23):15–16.

Browne, Joy
1973 The Used-Car Game: A Sociology of the Bargain. Lexington, Mass.: Heath.

Cooley, Charles Horton
1964 Human Nature and the Social Order. New York: Schocken Books.

Cleveland Plain Dealer
1980 "Bailbondsmen here feed on legal system, get fat on misery." August 3, Section A:1.

Davis, David Scott
1982 Deviance and Social Isolation: The Case of the Falsely Accused. Unpublished Ph.D. dissertation, Princeton University.

DeRhoda
1979 "Whither the bailbondsman." Law Journal 1:19.

Foote, Caleb (ed.)
1966 Studies in Bail. Philadelphia: University of Pennsylvania Press.

Freed, Donald and Patricia Wald
1964 "Bail in the United States: 1964." Working Papers for the National Conference on Bail and Criminal Justice, Washington, D.C.
Goffman, Erving
1963 Stigma. Englewood Cliffs, N.J.: Prentice-Hall.
Gold, Raymond L.
1964 "In the basement—the apartment-building janitor." Pp. 1–49 in Peter Berger (ed.), The Human Shape of Work. New York: Macmillan.
Goldfarb, Ronald
1965 Ransom: A Critique of the American Bail System. New York: Harper and Row.
Goldman, Marion S.
1981 "Book review of Robert Prus and Styllianos Irini, Hookers; Rounders, and Desk Clerks: The Social Organization of a Motel Community." Sociology of Work and Occupations 8:381–384.
Goldschalk, J. J.
1979 "Foreign labour and dirty work." The Netherlands' Journal of Sociology 15:1–11.
Hartnett, Catherine
1981 "The pawnbroker: banker of the poor?" Pp. 149–155 in Israel L. Barak-Glantz and C. Ronald Huff (eds.), The Mad, the Bad, and the Different: Essays in Honor of Simon Dinitz. Lexington, Mass.: Lexington Books.
Hughes, Everett C.
1951 "Work and self." Pp. 313–323 in John H. Rohrer and Muzafer Sherif (eds.), Social Psychology at the Crossroads. New York: Harper.
1964 "Good people and dirty work." Pp. 23–26 in Howard Becker (ed.), The Other Side. New York: Free Press.
Jacobs, James B. and Harold C. Retsky
1975 "Prison guard." Urban Life 4:5–29.
Killian, Lewis M.
1981 "The sociologists look at the Cuckoo's nest: the misuse of ideal types." The American Sociologist 16:230–239.
Lazar Institute
1981 Advisory Panel Meeting on Bail Bonding Study. Washington, D.C., April 10.
Lemert, Edwin
1953 "An isolation closure theory of check forgery." Journal of Criminal Law, Criminology, and Police Science 44(3):296–307.
Levine, S.
1913 The Business of Pawnbroking: A Guide and a Defense. New York: D. Halpern.
McAdoo, William
1905 Guarding a Great City. New York: Harper.
Perry, S. E.
1978 San Francisco Scavengers: Dirty Work and the Pride of Ownership. Berkeley: University of California Press.
Pine, V.
1977 Caretaker of the Dead: The American Funeral Director. New York: Irvington.

Robinson, E.
1935 The Structure of Competitive Industry. London: Nisbet.
Roth, J.
1962 "Bondsman looks back wistfully to days of reliable criminals." New York Times (September 20):35.
Sanson, Henry (ed.)
1881 Memoirs of the Sansons. Picadilly: Chatto and Windus.
Saunders, Conrad
1981 Social Stigma of Occupations: The Lower Grade Worker in Service Organizations. Westmead: Gower.
Schneider, Joseph and Peter Conrad
1980 "In the closet with illness: epilepsy, stigma potential and information control." Social Problems 28(1):32–44.
Seeman, Melvin
1972 "Alienation and engagement." Pp. 467–527 in Angus Campbell and Phillip E. Converse (eds.), The Human Meaning of Social Change. New York: Russell Sage.
Simoni, Joseph J. and Richard A. Ball
1977 "The Mexican medicine huckster: he must be doing something right." Sociology of Work and Occupations 4:343–365.
Smith, Reginald H. and Herbert B. Ehrmann
1974 "The Municipal Court in Cleveland." Pp. 26–59 in John Robertson (ed.), Rough Justice: Perspectives on Lower Criminal Courts. Boston: Little Brown.
Stonequist, Everett
1942 "The marginal character of the Jews." In Isacque Graeber and Steuart Brett (eds.), Jews in a Gentile world: The Problems of Anti-Semitism. Westport, Conn.: Greenwood.
Thomas, Wayne
1976 Bail Reform in America. Berkeley: University of California Press.
Thomas, William Isaac and Florian Znaniecki
1918 The Polish Peasant in Europe and America, Vol. 1. Chicago: University of Chicago Press.
U.S. Task Force on Law and Law Enforcement
1970 The Rule of Law: An Alternative to Violence. Nashville: Aurora Publishers.
Wice, Paul
1974 Freedom for Sale: A National Study of Pretrial Release. Lexington, Mass.: Lexington Books.
Wulbert, Roland
1965 "Inmate pride in total institutions." American Journal of Sociology 71(1):1–9.

Part 6 / Changing Deviance

Part 4 offered materials that demonstrate how a person's public identity becomes transformed into a "deviant" identity. Central to this process is the "status denunciation ceremony," in which a collective effort is made to place an institutional tag upon a person. This status-conferring process was especially evident in those articles dealing with the involuntary processing and incarceration of clients as mental patients. The articles also helped to underscore the fact that the institutional deviant has relatively little to say about his or her processing. It has been emphasized, too, that the identity-transformation process is generally rather routine.

How the labeled deviant actually perceives and responds to institutional processing is often difficult to judge. As we have seen, some will accept the label, while others will either reject or ignore it. The individual's response is critical in the alteration of a deviant identity—that is, in moving from a deviant to a nondeviant status, with the deviant label being removed during the process of change. For example, if an individual rejects an institutional label, he or she can expect to encounter various types of difficulties. The plight of McMurphy (discussed in the general introduction) offers an illustration of this. Not only did he reject the "sick role," but his resistance, when viewed from the institution's perspective, was taken as a sign that he needed help. In this instance, the prognosis for change—again from the institution's viewpoint (i.e., its theory of the office and associated diagnostic stereotypes)—was extremely poor. A patient may, however, accept the label and act in accordance with institutional expectations. Such patients thus become willing parties in the transformation process.

Even if individuals decide to conform to social norms, they will most certainly encounter numerous structural and individual barriers—barriers that often reduce the probability that they will elect to change their behavior. The ex-deviant, as I have noted in the general introduction, frequently experiences difficulty finding housing and employment, primarily because others, in general, continue to react to the person as a deviant. Institutional processing is very systematic and efficient in tagging individuals as deviants. The reverse process, however, is anything but systematic and efficient. Specifically, there are few, if any, institutional mechanisms that can be used to systematically remove deviant labels (and the associated stigma) from individuals. Thus, deviants are often left to fend for themselves. Obviously, giving ex-cons a bit of money and a suit of clothes, without helping them to deal with potential structural barriers (e.g., having to indicate they are ex-cons on job applications) and individual problems (e.g., feelings of low self-esteem) is not going to do much by way of "rehabilitating" them. A viable model of change, or "rehabilitation," must incorporate a concern for both individual and structural factors. Even this, however, is not enough.

Clearly, if the underlying images, conceptions, and categories of deviance are altered (as discussed in Part 1), then the picture of deviance and the deviant must undergo some corresponding changes. Analytically, it is useful to think in terms of the transformation of deviant categories, as well as the transformation of actors and structures. As an example, certain crimes may become decriminalized, and acts that were formerly perceived as deviant may become acceptable. The selections in this part explore possibilities such as these. The initial two pieces analyze how the content of prevailing conceptions and categories may be transformed. The next two selections examine how actors may attempt to transform their deviant identity. The final selections illustrate some of the ways in which deviant organizations, decision makers, and structures can be controlled, sanctioned, or even altered.

DEVIANT CONCEPTIONS AND CATEGORIES

A central theme in Part 1 was the idea that the reactions of social observers provide acts with meanings—that is, indicate whether the acts are deviant or nondeviant. (Duster's analysis of how drug use became criminalized offered an excellent account of this.) In "Reform the Law: Decriminalization," Samuel Walker provides a provocative analysis of how removing selected types of behavior from the statutes may affect the picture of crime and deviance. He begins by drawing most heavily upon the classic work by Morris and Hawkins, *The Honest Politician's Guide to Crime Control,* and notes that these authors propose to decriminalize acts in seven areas: (1) drunkenness, (2) narcotics and drug abuse, (3) gambling, (4) disorderly conduct and vagrancy, (5) abortion, (6) sexual behavior, and (7) juvenile delinquency. The rationale for decriminalizing these domains is predicated primarily upon three arguments: many of the existing laws, in their applications, are "criminogenic" (i.e., produce more crime); they overburden the justice system; and they violate individual rights. Walker's working proposition, and one that is centered on a major concern of his, is that "with the possible exception of heroin policy, decriminalization is simply irrelevant to the control of robbery and burglary." Hence, he is concerned mainly with what he views as being serious crime. In an effort to establish, as well as substantiate, the irrelevance of a linkage between most victimless crimes and the serious crimes of robbery and burglary, the author offers a balanced and insightful examination of the arguments and evidence associated with each of the areas listed by Morris and Hawkins. For example, in terms of the proposal to decriminalize most sexual activities (e.g., adultery, fornication, cohabitation, prostitution, and the like), he contends that many good arguments—some of which he reviews briefly—have been advanced for doing so. Walker does caution us, however, that decriminalization in a selected area may not reduce the ancillary crime connected with it. Customers may still be mugged or robbed before, during, or after their sexual encounter with a prostitute.

Patricia A. Adler and Peter Adler, in "Tinydopers: A Case Study of Deviant Socialization," offer another account of how an existing deviant or criminal category can undergo significant change. The authors focus on "tinydopers"—that is, marijuana-smoking children under nine years old. Adler and Adler are concerned initially with outlining the societal conditions that produced a "moral passage," or transformation, of marijuana's social and legal status from criminalization to relative legitimization. The authors are also interested in demonstrating what is likely to happen when smoking spreads to one of society's most sacred groups, children. The researchers present a five-stage model of social change that they feel captures the diffusion and legitimization of marijuana. For example, during Stage I (the 1940s), the "carriers" or users were what Adler and Adler term "stigmatized outgroups" (blacks). By Stage II (the 1950s), usage had spread to "ingroup deviants" (e.g., jazz musicians) who identified with the stigmatized outgroups. From there, usage spread to such "avant-garde ingroup members" as college students (Stage III, the 1960s), to such "normal ingroups members" as the middle class (Stage IV, the 1970s), and finally to such "sacred groups" as children (Stage V, from 1975 on). Adler and Adler maintain that the spread of deviance to Stage V can produce social revulsion and can trigger attempts to ban the behavior by children; this appears to be the case with respect to the tinydopers. Throughout, one can obtain an excellent feel for the moral passage of marijuana. Of interest, too, are the ways in which parents manage a potentially discrediting feature about their child. Some, for example, are concerned that their tinydoper will tell others and thus take certain precautions; other parents are relatively unconcerned.

DEVIANT ACTORS

As I have suggested, noninstitutional deviants (e.g., drug addicts and prostitutes) and institutional deviants (e.g., mental patients and delinquents) who elect to change their deviant behavior can expect to encounter a range of structural and individual roadblocks—roadblocks that may ultimately produce a relapse or further deviance.

Douglas Degher and Gerald Hughes, in "The Identity Change Process: A Field Study of Obesity," offer an identity change process model that can be used to analyze the ways in which a social actor may attempt to alter his or her behavior. They, similarly to the thrust of this book, focus on the notion of career shifts, and particularly those internal and external features or cues that may prompt a change in an actor's status. Their analysis is given to obesity. The authors note initially that obese or fat people frequently suffer in certain ways. Not only do the obese feel the brunt of a range of negative stereotypes but they may be discriminated against in various domains (e.g., in terms of college admissions, wages, and employment). The obese or fat label, the authors contend, can, in terms of Becker's description in Part 2, be viewed as a "master status," whereby people tend to respond to one's "fatness" and not to one's other status features or traits. The identity change process itself must be examined on two levels: the public and the private or internal. And in terms of the public dimension, two cognitive processes must be satisfied prior to the completion of an identity change: the involved must recognize the inappropriateness of his or her current status, as well as locate a new more appropriate status. Active (e.g., being teased or called chubby) and passive (e.g., standing on a scale) cues are important in this process. For example, they provide information about one's degree of fatness and, as such, impact on the two major internal components of "recognizing" and "placing." An actor may, in terms of the cues received, "recognize" that his or her current status is inappropriate. He or she may, also relative to the "placing" process, begin a search for a new, more appropriate status. The final stage in the process entails the acceptance of a new status. Acceptance of the new status, the researchers note, may entail becoming involved in weight reduction programs.

Thomas J. Schmid and Richard S. Jones, in "Suspended Identity: Identity Transformation in a Maximum Security Prison," present an interesting variant of the identity change process. Their attention is given to inmates incarcerated in a maximum security prison. Of interest are not only the ways in which inmates may suspend their preprison identities but how inauthentic prison identities may be constructed. They note initially that most inmates have little in common prior to their imprisonment; they also have little knowledge about what prison is like. However, inmates are required to come to grips with the fact of their incarceration. An inmate often finds himself trying to manage a dualistic self, trying to balance his "true" identity (i.e., his preprison identity) with his "false" identity (i.e., his prison identity). The researchers note that this separation of identities "represents two conscious and interdependent identity-preservation tactics, formulated through self-dialogue and refined through tentative interaction with others." Schmid and Jones present an excellent diagram illustrating the major features involved in the identity change process. They conclude by discussing how an inmate's postprison identity may be impacted along certain dimensions in various domains.

DEVIANT ORGANIZATIONS, DECISION MAKERS, AND STRUCTURES

As is evident throughout this book, it is the social actor—and usually a person who is relatively powerless—who becomes selected out and processed as a deviant by some type of people-processing or people-changing institution. As I have already argued, it is the actor who must alter behavior. Placing the burden for change exclusively upon the individual, however, effectively means that the decision makers and their organizations escape scrutiny. Yet there is solid evidence pointing to the need for such examinations. In Part 4, Scheff and Culver's data on the perfunctory treatment of involuntary mental patients and Jeffery's study of the indifferent handling of "rubbish" offer excellent cases in point. Policywise, an important message is also contained in research such as Scheff and Culver's: if an institution's underlying organizational structure (i.e., its theory of the office, diagnostic stereotypes, career lines, and staff socializing procedures) remains unaltered, then selected categories of clients can expect to be typed and treated in a routinized, stereotypical, and uncaring fashion. Predictably, if Scheff and Culver's involuntary mental patients continue to be processed on the basis of a working ideology that presumes mental illness, we can expect that these patients will be committed. Similarly, if low-income and minority students continue to be processed in accordance with a theory of the office that presumes differential ability, we can expect failure, dropouts, and youth deviance. This need for focusing on underlying structures and ideologies applies not only to such formal, bureaucratic entities as the mental institution and the school, but to other types of groupings and organizations as well. Watson's description of the content of the outlaw motorcyclist subculture (Part 2), Hunt and Manning's analysis of police lying (Part 4), Best and Luckenbill's discussion of the social organization of deviants (Part 5), and Chambliss' depiction of state-organized crime (Part 5) offer but a few examples underscoring the need for focusing on underlying organizational structures. In terms of a more specific illustration, if the values and associated normative configurations of the outlaw motorist subculture remain intact, recruits, once socialized, will exhibit the expected behavior and attitudes. If, however, significant change is to occur on the part of the motorcyclists, it must come initially from an overhauling of those components (values and norms) that are inculcated within the individual. The same applies with respect to those who process mental patients, disadvantaged students, and other perceived "societal misfits." Clearly, a different theory of the office, once effectively ingrained within the decision makers, would produce changes in client processing. As an example, if educators and counselors presume that *all* students have strong abilities, the need for sorting, categorizing, or stratifying students would be reduced substantially. Thus, in the analysis of change, attention must be given not only to the social actor but to the decision makers, the institutions, and the underlying theories of the office.

Brent Fisse and John Braithwaite, in "The Impact of Publicity on Corporate Offenders: The Ford Motor Company and the Pinto Papers," illustrate and document some of the difficulties involved in trying to control and regulate organizations and their decision makers who engage in what may be perceived as deviant activities. Their focus is corporate misconduct, and they contend initially that, even though corporate violence and crime are widespread, corporations are rarely prosecuted for such crimes as homicide or assault. Fisse and Braithwaite note that the Pinto trial in Indiana provided an important exception to this. The authors begin by describing the events that culminated in the actual trial. Briefly, the trial evolved as a result of a 1978 accident in which three women were burned fatally when their 1973 Pinto was rear-ended. Not only was a grand jury convened subsequently, but the hearing itself became centered primarily on the safety and location of the Pinto's fuel system—a system with the tank located just six inches in front of the rear bumper. As a result of this hearing, the National Highway and Traffic Safety Administration initiated a defect proceeding against Ford in April of 1978, and Ford countered by announcing a voluntary recall of all Pintos produced between 1971 and 1976. Events such as these, however, triggered a number of liability actions against Ford, the most notable of which was the Grimshaw suit that produced an award of $128.5 million in damages. The authors point out that, even though this suit was civil in nature, the awarding of punitive damages was based on the assumption that Ford's corporate leaders possessed knowledge about the dangers associated with the location of the Pinto's fuel tank and, hence, could be found liable in a criminal proceeding. Three indictments of reckless homicide were eventually returned against Ford. The trial itself attracted a great deal of media coverage, with much of it being of an adverse nature for Ford. Particularly damaging was the publication of "Pinto Madness," an award-winning article by Mark Dowie. A portion of this piece claimed that secret internal company documents showed that, in spite of tests demonstrating that crash-tests of Pintos traveling in excess of 25 miles per hour resulted in a ruptured fuel tank, no structural alterations were made. The needed improvement would have cost approximately $11 per car and saved 180 fiery deaths a year. One of the most significant elements of the trial was the fact that a corporate defendant was being tried. Even though an acquittal was reached, the trial did produce a range of financial and nonfinancial impacts. For example, because of the Pinto scare, Ford's market share dropped, along with the value of its stock. And in terms of nonfinancial effects, executives felt that their image and reputations had been tarnished. They also worried about the long-term impact the trial might have on sales, as well as the attempts at product and safety legislation that might be generated.

The last selection ("Rehabilitating Social Systems and Institutions") is from my book *Creating School Failure, Youth Crime, and Deviance.* I initially describe how legislators, practitioners, professionals, and others, with their rather strict and exclusive focus on the individual, help to perpetuate what I have termed a "medical-clinical-individualistic" model of change and treatment. I then offer evidence demonstrating how such a model frequently affects the social actor, who may elect to alter his or her behavior. Most significantly, people become caught between two worlds—the conforming and the nonconforming. Not only does this dilemma give rise to a great deal of anxiety and self-debate, but the actor soon learns that neither world is likely to change much. Thus, "the individual must weigh the costs and benefits that may ensue by virtue of involvement with one culture as opposed to another." Frequently—and due to such factors as peer pressure, as well as unsatisfactory experiences with former friends and family members—the actor will exhibit a relapse. Defining failure in *individual* terms and not in *structural-organizational* terms is associated with other serious limitations; most notably, this viewpoint protects the real culprits from scrutiny and analysis. In support of this thesis, I conclude with an analysis of how the educational system, by virtue of the way it is structured organizationally (i.e., its use of ability groups, tracks systems, and career lines), actually builds and perpetuates deviant careers for particularly vulnerable categories of students, such as black and low-income pupils. I also outline how, with the inculcation of a different theory of the office within educators, parents, and others, changes could be produced. These ideological and organizational alterations have implications for the rehabilitation of any social system or institution.

39 / Reform the Law: Decriminalization

SAMUEL WALKER

The "first principle" advanced by Norval Morris and Gordon Hawkins in the 1970 book, *The Honest Politician's Guide to Crime Control*, involved removing a broad range of crimes from the statutes. Decriminalization of certain types of behavior has long been a major item on the liberal crime control agenda. In his book *Crime and Punishment: A Radical Solution*, Aryeh Neier, then Executive Director of the ACLU, offered decriminalization as his most substantive crime reduction proposal.[1]

For liberals the problem is what Morris and Hawkins call the "overreach" of the criminal law. It covers too wide a range of human behavior. Too much of it expresses the moralistic concerns of particular groups who are offended by the behavior of others. Morris and Hawkins urge us to "strip off the moralistic excrescences on our criminal justice system so that it may concentrate on the essential." They propose decriminalization in seven general areas:

1. **Drunkenness.** Public drunkenness shall cease to be a criminal offense.
2. **Narcotics and drug abuse.** Neither the acquisition, purchase, possession, nor the use of any drug will be a criminal offense. The sale of some drugs other than by a licensed chemist (druggist) and on prescription will be criminally proscribed; proof of possession of excessive quantities may be evidence of a sale or of intent to sell.
3. **Gambling.** No form of gambling will be prohibited in the criminal law; certain fraudulent and cheating gambling practices will remain criminal.
4. **Disorderly conduct and vagrancy.** Disorderly conduct and vagrancy laws will be replaced by laws precisely stipulating the conduct proscribed and defining the circumstances in which the police should intervene.
5. **Abortion.** Abortion performed by a qualified medical practitioner in a registered hospital shall cease to be a criminal offense.
6. **Sexual behavior.** Sexual activities between consenting adults in private will not be subject to the criminal law. [In the following areas,] adultery, fornication, illicit cohabitation, statutory rape and carnal

knowledge, bigamy, incest, sodomy, bestiality, homosexuality, prostitution, pornography, and obscenity . . . the role of the criminal law is excessive.

7. **Juvenile delinquency.** The juvenile court should retain jurisdiction only over conduct by children which would be criminal were they adult.

THE RATIONALE

The rationale for decriminalization consists of three arguments. First, and of primary concern to us here, many of these laws are criminogenic. They produce crime through at least three different means: labeling, secondary deviance, and the creation of a crime tariff. According to labeling theory, the criminal process itself encourages criminal careers. Any contact with the system—arrest, prosecution, conviction, or incarceration—imposes a "criminal label" on the individual. The person internalizes the label and proceeds to act out the role, committing additional and more serious crimes. Decriminalization advocates argue that the laws covering essentially harmless behavior launch people onto criminal careers. Abolish those laws and these people will never become entangled in the criminal justice system to begin with. As a result, crime will be reduced.[2] The laws also create what is known as "secondary deviance." A person becomes addicted to heroin and then, because the drug is illegal and expensive, must turn to crime to support the habit. If addiction were handled as a medical problem, with appropriate treatment or maintenance programs, addicts would not have to rob and steal. Thus we would reduce much of the drug-related crime. Criminologists also refer to the "crime tariff" problem in this regard. Making a product illegal only drives up the price. Not only does this effect raise the amount of money the person needs to obtain illegally, but it encourages the development of criminal syndicates seeking to control the market. Thus, many decriminalization advocates charge that our gambling statutes are responsible for sustaining organized crime.

Overly broad criminal statutes undermine respect for the law. Prohibition is the classic example. The law made criminals out of millions of people who simply wanted a recreational drink. Today, it is argued that many young people lost respect for the law and the legal system by the illegal status of marijuana, a relatively harmless recreational drug.

In addition to actively generating more crime, the laws in question overburden the criminal justice system. Morris and Hawkins, along with many others, maintain that the police waste far too much time dealing with vagrancy, disorderly conduct, and public intoxication when they should be concentrating on serious crimes against people and property. Moreover, insofar as the gambling statutes sustain organized crime, they are also responsible for the most serious patterns of corruption in the criminal justice system.

The final decriminalization argument is that the laws violate individual rights. Much of the behavior covered by criminal statutes is a private matter: one's sexual preference or the decision to have an abortion, for example. As long as the behavior harms no one, it should not be criminalized. Most of the items on the Morris and Hawkins list are referred to as "victimless crimes."

There is room for debate on many of these issues. To what extent gambling should be legalized is an important social policy question, involving many considerations. Abortion is perhaps the most politically controversial moral issue in the United States today. Whether or not the drug addict is a "victim" is arguable. The debate between the libertarians, who wish to restrict the scope of the criminal law in order to enhance individual liberty, and the legal moralists, who argue that the law can and should reflect fundamental moral principles, has been going on for over a hundred years and will likely continue.

Here we are concerned with the control of serious crime. On the question of decriminalization, our position is:

> PROPOSITION 26: With the possible exception of heroin policy, decriminalization is simply irrelevant to the control of robbery and burglary.

Placing decriminalization at the center of a crime control policy, as Morris and Hawkins and Neier do, evades the issue. There are no easy answers to the problem of serious crime. Conservatives and liberals respond to this dilemma in different ways. Conservatives focus on serious crime but tend to propose unworkable solutions. Liberals tend to shift the subject and talk about social reforms that are not directly related to serious crime at all.

The one possible exception to the general irrelevance of decriminalization involves heroin policy. The connection between heroin addiction and crime is clear, although experts disagree about the nature and extent of that connection. Nonetheless, as we shall see, there is no consensus on the effective solution to the heroin problem. Decriminalization is only one possible alternative, and its efficacy is not clearly established.

VICTIMLESS CRIMES AND SERIOUS CRIME

To establish the irrelevance of the connection between most of the victimless crimes and the serious crimes of robbery and burglary we should examine each of the items on Morris and Hawkin's list.

Public drunkenness, disorderly conduct, and vagrancy are public nuisances rather than predatory crimes. They harm no one, even though they may offend the sensibilities of many people. Traditionally, these three crimes have consumed the bulk of police time and energy.[3] In the nineteenth century as many as 80 percent of all arrests were in these three categories, and they still make up the largest single group of arrests. In 1981, they accounted for 18.5 percent of all arrests, or as many as all eight of the Index crimes and three times as many as robbery and burglary.

The public nuisance arrests are indeed a burden on the police, the lower courts, and city jails. There are many good reasons for decriminalizing all three offense categories. From our standpoint, the question is whether or not this step would help reduce serious crime, as it potentially could in two different ways.

The most direct effect would take the form of more efficient police work. In theory, police would be freed from about 20 percent of their arrest work load and would be able to concentrate on the more serious crimes against people and property. There are two reasons why this shift in police priorities would not significantly reduce serious crime. In our discussion of the conservative proposal to add more cops and/or improve detective work, we found that there are some basic limits to the crime control capacity of the police. Decriminalization is simply the liberal means to the same end of making more cops available for serious crime. For all the same reasons, it will not achieve the intended results. In poorly managed departments the savings in officer time will not be effectively used. In well-managed departments, as we have already learned, more patrol and more detectives will not lower the crime rate.

To a great extent, the decriminalization of public nuisances has been occurring gradually over the past fifteen years as a result of two factors. First, courts and legislatures have decriminalized some of the offenses in question. In *Easter v. District of Columbia*, a U.S. District Court ruled that chronic alcoholism was a condition and not a crime. Meanwhile, a number of states have repealed their public intoxication statutes and some cities have replaced arrest with referral to detoxification programs. These steps reflect a growing consensus that criminalization is not the appropriate response to social and medical problems. The arguments of the decriminalization advocates, in other words, have found some acceptance.[4]

On a de facto basis, the police have shifted their priorities away from public nuisance offenses. The percentage of all arrests in the categories of public intoxication, disorderly conduct, and vagrancy fell from 39.7 percent in 1969 to 18.5 percent in 1981. It is unlikely that the number of drunks and unemployed vagrants has declined in those years. If anything, their numbers have probably increased. Instead, the police have simply shifted their priorities to devote more time to serious crime. The redirection effort was probably not the result of a formal policy directive from the chief. Rather, individual patrol officers, perhaps in consultation with their sergeants, made a common-sense judgment about what was important.[5]

Not everyone, however, supports this reordering of police priorities. George L. Kelling and James Q. Wilson argue that the police should devote more attention to the little nuisance problems that define the quality of life on the neighborhood level. Police should be more aggressive in keeping drunks off the street (or at least out of the neighborhood), for example, as a way of maintaining a sense of public safety among law-abiding residents. The police neglect of the small, "quality of life" issues, according to Kelling and Wilson, contributes to neighborhood deterioration.

The second way in which decriminalization of nuisance offenses might reduce serious crime is by negating the labeling effect. The theory is generally applied to juvenile delinquents—and even then its validity remains a matter of debate. The people who are arrested for public intoxication and vagrancy are not the kind who graduate to predatory crime. For the most part they are the chronic alcoholics and the chronically unemployed. Often in helpless condition, they are commonly the victims of crime. Police frequently arrest them, in fact, in order to provide them some protection from either the elements or potential muggers. Being arrested does not encourage them to become predatory criminals. They are not the young, healthy, and aggressive males who become career criminals. Decriminalization of public intoxication, disorderly conduct, and vagrancy may well be sound social policy; but it is not a solution to the problem of serious crime.

Much has happened since Morris and Hawkins recommended the decriminalization of abortion in 1970. Three years later the Supreme Court did just that in *Roe v. Wade.* One can debate the morality of abortion and the wisdom of the *Roe* decision as social policy. But it is hard to establish the connection between the old policy of criminal abortion and serious crime. There is nothing to suggest that a person is transformed into a robber or burglar because abortions are illegal. By the same token, the argument of many Right to Life advocates that abortion undermines the moral fabric of the nation, and thereby contributes to crime, is without foundation. Abortion is a supremely important social policy question, but it has no bearing on serious crime.

Much the same can be said for the proposal to decriminalize various sexual activities between consenting adults. The statutes are still filled with laws criminalizing adultery, fornication, cohabitation, statutory rape, homosexuality, and prostitution. Whether or not these activities are acceptable is a significant moral question. Good arguments can be advanced for removing them from their criminal status and, for the most part, police have accommodated themselves to changing moral standards by simply not enforcing them. Decriminalization, however, will not in any way reduce the level of predatory crime. The one possible exception is prostitution. A certain amount of ancillary crime accompanies this activity. Customers are occasionally mugged and robbed before or after their transactions with prostitutes. But those instances represent only a minor part of the total robbery picture.

A good case can be made that gambling sustains organized crime in America. Most experts on the subject agree that criminal syndicates generate not only a majority of revenues but their steadiest and most secure revenues from gambling. Our social policy of making many forms of gambling illegal creates a potentially lucrative area of enterprise for anyone willing to assume the risks of providing the necessary goods and services. The pernicious effects of criminal syndicates on our society are well known. Organized crime money is the major corruptive force in the criminal justice system and a significant corrupter in politics. Criminal syndicates also invest their money in legitimate businesses and, using their accustomed methods, pervert the free enterprise system. Organized crime does generate some violent crime, but these murders and assaults are directed against other members of the criminal syndicates. To be sure, some threats and actual violence are directed against nonmembers—for example, owners of legitimate businesses that the syndicates are attempting to take over. But this category represents at most a tiny fraction of the violent crimes in this country. Decriminalization of gambling may or may not be a wise social policy. It may or may not strike at the roots of organized crime, as many people believe. But it will not reduce the incidence of robbery and burglary.

THE HEROIN PROBLEM

The one area in which decriminalization might help reduce crime involves heroin. There is no question that heroin is a terrible problem in our society and that a lot of predatory crime is committed by heroin addicts. Decriminalization is one possible remedy for these related problems, but it is not a self-evident solution. There is considerable disagreement over three central points: the number of heroin addicts, the amount of crime committed by addicts, and whether methadone maintenance or some other form of treatment effectively reduces addiction and crime.

The drug problem, unfortunately, has attracted more than its share of crusaders and quacks. Much of the information put out by drug crusaders is grossly wrong. Sorting our way through the misinformation is a difficult task by itself.

The first question concerns the number of heroin addicts in the United States. Official estimates range from 200,000 to 900,000, with about half of them in New York City alone. Use of the term "addict" is part of the problem. Not everyone who uses heroin is physically addicted. Antidrug propagandists created the myth that even the smallest use results in addiction. But there are large numbers of "weekend chippers" who use heroin occasionally as just another recreational drug. There are also many regular users who are not truly addicted. Even among addicts, there are great differences in the intensity of the addiction and the amount of heroin needed. As we shall see, these differences are important in estimating the amount of crime committed by heroin addicts. For the sake of the argument, let us accept the lower estimates and assume that there are between 200,000 and 300,000 regular users of heroin, including addicts, in the country and that 40 percent to 50 percent of them are in New York City.[8]

The second question is the amount of crime that is the direct result of heroin addiction. Or, to put it another way, how much crime could be eliminated by an effective heroin control policy (leaving the exact policy open for the moment)? On this issue we must sort our way through some truly fantastic estimates. The Rand Corporation estimated in 1969 that heroin addicts were responsible for $2 billion to $5 billion worth of crime in New York City. Frightening estimates of this sort are routine in the drug control business. They bear little relationship to reality, however.

In the pages of *The Public Interest*, Max Singer performed a devastating critique of the Rand heroin/crime estimates. If there were 100,000 addicts in New York City who needed $30 a day to maintain their habit, they would have to raise $1.1 billion over the course of a year (100,000 × $30 × 365). But criminals must sell their stolen goods to fences, who give them at most 25 percent of actual value (Singer may have been overly generous; some goods yield only 10 percent of their value from fences). Thus, the total value of stolen property would be in the neighborhood of $4 to $5 billion in New York City alone. By looking at the figures for particular crimes, Singer found that amount to be utterly absurd. Retail sales in New York City totaled $15 billion annually, and if addicts were responsible for half of the estimated 2 percent inventory loss they would realize only $150 million during the year. Likewise, 500,000 burglaries at an average loss of $200 would yield the addicts another $100 million. In 1969, however, there were only 196,397 reported burglaries in New York City (or about 400,000 total burglaries, if we assume that only half were reported). The same absurdity applies to robbery. At an average take of $100 (high by most recent estimates), 800,000 robberies would yield the addicts $80 million. Unfortunately there were only 61,209 reported robberies, or an estimated 120,000 actual robberies in New York City in 1969. Singer concludes that addicts are responsible for, at most, only one-tenth the amount of crime attributed to them by the Rand report.[9]

How could the Rand report and most of the other drug experts be so wrong? Easy. You begin with a high estimate of heroin users and assume that all users are addicts. Then you multiply the result by a relatively high estimate of the price of satisfying an intense level of addiction each day. This calculation ignores some well-known facts about heroin usage. Not all users are addicts. Neither regular users nor addicts have the same daily need. Some addicts can meet their needs through lawfully gained income. The cases of the addicted physicians and musicians are well known. Some blue-collar and now even white-collar workers can continue to work while addicted. Many addicts meet their financial needs through prostitution, pimping, and drug dealing. Only some heroin addicts, then, must turn to predatory crime to feed their habits. They are indeed responsible for a lot of crime, but it is much less than most of the sensational estimates would have us believe.

A realistic estimate of the amount of crime committed by heroin addicts must take into account the fluctuating intensity of addiction. During a "run" or a period of heavy addiction, an addict/criminal may rob or steal six times as much as during a period of less intense addiction.[10] Estimates based on interviews with addicts who report their needs during peak periods will inevitably result in gross exaggerations of the total heroin/crime picture. In short, there is no such thing as the "average" heroin addict (even forgetting, for the moment, about the nonaddicted users) and, as we discussed in relation to the problem of estimating average offense rates for career criminals, no meaningful "average" amount of crime committed by addicts.

The question of whether heroin causes predatory street crime has been hotly debated. The drug crusaders traditionally paint a picture of the addict driven to crime by the need to supply his or her habit. In this scenario, heroin causes crime. Criminologists tend to take a different view. Research has indicated that among addicts/criminals, the first arrest preceded the first use of heroin by about a year and a half. Crime and heroin use are seen as two parts of a deviant lifestyle, without a strong causal relationship working in either direction. Many factors lead people into this deviant lifestyle, but criminologists have yet to isolate any one of them as taking priority over the others. From our perspective this lack of established causality signifies that the effective control of heroin (by whatever means) would not in and of itself keep substantially more people from entering lives of crime.[11]

We now turn to the question of decriminalization as a method of controlling heroin-related crime. It is only one of several alternatives available. Law enforcement strategies may be divided into two classes: "supply reduction" and "demand reduction."[12] The former attempts to reduce the amount of heroin available on the streets, either by interdicting importation or by cracking down on major dealers. Decades of law enforcement effort have proven this approach to be a will-of-the-wisp. The potential sources of supply are simply too numerous and there are too many people willing to take the risks of becoming importers and major dealers. A number of supply reduction campaigns may actually have backfired. Supply reduction, of course, raises the price of the commodity in question and thus may only force current addicts to increase their criminal activity to meet the higher price. Or it may cause drug users to turn to other drugs to meet their recreational or physical needs.

Nor does demand reduction appear to be any more promising. The most notable effort in this regard is the 1973 New York drug law. . . . Despite its Draconian penalties, the law did not reduce the level of drug usage in New York City. Deterring people from wanting heroin is not a realistic goal.[13]

These lines of reasoning bring us to decriminalization. Many thoughtful observers have argued, quite persuasively, that the criminalization of heroin use has done incalculable damage to our society and our criminal justice system. Criminal penalties have brought suffering to addicts, sustained criminal syndicates, corrupted the criminal justice system, and brought the law and law enforcement into disrepute by exposing their helplessness. As a policy, decriminalization does not mean a total legalization of and disregard for heroin. Advocates of decriminalization acknowledge that the drug is a terribly destructive commodity that requires control. Decriminalization usually means removing criminal penalties for its *use* but not for its sale and distribution. Thus, the individual addict would not face criminal penalties. Heroin trafficking, however, would remain a crime. At the same time, most decriminalization proposals call for some form of treatment or maintenance for the addict. Methadone is the most popular form of maintenance, although some experts propose maintaining addicts through medically prescribed heroin.

The story of methadone maintenance is another example of a familiar syndrome in the treatment literature: a new treatment is announced, its proponents claim amazing success rates amid great publicity, independent evaluations reveal that the successes are greatly exaggerated, and a powerful backlash sets in. In the case of methadone maintenance, Vincent Dole, Marie Nyswander, and Alan Warner claimed, in the pages of the December 1968 issue of the *Journal of the American Medical Association*, a 90 percent success rate in treating heroin addicts. After four years of treatment through methadone maintenance, 88 percent of their 750 addicts with criminal records remained arrest-free. By comparison, 91 percent of the group had had some jail experience before entering treatment. Only 5.6 percent of the group were arrested and convicted while in methadone treatment. Dole, Nyswander, and Warner professed to have saved New York City over $1 million per day in prevented crime. A year later, Dr. Francis Gearing, of Columbia University School of Public Health, asserted that after three years of methadone maintenance his group of heroin addicts had an arrest rate lower than that of the general population.[14]

The backlash was not long in coming. A reevaluation of the Dole, Nyswander, and Warner data showed that while 94 percent of the addicts had not been arrested in the year following treatment, only 80 percent had not been arrested the year before treatment—a drop of but 14 percent. Further studies indicated that many methadone programs were not careful to ensure enrollment of true addicts rather than occasional heroin users. Some provided methadone but no other treatment services. Levels of dosage varied widely. Not all programs monitored the behavior of their clients carefully to ensure that they were not selling their methadone. As is the case with so many evaluations in other forms of correctional treatment, evaluators failed to use adequate controls, and the resulting findings are not reliable. Arnold Trebach concludes that there are "no definitive answers in the 'scientific' studies." The backlash reached its apogee with Edward Jay Epstein's 1974 article, "Methadone: the Forlorn Hope." Appearing in *The Public Interest* in the same year that the magazine published Martinson's "What Works?" article, Epstein's article denounced methadone as a complete failure. Not only was there no evidence of its success but, in many respects, it was as damaging as heroin itself.[15]

The truth is that methadone maintenance is partially but not completely successful. John Kaplan estimates that it achieves permanent success with about 40 percent of the addicts who receive treatment. That may not seem like a terribly high success rate, but, Kaplan argues, it is "about as well as we can do." Methadone maintenance is "the most cost-effective treatment we have today" for this destructive drug that has resisted every form of control and treatment. With respect to crime, it appears that methadone maintenance reduces but does not eliminate criminal activity. In one California experiment, income from criminal activity dropped from $3,900 to $400 a year for one group of former addicts, and from $7,200 to $1,700 for another group. Another study by Dr. Paul Cushman found that arrest rates for addicts fluctuated from 3.1 per 100 person/years before addiction to 35.1 per 100 during addiction (confirming other data indicating that addicts do indeed commit large numbers of crimes). During methadone maintenance, arrest rates dropped from 5.9 per 100 and then rose to 9.0 per 100 after the clients were discharged from the program. We can view this "success" from different perspectives. Discharged clients were committing about three times as much crime after treatment as before addiction, but less than during their addiction period.[16]

As John Kaplan suggests, heroin is indeed "the hardest drug." It is the hardest not just in terms of its addictive powers but also because it has resisted all our attempts to control it. He suggests that decriminalization is the wisest approach to this terrible problem. But he has no illusions about its being a total cure. Decriminalization, with methadone maintenance and accompanying treatment, might make some difference. But it will neither completely reduce addiction nor eliminate heroin-related crime.

Notes

1. Norval Morris and Gordon Hawkins, *The Honest Politician's Guide to Crime Control* (Chicago: University of Chicago Press, 1970), chap. 1; Aryeh Neier, *Crime and Punishment: A Radical Solution* (New York: Stein and Day, 1976).
2. Edwin M. Schur, *Crimes without Victims* (Englewood Cliffs, N.J.: Prentice-Hall, 1965).
3. Raymond T. Nimmer, *Two Million Unnecessary Arrests* (Chicago: American Bar Foundation, 1971).
4. Nimmer, *Two Million Unnecessary Arrests.*
5. David E. Aaronson, C. Thomas Dienes, and Michael C. Mushneno, *Public Policy and Police Discretion* (New York: Clark Boardman, 1984).
6. George L. Kelling and James Q. Wilson, "Broken Windows: The Police and Neighborhood Safety," *Atlantic Monthly* 249 (March 1982), reprinted in James Q. Wilson, *Thinking about Crime*, rev. ed. (New York: Basic Books, 1983), chap. 5.
7. Nimmer, *Two Million Unnecessary Arrests*, chap. 2.
8. John Kaplan, *The Hardest Drug: Heroin and Public Policy* (Chicago: University of Chicago Press, 1983).
9. Max Singer, "The Vitality of Mythical Numbers," *The Public Interest* 23 (Spring 1971):3–9.
10. Kaplan, *The Hardest Drug*, pp. 55–57.

11. Kaplan, *The Hardest Drug*, p. 55.
12. Mark H. Moore, "Controlling Criminogenic Commodities: Drugs, Guns, and Alcohol," in James Q. Wilson, ed., *Crime and Public Policy* (San Francisco: ICS Press, 1983), pp. 125–144.
13. U.S. Department of Justice, *The Nation's Toughest Drug Law: Evaluating the New York Experience* (Washington, D.C.: U.S. Government Printing Office, 1978).
14. Arnold Trebach, *The Heroin Solution* (New Haven, Conn.: Yale University Press, 1982), pp. 259–260.
15. Edward Jay Epstein, "Methadone: The Forlorn Hope," *The Public Interest* 36 (Summer 1974).
16. Kaplan, *The Hardest Drug*, p. 222; Trebach, *The Heroin Solution*, p. 261.

40 / Tinydopers: A Case Study of Deviant Socialization

PATRICIA A. ADLER
PETER ADLER

Marijuana smoking is now filtering down to our youngest generation; a number of children from 0–8 years old are participating in this practice under the influence and supervision of their parents. This phenomenon, *tinydoping*, raises interesting questions about changes in societal mores and patterns of socialization. We are not concerned here with the desirability or morality of the activity. Instead, we will discuss the phenomenon, elucidating the diverse range of attitudes, strategems and procedures held and exercised by parents and children.

An examination of the history and cultural evolution of marijuana over the last several decades illuminates the atmosphere in which tinydoping arose. Marijuana use, first located chiefly among jazz musicians and ghetto communities, eventually expanded to "the highly alienated young in flight from families, schools and conventional communities" (Simon and Gagnon, 1968:60. See also Goode, 1970; Carey, 1968; Kaplan, 1971; and Grinspoon, 1971). Blossoming in the mid-1960s, this youth scene formed an estranged and deviant subculture offsetting the dominant culture's work ethic and instrumental success orientation. Society reacted as an angry parent, enforcing legal, social and moral penalties against its rebellious children. Today, however, the pothead subculture has eroded and the population of smokers has broadened to include large numbers of middle-class and establishment-oriented people.

Marijuana, then, may soon take its place with alcohol, its "prohibition" a thing of the past. These two changes can be considered movements of moral passage:

> Movements to redefine behavior may eventuate in a moral passage, a transition of the behavior from one moral status to another.... What is attacked as criminal today may be seen as sick next year and fought over as possibly legitimate by the next generation. (Gusfield, 1967:187. See also Matza, 1969; Kitsuse, 1962; Douglas, 1970; and Becker, 1963 for further discussions of the social creation of deviance.)

Profound metamorphoses testify to this redefinition: frequency and severity of arrest is proportionately down from a decade ago; the stigma of a marijuana-related arrest is no longer as personally and occupationally ostracizing; and the fear that using grass will press the individual into close contact with hardened criminals and cause him to adopt a deviant self-identity or take up criminal ways has also largely passed.

The transformation in marijuana's social and legal status is not intrinsic to its own characteristics or those of mood-altering drugs in general. Rather, it illustrates a process of becoming socially accepted many deviant activities or substances may go through. This research suggests a more generic model of social change, a sequential development characteristic of the diffusion and legitimation of a formerly unconventional practice. Five stages identify the spread of such activities from small isolated outgroups, through increasing levels of mainstream society, and finally to such sacred groups as children.[1] Often, however, as with the case of pornography, the appearance of this quasi-sanctioned conduct among juveniles elicits moral outrage and a social backlash designed to prevent such behavior in the sacred population, while leaving it more open to the remainder of society.

Most treatments of pot smoking in the sociological literature have been historically and subculturally specific (see Carey, 1968; Goode, 1970; Grupp, 1971; Hochman, 1972; Kaplan, 1971; and Simon and Gagnon, 1968), swiftly dated by our rapidly changing society. Only Becker's (1953) work is comparable to our research since it offers a general sequential model of the process for becoming a marijuana user.

The data in this paper show an alternate route to marijuana smoking. Two developments necessitate a modification of Becker's conceptualization. First, there have been many changes in norms, traditions and patterns of use since the time he wrote. Second, the age of this new category of smokers is cause for reformulation. Theories of child development proposed by Mead (1934), Erikson (1968), and Piaget (1948) agree that prior to a certain age children are unable to comprehend subtle transformations and perceptions. As we will see, the full effects and symbolic meanings of marijuana are partially lost to them due to their inability to differentiate between altered states of consciousness and to connect this with the smoking experience. Yet this does not preclude their becoming avid pot users and joining in the smoking group as accepted members.

Socialization practices are the final concern of this research. The existence of tinydoping both illustrates and contradicts several established norms of traditional childrearing. Imitative behavior (see Piaget, 1962), for instance, is integral to tinydoping since the children's desire to copy the actions of parents and other adults is a primary motivation. Boundary maintenance also arises as a consideration: as soon as their offspring can communicate, parents must instruct them in the perception of social borders and the need for guarding group activities as secret. In contrast, refutations of convention include the introduction of mood-altering drugs into the sacred childhood period and, even more unusual, parents and children get high together. This bridges, often to the point of eradication, the inter-generational gap firmly entrenched in most societies. Thus, although parents view their actions as normal, tinydoping must presently be considered as deviant socialization.

METHODS

Collected over the course of 18 months, our data include observations of two dozen youngsters between the ages of birth and eight, and a similar number of parents, aged 21 to 32, all in middle-class households. To obtain a complete image of this practice we talked with parents, kids and other involved observers (the "multiperspectival" approach, Douglas, 1976). Many of our conversations with adults were taped but our discussions with the children took the form of informal, extemporaneous dialogue, since the tape recorder distracts and diverts their attention. Finally, our study is exploratory and suggestive; we make no claim to all-inclusiveness in the cases or categories below.

THE KIDS

The following four individuals, each uniquely interesting, represent many common characteristics of other children and adults we observed.

"Big Ed": The Diaperdoper

Big Ed derives his name from his miniature size. Born three months prematurely, now three years old, he resembles a toy human being. Beneath his near-white wispy hair and toddling diapered bottom, he packs a punch of childish energy. Big Ed's mother and older siblings take care of him although he often sees his father who lives in a neighboring California town. Laxity and permissiveness characterize his upbringing, as he freely roams the neighborhood under his own and other children's supervision. Exposure to marijuana has prevailed since birth and in the last year he advanced from passive inhalation (smoke blown in his direction) to active puffing on joints. Still in the learning stage, most of his power is expended blowing air into the reefer instead of inhaling. He prefers to suck on a "bong" (a specially designed waterpipe), delighting in the gurgling sound the water makes. A breast fed baby, he will go to the bong for oral satisfaction, whether it is filled or not. He does not actively seek joints, but Big Ed never refuses one when offered. After a few puffs, however, he usually winds up with smoke in his eyes and tearfully retreats to a glass of water. Actual marijuana inhalation is minimal; his size renders it potent. Big Ed has not absorbed any social restrictions related to pot use or any awareness of its illegality, but is still too young to make a blooper as his speech is limited.

Stephanie: The Social Smoker

Stephanie is a dreamy four-year old with quite good manners, calm assurance, sweet disposition and a ladylike personality and appearance. Although her brothers are rough and tumble, Stephanie can play with the boys or amuse herself sedately alone or in the company of adults. Attendance at a progressive school for the last two years has developed her natural curiosity and intelligence. Stephanie's mother and father both work, but still find enough recreational time to raise their children with love and care and to engage in frequent marijuana smoking. Accordingly, Stephanie has seen grass since infancy and accepted it as a natural part of life. Unlike the diaperdoper, she has mastered the art of inhalation and can breathe the smoke out through her nose. Never grasping or grubbing for pot, she has advanced from a preference for bongs or pipes and now enjoys joints when offered. She revels in being part of a crowd of smokers and passes the reefer immediately after each puff, never holding it for an unsociable amount of time. Her treasure box contains a handful of roaches (marijuana butts) and seeds (she delights in munching them as snacks) that she keeps as mementos of social occasions with (adult) "friends." After smoking, Stephanie becomes more bubbly and outgoing. Dancing to records, she turns in circles as she jogs from one foot to the other, releasing her body to the rhythm. She then eats everything in sight and falls asleep—roughly the same cycle as adults, but faster.

When interviewed, Stephanie clearly recognized the difference between a cigarette and a joint (both parents use tobacco), defining the effects of the latter as good but still being unsure of what the former did and how the contents of each varied. She also responded with some confusion about social boundaries separating pot users from non-users, speculating that perhaps her grandmother did smoke it but her grandfather certainly did not (neither do). In the words of her father: "She knows not to tell people about it but she just probably wouldn't anyway."

Josh: The Self-gratifier

Everyone in the neighborhood knows Josh. Vociferous and outgoing, at age five he has a decidedly Dennis-the-Menace quality in both looks and personality. Neither timid nor reserved, he boasts to total strangers of his fantastic exploits and talents. Yet behind his bravado swagger lies a seeming insecurity and need for acceptance, coupled with a difficulty in accepting authority, which has led him into squabbles with peers, teachers, siblings and parents.

Josh's home shows the traditional division of labor. His mother stays home to cook and care for the children while his father works long hours. The mother is always calm and tolerant about her youngster's smart-alec ways, but his escapades may provoke an explosive tirade from his father. Yet this male parent is clearly the dominating force in Josh's life. Singling Josh out from his younger sister and brother, the father has chosen him as his successor in the male tradition. The parent had himself begun drinking and smoking cigarettes in his early formative years, commencing pot use as a teenager, and now has a favorable attitude toward the early use of stimulants which he is actively passing on to Josh.

According to his parents, his smoking has had several beneficial effects. Considering Josh a "hyper" child, they claim that it calms him down to a more normal speed, often permitting him to engage in activities which would otherwise be too difficult for his powers of concentration. He also appears to become more sedate and less prone to temper tantrums, sleeping longer and more deeply. But Josh's smoking patterns differ significantly from our last two subjects. He does not enjoy social smoking, preferring for his father to roll him "pinners" (thin joints) to smoke by himself. Unlike many other tinydopers, Josh frequently refuses the offer of a joint saying, "Oh that! I gave up smoking that stuff." At age five he claims to have already quit and gone back several times. His mother backs this assertion as valid; his father brushes it off as merely a ploy to shock and gain attention. Here, the especially close male parent recognizes the behavior as imitative and accepts it as normal. To others, however, it appears strange and suggests surprising sophistication.

Josh's perception of social boundaries is also mature. Only a year older than Stephanie, Josh has made some mistakes but his awareness of the necessity for secrecy is complete; he differentiates those people with whom he may and may not discuss the subject by the experience of actually smoking with them. He knows individuals but cannot yet socially categorize the boundaries. Josh also realizes the contrast between joints and cigarettes down to the marijuana and tobacco they contain. Interestingly, he is aggressively opposed to tobacco while favoring pot use (this may be the result of anti-tobacco cancer propaganda from kindergarten).

Kyra: The Bohemian

A worldly but curiously childlike girl is seven-year-old Kyra. Her wavy brown hair falls to her shoulders and her sun-tanned body testifies to many hours at the beach in winter and summer. Of average height for her age, she dresses with a maturity beyond her years. Friendly and sociable she has few reservations about what she says to people. Kyra lives with her youthful mother and whatever boyfriend her mother fancies at the moment. Their basic family unit consists of two (mother and daughter), and they have travelled together living a free life all along the West Coast and Hawaii. While Josh's family was male dominated, this is clearly female centered, all of Kyra's close relatives being women. They are a bohemian group, generation after generation following a hip, up-to-the-moment, unshackled lifestyle. The house is often filled with people, but when the visitors clear out, a youthful, thrillseeking mother remains, who raises this daughter by treating her like a sister or friend. This demand on Kyra to behave as an adult may produce some internal strain, but she seems to have grown accustomed to it. Placed in situations others might find awkward, she handles them with precocity. Like her mother, she is being reared for a life of independence and freedom.

Pot smoking is an integral part of this picture. To Kyra it is another symbol for her adulthood; she enjoys it and wants to do it a lot. At seven she is an accomplished smoker; her challenge right now lies in the mastery of rolling joints. Of our four examples, social boundaries are clearest to Kyra. Not only is she aware of the necessary secrecy surrounding pot use, but she is able to socially categorize types of people into marijuana smokers and straights. She may err in her judgment occasionally, but no more so than any adult.

STAGES OF DEVELOPMENT

These four and other cases suggest a continuum of reactions to marijuana that is loosely followed by most tinydopers.

From birth to around 18 months a child's involvement is passive. Most parents keep their infants nearby at all times and if pot is smoked the room becomes filled with potent clouds. At this age just a little marijuana smoke can be very powerful and these infants, the youngest diaperdopers, manifest noticeable effects. The drug usually has a calming influence, putting the infant into a less cranky mood and extending the depth and duration of sleep.

After the first one and a half years, the children are more attuned to what is going on around them: they begin to desire participation in a "monkey see, monkey do" fashion. During the second year, a fascination with paraphernalia generally develops, as they play with it and try to figure it out. Eager to smoke with the adults and older children, they are soon discouraged after a toke (puff) or two. They find smoking difficult and painful (particularly to the eyes and throat)—after all, it is not easy to inhale burning hot air and hold it in your lungs.

But continual practice eventually produces results, and inhalation seems to be achieved somewhere during the third or fourth year. This brings considerable pride and makes the kids feels they have attained semi-adult status. Now they can put the paraphernalia to work. Most tinydopers of this age are wild about "roach clips," itching to put their joints into them as soon as possible after lighting.

Ages four and five bring the first social sense of the nature of pot and who should know about it. This begins as a vague idea, becoming further refined with age and sophistication. Finally, by age seven or eight kids have a clear concept of where the lines can be drawn between those who are and aren't "cool," and can make these distinctions on their own. No child we interviewed, however, could verbalize about any specific effects felt after smoking marijuana. Ironically, although they participate in smoking and actually manifest clear physical symptoms of the effects, tinydopers are rationally and intellectually unaware of how the drug is acting upon them. They are too young to notice a change in their behavior or to make the symbolic leap and associate this transformation with having smoked pot previously. The effects of marijuana must be socially and consensually delineated from non-high sensations for the user to fully appreciate the often subtle perceptual and physiological changes that have occurred. To the youngster the benefits of pot smoking are not at all subtle: he is permitted to imitate his elders by engaging in a social ritual they view as pleasurable and important; the status of adulthood is partially conferred on him by allowing this act, and his desire for acceptance is fulfilled through inclusion in his parents' peer group. This constitutes the major difference in appreciation between the child and adult smoker.

PARENTS' STRATEGIES

The youth of the sixties made some forceful statements through their actions about how they evaluated the Establishment and the conventional American lifestyle. While their political activism has faded, many former members of this group still feel a strong commitment to smoking pot and attach a measure of symbolic significance to it. When they had children the question then arose of how to handle the drug vis-à-vis their offspring. The continuum of responses they developed ranges from total openness and permissiveness to various measures of secrecy.

Smoking Regularly Permitted

Some parents give their children marijuana whenever it is requested. They may wait until the child reaches a certain age, but most parents in this category started their kids on pot from infancy. These parents may be "worried" or "unconcerned."

Worried. Ken and Deedy are moderate pot smokers, getting high a few times a week. Both had been regular users for several years prior to having children. When Deedy was pregnant she absolutely refused to continue her smoking pattern.

> I didn't know what effect it could have on the unborn child. I tried to read and find out, but there's very little written on that. But in the *Playboy* Advisor there was an article: they said we advise you to stay away from all drugs when you're pregnant. That was sort of my proof. I figured they don't bullshit about these

> types of things. I sort of said now at least somebody stands behind me because people were saying, "You can get high, it's not going to hurt the baby."

This abstinence satisfied them and once the child was born they resumed getting high as before. Frequently smoking in the same room as the baby, they began to worry about the possible harmful effects this exposure might have on his physical, psychological and mental development. After some discussion, they consulted the family pediatrician, a prominent doctor in the city.

> I was really embarrassed, but I said, "Doctor, we get high, we smoke pot, and sometimes the kid's in the room. If he's in the room can this hurt him? I don't want him to be mentally retarded." He said, "Don't worry about it, they're going to be legalizing it any day now—this was three years ago—it's harmless and a great sedative."

This reassured them on two counts: they no longer were fearful in their own minds, and they had a legitimate answer when questioned by their friends.[2]

Ken and Deedy were particularly sensitive about peer reactions:

> Some people say, "You let your children get high?!" They really act with disgust. Or they'll say, "Oh you let your kids get high," and then they kind of look at you like, "That's neat, I think." And it's just nice to be able to back it up.

Ken and Deedy were further nonplussed about the problem of teaching their children boundary maintenance. Recognizing the need to prevent their offspring from saying things to the wrong people, they were unsure how to approach this subject properly.

> How can you tell a kid, how can you go up to him and say, "Well you want to get high, but don't tell anybody you're doing it"? You can't. We didn't really know how to tell them. You don't want to bring the attention, you don't want to tell your children not to say anything about it because that's a sure way to get them to do it. We just never said anything about it.

They hope this philosophy of openness and permissiveness will forestall the need to limit their children's marijuana consumption. Limits, for them, resemble prohibitions and interdictions against discussing grass: they make transgressions attractive. Both parents believe strongly in presenting marijuana as an everyday occurrence, definitely not as an undercover affair. When asked how they thought this upbringing might affect their kids, Deedy offered a fearful but doubtful speculation that her children might one day reject the drug.

> I don't imagine they'd try to abuse it. Maybe they won't even smoke pot when they get older. That's a big possibility. I doubt it, but hopefully they won't be that way. They've got potheads for parents.

Unconcerned: Alan and Anna make use of a variety of stimulants—pot, alcohol, cocaine—to enrich their lives. Considered heavy users, they consume marijuana and alcohol daily. Alan became acquainted with drugs, particularly alcohol, at a very early age and Anna first tried them in her teens. When they decided to have children the question of whether they would permit the youngsters to partake in their mood-altering experiences never arose. Anna didn't curtail her drug intake during pregnancy; her offspring were conceived, formed and weaned on this steady diet. When queried about their motivations, Alan volunteered:

> What the hell! It grows in the ground, it's a weed. I can't see anything wrong with doing anything, inducing any part of it into your body anyway that you possibly could eat it, smoke it, intravenously, or whatever, that it would ever harm you because it grows in the ground. It's a natural thing. It's one of God's treats.

All of their children have been surrounded by marijuana's aromatic vapor since the day they returned from the hospital. Alan and Anna were pleased with the effect pot had on their infants; the relaxed, sleepy and happy qualities achieved after inhaling pot smoke made childrearing an easier task. As the little ones grew older they naturally wanted to share in their parents' activities. Alan viewed this as the children's desire to imitate rather than true enjoyment of any effects:

> Emily used to drink Jack Daniels straight and like it. I don't think it was taste, I think it was more of an acceptance thing because that's what I was drinking. She was also puffing on joints at six months.

This mimicking, coupled with a craving for acceptance, although recognized by Alan in his kids, was not repeated in his own feelings toward friends or relatives. At no time during the course of our interview or acquaintance did he show any concern with what others thought of his behavior; rather, his convictions dominated, and his wife passively followed his lead.

In contrast to the last couple, Alan was not reluctant to address the problem of boundary maintenance. A situation arose when Emily was three, where she was forced to learn rapidly:

> One time we were stopped by the police while driving drunk. I said to Emily—we haven't been smoking marijuana. We all acted quiet and Emily realized there was something going on and she delved into it. I explained that some people are stupid and they'll harm you very badly if you smoke marijuana. To this day I haven't heard her mention it to anyone she hasn't smoked with.

As each new child came along, Alan saw to it that they learned the essential facts of life.

Neither Alan nor Anna saw any moral distinction between marijuana smoking and other, more accepted pastimes. They heartily endorsed marijuana as something to indulge in like "tobacco, alcohol, sex, breathing or anything else that brings pleasure to the senses." Alan and Anna hope their children will continue to smoke grass in their later lives. It has had beneficial effects for them and they believe it can do the same for their kids:

> I smoked marijuana for a long time, stopped and developed two ulcers; and smoked again and the two ulcers went away. It has great medicinal value.

Smoking Occasionally Permitted

In contrast to uninterrupted permissiveness, other parents restrict marijuana use among their children to specific occasions. A plethora of reasons and rationalizations lie behind this behavior, some openly avowed by parents and others not. Several people believe it is okay to let the kids get high as long as it isn't done too often. Many other people do not have any carefully thought-out notion of what they want, tending to make spur-of-the-moment decisions. As a result, they allow occasional but largely undefined smoking in a sporadic and irregular manner. Particular reasons for this inconsistency can be illustrated by three examples from our research:

1. *Conflicts between parents* can confuse the situation. While Stella had always planned to bring her children up with pot, Burt did not like the idea. Consequently, the household rule on this matter varied according to the unpredictable moods of the adults and which parent was in the house.
2. Mike and Gwen had trouble *making up their minds*. At one time they thought it probably couldn't harm the child, only to decide the next day they shouldn't take chances and rescind that decision.
3. Lois and David didn't waver hourly but had *changing ideas over time*. At first they were against it, but then met a group of friends who liked to party and approved of tinydoping. After a few years they moved to a new neighborhood and changed their lifestyle, again prohibiting pot smoking for the kids.

These are just a few of the many situations in which parents allow children an occasional opportunity to smoke grass. They use various criteria to decide when those permissible instances ought to be, most families subscribing to several of the following patterns:

Reward: The child receives pot as a bonus for good behavior in the past, present or future. This may serve as an incentive: "If you're a good boy today, Johnny, I may let you smoke with us tonight," or to celebrate an achievement already completed like "going potty" or reciting the alphabet.

Guilt: Marijuana can be another way of compensating children for what they aren't getting. Historically, parents have tried to buy their kids off or make themselves loved through gifts of money or toys but pot can also be suitable here. This is utilized both by couples with busy schedules who don't have time for the children ("We're going out again tonight so we'll give you this special treat to make it up to you") and by separated parents who are trying to compete with the former spouse for the child's love ("I know Mommy doesn't let you do this but you can do special things when you're with me").

Cuteness: To please themselves parents may occasionally let the children smoke pot because it's cute. Younger children look especially funny because they cannot inhale, yet in their eagerness to be like Mommy and Daddy they make a hilarious effort and still have a good time themselves. Often this will originate as amusement for the parents and then spread to include cuteness in front of friends. Carrying this trend further, friends may roll joints for the little ones or turn them on when the parents are away. This still precludes regular use.

Purposive: Giving marijuana to kids often carries a specific anticipated goal for the parents. The known effects of pot are occasionally desired and actively sought. They may want to calm the child down because of the necessities of a special setting or company. Sleep is another pursued end, as in "Thank you for taking Billy for the night; if he gives you any trouble just let him smoke this and he'll go right to bed." They may also give it to the children medicinally. Users believe marijuana soothes the upset stomach and alleviates the symptoms of the common cold better than any other drug. As a mood elevator, many parents have given pot to alleviate the crankiness young children develop from a general illness, specific pain or injury. One couple used it experimentally as a treatment for hyperactivity (see Josh).

Abstention

Our last category of marijuana smoking parents contains those who do not permit their children any direct involvement with illegal drugs. This leaves several possible ways to treat the topic of the adults' own involvement with drugs and how open they are about it. Do they let the kids know they smoke pot? Moreover, do they do it in the children's presence?

Overt: The great majority of our subjects openly smoked in front of their children, defining marijuana as an accepted and natural pastime. Even parents who withhold it from their young children hope that the kids will someday grow up to be like themselves. Thus, they smoke pot overtly. These marijuana smokers are divided on the issue of other drugs, such as pills and cocaine.

a. *permissive*—One group considers it acceptable to use any drug in front of the children. Either they believe in what they are doing and consider it right for the kids to observe their actions, or they don't worry about it and just do it.

b. *pragmatic*—A larger, practically oriented group differentiated between "smokable" drugs (pot and hashish) and the others (cocaine and pills), finding it acceptable to let children view consumption of the former group, but not the latter. Rationales varied for this, ranging from safety to morality:

> Well, we have smoked hashish around them but we absolutely never ever do coke in front of them because it's a white powder and if they saw us snorting a white powder there goes the drain cleaner, there goes baby powder. Anything white, they'll try it; and that goes for pills too. The only thing they have free rein of is popping vitamins.

Fred expressed his concern over problems this might engender in the preservation of his children's moral fibre:

> If he sees me snorting coke, how is he going to differentiate that from heroin? He gets all this anti-drug education from school and they tell him that heroin is bad. How can I explain to him that doing coke is okay and it's fun and doesn't hurt you but heroin is something else, so different and bad? How could I teach right from wrong?

c. *capricious*—A third group is irregular in its handling of multiple drug viewing and their offspring. Jon and Linda, for instance, claim that they don't mind smoking before their child but absolutely won't permit other drugs to be used in his presence. Yet in fact they often use almost any intoxicant in front of him, depending on their mood and how high they have already become.

In our observations we have never seen any parent give a child in the tinydoper range any kind of illegal drug other than marijuana and, extremely rarely, hashish. Moreover, the treatment of pot has been above all direct and open: even those parents who don't permit their children to join have rejected the clandestine secrecy of the behind-closed-doors approach. Ironically, however, they must often adopt this strategy toward the outside world; those parents who let it be known that they permit tinydoping frequently take on an extra social and legal stigma. Their motivation for doing so stems from a desire to avoid having the children view pot and their smoking it as evil or unnatural. Thus, to destigmatize marijuana they stigmatize themselves in the face of society.

CONCLUSIONS

Tinydoping, with its combined aspects of understandably innovative social development and surprising challenges to convention, is a fruitful subject for sociological analysis. A review of historical and cultural forces leading to the present offers insight into how and why this phenomenon came to arise. Essentially, we are witnessing the moral passage of marijuana, its transformation from an isolated and taboo drug surrounded by connotations of fear and danger, into an increasingly accepted form of social relaxation, similar to alcohol. The continuing destigmatization of pot fosters an atmosphere in which parents are willing to let their children smoke.

Marijuana's social transition is not an isolated occurrence, however. Many formerly deviant activities have gradually become acceptable forms of behavior. Table 1 presents a general model of social change which outlines the sequential development and spread of a conduct undergoing legitimization.

Particular behaviors which first occur only among relatively small and stigmatized outgroups are frequently picked up by ingroup deviants who identify with the stigmatized outgroup. In an attempt to be cool and avante-garde, larger clusters of ingroup members adopt this deviant practice, often for the sake of nonconformity as well as its own merits. By this time the deviant activity is gaining exposure as well as momentum and may spread to normal ingroup members. The final step is its eventual introduction to sacred groups in the society, such as children.

Becker's (1953) research and theory are pertinent to historical stages I and II. More recently, Carey (1968) and Goode (1970) have depicted stage III. To date, sociologists have not described stage IV and we are the first to portray stage V.

The general value of this model can be further illustrated by showing its application to another deviant activity which has followed a similar progression: pornography. Initially a highly stigmatized practice engaged in by people largely hidden from public view, it slowly became incorporated into a wider cross-section of the population. With the advent of *Playboy*, mainstream media entered the scene, resulting in the present proliferation of sexually-oriented magazines and tabloids. Recently, however, this practice passed into stage V; a violent societal reaction ensued, with moralist groups crusading to hold the sacred period of childhood free from such deviant intrusions.

Table 1 / Sequential Model of Social Change: The Diffusion and Legitimization of Marijuana

Stage		*Carriers*	
I	1940's	Stigmatized outgroup	Blacks
II	1950's	Ingroup deviants who identify with stigmatized outgroup	Jazz Musicians
III	1960's	Avant-garde ingroup members	College students and counterculture
IV	1970's	Normal ingroup members	Middle class
V	1975+	Sacred group	Children

Tinydoping has not become broadly publicly recognized but, as with pornography, the widespread (collective) softening of attitudes has not extended to youngsters. Rather, a backlash effect stemming from conventional morality condemns such "intrusions and violations of childhood" as repulsive. Thus, the spread of deviance to Group V prompts social revulsion and renewed effort to ban the behavior by children while allowing it to adults.

These data also recommend a re-examination of sociological theories about marijuana use. Becker's (1953) theory is in some ways timeless, illuminating a model of the actor which encompasses a dynamic processual development. It proposes an initiation process that precedes bona fide membership in a pot smoking milieu. Minimally, this includes: learning the proper techniques to ensure adequate consumption; perception of the drug's unique effects; association of these effects with the smoking experience, and the conceptualization of these effects as pleasurable. Symbolic *meaning* is crucial to this schema: through a "sequence of social experiences" the individual continually reformulates his attitudes, eventually learning to view marijuana smoking as desirable. The formation of this conception is the key to understanding the motivations and actions of users.

Accepting this model for the adult initiate, the present research has explored an historically novel group (tinydopers), describing a new route to becoming a marijuana user taken by these children. As has been shown, tinydopers are unable to recognize the psychological and physiological effects of pot or to connect them with having smoked. This effectively precludes their following Becker's model which accords full user status to the individual only after he has successfully perceived the effects of the drug and marked them as pleasurable. Our research into child perception relied mostly on observation and inference since, as Piaget (1948) noted, it is nearly impossible to discover this from children; the conceptual categories are too sophisticated for their grasp. That the marijuana affects them is certain: giddy, they laugh, dance and run to the refrigerator, talking excitedly and happily until they suddenly fall asleep. But through observations and conversations before, during and after the intoxicated periods, tinydopers were found to be unaware of any changes in themselves.

Their incomplete development, perceptually, cognitively and interactionally, is the cause of this ignorance. According to the socialization theories of Mead (1934), Erikson (1968), and Piaget (1948), children of eight and under are still psychologically forming, gradually learning to function. Piaget particularly notes definitive cognitive stages, asserting that conservation, transformation and classification are all too advanced for the tinydoper age bracket. According to Mead (see also Adler and Adler, 1979), the essence lies in their lack of mature selves, without which they cannot fully act and interact competently. The ages (8–9) seem to be a decisive turning point as youngsters change in internal psychological composition and become capable of *reflecting* on themselves, both through their own eyes and those of the other. (Mead argues that this is possible only after the child has completed the play, game and generalized other stages and can competently engage in roletaking.) Hence, before that time they cannot genuinely recognize their "normal selves" or differentiate them from their "high selves." Without this perception, the effects of marijuana are held to those created by the parents, who frame the experience with their own intentional and unintentional definitions of the situation. Thus, tinydopers become marijuana users almost unconsciously, based on a decision made by others. Moreover, the social meanings they associate with its use are very different than those experienced by adult initiates.

How does this new practice correspond to conventional modes of child-rearing? One traditional procedure we see reaffirmed is imitative behavior (see Piaget, 1962), through which the child learns and matures by copying the actions of significant adult models. Several of the illustrative cases chosen show particularly how directly the youngsters are influenced by their desire to behave and be like older family members and friends. They have two aspirations: wanting to be accorded quasi-adult status and longing for acceptance as members of the social group. Parents have corresponding and natural positive feelings about inculcating meaningful beliefs and values into their offspring. Teaching boundary maintenance is also a necessary adjunct to allowing tinydoping. Marijuana's continued illegality and social unacceptability for juveniles necessitate parents ensuring that information about pot smoking is neither intentionally nor accidentally revealed by youngsters. Children must early learn to differentiate between members of various social groups and to judge who are and are not appropriate to be told. This is difficult because it involves mixing positive and negative connotations of the drug in a complex manner. Valuable parallels for this contradictory socialization can be found in child use of alcohol and tobacco, as well as to families of persecuted religious groups (i.e., Marrano Jews in 15th century Spain, covert Jews in Nazi Germany and possibly Mormons in the 19th century). Members of these enclaves believed that what they were teaching their offspring was fundamentally honorable, but still had to communicate to the younger generation their social ostracization and the need to maintain some barriers of secrecy.

Juxtaposed to those aspects which reproduce regular features of socialization are the contradictory procedures. One such departure is the introduction of mood-altering intoxicants into the sacred childhood period. Tinydoping violates the barriers created by most societies to reserve various types of responsibilities, dangers and special pleasures (such as drugs and sex) for adults only. Yet perhaps the most unusual and unprecedented facet of tinydoping socialization observed is the intergenerational bridging that occurs between parent and child. By introducing youngsters into the adult social group and having them participate as peers, parents permit generational boundaries to become extremely vague, often to the point of nonexistence. Several cases show how children have come to look at parents and other adults as friends. This embodies extreme variance from cultures and situations where parents love and treasure their children yet still treat them unequally.

How then can tinydoping be compared to traditional childrearing practices and habits? Existing indicators suggest both similarity and divergence. The parents in this study consider marijuana a substance they overwhelmingly feel comfortable with, regard as something "natural" (i.e., Alan and Anna), and would like their progeny to be exposed to in a favorable light. To them, tinydoping represents a form of normal socialization within the context of their subcultural value system. From the greater society's perspective, however, the illegality of the behavior, aberration from conventional childrearing norms and uncertain implications for futurity combine to define tinydoping as deviant socialization.

Notes

1. The period of childhood has traditionally been a special time in which developing adults were given special treatment to ensure their growing up to be capable and responsible members of society. Throughout history and in most cultures children have been kept apart from adults and sheltered in protective isolation from certain knowledge and practices (see Aries, 1965).

2. Particularly relevant to these "justifications" is Lyman and Scott's (1968) analysis of accounts, as statements made to relieve one of culpability. Specifically, they can be seen as "denial of injury" (Sykes and Matza, 1957) as they assert the innocuousness of giving marijuana to their child. An "excuse" is further employed, "scapegoating" the doctor as the one really responsible for this aberration. Also, the appeal to science has been made.

References

Adler, Peter and Patricia A. Adler
1979 "Symbolic Interactionism," in Patricia A. Adler, Peter Adler, Jack D. Douglas, Andrea Fontana, C. Robert Freeman and Joseph Kotarba, An Introduction to the Sociologies of Everyday Life, Boston: Allyn and Bacon.
Aries, Phillipe
1965 Centuries of Childhood: A Social History of Family Life, New York: Vintage.
Becker, Howard S.
1953 "Becoming a Marijuana User," American Journal of Sociology, 59, November.
1963 Outsiders, New York: Free Press.
Carey, James T.
1968 The College Drug Scene, Englewood Cliffs: Prentice-Hall.
Douglas, Jack D.
1970 "Deviance and Respectability: The Social Construction of Moral Meanings," in Jack D. Douglas (ed.), Deviance and Respectability, New York: Basic Books.
Douglas, Jack D.
1976 Investigative Social Research, Beverly Hills: Sage.
Erikson, Erik
1968 Identity, Youth and Crisis, New York: Norton.

Goode, Erich
1970 The Marijuana Smokers, New York: Basic Books.
Grinspoon, Lester
1971 Marihuana Reconsidered, Cambridge: Harvard University Press.
Grupp, Stanley E. (ed.)
1971 Marihuana, Columbus, Ohio: Charles E. Merrill.
Gusfield, Joseph R.
1967 "Moral Passage: The Symbolic Process in Public Designations of Deviance," Social Problems, 15, II, Fall.
Hochman, Joel S.
1972 Marijuana and Social Evolution, Englewood Cliffs: Prentice-Hall.
Kaplan, John
1971 Marihuana: The New Prohibition, New York: Pocket.
Kitsuse, John I.
1962 "Societal Reactions to Deviant Behavior," Social Problems, 9, 3, Winter.
Lyman, Stanford and Marvin B. Scott
1968 "Accounts," American Sociological Review, 33, 1.
Matza, David
1969 Becoming Deviant, Englewood Cliffs: Prentice-Hall.
Mead, George H.
1934 Mind, Self and Society, Chicago: The University of Chicago Press.
Piaget, Jean
1948 The Moral Judgment of the Child, New York: Free Press.
1962 Play, Dreams and Imitation in Childhood, New York: Norton.
Simon, William and John H. Gagnon
1968 "Children of the Drug Age," Saturday Review, September 21.
Sykes, Gresham and David Matza
1957 "Techniques of Neutralization," American Sociological Review, 22, December.

41 / The Identity Change Process: A Field Study of Obesity

DOUGLAS DEGHER
GERALD HUGHES

Becker = label

The interactionist perspective has come to play an important part in contemporary criminological and deviance theory. Within this approach, deviance is viewed as a subjectively problematic identity rather than an objective condition of behavior. At the core is the emphasis on "process" rather than on viewing deviance as a static entity. To paraphrase vintage Howard Becker, "... social groups create deviance by making the rules whose infraction constitutes deviance. Consequently, deviance is not a quality of the act... but rather a consequence of the application by others of rules and sanctions to an offender" (Becker, 1963, p. 9). Attention is focused upon the *interaction* between those being labeled deviant and those promoting the deviant label. In the interactionist literature, emphases are in two major areas: (a) the conditions under which the label "deviant" comes to be applied to an individual and the consequences for the individual of having adopted that label (Tannenbaum, 1939; Lemert, 1951; Kitsuse, 1961, p. 247; Goffman, 1963; Baum, 1987, p. 96; Greenberg, 1989, p. 79), and/or (b) the role of social control agents[1] in contributing to the application of deviant labels (Becker, 1963; Piliavin & Briar, 1964, p. 206; Cicourel, 1968; Schur, 1971; Conrad, 1975, p. 12).

Much of this literature frequently assumes that once an individual has been labeled, the promoted label and attendant identity is either internalized or rejected. As Lemert proposes, the shift from primary to secondary deviance is a categorical one, and is primarily a response to problems created by the societal reaction (Lemert, 1951, p. 40).

What is most often neglected is an examination of the mechanistic features of this identity shift. Our focus is on this "identity change process," which is what we have chosen to call this identity shift. Of interest is how individuals come to make some personal sense out of proffered labels and their attendant identities.

METHODOLOGY

The primary methodological tool employed to construct our identity change process model comes from "grounded" analysis (Glaser & Strauss, 1967; Glaser, 1978; Bigus, Hadden, & Glaser, 1982). This method is particularly appropriate when, as in the present case, little prior theoretical work on the phenomenon exists. As Glaser and Strauss contend, "whether or not there is previous speculative theory, discovery gives us a theory that 'fits or works' in a substantive or formal area . . . since the theory has been derived from research data, not deduced from logical assumptions about it" (Glaser & Strauss, 1967, pp. 29–30).

The "grounded theory" method can be described as a set of comparative analytic procedures by which a theoretical model may be inductively generated from data. The emphasis in this approach is on identifying and describing the fundamental social processes that are occurring within a substantive setting. Through the systematic application of a set of coding procedures, substantive regularities are transformed into conceptual categories of the fundamental process(es). In turn, these conceptual categories constitute the framework of the emerging theoretical model. By returning to new subsets of the data, the researcher can obtain intraresearch verification of the emerging model, as well as new information for the elaboration and modification of the framework. This comparison process is continued until the model is able to subsume all the theoretical variation that exists within the data. At that point, "theoretical saturation" (Glaser & Strauss, 1967, p. 61) has been achieved, and the process is complete.

The model presented in this paper emerged from comments and codes appearing in interviews with obese members of a weight reduction organization that had weekly meetings. The frequency of attendance allowed us to consider the members typical, and allowed us to suggest that major issues of obesity are trans-situational and temporally durable. If obesity disappeared tomorrow, we would still be able to apply the generic concepts generated from our data to make statements about the process of "identity change." As suggested by Hadden, Degher, and Fernandez, our focus is on process rather than on unit characteristics of social phenomena (Hadden, Degher, & Fernandez, 1989, p. 9). This provides us with insights that have import for major issues in sociological theory.

SITE SELECTION

Because obese individuals suffer both internally (negative self-concepts) and externally (discrimination), they possess what Goffman refers to as a "spoiled identity" (Goffman, 1963). This seems to be the case particularly in contemporary America with what may be described as an almost pathological emphasis on fitness. The boom in health clubs, sales of videotapes on fitness, diet books, and so forth promote a definition of the "healthy" physical presence. As Kelly (1990) sees it, the boom in physical fitness in the mid-1980s is an attempt by many people to create a specific image of an ideal body. Thus, body build becomes a crucial element in self-appraisal. Consequently, fat people are an ideal strategic group within which to study the "identity change process."

One of the most significant social consequences of obesity is that it is a condition about which many negative stereotypes exist. Studies of school-age children have consistently found that the overweight child is the least liked, has the fewest friends, and is attributed the greatest number of negative personality characteristics (Staffieri, 1967, p. 101; Lerner, 1969, p. 137; Caskey & Felder, 1971, p. 251; Lerner & Gellert, 1969, p. 456; Lerner & Schroeder, 1971, p. 538; Dion & Berscheid, 1974, p. 1; Penick & Stunkard, 1975, p. 17).

In response to the negative externally held stereotypes, most obese individuals have a poor self-concept and suffer from low self-esteem (Alexander, 1968, p. 3048; Cahnman, 1968, p. 283; Wadden, Foster, & Brownell, 1984, p. 1104; Schumaker, Krejci, & Small, 1985, p. 1147; Mendelson & White, 1985, p. 90; Stein, 1987, p. 77; Martin, Hausley, & McCoy, 1988, p. 879; Pauley, 1989, p. 713).

Obese people are not only the subject of negative stereotypes, they are also actively discriminated against in college admissions (Canning & Mayer, 1966, p. 1172), pay more for goods and services (Petit, 1974), received prejudicial medical treatment (Maddox, Back, & Liederman, 1968, p. 287; Maddox & Liederman, 1969, p. 214), are treated less promptly by salespersons (Pauley, 1989, p. 713), have higher rates of unemployment (Laslett & Warren, 1975, p. 69), and receive lower wages (Register, 1990, p. 130). The obese label is one that seems to clearly fit Becker's description of a "master status," that is

> Some statuses in our society, as in others, override all other statuses and have a certain priority . . . the status deviant (depending on the kind of deviance) is this kind of master status . . . one will be identified as a deviant first, before other identifications are made. (Becker, 1983, p. 33)

Obese people are "fat" first, and only secondarily are seen as possessing ancillary characteristics.

The site for the field observations had to meet two requirements (a) it had to contain a high proportion of obese, or formerly obese individuals; and (b) these individuals had to be identifiable by the observer. The existence of a large number of national weight control organizations (a) whose membership is composed of individuals who have internalized an obese identity; and (b) who emphasize a radical program of identity change, make these organizations an excellent choice as strategic sites for study and analysis.

The local franchise chapter of one of these national weight loss organizations satisfied both of our requirements, and was selected as the site for our study.

Attendance at the weekly meetings of this national weight control group is restricted to individuals who are current members of the organization. Since one requirement for membership is that the individual be at least 10 pounds over the maximum weight for his or her sex and height (according to New York Life tables), all of the people attending the meetings are, or were, overweight, and a high proportion of them are, or were, sufficiently overweight to be classified as obese.[2]

During the period of the initial field observations, the weekly membership of the group varied from 30 to 100 members, with an average attendance of around 60 members. Although there was a considerable turnover in membership, the greatest part of this turnover consisted of "rejoins" (individuals who had been members previously, and were joining again).

Although we have no quantitative data from which to generalize, the group membership appeared to represent a cross section of the larger community. The group included both male and female members, although females did constitute about three fourths of the membership. Although the membership was predominantly white, a range of ethnicities, notably Hispanic and Native American, existed within the group. The majority of the members appeared to fall within the 30 to 50 age range, although there was a member as young as 11, and one over 70.

DATA COLLECTION

Two types of data were gathered for this study: field observations and in-depth interviews. The field observations were performed while attending meetings of a local weight control organization. The insights gained from these observations were used primarily to develop interview guides. There were two major sources of observation during the meeting itself.[3] The observations were recorded in note form and served to provide an orientation for the subsequent interviews. The goal during this period of observation was to gain insight into the basic processes of obesity and the obese career.

The in-depth interviews were carried out with 29 members from the local group. The interviews were solicited on a voluntary basis, and each individual was assured anonymity. The interviewees were representative of the group membership. Although most were middle- aged, middle-income, white females, various age groups, ethnicities, marital statuses, genders, and social classes were presented.

These interviews lasted in length from $\frac{1}{2}$ to $2\frac{1}{2}$ hours, with the average interview being about 1 hour and 15 minutes in duration. The interviews produced almost 40 hours of taped discussion, which yielded more than 600 pages of typed transcript for coding.

ANALYSIS

The analytic technique used upon the interview data corresponds roughly to the method developed by Glaser and Strauss (1967) for generating "grounded theory." This approach consists of a series of steps for systematically codifying qualitative data. These steps involve (a) substantive coding; (b) theoretical coding; and (c) writing and sorting memos. As Glaser and Strauss wrote, "Joint collection, coding, and analysis of data is the underlying operation. The generating of theory, coupled with the notion of theory as process, requires that all three operations be done together as much as possible" (Glaser & Strauss, 1967, p. 43). We believe the combination of techniques used yielded a substantial range of data on overweight individuals. Based on our data, it is possible to make legitimate generalizations about the process involved in the construction of a "fat identity."

THE IDENTITY CHANGE PROCESS

In conceptualizing the "identity change" process, the concept of "career" was employed. As Goffman notes, "career" refers, "...to any social strand of any person's course through life" (Goffman, 1961, p. 127). In the present paper, our concern is the change process that takes place as individuals come to see definitions of self in light of specific transmitted information.

An important aspect of this career model is what Becker referred to as "career contingencies," or "...those factors on which mobility from one position to another depends. Career contingencies include both the objective facts of social structure, and changes in the perspectives, motivations, and desires of the individual" (Becker, 1962, p. 24).

Thus, the "identity change" process must be viewed on two levels: a public (external) and a private (internal) level. As Goffman has stated, "One value of the concept of career is its twosidedness. One side is linked to internal matters held dearly and closely, such as image of self and felt identity; the other side concerns official position, jural relations, and style of life and is part of a publicly acceptable institution complex" (Goffman, 1961, p. 127).

On the public level, social status exists as part of the public domain; social status is socially defined and promoted. The social environment not only contains definitions and attendant stereotypes for each status, it also contains information, in the form of *status cues,* about the applicability of that status for the individual.

On the internal level, two distinct cognitive processes must take place for the identity change process to occur: first, the individual must come to recognize that the current status is inappropriate; and second, the individual must locate a new, more appropriate status. Thus, in response to the external status cues, the individual comes to recognize internally that the

Figure 1 / Visualization of the Identity Change Process (ICP)

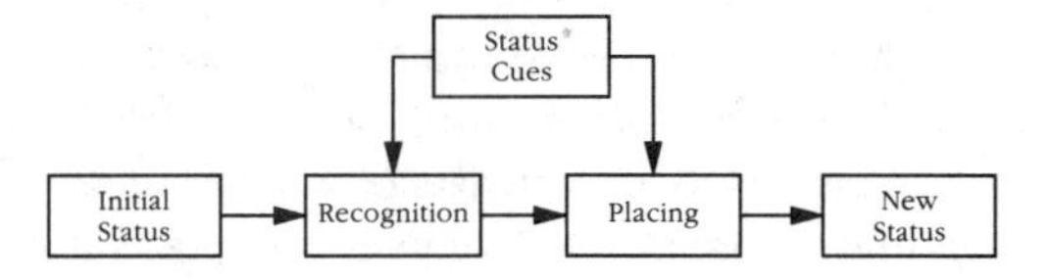

initial status is inappropriate; and then he or she uses the cues to locate a new, more appropriate status. The identity change occurs in response to, and is mediated through, the status cues that exist in the social environment (Figure 1).

STATUS CUES: THE EXTERNAL COMPONENT

Status cues make up the public or external component of the identity change process. A status cue is some feature of the social environment that contains information about a particular status or status dimension. Because this paper is about obesity, cues of interest are about "fatness." Such status cues provide information about whether or not the individual is "fat," and if so, how "fat."

"Recognizing" and "placing" comprise the internal component of the identity change process and occur in response to, and are mediated through, the status cues that exist in the social environment. In order to fully understand the identity change process, it is necessary to explain the interaction between outer and inner processes (Scheff, 1988, p. 396), or in our case, external and internal components of the process.

Status cues are transmitted in two ways: actively and passively. Active cues are communicated through interaction. For example, people are informed by peers, friends, spouses, etc., that they are overweight. The following are some typical comments that occurred repeatedly in the interviews in response to the questions, "How did you know that you were fat?"

> I was starting to be called chubby, and being teased in school.
>
> When my mother would take me shopping, she'd get angry because the clothes that were supposed to be in my age group wouldn't fit me. She would yell at me.
>
> Well, people would say, "When did you put on all your weight, Bob?" You know, something like that. You know, you kind of get the message, that, you know, I put on weight.

A second category of cues might accurately be described as passive in form. The information in these cues exists within the environment, but the individual must in some way be sensitized to that information. For example, standing on a scale will provide an individual with information about weight. It is up to the individual to get on the scale, look at the numbers, and then make some sense out of them. Other passive cues might involve seeing one's reflection in a mirror, standing next to others, fitting in chairs, or, as frequently mentioned by respondents, the sizing of clothes. The comments below, all made in response to the question, "How did you know that you were fat?" are representative of passive cue statements.

> I think that it was not being able to wear the clothes that the other kids wore.

> How did I know? Because when we went to get weighed, I weighed more than my, uh, a girl my height should have weighed, according to the chart, according to all the charts that I used to read. That's when I first noticed that I was overweight.

> I would see all these ladies come in and they could wear size 11 and 12, and I thought, Why can't I do that? I should be able to do that.

Both active and passive cues serve as mechanisms for communicating information about a specific status. As can be seen from the data, events occur that force the individual to evaluate his or her conceptions of self.

RECOGNIZING

The term "recognizing" refers to the cognitive process by which an individual becomes aware that a particular status is no longer appropriate. As shown in Figure 1, the process assumes the individual's acceptance of some initial status. For obese individuals, the initial status is that of "normal body build."[4] This assumption is based on the observation that none of our interviewees assumed that they were "always fat." Even those who were fat as children could identify when they became aware that they were "fat." Through the perception of discrepant status cues, the individual comes to recognize that the initial status is inappropriate. It is possible that the person will perceive the discrepant cues and will either ignore or reject them, in which case the initial status is retained. The factors regulating such a failure to recognize are important, but are not dealt with in this paper. Further research on this point is called for.

Status cues are the external mechanisms through which the recognizing takes place, but it is paying attention to the information contained in these cues that triggers the internal cognitive process of recognizing.

An important point is that the acceptance (or rejection) of a particular status does not occur simply because the individual possesses a set of objective characteristics. For example, two people may have similar body builds, but one may have a self-definition of "fat" whereas the other may not. There appears to be a rather tenuous connection between objective condition and subjective definition. The following comments are supportive of this disjunction.

> I was really, as far as pounds go, very thin, but I had a feeling about myself that I was huge.

> Well, I don't remember ever thinking about it until I was about in eighth grade. But I was looking back at pictures when I was little. I was always chunky, chubby.

This lack of necessary connection between objective condition and subjective definition points up an important and frequently overlooked feature of social statuses: the extent to which they are *self-evident*. Self-evidentiality refers to the degree to which a person who possesses certain objective status characteristics is *aware* that a particular status label applies to them.[5]

Some statuses possess a high degree of evidentiality: gender identification is one of these.[6] On the other hand, being beautiful or intelligent is somewhat non-self-evident. This is not to imply that individuals are either ignorant of these statuses or of the characteristics upon which they are assigned. People may know that other people are intelligent, but they may be unaware that the label is equally applicable to them.

One idea that emerged quite early from the interviews was that being "fat" is a relatively non-self-evident status. Individuals do not recognize that "fat" is the description that applies to them.[7] The objective condition of being overweight is not sufficient, in itself, to promote the adoption of a "fat" identity. This non-self-evidentiality is demonstrated in the following excerpts.

> I think that I just thought that it was a little bit here and there. I didn't think of it, and I didn't think of myself as looking bad. But you know, I must have.

> I have pictures of me right after the baby was born. I had no idea that I was that fat.

The self-evidentiality of a status is important in the discussion of the identity change process. The less self-evident a status, the more difficult the recognizing process becomes. Further, because recognition occurs in response to status cues, the self-evidentiality of a status will influence the type of cues that play the most prominent role in identity change.

A somewhat speculative observation should be made about status cues in the recognizing process. For our subjects, recognizing occurred primarily through active cues. When passive cues were involved, they typically were highly visible and unambiguous. In general, active cues appear to be more potent in forcing the individuals's attention to the information that the current status is inappropriate. The predominance of these active cues is possibly a consequence of the relatively non-self-evident character of the "fat" status. It is probable that the less self-evident a status, the more likely that the recognizing process will occur through active rather than passive cues.

Once the individual comes to recognize the inappropriateness of the initial status, it becomes necessary to locate a new, more appropriate status. This search for a more appropriate status is referred to as the "placing" process.[8]

PLACING

Placing refers to a cognitive process whereby an individual comes to identify an appropriate status from among those available. The number of status categories along a status dimension influences the placing process. A status dimension may contain any number of status categories. If there are only two status dimensional categories, such as in the case of gender, the placement process is more or less automatic. When individuals recognize that they do not belong in one category, the remaining category becomes the obvious alternative. The greater the number of status categories, the more difficult the placing process becomes.

The body build dimension contains an extremely large number of categories. When an individual recognizes that he or she does not possess a "normal" body build, there are innumerable alternatives open. The knowledge that one's status lies toward the "fat" rather than the "thin" end of the continuum still presents a wide range of choices. In everyday conversation, we hear terms that describe these alternatives: chubby, porky, plump, hefty, full-figured, beer belly, etc. All are informal descriptions reflecting the myriad categories along the body build dimension.

> I wasn't real fat in my eyes. I don't think. I was just chunky.
>
> Not fat. I didn't exactly classify it as fat. I just thought, I'm, you know, I am a pudgy lady.
>
> I don't think that I have ever called myself fat. I have called myself heavy.

Even when individuals adopt a "fat" identity, they attempt to make distinctions about how fat they are. Because being fat is a devalued status, individuals attempt to escape the full weight of its negative attributes while still acknowledging the non-normal status. The following responses exemplify this attempt to neutralize the pejorative connotations of having a "fat" status. The practice of differentiating one's status from others becomes vital in managing a fat identity.

Q: How did you know that you weren't *that* fat?
A: Well, comparing myself to others at the time, I didn't really feel that I was that fat. But I knew maybe because they didn't treat me the same way they treated people who were heavier than me. You know, I got teased lightly, but I was still liked by a lot of people, and the people that were heavy weren't.

As is apparent from this excerpt, the individual neutralized self-image by linking "fatness" with the level of teasing done by peers.

NEW STATUS

The final phase of the identity change process involves the acceptance of a new status. For our informants, it was the acceptance of a "fat" status, along with its previously mentioned pejorative characterizations.[9]

> I hate to look in mirrors. I hate that. It makes me feel so self-conscious. If I walk into a store, and I see my reflection in the glass, I just look away.

> We'd go somewhere and I would think, "I never look as good as everybody else." You know everybody always looks better. I'd cry before we'd go bowling because I'd think, "Oh, I just look awful."

As is clear, the final phase of the identity change process involves the internalization of a negative (deviant) definition of self. For many fat people accepting a new status means starting on the merry-go-round of weight reduction programs.[10] Many of these programs or organizations attempt to get members to accept a devalued status fully, and then work to change it. Consequently, individuals are forced to "admit" that they are fat and to "witness" in front of others.[11] The new identity becomes that of a "fat" person, which the weight reduction programs then attempt to transform. A further analysis of the impact of informal organizations on the identity change process will be attempted in another paper.

CONCLUSION

In this paper, we have attempted a fill a void within the interactionist literature by presenting an inductively generated model of the identity change process. The proposed model treats the change process from a career focus, and thus addresses both the external (public) and the internal (cognitive) features of the identity change.

We have suggested that the adoption of a new status takes place through two sequential cognitive processes, "recognizing" and "placing." First, the individual must come to recognize that a current status is no longer appropriate. Second, the individual must locate a new, more appropriate status from among those available. We have further suggested that these internal or cognitive processes are triggered by and mediated through status cues, which exist in the external environment. These cues can be either active or passive. Active cues are transmitted through interaction, whereas passive cues must be sought out by the individual.

We also found a relationship between the evidentiality of the status, that is, how obvious that status is to the individual, and the role of the different types of cues in the identity change process. Finally, we have suggested that the adoption of a new status is a trigger for further career changes.

Although the model presented in this paper was generated inductively from field data on obese individuals, we are confident that it may be fruitfully applied to the study of other deviant careers. It seems particularly appropriate where the identity involved has a low degree of self-evidentiality.

In addition, we feel that the focus upon the different types of status cues and their differing roles in the recognizing and placing processes can lead to a better understanding of how institutionally promoted identity changes occur.

Notes

1. Included here is research on both rule creators and rule enforcers. We have not made an attempt to analytically separate the two types of investigation.

2. Some of the members had successfully lost their excess weight. When these people were present at a meeting, a leader was careful to introduce them to the other members of the class and to tell how much weight they had lost. This was done to uphold their claim to acceptance by the other group members.

3. Access to this information was gained from an "insider" perspective because one of the researchers was well known among the membership, being an "off and on" member of the organization for 3 years. Thus, he was not confronted with the problem of gaining entry into a semi-closed social setting. Similarly, because the observer had "been an ongoing participant of the group," he did not have to desensitize the other members of the group to his presence.

4. It is important to note that this process can operate generically. That is, it is not only applicable to the "identity change" from a "normal" to a "deviant" identity, but can encompass the reverse process as well. In a forthcoming project, we will use the process to analyze how various rehabilitation programs attempt to get individuals back to the initial status.

5. This concept is different in an important way from what Goffman calls "visibility." He uses the term to refer to, "...how well or how badly the stigma is adapted to provide means of communicating that the individual possesses it" (Goffman, 1963, p. 48). The focus of the concept is on how readily the social environment can identify that the individual possesses a stigmatized trait. The concept of self-evidentiality deals with how readily the individual can internalize possession of the stigmatized trait. The focus is upon the actor's perceptions, not on the audience.

6. We are referring here to the physiological description of being male or female. We realize that sex roles are much less self-evident.

7. Conversely, a number of individuals thought of themselves as "fat" or "obese," and were objectively "normal." In this case, the existence of objective indicators was insufficient to prevent the individual from adopting a "fat" identity.

8. In some instances, recognizing and placing occur simultaneously. This is especially true when the cue involved is an active one, and contains information about both the initial and new statuses. For example, if peers call a child "fatty," this interaction informs the child that the "normal" status is inappropriate. At the same time, it informs the child that being "fat" is the appropriate status. Even here however, the individual must recognize before it is possible to place.

9. This phase corresponds closely to that presented in much of the "subcultural" research. (See Schur, 1971; Becker, 1963; Sykes & Matza, 1957, p. 664.)

10. Weight Watchers, TOPS, Overeaters Anonymous, Diet Center, and OptiFast are typical examples of this type of program.

11. By witnessing, we are referring to the process whereby individuals come to renounce in front of others, a former self and former behaviors associated with that self. Some religious groups, Synanon, Alcoholics Anonymous, etc., seem to encourage this type of degradation of self.

References

Alexander, W. R. (1968). A study of body types, self image, and environmental adjustment in freshman college women. *Dissertation Abstracts,* 2B(8A):3048.

Baum, L. (1987, August 3) Extra pounds can weigh down your career. *Business Week*, p. 96.
Becker, H. S. (1963). *Outsiders: Studies in the sociology of deviance*. New York: Free Press.
Bigus, O. E., Hadden, S. C., & Glaser, B. G. (1982). The study of basic social processes. In P. Smith, J. Manning, & B. Robert (Eds.), *Handbook of social science method: Qualitative methods*. New York: Irving.
Cahnman, W. J. (1968). The stigma of obesity. *Sociological Quarterly*, 9 (Summer), 283–299.
Canning, H. & Mayer, J. (1966). Obesity: Its possible effects on college acceptance. *New England Journal of Medicine*, 275(24); November, 1172–1174.
Caskey, S., & Felker, D. W. (1971). Social stereotyping of female body image by elementary school age girls. *Research Quarterly*, 42(3); October, 251–253.
Cicourel, A. (1968). *The social organization of juvenile justice*. New York: Wiley.
Conrad, P. (1975). The discovery of hyperkinesis: Notes on the medicalization of deviant behavior. *Social Problems*, 23,(1); October, 12–21.
Dion, K., & Berscheid, E. (1984). Physical attractiveness and peer perception among children. *Sociometry*, 37(1): 1–12.
Glaser, B. G. (1978). *Theoretical sensitivity*. San Francisco: Sociology Press.
Glaser, B. G., & Strauss, A. L. (1967). *The discovery of grounded theory: Strategies for qualitative research*. Chicago: Aldine.
Goffman, E. (1961). *Asylums*. Garden City, NY: Anchor.
Goffman, E. (1963). *Stigma: Notes on the management of spoiled identity*. Englewood Cliffs, NJ: Prentice-Hall.
Greenberg, D. (1989). The antifat conspiracy. *New Scientist*, 22, (April 22): 79.
Hadden, S. C., Degher, D., & Fernandez, R. (1989). Sports as a strategic ethnographic arena. *Arena Review*, 13(1): 9–19.
Kelly, J. R. (1990). *Leisure* (2nd ed.). Englewood Cliffs, NJ: Prentice-Hall.
Kitsuse, J. (1962) Societal Reactions to deviant behavior: Problems of theory and method. *Social Problems*, 9 (Winter): 247–256.
Laslett, B., & Warren, C. A. B. (1975). Losing weight: The organizational promotion of behavior change. *Social Problems*, 23(1): 69–80.
Lemert, E. (1951). *Social Pathology*. New York: McGraw-Hill.
Lerner, R. M. (1969). The development of stereotyped expectancies of body build behavior relations. *Child Development*, 40(1): 137–141.
Lerner, R. M., & Gellert, E. (1969). Body building identification, preferences, and aversions in children. *Developmental Psychology*, 5(3): 456–462.
Lerner, R. M., & Schroeder, C. (1971). Physique identification, preferences, and aversion in kindergarten children. *Developmental Psychology*, 5(3): 538.
Maddox, G. L., Back, K. W., & Liederman, V. (1968). Overweight as social deviance and disability. *Journal of Health and Social Behavior*, 9(4): 287–298.
Maddox, G. L., & Liederman, V. (1969). Overweight as a social disability with medical implications. *Journal of Medical Education*, 9(4): 287–298.
Martin, S., Housely, K., & McCoy, H. (1988). Self-esteem of adolescent girls as related to weight. *Perceptual and Motor Skills*, 67: 879–884.
Mendelson, B. K., & White, D. R. (1985). Development of self-body-esteem in overweight youngsters. *Developmental Psychology*, 21: 90–96.
Pauley, L. L. (1989). Customer weights as a variable in salespersons' response time. *Journal of Social Psychology*, 129: 713–714.

Penick, S. B., & Stunkard, A. J. (1975). Newer concepts of obesity. In B. Q. Hefen (Ed.), *Overweight and obesity: Causes, fallacies, treatment* (pp. 17–26). Provo, UT: Brigham Young University Press.

Petit, D. W. (1974). The ills of the obese. In G. A. Gray & J. E. Bethune (Eds.), *Treatment and management of obesity*. New York: Harper & Row.

Piliavin, I., & Briar, S. (1964). Police encounters with juveniles. *American Journal of Sociology*, (September): 206–214.

Register, C. A. (1990). Wage effects of obesity among young workers. *Social Science Quarterly*, 71 (March): 130–141.

Scheff, T. (1988). Shame and conformity: The deference emotion system. *American Journal of Sociology*, 53 (June): 395–406.

Schumaker, J. F., Krejci, R. C., & Small, L. (1985). Experience of loneliness by obese individuals. *Psychological Reports*, 57(2): 1147–1154.

Schur, E. M. (1971). *Labeling deviant behavior: Its sociological implications*. New York: Harper & Row.

Staffieri, J. R. (1967). A study of social stereotypes of body image in children. *Journal of Personality and Social Psychology*, 7(1): 101–104.

Stein, R. F. (1987). Comparison of self-concept of non-obese and obese university junior female nursing students. *Adolescence*, 22 (Spring): 77–90.

Sykes, G., & Matza, D. (1957). Techniques of neutralization: a theory of delinquency. *American Sociological Review*, (December): 664–670.

Tannenbaum, F. (1939). *Crime and the community*. New York: Columbia University Press.

Wadden, T. A., Foster, G. D., & Brownell, K. D. (1984). Self-concept in obese and normal weight children. *Journal of Consulting and Clinical Psychology*, 52 (December): 1104–1105.

42 / Suspended Identity: Identity Transformation in a Maximum Security Prison

THOMAS J. SCHMID
RICHARD S. JONES

The extent to which people hide behind the masks of impression management in everyday life is a point of theoretical controversy (Goffman 1959; Gross and Stone 1964; Irwin 1977; Douglas et al. 1980; Douglas and Johnson 1977; Messinger et al. 1962; Blumer 1969, 1972). A variety of problematic circumstances can be identified, however, in which individuals find it necessary to accommodate a sudden but encompassing shift in social situations by establishing temporary identities. These circumstances, which can range from meteoric fame (Adler and Adler 1989) to confinement in total institutions, place new identity demands on the individual, while seriously challenging his or her prior identity bases.

A prison sentence constitutes a "massive assault" on the identity of those imprisoned (Berger 1963: 100–101). This assault is especially severe on first-time inmates, and we might expect radical identity changes to ensue from their imprisonment. At the same time, a prisoner's awareness of the challenge to his identity affords some measure of protection against it. As part of an ethnographic analysis of the prison experiences of first-time, short-term inmates, this article presents an identity transformation model that differs both from the gradual transformation processes that characterize most adult identity changes and from such radical transformation processes as brainwashing or conversion.

Data for the study are derived principally from ten months of participant observation at a maximum security prison for men in the upper midwest of the United States. One of the authors was an inmate serving a felony sentence for one year and one day, while the other participated in the study as an outside observer. Relying on traditional ethnographic data collection and analysis techniques, this approach offered us general observations of hundreds of prisoners, and extensive fieldnotes that were based on repeated, often daily, contacts with about fifty inmates, as well as on personal relationships established with a smaller number of inmates. We subsequently

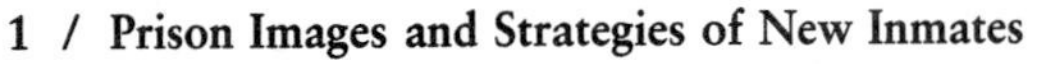

1 / Prison Images and Strategies of New Inmates

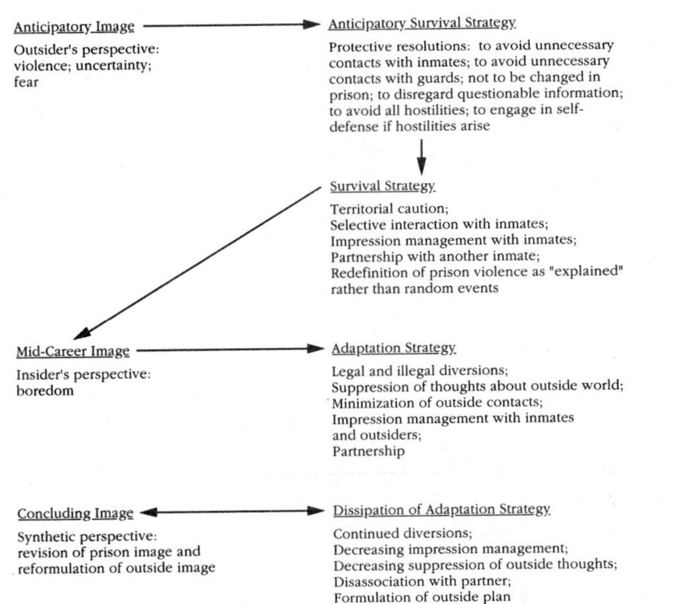

returned to the prison to conduct focused interviews with other prisoners; using information provided by prison officials, we were able to identify and interview twenty additional first-time inmates who were serving sentences of two years or less. See Schmid and Jones (1987) for further description of this study.

Three interrelated research questions guided our analysis: How do first-time, short-term inmates define the prison world, and how do their definitions change during their prison careers? How do these inmates adapt to the prison world, and how do their adaptation strategies change during their prison careers? How do their self-definitions change during their prison careers? Our analyses of the first two questions are presented in detail elsewhere (Schmid and Jones 1987, 1990); an abbreviated outline of these analyses, to which we will allude throughout this article, is presented in Figure 1. The identity transformation model presented here, based on our analysis of the third question, is outlined in Figure 2.

PREPRISON IDENTITY

Our data suggest that the inmates we studied have little in common before their arrival at prison, except their conventionality. Although convicted of felonies, most do not possess "criminal" identities (cf. Irwin 1970: 29–34). They begin their sentences with only a vague, incomplete image

2 / Suspended Identity Dialectic

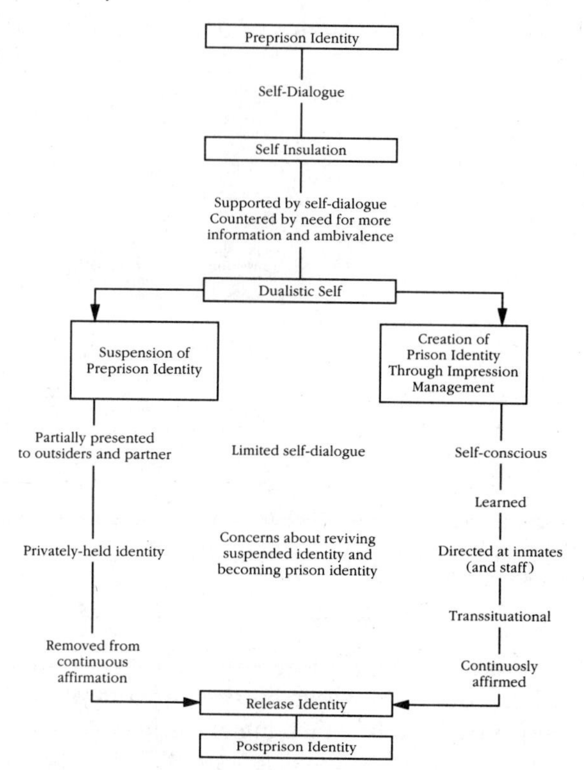

(Boulding 1961) of what prison is like, but an image that nonetheless stands in contrast to how they view their own social worlds. Their prison image is dominated by the theme of violence: they see prison inmates as violent, hostile, alien human beings, with whom they have nothing in common. They have several specific fears about what will happen to them in prison, including fears of assault, rape, and death. They are also concerned about their identities, fearing that—if they survive prison at all—they are in danger of changing in prison, either through the intentional efforts of rehabilitation personnel or through the unavoidable hardening effects of the prison environment. Acting on this imagery (Blumer 1969)—or, more precisely, on the inconsonance of their self-images with this prison image—they develop an anticipatory survival strategy (see Figure 1) that consists primarily of protective resolutions: a resolve to avoid all hostilities; a resolve to avoid all nonessential contacts with inmates and guards; a resolve to defend themselves in any way possible; and a resolve not to change, or to be changed, in prison.

A felon's image and strategy are formulated through a running self-dialogue, a heightened state of reflexive awareness (Lewis 1979) through which he ruminates about his past behavior and motives, and imaginatively projects himself into the prison world. This self-dialogue begins shortly after his arrest, continues intermittently during his trial or court hearings, and becomes especially intense at the time of his transfer to prison.

> You start taking a review—it's almost like your life is passing before your eyes. You wonder how in the heck you got to this point and, you know, what are—what's your family gonna think about it—your friends, all the talk, and how are you going to deal with that—and the kids, you know, how are they gonna react to it?... All those things run through your head.... The total loss of control—the first time in all my life that some other people were controlling my life.

* * *

> My first night in the joint was spent mainly on kicking myself in the butt for putting myself in the joint. It was a very emotional evening. I thought a lot about all my friends and family, the good-byes, the things we did the last couple of months, how good they had been to me, sticking by me. I also thought about my fears: Am I going to go crazy? Will I end up fighting for my life? How am I going to survive in here for a year? Will I change? Will things be the same when I get out?

His self-dialogue is also typically the most extensive self-assessment he has ever conducted; thus, at the same time that he is resolving not to change, he is also initiating the kind of introspective analysis that is essential to any identity transformation process.

SELF-INSULATION

A felon's self-dialogue continues during the initial weeks and months of his sentence, and it remains a solitary activity, each inmate struggling to come to grips with the inconsonance of his established (preprison) identity and his present predicament. Despite the differences in their preprison identities, however, inmates now share a common situation that affects their identities. With few exceptions, their self-dialogues involve feelings of vulnerability, discontinuity, and differentiation from other inmates, emotions that reflect both the degradations and deprivations of institutional life (cf. Goffman 1961; Sykes 1958; and Garfinkel 1956) and their continuing outsiders' perspective on the prison world. These feelings are obviously the result of everything that has happened to the inmates, but they are something else as well: they are the conditions in which every first-time, short-term inmate finds himself. They might even be called the common attributes of the inmates' selves-in-prison, for the irrelevance of their preprison identities within the prison world reduces their self-definitions, temporarily, to the level of pure emotion.[1] These feelings, and a consequent emphasis on the "physical self" (Zurcher 1977: 176), also constitute the essential motivation for the inmates' self-insulation strategies.[2]

An inmate cannot remain wholly insulated within the prison world, for a number of reasons. He simply spends too much of his time in the presence of others to avoid all interaction with them. He also recognizes that his prison image is based on incomplete and inadequate information, and that he must interact with others in order to acquire first-hand information about the prison world. His behavior in prison, moreover, is guided not only by his prison image but by a fundamental ambivalence he feels about his situation, resulting from his marginality between the prison and outside social worlds (Schmid and Jones 1987). His ambivalence has several manifestations throughout his prison career, but the most important is his conflicting desires for self-insulation and for human communication.

MANAGING A DUALISTIC SELF

An inmate is able to express both directions of his ambivalence (and to address his need for more information about the prison) by drawing a distinction between his "true" identity (i.e., his outside, preprison identity) and a "false" identity he creates for the prison world. For most of a new inmate's prison career, his preprison identity remains a "subjective" or "personal" identity while his prison identity serves as his "objective" or "social" basis for interaction in prison (see Weigert 1986; Goffman 1963). This bifurcation of his self (Figure 2) is not a conscious decision made at a single point in time, but it does represent two conscious and interdependent identity-preservation tactics, formulated through self-dialogue and refined through tentative interaction with others.

First, after coming to believe that he cannot "be himself" in prison because he would be too vulnerable, he decides to "suspend" his preprison identity for the duration of his sentence. He retains his resolve not to let prison change him, protecting himself by choosing not to reveal himself (his "true" self) to others. Expressions of a suspension of identity emerged repeatedly and consistently in both the fieldwork and interview phases of our research through such statements as

> I was reserved.... I wouldn't be very communicative, you know. I'd try to keep conversation to a minimum.... I wasn't interested in getting close to anybody... or asking a lot of questions. You know, try to cut the conversation short... go my own way back to my cell or go to the library or do something.

* * *

> I didn't want nobody to know too much about me. That was part of the act.

An inmate's decision to suspend his preprison identity emanates directly from his feelings of vulnerability, discontinuity and differentiation from other inmates. These emotions foster something like a "proto-sociological attitude" (Weigert 1986: 173; see also Zurcher 1977), in which new inmates find it necessary to step outside their taken-for-granted preprison identities. Rather than viewing these identities and the everyday life experience in which they are grounded as social constructions, however, inmates see the *prison* world as an artificial construction, and judge their "naturally occurring" preprison identities to be out of place within this construction. By attempting to suspend his preprison identity for the time that he spends in prison an inmate believes that he will again "be his old self" after his release.

While he is in confinement, an inmate's decision to suspend his identity leaves him with little or no basis for interaction. His second identity tactic, then, is the creation of an identity that allows him to interact, however cautiously, with others. This tactic consists of his increasingly sophisticated impression management skills (Goffman 1959; Schlenker 1980), which are initially designed simply to hide his vulnerability, but which gradually evolve into an alternative identity felt to be more suitable to the prison world. The character of the presented identity is remarkably similar from inmate to inmate:

> Well, I learned that you can't act like—you can't get the attitude where you are better than they are. Even where you might be better than them, you can't strut around like you are. Basically, you can't stick out. You don't stare at people and things like that. I knew a lot of these things from talking to people and I figured them out by myself. I sat down and figured out just what kind of attitude I'm going to have to take.

* * *

> Most people out here learn to be tough, whether they can back it up or not. If you don't learn to be tough, you will definitely pay for it. This toughness can be demonstrated through a mean look, tough language, or an extremely big build.... One important thing is never to let your guard down.

An inmate's prison identity, as an inauthentic presentation of self, is not in itself a form of identity transformation but is rather a form of identity construction. His prison identity is simply who he must pretend to be while he is in prison. It is a false identity created for survival in an artificial world. But this identity nonetheless emerges in the same manner as any other identity: it is learned from others, and it must be presented to, negotiated with, and validated by others. A new inmate arrives at prison with a general image of what prisoners are like, and he begins to flesh out this image from the day of his arrival, warily observing others just as they are observing him. Through watching others, through eavesdropping, through cautious conversation and selective interaction, a new inmate refines his understanding of what maximum security prisoners look like, how they talk, how they move, how they act. Despite his belief that he is different from these other prisoners, he knows that he cannot appear to be too different from them, if he is to hide his vulnerability. His initial image of other prisoners, his early observations, and his concern over how he appears to others thus provide a foundation for the identity he gradually creates through impression management.

Impression management skills, of course, are not exclusive to the prison world; a new inmate, like anyone else, has had experience in the creation of his prison identity. He has undoubtedly even had experience in presenting a "front" to others, and he draws upon his experience in projecting the very attributes—strength, stoicism, aplomb—required by his prison identity. Impression management in prison differs, however, in the totality with which it governs interactions and in the perceived costs of failure: humiliation, assault, or death. For these reasons the entire impression management process becomes a more highly conscious endeavor. When presenting himself before others, a new inmate pays close attention to such minute details of his front as eye contact, posture, and manner of walking:

> I finally got out of orientation. I was going out with the main population, going down to get my meals and things. The main thing is not to stare at a bunch of people, you know. I tried to just look ahead, you know, not stare at people. 'Cause I didn't really know; I just had to learn a little at a time.

* * *

> The way you look seems to be very important. The feeling is you shouldn't smile, that a frown is much more appropriate. The eyes are very important. You should never look away; it is considered a sign of weakness. Either stare straight ahead, look around, or look the person dead in the eyes. The way you walk is important. You shouldn't walk too fast; they might think you were scared and in a hurry to get away.

To create an appropriate embodiment (Weigert 1986; Stone 1962) of their prison identities, some new intimates devote long hours to weightlifting or other body-building exercises, and virtually all of them relinquish their civilian clothes—which might express their preprison identities—in favor of the standard issue clothing that most inmates wear. Whenever a new inmate is open to the view of other inmates, in fact, he is likely to relinquish most overt symbols of his individuality, in favor of a standard issue "prison inmate" appearance.

By acting self-consciously, of course, a new inmate runs the risk of exposing the fact that he *is* acting. But he sees no alternative to playing his part better; he cannot "not act" because that too would expose the vulnerability of his "true" identity. He thus sees every new prison experience, every new territory that he is allowed to explore, as a test of his impression management skills. Every nonconfrontive encounter with another inmate symbolizes his success at these skills, but it is also a social validation of his prison identity. Eventually he comes to see that many, perhaps most, inmates are engaging in the same kind of inauthentic presentations of self (cf. Glaser and Strauss 1964). Their identities are as "false" as his, and their validations of his identity may be equally false. But he realizes that he is powerless to change this state of affairs, and that he must continue to present his prison identity for as long as he remains in prison.

A first-time inmate enters prison as an outsider, and it is from an outsider's perspective that he initially creates his prison identity. In contrast to his suspended preprison identity, his prison identity is a *shared* identity, because it is modeled on his observations of other inmates. Like those of more experienced prisoners, his prison identity is tied directly to the social role of "prison inmate" (cf. Scheff 1970; Solomon 1970); because he is an outsider, however, his prison identity is also severely limited by his narrow understanding of that role. It is based on an outsider's stereotype of who a maximum security inmate is and what he acts like. It is, nonetheless, a *structural* identity (Weigert 1968), created to address his outsider's institutional problems of social isolation and inadequate information about the prison world.

By the middle of his sentence, a new inmate comes to adopt what is essentially an insider's perspective on the prison world. His prison image has evolved to the point where it is dominated by the theme of boredom rather than violence. (The possibility of violence is still acknowledged and feared, but those violent incidents that do occur have been redefined as the consequences of prison norm violations rather than as random predatory acts; see Schmid and Jones 1990.) His survival strategy, although still extant, has been supplemented by such general adaptation techniques as legal and illegal diversionary activities and conscious efforts to suppress his thoughts about the outside world (Figure 1). His impression management tactics have become second nature rather than self-conscious, as he routinely interacts with others in terms of his prison identity.

An inmate's suspension of his preprison identity, of course, is never absolute, and the separation between his suspended identity and his prison identity is never complete. He continues to interact with his visitors at least partially in terms of his preprison identity, and he is likely to have acquired at least one inmate "partner" with whom he interacts in terms of his preprison as well as his prison identity. During times of introspection, however—which take place less frequently but do not disappear—he generally continues to think of himself as being the same person he was before he came to prison. But it is also during these periods of self-dialogue that he begins to have doubts about his ability to revive his suspended identity.

> That's what I worry about a lot. Because I didn't want to change.... I'm still fighting it, 'cause from what I understood, before, I wasn't that bad—I wasn't even violent. But I have people say stuff to me now, before I used to say "O.k., o.k."—but now it seems like I got to eye them back, you know.

* * *

> I don't know, but I may be losing touch with the outside. I am feeling real strange during visits, very uncomfortable. I just can't seem to be myself, although I am not really sure what myself is all about. My mind really seems to be glued to the inside of these walls. I can't even really comprehend the outside. I haven't even been here three months, and I feel like I'm starting to lose it. Maybe I'm just paranoid. But during these visits I really feel like I'm acting. I'm groping for the right words, always trying to keep the conversation going. Maybe I'm just trying to present a picture that will relieve the minds of my visitors, I just don't know.

* * *

> I realized that strength is going to be an important factor whether I'm going to turn into a cold person or whether I'm going to keep my humanitarian point of view. I knew it is going to be an internal war. It's going to take a lot of energy to do that.... I just keep telling myself that you gotta do it and sometimes you get to the point where you don't care anymore. You just kinda lose it and you get so full of hate, so full of frustration, it gets wound up in your head a lot.

At this point, both the inmate's suspended preprison identity and his created prison identity are part of his "performance consciousness" (Schechner 1985), although they are not given equal value. His preprison identity is grounded primarily in the memory of his biography (Weigert 1986) rather than in self-performance. His concern, during the middle of his sentence, is that he has become so accustomed to dealing with others in terms of his prison identity—that he has been presenting and receiving affirmation of this identity for so long—that it is becoming his "true" identity.[3]

An inmate's fear that he is becoming the character he has been presenting is not unfounded. All of his interactions within the prison world indicate the strong likelihood of a "role-person merger" (Turner 1978). An inmate views his presentation of his prison identity as a necessary expression of his inmate status. Unlike situational identities presented through impression management in the outside world, performance of the inmate role is transsituational and continuous. For a new inmate, prison consists almost exclusively of front regions, in which he must remain in character. As long as he is in the maximum security institution, he remains in at least partial view of the audience for which his prison identity is intended: other prison inmates.[4] Moreover, because the stakes of his performance are so high, there is little room for self-mockery or other forms of role distance (Ungar

1984; Coser 1966) from his prison identity, and there is little possibility that an inmate's performance will be "punctured" (Adler and Adler 1989) by his partner or other prison acquaintances. And because his presentation of his prison identity is continuous, he also receives continuous affirmation of this identity from others—affirmation that becomes more significant in light of the fact that he also remains removed from day-to-day reaffirmation of his preprison identity by his associates in the outside world. The inauthenticity of the process is beside the point: Stone's (1962: 93) observation that "one's identity is established when others *place* him as a social object by assigning him the same words of identity that he appropriates for himself or *announces*" remains sound even when both the announcements and the placements are recognized as false.

Standing against these various forms of support for an inmate's prison identity are the inmate's resolve not to be changed in prison, the fact that his sentence is relatively brief (though many new inmates lose sight of this brevity during the middle of their careers) and the limited reaffirmation of his preprison identity that he receives from outsiders and from his partner. These are not insubstantial resources, but nor do they guarantee an inmate's future ability to discard his prison identity and revive the one he has suspended.

IDENTITY DIALECTIC

When an inmate's concerns about his identity first emerge, there is little that he can do about them. He recognizes that he has no choice but to present his prison identity so, following the insider's perspective he has now adopted, he consciously attempts to suppress his concerns. Eventually, however, he must begin to consider seriously his capacity to revive his suspended identity; his identity concerns, and his belief that he must deal with them, become particularly acute if he is transferred to the minimum security unit of the prison for the final months of his sentence.[5] At the conclusion of his prison career, an inmate shifts back toward an outsider's perspective on the prison world (see Figure 1); this shift involves the dissipation of his maximum security adaptation strategy, further revision of his prison image, reconstruction of an image of the outside world, and the initial development of an outside plan.[6] The inmate's efforts to revive his suspended identity are part of this shift in perspectives.

It is primarily through a renewed self-dialogue that the inmate struggles to revive his suspended identity—a struggle that amounts to a dialectic between his suspended identity and his prison identity. Through self-dialogue he recognizes, and tries to confront, the extent to which these two identities really do differ. He again tries to differentiate himself from maximum security inmates.

> There seems to be a concern with the inmates here to be able to distinguish... themselves from the other inmates. That is—they feel they are above the others.... Although they may associate with each other, it still seems important to degrade the majority here.

And he does have some success in freeing himself from his prison identity.

> Well, I think I am starting to soften up a little bit. I believe the identity I picked up in the prison is starting to leave me now that I have left the world of the [maximum security] joint. I find myself becoming more and more involved with the happenings of the outside world. I am even getting anxious to go out and see the sights, just to get away from this place.

But he recognizes that he *has* changed in prison, and that these changes run deeper than the mask he has been presenting to others. He has not returned to his "old self" simply because his impression management skills are used less frequently in minimum security. He raises the question—though he cannot answer it—of how permanent these changes are. He wonders how much his family and friends will see him as having changed. As stated by one of our interview respondents:

> I know I've changed a little bit. I just want to realize how the people I know are going to see it, because they [will] be able to see it more than I can see it.... Sometimes I just want to go somewhere and hide.

He speculates about how much the outside world—especially his own network of outside relationships—has changed in his absence. (It is his life, not those of his family and friends, that has been suspended during his prison sentence; he knows that changes have occurred in the outside world, and he suspects that some of these changes may have been withheld from him, intentionally or otherwise.) He has questions, if not serious doubts, about his ability to "make it" on the outside, especially concerning his relationships with others; he knows, in any case, that he cannot simply return to the outside world as if nothing has happened. Above all, he repeatedly confronts the question of who he is, and who he will be in the outside world.

An inmate's struggle with these questions, like his self-dialogue at the beginning of his prison career, is necessarily a solitary activity. The identity he claims at the time of his release, in contrast to his prison identity, cannot be learned from other inmates. Also like his earlier periods of self-dialogue, the questions he considers are not approached in a rational, systematic manner. The process is more one of rumination—of pondering one question until another replaces it, and then contemplating the new question until it is replaced by still another, or suppressed from his thoughts. There is, then, no final resolution to any of the inmate's identity questions. Each inmate confronts these questions in his own way, and each arrives at his own understanding of who he is, based on this unfinished, unresolved self-dialogue. In every case, however, an inmate's release identity is a synthesis of his suspended preprison identity and his prison identity.[7]

POSTPRISON IDENTITY

Because each inmate's release identity is the outcome of his own identity dialectic, we cannot provide a profile of the "typical" release identity. But our data do allow us to specify some of the conditions that affect this outcome. Reaffirmations of his preprison identity by outsiders—visits and furloughs during which others interact with him as if he has not changed—provide powerful support for his efforts to revive his suspended identity. These efforts are also promoted by an inmate's recollection of his preprison identity (i.e., his attempts, through self-dialogue, to assess who he was before he came to prison), by his desire to abandon his prison identity, and by his general shift back toward an outsider's perspective. But there are also several factors that favor his prison identity, including his continued use of diversionary activities; his continued periodic efforts to suppress thoughts about the outside world; his continued ability to use prison impression management skills; and his continuing sense of injustice about the treatment he has received. Strained or cautious interactions with outsiders, or unfulfilled furlough expectations, inhibit the revival of his preprison identity. And he faces direct, experiential evidence that he has changed: when a minimum security resident recognizes that he is now completely unaffected by reports of violent incidents in maximum security, he acknowledges that he is no longer the same person that he was when he entered prison. Turner (1978: 1) has suggested three criteria for role-person merger: "failure of role compartmentalization, resistance to abandoning a role in the face of advantageous alternative roles, and the acquisition of role-appropriate attitudes"; at the time of their release from prison, the inmates we studied had already accrued some experience with each of these criteria.

Just as we cannot define a typical release identity, we cannot predict these inmates' future, postprison identities, not only because we have restricted our analysis to their prison experiences but because each inmate's future identity is inherently unpredictable. What effect an ex-inmate's prison experience has on his identity depends on how he, in interaction with others, defines this experience. Some of the men we have studied will be returned to prison in the future; others will not. But all will have been changed by their prison experiences. They entered the prison world fearing for their lives; they depart with the knowledge that they have survived. On the one hand, these men are undoubtedly stronger persons by virtue of this accomplishment. On the other hand, the same tactics that enabled them to survive the prison world can be called upon, appropriately or not, in difficult situations in the outside world. To the extent that these men draw upon their prison survival tactics to cope with the hardships of the outside world—to the extent that their prison behavior becomes a meaningful part of their "role repertoire" (Turner 1978) in their everyday lives—their prison identities will have become inseparable form their "true" identities.

THE SUSPENDED IDENTITY MODEL

As identity preservation tactics, an inmate's suspension of his preprison identity and development of a false prison identity are not, and cannot be, entirely successful. At the conclusion of his sentence, no inmate can ever fully revive his suspended identity; he cannot remain the same person he was before he came to prison. But his tactics do not fail entirely either. An inmate's resolve not to change, his decision to suspend his preprison identity, his belief that he will be able to revive this identity, and his subsequent struggle to revive this identity undoubtedly minimize the identity change that would otherwise have taken place. The inmate's tactics, leading up to his suspended identity dialectic, constitute an identity transformation process, summarized in Figure 2, that differs from both the gradual, sequential model of identity transformation and models of radical identity transformation (Strauss 1959). It also shares some characteristics with each of these models.

As in cases of brainwashing and conversion, there is an external change agency involved, the inmate does learn a new perspective (an insider's perspective) for evaluating himself and the world around him, and he does develop new group loyalties while his old loyalties are reduced. But unlike a radical identity transformation, the inmate does not interpret the changes that take place as changes in a *central* identity; the insider's perspective he learns and the new person he becomes in prison are viewed as a false front that he must present to others, but a front that does not affect who he really is. And while suspending his preprison identity necessarily entails a weakening of his outside loyalties, it does not, in most cases, destroy them. Because he never achieves more than a marginal status in the prison world, the inmate's ambivalence prevents him from accepting an insider's perspective too fully, and thus prevents him from fully severing his loyalties to the outside world (Schmid and Jones 1987). He retains a fundamental, if ambivalent, commitment to his outside world throughout his sentence, and he expects to reestablish his outside relationships (just as he expects to revive his suspended identity) when his sentence is over.

Like a religious convert who later loses his faith, an inmate cannot simply return to his old self. The liminal conditions (Turner 1977) of the prison world have removed him, for too long, from his accustomed identity bearings in everyday life. He does change in prison, but his attempts to suspend and subsequently revive his preprison identity maintain a general sense of identity continuity for most of his prison career. As in the gradual identity transformation process delineated by Strauss (1959), he recognizes changes in his identity only at periodic "turning points," especially his mid-career doubts about his ability to revive his suspended identity and his self-dialogue at the end of his sentence. Also like a gradual identity transformation, the extent of his identity change depends on a balance between the situational adjustments he has made in prison and his continuing commitments to the outside world (Becker 1960, 1964). His identity depends, in other words, on the outcome of the dialectic between his prison identity and his suspended preprison identity.

The suspended identity model is one component and a holistic analysis of the experiences of first-time, short-term inmates at a specific maximum security prison. Like any holistic analysis, its usefulness lies primarily in its capacity to explain the particular case under study (Deising 1971). We nonetheless expect similar identity transformation processes to occur under similar circumstances: among individuals who desire to preserve their identities despite finding themselves involved in temporary but encompassing social situations that subject them to new and disparate identity demands and render their prior identities inappropriate. The suspended identity model presented here provides a basis for further exploration of these circumstances.

Acknowledgments

We wish to thank Jim Thomas, Patricia A. Adler and the reviewers of *Symbolic Interaction* for their useful comments and suggestions.

Notes

1. This is a matter of some theoretical interest. Proponents of existential sociology (cf. Douglas and Johnson 1977) view feelings as the very foundation of social action, social structures, and the self. From this theoretical framework, a new inmate would be viewed as someone who has been stripped to that core of primal feelings that constitutes his existential self; the symbolic constructions of his former world, including his cognitive definition of himself (learned from the definitions that others hold of him) are exposed as artificial, leaving the individual at least partially free to choose for himself what he wants to be and how he wants to present himself to others. Whether or not we view the feelings of vulnerability, discontinuity, and differentiation as the core of an inmate's self, or even as attributes of his self, we must note that the inmate does not reject his earlier self-image (or other symbolic constructions) as artificial. He continues to hold on to his preprison identity as his "true" self and he continues to view the outside world as the "real" world. It is the prison world that is viewed as artificial. His definitions of the outside world and the prison world do change during his prison career, but he never fully rejects his outsider's perspective.

2. There are four principal components to the survival strategies of the inmates we studied, in the early months of their prison sentences. "Selective interaction" and "territorial caution" are essentially precautionary guidelines that allow inmates to increase their understanding of the prison world while minimizing danger to themselves. "Partnership" is a special friendship

bond between two inmates, typically based on common backgrounds and interests (including a shared uncertainty about prison life) and strengthened by the inmates' mutual exploration of a hostile prison world. The fourth component of their strategies, impression management, is discussed in subsequent sections of this article.

3. Clemmer (1958: 299) has defined "prisonization" as the "taking on in greater or less degree of the folkways, mores, customs, and general culture of the penitentiary." Yet new inmates begin to "take on" these things almost immediately, as part of the impression they are attempting to present to other inmates. Thus, we would argue instead that prisonization (meaning assimilation to the prison world) begins to occur for these inmates when their prison identities become second nature—when their expressions of prison norms and customs are no longer based on self-conscious acting. A new inmate's identity concerns, during the middle of his sentence, are essentially a recognition of this assimilation. For other examples of problems associated with double identity, see Warren and Ponse (1977) and Lemert (1967); Adler and Adler (1989) describe self-diminishment problems, as well as self-aggrandizement effects, that accompany even highly valued identity constructions.

4. This finding stands in contrast to other works on total institutions, which suggest that inmates direct their impression management tactics toward the staff. See, for example, Goffman (1961: 318) and Heffernan (1972; chapter VI). First-time, short-term inmates certainly interact with guards and other staff in terms of their prison identities, but these personnel are neither the primary source of their fear nor the primary objects of their impression management. Interactions with staff are limited by a concern with how other inmates will define such interactions; in this sense, presentation of a new inmate's prison identity to staff can be viewed as part of the impression he is creating for other inmates.

5. Not all prisoners participate in this unit; inmates must apply for transfer to the unit, and their acceptance depends both on the crimes for which they were sentenced and staff evaluation of their potential for success in the unit. Our analysis focuses on those inmates who are transferred.

6. There are three features of the minimum security unit that facilitate this shift in perspectives: a more open physical and social environment; the fact that the unit lies just outside the prison wall (so that an inmate who is transferred is also physically removed from the maximum security prison); and greater opportunity for direct contact with the outside world, through greater access to telephones, an unrestricted visitor list, unrestricted visiting hours and, eventually, weekend furloughs.

7. This is an important parallel with our analysis of the inmate's changing prison definitions: his concluding prison image is a synthesis of the image he formulates before coming to prison and the image he holds at the middle of his prison career; see Schmid and Jones 1990.

References

Adler, Patricia A. and Peter Adler. 1989. "The Gloried Self: The Aggrandizement and the Constriction of Self." *Social Psychology Quarterly* 52:299–310.

Becker, Howard S. 1960. "Notes on the Concept of Commitment." *American Journal of Sociology* 66:32–40.

——. "Personal Change in Adult Life." 1964. *Sociometry* 27:40–53.

Berger, Peter L. 1963. *Invitation to Sociology: A Humanistic Perspective.* Garden City, NY: Doubleday Anchor Books.

Blumer, Herbert. 1972. "Action vs. Interaction: Review of *Relations in Public* by Erving Goffman." *Transaction* 9:50–53.

——. 1969. *Symbolic Interactionism: Perspective and Method,* Englewood Cliffs, NJ: Prentice-Hall.

Boulding, Kenneth. 1961. *The Image.* Ann Arbor: University of Michigan Press.

Clemmer, Donald. 1958. *The Prison Community.* New York: Holt, Rinehart and Winston.

Coser, R. 1966. "Role Distance, Sociological Ambivalence and Traditional Status Systems." *American Journal of Sociology* 72:173–187.

Deising, Paul. 1971. *Patterns of Discovery in the Social Sciences.* Chicago: Aldine-Atherton.

Douglas, Jack D., Patricia A. Adler, Peter Adler, Andrea Fontana, Robert C. Freeman, and Joseph A. Kotarba. 1980. *Introduction to the Sociologies of Everyday Life.* Boston: Allyn and Bacon.

Douglas, Jack D. and John M. Johnson. 1977. *Existential Sociology.* Cambridge: Cambridge University Press.

Garfinkel, Harold. 1956. "Conditions of Successful Degredation Ceremonies." *American Journal of Sociology* 61:420–424.

Glaser, Barney G. and Anselm L. Strauss. 1964. "Awareness Contexts and Social Interaction." *American Sociological Review* 29:269–279.

Goffman, Erving. 1961. *Asylums.* Garden City, NY: Doubleday Anchor Books.

——1959. *The Presentation of Self in Everyday Life.* Garden City, NY: Doubleday Anchor Books.

——1963. *Stigma: Notes on the Management of Spoiled Identity.* Englewood Cliffs, NJ: Prentice-Hall.

Gross, Edward and Gregory P. Stone. 1964. "Embarrassment and the Analysis of Role Requirements." *American Journal of Sociology* 70:1–15.

Heffernan, Esther. 1972. *Making It in Prison: The Square, the Cool and the Life.* New York: Wiley-Interscience.

Irwin, John. 1970. *The Felon.* Englewood Cliffs, NJ: Prentice-Hall.

——. 1977. *Scenes.* Beverly Hills: Sage.

Lemert, Edwin. 1967. "Role Enactment, Self, and Identity in the Systematic Check Forger." Pp. 119–134 in *Human Deviance, Social Problems and Social Control.* Englewood Cliffs, NJ: Prentice-Hall.

Lewis, David J. 1979. "A Social Behaviorist Interpretation of the Median I." *American Journal of Sociology* 84:261–287.

Messinger, Sheldon E., Harold Sampson, and Robert D. Towne. 1962. "Life as Theater: Some Notes on the Dramaturgic Approach to Social Reality." *Sociometry* 25:98–111.

Schechner, Richard. 1985. *Between Theater and Anthropology.* Philadelphia: University of Pennsylvania Press.

Scheff, Thomas. 1970. "On the Concepts of Identity and Social Relationships" Pp. 193–207 in *Human Nature and Collective Behavior,* edited by T. Shibutani. Englewood Cliffs, NJ: Prentice-Hall.

Schlenker, B. 1980. *Impression Management: The Self Concept, Social Identity and Interpersonal Relations.* Belmont, CA: Wadsworth.

Schmid, Thomas and Richard Jones. 1987. "Ambivalent Actions: Prison Adaptation Strategies of New Inmates." American Society of Criminology, annual meetings, Montreal, Quebec.

Schmid, Thomas and Richard Jones. 1990. "Experiential Orientations to the Prison Experience: The Case of First-Time, Short-Term Inmates." Pp. 189–210 in *Perspectives on Social Problems,* edited by Gale Miller and James A. Holstein. Greenwich, CT: JAI Press.

Solomon, David N. 1970. "Role and Self-Conception: Adaptation and Change in Occupations." Pp. 286–300 in *Human Nature and Collective Behavior,* edited by T. Shibutani. Englewood Cliffs, NJ: Prentice-Hall.

Stone, Gregory P. 1962. "Appearance and the Self." Pp. 86–118 in *Human Behavior and Social Processes,* edited by Arnold Rose. Boston: Houghton Mifflin.

Stauss, Anselm L. 1959. *Mirrors and Masks: The Search for Identity*. Glencoe: The Free Press.

Sykes, Gresham. 1958. *The Society of Captives: A Study of a Maximum Security Prison*. Princeton: Princeton University Press.

Turner, Ralph H. 1978. "The Role and the Person." *American Journal of Sociology* 84:1–23.

Turner, Victor. 1977. *The Ritual Process: Structure and Anti-Structure*. Ithaca, NY: Cornell University Press.

Ungar, Sheldon. 1984. "Self-Mockery: An Alternative Form of Self-Presentation." *Symbolic Interaction* 7:121–133.

Warren, Carol A. and Barbara Ponse. 1977. "The Existential Self in the Gay World." Pp. 273–289 in *Existential Sociology*, edited by Jack D. Douglas and John M. Johnson. Cambridge: Cambridge University Press.

Weigert, Andrew J. 1986. "The Social Production of Identity: Metatheoretical Foundations." *Sociological Quarterly* 27:165–183.

Zurcher, Louis A. 1977. *The Mutable Self*. Beverly Hills: Sage.

43 / The Impact of Publicity on Corporate Offenders: The Ford Motor Company and the Pinto Papers

BRENT FISSE
JOHN BRAITHWAITE

THE PINTO TRIAL

Prevalent as corporate "violence" is,[1] corporations are rarely prosecuted for homicide or assault. The Pinto trial in Indiana provided a dramatic exception, for it involved the spectacle of one of America's largest corporations, the Ford Motor Company, being charged with reckless homicide, not by knife or gun but by fire.

The trial arose from an accident in August 1978 in which three young women were fatally burned when their 1973 Ford Pinto burst into flames after being rear-ended by a Chevrolet van. The fuel tank of the Pinto ruptured in the collision, gasoline entered the passenger compartment as the car crumpled, and fire exploded instantaneously.

Grand jury proceedings were launched, there being much doubt as to the safety of the Pinto fuel system. Over the previous year the media had criticized the location of the fuel tank, which was positioned six inches forward of the rear bumper. As a result, the National Highway and Traffic Safety Administration [NHTSA] had initiated defect proceedings in April 1978, and in June Ford had announced a voluntary recall of all Pintos manufactured between 1971 and 1976.[2] Moreover, these events aroused product liability actions against Ford, most notably the *Grimshaw*[3] suit in which damages of $128.5 million were awarded, including a record $125 million in punitive damages (later reduced to $3 million). Although the suit in *Grimshaw* was civil, the award of punitive damages depended upon a finding of corporate knowledge about the danger of the Pinto fuel tank location, and this in turn suggested that Ford might be found at fault in criminal proceedings for unlawful homicide.

The grand jury returned three indictments of reckless homicide, an offense recently enacted under Indiana's criminal code.[4] A pre-trial skirmish ensued wherein Ford attacked the indictments on a variety of grounds, including the application of the reckless homicide offense to corporate persons[5] and the constitutional difficulty raised by the allegations of reckless conduct by Ford at times prior to the creation of the offense. The indictments stood. It was held that corporations could commit reckless homicide under Indiana law and unconstitutional retroactivity was avoidable if the recklessness alleged was deemed to be that Ford had knowingly failed to rectify the Pinto danger after the new offense became law.

The resulting trial revolved around three issues. First, had Ford been aware of an unjustifiable danger in the design of the Pinto? Second, had Ford failed substantially to rectify any such unjustifiable danger? Third, in any event, was the closing speed between the van and the Pinto low enough that a small car could reasonably have been expected not to leak fuel? For the prosecution to succeed, each of these questions had to be resolved affirmatively beyond reasonable doubt.

The main obstacle confronting the prosecution on the first issue was the non-admission of much evidence. Many of the so-called "Pinto Papers"—internal documents about engineering and safety matters—were ruled inadmissible, some because Ford refused to stipulate their authenticity, others because they related to the 1971 and 1972 Pinto and not the 1973 car in which the victims had suffered their fatal burns.[6] The most critical document excluded was a highly unfavorable NHTSA report of fuel leakage rates from crash-tested Pintos and GM Vegas, the ground of exclusion being that only 1971 and 1972 Pintos had been tested, whereas some improvements had been made for the 1973 model (according to Ford, these improvements raised the speed of barrier-crash survivability from "around" 20 m.p.h. to above 20 m.p.h.).[7] Surprisingly, the prosecution never asked NHTSA to perform tests on the 1973 model (Ford has suggested that this possibly was because the results were expected to be unfavorable to the prosecution's case).[8]

The prosecution also ran into difficulty over the second issue. Had Ford failed substantially to rectify any danger in the design of the Pinto? To begin with, the relevant time span was the 41-day period between the commencement of the new reckless homicide offense and the date of the fatal accident subject to prosecution; the diligence of Ford prior to that period was not in issue. Furthermore, during the two months between Ford's recall announcement and the accident, NHTSA had been regulating the recall and there was no evidence of undue delay or neglect on the part of Ford.[9]

Third, was the closing speed between the van and the Pinto so high that no small car could reasonably have been expected not to leak fuel? The contention of the prosecution was that the closing speed was no more than 35 m.p.h. (several eye-witnesses so asserted) and that this speed was insufficiently high to cause fuel leakage in a small car of adequate design. Late in the trial the defense produced two witnesses who testified that, just before the driver of the Pinto died in hospital, she had mentioned stopping just before the crash occurred.[10] If this were true, the closing speed would have been approximately 50 miles per hour, a speed of impact that no small car fuel tank could be expected to withstand. To highlight the point, the defense showed films of specially arranged crash tests in which a similar van hit a 1973 Pinto and other makes of cars at 50 m.p.h. All of the cars struck suffered substantial fuel leakage.[11]

After 25 hours of deliberation stretched over four days, the jury returned a verdict of not guilty. Its members' reasons for acquitting Ford were aired at a press interview arranged by the trial judge at the conclusion of proceedings. Although there was no consensus as to the safety of the Pinto or the closing speed of the vehicles at the time of the accident, it was agreed that the prosecution had not proven reckless failure by Ford to rectify any danger which may have existed in the Pinto's fuel system.[12]

PUBLICITY AND COUNTERPUBLICITY

The Pinto trial attracted intensive media coverage, partly because there had been much advance publicity, and partly because the idea of a corporation committing reckless murder was no longer merely political rhetoric but living law.[13]

The adverse publicity began in earnest with "Pinto Madness,"[14] an award-winning article by Mark Dowie in the September 1977 *Mother Jones* magazine; this, Ford executives lamented to us, was "the real watershed." The article claimed that internal company documents (the "Pinto Papers") showed that "Ford has crash-tested the Pinto at a top-secret site more than 40 times and that *every* test made at over 25 m.p.h. without special structural alteration of the car has resulted in a ruptured fuel tank." It also contended that none of the protective modifications tested had been incorporated in production-line Pintos, reference being made to an internal cost-benefit study[15] in 1973. The gist of this particular study was represented as follows:

$11 VS. A BURN DEATH
Benefits and Costs Relating to Fuel Leakage
Associated with the Static Rollover
Test Portion of FMVSS 208

Benefits

Savings: 180 burn deaths, 180 serious burn injuries, 2,100 burned vehicles.
Unit cost: $200,000 per death, $67,000 per injury, $700 per vehicle
Total benefit: (180 × $200,000) + (180 × $67,000) + (2100 × $700) = $49.5 million.

Costs

Sales: 11 million cars, 1.5 million light trucks.
Unit cost: $11 per car, $11 per truck.
Total cost: (11,000,000 × $11) + (1,500,000 × $11) = $137 million.[16]

The implication was that Ford had deliberately chosen not to make "an $11-per-car improvement that would prevent 180 fiery deaths a year."[17] These were the allegations which stuck in the mind of the state trooper at the scene of the Elkhart accident, and prompted him to take active steps toward prosecution.[18]

Soon thereafter the *Grimshaw* suit was decided. A "major spout" of adverse publicity resulted from the record award of $125 million in punitive damages and, more significantly, from the evidence relied upon to establish that Ford had consciously and willfully disregarded the safety of Pinto owners. As a result, the Pinto became infamous, even overseas.[19]

Then came the much-publicized NHTSA defect notice in May 1978.[20] After completing an initial investigation into the Pinto (an investigation provoked by the *Mother Jones* article), NHTSA advised Ford that there has been "an initial determination of the existence of a safety-related defect" in the 1971–1976 Pintos.[21]

It was the trial, however, which drew the most publicity. The horrific nature of the deaths, the sinister reputation of the Pinto Papers, the novelty of the charge of corporate homicide, and the flamboyance of chief counsel on both sides made the event a theatrical occasion. Throughout the two months of the trial a group of about 50 reporters, producers, cameramen, and technicians stayed on location to cover the proceedings. Their output was prodigious, largely because prosecution and defense supplied them with an abundance of newsworthy lines, including the prosecution's chilling opening allegation that Ford "deliberately chose profit over human life" and "totally disregarded" repeated warnings from its engineers.[22] Ultimately, the trial became the subject of a book by Lee Strobel, a reporter who covered the event for the *Chicago Tribune*.[23]

A notable feature of the publicity about the Pinto trial was that a *corporate* defendant held the limelight. As was repeatedly stressed in the media, it was the first case in which a corporation had been charged with unlawful homicide in the context of product liability,[24] and the indictment for reckless homicide as opposed to merely manslaughter added an additional element of novelty. Moreover, no Ford personnel were tried with the company itself, the prosecutor's explanation being that "Ford Motor Co., the corporation itself, was all that Elkhart County could handle. To go further, and take the next step, which may be individuals, [would have to be taken by] somebody with far more resources than we have. . . ."[25] Accordingly, those who followed the trial were presented squarely with a question of corporate blameworthiness.[26]

Despite the acquittal of Ford in the Pinto trial, adverse publicity continued. Although the decision was generally considered to be correct, given the particular facts of the case, it did not resolve the basic doubts surrounding the safety of the Pinto. Thus, in one widely-publicized comment on the jury's verdict, Clarence Ditlow, a leading critic of the motor industry, revived the issue of blameworthiness:

> In view of the judge's restrictions against the introduction of supporting evidence, but letting in the Ford crash tests, I felt the decision was preordained. However, in the next case, with a better judge or with a different striking vehicle, I feel sure Ford or any other manufacturer would be convicted.[27]

Faced by the adverse publicity outlined above, Ford became involved in three counterpublicity exercises of note: a press release in response to the *Mother Jones* article, a voluntary recall in response to the NHTSA defect notice, and the trial itself.

In response to the *Mother Jones* article, Ford issued an eight-page release. The main counterclaims stressed in this press release were threefold:

a. statistically, the Pinto was not involved in an unusually high proportion of fire-related deaths;

b. internal Ford documents (i.e., the Pinto Papers) relied upon by *Mother Jones* related neither to the Pinto models subject to criticism nor to rear-end impact protection, but concerned either later models or prospective federal vehicle safety standards; and

c. autos and their makers should be judged by the standards applicable at the time, rather than in light of ideas for future improvements.

In conclusion, it was argued that:

> ...the Ford Pinto does not pose any undue hazard to its occupants as [*Mother Jones*] tries to contend. Although absolute travelling safety cannot be guaranteed in any car, [government statistics] show that the performance of the Pinto's fuel-tank system in actual accidents appears to be superior to that which might be expected of cars of its size and weight.[28]

A second counterpublicity measure was the recall of the 1971–1976 Pintos shortly after the NHTSA defect notice. The press release announcing the recall indicated Ford's disagreement with the NHTSA finding that the Pinto was unsafe, but nonetheless offered the promise of "modifications" designed to "reduce significantly" the risk of fire if the cars were hit from the rear. As one executive testified at the Indiana trial, the recall was seen as an important public relations exercise:

> The corporation had been subjected to allegations of a problem unique to the Pinto, and this obviously was damaging our public reputation, and the attitude of the public. It had become a critical problem for the company, a reputational problem.... On balance, it was felt that if we could reach an agreement with NHTSA [on a recall], it would reassure the owners and the public of the company's good intentions in the matter.[29]

In effect, although not by admitted intention, the recall avoided a full-scale NHTSA hearing and reduced the obvious risk of further adverse publicity (however, the recall did provoke Nader into issuing a press statement vilifying Henry Ford II).[30] At this time, it should be remembered, Ford had no other small car to offer in the immediate future; in the words of one of our respondents, "we had to keep the Pinto alive for two years."

Subsequently, the Pinto trial provided Ford with a far better opportunity to defend itself publicly, and full advantage was taken of it. As an initial precaution, an opinion poll was conducted to test the reaction of potential jurors in the areas where the accident occurred;[31] the results being unfavorable, a change of venue was obtained (from Elkhart to Winamac, Indiana). When the trial began, a senior public relations officer was assigned to follow press reactions, to keep reporters abreast of Ford's stand, and to tackle those "not giving us a fair break."[32] Above all, Ford staged a showcase defense, meticulously prepared by a team of lawyers and brilliantly presented by James Neal, an accomplished trial counsel of Watergate fame. As well as winning over the jurors at the trial, Neal's presentation was deliberately aimed at the general public. It repeatedly portrayed Ford as an All-American institution which, far from being an inhuman reckless murderer, was peopled by executives who not only were sensitive to the issue of safety, but also were prepared to provide Pintos for the use of their own families.[33]

After the acquittal, Ford considered mounting a public relations campaign, but no serious steps were taken in this direction, largely because the media was believed to be preoccupied with immediate events; "news a day late is no news." This belief, we were told, was founded partly on experience: some information had been provided to reporters without evoking any sign of interest. Accordingly, Ford let the matter rest with a statement by its new chairman, Philip Caldwell, that "there must be responsibility on the part of those who use products as well as on the part of those who manufacture them."[34] Others, however, were quick to come to Ford's side. Most notably, General Motors issued a congratulatory press release, and one of Ford's defense counsel for the trial published a sympathetic series of articles in the *National Law Journal*.[35]

Looking back over the Pinto trial, the Ford executives with whom we spoke regarded being prosecuted as a blow which could have been struck against any company in the auto-manufacturing business and, indeed, many companies in other industries as well. They resented the difficulty they experienced in getting Ford's side of the story into the media, especially the company's position that the cost-benefit study related to a proposed federal safety standard, and not to the actual design of the Pinto. It was said that Strobel, the author of *Reckless Homicide: Ford's Pinto Trial*, had written a distorted account because he had never approached Ford to check out the facts. These reflections ended on a sweeter note, however, because *Fortune* had smiled. A recent article in the magazine had excluded Ford from its list of 100 leading corporate criminals, presumably because the company had been vindicated by the acquittal at Winamac.[36]

FINANCIAL IMPACTS

The adverse publicity before and during the Pinto trial did have an impact on Ford's sales and profitability, and stock prices may also have suffered. Sales of the Pinto dropped sharply at first but later recovered. As a result of the "Pinto Madness" scare in 1977–1978, its share of the market was cut from 11–12 percent to 6.7 percent.[37] The car was then facelifted for the 1980 model year, and an advertising campaign stressed the price advantage the Pinto had over imports. The share of the market then climbed back to 9.7 percent.[38] We were informed that the path back had not been blocked by any criticism of the Pinto by competitors ("they were rooting for us on the footing that, but for the grace of God, there go I") or by any bans on government purchases (the last 4,000 Pintos were bought by the U.S. government for the Postal Service). At the same time, the recovery had not really been Ford's doing alone; the crisis in Iran had resulted in an upsurge in demand for small cars generally. Within 30 days of the onset of that crisis there had been a significant switch in consumer preference from large to small cars (in 1980 the number of Pintos produced increased by 125,000 to 325,000). This being so, why had the Pinto been discontinued in 1980? Contrary to rumor, it was insisted that the production of the Pinto had not been stopped as a result of the publicity about safety, but because the car had come to the end of its planned 10-year cycle.

Despite overall sales of 2.9 million, however, the Pinto was not a profitable car. As Ford's chairman recently bemoaned in corporates: "I just wish we had been able to get a better balance between the incomings and the outgoings."[39] Apart from loss of revenue through a fall in sales, and the cost of the 1978 recall, considerable legal costs were incurred in the criminal trial and in civil damages actions. The legal costs associated with the criminal trial were never disclosed by Ford, but the figure often guessed was $1 million;[40] the amount paid out in civil damages remains confidential. By no means can all of these costs be attributed to the adverse publicity surrounding the Pinto, but that publicity did induce Ford to spare no expense in staging its defense at the criminal trial and undoubtedly contributed to the onset of civil claims and to Ford's willingness to settle them. It is noteworthy that Ford's associate counsel in charge of litigation felt that the publicity about the deaths of three young women in the homicide case "made it very difficult for us to get a fair trial almost anywhere on a Pinto case."[41] After the acquittal in the criminal trial, the flow of civil claims dropped to a trickle and a case proceeding to trial in December 1980 was won by the company.[42]

Apart from the impact upon the sales and profitability of the Pinto, the effects of the publicity were felt generally in the market share of other cars sold by Ford. During the period of the trial, Ford sales declined 30.6 percent whereas General Motors and Chrysler suffered smaller declines of

7.2 percent and 26 percent respectively.[43] At least part of this decline was attributed to the adverse publicity. As one spokesman informed us, "management here believe that the Pinto adverse publicity has raised questions about our product quality generally and is one of the reasons for our declined market share in the last two years."

The impact on stock market prices was far more difficult to gauge. We were told by one senior executive that "the general reaction is that nobody knows what the hell the stock market is doing; I can't remember anyone saying that the market went up or down in response to the acquittal or the indictment." He also said that he could not remember any impact, favorable or unfavorable, of the *Grimshaw* case.

We then spoke to Ford's investor-relations officer. Ford's stock had generally traded in the range of $40–$50 during the 1960s and 1970s but more recently there had been a precipitous drop to the $22 mark. Throughout 1980 and late 1979, Ford stocks consistently traded well below the prices prevailing during the previous four years. However, there had been no apparent connection between any attacks on Ford during the Pinto trial and any drop in the price of Ford stock on particular days. The market was so irrational that it was impossible to explain particular changes in stock market prices except where the causes were blatant. He pointed out that Ford's stock price had dropped on the day of the acquittal in the Pinto trial whereas it had gone up after the announcement of a quarterly loss and a substantial reduction in dividend. Nonetheless, the Pinto publicity was considered to have had an adverse effect over the period during which Ford's stocks had dropped in price. "It had an effect on our image and therefore on our ability to sell cars and trucks; in turn, it affected our profitability and hence had an effect on our stock price."

These financial impacts should be seen in perspective. All of the executives with whom we spoke stressed that the loss threatened by the sudden switch in preference from large to small cars (a switch precipitated by the crisis in Iran) had transcended any of the other problems facing the company, especially since Ford then had no car to match the Japanese subcompacts. Adverse publicity, particularly as extreme as that in the Pinto case, is much less likely than fines to be written off as a minor cost of doing business, but it can be pushed into the background by a force majeure.[44]

NON-FINANCIAL IMPACTS

The adverse publicity leading up to and surrounding the Pinto trial had four main non-financial impacts: tarnishing of Ford's corporate image, lowering of personal reputation of executives, creating worry about possible longer-term effects on sales, and arousing concern about legislative implications.

The image-blackening effect of the Pinto trial and the prior adverse publicity was considerable. Numerous newspaper accounts of the Pinto story spoke explicitly of its detracting from Ford's corporate reputation,[45] and then pressure to save that reputation in large part accounted for the effort which the company put into defending itself against the reckless homicide charges. Just how great that pressure was is apparent from the results of one survey of consumer opinion undertaken soon after the indictments: 38 percent of the persons surveyed had heard that Ford cars were unsafe (cp. 6 percent re GM cars; 4 percent re imports; and 1 percent re American Motors cars) and 47 percent of those under 35 years of age had heard or read negative comments.[46] Moreover, there was Henry Ford II's famous quote: "The lawyers would shoot me for saying this, but I think there's some cause for the concern about the car. I don't even listen to the cost-figures—we've got to fix it."[47]

The attack upon Ford's corporate image radiated out to executives. This is how Strobel saw the impact:

> Even though no executives were formally charged, prosecutors had to present evidence that the car had been defectively designed and that the corporation had been reckless in failing to warn consumers. A corporation acts through its executives, and so the prosecutors, in effect, would be trying individual members of Ford management for their decisions regarding the Pinto. Ford executives, accustomed to receiving community respect commensurate with their high social status and lucrative salaries, cringed at such a degrading possibility. Even if they felt they had done nothing wrong, the idea of undergoing public interrogation and being the target of a prosecutor's allegations and insinuations was a humiliating thought.[48]

"Cringed," however, is much too strong a word, for although the executives felt themselves assailed (for example, the chief engineer felt under an obligation to explain to his family why he considered Ford not to be a murderer), their attitude was described to us as being one of willingness and anxiety to have the opportunity "to set the record straight." Furthermore, the reflection was offered that persons working for auto-makers in Detroit were essentially members of one big family, whereas personnel employed by Lockheed during the bribery scandal had far less collegiate insulation; unlike the car industry in Detroit, aerospace has no real home.

Also significant was the worry occasioned about long-term sales. Shortly after the indictments, Ford's associate general counsel for litigation admitted that "publicity has called into question the design of the Pinto and that has a tendency to rub off on other areas as people are apt to wonder: 'If there's a problem with the Pinto, there might be a problem in other areas.' "[49] Ford's sensitivity on this issue was particularly acute since its executives worried that adverse publicity from the Pinto trial could trigger sales resistance to the new Escort, a car essential to the company's recovery in the early 1980s; in the words of Henry Ford II,

> Everything hangs on the success of that car—it sure does. It has to do *everything* by itself for 1981 and 1982. We'll have to sell every one we can make to... support the profitable end of the line.[50]

Moreover, it was feared that a dramatic downturn in Pinto sales would increase Ford's fleet fuel economy average above that required by the Energy Policy and Conservation Act of 1975, thereby forcing the company to restrict sales of its new full-size models.[51]

A further non-financial impact was concern about legislative implications. Although no safety standard governing resistance to rear-end collisions resulted from the Pinto trial or the publicity which inspired it (a new standard had been introduced in 1977 prior to that publicity), the Pinto case was relied upon to support a federal Bill requiring corporate managers to dislose life-threatening defects in any of their company's products.[52] The statute proposed was not enacted, but the prospect was anathema to business because of the possibility of severe individual criminal liability and the danger of being forced to provide information which could provoke costly civil damages claims.[53]

REFORMS

Shaken by the adverse publicity over the Pinto, Ford instituted several reforms in the areas of safety and legal self-protection. No changes were made in the fuel storage system of the Pinto after the recall for modifications in 1978, and the fuel tank of the new Escort, a front-wheel drive car, had always been planned to sit ahead of the rear wheels. As to law reform, Ford's acquittal muffled any calls for change.

In the area of safety, it was felt within Ford that one contributing factor in the Pinto crisis had been the pressure placed upon the design and engineering staff by the then president, Lee Iacocca, that the car had to weigh under 2000 pounds and cost less than $2,000.[54] The edict, according to one executive we interviewed, was the toughest Ford had ever experienced with a new vehicle. There was also limited time for design and retooling. Today, these areas are covered by a major policy directive of June 1979: "Targets will be selected in sufficient time for all company activities to achieve the desired DQR [Durability, Quality, and Reliability] end result."[55] This policy directive was backed by considerable pruning and grafting of decision trees within the organization, the aim being to ensure that management would look beforehand at points of no return. In addition, there was an increase in engineering and research staff, and several positions were upgraded.

The document setting out the new policy directive, Policy Document F-1, sought to establish the importance of durability, quality, and reliability by stressing the relevance of these goals to how Ford fared competitively. It was explained to us that the problem within the organization was to convince people that there was no justification for sacrificing safety in the name of profit. The real solution to this problem was to elevate safety to a high level, "DQR" being a designation which minimized the risk of association with Ford's unsuccessful "Life Guard" campaign to sell safety in the 1950s.

It was readily conceded by those with whom we spoke that the new policy directive was subject to the pressures of time, cost, and survival. Time was always a problem in the planning, design, and manufacture of cars. Consumer preferences were fickle, whereas car production was necessarily governed by routine. In the car industry, flexibility had always been delicately balanced against rigidity and certainty. Admittedly, the Japanese had adjusted to this tension by opting for long-term planning and sticking to their plans, but in the American context that was considered to be a recipe for disaster. In terms of cost, it was stressed that mammoth expenses were involved in retooling and that, once a car had been put on the market, there was little room to adjust the trade-off between safety and profitability. Above all, the first aim of the company was to survive. It was all very well talking about safe cars, but there was no future in losses; the business of automobile manufacturers was not to make "museum pieces."

The other significant area of organizational reform was that of legal self-protection. The main impact of the Pinto trial, according to product liability specialists at Ford, was to ignite their desire to provide effective legal protection against exposure to liability. A new procedure was instituted for recording the background to safety and engineering decisions; the aim of the fuller documentation was to enable the company to defend itself more adequately in any future litigation.

Although the Pinto was a rough ride for Ford and led to some internal revisions within the company, legislative reform did not ensue. Calls for tougher regulation of auto safety were muted by the acquittal at Winimac.[56] It cannot be said, however, that the trial provided the public with the information required to make an informed choice about the need for reform.

The Pinto trial, although widely heralded as a passion play about the riskiness of Ford engineering and design, turned out to be a great disappointment. The relevant offense was defined in terms of recklessly causing death, and the trial therefore necessarily focused on issues directly connected with the particular deaths subject to prosecution. This meant that information about the safety and engineering decisions behind the Pinto was irrelevant unless it related to the 1973 Pinto involved in the death of the three young women. Moreover, any question of reckless engineering or non-rectification of faults was overshadowed by the question of whether the closing speed of the van that struck the Pinto was so high that the fuel tank of any small car would have been ruptured. As a result, the rights or wrongs of the Pinto Papers were never effectively canvassed at the trial.

Not surprisingly, the trial confused rather than clarified lay perceptions of the dangers of Ford's policy and the safety of the Pinto. For instance, after Ford had been acquitted, the foreman of the jury disclosed that "We just felt that the state never presented enough evidence to convince us that Ford was guilty," but added that he wouldn't buy a Pinto himself, although he would not be averse to a gift of one. "I wouldn't feel safe but I'd drive it."[57] So, from the standpoint of community education or sociodrama[58] the trial was a dismal flop. It failed to clarify, much less resolve, the issues that should have been of real concern to the public.

This bears out the point that criminal trials and their attendant publicity inadequately inform public choices about corporate decision-making if the focus of attention is an offense defined in terms of causing harm as opposed to taking an unacceptable *risk*.[59] Harm-causing offenses are oriented towards idiosyncratic results rather than underlying problems of risk-taking. Guido Calabresi has made this clear in his discussion of road-accident compensation policy:

> The effect of case-by-case decisions is to center on the particular or unusual cause of an accident. If one asks, as case-by-case determinants tend to do, "What went wrong in this case?" the answer will most likely center on the peculiar cause. Yet here is a very good argument for the notion that the cheapest way of avoiding accident costs is not to attempt to control the *unusual* event but rather to modify a recurring event. It may be that absentmindedness is a cause of one particular accident, too much whiskey the cause of another, and drowsiness the cause of a third. But it may also be that a badly designed curve or inadequate tires are causes of each of these as well. The fault system, because it centers on the possible *particular* cost avoider, is very likely to ignore the recurring cost avoider and hence fail altogether to consider some potential cheapest cost avoiders such as highway builders or tiremakers.[60]

In the absence of an offense defined in terms of manufacturing an unjustifiably dangerous product, questions of acceptable risk of the kind raised by the Pinto Papers will rarely be the central subject of inquiry in the context of corporate offenses against the person. This is unsatisfactory, not only because of the danger of a serious underlying risk being concealed from society, but also because it may do more harm than good not to face up to the need for studies of the costs of improving product safety in matters such as that for which Ford was pilloried.[61]

Notes

1. John Monahan and Raymond W. Novaco, "Corporate Violence: A Psychological Analysis," in Paul Lipsitt and Bruce Sales, eds., *New Directions in Psycholegal Research* (New York: Van Nostrand, 1980):3–25.
2. *New York Times*, June 10, 1978, p. 1.
3. *Grimshaw* v. *Ford Motor Co.*, No. 197761 (Superior Court, Orange County, Ca., 1978).
4. Ind. Code, 35-42-1-5 (Supp. 1978).
5. See generally Comment, "Corporate Homicide: A New Assault on Corporate Decision-Making," *Notre Dame Law Review* 54 (1979):911–924; Comment, "Corporate Criminal Liability for Homicide: The Controversy Flames Anew," *California Western Law Review* 17

(1981):465–492; Comment, "Corporate Homicide: The Stark Realities of Artificial Beings and Legal Fictions," *Pepperdine Law Review* 8 (1981):367–412.

6. *Chicago Tribune*, March 14, 1980.

7. Lee Strobel, *Reckless Homicide: Ford's Pinto Trial* (South Bend, Ind.: And Books, 1980), pp. 151–152.

8. *New York Times*, April 4, 1980, p. 8.

9. Strobel, *Reckless Homicide*, pp. 221, 223–225.

10. *New York Times*, February 14, 1980, p. 20; *Wall Street Journal*, March 14, 1980, p. 7.

11. Strobel, *Reckless Homicide*, Ch. 20.

12. Ibid., pp. 267–270.

13. See further Victoria Lynn Swigert and Ronald A. Farrell, "Corporate Homicide: Definitional Processes in the Creation of Deviance," *Law & Society Review* 15 (1980):161–182.

14. Mark Dowie, "Pinto Madness," *Mother Jones*, September/October 1977:2–13.

15. E. S. Grush and C. S. Saunby, *Fatalities Associated with Crash-Induced Fires and Fuel Leakages* (internal document, Ford Motor Company, 1973).

16. Dowie, "Pinto Madness," p. 7. See also Strobel, *Reckless Homicide*, pp. 89–90.

17. Dowie, "Pinto Madness," p. 7.

18. Strobel, *Reckless Homicide*, pp. 19, 28.

19. See, e.g., *National Times* (Australia), February 27–March 4, 1978; Strobel, *Reckless Homicide*, p. 66.

20. *New York Times*, May 4, 1978, p. 22.

21. Strobel, *Reckless Homicide*, p. 23.

22. *Wall Street Journal*, January 16, 1980.

23. Strobel, *Reckless Homicide*.

24. *Washington Star*, March 13, 1980.

25. *Los Angeles Times*, January 8, 1980.

26. By contrast, in the electrical equipment conspiracies, corporate blameworthiness took second place to the jail sentences handed out to individual actors.

27. *Los Angeles Times*, March 14, 1980.

28. Ford Motor Company, Press Release, August 29, 1977, p. 8. This release appears to have received little press coverage: see Swigert and Farrell, "Corporate Homicide," p. 175.

29. Strobel, *Reckless Homicide*, p. 217. See also *New York Times*, February 21, 1980, p. 16.

30. *Chicago Tribune*, August 26, 1978.

31. Bruce Mays, "Hans Zeisel: The Time of His Life," *Student Lawyer*, April 1980:22–39, pp. 23, 37.

32. Strobel, *Reckless Homicide*, p. 104. An additional function was to offer selected news items for distribution to media unrepresented by a reporter at the trial: Ibid., p. 120.

33. Strobel, *Reckless Homicide*, pp. 185, 203–212; *New York Times*, February 20, 1980, p. 16.

34. *Los Angeles Times*, March 14, 1980.

35. *Detroit Free Press*, March 14, 1980; Malcolm E. Wheeler, "In Pinto's Wake, Criminal Trials Loom for More Manufacturers," *National Law Journal*, October 6, 1981:27–28 (first of five-part series). See also Richard A. Epstein, "Is Pinto a Criminal?," *Regulation*, March–April 1980:15–21.

36. Irwin Ross, "How Lawless are Big Companies?," *Fortune*, December 1, 1980:56–64.

37. *Advertising Age*, April 7, 1980. Ford used car prices were also severely affected: *Houston Post*, September 15, 1978.

38. *Advertising Age*, April 7, 1980.

39. Ibid.

40. *New York Times*, February 17, 1980, section IV, p. E9.

41. *New York Times*, June 10, 1979, p. 26. See also Strobel, *Reckless Homicide*, p. 41.

42. *Yarborough* v. *Ford Motor Co.*, Civil No. 80 CI 409 (Dist. Ct., 45th Judicial District, Texas, 1980).

43. *Indianapolis News*, March 15, 1980. See also John B. Schnapp, *Corporate Strategies of Automotive Manufacturers* (Lexington, Mass.: Lexington Books, 1979), p. 48.

44. Cf. Christopher D. Stone, *Where the Law Ends: The Social Control of Corporate Behavior* (New York: Harper & Row, 1975), pp. 39–40.

45. *Wall Street Journal*, October 1, 1979, pp. 1, 39; *New York Times*, June 10, 1979, p. 26.
46. Strobel, *Reckless Homicide*, pp. 40–41.
47. *Washington Post*, August 26, 1978; Walter Guzzardi, Jr., "Ford: The Road Ahead," *Fortune*, September 11, 1978:36–48, p. 42.
48. Strobel, *Reckless Homicide*, p. 41.
49. *New York Times*, June 10, 1979, p. 26.
50. Guzzardi, "Ford: The Road Ahead," p. 42.
51. *Houston Post*, September 25, 1978.
52. H.R. 7040 (1980); U.S.H.R., Subcommittee on Crime of the Committee on the Judiciary, *Corporate Crime*, 96th Cong., 2nd Sess., 1980. See also *New York Times*, March 16, 1980, section IV, p. 20.
53. Cf. W. Allen Spurgeon and Terence P. Fagan, "Criminal Liability for Life-Endangering Corporate Conduct," *Journal of Criminal Law & Criminology* 72 (1981):400–433.
54. Strobel, *Reckless Homicide*, p. 79.
55. Ford, *Policy Document F-1* (Dearborn, Mich.: Ford, 1979).
56. But note that the Pinto case was one of several instanced in support of a federal bill requiring corporate managers to disclose the existence of life-threatening defects to the relevant enforcement agency: Subcommittee on Crime, *Corporate Crime*, pp. 8–11. See also *New York Times*, March 16, 1980, section IV, p. 20.
57. *Buffalo Evening News*, March 14, 1980.
58. See generally Hugh Dalziel Duncan, *Symbols in Society* (New York: Oxford University Press, 1968).
59. See generally Stephen J. Schulhofer, "Harm and Punishment: A Critique of Emphasis on the Results of Conduct in the Criminal Law," *University of Pennsylvania Law Review* 122 (1974):1497–1607; Christopher D. Stone, "The Place of Enterprise Liability in the Control of Corporate Conduct," *Yale Law Journal* 90 (1980):1–77.
60. Guido Calabresi, *The Costs of Accidents: A Legal and Economic Analysis* (New Haven, Conn.: Yale University Press, 1970), p. 256.
61. See generally Jonathan D. Glover, *Causing Death and Saving Lives* (New York: Penguin, 1977); Richard T. DeGeorge, "Ethical Responsibilities of Engineers in Large Organizations," *Business & Professional Ethics Journal* 1 (1981):1–14; Rachel Dardis and Claudia Zent, "The Economics of the Pinto Recall," *Journal of Consumer Affairs* 16 (1982):261–277.

44 / Rehabilitating Social Systems and Institutions

DELOS H. KELLY

One fact that should be apparent now is that as long as failure, criminal, and deviant values and traditions exist, we will obtain outcomes commensurate with these phenomena. Correlatively, getting tough on crime and delinquency, for example, will not begin to get the job done, primarily because... those normative structures, conditions, and environments that guarantee the continued production of perceived deviation will remain virtually unchanged. Predictably, then, individuals will become exposed to and recruited out to play the role of the school failure, the young criminal, and the deviant. And some willing or unwilling recruits will... participate at times or drop out, while others will become regular members. These are some of the inescapable and basic facts the practitioners must begin to come to grips with. Unfortunately,... the efforts of these individuals (as well as the legislators, the policy makers, the professionals, and others) often do nothing more than to help perpetuate a medical-clinical-individualistic model of change and treatment. Thus, instead of looking within society to explain deviation, they look within the individual. Thereafter, the individual is taught how to cope or perhaps even feel good about himself or herself. And for some, a strategy of this type may work. For most, however, the efforts not only fail but the individuals experience a relapse; this is certainly understandable and most predictable.

THE CLINICAL MODEL REVISITED, OR BLAMING THE INDIVIDUAL

What the practitioners and others do not seem to recognize is that behavior viewed as criminal or deviant to them may be perceived as being acceptable and *normal* to the individual. In fact,... nonconformity is often the demanded response on the part of a group member. It may be recalled, for example, that Miller's gang boys received positive sanctions and rewards when they acted in accordance with the "focal concerns" (e.g., fighting and getting into trouble). Moreover, failure to conform, Miller claimed, would have probably resulted in exclusion from the gang. Similarly, Reiss', Cohen's, and Hargreaves' delinquent males were expected to live up to the values and normative systems they were immersed in. The same held for the nudists, prostitutes, mental patients, and the like. Observations such as these contain an underlying message: Efforts at change focused exclusively upon the individual are usually doomed from the start, mainly because the policy makers and the practitioners fail to recognize that most individuals are actually responding normally to their own *immediate* world. Thus, and even though people are removed, treated, or incarcerated, they do, upon their return, become a part of that environment once again. Quite clearly, Weinberg's nudists, Bryan's prostitutes, Scheff's mental patients, and Wallace's skid rowers may leave; however, they must, upon their return, conform to the existing normative structure.[1] In a very real sense, the labeled deviants, criminals, delinquents, failures, and others become caught between two worlds: the conforming and the nonconforming; this dilemma creates some obvious problems for individuals so situated. If, for example, an actor elects to go straight, he or she runs the risk of being defined as a deviant and perhaps even rejected by his or her peers. On the other hand, conformity to group norms and values may produce further contact with social control agencies. What this often means is that the individual must weight the costs and benefits that may ensue by virtue of involvement with one culture as opposed to another. Ray's (1961) research on abstinence and relapse cycles among heroin addicts offers an excellent illustration of how these processes frequently operate.

Ray (1961:133) notes initially that the social world of addiction, like any other world (e.g., the world of nudism or prostitution), can be characterized by its organizational and cultural elements (e.g., its argot or language, market, pricing system). Not only this but commitment to the addict world provides the member with a major status and associated identity. Addiction, however, often means that the addict will come to assume or exhibit other secondary status features. For example, as the habit grows, most efforts will be oriented toward obtaining drugs. Thus one may become careless about his or her appearance and cleanliness, and this frequently means that non-addicts will begin to label the addict as a "bum," "degenerate," or lacking "will power." Of significance here, at least as far as the potential for change is concerned, is Ray's (1961:134) observation that even though the addict is *aware* that he or she is being judged in terms of these secondary characteristics or definitions and may, therefore, try to *reject* or shed the labels, it is virtually impossible to do so, primarily because most interactions and institutional experiences operate in such a manner as to ratify the labels or definitions that have been applied to the addict. In fact, incarceration in correctional and mental facilities plays a most important role in the ratification process, particularly in view of the fact that contacts with non-addicts and their values often produce significant changes in one's identity or view of self. Ray (1961:133) comments on how the inmate and others may react to institutionalization:

> The addict's incarceration in correctional institutions has specific meanings which he finds reflected in the attitudes toward him by members of non-addict society

> and by his fellow addicts. Additionally, as his habit grows and the demands for drugs get beyond any legitimate means of supply, his own activities in satisfying his increased craving give him direct experiential evidence of the criminal aspects of self. These meanings of self as a criminal become internalized as he begins to apply criminal argot to his activities and institutional experiences....

In effect, the inmate often accepts the criminal label and begins to act accordingly (i.e., becomes a career criminal); this same type of situation exists relative to the mental institution. However, instead of promoting the ideology that the client is criminal, the operating assumption is that the addict is psychologically inadequate or deficient. Thus, attempts are made to treat the individual's mind, usually through the use of some kind of counseling or group therapy. Contacts with psychiatric or psychological personnel produce another effect: They remind the addict that the institution and its staff view him or her as being mentally ill. In the words of one addict (Ray, 1961:134):

> When I got down to the hospital, I was interviewed by different doctors and one of them told me, "you now have one mark against you as crazy for having been down here." I hadn't known it was a crazy house. You know regular people [non-addicts] think this too.

And like the criminal, the addict may eventually accept the identity that is being imputed to him or her. Acceptance of this new status, as well as its associated labels, does reduce the odds that a cure can be effected, primarily because the addict becomes further entrenched within the addict and other (perceived) deviant cultures (e.g., the inmate).

Even though the overall prognosis for change is certainly poor, some addicts will experience a cure (i.e., remain free of drugs). The most likely candidates are drawn from the ranks of those addicts who, for some reason (e.g., incarceration), begin to question their addict identity, as well as the values of the drug world. Ray (1961:134) has stated this most succinctly:

> An episode of cure begins in the *private thoughts* of the addict rather than in his overt behavior. These deliberations develop as a result of experience in specific situations of interaction with *important others* that cause the addict to experience social stress, to develop some feeling of alienation from or dissatisfaction with his present identity, and to call it into question and examine it in all of its implications and ramifications. In these situations the *addict engages in private self-debate* in which he juxtaposes the values and social relationships which have become immediate and concrete through his addiction with those that are sometimes only half remembered or only imperfectly perceived. [Italics mine.]

Such questioning or self-debate may begin because of some kind of institutional contact (e.g., confinement in a hospital or correctional facility). It may also occur as a result of what Ray (1961:135) has termed a "socially disjunctive experience" with other addicts (e.g., an addict may be sent to buy drugs but never returns). More typically, however, the analysis of self or introspection emerges by virtue of some type of interaction or experience with a non-addict and/or the non-addict world; these provide the major catalytic elements for change (Ray, 1961:135).

Once withdrawal has been completed and a decision has been made to abstain (i.e., to structure an abstainer identity), the former addict is confronted immediately with some serious identity and self-image problems. During this initial period, Ray (1961:136) maintains that the individual becomes locked in a "running struggle" with problems of social identity. He or she is not sure of self; however, certain expectations are held about the future and its possibilities. Thus, the early stages of a cure are often characterized by substantial ambivalence; this is produced by the abstainer's efforts to find out where he or she stands relative to the addict and non-addict groups. Such ambivalence or lingering uncertainty may, according to Ray (1961:136), manifest itself through the type of pronouns used in discussions of addicts and their world (e.g., the use of "we" and "they" to refer to non-addicts as opposed to addicts), as well as in terms of how the attempted abstainer speaks of self (e.g., he or she may preface a statement with "When I was an addict. . . . ").

Whether a former addict will continue to remain abstinent is, however, problematic. And critical to the success of any cure appears to be the role played by significant others (e.g., family members, spouses, friends, etc.). As Ray (1961:136) puts it: ". . . Above all, he appears to desire ratification by significant others of his newly developing identity, and in his interactions during an episode of abstinence he expects to secure it." Stated somewhat differently, if others are generally supportive and caring, the chances are much greater that an abstainer identity can be built and perhaps maintained. Probably most important to the successful completion of this process are the reactions of one's immediate family members. If, as a result of perceived positive changes on the part of the individual (e.g., obtaining and keeping a job, improving appearance, professing an allegiance to non-addict values), the family's attitudes undergo modification, the probability of a long-term cure appears more likely (Ray, 1961:136). At this point Ray (1961:137) stresses the fact that attitudinal changes, whether they occur on the part of the abstainer or the family, are usually not enough to produce a cure. Rather, professed commitment to the non-addict life style and its values "must be grounded in action." In other words, the abstainer must, in his or her interactions with the non-addicts, be allowed to actually occupy and play out the role of the non-addict; this not only helps to strengthen one's image as an abstainer but it also provides an opportunity whereby the non-addict values and perspectives can be learned and shared. Failure to satisfy this latter condition, it can be noted, increases the likelihood of a relapse. And a relapse is most apt to occur when the expectations held of self and others are not met. As Ray (1961:137) puts it:

> The tendency toward relapse develops out of the meanings of the abstainer's experiences in social situations when he develops an image of himself as so-

> cially different from non-addicts, and relapse occurs when he redefines himself as an addict. When his social expectations and the expectations of others with whom he interacts are not met, social stress develops and he is required to re-examine the meaningfulness of his experience in non-addict society and in so doing question his identity as an abstainer. This type of experience promotes a mental realignment with addict values and standards....

Ray (1961:137) notes that relapse or re-addiction is most likely to occur during the initial period following physical withdrawal; this is the time in which the addict becomes actively engaged in the "running struggle" or battle with identity problems (i.e., he or she engages in a great deal of self-debate). Coupled with this is the fact that the addict identity, values, life style, and experiences are still most immediate, while these same elements of the non-addict world are often unclear or hazy. A situation such as this (i.e., pressing identity problems, familiarity with the addict world, and a corresponding unfamiliarity with the non-addict society), however, places the individual in an especially vulnerable position and, predictably, many former addicts or attempted abstainers will, as a result of pressure by other addicts, relapse. The possibility of this occurring appears noticeably great when the social expectations and reactions of addicts are such that the individual finds it virtually impossible to identify with or even act out any significant non-addict roles. Other addicts may, according to Ray (1961:137), dislike any attempt at presenting a "square" image of self, and they may begin to view the individual as being peculiar or strange. Thus, the perceived "deviant" will be pressured to conform.

Ray (1961:138) makes an important point to the effect that relapse is not necessarily due to one's associations. Rather, it is a function of how the individual evaluates self relative to the social situations he or she encounters. For example, some abstainers will have contacts with former addicts and still maintain their abstainer identity, while others will redefine themselves as addicts and move back into the fold. Similarly, some ex-addicts will associate with non-addicts and stay abstinent, while others will reject the abstainer role and then reassume the addict role. Predicting which outcome is most likely is difficult; however, if the abstainer is pressured by other addicts to conform and if, further, he or she is not allowed to assume a non-addict status, the probability of relapse is high. The same applies to associations with non-addicts. In fact, unsatisfactory experiences with non-addicts often contribute heavily to a lack of cure, and particularly those interactional situations and associated exchanges which operate in such a manner as to keep the individual locked into his or her addict role (Ray, 1961:138). Stated more simply, the abstainer may try to move from an addict to a non-addict status, and correspondingly, he or she expects others to accept, as well as ratify, the attempted status change. And when this acceptance is not forthcoming (e.g., significant others may continue to refer to the individual in terms of his or her prior addict identity and status), questions about one's identity and status begin to emerge. Ray (1961:138–139) offers the comments of an addict who experienced this type of treatment:

> My relatives were always saying things to me like "Have you really quit using that drug now?" and things like that. And I knew that they were doing a lot of talking behind my back because when I came around they would stop talking but I overheard them. It used to burn my ass.

A person such as this would probably be an excellent candidate for relapse. Relapse itself entails movement back into the addict world. It also involves some resocializing of the individual. In the words of Ray (1961:139):

> [Reentry] requires a recommitment to the norms of addiction and limits the degree to which he may relate to non-addict groups in terms of the latter's values and standards. It demands participation in the old ways of organizing conduct and experiences and, as a consequence, the readoption of the secondary status characteristics of addiction. He again shows a lack of concern about his personal appearance and grooming. Illicit activities are again engaged in to get money for drugs, and as a result the possibility of more firmly establishing the criminal aspect of his identity becomes a reality.

Thus, complete resocialization not only demands a recommitment to the values of the addict world but it also requires a redefinition of self as an addict.

What may not be recognized from research such as the preceding is that a medical-clinical-individualistic model of change is very much in evidence. Understandably, then, if a change in personal and public identity, attitudes, or behavior is to occur, it must come from within the individual. It is he or she who must make the move. And even if, because of some socially disjunctive experience or personal crisis, a person begins to question or redefine his or her present deviant identities, he or she must attempt to operate in two worlds: the conforming and the nonconforming; this produces some obvious difficulties relative to any attempt to structure and maintain a non-deviant personal and public identity. Not only will deviant peers often pressure the "deviant" to conform to their values and associated normative system, but similar requests or demands will be made by selected non-deviants. In fact, the responses of, as well as interactions with, generalized (e.g., hospital and correctional staff) and significant (e.g., family) others are an especially important ingredient in the success or failure of any attempted cure or rehabilitation. Are these others willing to alter their perceptions of the deviant (i.e., begin to view him or her as nondeviant or conformist)? Equally critical, is the labeled or perceived deviant allowed to actually occupy and act out the role of a non-deviant, or is he or she kept effectively locked into a deviant status? In most cases, the evidence on these matters exhibits a mistakenly clear pattern: Not only are people unwilling to modify their views and expectations of those deviants and/or ex-deviants who are trying to restructure their complement of identities, but the "straights" also fail to provide any realistic opportunities whereby the perceived "misfits" can learn, or perhaps even relearn, the conventional, non-deviant roles; this unwillingness or reluctance to change can be used to highlight the most basic flaw of virtually all treatment and change programs. Specifically, environments, values, and normative systems remain unchanged. What this means with respect to theory and practice is that the legislators, law enforcement personnel, practitioners, therapists, and others either generally neglect or else ignore those factors, conditions, and influences responsible for producing deviant outcomes and, instead, concentrate on the actor. And, predictably, failure becomes defined in *individual* terms and not in *structural-organizational* terms. Obviously, blaming the individual is a much easier task than blaming the system.

REHABILITATING SOCIAL SYSTEMS AND INSTITUTIONS

Unfortunately, blaming the individual does nothing more than to protect the real culprits. If... a student is designated as a potential failure or delinquent and placed in a non-academic or delinquent career line, that pupil will, in more cases than not, live up to such expectations. Yet, instead of charging the educators and their system with malfeasance, we indict the academic failure or "misfit" and build a case against him or her. And not only will the student be convicted, so to speak, but the guilty parties escape prosecution and conviction.

What people at all levels must begin to recognize, however, is that failure, alienation, delinquency, misconduct, dropout, and so on are guaranteed products of the school. Another way of saying this is that the educational system's underlying organizational structure is geared to produce these outcomes and others.... Thus, and most predictably, students will be assigned to deviant career lines and they will, once socialized, exhibit attitudes and behaviors commensurate with their status; this, as I have stressed, also applies to any other social system an actor may become a part of (e.g., the nudist or skid row culture). The point that must be emphasized at this stage is, therefore, basic, yet most fundamental: If school failure, youth crime, and deviance are to be reduced significantly, then the organizational structure of the educational system must be attacked and altered radically. Eliminating deviant career lines (e.g., low ability groups or tracks) would be an important and necessary first step. Changing the *content* of some of the values of the school's existing subcultures or social systems would constitute another. If, for example, the anti-academic values of Hargreaves' delinquent subculture were replaced with those of the academic, the patterns of school failure, misconduct, and petty delinquency would look much different. In fact, not only would there be a sharp reduction in outcomes such as these, but an educational environment with a *common* set of academic values would have been created. Altering the value structure in this manner would, however, require other basic changes. Most dramatically, educators, school administrators, and others would be required to question the presumed validity of the success-fail philosophy that guides their interactions with students. Stated more simply, instituting a common set of values would eliminate the need for deviant career lines and this strategy would, in turn, require the development of a new working ideology—one that is based upon *the presumption of ability*. Translating this official perspective (i.e., the belief that *all* children and students possess ability and can perform) into action would not be easy, nor necessarily successful, primarily because changes would be required at all levels, regardless of whether focus is given to educators, parents, or others. In effect, we are dealing with a problem with deep societal roots.

Even though the existing theory and evidence actually call for a total revamping or restructuring of society, the probability of this occurring in either the short- or long-run is, admittedly, most remote. Nor should one expect much to happen within the educational system. Not only is the success-fail philosophy embedded deeply within the organizational structure of the school, but the educators, the administrators, and the students have been indoctrinated with this ideology. Most parents, as I argued, have also been socialized to believe in the current educational philosophy (i.e., they follow the belief that some students have ability, while others have little or none). Thus, parents, like the educators, must be a part of any plan to change the present situation.

Given the prospects for change, then it becomes an easy task to advance the argument that nothing can be done about those conditions responsible for producing *careers* of failure, youth crime, and deviance. And most do, in fact, argue along these lines. Such reasoning is, however, faulty and, even more basic, it fails to address the cold, hard facts. In this respect, the evidence is crystal clear: Institutions, by virtue of the way they are structured and intersect with each other, are geared to produce our failures, our delinquents, and our young criminals. The most graphic representation of this would have to be my analysis of how the educational system builds, maintains, and perpetuates a variety of deviant careers and identities—careers and identities that are often reinforced, strengthened, and solidified by a range of social control agencies and their agents. What evidence of this type points to, once again, is the need for structural-organizational change.

If change is to come about, then I believe that it must begin with the educational system. Not only is this one of our basic institutions but most children spend at least ten years or more within the system; they also spend many hours each day in school. The same does not exist with respect to many families or the community. Thus, the school probably represents the most stable environment in which to impact; this should not be taken to mean that the family units or peer networks should be ignored. On the contrary, they must be involved. Ideally, changes in the structure and process of schooling should emanate out to these elements.

Although most educators find very little wrong with the way they go about educating students, I have argued that they and their organization actually help to create many of the problems they would like to get rid of. And the basic problem is structural in nature. Stated most bluntly, the educators, parents, and others have bought the script, along with all of its value-laden stereotypes. The script must be rewritten. Hence, my initial call for the introduction of an educational philosophy predicated upon the presumption of ability—a theory of the office or working ideology that would, as I pointed out, eliminate the need for such sorting machines as ability groups, tracks, and streams; this, in turn, would require the elimination of the diagnostic stereotypes that characterize the *deviant* or non-academic career lines. In a sense, the school and its agents must begin to make it extremely difficult for the student to fail.

A new ideology and its corresponding diagnostic stereotypes call for some obvious desocialization and resocialization of present, as well as future, educators; this could be accomplished through a variety of methods. For example, teachers and other educational personnel would be required to attend seminars or workshops where they could be educated in terms of how the school, by virtue of its action or inaction, can help in the production of deviant careers and identities. Also, future educators of all types would not receive their credentials or even be allowed to teach until they had completed a set of mandatory courses dealing with basic issues, concepts, and processes... (e.g., courses which sensitize them to the way in which conflicting perspectives, such as the clinical versus the social system, affect the identifying and processing of clients; how and why career lines and subcultures may originate; how teachers can perpetuate academic stereotypes; how teachers may initiate status degradation ceremonies; how teachers may destroy a student's identity and self-image, and so on).

Additional strategies could be provided (e.g., implementing a range of institutional sanctions that would be used to deal with those who fail to comply with the new working ideology); however, what needs to be stressed at this stage is that parents, peers, and others must also be desocialized and resocialized accordingly. Obviously, and as with respect to the educational arena, the probability of producing noticeable change is low. Still, the logic and evidence point to such a need.

One of the basic problems with most families is that they have placed too much faith in the educational system and its agents. The guiding assumption is that, somehow, the educators really know what is best for their children; this, I contend, is not only a fallacious view but actually does nothing more than to give free rein to the educators. Thus, and predictably, it should not be surprising to find them operating on the basis of stereotypic notions about ability—the very same stereotypes that are, as we have seen, used to select out students for placement in deviant career lines. The responses on the part of the parents and the educators are certainly understandable, particularly in view of the fact that both have, as a result of their formal and informal socializing experiences, been indoctrinated with the success-fail philosophy. A major outcome of this socialization is that parents, peers, students, and others are taught not to question the educational decision makers.... In effect, whenever a parent questioned a decision, he or she was "cooled out" by the counselor.

Parents, like the educators and all others, should be resocialized. And as a start, they must become aware and begin to question and challenge the presumed validity of the success-fail philosophy, as well as each and every decision that is rendered on the behalf of their children. Parents must also begin to recognize that they can have a direct say in terms of how their children are handled by the educational decision makers. The same applies with respect to students; they, too, must begin to heighten their "consciousness" and become aware of what is actually happening at the hands of the educators. As an illustration, and in the area of career decisions, options must be presented to all—options, I might add, that are not only available for all to achieve but options that are actually attainable. For example, pupils must be apprised of what it takes to become a doctor, lawyer, professor, dentist, and the like, and they must be encouraged to pursue options such as these if they so choose; this strategy would not produce a glut of professionals. Some students, once the requirements and the nature of the occupations are spelled out, will elect to follow other career routes. The point that must be emphasized, however, is that career options must be *genuine* options and the choice factor must be *real*. And to be effective, information relative to careers and the right of choice must be presented at the earliest possible stage. Waiting until the junior or senior year is often too late, and this is especially so for those who have been processed as non-college material. The educational and occupational prospects of these students have already been damaged seriously; this does not mean that these individuals should be written-off. Quite the contrary, they, too, like the educators and the parents, could be retrained and resocialized. Admittedly, the task would be onerous, primarily because we would be required to undo what has taken many years to produce. Another way of saying this is that it takes a great deal of time and effort to produce a *good* non-college-bound product, failure, drop-out, delinquent, criminal, and so on. Hence, we should not expect any instant cures or miracles.

SOME FINAL COMMENTS

Yet... this is exactly what the people are looking for. Thus, demands are being made continually for more laws, longer sentences, more cells, and the like—demands that are predicated firmly upon the belief that if we really crack down on crime, this will solve the problem. Unfortunately, the call for the use of "quick-fix" or "band-aid" solutions or measures will not begin to get the job done. As an illustration, we can incarcerate more people for longer periods of time; however, this will only aggravate the situation, primarily because we will have an even greater number of individuals operating under the brunt of stigmatizing labels—labels that will certainly mitigate against the probability that one will elect to go straight; this, it may be recalled, was one of the basic messages offered by Ray's research. In effect, addicts found it very difficult to structure and maintain an abstainer identity, both in the personal and public sense. Not only did they experience difficulty with the other addicts but non-addicts continued to respond to them as addicts. Equally important, the attempted abstainer was not allowed to assume nor act out the non-addict role. And predictably, most relapsed and moved back into the addict world. The same situation holds for the rest of society's deviants or ex-deviants; they, too, may try to build a non-deviant personal and public identity, and a few will actually succeed in doing so. All, however, will soon learn that society does not look too kindly upon its deviators, and they will also come to realize that structures, environments, and traditions are relatively unchanging. And, as I have argued rather repeatedly, if change is to occur, it must come from within the individual. It is he or she who must be rehabilitated.

Probably the most curious, as well as perplexing, feature of such a position or argument concerns the failure of the proponents to recognize the fact that most behavior, however defined, emerges out of a group or social psychological context; this holds regardless of whether we are focusing on the family, the peer group, the gang, the skid row culture, the nudist society, or the homosexual subculture. Thus, an ideology such as the preceding (i.e., promoting the notion of individual failure, pathology, or deficiency) must be viewed as being eminently uninformed, unsubstantiated, and most unscientific. It also contains some potentially damaging, as well as dangerous, features. For example, when we get down to the point of actually doing something about failure, crime, or deviance, we stop being sociologists or social scientists and become psychiatrists, psychologists, or some other type of clinician. Henceforth, we neglect the value and normative systems of which one is or has been implicated in—the very same structures that have given definition and shape to the person's behavior, identities, and self-image—and go to work on the mind; this is a most unfortunate and unproductive strategy, and it becomes especially so when considered in the light of the logic, theory, and evidence pointing to the need for rehabilitating some social systems and institutions. The best illustrations in support of this need, at least as found in this book, would have to be the evidence indicating how the *disadvantaged* or *powerless* (broadly defined) are frequently perceived and responded to by our schools, our mental institutions, our police departments, our courts, and our parole units. It is not a pretty sight.

Promoting the ideology of individual failure or deficiency is associated with other, equally subtle and pernicious, effects. Most prominently, focusing in on the individual deflects our attention away from the real problems. If, for example, people buy the arguments—and many certainly do—that school failure is an individual problem, that gang behavior is a function of a disturbed psyche, or that homosexuality and prostitution are manifestations of some type of genetic or biological abnormality, then the search for the actual causes or origins of these behaviors stops; this, too, is an unfortunate state of affairs. In effect, and as I have also argued, blaming the individual is and continues to be a very handy and effective political smokescreen. If, for example, the politicians, educators, and law enforcement officials can blame the individual, then they do not have to deal with the basic fact that the schools can, by virtue of the way they dispense education, contribute very heavily to the production of careers in failure, dropout, crime, deviance, and so on; nor do they have to deal with the fact that gang activity, when analyzed in terms of the normative systems that produce and demand such behavior, is often viewed as normal behavior by its members. This should not be taken to mean that violence should be tolerated. It should not. What these statements do mean is that we *have* some good evidence available to us. Being able to develop and implement programs on the basis of this information is where the difficulty comes in. How many politicians, for example, are willing to indict the educational or law enforcement system? Concomitantly, how many would be willing to provide the necessary funds for the restructuring of the educational system, as well as for the retraining of educational personnel, parents, and others? Quite obviously, none, if they are concerned with enhancing their political careers, would dare to venture into these areas; these are politically hot issues. Yet, and as I have illustrated, changes are needed—changes that could, in fact, be made. And changes that would make a difference.

Finally, failure to address the structural-organizational sources of crime, delinquency, and deviance only gives further credence to a clinical-medical model of explanation; this, too, is associated with some detrimental consequences. Most significantly, it not only allows for the continued perpetuation of myths about the nature and extent of social deviance but, in a related sense, it also provides the basis upon which many irresponsible statements are made. Like my comments relative to the school, there is, however, a way out. As a start, people should not be allowed to make statements about crime until they have studied it thoroughly and begin to know something about it; this holds for the politicians, the social scientists, the practitioners, and others. As an illustration, campaigning on the basis of a "lock them up" or "get tough on crime" plank will certainly produce the votes; however, such a platform, even if translated into policy, will not make a substantial dent in crime. Crime, whatever its variety, is, as I have demonstrated, more complex than this. And the basic flaw with an ideology or mentality such as this is that it is much too simplistic and clinical in nature. It also, as I have stressed rather repeatedly, fails to incorporate a direct and systematic concern for those factors, conditions, and environments that have actually given shape to the behavior or behaviors under scrutiny. Structures thus remain intact. . . .

Note

1. For a more complete discussion of the works mentioned thus far, see Chapter 5 in D. H. Kelly, *Creating School Failure, Youth Crime, and Deviance*. Los Angeles: Trident Shop, 1982.

Reference

Ray, M. B. 1961 "The cycle of abstinence and relapse among heroin addicts." *Social Problems* 9:132–140.

Acknowledgments *(cont'd)*

J. Mark Watson, "Outlaw Motorcyclists: An Outgrowth of Lower Class Cultural Concerns," reprinted from DEVIANT BEHAVIOR 2 1980, pp. 31–48, by permission.

Gresham M. Sykes and David Matza "Techniques of Neutralization: A Theory of Delinquency," reprinted from AMERICAN SOCIOLOGICAL REVIEW, 22, 1957, pages 666–670, by permission.

Diana Scully and Joseph Marolla, "Convicted Rapists' Vocabulary of Motive: Excuses and Justifications," © 1984 by the Society for the Study of Social Problems. Reprinted from *Social Problems,* Vol 31, No. 5, June 1984, pp. 530–544 by permission of the University of California Press Journals.

Robert K. Merton, "Social Structure and Anomie," reprinted from AMERICAN SOCIOLOGICAL REVIEW, 3, 1938, pages 672–682, by permission.

Richard A. Cloward and Lloyd E. Ohlin, "Differential Opportunity and Delinquent Subcultures," reprinted with the permission of The Free Press, a Division of Macmillan, Inc. from DELINQUENCY AND OPPORTUNITY by Richard A. Cloward and Lloyd E. Ohlin. Copyright © 1960 by The Free Press; copyright renewed 1988 by Richard E. Cloward and Lloyd E. Ohlin.

Jeffrey H. Reiman, "A Radical Perspective on Crime," reprinted with the permission of Macmillan Publishing Company from THE RICH GET RICHER AND THE POOR GET PRISON by Jeffrey H. Reiman. Copyright © 1970 by Macmillan Publishing Company.

William J. Chambliss, "A Sociological Analysis of the Law of Vagrancy," © 1964 by the Society of the Study of Social Problems. Reprinted from *Social Problems,* Vol. 12, No. 1, Summer 1964, pp. 67–77, by permission.

Travis Hirschi, "A Control Theory of Delinquency," pages 16–26. Copyright © 1969 The Regents of the University of California.

Neal Shover and David Honaker, "The Socially Bounded Decision Making of Persistent Property Offenders," (Howard Journal of Criminal Justice, forthcoming). Reprinted by permission of the Howard League.

Edwin M. Lemert, "Primary and Secondary Deviation," from Edwin M. Lemert, SOCIAL PATHOLOGY, New York: McGraw-Hill, 1951. Reprinted by permission.

Howard S. Becker, "Career Deviance," reprinted with permission of The Free Press, a Division of Macmillan, Inc. from OUTSIDERS by Howard S. Becker. Copyright © 1963 by The Free Press.

Joseph W. Schneider and Peter Conrad, "In the Closet with Illness: Epilepsy, Stigma Potential and Information Control," © 1980 by the Society for the Study of Social Problems. Reprinted from *Social Problems,* Vol. 28, No. 1, October 80, pp. 32–44 by permission.

Rose Weitz, "Living with the Stigma of AIDS," reprinted from QUALITATIVE SOCIOLOGY, 13:1 (Spring 1990), pp. 23–38, with permission.

Joan K. Jackson, "The Adjustment of the Family to the Crisis of Alcoholism," reprinted from QUARTERLY JOURNAL OF STUDIES IN ALCOHOL, 15:562–586, 1954, by permission.

Kathleen J. Ferraro and John M. Johnson, "How Women Experience Battering: The Process of Victimization," © 1983 by the Society for Study of Social Problems. Reprinted from *Social Problems,* Vol 30, No. 3, February 1983, pp. 325–335 by permission.

Thomas J. Scheff and Daniel M. Culver, "The Societal Reaction to Deviance: Ascriptive Elements in the Psychiatric Screening of Mental Patients in a Midwestern State," © 1964 by the Society for the Study of Social Problems. Reprinted from *Social Problems,* Vol. 11, No. 4, Spring, 1964, pp. 401–413, by permission.

Roger Jeffery, "Normal Rubbish: Deviant Patients in Casualty Department," reprinted from SOCIOLOGY OF HEALTH AND ILLNESS, Vol 1, No 1, pp. 90–107, by permission.

Gary T. Marx, "Ironies of Social Control: Authorities as Contributors to Deviance through Escalation, Nonenforcement, and Covert Facilitation," © 1981 by the Society for the Study of Social Problems. Reprinted from *Social Problems,* Vol 28, No. 3, February 1981, pp. 221–233 by permission.

Jennifer Hunt and Peter K. Manning, "The Social Context of Police Lying," *Symbolic Interaction,* 14:1 (Spring, 1991), pp. 51–70; reprinted by permission.

Jack W. Spencer, "Accounts, Attitudes, and Solutions: Probation Officer–Defendant Negotiations of Subjective Orientations," © 1983 by the Society for the Study of Social Problems. Reprinted from *Social Problems,* Vol. 30, No. 5, June 1983, pp. 570–581 by permission.

Jacqueline P. Wiseman, "Court Responses to Skid Row Alcoholics," From Jacqueline P. Wiseman, STATIONS OF THE LOST. Englewood Cliffs: Prentice Hall, 1970. Reprinted by permission of the University of Chicago Press.

Erving Goffman, "The Moral Career of the Mental Patient," reprinted from PSYCHIATRY, 22:123–142, 1959, by permission.

Bradley J. Fischer, "Illness Career Descent in Institutions for the Elderly," reprinted from QUALITATIVE SOCIOLOGY, 10:2 (Summer 1987), pp. 132–145, by permission.

Joel Best and David F. Luckenbill, "The Social Organization of Deviants," reprinted from SOCIAL PROBLEMS, 28:1, October 1980, by permission.

David F. Luckenbill, "Deviant Career Mobility: The Case of Male Prostitutes," © 1986 by the Society for the Study of Social Problems. Reprinted from *Social Problems,* vol. 33, No. 4, April, 1986, pp. 283–296 by permission.

Shiegla Murphy, Dan Waldorf, and Craig Reinarman, "Drifting into Dealing: Becoming a Cocaine Seller," reprinted from QUALITATIVE SOCIOLOGY, 13:4, (Winter 1990), by permission.

Barbara Sherman Heyl, "The Madam as Teacher: The Training of House Prostitutes," Chapter 5, pages 113–128 in Barbara Sherman Heyl, THE MADAM AS ENTREPRENEUR. New Brunswick: Transaction Books, 1979. Reprinted by permission.

William J. Chambliss, "State-Organized Crime," reprinted by permission of the American Society of Criminology.

Andrew Szasz, "Corporations, Organized Crime, and the Disposal of Hazardous Waste: An Examination of a Criminogenic Regulatory Structure," reprinted by permission of the American Society of Criminology.

William E. Thompson, "Handling the Stigma of Handling the Dead: Morticians and Funeral Directors," reprinted from DEVIANT BEHAVIOR 12 1991, pp. 403–429, by permission.

David S. Davis, "Good People Doing Dirty Work: A Study of Social Isolation," reprinted from *Symbolic Interaction,* 7:2, "Good People Doing Dirty Work: A Study of Social Isolation," pp. 233–247, by permission.

Samuel Walker, "Reform the Law: Decriminalization," from *Sense and Nonsense about Crime: A Policy Guide* by Samuel Walker. Copyright © 1985 by Wadsworth, Inc. Reprinted by permission of Brooks/Cole Publishing Company, Pacific Grove, CA 93950.

Patricia A. Adler and Peter Adler, "Tinydopers: A Case Study of Deviant Socialization," reprinted from *Symbolic Interaction,* 1:2 (Spring, 1978), pp. 90–105, by permission.

Douglas Degher and Gerald Hughes, "The Identity Change Process: A Field Study of Obesity," reprinted from DEVIANT BEHAVIOR 12 1992, pp. 385–401, by permission.

Thomas J. Schmid and Richard S. Jones, "Suspended Identity: Identity Transformation in a Maximum Security Prison," reprinted from *Symbolic Interaction,* 14:4 (Winter, 1991), pp. 415–432, by permission.

Brent Fisse and John Braithwaite, "The Impact of Publicity on Corporate Offenders: The Ford Motor Company and the Pinto Papers," reprinted from THE IMPACT OF PUBLICITY ON CORPORATE OFFENDERS by Brent Fisse and John Braithwaite by permission of the State University of New York Press.

Delos H. Kelly, "Rehabilitating Social Systems and Institutions," from CREATING SCHOOL FAILURE, YOUTH CRIME, AND DEVIANCE by Delos H. Kelly, Los Angeles: Trident Shop, 1982. Copyright © by Delos H. Kelly.